Game AI Pro 3

Game AI Pro 3
Collected Wisdom of Game AI Professionals

Edited by
Steve Rabin

CRC Press
Taylor & Francis Group
Boca Raton London New York

CRC Press is an imprint of the
Taylor & Francis Group, an **informa** business

AN A K PETERS BOOK

CRC Press
Taylor & Francis Group
6000 Broken Sound Parkway NW, Suite 300
Boca Raton, FL 33487-2742

© 2017 by Taylor & Francis Group, LLC
CRC Press is an imprint of Taylor & Francis Group, an Informa business

No claim to original U.S. Government works

Printed on acid-free paper

International Standard Book Number-13: 978-1-4987-4258-0 (Hardback)

Visit the Taylor & Francis Web site at
http://www.taylorandfrancis.com

and the CRC Press Web site at
http://www.crcpress.com

Printed and bound in the United States of America by Sheridan

Contents

Section II   Architecture

Section III   Movement and Pathfinding

Section IV   Tactics and Strategy

Section V   Character Behavior

Section VI   Odds and Ends

Preface

Welcome to an all new volume of *Game AI Pro*! As with each book in this series, I am proud to deliver brand new material from 50 of the top developers and researchers in the field of game AI. With 42 chapters of innovative techniques and algorithms, I am humbled at the goodwill and sharing of wisdom that this work represents. This book is a testament to the generous community of game AI developers as well as the larger game development community. Everyone involved in this effort believes that sharing information is the single best way to rapidly innovate, grow as developers, and continue to move the game industry forward. We sincerely hope that you will benefit from the insights and wisdom held within this book.

This book is divided into six primary sections. In the first section, "General Wisdom," we have a selection of techniques that generally apply to all games. In the "Architecture" section, we further explore modern architectures such as behavior trees and share architectures used in top games such as *FINAL FANTASY XV*, the *Call of Duty* series, and the *Guild Wars* series. In the "Movement and Pathfinding" section, we explore ways to better smooth paths, avoid obstacles, and navigate 3D space, and present cutting-edge techniques to speed up A* and Dijkstra. The "Tactics and Strategy" section focuses largely on combat decisions made in a wide variety of genres such as RTS, RPG, MOBA, strategy, and tower defense games. In the "Character Behavior" section, we look at individual AI behavior such as character interactions, modeling knowledge, efficient simulation, difficulty balancing, and making decisions with case studies from both commercial games (*Paragon*, *Dragon Age Inquisition*, and *FINAL FANTASY XV*) and indie games (*Project Highrise* and *Talk of the Town*). Finally, we end with the "Odds and Ends" section that contains chapters on specialized AI topics ranging from recommendation systems to random number generation and procedural content generation.

Right now, the game AI community is larger than ever and I want to invite you to discover all of the wonderful resources that are available. In addition to reading about new game AI techniques in the "Game AI Pro" book series, there are annual conferences, which are academic and developer centric, all over the globe. Organized by developers, there is the GDC AI Summit in San Francisco and the Game/AI Conference in Europe.

Organized by academia, there is the AAAI Conference on Artificial Intelligence and Interactive Digital Entertainment (AIIDE) and the IEEE Conference on Computational Intelligence and Games. Outside of events, there are two communities that have also sprung up to help developers. The AI Game Programmers Guild is a free professional group with more than 500 worldwide members (http://www.gameai.com), and there is a wonderful community of hobbyists and professionals at AiGameDev.com. We warmly welcome you to come and hang out with us at any one of these conferences or participate in one of our online communities!

Web Materials

Example programs and source code to accompany the chapters are available at http://www.gameaipro.com.

General System Requirements

The following are required to compile and execute the example programs:

- The DirectX August 2009 SDK
- DirectX 9.0 compatible or newer graphics card
- Windows 7 or newer
- Visual C++ .NET 2012 or newer

Updates

Example programs and source code will be updated as needed.

Comments and Suggestions

Please send any comments or suggestions to steve.rabin@gmail.com.

Acknowledgments

Game AI Pro 3 required a huge team effort to come together. First, I humbly thank the five section editors for the excellent job they did in selecting, guiding, and editing the contributions in this book. The section editors were as follows:

- Neil Kirby—General Wisdom
- Alex Champandard—Architecture
- Nathan R. Sturtevant—Movement and Pathfinding
- Damián Isla—Character Behavior
- Kevin Dill—Tactics and Strategy; Odds and Ends

The wonderful cover artwork has been provided courtesy of Epic Games from the multiplayer online battle arena game *Paragon*. Two chapters covering techniques from this game appear in this book: *Being Where It Counts: Telling Paragon Bots Where to Go* and *Paragon Bots: A Bag of Tricks*.

The team at CRC Press and A K Peters have done an excellent job, making this whole project happen. I want to thank Rick Adams, Jessica Vega, and the entire production team, who took the contributions and carefully turned them into this book.

Special thanks go to our families and friends, who have supported us and endured the intense production cycle that required long hours, evenings, and weekends.

About the Editors

Alex Champandard is the founder of AiGameDev.com, the largest online hub for artificial intelligence in games. He has worked in the industry as a senior AI programmer for many years, most notably for Rockstar Games where he also worked on the animation technology of *Max Payne 3*. He regularly consults with leading studios in Europe, most notably at Guerrilla Games on the multiplayer bots for *KillZone 2 & 3*. Alex is also the event director for the Game/AI Conference, the largest independent event dedicated to AI in games.

Kevin Dill is a member of the senior technical staff at Lockheed Martin Rotary & Missions Systems and the chief architect of the Game AI Architecture. He is a veteran of the game and military simulation industries with more than 15 years' experience, and has worked on AI for everything from games (including several major hits, such as *Red Dead Redemption*, *Iron Man*, and *Zoo Tycoon 2*) to military training to emotive avatars. His professional interests include improved techniques for behavior specification, tactical and strategic AI, spatial reasoning, and believable characters. He was the technical editor for *Introduction to Game AI* and *Behavioral Mathematics for Game AI*, and a section editor for "AI Game Programming Wisdom 4" and the "Game AI Pro" series. He is a prolific author and speaker, and has taught at Harvard University, Cambridge, Massachusetts, Boston University, Boston, Massachusetts, and Northeastern University, Boston, Massachusetts.

Damián Isla has been working on and writing about game technology for more than a decade. He is a cofounder of the indie game studio, The Molasses Flood, and was previously the president of Moonshot Games, where he directed *Third Eye Crime*, an innovative AI-based stealth/puzzle/telepathy game. Before joining Moonshot, Damián was the AI and Gameplay engineering lead at Bungie Studios, where he was responsible for the AI in the mega-hit first-person shooters *Halo 2* and *Halo 3*. He also contributed to the AI of *Bioshock: Infinite*, and to the early development of *Destiny*.

Neil Kirby cofounded the IGDA Foundation and serves on its board. He oversees the Eric Dybsand AI Memorial Scholarship to GDC that is awarded each year and works with the IGDA Foundation Scholars and Ambassadors programs.

Neil is a section editor in the "Game AI Pro" book series. He is the author of *An Introduction to Game AI*. His other publications include articles in volumes I, II, and IV of *AI Game Programming Wisdom*. He cowrote "Effective Requirements Traceability: Models, Tools and Practices" for the *Bell Labs Technical Journal*. His 1991 paper, "Artificial Intelligence without AI: An evolutionary Approach," may well show the first use of what is now known as "circle strafing" in a game. His other papers and presentations can be found in the proceedings of the Computer Game Developers Conference from 1991 to present as well as the 2003 Australian Game Developers Conference.

He is a member of technical staff at Nokia. He currently develops .NET solutions used to support requirements traceability. He also provides software architecture consulting services. His previous assignments have included building speech recognition software and teaching at the university level. He has been the head judge of The Ohio State University's Fundamentals of Engineering Honors robot competition for many years.

Neil holds a master's degree in computer science from The Ohio State University, Columbus, Ohio. He lives with his spouse in central Ohio. There he chairs his local village planning commission and volunteers for the historical society.

Steve Rabin has been a key figure in the game AI community for more than a decade and is currently a principal software engineer at Nintendo Technology Development. After initially working as an AI engineer at several Seattle startups, he managed and edited seven game AI books in the "Game AI Pro" series and the "AI Game Programming Wisdom" series. He also edited the book *Introduction to Game Development* and has more than two dozen articles published in the "Game Programming Gems" series. He has been an invited keynote speaker at several AI conferences, founded the AI Game Programmers Guild in 2008, and founded the GDC AI Summit where he has been a summit adviser since 2009. Steve is a principal lecturer at the DigiPen Institute of Technology, Redmond, Washington, where he has taught game AI since 2006. He earned a BS in computer engineering and an MS in computer science, both at the University of Washington, Seattle, Washington.

Nathan R. Sturtevant is an associate professor of computer science at the University of Denver, Denver, Colorado, where he works on AI and games. He began his games career working on shareware games as a college student in the mid-1990s, and returned to the game industry to write the pathfinding engine for *Dragon Age: Origins*. In addition to his work collaborating with the game industry (through work on "Game AI Pro" books, speaking at GDC, and other projects), Nathan guides capstone game projects at the University of Denver and develops games in his free time.

Contributors

Kyle Anderson has written games for everything from cell phones and PCs to low-level hardware controllers for motion-activated exergaming equipment. He is currently interested in all things VR. Kyle is the lead programmer at Shikigami Games.

Nicolas A. Barriga is a PhD candidate at the University of Alberta, Edmonton, Canada. He earned BSc (engineering) and MSc degrees in informatics engineering at Universidad Técnica Federico Santa María, Valparaíso, Chile. After a few years working as a software engineer for Gemini and ALMA astronomical observatories, he came back to graduate school and is currently working on state and action abstraction mechanisms for RTS games.

Daniel Brewer graduated from University of Natal Durban, South Africa, in 2000 with a BSc (engineering) in electronic engineering focusing on artificial intelligence, control systems, and data communications. He worked at Cathexis Technologies for six years, as a software engineer writing software for digital surveillance systems, where he was responsible for operating system drivers for PCI video capture cards, image capture scheduling, video compression, and image processing algorithms such as motion detection, people counting, and visual camera tamper detection. He moved to Digital Extremes in 2007 where he is the lead AI programmer and has worked on several titles including *Dark Sector* (March 2008), *BioShock 2* multiplayer (February 2010), and *The Darkness II* (February 2012), *Halo 4* multiplayer DLC packages (2012), and *Warframe* (2013).

Michael Buro is a professor in the computing science department at the University of Alberta, Edmonton, Canada. He received his PhD in 1994 for his work on *Logistello*—an Othello program that defeated the reigning human World champion 6-0. His current research interests include heuristic search, pathfinding, abstraction, state inference, and opponent modeling applied to video games and card games. In these areas, Michael and his students have made numerous contributions, culminating in developing fast geometric pathfinding algorithms and creating the World's best Skat playing program and one of the strongest *StarCraft: Brood War* bots.

David Churchill is the lead AI programmer for Lunarch Studios on the online strategy game, *Prismata*. He completed his PhD in computing science at the University of Alberta, Edmonton, Canada, in the area of artificial intelligence for video games, specifically in real-time heuristic search techniques for *StarCraft*. Since 2011, he has been the organizer of the AIIDE *Starcraft* AI Competition, and won the competition in 2013 with his entry UAlbertaBot.

Christopher Dragert received his PhD in computer science from McGill University, Montréal, Canada. His research focused on the application of software engineering techniques to the development process of game AI, with work being published at top academic conferences, including AIIDE, FDG, FSE, and GAS. Recently, he spoke at GDC 2016 and authored a chapter in the recent book *Computer Games and Software Engineering.* Chris is currently employed at Ubisoft Toronto as an AI programmer on *Watch Dogs 2*.

Anthony Francis, by day, studies human and other minds to create intelligent machines and emotional robots; by night, he writes urban fantasy and draws comic books. His work explores deep learning for robotic control at Google Research. He earned his PhD at Georgia Institute of Technology, Atlanta, Georgia, studying contextual memory for information retrieval, but also worked on emotional long-term memory for robot pets, a project documented on the Google Research blog as "Maybe your computer just needs a hug." Anthony is best known for his "Skindancer" series of urban fantasy novels featuring magical tattoo artist Dakota Frost, including the award-winning *Frost Moon* and its sequels *Blood Rock* and *Liquid Fire*. Anthony lives in San Jose with his wife and cats, but his heart will always belong in Atlanta. You can follow Anthony online at http://www.dresan.com/

David "Rez" Graham is a senior AI programmer currently working independently on a self-funded unannounced project. Before that, he was the director of game programming at the Academy of Art University's School of Game Development, San Francisco, California, where he built the entire game programming curriculum from scratch. He has worked in the game industry as an engineer since 2005, spending most of that time working on various kinds of AI, from platformer enemy AI to full simulation games. Most recently, he was the lead AI programmer on *The Sims 4* at Maxis. Before that, he worked at PlayFirst, Slipgate Ironworks, Planet Moon Studios, and Super-Ego Games. He is the coauthor of *Game Coding Complete* (4th edition), has two articles in *Game AI Pro*, and regularly speaks at the Game Developers Conference. Rez spends his free time acting and running tabletop RPGs.

Fabien Gravot made his debut in the game industry in 2011 as an AI researcher with Square Enix. He has worked on a navigation mesh solution for both *FINAL FANTASY XIV: A REALM REBORN* and *FINAL FANTASY XV*. Previously, he had been working on robot AI and autonomous driving. He thought that games were less risky than moving one ton of metal with his program. He received his PhD in computer science from the Paul Sabatier University, Toulouse, France, in 2004.

Ingimar Hólm Guðmundsson is an AI engineer at Square Enix and is focused on character motion, simulations, and workflow tools. His current project is *FINAL FANTASY XV*, a Japanese role-playing game that takes players on a journey of four friends, as their kingdom is threatened and potentially lost. Ingimar has worked on numerous titles in the video game industry, most notably the BAFTA award winning, *Total War: Shogun 2* (2011) by Creative Assembly, where he was the battle AI programmer responsible for the real-time battle strategies. Previously he worked on other *Total War* games, such as *Napoleon: Total War* (2010), and *Empire: Total War* (2009), which was his first foray into the game industry. Ingimar has a master's degree in applied artificial intelligence from the University of Exeter, Exeter, the United Kingdom, and an undergraduate degree in physics from the University of Iceland, Reykjavík, Iceland.

Sebastian Hanlon is a programmer-turned-designer who has been with BioWare Edmonton since 2006. His shipped game credits include *Dragon Age: Origins*, *Dragon Age II*, *Dragon Age: Inquisition*, *Mass Effect 2*, and *Mass Effect 3*. Sebastian holds a BSc and an MSc in computer science from the University of Lethbridge, Lethbridge, Canada.

Jurie Horneman has been programming, designing, and producing games since 1991, at companies such as Rockstar Games, Blue Byte Software, and Thalion Software. He has a strong interest in the intersection of game design, programming, and storytelling.

Ian Horswill is an associate professor of computer science at Northwestern University, Evanston, Illinois, where he teaches and does research on interactive entertainment technologies and cognitive modeling for virtual characters. He received his PhD in computer science from the Massachusetts Institute of Technology, Cambridge, Massachusetts, in 1993, is an associate editor of *IEEE Transactions of Computational Intelligence and AI in Games*, is a past chair of the standing committee of the "AAAI Symposium" series, and has spoken at both the Education and AI Summits at GDC.

Éric Jacopin is a professor at the French Military Academy of Saint-Cyr, Guer, France where he headed the Computer Science Research Laboratory from 1998 to 2012; this includes teaching Turing machines, war games and project management, and the management of international internships for computer science cadets. His research has been in the area of AI Planning for the past 25 years, not only from the viewpoint of artificial intelligence but also from everyday life and gaming perspectives. He received his PhD (1993) and his habilitation to direct research (1999), both from the Pierre and Marie Curie University (Paris VI), Paris, France.

Sumeet Jakatdar is the lead AI engineer at Treyarch/Activision Blizzard, Santa Monica, California, and has been working there for more than 9 years. He has been involved in developing AI for some of the Activision's most popular first-person shooter games. During his years as an AI developer, he has worked on gameplay programming, level design, behavior, animation systems, and networking. Before joining the industry in 2007, he received MS degree in computer science from University of Southern California, Los Angeles, California.

Chris Jenner obtained his PhD in 1998 from the University of Newcastle upon Tyne, the United Kingdom. He has been working as a programmer in the game industry since 1999, in the studio that is now known as Ubisoft Reflections, and have worked on *Driver 2*, *Stuntman*, *Driver 3*, *Driver Parallel Lines*, *Driver San Francisco*, *Just Dance 3*, *Just Dance 4*, *The Crew*, *Assassins Creed: Syndicate*, and *The Division*.

Eric Johnson is a senior AI engineer in the Advanced Technology Division of SQUARE ENIX, developing the AI systems for *KINGDOM HEARTS III*. Before joining the industry in 2008, Eric received his master's degree in artificial intelligence from the Georgia Institute of Technology, Atlanta, Georgia, focusing on case-based reasoning for real-time strategy games. In addition to SQUARE ENIX, Eric has developed AI systems at CCP, KIXEYE, and LucasArts.

Matthew W. Johnson joined Square Enix in 2013 after completing his PhD in data analytics and data mining. He develops various AI techniques and tools used in the production of *FINAL FANTASY XV*. Before *FINAL FANTASY*, he did research in educational data mining and personalized learning systems known as intelligent tutoring systems.

Tomoki Komatsu graduated from Tohoku University, Sendai, Japan, and completed the master's degree in computer science. Then he started his career as an AI Engineer at SQUARE ENIX in 2014. He developed the Monster AI and supported the development of the tools for *FINAL FANTASY XV*.

Mark Langerak is the principal software engineer at Microsoft, where he works on augmented reality applications and computer vision technologies for the HoloLens platform. Mark has been in the game industry since the early 1990s. Before joining Microsoft, he worked at Microprose, Sony/Psygnosis, Sega, DreamWorks Interactive, Maxis, Electronic Arts, and Pandemic Studios, in graphics engineer, lead programmer, and technical director roles.

Mike Lewis entered the game industry as a programmer in early 2002, and has spent most of the intervening years focusing on game AI and surrounding technologies. He has lectured at the Game Developers Conference and published articles in previous volumes of *Game AI Pro*. Currently, Mike calls ArenaNet, LLC, home, where he tirelessly schemes to bring better AI to the world of massively multiplayer online gaming.

John Manslow started writing games on his Vic-20 as a teenager and gradually became more and more interested in smart AI. Having completed a degree and then a PhD in the subject, he joined Codemasters as the AI specialist in their R&D team, where he worked on several projects to bring the next generation AI to Codemasters' games. Since then, John has worked for several companies outside the industry but has remained focused on AI and statistical analytics.

Eric Martel has been developing games for more than 15 years. He has worked on numerous franchises such as *Far Cry*, *Assassin's Creed*, and *Thief*. He is the published author of "An Analysis of *Far Cry: Instincts'* Anchor System" in AI Game Programming Wisdom 3 and "Tips and Tricks for a Robust Third Person Camera System" in *Game AI Pro*.

He is currently a lead AI programmer at Ubisoft Québec studio where he recently worked on *Assassin's Creed Syndicate*.

Michael Mateas is the codirector of Expressive Intelligence Studio and the director of the Center for Games and Playable Media at the University of California, Santa Cruz, California. His research in game AI focuses on enabling new forms of gameplay through innovative AI solutions. The Expressive Intelligence Studio has ongoing projects in autonomous characters, interactive storytelling, game design support systems, AI models of creativity, and automated game generation. With Andrew Stern, Michael created *Façade*, which uses AI techniques to combine rich autonomous characters with interactive plot control to create the world's first, fully produced, real-time, interactive drama. Michael received his PhD in computer science from Carnegie Mellon University, Pittsburgh, Pennsylvania.

Kousuke Namiki joined FROM SOFTWARE in 2009 and worked on *STEEL BATTALION* and *Monster Hunter Diary: Poka Poka Airou Village*. He has been with SQUARE ENIX since 2012 as an AI programmer developing Luminous Studio. Now he is engaged in the development of enemy character AI for *FINAL FANTASY XV*.

Shintaro Minamino graduated from a game development technical college in Japan in 2005, and has been an engineer at Square Enix Japan since 2012. His most recent work has focused on the asset building pipeline and game metrics system for *FINAL FANTASY XV*. He has been a leader of the Engineering Department of Computer Entertainment Developers Conference (CEDEC) since 2012. Before joining Square Enix, he worked for seven years (2005–2012) on numerous game titles at Polygon Magic, Inc. Japan, where he was also the leader of the R&D section of GeePlus, Inc., Polygon Magic's child company.

Youichiro Miyake is the lead AI researcher at Square Enix, working as the leader of the AI unit for the next-generation game engine Luminous Studio. He is the chairman of the IGDA JAPAN SIG-AI and a board member of DiGRA JAPAN. He has been developing and researching game AI since 2004. He developed the technical design of AI for the following game titles: *Chromehounds* (2006, Xbox 360), *Demon's Souls* (2009, PlayStation 3), and *Armored Core V* (2012, Xbox 360, PlayStation 3), developed by FromSoftware. At Square Enix, he was engaged in the AI development of *FINAL FANTASY XIV: A Realm Reborn*. At present, he is developing AI in *FINAL FANTASY XV* as the lead AI technical architect. He has published papers and books about game AI technologies and has given many lectures at universities and conferences. He was a keynote speaker of GAMEON ASIA 2012 and a game AI course speaker in SIGGRAPH ASIA 2015. His paper "Current Status of Applying Artificial Intelligence in Digital Games" will be published in the *Handbook of Digital Games and Entertainment Technologies* by Springer.

Sergio Ocio Barriales has been working in the game industry since 2005. He received his PhD in 2010 from the University of Oviedo, Asturias, Spain, with his thesis about hinted-execution behavior trees. He has worked on the AI for numerous major titles, such as *Driver San Francisco*, *Splinter Cell: Blacklist*, *DOOM*, and *Watch_Dogs 2*. He joined the team at Hangar 13 as a lead AI engineer in 2016, where he continues pushing character AI forward.

Graham Pentheny is an independent game developer from Cambridge, Massachusetts. He currently runs the local Boston Unity3D user group and does engineering work and consultation with various local studios. Previously, he worked with Dr. Jeff Orkin on conversational AI systems at Giant Otter, led AI and engine development at Subatomic Studios, and is credited on the *Fieldrunners* tower defense games. He received a BS in both computer science and interactive media and game development from Worcester Polytechnic Institute, Worcester, Massachusetts. (grahamboree.com)

Prasert Prasertvithyakarn is the lead game designer for *FINAL FANTASY XV* and is responsible for the game's AI main player characters. He was the leader of the enemy team in *MAJIN AND THE FORSAKEN KINGDOM* (2010, Xbox360, PlayStations3) at GAME REPUBLIC INC. before joining SQUARE ENIX in 2010.

Gijs-Jan Roelofs is the AI and lead programmer at Goldhawk Interactive where he has, among other projects, worked on the "Xenonauts" series. He is also the founder of CodePoKE, an independent game development company aimed at innovative applications of AI in games that cooperates with the Department of Knowledge Engineering at Maastricht University, Maastricht, the Netherlands. His passion for AI was ignited by Professor Mark Winands and the emergence of MCTS during his time in Maastricht. He is currently working on techniques for procedural generation of narratives, and tactical AI using MCTS.

Jeff Rollason is an AI developer who currently heads, and is a cofounder of, AI Factory Ltd, a company with an estimated 200 million users (including more than 129 million Android downloads). AI Factory was founded in 2003 with the premise of creating modular AI and games that would be licensed to third parties. The business has been very successful, with clients such as Microsoft. AI Factory's game engines appear in consoles, PCs, in-flight entertainment, and mobile devices. In addition to his work at AI Factory, Jeff has worked for 17 years in academia, including teaching core computer architecture courses at King's College London, the United Kingdom. He has published in numerous journals and books, including the journal *Artificial Intelligence*. His programs have also competed in computer tournaments for Chess, Go, and particularly Shogi (Japanese Chess), where his program *Shotest* twice ranked third in the world.

James Ryan is a PhD student of computer science at the University of California, Santa Cruz, California, working with the Expressive Intelligence Studio. He earned his BA in linguistics and MS in health informatics (with a minor in cognitive science) at the University of Minnesota, Minneapolis, Minnesota. His current research agenda spans two main topics: building autonomous agents who construct personal narratives out of their subjective experience in simulated worlds, and developing new technologies for freeform conversational interaction in games (by integrating systems for dialog management, natural language generation, and natural language understanding).

Kazuya Shimokawa researched and developed Computer Go AI in his master course at the University of Electro-Communications, Tokyo, Japan. He has been with SQUARE ENIX since 2013. At present, he is developing AI in *FINAL FANTASY XV* and was part of the team that developed Luminous Studio Tools.

Youji Shirakami has worked as a programmer in SQUARE ENIX since 2005. Before that, he worked as an engineer for transportation systems. He was engaged in the development of *Seiken Densetsu FRIENDS of MANA* (Mobile), *KINGDOM HEARTS* (Mobile), and *FINAL FANTASY TYPE-0* (PSP). His current tasks include implementation of the AI Graph Editor and character AI development.

Hendrik Skubch joined Square Enix in Japan in 2013 as an AI researcher, where he develops generic AI technologies for all aspects of game AI. In 2014, he joined a focused effort on *FINAL FANTASY XV* as a senior AI engineer. Before entering the game industry, he researched cooperative robotics and led a robotic soccer team within the RoboCup initiative. He received his PhD for work on robotic teams in 2012 from the University of Kassel, Kassel, Germany.

Marius Stanescu is a PhD candidate at the University of Alberta, Edmonton, Canada. He completed his MSc in artificial intelligence at University of Edinburgh, Edinburgh, the United Kingdom, in 2011, and became a researcher at the Center of Nanosciences for Renewable & Alternative Energy Sources of University of Bucharest, Bucharest, Romania, in 2012. Since 2013, he has been helping organize the AIIDE StarCraft Competition. Marius' main areas of research include machine learning, AI, and RTS games.

Ben Sunshine-Hill is the lead developer of Havok AI. He holds a PhD in computer science from the University of Pennsylvania, Philadelphia, Pennsylvania, for his work in perceptually driven simulation. He once saw a really cool-looking cow.

Joudan Tatsuhiro has been with SQUARE ENIX since 2011. He was engaged in the development at Luminous Studio, especially for tools. He has been developing buddy AI within the *FINAL FANTASY XV* team, especially for the meta-AI system that controls them.

Matthew Viglione is a cofounder of SomaSim, a Chicago-based indie studio founded in 2013 to create simulation games. He has extensive experience in creative direction, writing, and graphic design. Before starting SomaSim, Matthew was the director of communications for Catholic Charities in San Francisco, California.

Cody Watts is a programmer and professional game developer. Since 2010, he has been working at BioWare Edmonton, where he is variously described by his coworkers as "a freaking genius" and "a space wizard ninja." While at BioWare, Cody has contributed to such AAA titles as *Dragon Age: Origins*, *Dragon Age II*, *Dragon Age: Inquisition* and *Mass Effect: Andromeda*. Cody holds a BSc and an MSc in computer science from the University of Calgary, Calgary, Canada, but more importantly, he beat *SpaceChem*—and that is *way* harder than defending a master's thesis. Follow Cody's latest adventures at www.codywatts.com.

Ben G. Weber is a senior data scientist at Electronic Arts (EA), where his current focus is on improving the computing infrastructure and workflows used by the data science and analytics teams. He received his PhD in computer science from University of California, Santa Cruz, California, where he studied Game AI and machine learning. Before joining EA, Ben worked as a user research analyst at Microsoft Studios and directed the BI and analytics team at Daybreak Games.

Baylor Wetzel has degrees in psychology and computer science and until recently taught artificial intelligence and English at a major university. When not making NPCs behave properly for others, he enjoys designing and writing dialog for his own story-rich indie games. Baylor currently works as a game designer at indie game studio Shikigami Games.

Takanori Yokoyama has worked as a game programmer in the game industry since 2004. He has been especially interested in game AI and implemented it for many game titles including *ENCHANT ARMS* (2006, Xbox360), *CHROME HOUNDS* (2006, Xbox360), and *Demon's Souls* (2009, PlayStation3) developed by FROM SOFTWARE. He is now working as an AI engineer at SQUARE ENIX.

David Young is a senior software engineer at Activision Treyarch, specializing in AI and animation systems, and he previously shipped both *Call of Duty Black Ops II* and *Black Ops III*. Before working in the game industry, David started his career at the NASA (National Aeronautics and Space Administration) Deep Space Network and later went on to work on the Curiosity rover mission at the NASA Jet Propulsion Laboratory, Pasadena, California. Currently, David is simultaneously pursuing a PhD at the University of Southern California, Los Angeles, California, focusing on real-time hair simulation techniques.

Mieszko Zieliński has worked in the game industry throughout his professional life—that is close to 13 years at the time of writing—most of which focused on game AI. For the past eight years, he has been with Epic Games, with the past five spent on leading the AI system development in Unreal Engine 4. He has recently been micromanaging Paragon bots, which he found a very refreshing activity after the time spent on working for generic AI systems.

Robert Zubek is a game developer and cofounder at SomaSim, a Chicago-based indie studio founded in 2013 to create simulation games. Previously, he built large-scale online social games at Zynga, MMO game and analytics infrastructure at Three Rings Design, and console games at Electronic Arts/Maxis. Before joining the industry, he specialized in artificial intelligence and robotics research. Robert holds a PhD in computer science from Northwestern University, Evanston, Illinois, where he also received his previous computer science degrees.

SECTION I
General Wisdom

1

The Illusion of Intelligence

Steve Rabin

1.1 Introduction

The secret is out. Game AI is seldom about any deep intelligence but rather about the illusion of intelligence. Often we are trying to create believable human behavior, but the actual intelligence that we are able to program is fairly constrained and painfully brittle. Yet, we struggle to put up a good show and strive to keep up the illusion.

Well, maybe we should be a little more purposeful and directly work on propping up the illusion, instead of shoring up the crumbling intelligence. Maybe there are tricks that we can use to fool the players into *believing* there is real intelligence there. Instead of working toward patching up the actual intelligence, perhaps we should also consciously work toward promoting the appearance of intelligence.

In fact, if you do not work on the illusion side of the equation, you are likely failing to do your job. Expectations play a huge role in how humans perceive the world, and if expectations are not properly managed, then even truly human-level intelligent behavior might be perceived as incompetent and decidedly nonhuman.

This chapter aims to accomplish two things. To start, we will explain why it is scientifically possible to trick players into believing there is real intelligence. Then, we will look at six concrete ways to perpetuate the illusion of intelligence in the eyes of the player.

1.2 Why the Illusion Works

There are three things that work to make players very susceptible to the illusion. First, players want to believe that there are glimmers of real human-level intelligence in their games. Second, humans have this desire to anthropomorphize nonhuman entities, seeing human traits and emotions where there are none. Third, expectations can easily become reality in the mind of the player.

1.2.1 Players Want to Believe

We have the perfect audience to make this work. The players want to believe—in fact, they are willing participants in the illusion. They want to believe that the fake video game characters have human-like qualities. The players are incredibly forgiving as long as the virtual humans do not make any glaring mistakes. Players simply need the right clues and suggestions for them to share and fully participate in the deception.

1.2.2 Eagerly Ready to Anthropomorphize

When people talk about a thing or creature as if it were human, they are anthropomorphizing it. Anthropomorphism appears to happen naturally as we see things all around us that remind of human traits, emotions, or intentions. Your computer hates you, your car is temperamental, and your recently picked flowers are starting to look sad.

One theory put forth by neuroscientists is that similar parts of the brain are involved when we think about both human and nonhuman entities (Gazzola et al. 2007). This suggests that anthropomorphism is the result of using similar processes as when we think about people. It is a sort of a misattribution effect that is perhaps hardwired into our brains.

Another theory is that when people try to understand incomprehensible behavior, they often apply familiar human traits to make sense of the situation (Waytz et al. 2010). So when a human-like entity in a game exhibits any kind of behavior, human-like traits are the first template we try to apply. How can we understand this behavior? Well, let us try applying human behavior and see if that explains what we are seeing. When this happens, the confounding of actual human intelligence with AI is greatly enhanced.

And here we are, as video game developers, presenting human-looking avatars that animate, move, and speak similar to humans. Anthropomorphism is a welcome effect that encourages the illusion.

1.2.3 The Power of Expectations

Expectations powerfully control how we experience the world. For example, if you believe a bottle of wine is very expensive, you will not only think the wine tastes better, but your actual enjoyment will be more. Researchers at Caltech and Stanford presented people with a $45 bottle of wine and a $5 bottle of wine. Using brain-imaging techniques, they found that the human brain actually *experiences more pleasure* when the participants believed they were drinking the expensive wine versus the cheap wine, even though both were the same (Plassmann et al. 2008). This is not people reporting that the wine was tastier—neurologically, the brain actually experienced more pleasure.

Similarly, the placebo effect is a real phenomenon in humans that likely works on the same mechanism of expectations. A *placebo* is a medically ineffective treatment for a medical condition that is intended to deceive the patient. If we give a person this ineffective treatment, the person will often have a perceived or actual improvement. This is called the *placebo effect* or *placebo response*. Brain-imaging techniques have shown that placebo causes real physiological changes in the brain that are measurable (Lieberman et al. 2004). The effect is attributed to the perceptions and expectations of the patient (Kirsch 1985).

Clearly, expectations can have a powerful effect on what we experience. This further emphasizes that managing player expectations can have a significant effect on promoting the illusion of intelligence.

1.3 Selling the Illusion

Now that we understand why the illusion works and how it is reinforced, our goal is to further encourage and nurture the illusion. This can be done through expectations and performance.

1.3.1 Promoting the Quality of the AI

One simple way to manage expectations is to simply tell the player about the strengths of the AI. Over the years, several games have chosen to tout the quality of their game's AI in press releases, interviews, and box art.

A positive example of this is from 2006 when the game *The Elder Scrolls IV: Oblivion* heavily promoted their Radiant AI system, which was subsequently used on *The Elder Scrolls V: Skyrim, Fallout 3, Fallout: New Vegas*, and *Fallout 4*. Similarly, the series *Left 4 Dead* let players know that an AI director was helping craft the tension and experience. When players have heard about or can even name the technology behind the game, then that is evidence it could be really good.

An example where this did not work out as well was *Madden NFL 98* that bragged in a press release about their liquid AI system used to make their video football players move and flow like water. This partly backfired due to the weak analogy, since water is not very intelligent. However, the worst blowback came from a competing football game, *NFL GameDay 98*, that snidely commented in a Next Generation magazine interview that "Liquid AI is the stuff that ran down EA's leg when they saw *GameDay*."

A subtle use of managing expectations is to use hints during loading screens to highlight aspects of the AI. If the AI is considering several aspects to make a particular decision, perhaps mention this to the player as part of a tip. It will make the player more aware of how the AI is responding, and it might make both the AI and the game seem more interesting.

If your game is doing something truly remarkable, then there might be value in letting players know. However, you need to be confident that you can deliver and not have it backfire.

1.3.2 Perform with Animation and Dialog

The AI must give the performance of its short lifetime if it wants to impress. The chief way this is done is through subtle animation and dialog. Unfortunately, this is frustrating for most game AI programmers because they do not directly create the animations or the dialog. The best they can do is make compelling arguments to management that these assets should be created. However, this is so important that it really does need to become a priority.

To understand how important this is, let us work through a very short thought experiment. Imagine all of the ways that the player comes to understand and experience an AI character. Let us call this the *vocabulary* of the AI. The vocabulary consists of every dialog clip, every grunt, every animation, every movement, and every interaction. Imagine that an AI character had only two sound clips (an attack grunt and a death cry) and had only four animations (idle, walk, attack, and die). The vocabulary of this particular AI is severely stunted, ironically, with the most interesting behavior happening when it dies. There is virtually no way you can convey a deeply intelligent AI with such a limited vocabulary.

Fortunately, one way to programmatically add to an AI's vocabulary is with the head look. If the AI's head and gaze can be controlled directly, then you as an AI programmer can wield great power. With head control, you now have the ability for the AI to notice things, compare objects in the environment, anticipate actions, and truly seem aware. Let us illustrate this with a simple scenario. An AI has two enemies to fight: left bad guy and right bad guy. After running a complex evaluation, the AI decides it is best to fight the left bad guy. Fighting ensues, but the problem is that the subtleties of the decision were both instantaneous and hidden. However, what if the AI spends a second looking at each enemy and sizes them up before attacking the left bad guy. What if during the fight with the left bad guy, the AI occasionally looks back at the right bad guy to keep an eye on him. This can telegraph deep intelligence to the player for something that the AI instantaneously chose and is no longer concerned with. However, it is the showmanship of the situation that will convey a conscious and relatable AI character.

Another element of animation that programmers have control over is speed. Fast movements convey being upset, agitated, confused, and nervous. Slow movements convey being relaxed, calm, and in control over the situation. These are all very human adjectives that we might want the player to liberally apply to our AI characters.

In the right situation, one of the best reactions to play might be one that is completely ambiguous. Consider this stroke of genius from the 2005 game *Façade*. In *Façade*, there were two AI characters who would respond to free-form text entered by the player. When the AI inevitably did not understand a player statement or knew that the statement was of questionable moral content, one of the AI characters might respond simply with a raised eyebrow. The genius of this choice is that the interpretation is left up to the player, because it is an ambiguous reaction. However, it is the perfect time for the player to project all kinds of human properties and thought processes onto the AI, furthering the illusion.

One of the truly great secrets in game AI is to use dialog between AI characters to emphasize and sell the intelligence. The first prominent example of this was in *F.E.A.R.* where pursuing AI guards would converse with each other, remarking, "Where did the player go?" and responding with, "He is behind the boxes!" All of a sudden, not only were the guards hunting down the player, but they were working together! The surprising thing was that this was all smoke and mirrors. An AI module simply monitored what was happening and called for these dialog moments as they fit the moment (Orkin 2015). It is a great technique that has been used many times since in games such as *The Last of Us*.

1.3.3 Stop Moving Like a Robot

Although it is crucial to have an adequate vocabulary, the quality of the movement is the other aspect that needs careful attention. If the AI movement is not smooth and lifelike, then the illusion will start to wear thin.

This is where knowledge of animation techniques, such as anticipation, ease-in, and ease out, can really help. Your goal is to make the movement fluid and credible. Work to identify jarring movements and eliminate them. Discontinuous movement is incredibly unnatural and draws attention to the inauthenticity of the situation. Be very sensitive to this when there are collisions. Sometimes, it is much better to briefly allow object penetration, thus avoiding hard collisions and discontinuous movement.

Reaction times are another key area that has the potential to destroy the illusion. Humans are incapable of instantaneous reaction. The fastest a hyperfocused human can react is 0.2 seconds with mental comparisons requiring a bare minimum of 0.4 seconds (Rabin 2015). Use these times as the baseline to always delay the results of a decision. However, realize that distracted or unfocused characters would have much longer reaction times.

A final aspect of movement that should be mentioned is that your AI should stop pursuing the player relentlessly, similar to a terminator. Intelligent creatures sometimes stop, they reflect, they hesitate, they reconsider, they second-guess themselves, they size up their opponent, and they pause. Movement is an indication of deeper thought processes, and variations in movement can convey all of these thoughts and more. In addition, enemies that temporarily back off are much more enjoyable adversaries. This is an old advice that was well known even during the early 1980s, as shown by the wave-patterned attack/retreat behavior of ghosts in *Pac-Man*.

1.3.4 Have a Reason to Exist

AI characters need to stop standing around waiting for the player to approach. Characters with nothing to do are a clear signal that the AI is fake and has no real purpose. AI characters should have a reason to exist beyond the player.

For each AI character, this can be as simple as figuring out their backstory, and why they are in their current situation. What is their agenda for today? By giving each AI its own motivations (beyond its interactions with the player), it can make each character feel more connected to the game world. After all, the game world is their home and reality. If it makes sense, it will be much more natural and realistic to the player.

1.3.5 Project a Strong Personality

Personality is the culmination of all the properties of an intelligent character. It implies the entire existence of the character up until the point you interact with it: where it was born, how it grew up, and how it interacts with its reality. It exudes emotions, motives, purpose, and competence. Personality implies incredible depth and authenticity.

Because personality has such power and influence, a carefully crafted personality can convincingly convey there is something beneath the surface of your characters, whether there is or not. Personality can be used as a shell around your character to imply humanistic qualities that are simply an illusion. How you leverage this tool can completely change how your players feel about the game.

In addition, a strong personality goes a long way to covering up any inconsistencies in the behavior or logic of a character. Strong personalities can be irrational and unpredictable, allowing incredible leeway in how players might critique their actions.

1.3.6 React Emotionally on Demand

Some programmers have this weird obsession with trying to get game AI to simulate emotions. This seems to stem from the belief that if an AI was truly sad, angry, or happy, then maybe it might finally convince players that some deep kind of intelligence was actually there. This can be equated to the practice of method acting, where an actor will immerse themselves in the character, and through this process, it is hoped that authenticity will emanate out of their performance. It seems to be an unfounded belief that if an AI truly feels emotions, perhaps it will pervade the AI's behavior, and maybe the player will notice.

Without simulating everything that makes up human-level intelligence, this approach for the purposes of games appears misguided. The more straightforward approach would be to directly convey emotions as directly demanded by the situation and the environment. For example, if surrounded by overwhelming forces, fear would be a good emotion to directly convey. Fear does not need to emanate from a simulation within the character; it can be directly shown through dialog and animation when the situation calls for it. If a creature calculates that it is doomed, it should give a performance that matches the situation, conveying a fear of death.

Players can only see an AI's behavior, not what is being simulated. If you want to make an AI appear emotional, then directly show that specific emotion in the correct situations. This can have a dramatic effect on how the player feels toward the AI.

1.4 Conclusion

In this chapter, we looked at the importance of promoting the illusion of intelligence. It is not enough for game AI characters to actually have intelligence, but there is a need and obligation to actively sell the illusion. Luckily, there are many things helping us out, such as players who are willing participants, unconscious anthropomorphism, and the power of setting expectations.

Fortunately, there are many levers that we have in order to promote the illusion of intelligence. We covered six main areas: promoting the quality of the AI, perform with animation and dialog, stop moving like a robot, have a reason to exist, project a strong personality, and react emotionally on demand. With many of these tricks up your sleeve, you should not only be able to sell the illusion, but master it.

References

Gazzola, V., Rizzolatti, G., Wicker, B., and Keysers, C. 2007. The anthropomorphic brain: The mirror neuron system responds to human and robotic actions. *NeuroImage*, 35, 1674–1684.

Kirsch, I. 1985. Response expectancy as a determinant of experience and behavior. *American Psychologist*, 40 (11), 1189–1202.

Lieberman, M. D., Jarcho, J. M., Berman, S., Naliboff, B. D., Suyenobu, B. Y., Mandelkern, M., and Mayer, E. A. 2004. The neural correlates of placebo effects: A disruption account. *Neuroimage*, 22, 447–455.

Orkin, J. 2015. Combat dialog in FEAR: The illusion of communication. In *Game AI Pro 2*, ed. S. Rabin. Boca Raton, FL: CRC Press.

Plassmann, H., O'Doherty, J., Shiv, B., and Rangel, A. 2008. Marketing actions can modulate neural representations of experienced pleasantness. *Proceedings of the National Academy of Sciences USA*, 105, 1050–1054.

Rabin, S. 2015. Agent reaction time: How fast should an AI react? In *Game AI Pro 2*, ed. S. Rabin. Boca Raton, FL: CRC Press.

Waytz, A., Morewedge, C. K., Epley, N., Monteleone, G., Gao, J. H., and Cacioppo, J. T. 2010. Making sense by making sentient: Effectance motivation increases anthropomorphism. *Journal of Personality and Social Psychology*, 99 (3), 410–435.

2

Creating the Past, Present, and Future with Random Walks

John Manslow

2.1 Introduction

Randomness plays an important role in many games by adding replay value and forcing the player to adapt to unpredictable events. It often takes the form of variables with values that change gradually but randomly with time and hence perform what are technically known as random walks. Such variables might affect visibility or cloud cover in a weather simulation, the mood of an NPC, the loyalty of a political faction, or the price of a commodity. This chapter will describe the statistical properties of normally distributed random walks and will show how they can be shaped and manipulated so that they remain unpredictable while also being subject to scripted constraints and responsive to player interaction.

We begin by describing how to generate a simple random walk and discuss some of its limitations. We then show how to overcome those limitations using the walk's statistical properties to efficiently sample from it at arbitrary points in its past and future. Next, we discuss how to fix the values of the walk at specific points in time, how to control the general shape of the movement of the walk between them, and how to limit the walk to a specific range of values. Finally, we describe how to generate random walks with arbitrary probability distributions and to allow for player interaction. The book's web site contains spreadsheets and C++ source code for all the techniques that are described in this chapter.

2.2 Problems with a Basic Random Walk

One simple way to generate a random walk is to initialize a variable, say x, to some desired starting value x_0, and then, on each step of the simulation of the game world, add a sample from a normal distribution (a bell curve). This process is fast and efficient and produces values of x that start at x_0 and then randomly wander around, perhaps ending up a long way from the starting point or perhaps returning to a point close to it.

This approach is not without its problems, however. For example, how can we work out what the value of x will be two days from now? Equivalently, what value should x be at right now, given that the player last observed it having a particular value two days ago? Perhaps we are simulating the prices of commodities in a large procedurally generated universe, and the player has just returned to a planet that they last visited two days ago. This is the problem of extrapolating a random walk.

2.3 Solving the Extrapolation Problem Using Statistical Methods

One way to solve the extrapolation problem is to quickly simulate the missing part of the random walk. However, this might be computationally infeasible or undesirable, particularly if we are modeling a large number of random walks simultaneously, as might be the case if they represent prices in a virtual economy. Fortunately, we can use statistical methods to work out exactly how x will be distributed two days after it was last observed based only on the last observed value. Specifically, the central limit theorem tells us that if x had the value x_0 at time t_0, then at time t, x will be distributed as

$$p(x) \sim N\left(x_0, (t-t_0)\sigma_{xx}^2\right) \tag{2.1}$$

This is a normal distribution with the following two characteristics: it has mean x_0, which is the last observed value; and variance $(t - t_0)\sigma_{xx}^2$, where $t - t_0$ is the time since the last observation; and σ_{xx}^2 is a parameter that controls how quickly the walk can wander away from the starting point. In fact, since the distribution is normal, we know that x will lie in a range of approximately $x_0 \pm 1.96\sqrt{(t-t_0)\sigma_{xx}^2}$ about 95% of the time. Figure 2.1a shows a random walk generated using Equation 2.1 with x_0 equal to 90 and σ_{xx}^2 equal to one.

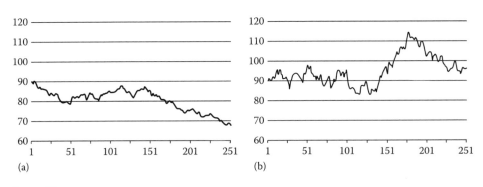

Figure 2.1

(a) shows 250 steps of a random walk generated using the extrapolation equation and (b) shows the effect of increasing σ^2_{xx}.

Figure 2.1b shows how increasing the value of σ^2_{xx} to five makes the walk wander about much more rapidly.

Of course, we need to select a specific value for x, and that can be done by sampling from $p(x)$. Although this produces a value of x that is technically not the same as the one that would have been produced by simulating two days' worth of random walk, it is impossible for the player to tell the difference because the true value and the sampled value have identical statistical properties given the player's limited state of knowledge about how the numbers are generated.

Equation 2.1 actually provides us with a much better way of generating random walks than the naive approach that was mentioned earlier. In particular, because $t - t_0$ represents the time between successive samples, it allows us to update the random walk in a way that is invariant to changes in the real times of steps in the simulation of the game world; the statistical properties of the walk will remain the same even if the times between updates are irregular or different on different platforms.

To generate a random walk using Equation 2.1, first pick an initial value for x_0 for use in $p(x)$, and then sample from $p(x)$ to get the next value, x_1. The value x_1 can then be used in place of x_0 in $p(x)$, and x_2 can be sampled from $p(x)$. Next, use x_2 in place of x_1 in $p(x)$ and sample x_3, and so on. In each case, the time interval should be the time between the observations of the random walk and hence might be the times between updates to the game world but might also be arbitrary and irregular intervals if the player does not observe the value of the walk on every tick of the game engine.

An interesting feature of Equation 2.1 is that it is time reversible and hence can be used to generate values of x in the past just as easily as ones in the future. Consider if a player visits a planet for the first time and needs to see a history of the price of a commodity. Equation 2.1 can be used to generate a sequence of samples that represent the price history. This is done in exactly the same way as when samples are generated forward in time except that x_1 would be interpreted as preceding x_0, x_2 would be interpreted as preceding x_1, and so on.

Although having the ability to extrapolate random walks forward and backward in time is extremely useful, we often need to do more. What happens, for example, if the player has observed the value of a variable but we need to make sure that it has some other specific value in one hour from now? This situation might arise if a prescribed event is due to occur—perhaps a war will affect commodity prices, or there will be a thunderstorm for which we need thick cloud cover. Since we now have two fixed points on the walk—the most recently observed value and a specified future value—it is no longer good enough to be able to extrapolate—we must interpolate.

2.4 Using Interpolation to Walk toward a Fixed Point

Now that we can generate samples from a random walk that are consistent with a single fixed value, we have everything we need to interpolate between two fixed values—we just need to generate samples that are consistent with both. We do this by calculating the probability distributions for x with respect to each of the fixed values and then multiply them together. As Equation 2.1 represents a normal distribution, we can write down the probability distribution for interpolated points quite easily:

$$
p(x) \sim N\left(\left(\frac{x_0}{(t-t_0)\sigma_{xx}^2} + \frac{x_n}{(t_n-t)\sigma_{xx}^2}\right) \middle/ \left(\frac{1}{(t-t_0)\sigma_{xx}^2} + \frac{1}{(t_n-t)\sigma_{xx}^2}\right),\right.
$$

$$
\left. 1 \middle/ \left(\frac{1}{(t-t_0)\sigma_{xx}^2} + \frac{1}{(t_n-t)\sigma_{xx}^2}\right)\right)
$$

(2.2)

Here x_0 is the first specified value, which occurs at time t_0; x_n is the second, which occurs at t_n; and x is the interpolated value of the walk at any time t. As before, in order to obtain a specific value for x, we need to sample from this distribution. Interpolated values of x are guaranteed to start at x_0 at time t_0, to randomly wander around between t_0 and t_n, and to converge to x_n at time t_n. Interpolation therefore makes it possible to precisely determine the value of the walk at specific points in time while leaving it free to wander about in between.

To generate a walk using Equation 2.2, use x_0 and x_n to sample from $p(x)$ to generate the next value of x and x_1. Next, use x_1 in place of x_0 and sample again from $p(x)$ to generate x_2, and so on—this can be done either forward or backward in time. The interpolation equation has fractal properties and will always reveal more detail no matter how small the interpolated interval. This means that it can be applied recursively to solve problems like allowing the player to see a 25-year history of the price of a particular commodity while also allowing him to zoom in on any part of the history to reveal submillisecond price movements.

2.5 Restricting the Walk to a Fixed Range of Values

One potentially undesirable feature of the random walk that has been described so far is that, given enough time, it might wander arbitrarily far from its starting point. In practice, however, we usually want it to take on some range of reasonable values, and this can easily be done by adding a statistical constraint that specifies that the values of x must, over an infinite amount of time, follow a particular probability distribution. If we choose a normal distribution with mean x^* and variance σ^{*2} to keep the math simple, the equation for extrapolating becomes

$$p(x) \sim N\left(\left(\frac{x_0}{(t-t_0)\sigma_{xx}^2} + \frac{x^*}{\sigma^{*2}}\right) \middle/ \left(\frac{1}{(t-t_0)\sigma_{xx}^2} + \frac{1}{\sigma^{*2}}\right), 1 \middle/ \left(\frac{1}{(t-t_0)\sigma_{xx}^2} + \frac{1}{\sigma^{*2}}\right)\right) \quad (2.3)$$

and the equation for interpolating becomes

$$p(x) \sim N\left(\frac{\left(\dfrac{x_0}{(t-t_0)\sigma_{xx}^2} + \dfrac{x^*}{\sigma^{*2}} + \dfrac{x_n}{(t_n-t)\sigma_{xx}^2}\right)}{\left(\dfrac{1}{(t-t_0)\sigma_{xx}^2} + \dfrac{1}{\sigma^{*2}} + \dfrac{1}{(t_n-t)\sigma_{xx}^2}\right)}, 1 \middle/ \left(\frac{1}{(t-t_0)\sigma_{xx}^2} + \frac{1}{\sigma^{*2}} + \frac{1}{(t_n-t)\sigma_{xx}^2}\right)\right) \quad (2.4)$$

A walk generated according to these equations is subject to a soft bound in the sense that it will lie in the range $x^* \pm 1.96\sqrt{\sigma^{*2}}$ about 95% of the time but will occasionally wander a little further, exceeding $x^* \pm 6.11\sqrt{\sigma^{*2}}$ with a probability of less than one in a billion. Figure 2.2a shows a random walk generated according to Equation 2.3 with x^* equal to 90 and σ^{*2} equal to 100.

If it is necessary to be absolutely certain that the walk will stay between fixed bounds, then it is better to use the unconstrained extrapolation and interpolation equations and postprocess the values they generate. If this is done by reflecting the walk off the bounds whenever it encounters them, the walk will retain the important statistical property that its behavior is invariant to the time steps that are used to generate it. To see how this works in practice, consider generating a random walk that must be constrained to lie between zero and one.

This can be done by generating a dummy variable x^* using the unconstrained extrapolation and interpolation equations but presenting a value x to the player that is derived according to the following rules:

```
if floor(x*) is even then x=x*-floor(x*)
otherwise x=1-x*+floor(x*).
```

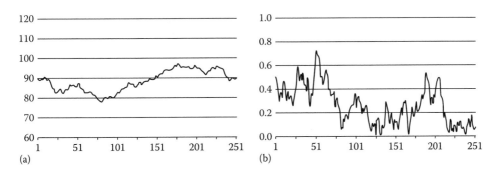

(a)   (b)

Figure 2.2

(a) shows a random walk that is soft bounded to have a normal distribution with $x^* = 90$ and $\sigma^{*2} = 100$ and (b) shows a random walk that is hard bounded to lie between zero and one.

x will perform the required random walk between the bounds zero and one, and in the long term will tend toward a uniform distribution. Figure 2.2b shows a random walk between the bounds zero and one that was generated using this technique. If we simply require x to be nonnegative, it is sufficient to take the absolute value of x^*; doing so will produce a random walk that is always nonnegative that will also, in the long term, tend toward a uniform distribution.

2.6 Manipulating and Shaping the Walk with Additive Functions

We have so far described how a random walk can be manipulated by using the interpolation equation with one or more fixed points. Interpolation guarantees that the walk will pass through the required points but it gives us no control over what it does in between—whether it follows roughly a straight line, roughly a curve, or makes multiple sudden jumps. Sometimes we want exactly that kind of control, and one way to achieve it is simply to add the random walk to another function that provides the basic form of the walk that we want. In this way, the random walk is just adding random variability to disguise the simple underlying form.

Consider a game where we have a commodity with a price of 90 credits that must rise to 110 credits in one hour from now. We could simply do this by using the interpolation equation and letting the walk find its own way between the two fixed price points, as shown in Figure 2.3a. Alternatively, we could choose a function that starts at 90 credits and rises to

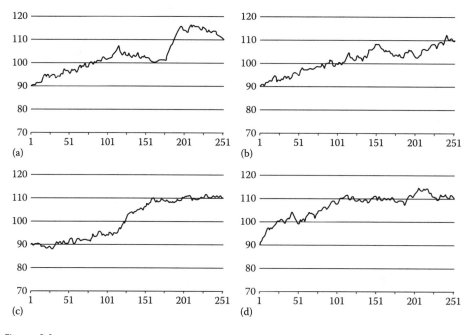

Figure 2.3

(a) shows the result of using the basic interpolation equation to generate a random walk from 90 to 110 in 250 steps, (b) shows the result of using a linear function to shape the walk, (c) shows the result of using the smoothstep function, and (d) shows the result of using the quarter circle function.

110 credits and provides us with the basic shape of the movement we want and add to it a random walk that is bounded by the interpolation equation to start and end at zero.

For example, we might want the price to move roughly linearly between the fixed points so we would use the linear function

$$x = 90(1-t)+110t \tag{2.5}$$

to provide the basic shape. Here, for convenience, t has been scaled so that it has the value zero at the start of the hour and one at the end. By adding the random walk to values of x generated by this formula and using the interpolation formula to generate the random walk in such a way that it starts and ends at zero, the sum of x and the random walk will be 90 at the start of the hour, 110 at the end, and move roughly linearly in between but with some random variation, as shown in Figure 2.3b.

Of course, we do not always have to use a linear function to provide the basic form. Other useful functions are the step function, which produces a sudden jump, the smooth-step function

$$x = 90 + 20(3t^2 - 2t^3) \tag{2.6}$$

which provides a smoothly curving transition, and the quarter circle function

$$x = 90 + 20\sqrt{1-(1-t)^2} \tag{2.7}$$

which rises rapidly at first and then levels out. Random walks based on the smoothstep and quarter circle functions are shown in Figure 2.3c and d respectively.

2.7 Using Additive Functions to Allow for Player Interaction

We now know how to extrapolate and interpolate random walks and bend and manipulate them in interesting ways, but how can we make them interactive so that the player can influence where they go? Fortunately, player interaction is just another way in which random walks are manipulated and hence all of the techniques that have already been described can be used to produce player interaction.

For example, the player might start a research program that produces a 25% reduction in the basic cost of a particular weapon class over the course of 15 minutes. This effect could be produced by simulating the price using a random walk with zero mean added to a function that represents the average price, which declines by 25% during the course of the research program. This will produce a price that randomly wanders around but is typically 25% lower once the research program has completed than it was before it was started.

Similarly, a player might sell a large quantity of a particular commodity, and we might want to simulate the effect of a temporary excess of supply over demand by showing a temporary reduction in its price. This could be done either by recording an observation of an artificially reduced price immediately after the sale and generating future prices by extrapolation or by subtracting an exponentially decaying function from the commodity's price and allowing the randomness of the walk to hide the function's simple form.

In the case of the research program, we must permanently record the action of the player, and its effect on price because the effect was permanent. In the case of the excess of supply over demand, the effect is essentially temporary because the exponential decay will ensure that it will eventually become so small that it can be ignored, at which point the game can forget about it unless it might need to create a price history at some point in the future.

2.8 Combining Walks to Simulate Dependent Variables

We have so far discussed how to generate independent random walks and provided a simple set of tools for controlling and manipulating them. In practice, we might need to generate random walks that are in some way related: perhaps we need two random walks that tend to go up and down at the same time, or one that tends to go up when another goes down or vice versa. These effects can easily be achieved by adding and multiplying random walks together and through the use of dummy variables.

Imagine that we need to simulate the prices of electronics and robotics products. Since electronics products are a core component of robotics products, we would expect the price of robotics products to increase if the price of electronics products increased—but not for either price to track the other exactly. This effect can be achieved by modeling the price of electronics products using a random walk and then using another random walk to model a dummy variable that represents either the difference in the prices of electronics and robotics products or their ratio.

If we decide to use a dummy variable to represent the difference between the prices, we could use a random walk with an x^* of 100 and σ^{*2} of 100 to model the price of electronics products and a walk with x^* of 25 and σ^{*2} of 100 to model the difference in the price of electronics products and robotics products. Since the price of robotics products would be the sum of the values of these two random walks, it would itself be a random walk, and it would have an x^* of 125 and an σ^{*2} of 200 and would tend to increase and decrease with the prices of electronics products, as shown in Figure 2.4.

Combinations of random walks can be made arbitrarily complex. The price of a space-craft, for example, could be a weighted sum of the prices of its various components plus the value of a dummy variable that represents the deviation of the actual sale price from the total cost of its components. In general, if a random walk is formed by a sum of N

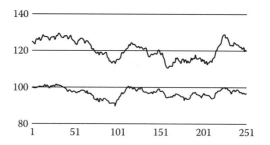

Figure 2.4

The lower random walk has $x^* = 100$ and $\sigma^{*2} = 100$ and represents the price of electronics products. The upper random walk is the sum of the lower random walk and another with $x^* = 25$ and $\sigma^{*2} = 100$ and represents the price of robotics products.

2. Creating the Past, Present, and Future with Random Walks

component random walks $x_1 \ldots x_N$ with means $x^*_1 \ldots x^*_N$ and variances $\sigma^{*2}_1 \ldots \sigma^{*2}_N$, which have weights $w_1 \ldots w_N$ in the sum, it will have mean

$$x^* = \sum_{n=1}^{N} w_n x^*_n \qquad (2.8)$$

and variance

$$\sigma^{*2} = \sum_{n=1}^{N} w_n^2 \sigma^{*2}_n \qquad (2.9)$$

It could be the case that the player can observe the values of all, some, or none of the components in the sum. We might, for example, want to make the prices of a commodity in a space simulation more similar in star systems that are closer together, and one way to do that is to use a dummy variable in each system to represent a dummy price that the player cannot observe. The price that the player would see in any particular system would then be the weighted sum of the dummy prices of neighboring systems with larger weights being assigned to closer systems. It is interesting to note that if one of the components in Equation 2.8 has a negative weight, then it produces a negative correlation; that is, when its value increases, it will tend to reduce the value of the sum. This can be useful when walks represent mutually competing interests such as the strengths of warring empires.

2.9 Generating Walks with Different Probability Distributions

If a random walk is generated according to the soft-bounded extrapolation equation, the values it takes will, over a long period of time, have a normal distribution with mean x^* and variance σ^{*2}. This is perfect for most applications, but we will occasionally want to generate a walk with a different distribution. For example, share prices have been modeled using log-normal distributions, and we can easily generate a log-normally distributed random walk by interpreting the extrapolation equation as modeling the natural logarithm of the share price and producing the actual price by applying the exponential function.

More generally, the inverse transformation method is often used to convert a random variable that is uniformly distributed between zero and one to another random variable with a particular target distribution by applying a nonlinear transformation. For example, taking the natural logarithm of a random variable that is uniformly distributed between zero and one produces a random variable that has an exponential distribution that can be used to realistically model the times between random events.

Although the random walks that have been described in this chapter have normal distributions, they can be made uniformly distributed by hard bounding them to a fixed interval, as was described earlier, or by transforming them using the cumulative normal distribution function. Specifically, if a sample x from a random walk has mean x^* and variance σ^{*2}, we can compute the variable

$$y = F\left(x, x^*, \sigma^{*2}\right) \qquad (2.10)$$

where F is the cumulative normal distribution function. The variable y will be uniformly distributed between zero and one and hence can be used with the inverse transformation method to generate random walks with a wide range of distributions. For example, a linear transformation of y can be used to produce a random walk that is uniformly distributed over an arbitrary range of values, while taking the natural logarithm produces a walk with an exponential distribution. It should be noted that, when the inverse transformation method is used to change a random walk's distribution, the sizes of the steps taken by the walk will not be independent of its value. A walk that is bounded by the inverse transformation method to lie in the range zero to one, for example, will take smaller steps when its value is close to its bounds than when it is far from them.

2.10 Solving the Persistence Problem with Procedural Generation

At the heart of a computer-generated random walk lies a random number generator that can be made to produce and reproduce a specific sequence of numbers by applying a seed. By recording the seed values that were used in constructing parts of a random walk, those parts can be exactly reconstructed if and when required. For example, if a player visited a planet for the first time and looked at the history of the price of a commodity over the last year, that history could be created by seeding the random number generator with the time of the player's visit and then applying the extrapolation equation backward in time. If the player returned to the planet a couple of months later and looked at the same history, it could easily be reconstructed based only on the original seed, and hence the history itself would not need to be stored. This is a major benefit, particularly in large open world games that contain many random walks with detailed and observable histories.

2.11 Conclusion

This chapter has provided a selection of simple but powerful techniques for generating and manipulating random walks. The techniques make it possible to exploit the unpredictability and replay value that randomness adds while also providing the control that is necessary to allow it to be both scripted and interactive when necessary. Spreadsheets and C++ classes that demonstrate the key concepts that are described in this chapter have been provided to make it as easy as possible to apply them in practice.

3

Logging Visualization in *FINAL FANTASY XV*

Matthew W. Johnson, Fabien Gravot, Shintaro Minamino, Ingimar Hólm Guðmundsson, Hendrik Skubch, and Youichiro Miyake

3.1 Introduction

Data analytics have had a variety of uses in the gaming industry, most commonly in online games and the mobile market. However, in the development of *FINAL FANTASY XV*, an action style Role Playing Game (RPG), we have found an additional use for data logging combined with visualization. One challenge we face with a large team, measuring in the hundreds working across the globe, is ensuring quality game data. In an ideal scenario, the game's design and tools would be well defined, and accurate data would be ensured at the time of authoring. However, games often have changing requirements, new features, and new fun and exciting ideas introduced during the development process. These aspects can make it difficult to know precise boundaries of still-developing areas of a game. Nevertheless, ensuring quality game data is still an important problem that all teams address with varying techniques. Furthermore as the project scale continues to grow, additional quality assurance challenges are introduced.

We address these issues in *FINAL FANTASY XV* through a comprehensive logging and data analysis toolset. We log various aspects of the game in a database and use a web-based front end for analysis. This enables us to investigate movement issues, monitor event distributions in both time and space, and observe changes in the navigation mesh over time. Conceptually, our approach enables similar analysis options as done by Thorzen for *The Witcher 3* (Thorzen 2015). However, Thorzen directly populated a database with content information in order to find problematic data, while we are logging gameplay information to a database and analyzing that data.

In this chapter, we will describe the architecture we used and the reasons behind the choices we made, will look at the three main uses of our tool, and will discuss some of the future work we plan. By leveraging data visualization, we found that identifying potential issues, even in large worlds with lots of data, was easy and convenient for designers and developers. Additionally, the logging system was not intrusive and had no adverse effects to the gameplay experience and provided meaningful insight to our team.

3.2 Architecture

The architecture for this system was influenced by two main goals: (1) minimize impact on game performance at all costs and (2) allow both designers and developers capabilities to analyze the data via web browser. Since we log a lot of data, effectively searching through it is important. Conveniently, these goals can be achieved with off-the-shelf database and web technologies. Our implementation employs MongoDB as our database and NodeJS as our web server. These meet the requirements while also allowing substantial flexibility during the development of our visualization tool (MongoDB 2016, NodeJS 2016).

3.2.1 Logging

In order to minimize the logging's impact on performance, it needed to be fast and non-blocking. A logging system that affects frame rate or causes gameplay issues is more harmful than it is helpful. We implemented a nonintrusive logging system by doing most of the heavy computation via a process that can run on a different computer, which is important when playtesting on a console. In our case, the theoretical maximum bandwidth was 80 Mbps, which is a data volume limitation, but all the data described in this chapter did not reach this limit.

In Figure 3.1, there are three main components. The game and application logger make up the first component, which executes on the gaming console. The next component is the log aggregator, which we will cover momentarily. The final component is the client side view, for which we support a couple of options.

We will come back to Figure 3.1, but for now let us focus on the logging system, which is compiled into the game's runtime. As the player experiences the game, a variety of different events contain log statements that save data to the logging system. Figure 3.2 shows

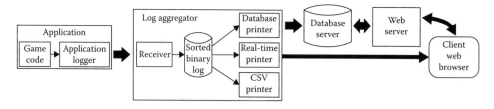

Figure 3.1

Data flow from game to web browser visualization.

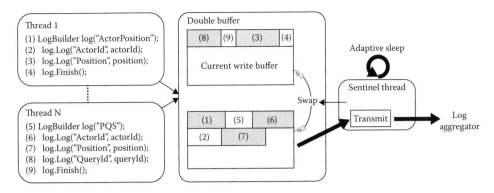

Figure 3.2

Logging library implementation pipeline shows multithreaded logging process.

Table 3.1 Elementary Data Chunk for Logging

Context Id	Unique Id for one log
Action Id	Identify the chunk role
Name Id	String to identify the data inside the database
Type Id	Type of the binary data
Data	Array of the binary data

the logging system's architecture. A single log entry can be arbitrarily complex and is composed of multiple elementary data chunks described in Table 3.1. Each chunk in the same log entry shares the same context ID, which is generated by atomic increment. Figure 3.2 shows two log entries, comprised of nine total chunks. As an example, when a player takes damage or an NPC activates a script, the system generates a context ID for that event and tags the relevant data chunks in the log. Since these events can happen simultaneously, the log system executes on multiple threads and writes to a double buffer. When a buffer fills, it is swapped out and sent to the sentinel. The sentinel accumulates data and adaptively sends it to the log aggregator over TCP/IP. The sentinel adapts to the rate of data commits to the aggregator, which is a function of how much data are coming in from the buffer. Based on the data-logging rate, the sentinel will send data between once per second to ten times per second. Furthermore, the sentinel also sends its own statistics to the log aggregator, so that system can also be monitored and tuned for performance.

Writing a chunk is a three-step process:

1. *Reserve*: Increase the number of users of the buffer, and reserve the memory needed for writing the whole chunk. This is normally a nonlocking function because it only increments the buffer's atomic variables. If there is not enough memory, then we have to block until the next buffer swap.
2. *Write*: Save the data.
3. *Finish*: Reduce the number of users of the buffer. The sentinel will wait until the buffer is unused before sending the data via TCP/IP.

The sentinel is working on its own thread and regularly wakes up to swap the buffer and send the logged data to the log aggregator via TPC/IP. The update frequency varies based on the rate of data sent. What is more, the statistics of this adaptive sleep are also logged and can be used to further tune the algorithm.

3.2.2 The Log Aggregator

Returning to Figure 3.1, the next component is the log aggregator. Since the logging system receives chunks for different log entries from multiple threads, essentially nothing is in a desirable order. The log aggregator's role is to fix this issue so that data are easier to store, manipulate, visualize, and understand. The aggregator performs another important task, which is offloading parts of the processing done by the runtime in order to minimize performance impact. Once the chunks are ordered per log entry, they can be used by one of the several printers.

We currently have three different printers:

- *The CSV printer*: Parses binary data to a CSV file. Useful for debugging or local tests.
- *The database printer*: The most useful of the three, it stores data inside a global database. It parses the binary to JSON and makes it ready for later analysis. This printer also has a local buffer, which is used to reduce network congestion on the database server.
- *The real-time printer*: Similar to the database printer since its output format is identical (JSON), uses a different protocol, based on web server push notification technology (i.e., "web socket"). This printer provides streaming data, which provides nearly real-time updates on the client web browser. With this printer, we are able to display the player and enemies on a 2D map while playing the game, which is useful for analyzing and tuning the AI.

3.2.3 The Data Format

Although the logging system allows an arbitrarily complex log, we still need to be able to analyze it. Consequently, we defined several standard log headers. A log header is generated with a class wrapper around the data, which will generate the common elements.

One of these shared data formats is the session header. The session identifies a game play experience. Each session is stored in a different database collection. The session header is explained in Table 3.2 and allows filtering for which data collection

Table 3.2 Common Headers Used for Logging Sessions

Machine name	(Computer Machine ID—physical hardware)
Session Id	Unique ID for this execution of the game
User	(Windows login of user)
Start time	Time stamp of session play starting
Binary name	Vs—Solution name
Binary version	Change list number from Versioning Software
Configuration	(Visual studio Build Configuration—Release/Debug/etc.)
Platform	PS4, Xbox, PC

will be used for further analysis. For example, if a developer was interested in looking at data generated from a specific tester at a specific time that a particular artifact occurred, then they can more easily investigate the parameters logged around that issue.

In addition, all logs share a common header with the game time, a position (used for spatial analysis), and the corresponding agent Id. These common headers offer format consistency for the front-end methods.

3.2.4 Data Analysis

Data analysis is done through the database printer and accessed through a web front end written in JavaScript. A separate front end interacts directly with the log aggregator for real-time updates via the real-time printer. Accessing the database is a two-step process: first determine the sessions that are to be analyzed, then retrieve the data you are interested in and aggregate the session results.

Our visualization toolset supports a variety of visualizations, which can be split into two broad categories: spatial analysis and statistical analysis. Spatial analysis visualizations project the data on a 2D map via Leaflet and provides a Google map-like user experience for exploring spatial data in the world of *FINAL FANTASY XV* (Leaflet 2016). Statistical analysis uses more traditional visualization techniques, such as bar charts and histograms, to allow us to investigate nonspatial characteristics in our data, for example, temporal distributions of particular events.

3.3 Statistical Analysis

Different views were developed for displaying event information, which we were interested in tracking. The web client was implemented in JavaScript and data-driven documents (D3) (D3 2016). The first view we made available is a histogram of data gathered from our point querying system described in later chapters of this book. The team was interested in tracking the amount of use the system had and in which sections of the game. Figure 3.3 shows the different play sessions logged on the left-hand side, with the corresponding histogram on the right. In this example session, we can see that the Ambient Spawn Query, a query responsible for spawning NPCs, is occurring nearly 700 times during this play session. In this example, it is easy to recognize the effects of entering a large town with a high number of agents being spawned into the scene. This type of visualization makes it convenient to recognize potential bugs related to our point querying system.

We developed a separate view for monitoring the distribution of executed character dialogues. When certain events happen in the game, one of many dialogue events can be triggered, and these events are separated into groups. In Figure 3.4, we see six different dialogue groups, each with multiple dialogues. By presenting this information in a bar chart ordered by group and frequency, we can easily monitor potential issues that may exist in our dialogue system. With this grouped histogram view, it is easy to see that one script in our first group occurs more often than intended, and the parameters for that script may need review. Visualization makes identifying these cases easy and convenient for designers and developers.

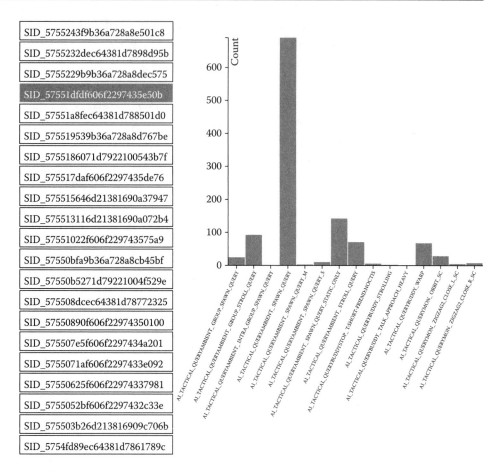

Figure 3.3

A histogram of our point querying system logging all queries and their frequencies.

3.4 Spatial Analysis

The statistical analyses are interesting, but the 2D map is arguably the more exciting use of this system. We used Leaflet, an open-source JavaScript map library to create an interactive 2D map of the *FINAL FANTASY XV* world. The library supports features like drawing points, adding tool tips, displaying heat maps, and zoom levels. The range of possibilities is large, and we continue to find new uses.

The first step is to load the appropriate data into Leaflet in order to create our 2D map. The basic process is to generate a series of top–down orthographic camera screen shots. The camera moves along a grid and captures the necessary images. Next, high-level zoom images are generated by downscaling and merging those screen shots. By performing this process, we enable mouse-wheel zoom on the world through a web browser. Once the data loads, we can begin exploring the world.

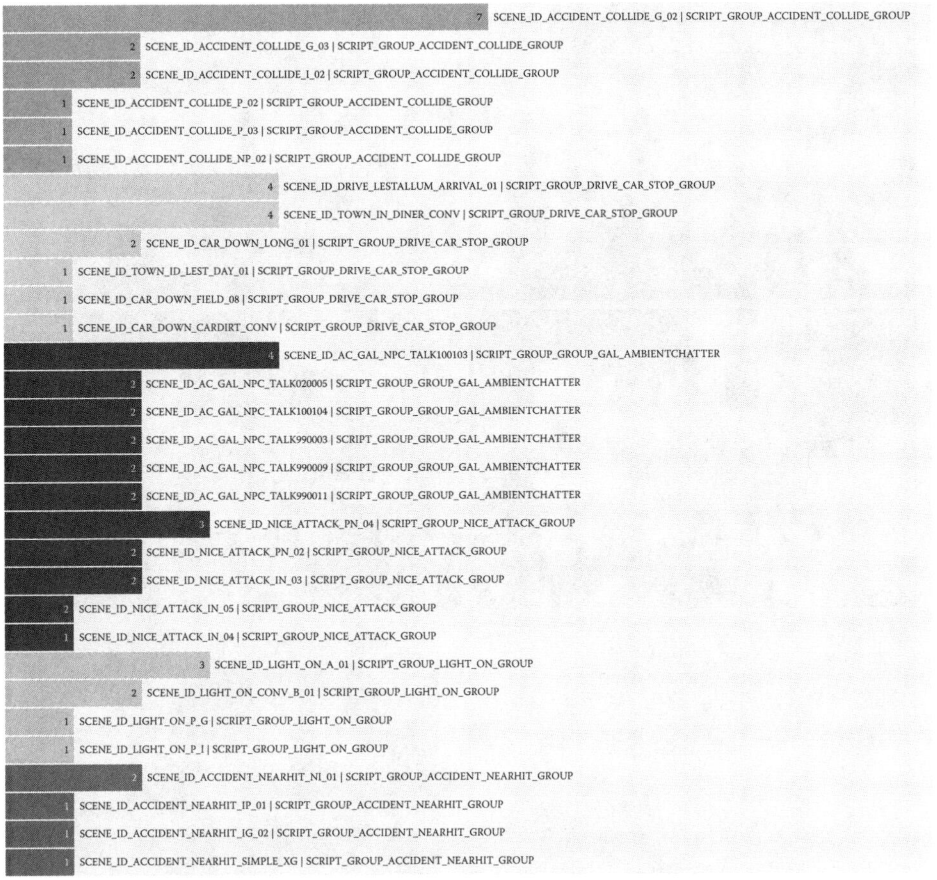

Figure 3.4

A grouped histogram view showing one script executing more often than intended.

3.4.1 Two-Dimensional Navigation Mesh Map

Any type of screenshot could be used in this process, but rather than using game screenshots, we used images of the game's navigation mesh. This provided us with several benefits. First, for quality assurance purposes when our navigation mesh data are being built, we were also generating the 2D map screenshots. In addition to this, the process is automatic, making it convenient to use. Next, by using the navigation mesh, we can ignore geometry that may obstruct a top–down view, such as trees or buildings. Finally, the navigation mesh covers all the areas in which NPCs and the player can travel allowing us to focus on areas that are contained in the game play portions of the world. We export not one but several maps at the same time, shown in Figure 3.5.

In Figure 3.5, there are six different uses of the leaflet visualization. These are: (a) connectivity mesh, (b) large monster navigation mesh, (c) nonfiltered mesh, (d) filtered navigation mesh, (e) difference image, and (f) zoomed in section of map shown in (d). We will handle them out of order, starting with the nonfiltered map.

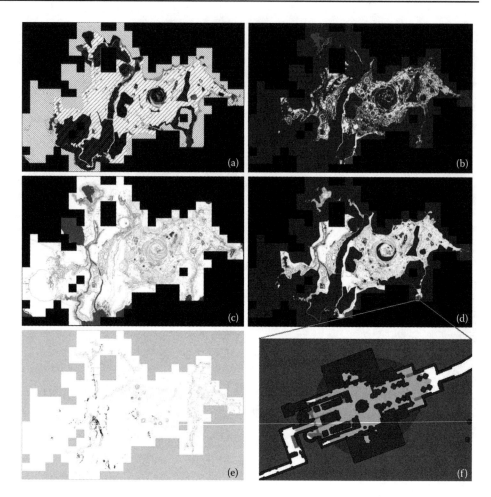

Figure 3.5

Leaflet map visualization of the navigation mesh of the *FINAL FANTASY XV* world. (a) connectivity mesh, (b) large monster navigation mesh, (c) nonfiltered mesh, (d) filtered navigation mesh, (e) difference image, and (f) zoomed in section of map shown in (d).

3.4.1.1 Nonfiltered Mesh

Figure 3.5c shows the whole set of auto-generated navigation meshes. In the live tool, the map's colors have meaning, which represent polygon flags such as water for sea monsters or ceiling heights for flying creatures. The other figures show subsets of this set.

3.4.1.2 Connectivity Mesh

Figure 3.5a shows the navigation mesh's walking connectivity. For adjacent regions with differing patterns in the image, it means agents are incapable of path planning between them because the regions are not connected. In the web tool, these regions are depicted with differing colors. This allows us to quickly check for invisible walls or unintentional holes in the mesh. We can also confirm whether an agent should be able to walk between two points or not. Navigation mesh generation is an automated process, based on a variety of rules (angle of a slope, *step-height* of a character, etc.). Depending on how the world is edited, otherwise-connected regions can become disconnected and vice versa. This tool lets us confirm mesh accuracy as the world map evolves.

3.4.1.3 Filtered Meshes

The generated mesh has navigation mesh above the sea, over roof tops, and even inside big rocks, anywhere it is possible to for an agent to stand. To avoid this, a common solution is to use a seed point. Only areas connected to the seed point will be kept. By using the walk connectivity shown in Figure 3.5a, we can generate Figure 3.5d, which is the filtered mesh that is used in the game for humanoid characters.

Figure 3.5b is similar to Figure 3.5d but with a different archetype. It is really useful to be able to check the map for the different archetypes. Different characters have different sizes, different step heights, and so on, and so Figure 3.5d is the navigation mesh, which is available for humans. Figure 3.5b on the other hand is for large creatures, namely the Behemoth. The Behemoth is one of *FINAL FANTASY XV*'s largest creatures, and it requires a lot of space in order to walk about, making its navigable area smaller than a human's. The white area in these images is where agents, whether human or behemoth, can go.

3.4.1.4 Difference Image

Lastly, Figure 3.5e is a difference map showing the difference between two subsequent versions of the world's navigation mesh. White regions in this image are the same as previous versions. Dark areas are places where changes occurred. This allows designers and developers to monitor changes over time, which can make it easy to confirm errors when AI behavior suddenly or unexpectedly changes in one area of the map.

Figure 3.5f depicts a zoomed version of a small region shown in the bottom of 3.5d, the interior of a large building.

3.4.2 Heat Map Visualization

Heat maps are an effective and convenient method for displaying density information over a 2D map. One example of heat map use was tracking the player's position to monitor map coverage by the quality assurance team. Here, however, we describe an interesting feature related to data packaging.

In *FINAL FANTASY XV*, we have numerous animations and data variations depending on a character's age, culture, and other characteristics. As we cannot load all possible animations into memory, we must know which ones to preload and where. We used the log data to display a heat map of animation IDs. This allowed designers to check for inconsistencies and rarely used animations, which helped to package animations into the relevant areas. Figure 3.6 shows an example of such a heat map.

Figure 3.6

Heat map visualization of events being executed by NPCs in a small town.

3.5 Conclusion

Interactive visualization techniques like the ones described here have improved the efficiency of developing large-scale video games. A number of characteristics from the game are collected and analyzed during the development process, which has made debugging and investigation of data issues more efficient. Map tools, like Leaflet, also enable us to monitor spatial issues that might arise in the game. These types of tools are particularly exciting because their future potential is just starting to be explored.

References

Data Driven Documents [Computer Software]. (2016). Retrieved from https://d3js.org/
Leaflet [Computer Software]. (2016). Retrieved from https://leafletjs.com/
MongoDB [Computer Software]. (2016). Retrieved from https://www.mongodb.com
NodeJS [Computer Software]. (2016). Retrieved from https://nodejs.org/en/
Thorzen, M. (2015). Content optimization pipeline for an open world game, GDC 2015.

4

What You See Is Not What You Get
Player Perception of AI Opponents

Baylor Wetzel and Kyle Anderson

4.1 Introduction

For many, even in the game development community, the goal of AI development is to make the "winningest" AI that one can from the perspective of the developer, which sounds like a reasonable goal. From the perspective of the person spending money to buy the game, of course, an unbeatable AI is not such a great idea. The player just wants to have fun.

If we want to make an AI that the player appreciates, we need to understand how the player sees the AI. So we decided to do exactly that. A group of players played a turn-based strategy game against two dozen AI opponents; ranked them on difficulty, realism, and fun; and explained what they believed each AI's strategy was. Among the findings, players are bad at determining AI's strategies and detecting randomness and cheating. Perceived difficulty correlated highly with realism, but actual difficulty's correlation was only moderate. Complex techniques often achieved higher scores but seemed no more difficult, realistic, or fun to players than significantly simpler AIs. No factor correlated highly with how much players enjoyed playing a particular opponent.

4.2 The Game

We have made AI opponents, NPCs, and systems for a wide variety of genres, and we know that different genres have different AI requirements. Our goal was to learn something universal, but our test had to be grounded in a specific game. We wanted something where the AI controlled an opponent since it allowed the player to test the AI more. We wanted something where the AI lasted more than a few seconds (this turns out to be shockingly rare). We wanted the AI to have a lot of choices since it gave the player more opportunity to study the AI. We wanted symmetric game play and equal resources, by which we mean that, just like in chess and very much unlike most boss battles, we wanted both the human and the AI to have the same options and chances of winning. We reasoned that if the player faces the same decisions as the AI, then the player more easily understands the AI's reasoning. In perhaps our most controversial decision, we decided we wanted a game where time was not a factor; our belief being that a player facing a clock has less time to worry about what the AI is thinking.

In the end, we decided to build a turn-based strategy game. We based our game on the combat portion of *Heroes of Might & Magic*, a well-balanced game giving players and the AI many strategic options.

In our game, each player controls 10 armies, where an army is a stack of units of the same type. The player picks among 46 types of units such as elf, devil, hydra, crusader, ice dragon, and bone dragon. Unit properties included obvious candidates such as health, damage range, attack, and defense (damage multiplier and divisor, respectively) as well as speed (controls which unit goes first), damage types (fire, poison, etc.), their resistances, and, finally, cost. Each player gets the same amount of money to purchase their armies. In our test, however, we required both sides to use random armies each game, again in the belief that it would force the player to think more about their—and the AI's—strategy.

As in *Heroes*, there are damage-over-time attacks, some units that are strongly biased to offense or defense and some units that are significantly stronger than others. It is not uncommon to see 500 imps fight one black dragon. Who the AI decides to attack is a clue to the AI's goals and thought process, and we want to know if the player can figure out what the AI is thinking. As area of effect attacks, favored by bosses in boss battles across the world, show little of an AI's intelligence, we removed them from the game.

For those familiar with *Heroes of Might & Magic*, we made a few other changes to simplify the game; removing morale modifiers and adding and tweaking a few units to better support balance and strategy use. The most significant change is that we removed movement and thus any need for spatial reasoning—units fought from where they stood and could attack any other unit. This allowed players to have more choices of who to attack, again allowing players to have more opportunities to examine the AI's reasoning. We tried to give the player every opportunity to see the AI's decision-making in action.

As in *Heroes*, aside from damage range, there is no randomness in the game. Units do not miss. This places the focus on decision-making (important for this study) and deemphasizes the effects of luck.

To summarize our game, both sides are given a random set of units. The AI has to decide which of it its armies to employ and which enemy armies to attack. The armies vary significantly in size, strength, and defense. They potentially employ elemental attacks and resistances as well as damage-over-time effects. The player cannot see the AI's thought process, but they do see the AI make dozens of decisions each game and have ample time to see and think about those decisions.

4.3 AI Design Goals

Before we can conduct experiments on what the player does and does not notice and appreciate in an AI opponent, we need to decide what is important to us as AI designers in developing an AI. We decided on a few things. For the player, we care about the AI's overall competence, visible error rate, visible error severity, and the player's perception of the AI. For the developer, we care about the AI's complexity and implementation difficulty. The AIs we created for the experiment were designed with these goals in mind.

For us, player perception meant the player's opinion of the AI's difficulty and realism and how much fun it is to play against. As part of this, we created AIs that exhibited certain common human behaviors (persistence and revenge, explained in the next section). We also created AIs that attempted to subtly allow the player to win. One thing we did not include was AIs with deep and somewhat irrational personalities. As is discussed in the results section, this did not prevent players from believing we had. A scientific investigation of how personality characteristics affect a player's perception of an AI agent is an interesting topic for a future experiment.

Complexity refers to how complicated an AI's programming is. Although not commonly used in commercial games, it is common for programmers to consider using techniques such as deep learning, game theory, Markov chain Monte-Carlo simulations, and genetic algorithms. Implementation difficulty refers to how hard it is to construct an AI. A complex AI does not necessarily take a long time (especially if one uses a library). A simple AI that uses a lot of variables might take little time to create but a significant amount of time to tune. For both factors, the relevant question is, "do players notice, appreciate, or care about the AI technique or complexity?" Put another way, games are not cheap to make, are we spending our time and money on the right things?

By overall competence, we mean how often does it win? Visible error rate refers to mistakes the AI makes that the player notices. By visible error severity, we do not mean that the AI makes a mistake that causes it to lose the game, we mean that the AI makes a mistake that causes the player to think, "Wow, this AI is really stupid." If an AI opponent beats a player but makes an incredibly stupid mistake that no human would make, would the player be impressed or would they focus on the incredibly dumb error? We first seriously considered this issue when a billiards AI which one of the authors played against made a difficult shot that only a very good player could make; then missed three simple shots, which any amateur could make. The AI made the wrong types of errors, forcefully reminding the player that he or she was just playing a computer and causing him or her to never play the game again. Those sorts of mistakes are perhaps more obvious in a billiards game than a turn-based strategy game, but it is an issue that game AI developers in all genres should think about.

4.4 Visible AI Traits

What can the player tell about their AI opponent? We certainly do not expect players to notice or care whether the AI was implemented using a behavior tree, influence map, or some form of deferred, time-sliced AI technique. But what do we expect them to notice? This important design question influences the types of AIs we want to make. For this experiment, we decided on eight properties of an AI opponent: use of available information, use of direct versus summary information, technique complexity, predictability, strategy obviousness, persistency, revenge, and hustling.

4.4.1 Available Information

When we talk about whether an AI uses the available information, we are talking about how many relevant and available pieces of information the AI chooses to use. A strategy such as *Attack the Enemy with the Highest Attack Score* only requires one piece of information. *Attack the Enemy You Can Do the Most Damage To* requires at least two—the amount of damage you can do and the defensive ability of the enemy. *Attack the Enemy You Can Kill This Turn* requires at least three—the damage you can do, the enemy's defensive ability, and the enemy's current health. If the targeting strategy accounts for damage type (e.g., using fire attacks against wooden enemies or avoiding using poison attacks on metal enemies), two more pieces of information are required. If every game AI used all available, relevant information, it would not be worth measuring in this experiment, but we have played with enough triple-A game AIs that fought fire with fire (or fire-resistant creatures with fire attacks) to know better.

4.4.2 Direct versus Summary Information

Assuming it knows how, an AI can calculate how powerful a given enemy is by using low-level information about the unit. For example, unit strength might be determined by its attack, defense, and starting health. These values are easy to compare across units. Information such as which unit attacks first is harder to weigh relative to health and attack strength. Special abilities (depending on the ability) can be hard to evaluate. For example, if a unit in a first person shooter has a 10% chance of not consuming ammunition when attacking, does that make them stronger or weaker than a similar unit with 5% more health? The AI designer could create a complicated formula that accounts for all of the relevant factors and then balances the weights of each term, or they could take the fast and easy approach of using something that presumably summarizes all that information such as the unit's cost. Want to attack the most dangerous enemy? Attack the one that costs the most. Not all games have unit cost, but some have level and in others maximum health is a decent proxy for overall unit strength. This is what we mean by use of direct versus summary information. Using summary information is easier and potentially captures the values of hard to weigh factors such as special abilities that would otherwise take a lot of time (and therefore money) to properly weigh. It might (or might not) result in a less capable AI but the important question is, will the player notice?

4.4.3 Technique Complexity

Technique complexity refers to how complicated an AI technique is. A complex technique might be complicated because it uses a complex formula, or it might be complex because it uses a fancy AI technique. A simple technique, in contrast, is probably simple because it only took a few minutes to think up and implement. The latter has a variety of advantages ranging from taking less time to implement (and therefore less chance of missing a deadline) and less cost (because it takes less time to implement) to being easier to debug. The downside is that the AI might be dumber and dumber, AI opponents might be less fun to play against. This assumes that the player can tell the difference between a fancy AI and a simple one, which was one of the questions in this experiment.

4.4.4 Predictability

Predictability refers to how predictable an AI's actions are. Strategy obviousness refers to how easy it is to explain what the AI is doing. If an AI picks its targets at random, the AI's actions are essentially impossible to predict, but the AI's target selection strategy is obvious. This experiment checks that supposition.

4.4.5 Persistency

Persistency refers to the AI's tendency to stick with a choice. An AI that selects an enemy and never let them go is persistent. An AI that switches targets every turn is not. We ran this experiment multiple times over the course of a year. Earlier versions of this test showed that humans tended to be persistent, and an AI that switched targets too frequently was seen as "computery." We added this trait after those early tests.

4.4.6 Revenge

Another human-like trait was revenge. Human players who were attacked by a given enemy tended to focus on that enemy, punishing it for attacking them. Adding this behavior to an AI is quick and easy. In theory, it gives the AI more personality and makes it appear more human.

4.4.7 Hustling

We use the term hustling instead of cheating because the intention behind the two is different. When we say someone is cheating, we often mean they are trying to get a win they did not earn to immediately benefit themselves. When we say a person is hustling you, we often mean the person is pretending to be worse than they are, actively managing the game so that when you lose, it is only by a little and you feel like you almost had it. When we use the term hustling in game AI, we are talking about an AI opponent who makes small, undetectable but plausible changes that result in the player just barely winning. We have two goals: the player must believe the AI is trying its best and feel accomplished when they beat the AI. We do not want the AI to make visible errors and, if the AI is so far ahead that there is no way for the player to win, we want the AI to ruthlessly crush the player so that when they finally do beat the AI, they feel like they beat a worthy opponent. For some of our AIs, hustling was done by shaving dice rolls when the AI was significantly ahead (e.g., if it normally does 20–40 points of damage, lower the range to 20–30). Others also picked the second best target if that target was also reasonable (within 20% of the value of the top ranked target). One AI switched strategies to a second, still good, strategy if it was too far ahead. It is OK (and often computationally efficient, which is important when you have limited computational resources) to cheat, but it is critical that the AI not get caught cheating. If done correctly, the player should not notice that the AI is cheating but should feel like they won all on their own.

4.5 The AIs We Created

We tried to create AI opponents who varied both across the aforementioned AI properties and within them (e.g., multiple low-complexity techniques). In the end, we created 51 AI opponents, although only 22 were used in these experiments.

The most complicated AIs were *PowerCalculationFancy*, which used a complicated, manually tuned formula, and *TeamDamageMonteCarlo*, which used simulations to calculate how much collective damage the enemy team could do before and after a given target was attacked. Less complicated AIs included *HighestStackHealth*, which picks the enemy army whose combined health is the highest, and *HighestStackAdjustedHealth*, which picks the enemy army whose combined health times their defense is the highest. Low-complexity AIs included *Alphabetical* and *LongestName*, which chose enemies based on their names. These were obviously not written to be good AIs, but they are good tests of whether players can figure out what an AI is thinking. They also provide a floor on AI performance, making it easier to evaluate more serious AI approaches.

HighestStackCost uses unit cost as a proxy for power, attacking the stack whose units cost the most. *PersistentHighestStackHealth* and *PersistentHighestStackCost* pick a target by health and cost, respectively, then stay on that target until they are destroyed. *IndividualRevenge* attacks the first unit that attacks them and stays on them until they are defeated. In *TeamRevenge*, every AI attacks the first enemy to attack any of them.

RandomBot attacks random enemies. *TK* attacks random teammates (it is not a very good AI). *TopDown* attacks the army closest to the top of the screen. We created these AIs as a baseline of how well players could infer an AI's strategies. *Wolf's* strategy was to pick off the weak and damaged, which was implemented by attacking at random until a unit falls below 50%, at which point every AI army attacks that unit. *Gentleman* only picks on enemies its size (where size = level; if there are none, it picks on bigger enemies and, as a last resort, smaller ones). *AlternatingStrategies* switches between the strategies of *HighestStackCost* and *HighestUnitHealth*. *PingPong* assigns each enemy a score and chooses one of the top ones, the one chosen being random but weighted by their score.

When *ShareBear* has an army that has damage-over-time effect, it looks for enemy units not already affected by it (damage-over-time damage does not stack in the game). If there are none, it attacks the stack that does the most damage.

HighestStackAdjustedHealthManaged, *HighestStackCostManaged*, *PowerCalculationFancy*, and *TeamDamageMonteCarloManaged* are hustling AIs. They determine how well they are doing relative to the player and nerf their die rolls when too far ahead. They never improve their chances since players are more likely to notice (and complain) when an AI does better than normal than when they do worse. *TeamDamageMonteCarloManaged* also switches strategies to the still pretty good *HighestStackAdjustedHealth* if it is too far ahead.

4.6 The Test

This experiment was repeated four times, but the results reported here come from the final iteration, which was conducted with 12 game design students. It is not a huge sample size but given the qualitative nature of some of the data, the consistency with earlier results, and the resources we had available, it is not a bad one.

Subjects were asked to play multiple games against each of 22 AI opponents, tracking their wins. All games were played on the same day, and the order of opponents was randomized. After each set of games, they rated the AI opponent on fun, realism, and difficulty on a five-point scale. They also wrote a short explanation of what they felt the AI's strategy was.

4.7 The Numbers

We will start with how well the AIs did. Table 4.1 shows how many games each AI won. The top scoring AI was *ShareBear*, whose distinguishing feature is that if it has an army capable of doing damage-over-time (DoT) attacks, it targets enemy armies not currently suffering from a DoT effect. Otherwise, it attacks the army that does the most collective damage (but does not take into account the army's attack score, making the metric misleading). The next highest scoring AI used a hand-tuned formula that took into account a number of variables. Doing roughly as well was a one-move look-ahead Monte-Carlo algorithm. The worst performing AIs used nonsense strategies such as attacking armies based on their name, order on the screen, or simply selecting ones at random.

It is unclear what to make of the performance of the hustling algorithms. *PowerCalculationFancy* won 71% of its games, whereas *PowerCalculationFancyManaged*

Table 4.1 Actual Difficulty of AI Opponents

Rank	AI	Wins
1	ShareBear	76%
2	PowerCalculationFancy	71%
3	TeamDamageMonteCarlo	70%
4	PowerCalculationFancyManaged	57%
5	HighestStackCostManaged	54%
6	HighestStackCost	52%
	PingPong	52%
7	IndividualRevenge	38%
8	HighestStackHealth	37%
	PersistentHighestStackCost	37%
9	AlternatingStrategies	33%
	HighestStackAdjustedHealthManaged	33%
10	PersistentHighestStackHealth	30%
	TeamDamageMonteCarloManaged	30%
11	HighestStackAdjustedHealth	28%
12	Alphabetical	26%
13	LongestName	23%
	Randombot	23%
14	Wolf	22%
15	Topdown	13%
16	TK	9%
17	TeamRevenge	7%

Table 4.2 Perceived Difficulty of AI Opponents

Rank	AI	Score	Actual Difficulty	
			Wins	Rank
	HighestStackAdjustedHealthManaged	3.6	33%	9
2	HighestStackAdjustedHealth	3.5	28%	11
	IndividualRevenge	3.5	38%	7
	PersistentHighestStackCost	3.5	37%	8
	PersistentHighestStackHealth	3.5	30%	10
	RandomBot	3.5	23%	13
	TeamDamageMonteCarlo	3.5	70%	3
	TeamDamageMonteCarloManaged	3.5	30%	10
3	TeamRevenge	3.4	7%	17
4	HighestStackCost	3.3	52%	6
	Topdown	3.3	13%	15
5	LongestName	3.2	23%	13
	PingPong	3.2	52%	6
	PowerCalculationFancy	3.2	71%	2
	Wolf	3.2	22%	14
6	AlternatingStrategies	3.1	33%	9
	HighestStackCostManaged	3.1	54%	5
	HighestStackHealth	3.1	37%	8
7	TK	3	9%	16
	Alphabetical	3	26%	12
	ShareBear	3	71%	1
8	PowerCalculationFancyManaged	2.8	54%	4

won 57%. Given that the goal of a hustling AI is to put up enough of a fight to give a competent player a challenge without constantly winning, a 57% win rate is close to what we were hoping for. In every instance, the hustling version of an algorithm won fewer games than the nonhustling version, but in the case of the Monte-Carlo algorithm, it dramatically underperformed, 30% versus 70%.

The scores for perceived difficulty (Table 4.2) are far less spread out, with all but one of the AIs scoring between 3.0 and 3.6 on a five-point scale and more than a third scoring between 3.5 and 3.6. The hustling AIs were seen by players to be just as difficult as the nonhustling version, even though the actual scores show otherwise, implying that the players did not notice that the AIs were cheating for the player's benefit. Interestingly, the top scoring AI was perceived as the second easiest AI to beat while the second hardest AI was perceived to be the same difficulty as the AI that attacked units based on how long their names were.

Table 4.3 shows how realistic the players felt each AI was, and Table 4.4 shows how much they enjoyed playing each one. Of interest is that *LongestName*, a strategy that is utterly absurd, which ranked fourth for realism and fifth for fun. *Alphabetical* ranked sixth and seventh, respectively. We think we can explain why and do so in the next section.

Table 4.3 Perceived Realism of AI Opponent

Rank	AI	Score
1	PersistentHighestStackCost	3.8
	TeamDamageMonteCarlo	3.8
2	HighestStackHealth	3.7
	PowerCalculationFancy	3.7
	ShareBear	3.7
3	HighestStackCostManaged	3.6
4	LongestName	3.5
	PowerCalculationFancyManaged	3.5
5	TeamRevenge	3.4
6	Alphabetical	3.3
	HighestStackAdjustedHealthManaged	3.3
	HighestStackCost	3.3
	TopDown	3.3
7	AlternatingStrategies	3.2
	PersistentHighestStackHealth	3.2
	PingPong	3.2
	RandomBot	3.2
	TeamDamageMonteCarloManaged	3.2
8	HighestStackAdjustedHealth	3.1
	IndividualRevenge	3.1
9	wolf	3.0
10	TK	1.2

The earlier tables contained a few surprises but not as many as Table 4.5. Table 4.5 shows how many subjects were able to determine each AI's strategy. Full points were given if they described something roughly similar to one of the main points of the AI's strategies and partial credit if they described a relevant, if not core, aspect of the strategy. We were rather lenient on grading but even so, and despite all the opportunities the players had to study the AI opponents, strategy recognition was nearly nonexistent. The only two AIs whose strategies were discovered by the majority of the players were *TK*, which attacked its own teammates, and *TopDown*, which attacked the army closest to the top of the screen. The first has a unique, memorable, and shocking behavior, whereas the second leverages the player's spatial reasoning ability (which this experiment seems to show plays a major role in reasoning even in domains where it should not be relevant). 83% of players were unable to recognize an AI that was literally nothing more than a random number generator.

It is our opinion that this is an important finding—players have no idea what your AI is doing. We did not expect players to recognize a Monte-Carlo algorithm in action. We feel it is important but unsurprising that players could not differentiate between fancy AI (*PowerCalculationFancy*), simple AI (*HighestStackHealth*), and AI using indirect measures (*HighestStackCost*). We hoped players could not tell the difference between AIs that were trying their hardest and those that were intentionally throwing the game to make the player feel more competent. But we were surprised that players were completely unable to

Table 4.4 Enjoyment of AI Opponent

Rank	AI	Score
1	HighestStackAdjustedHealthManaged	3.6
2	HighestStackAdjustedHealth	3.5
	IndividualRevenge	3.5
	PersistentHighestStackCost	3.5
	PersistentHighestStackHealth	3.5
	RandomBot	3.5
	TeamDamageMonteCarlo	3.5
	TeamDamageMonteCarloManaged	3.5
3	TeamRevenge	3.4
4	HighestStackCost	3.3
	TopDown	3.3
5	LongestName	3.2
	PingPong	3.2
	PowerCalculationFancy	3.2
	Wolf	3.2
6	AlternatingStrategies	3.1
	HighestStackCostManaged	3.1
	HighestStackHealth	3.1
7	Alphabetical	3.0
	ShareBear	3.0
	TK	3.0
8	PowerCalculationFancyManaged	2.8

detect even blatant and intentionally human-like behaviors such as having an entire team focus on the first person to attack them (*TeamRevenge*), nor could they tell when an AI was changing strategies (*AlternatingStrategies*).

(An aside: While the average player might be unable to quickly determine an AI's strategy and is likely uninterested in conducting experiments to puzzle it out, The Internet is a large place and if your game has enough players, eventually someone will figure it out and publish it somewhere. We leave it to you to decide whether that is a bad thing or, perhaps, an opportunity to add Easter eggs for your more highly motivated players.)

Table 4.6 shows how the various measurements are correlated. Correlation scores are on a scale of 1 to −1, with 1 meaning they move together perfectly, −1 meaning they move in opposite directions, and 0 meaning there is no connection between them. Note that strategy recognition correlations are omitted because players were unable to recognize all but two strategies, making the analysis meaningless.

Perceived difficulty strongly correlates with everything but fun. Actual difficulty strongly correlates with perceived difficulty and moderately correlates with realism. In both cases, difficulty correlated with realism. This is perhaps in keeping with anecdotal findings from others that making an enemy more difficult made the AI appear more intelligent. Fun, unfortunately, did not correlate with anything. How much one enjoys playing against an AI opponent appears to be independent of how difficult or realistic the AI is.

Table 4.5 Player Recognition of AI Strategies

Rank	AI	Correct	Partial	Score
1	TK	12	0	1.00
2	TopDown	9	1	0.79
3	RandomBot	2	0	0.17
4	ShareBear	1	2	0.17
5	PersistentHighestStackCost		4	0.17
6	HighestStackAdjustedHealth		1	0.04
	PersistentHighestStackHealth		1	0.04
	TeamDamageMonteCarloManaged		1	0.04
7	Alphabetical			0.00
	AlternatingStrategies			0.00
	HighestStackAdjustedHealthManaged			0.00
	HighestStackCost			0.00
	HighestStackCostManaged			0.00
	HighestStackHealth			0.00
	IndividualRevenge			0.00
	LongestName			0.00
	PingPong			0.00
	PowerCalculationFancy			0.00
	PowerCalculationFancyManaged			0.00
	TeamDamageMonteCarlo			0.00
	TeamTevenge			0.00
	Wolf			0.00

Table 4.6 Correlation between Measurements

	Perceived Difficulty	Actual Difficulty	Realism	Fun
Perceived Difficulty	1.00	0.80	0.81	0.04
Actual Difficulty	0.80	1.00	0.54	−0.19
Realism	0.81	0.54	1.00	0.18
Fun	0.04	−0.19	0.18	1.00

4.8 The Explanations

Players determined an AI's strategy by studying which of the player's armies they attacked each turn. We were interested in two things. First, did they have enough information to determine properties of the AI such as its strategy and the complexity of that strategy? Second, what did they think the strategies were?

To understand the player's reasoning, it helps to have an example. Assume that the player has the armies shown in Table 4.7. They play four opponents who, on the first turn, attack their armies in the order specified in Table 4.8.

Maximum damage is the base damage done by one unit. Adjusted damage is computed as the unit damage times the number of units times the attack score. Inflicted damage in combat is adjusted damage divided by the target's defense.

Table 4.7 An Example Set of Armies Owned by a Player

# Units	Army	Unit Cost	Health	Maximum Damage	Attack	Defense	Speed
4	Black Dragon	8,000	400	160	50	60	7
6	Ice Dragon	4,000	300	70	50	50	4
1	Dwarf	33	12	3	11	11	3
1,650	Imp	20	7	2	10	10	6
80	Minotaur	200	70	10	16	16	6
12	Monk	500	50	20	30	22	5

Table 4.8 The Order in which a Player's Armies were Attacked by the Opponent

Opponent A	Opponent B	Opponent C	Opponent D	Opponent E
Black Dragon	Imp	Imp	Monk	Black Dragon
Ice Dragon	Black Dragon	Minotaur	Ice Dragon	Ice Dragon
Monk	Ice Dragon	Black Dragon	Minotaur	Minotaur
Minotaur	Minotaur	Ice Dragon	Black Dragon	Dwarf
Dwarf	Monk	Monk	Imp	Monk
Imp	Dwarf	Dwarf	Dwarf	Imp

Since we are only looking at the first turn of combat, we cannot determine some of the AI properties described in the previous section. We omit revenge, persistency, guided randomness, and hustling, but there is still information that both we and the players can glean and valuable points to make. (A multiarmy, multiturn example illustrates poorly in book form.)

Take a few seconds to see if you can figure out what the strategy of opponent A is. In doing so, you are placing yourself in the mind of the player and experiencing the game the way the way they are (just as you have Table 4.7, the players had a spreadsheet of all unit values). Is there an obvious explanation for why the AI chose the armies they did? The answer is probably "yes." In fact, there are probably several, a point we will come back to in a minute. Many of the players wrote "They are selecting the strongest," which is true, depending on how you define strongest. In this case, Opponent A picks the armies whose units have the highest maximum damage score.

Opponent B is less obvious. Take a second to think about what the AI might be thinking. You might notice that the AI no longer picks the dragons first, it picks the imps, which are the weakest units in the game. Why? If you look over the army details, you would likely notice just how many imps are there. While an individual imp only does two points of damage, the stack of imps does a cumulative 3,300 points of damage, five times what the black dragons do (4 ∗ 160 = 640).

Opponent C's attack order is slightly different than Opponent B's. As mentioned above, the actual damage an army does is the unit damage (Opponent A) multiplied by the number of units to get the stack damage (Opponent B) multiplied by the unit's attack score to get the adjusted damage. Opponent C uses this formula. Just because this strategy is reasonable, simple, and straight forward does not mean players will figure it out. Nor should we expect them to. Although more complex than Opponent B's strategy, it produces almost exactly the same results. It also presents the exact same results as the AIs *Stack Cost*, *Adjusted Stack Health*, *PowerCalculationFancy*, and potentially others (e.g., *TeamDamageMonteCarlo*). Moreover, in fact, no player was able to determine the strategy of any of these AIs.

What are the lessons here? One might be that players are simply not perceptive, deep thinking, or creative, even in environments where they are told to study the AI (we will come back to this theory in a bit). Another might be that reasonable and perhaps semireasonable strategies tend to come to the same conclusions. A corollary is that complicated strategies using multiple variables that require a lot of tuning might not produce results that the player will notice or appreciate. Another lesson might be that, in many games, traits are correlated. Powerful units such as dragons tend to have high health, attack, and damage, whereas weak units such as dwarves are relatively low on all of these. A corollary is that the AI might not have much information to exploit unless game designers intentionally put in units with unusual sets of values. We did that in this experiment by making units that had extremely high attack relative to health and defense and vice versa for the sole purpose of giving players and the AI more strategy options; an intelligent AI is wasted on a game whose design does not allow the AI to be clever.

The strategy used by Opponent D is not readily apparent from this snapshot. The attack order here is random. There is no other strategy—the AI is literally a random number generator. After several rounds of switching targets with no apparent reason, it is obvious that this AI has no strategy. Or so we thought. 83% of players were unable to tell the AI was acting randomly. This was especially surprising as other AIs with consistent strategies were routinely accused of being random. *RandomBot* was actually rated one of the least random AI opponents.

Before discussing Opponent E, let us discuss some of the strategy guesses that we received from players. Although far from exhaustive, several representative ones are listed in Table 4.9 (Note: The table does not include answers of the form "I do not know," which was common for almost all AIs).

A few observations:

1. Few players correctly guessed any portion of what AI was doing.
2. Different players often had very different impressions of the AIs (e.g., *HighestStack-Health* was said to "go for tough guys" by one player and "shoot the group with the most guys" by another; "groups with the most guys" tend to have weak units because one cannot afford large numbers of tough units).
3. More than half the AIs were accused of having no strategy and just behaving randomly.
4. One of the AIs that did not cheat was accused of blatant cheating. One of the AIs that cheated in the player's favor was accused of blatant cheating against the player.
5. Nonsense AIs are believed to be acting intelligently.
6. Many of the AIs were said to intentionally spread poison throughout the team in order to weaken them over the long run. This was often considered to be the AIs' only strategy. Despite this, only one of the 22 AIs knew how to use DoT attacks such as poison, and none of the AIs used them if they did not have units that could perform them (units were chosen at random, and only two of the 42 units had them).
7. Described strategies sometimes ascribed personality and prejudices to the AI.

Table 4.9 Examples of AI Strategies as Determined by Players (Spelling Left Unchanged)

AI	Strategy	Comments
Alphabetical	Select unit by name	• Takes out units by base strength • Attack the advatar with the highest attack • Spread damage around ot lower my dps • Take out the strongest one by one
HighestStackCost	#units * cost	• Attacks the stacks with the highest attack • Attack the advatar with highest def • Poison and take out the strongest
HighestStackCost Managed	#units * cost Lowers its damage dice rolls when player is significantly behind	• Randomly attacking groups • Attacks highest stacked with his front monsters and loweest stacked with there back monsters • It mimics the first two attacks from the opposing team and then generates a random attack pattern
HighestStackHealth	#units * health	• Shoot the group with the most guys • Go for tough guys • This AI likes punching babies
PersistentHighestStack Health	#units * health Stick with enemy until it dies	• Killing the lowest costing creatures first • This AI attacks the group with the highest amount of units • Attack strongest first • Takes out dot first then strong mid then strongest guy
HighestStackAdjusted Health	#units * health * defense	• Appears to attack randomly • Randomly choose 1 of the top 3 highest total life • Attacks the units with the most speed • It kills everything in one or two hits regardless of the stats
IndividualRevenge	Attack first enemy that attacks it	• Random • Wittle down the big hitters • DoT uses poison units to attack my weakest units. Chaos would attack power units • Goes after middle strongest and spreads the damage • Attacks based on what type of unit it is, only attacks all Ice Wolves etc. Then moves to the next unit
LongestName	Attack enemy with longest name	• Attacks the stack with the most health • Attacking the highest dps • Focus fire • Strongest, then strongest DoT, then Strongest big group
RandomBot	Select enemies at random	• Attack the advatar with highest def • Spreads damage among all enemies' attacks strongest and works way down spreading damage • This AI attacks two lowest staked creatures than two highest stack creatures

(Continued)

AI	Strategy	Comments
TeamDamage MonteCarlo	Use one-turn look ahead with Monte-Carlo Algorithm	• This AI takes very randomly • Appears to be a cheating AI that attacks too many times per turn • Attacked all ranged first and then attacked at random • Take out the highest attack the slowest
TeamDamage MonteCarloManaged	Use one-turn look ahead with Monte-Carlo Algorithm. If winning, switch to adjusted stack health strategy	• I do not have a clue, the AI must be pulling a random creature out of its hat to attack • Random flailing • Cheating AI seems to attack too many time per turn • hates medusa's bandits and orcs, do not even mention hydras • This AI took me out behind the wood shed!
TeamRevenge	All armies focus on first enemy to attack to attack any of them	• Appears to attack randomly • Attack the highest costing creature, then the third lowest, repeat step one then two • It attacks the celestial characters like the angels and the monks first

It is the last point we find the most interesting. Perhaps we are bad game designers, but it did not occur to us to give the AIs personality, which, in retrospect, seems at odds with our goals—players, being human, are designed to be good at inferring motivations, intentions, prejudices, and personality quirks—not mathematical formulas and optimizations. Many of our players saw personality in our AIs where none existed. One player believed that *HighestStackCostManaged* was copying their moves. *TeamRevenge* was said to prefer attacking holy characters such as angels and monks. *TeamDamageMonteCarloManaged* apparently hates medusas, bandits, orcs, and hydras. In the *Heroes* games, every unit belongs to a type (life, order, nature, etc.), and these are all chaos monsters. Chaos monsters are apparently treated specially by *IndividualRevenge*, who was said to use their chaos armies to attack the player's most powerful units while the rest spread poison among their army.

It is not clear why players believed these things, which is bad because it means it is out of the game designer's control. In some cases, however, the reason for the player's perception makes sense. *IndividualRevenge* was said to have to be out for ice wolves. In truth, ice wolves are the fastest unit in the game and thus attacks first. Since *IndividualRevenge* attacks the first unit that attacks it, it makes sense that it would attack ice wolves when they are present. The behavior is not personal, simply an artifact of strategy and speed scores, but the player does not see revenge, they see an AI with an unreasonable hatred of their beloved dogs.

This brings us back to Opponent E. Take a look at the order of armies the AI attacked. The AI starts with black dragons and ice dragons before working its way down to monks and imps. When asked what strategy the AI was following, the player explained to me that the AI hated dragons. They then went on to explain a very vivid backstory for the AI that involved their family being killed by dragons when they were young and their subsequent quest to rid the world of them. The actual AI strategy was to pick targets based on how long their names were. Dragon, however, is not a short word, and fantasy convention says dragon names should have modifiers—black dragon, green dragon, ice dragon, bone dragon, chaos dragon, and so on. As a result, all dragons had names longer than all other units and *LongestName* therefore did indeed have a bias for dragons. This personality might not have been apparent had we not had dragons in the game (the order minotaur, dwarf, and monk lacks the cohesive story that black dragon, bone dragon, and ice dragon have). Sometimes character is an accidental byproduct of other, seemingly unimportant game design decisions.

4.9 Conclusion

Through this experiment, we learned a few things about players and a few things about ourselves. We will not argue that all of these things are true for all games, and we would love to hear from other developers about what works for their games. We believe there are a lot of interesting lessons here that apply to a wide variety of games, and savvy game designers will know which ones are likely to be helpful to their games.

Players are not particularly good at estimating the difficulty of an AI opponent. They get the general order OK (but not great; the AI that won the most was considered one of the easiest to beat) but tend to think all but the worst AI are of roughly equal difficulty whereas the win/loss records suggest quite the opposite. Being a turn-based strategy, one would assume the player had ample opportunity to study the AI's ability. This is less likely to be true in fast paced in-games; although in many other game types, enemies are not more difficult because they are more intelligent, they are more difficult because they have more health, weapons, and so on. So perhaps we should say that players are not particularly good at telling how intelligent their opponent is.

Is it worth investing time in complicated AIs? The news is mixed. The most complicated AIs performed better than simple AIs, and the simple AIs outperformed the truly ridiculous AIs. However, players did not seem to notice. An AI that chose actions at random was rated by players as one of the most difficult AI opponents, tying with the Monte-Carlo algorithm and placing significantly ahead of the top two scoring AIs.

Perceived difficulty correlated highly with realism—if players thought an AI was difficult (or, as we said earlier, more intelligent), they also thought it was more realistic. Unfortunately, the correlation between actual difficulty and realism was not as high. As a result, it is hard to know how to interpret this. Do players feel like a given AI is more realistic because they believe, erroneously, that it is more intelligent, or do they believe it is more difficult and intelligent than it is because it seemed realistic?

We added two human-like traits to AI opponents: revenge and persistency. We also had an AI (Wolf) that changed tactics when a unit was seriously wounded, all units pouncing on the weakened enemy to finish it off. Each of these behaviors came from human studies on player personality. None of the AIs with these human-like traits scored highly on realism. The AI considered the most realistic was a Monte-Carlo-based algorithm that was arguably the least human-like AI in the test. We are not sure what this says about how players perceive realism. Perhaps the player's inability to understand what the AI was thinking left them little else to base realism on than how hard (they thought) it was to beat.

As perhaps comes as no surprise to anyone, players are not very good at detecting cheating. No player commented on the several AI opponents who routinely cheated in their favor, but several were quite vocal about how much the AI cheated to beat them, even though no such AI existed.

How good are players at inferring an AI opponent's strategy? Horrible, it turns out. We did not expect them to know whether an AI was basing its decision on cost or health, but they showed very little insights into any aspect of the AI's reasoning, even when the AI followed simple, consistent rules. We looked for patterns in qualitative measures such as "this AI is more random than others," "this AI uses a more sophisticated technique," "this AI considers several factors," and "this AI is as dumb as a rock" but did not find them. Between the player's inability to accurately gauge an opponent's difficulty/intelligence or understand the AI's strategy, we found no evidence that the players we tested appreciate the amount of effort AI designers put into making an AI opponent, at least not the effort put into making the AI intelligent.

Although we did not attempt to measure it, it is our belief (and the belief of many others over the decades) that players appreciate effort put into AI if it is the right kind of effort. It is common to hear that players loved an AI's external signs of intelligence, meaning the AI said out loud what it was thinking. Many players might not recognize or appreciate an AI that flanks them (the AI behaving intelligently), but they do appreciate when an AI explicitly shouts "let's flank them" (the AI claiming it is behaving intelligently). In game AI, words sometimes speak louder than actions. Our experience in other games with emotional characters suggests players react strongly to NPCs that cry, laugh, shiver, and otherwise outwardly show signs of thinking. We suspect that if we had included an AI that said before each attack "attack the wolves, their speed is a threat to us" or "we can finish off that giant, everyone focus on him," it would have been perceived as significantly more intelligent than the others. We think players appreciate intelligence; the tests here simply indicate that they do not seem to be very good at recognizing it. Perhaps the lesson to take away is that it is the AI designer's job to make sure they do not miss it.

What makes a game fun, at least when it comes to an AI opponent? We do not know. In this experiment, how much the player enjoyed playing a particular AI opponent did not correlate with actual or perceived difficulty or intelligence, nor did it correlate with how realistic the opponent was considered. It also did not correlate with the player's ability to recognize, understand, or appreciate the AI's strategy because the players could not. Hustling AIs that tried to give the player a chance to win without letting them know are placed in the top two spots for fun AI, but hustlers are also placed in two of the three bottom spots so it clearly is not that. It truly surprised us that a random AI tied for second as the most fun AI. Our initial thought was that the game we used must be poorly designed if a random AI is seen as just as viable as purposeful ones, but we reminded ourselves that our test bed is based on one of the most popular games in history.

This brings us to our final observation—players invent stories for the nonplayer-controlled characters in the game. They see cheating, bias, motivations, and desires where none exist. And while we did not capture it in our spreadsheets, anecdotally it seemed that players enjoyed the game more when they felt their opponent had that level of personality. If we wanted the player to have more fun, perhaps we should worry less about optimizing the AI for winning and worry more about giving it the appearance of desires, motivations, biases, and back stories.

5

Six Factory System Tricks for Extensibility and Library Reuse

Kevin Dill

5.1 Introduction

These days, many games employ a data-driven AI. In other words, the decision-making logic for the AI is not hardcoded in C++ but instead is placed in a configuration file (generally using XML or some similar format) and loaded at runtime. This file generally specifies the configuration of a variety of different types of polymorphic objects.

The standard solution for instantiating polymorphic objects while maintaining loose coupling between the object's implementation and its owner is the *factory* pattern (Gamma et al. 1995). Not all factory implementations are equal, however. This chapter presents tricks and lessons learned from the factory system for the Game AI Architecture (GAIA), with a strong emphasis on providing actual implementation details that you can use. GAIA is discussed in detail in a later chapter of this book (Dill 2016); this chapter focuses specifically on its factories and on aspects of those factories that are worthy of reuse. Specific topics include:

- A brief overview of both the factory pattern and the design requirements that drove our implementation.
- Trick #1: Abstracting the data format.
- Trick #2: Encapsulating the information objects will need to initialize themselves.
- Trick #3: A consistent approach for object construction and initialization.
- Trick #4: The injection of code from outside of the AI library.
- Trick #5: The use of templates and macros to standardize factory definitions.
- Trick #6: Using global object configurations to remove duplication from the data.

After implementing the ideas contained here, you will have a factory system that:

- To the greatest extent possible, eliminates code duplication. This greatly simplifies debugging and maintenance, as well as reducing the chance that a bug will be introduced in the first place.
- Makes it easy to add new factories (one line of code) or to add new objects to an existing factory (two lines of code).
- Provides a powerful, consistent, easy-to-use mechanism for instantiating and initializing the objects being constructed.
- Is decoupled from the data format, so you can switch formats without rewriting anything else.
- Allows code from external libraries (such as the game engine) to be injected into the AI library without creating dependencies on the external library (critical for AI library reuse).
- Enables reuse within the configuration (i.e., the XML).

5.2 Background

GAIA is a modular AI architecture that is designed to be (a) extensible, meaning that as new capabilities are needed, they can easily be added and (b) reusable, meaning that the architecture can be quickly and easily ported from project to project, including across different game engines (and even to things that are not game engines, like high fidelity military simulations). Both of these requirements have implications for the factory implementation. In order to understand them, however, we first need to understand what factories are, what conceptual abstractions and modular objects are, and how they interact.

5.2.1 The Factory Pattern

The factory pattern gives us a way to instantiate polymorphic objects from data without exposing the type of the object outside of the factory itself. To break that down, imagine that your configuration contains regions that are used for triggers, spawn volumes, and other similar purposes. Your designers want more than one way to define a region, however, so they have you implement a "circle" region (takes a center point and radius), a "rectangle" region (takes two sides of an axis-aligned rectangle), and a "polygon" region (takes an arbitrary sequence of vertices and creates a closed polygon from them).

In data, each type of region needs to be defined differently, because they require different arguments. In code, however, we do not want to have special case logic for each type of region in each place they are used. Not only would this result in a huge amount of duplicate code, but it would be a complete nightmare if the designers requested a new type of region late in the project! Instead, we define a base class for all of our regions that provides the interface for all types of regions (with pure virtual functions like GetRandomPoint() and IsInRegion()). Code which uses regions can simply interact with that interface. Thus, for example, each nonplayer character (NPC) might have a spawner, defined in data, which specifies the region where the NPC should spawn. That spawner could use any type of region, but the spawner code works with the base class (i.e., the interface) so that it does not have to know or care which specific type of region a particular NPC is using.

This still leaves a problem, however. All of the places in code that use regions need to be able to create a region object of the appropriate subclass (rectangle, circle, etc.), as specified in the data, but we do not want them to have to know the particular type of region that is being created, nor do we want to have to duplicate the code for creating and loading in a region of the correct type. We solve this by creating a *region factory*, which is responsible for looking at the data, determining the type of region, creating an object of the appropriate subclass (a.k.a. *instantiating* it), initializing that object using the values stored in the data (the center and radius for the circle, the two sides for the rectangle, etc.), and then returning the object using the interface's type. Internally, factories are typically just giant if-then-else statements, so a naïve implementation of the region factory might look like Listing 5.1.

Listing 5.1. A naïve implementation of a region factory.

```
AIRegionBase*
AIRegionFactory::Create(const TiXmlElement* pElement) {
    // Get the type of region we want to create
    std::string nodeType = pElement->Attribute("Type");

    // Create a region of the specified type
    AIRegionBase* pRegion = NULL;
    if (nodeType == "Circle") {
        pRegion = new AIRegion_Circle(pElement);
    } else if (nodeType == "Rectangle") {
        pRegion = new AIRegion_Rect(pElement);
    } else if (nodeType == "Polygon") {
        pRegion = new AIRegion_Poly(pElement);
    }

    return pRegion;
}
```

5.2.2 Conceptual Abstractions and Modular Components

GAIA defines *conceptual abstractions*, which represent the different fundamental types of objects that make up our AI, and *modular components*, which are specific implementations of their respective abstractions. In other words, the conceptual abstraction is the interface, and the modular components are the subclasses which implement that interface. The region, discussed in the previous section, is one example of a conceptual abstraction, and the rectangle, circle, and polygon regions are different types of modular components that implement that abstraction. GAIA contains many other conceptual abstractions (targets and actions, to name just two), and each type of conceptual abstraction has many different types of modular components. Each conceptual abstraction has its own factory, which knows how to instantiate all of its modular components. Thus the region factory instantiates all of the different types of regions, the target factory instantiates all of the targets, and so on.

5.2.3 Extensibility

One of the primary design goals of GAIA (and a key advantage of Modular AI) is that it is *extensible*. In other words, we need to be able to rapidly and safely add new types of modular components to meet new requirements from design. Furthermore, we also need to be able to add new types of conceptual abstractions as we discover new reusable concepts that can improve the way in which we build our AI. Finally, because we expect to have quite a few different conceptual abstractions (currently, there are 12), and each conceptual abstraction can define the interface for a lot of different types of modular components (in some cases, dozens), we want to ensure that there is as much consistency and as little code duplication as possible either within a given factory (as it handles the different types of modular components) or between the factories for different conceptual abstractions.

Trick #3 discusses how we support the addition of new types of modular components and minimize code duplication in their instantiation, while Trick #5 discusses how we add new types of conceptual abstractions and minimize code duplication between factories.

5.2.4 Reuse

GAIA was designed to be used like middleware. In other words, it is an independent code library that can be plugged in and used with any project, on any game engine. In order to make it easy to decouple GAIA from a particular application (such as a game) and reuse it on another, GAIA cannot have any dependencies on the application.

Conceptual abstractions provide one way to do this. Continuing our spawning example, imagine that the selection of a spawn position is part of a decision that is made inside of GAIA. However, the designers want a custom type of region that is game-specific. Our custom region can be implemented in the game engine but inherit from the AIRegionBase interface (which is part of GAIA). The rest of GAIA can then access it via the interface without any dependencies on the game-specific code. This example may seem a bit contrived—how often will a region implementation be game-specific? The answer is, "more often than you might think." That aside, there are other conceptual abstractions that are much more often game-dependent. Actions, for example, are modular components that are executed as a result of the AI's decisions. The vast majority of them (move, shoot, play an animation, speak a line of dialog, etc.) need to call into the game engine. These actions are injected into GAIA in exactly the same way as our hypothetical game-specific region.

There is still a problem, however. We need some mechanism for the factories to be able to instantiate application-specific modular components, but the factories are part of GAIA, not the application! Thus we need to be able to add application-specific components to the factory without adding dependencies on the application or disturbing the code that instantiates all of the modular components that are built into GAIA. The solution to this problem is the subject of Trick #4, while Tricks #1 and #2 discuss other ways to make reuse of the AI library easier. Finally, Trick #6 discusses reuse of data, rather than code.

5.3 Trick #1: Abstracting the Data Format

The first thing to keep in mind as you design your load system is that the format of your configuration may change. For example, the factory in Listing 5.1 uses a `TiXmlElement`, which is an object from Tiny XML (a popular open-source XML parser [Thomason n.d.]). The problem with depending on a specific implementation like this, or even depending on a specific format like XML, is that over time you might discover that XML is too verbose, or that the publisher requires you to use a binary data format, or that the designers are more comfortable working in JSON or YAML, or that some project wants to use an application-specific format, or that your favorite XML parser does not compile using the archaic version of GCC that some application requires, or that its implementation does not meet your stringent memory management requirements, or... you get the idea. Consequently, the format of your data (and the code to parse it) should be wrapped so that it can be replaced in a single location rather than having to chase its tendrils through the entire application. Ideally, it should be treated like any other conceptual abstraction – that is, define the parser interface and provide one or more implementations that ship with the AI library, but also allow the application to define its own parser if needed. This allows the AI library to support project-specific data formats without adding dependencies on the project.

In GAIA, we parse all of the configurations when the application is loaded and store them internally as `AISpecificationNodes`. Specification nodes have a *name* (the label from the XML node), a *type* (the type attribute from the XML node), and *attributes* and *subnodes* (the remaining attributes and subnodes from the XML). This is a pretty thin wrapper, but it gives us enough leverage to support JSON or YAML, for example.

Wrapping the data in this way provides another major benefit as well. Because we control the representation, we can control the way it is accessed. Thus, instead of exposing the data in a raw format, we provide a host of functions that allow you to get data of different types. This includes functions that read in simple types (floats, integers, Booleans, [x, y, z] positions, etc.) as well as abstract types (i.e., conceptual abstractions such as regions). As a result, we can do things such as:

- Standardize the way configurations are formatted so that it will be consistent for all modular components (e.g., Booleans must be "`true`" or "`false`", not "`yes`" or "`no`", and positions are specified using separate x, y, and z attributes rather than a single attribute that provides all three values).
- Check for errors in the data format (e.g., ensure that a parameter that is supposed to be a float is actually a valid number and not, for example, "`12.2.4`").
- Standardize default values (e.g., a position that does not specify z will have it set to 0).
- Provide conventions for specifying particular values (e.g., we allow both "`FLT_MAX`" and "`-FLT_MAX`" as floating point numbers, since both are important in the way our AI is specified).
- Provide a consistent set of conventions for handling the situation where values are missing or of the wrong type (e.g., the code requests a particular attribute as a float, but that attribute was not specified or is a nonnumeric string such as "`true`").

5.4 Trick #2: Encapsulating the Initialization Inputs

Initializing a modular component often requires more than just that component's specification node. For example, for a component in an AI for NPCs, the component may need access to the NPC it is a part of, or to a shared blackboard used by all of that NPC's AI components. What is more, even if a specific modular component does not need these things, other components that share the same conceptual abstraction might, or might contain components that do, so we want to pass all of the necessary metadata through every object's initialization regardless of whether we think it is going to be needed or not.

The simple solution is to wrap all of the initialization inputs (including the specification node) into a single object—in GAIA, it is the `AICreationData`. Each creation data is *required* to contain an `AISpecificationNode` and a pointer to the `AIActor` that represents the NPC that this component helps to control, as well as a variety of other required and optional metadata.

One nice thing about this approach (i.e., encapsulating all of the metadata in an `AICreationData`) is that it gives us a place to hang our hat as we add shared data and capabilities to the factory system. For example, there will often be cases where the application needs to pass application-specific data to its application-specific components. The application might have its own blackboard that handles things like line-of-sight queries (so that it can control the rate at which they happen), and it might implement a specialized line-of-sight AI component that makes use of these queries, for instance. This line-of-sight component needs access to the application's blackboard, but it is created by the AI library's factory, so the application blackboard needs to be added to the `AICreationData`. There are a number of possible ways to handle this. The one that GAIA uses is to have the `AICreationData` include a pointer to an AICreationData_App, which is just an empty base class that the application can subclass off to inject its custom data. Another (arguably better) solution would be to allow the application to create a subclass of the `AICreationData` and place application-specific values there.

Other examples of the usefulness of the `AICreationData` can be found in some of the tricks below.

5.5 Trick #3: Consistent Object Construction and Initialization

One mistake that we made when implementing GAIA is that we allowed every factory to use its own approach for initializing the objects. Our earliest factories worked like the one shown in Listing 5.1—that is, they simply passed the `TiXmlElement`, or the `AISpecificationNode`, or the `AICreationData` (depending on how early they were) into the constructor of the object being created.

As development progressed, however, we discovered that there were features we wanted to support in our factories that simply were not possible with this approach, so over time we started to have a variety of different approaches used by different factories, or even by different types of modular components in a single factory. This resulted in a mess that, while manageable if you understand the code, is highly confusing to engineers who are trying to integrate GAIA into a new application. Consequently, we have worked out a robust approach to object construction and initialization, and are slowly converting the entire library to use it. This approach has four basic steps:

1. Instantiate the object.
2. Optionally run a preload function on the object, which allows default values to be set by the object's owner before it is initialized.
3. Initialize the object from the creation data.
4. Check if the initialization succeeded. If so, return the object. Otherwise, delete it and return NULL.

In order to ensure that this four-step process is applied consistently, we implemented it as part of the AICreationData, as shown in Listing 5.2. This implementation

Listing 5.2. Using the AICreationData to instantiate and initialize objects.

```
class AICreationData {
public:
    // Not shown: Accessors and storage for the metadata from
    // trick #2.
    ...

    // The PreLoadCallback is called by ConstructObject()
    // after the object has been instantiated but before it
    // is initialized.
    typedef void (*PreLoadCallback) (AIBase* object);
    void SetPreLoadFunction(PreLoadCallback pFunction) {
        m_pPreLoadFunction = pFunction;
    }

    // Construct an object of the specified type, using this
    // creation data to initialize it.
    template<class T>
    T* ConstructObject() const {
        T* pObject = new T;

        if (m_pPreLoadFunction)
            m_pPreLoadFunction(pObject);

        bool bSuccess = pObject->Init(*this);
        if (!bSuccess) {
            // Print an error in the log!
            AI_ERROR ("Failed to initialize object of type "
                    "'%s'", GetNode().GetType().c_str());

            delete pObject;
            pObject = NULL;
        }

        return pObject;
    }
};
```

passes the preload function in as an argument, which has fairly arcane syntax. It also relies on the fact that all of our modular components inherit from AIBase (which is the base class of all of their interfaces). If we were starting over, we would probably address both of these issues by using a functor object for preload, but the details of that improvement are beyond the scope of this chapter (especially since it has not been implemented yet!).

Listing 5.3 shows the Create() method with all improvements. Notice that this function is still just as concise as Listing 5.1. Adding a new type of modular object just means adding another clause to the if-then-else, which amounts to two lines of code. Also note that while the creation data supports preload functions, the factory itself does not use them. If it is used, the preload function is set by the owner of the object the factory is creating and is generally used to specify default values.

Listing 5.3. The region factory's Create() function, with all improvements.

```
AIRegionBase*
AIRegionFactory::Create(const AICreationData& cd) {
    // Get the type of region we want to create
    const AIString& nodeType = cd.GetNode().GetType();

    // Create a region of the specified type
    AIRegionBase* pRegion = NULL;
    if (nodeType == "Circle") {
        pRegion = cd.ConstructObject<AIRegion_Circle>();
    } else if (nodeType == "Rectangle") {
        pRegion = cd.ConstructObject<AIRegion_Rect>();
    } else if (nodeType == "Polygon") {
        pRegion = cd.ConstructObject<AIRegion_Poly>();
    }

    return pRegion;
}
```

5.6 Trick #4: Injecting External Code into the AI

The tricks up to this point have focused on the process of instantiating objects. The remainder of the tricks will focus on other aspects of the factory system.

The next issue we address is the need to inject application-specific code into the AI library without creating any AI dependencies on the application. This is especially important for a library that is expected to be reused across many projects, but even within a single project it can be awfully nice to have the AI cleanly decoupled from the game.

We accomplish this by allowing the game to add custom object creators to the factories. We call these object creators *constructors*, although they should not be confused with a class's constructor function. A constructor is a sort of mini-factory that knows how to instantiate some subset of the modular components for a particular conceptual abstraction. The GAIA library includes a *default constructor* for each conceptual abstraction. That default constructor is responsible for instantiating the modular components built into the core library. Applications can also implement their own constructors and add them to the factory. Like most things in GAIA, the constructors all share a common base class that defines their interface, and the factory only interacts with that interface, so application-specific dependencies in the constructor will not place any requirements on GAIA.

To give a concrete example, let us return to our region factory. We built three types of regions into our AI library, as you will recall: the circle, rectangle, and polygon regions. Imagine that our game requires custom regions that are tied to specific navmesh nodes, or that our game has custom mechanics for underwater movement and has to have regions that reflect those mechanics, or that our game supports multi-story structures such as parking garages. We need to be able to add game-specific regions that know how to properly use the game-specific concepts that define the regions' location and extent.

In order to handle this, we first implement one or more game-specific region classes, all inheriting from AIRegionBase (as do the circle, rectangle, and polygon regions). Note that GAIA cannot depend on the game, but it is fine for the game to depend on GAIA, so there is no problem with including AIRegionBase.h in our game-specific code (if this were not true, the game would not be able to use GAIA at all). Next, we implement a game-specific region constructor that knows how to create our game-specific regions. The game-specific region constructor does *not* have to know how to create the circle, rectangle, or polygon regions—those are already handled by the default constructor that is built into the AI library. Finally, when the game is initialized, before anything is loaded, we add the game-specific region constructor to the region factory. Then, when a region is read in from the data the region factory goes down its list of constructors and calls the Create() function on each one until it finds a constructor that successfully returns a non-NULL region. If the region is game-specific, then it will be returned by the game-specific constructor. If it is one of the core types (like circle or rectangle) then it will be returned by the default constructor.

One other trick that only comes up very rarely, but is easy to support with constructors, is that occasionally a project will want to replace the built-in implementation of some modular component with a custom version. For example, imagine that your AI library is used by a project that specifies positions using something other than (x, y, z) triplets (this is not a completely contrived example—one of the projects that uses GAIA has this problem, although this is not how we solved it). You still want to have rectangle, circle, and polygon regions, but the built-in regions will not work for you. You can solve this by implementing project-specific circle, rectangle, and polygon regions that are instantiated by the project-specific constructor. When the factory goes through its constructors, it does so in reverse order of the order they were added, so the custom constructors will be checked first and the default constructor will be checked last. Thus when the custom constructor is checked and successfully returns a region with a type of "Circle", for example, the factory stops checking the remaining constructors, so the project-specific type will be used in place of the one built into the AI library.

In the interests of reducing duplication in this chapter (just as we do in our code), we will refrain from providing a code listing showing the region factory for this trick. The implementation of these ideas can be found along with the ideas from the next trick in Listings 5.4 and 5.5.

```
template<class T>
class AIConstructorBase {
public:
    virtual ~AIConstructorBase() {}

    // Attempts to create an object from the creation data.
    // Pure virtual so that child classes will be forced to
    // implement it.
    virtual T* Create(const AICreationData& cd) = 0;
};

template<class T>
class AIFactoryBase {
public:
    virtual ~AIFactoryBase();

    // Add a custom constructor. Takes ownership.
    void AddConstructor(AIConstructorBase<T>* pCnstr) {
        m_Constructors.push_back(pCnstr);
    }

    // Looks through all the constructors for one that can
    // create a region. Any constructor which doesn't know
    // how to handle an object of the creation data's type
    // should simply return NULL.
    T* Create(AICreationData& cd);

private:
    std::vector<AIConstructorBase<T>*> m_Constructors;
};

template<class T>
T* AIFactoryBase<T>::Create(AICreationData& cd) {
    T* pRetVal = NULL;

    // NOTE: Pay attention to the stop condition - we break
    // out as soon as we find a constructor that can handle
    // this creation data. We want to try them in the
    // reverse order from which they were added, so loop
    // backwards.
    for (int i = (int)m_Constructors.size() - 1;
         !pRetVal && (i >= 0); --i)
    {
        pRetVal = m_Constructors[i]->Create(cd);
    }

    if (!pRetVal)
        AI_ERROR_CONFIG("Factory failed to create an object "
                        "of type '%s'.",
                        cd.GetNode().GetType());

    return pRetVal;
}
```

Listing 5.5. The region factory when a templatized base class is used.

```
class AIRegionBase;

class AIRegionConstructor_Default
    : public AIConstructorBase<AIRegionBase> {
public:
    virtual AIRegionBase* Create(const AICreationData& cd);
    };

class AIRegionFactory
    : public AIFactoryBase<AIRegionBase>
    , public AISingletonBase<AIRegionFactory> {
public:
    AIRegionFactory() {
        AddConstructor(new AIRegionConstructor_Default);
    }
};
```

5.7 Trick #5: Using Templates and Macros to Standardize Factory Definitions

The approach in Trick #4 gives us a strong basis for our factories, but we do not want to have to copy-and-paste all of the code to implement it for every different conceptual abstraction—if we do, it is virtually guaranteed that the factories will diverge over time (and indeed, in GAIA they did). This quickly becomes a maintenance nightmare, as each factory is mostly the same but ever-so-slightly different than all the others.

Looking more closely, the only major differences between the region factory and another factory (such as the action factory or the target factory) are:

1. The type of object they create (`AIRegion` vs. `AITarget` or `AIAction`).
2. The implementation of the default constructor's `Create()` function (which has to actually instantiate objects of the appropriate types).

As a first step, then, we can use C++ templates that take the type of the object being created and handle most of the duplication. The result is shown in Listing 5.4.

With this done, the declaration of the region factory becomes much shorter, as shown in Listing 5.5. Of note, as this listing shows, GAIA's factories are also singletons. The singleton pattern is beyond the scope of this chapter, but it is well known and GAIA is not doing anything horribly unusual with it.

Listing 5.5 is quite good, but there is still a lot of code there. We are going to add new conceptual abstractions from time to time, and we want this to be as simple as possible. With C++ macros we can. Macro programming is painful, but the macros we need are fairly simple, and we only need to implement them once (and you, lucky reader, can benefit from our example).

The first step is to write a macro that can construct the code in Listing 5.5, but can substitute other words in place of "Region." Thus we could pass "Action" or "Target" into the macro to get the action factory or the target factory. That macro is shown in Listing 5.6.

```
#define DECLARE_GAIA_FACTORY(_TypeName)                              \
class AI##_TypeName##Base;                                           \
                                                                    \
class AI##_TypeName##Constructor_Default                            \
    : public AIConstructorBase<AI##_TypeName##Base> {              \
public:                                                             \
    virtual AI##_TypeName##Base*                                   \
        Create(const AICreationData& cd);                         \
};                                                                 \
                                                                    \
class AI##_TypeName##Factory                                        \
    : public AIFactoryBase<AI##_TypeName##Base>                    \
    , public AISingletonBase<AI##_TypeName##Factory> {            \
public:                                                             \
    AI##_TypeName##Factory() {                                     \
        AI##_TypeName##Constructor_Default* pDefault =            \
            new AI##_TypeName##Constructor_Default;               \
                                                                    \
        AddConstructor(pDefault);                                 \
    }                                                              \
};
```

Next, we define a macro that calls other macros, and passes in the name of each conceptual abstraction to each one. Listing 5.7 shows what this macro would look like if we had only region, action, and target conceptual abstractions, along with the call into it that actually creates the factories using the macro from Listing 5.6.

Listing 5.7. The `GAIA_EXECUTE_FACTORY_MACRO` macro.

```
#define GAIA_EXECUTE_FACTORY_MACRO(_FACTORY_MACRO)                  \
    _FACTORY_MACRO(Action)                                         \
    _FACTORY_MACRO(Region)                                         \
    _FACTORY_MACRO(Target)

GAIA_EXECUTE_FACTORY_MACRO(DECLARE_GAIA_FACTORY);
```

The `GAIA_EXECUTE_FACTORY_MACRO` is also used to define the singleton object for each factory, and to add the conceptual abstraction into the global object manager (global objects are the subject of Trick #6). Thus, when we want to add a new type of conceptual abstraction to GAIA, all that we need to do is add the name of the abstraction to the `GAIA_EXECUTE_FACTORY_MACRO`, and then implement the `Create()` function for the default constructor. Everything else—all of the infrastructure to create the factory, make it a singleton, and support its global storage—is created auto-magically by the macros. This is a huge boon, especially since we only add new conceptual abstractions very rarely (maybe once every year or two at this point), so it saves us from having to remember all the different places that changes would need to be made when we do.

　　　　　　　　　　　　　　　　　　5. Six Factory System Tricks for Extensibility and Library Reuse

5.8 Trick #6: Global Object Configurations

Duplication can be as much of a problem in the configuration as it is in the code. For example, imagine that we have a region which defines a spawn volume for a whole bunch of different NPCs. We do not want to have to copy-and-paste this region into every NPC configuration—if nothing else, it is likely to change as the designers tune the game, and we do not want to have to hunt down all the copies in order to change it!

Global object configurations allow us to define a configuration for a particular object once, and then use it elsewhere just as if we had copy-and-pasted it into place. We can do this for any conceptual abstraction—so we can have global regions, global targets, global actions, and so on. In the configuration file, we place the globals in a special node, named for the type of conceptual abstraction (`RegionDefinitions`, `TargetDefinitions`, `ActionDefinitions`, etc.). Each global configuration has to be given a unique name, which is used to look it up elsewhere. For example, we might have two Circle regions that represent spawn zones for friendly and enemy troops:

```
<RegionDefinitions>
  <Region Name="FriendlySpawnRegion"
          Type="Circle" Center="(0,0,0)" Radius="100"/>
  <Region Name="EnemySpawnRegion"
          Type="Circle" Center="(300,0,0)" Radius="100"/>
</RegionDefinitions>
```

We can then refer to these regions using the special type "Global" and the unique name, as follows:

```
<Region Type="Global" Name="EnemySpawnRegion"/>
```

In order to make this work, we need two things. First, we need a global object manager, which is a singleton. When the configurations are parsed, the global object manager is responsible for reading in all of the global definition nodes (such as the `RegionDefinitions` node) and storing away all of the global configurations. Second, the templatized `Create()` function in the `AIFactoryBase` class from Listing 5.4 needs to be extended, so that it resolves any globals before invoking the constructors. The modified function definition is shown in Listing 5.8.

Listing 5.8. The `AIFactoryBase`'s `Create()` function with support for globals.

```
template<class T>
T* AIFactoryBase<T>::Create(AICreationData& cd) {
    T* pRetVal = NULL;

    // Check if this is a global, and if so use the
    // specification node stored on the global manager.
    const AISpecificationNode& node = cd.GetNode();
    const AIString& nodeType = node.GetType();
    if (nodeType == "Global") {
```

(Continued)

```
        AIString globalName =
            node.GetAttributeString("Name");

        const AISpecificationNode* pActualNode =
            AIGlobalManager::Get().Find(globalName);

        if (!pActualNode) {
            AI_ERROR("Factory does not have a definition "
                    "for a global object named '%s'.",
                    globalName.c_str());
        } else {
            // Set the node on the creation data to the
            // actual node for this global, create the
            // object, then set the node on the creation
            // data back to its previous value.
            cd.SetNode(*pActualNode);
            pRetVal = Create(cd);
            cd.SetNode(node);

            return pRetVal;
        }
    }

    // The rest is the same as Listing 4.
    ...
}
```

5.9 Conclusion

In this chapter we covered a number of different tricks that have been learned through
the hard work of fixing mistakes and refactoring of the factory system for our reusable
AI library, GAIA. Together, these tricks provide a consistent approach for specifying and
initializing objects across all of our factories, allow us to decouple the AI library from the
rest of the game, unify the factory code so that new factories (along with all of their support structures) can be created with a single line of code, and greatly reduce the duplication
both within the factory code and also within the configurations themselves. The result is a
factory system that supports our goals of extensibility (new modular components can be
added with two lines of code, and new conceptual abstractions can be added with only one)
and reuse (the AI library is cleanly decoupled from the rest of the game, allowing us to reuse
the AI library with impunity).

References

Dill, K. 2016. Modular AI. In *Game AI Pro 3*, ed. S. Rabin. Boca Raton, FL: CRC Press,
    pp. 87–114.
Gamma, E., R. Helm, R. Johnson, and J. Vlissides. 1995. *Design Patterns: Elements of
    Reusable Object-Oriented Software*. Boston, MA: Addison-Wesley, pp. 107–116.
Thomason, L. n.d. TinyXML Main page. http://www.grinninglizard.com/tinyxml/ (accessed
    June 10, 2016).

6

Debugging AI with Instant In-Game Scrubbing

David Young

6.1 Introduction

Catching AI in the act of making a wrong decision is vital in understanding what logic error occurred and what the root cause of the problem was. Unfortunately, the time between seeing a decision acted out and the actual act of making that decision can mean that all relevant information has already been discarded. Ideally if the entire game simulation could be rewound to the exact moment in time when the error occurred, it would make notoriously difficult problems to debug, trivial to understand why they occurred.

Game engines have typically made reproducing these types of problems easier using deterministic playback methods (Dickinson 2001), where the entire state of the game simulation can jump back in time and resimulate the same problem over and over (Llopis 2008). Unfortunately, retrofitting determinism into an engine which currently is not deterministic is nontrivial and requires meticulous upkeep to prevent inadvertently breaking determinism.

Luckily, debugging AI decision-making and animation selection after the fact does not mandate resimulation or even reproduction of the issue. Using an in-game recorder system provides all the flexibility necessary to record all relevant data as well as allowing the visual representation of the game simulation to be stepped back and forth in time to understand when, where, and why the error occurred. This chapter will lay out the architecture of the in-game recorder system used internally in the creation of AAA games developed by Activision Treyarch.

6.2 In-Game Recorder

At a high level, an in-game recorder is a relatively straightforward concept; after each simulation frame finishes, iterate through every game object and record the minimal amount of data necessary to reproduce the exact visual state of the object. To replay recorded data, pause the game simulation, and restore all recorded data of each recorded game object from a single simulation frame. In order for a recorder system to be practically useful though during development, other real-world considerations must be met. The recording of object data must have minimal to no impact on the speed of the game simulation, the memory requirements of the system must be fixed, and the recording of object data must have no impact on the outcome of simulating objects. With these requirements in mind, the remainder of the chapter will detail each of the main components used to create an in-game recording system, as well as the practical uses of debugging AI using recorded debug information in tandem with navigating through playback, also known as scrubbing through playback.

6.2.1 Recorder Architecture

The most fundamental building blocks of recorder data are individual packets of data stored about recorded game objects. After a single frame of the game simulation finishes, a single packet of recorder data is constructed per object storing information such as position, orientation, joint matrices, and visibility. The entirety of all packets recorded per simulation frame will fluctuate and are collectively stored within a frame of recording data. Each recorded frame is timestamped with the absolute time of the simulation as well as the relative time between the last recorded frame to facilitate quick retrieval and accurate playback.

All recorded frames of simulation are stored and managed by a single recorder manager, which provides the interface between interacting with the recorder system as well as updating each subsystem to record object data. The manager internally stores a fixed-sized memory buffer which allocates and deallocates the memory consumed per packet and per frame of recorder data. When no additional free memory is available for allocation within the memory buffer, the oldest recorded frames of data are freed in order to allocate enough memory necessary to store a new frame's worth of packet data.

The responsibility of serializing recorder data is left to individual record handler object implementations that only serialize record data based on the type of object they are classified for. In practice, only a few varieties of record handlers as necessary to cover recording animated models, first person view models, player characters, and player cameras. To handle the playback of recorded data, playback handler objects implement deserialization functionality based on the type of object they are classified for. Typically, there is a one-to-one mapping of record handlers and playback handlers registered for use by the recorder.

The last component of the system deals with the user's interaction during record playback. A specialized controller implementation overrides the systems default controller implementation when recorder playback is enabled. The controller's button scheme is configured to provide access for free cam movement as well as rewinding, fast forwarding, and stepping through individual frames of recorded data. Additionally, the controller scheme allows for selecting particular objects of interest to limit rendering of additional debug information from superfluous objects. Figure 6.1 shows the

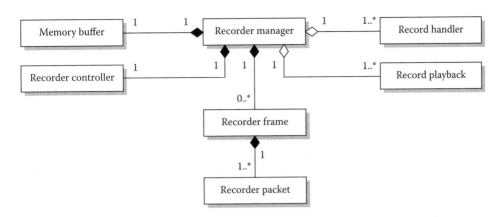

Figure 6.1

High-level class diagram of the recorder architecture.

high-level relationships between each subsystem of the recorder's architecture as well as the ownership of internal data used by the system.

6.3 Recording Data Primitives

Since a recorder is only a visualization of the past, when constructing primitive packet data, only the minimal visual information needed to reconstruct the state of the game object is necessary to be serialized. Typically, at a minimum, this piece of data includes the game object id, the type of the object, the position of the object, and if the object is targetable during recorder playback. Figure 6.2 shows examples of different types of recorder packet information based on what type of primitive is being recorded.

Looking at a particular packet type, the `RecorderModelPacket`, let us dissect what exact information is being stored per game object. The first data member stored about the game model is a unique identifier representing the game object available throughout

RecorderModelPacket
+id: int
+type: int
+next: *RecorderPacket
+targetable: bool
+position: vector3d
+angles: quaternion
+bones: matrix[]

RecorderBoxPacket
+id: int
+type: int
+next: *RecorderPacket
+targetable: bool
+position: vector3d
+angles: quaternion
+min: vector3d
+max: vector3d
+color: vector3d

RecorderTextPacket
+id: int
+type: int
+next: *RecorderPacket
+targetable: bool
+position: vector3d
+angles: quaternion
+text: char[]
+color: vector3d

Figure 6.2

Example data structures of different recorder packet types.

the engine. Although no information about the particular model is stored in the packet, retrieval of this information is available with the use of the unique id. The next field stored defines what type of object the id corresponds to and is similarly used through the engine to classify specific game objects.

A pointer to the next packet is stored within each recorder packet to form a singly linked list of all packet data within a frame. A singly linked list of packets is used as the internal data structure for recorder frames since individual packets can have varying sizes depending on the game object they are serializing. For instance, recording model data is dependent on the number of bones a particular model has, which varies model to model even though the game object type is the same.

The next field represents if the model should be selectable to toggle additional recorded debug information during recorder playback. The position field is self-explanatory and represents the current position of the object within the world. The angles field represents the current orientation of the model. The last field represents the current orientation and position of all skeletal bones the model has. If the model has no skeletal bones, this field is left null; otherwise an array of bone matrices is stored. Although it may seem counterintuitive to store a verbose representation for a game object's entire skeleton, storing animated bone matrices is preferable to storing animation data directly in order to account for physically driven or inverse kinematic bone constraints.

In addition to storing game object data, the recorder provides storing additional debug only primitives, which provide much of the debug capabilities of using a recorder system. Exposing a multitude of debug primitives such as lines, spheres, boxes, polygons, and text primitives associated with specific game objects allow for easily visualizing the underlying decision-making structures of an AI system. During normal game simulation, rendering the same debug primitives submitted to the recorder allows for identical debug capabilities during runtime as well as when scrubbing through recorder playback.

While recording every game object in this manner can be extremely useful during development, selectively recording only game objects of interest can greatly extend the amount of recording time allotted by the fixed memory budget. The use of recorder channels' facilities allowing users to select what type of objects should be recorded at any given time within the system. Each game object type can be classified to belong in one or more channel classifications such as AI, animation, script, and fx. Debug primitives can also specify which channel they should belong to so they appear appropriately when debugging specific systems such as animation or scripting.

6.3.1 Record Handlers

Since each game object type typically has dramatically different requirements for serializing visual representation, the recorder exposes a simple interface to implement different record handlers. A record handler primarily serves two different functions within the recorder: calculating the amount of memory required for any specific game object instance as well serializing the game object type within the specified allocated memory. Each record handler instance is in turn registered with the recorder specifying the type of game object the handler is able to serialize.

```
int GetRecordSize(entity* gameObject);
void Record(replay_packet* memory, entity* gameObject);
```

When a game object is being processed by the recorder for serialization, the corresponding record handler is first queued about the amount of memory required to construct a replay packet of information about the game object. If enough free memory exists within the memory buffer, the recorder will immediately call `Record` passing in the requested memory; otherwise the recorder must first deallocate the oldest recorded data within the memory buffer until the requested size can be allotted.

Decoupling serialization from the recorder's main responsibilities allows for extending the recorders support for new game object types within the game engine without having to modify the recorder system itself. In particular, new game object types are easily implemented by creating a new record handler and assigning an instance of the record handler during recorder registration.

One area to note though is the opaque nature of the record handler memory system. Replay packet memory passed into the `Record` function is merely uninitialized memory passed from the recorder's memory buffer. The recorder itself only knows how to interpret the initial recorder packet fields: id, type, next, targetable, position, and angles shared between all record packets but does not know how to interpret the remaining additional memory within varying packet types. The record handler must work in tandem with the playback handler in order to properly interpret the additional memory.

6.4 Recording Simulation Frames

All recorder packets from a single simulation frame are stored within a single recorder frame structure. Figure 6.3 shows the data structure of a typical recorder frame instance. Looking at the fields of a recorder frame, the first field, id, represents the unique identifier of the recorder frame. The next two fields store pointers to the previous recorded frame as well as the next recorder frame if one exists. Since frame time may vary and correctly associating a recorded frame to a specific timestamp is critical within the recorder system both the absolute time of the simulation as well as the delta time since the last recorded frame are stored in order to play back recorded frames with the same consistence as the original user experienced. The last field, packets, points to the head of the singly linked list of recorder packet data that are associated with the frame. As traversal of packet data is always linear, a linked list was sufficient for fast access times.

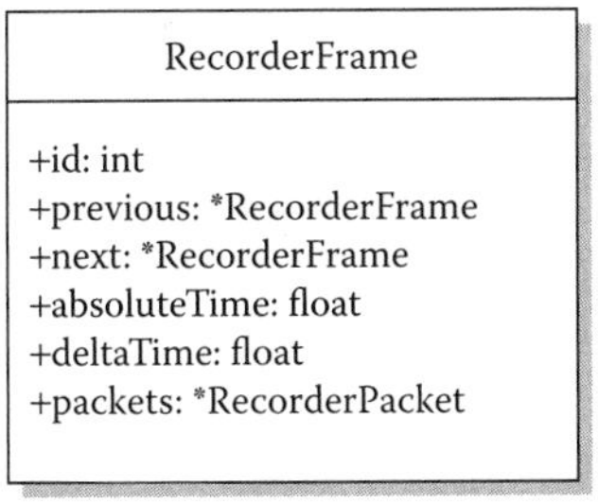

RecorderFrame
+id: int
+previous: *RecorderFrame
+next: *RecorderFrame
+absoluteTime: float
+deltaTime: float
+packets: *RecorderPacket

Figure 6.3

Recorder frame data structure.

Managing each simulation frame of recorder data primarily focuses around fast access of adjacent frame data when traversing frames forward or backward in time. Each newly recorded frame of data stores a head pointer to the first packet of recorder data as well as a pointer to the previous and next address of additional simulation frame recordings. Using a doubly linked list data structure allows for minimal upkeep when frames are added or destroyed since new frames are always added to the beginning of the list, and deleting frames are pruned from the tail end of the list.

To enable proper playback of recorded frames, storing both the absolute time of the game world as well as the delta time since the last frame was recorded provides the ability for determining which recorded frame of data represents any specific moment of time within the game world as well as accounting for variances in time step. Even though most game simulations run at fixed time steps, the actual amount of time for a simulation frame may exceed the allotted time budget. Storing a relative delta time within each frame allows for replaying data at the same rate as the original capture rate.

Even though both an absolute and relative timestamp is stored, other system's interactions with the recorder are done strictly based on game time for simplicity. Calculating the correct game time utilizes the stored absolute times within each frame of data, while scrubbing backward and forward in time utilizes only the delta time stored within a frame.

6.4.1 Recorder Manager

Managing the recorder system revolves around two distinct responsibilities, recording data after a simulation frame through a standard polling update loop and replaying recorded data when scrubbing through recorded frames. Figure 6.4 shows the high-level class diagram of the recorder manager's member data and external interface.

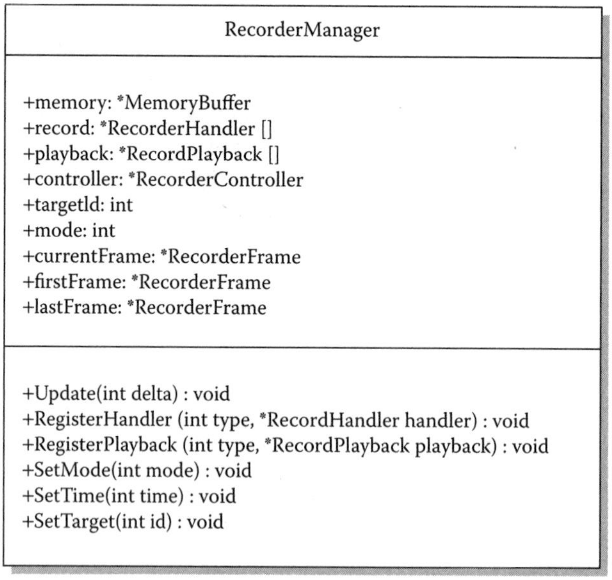

```
┌──────────────────────────────────────────────────────────┐
│                    RecorderManager                       │
├──────────────────────────────────────────────────────────┤
│ +memory: *MemoryBuffer                                   │
│ +record: *RecorderHandler []                             │
│ +playback: *RecordPlayback []                            │
│ +controller: *RecorderController                         │
│ +targetId: int                                           │
│ +mode: int                                               │
│ +currentFrame: *RecorderFrame                            │
│ +firstFrame: *RecorderFrame                              │
│ +lastFrame: *RecorderFrame                               │
├──────────────────────────────────────────────────────────┤
│ +Update(int delta) : void                                │
│ +RegisterHandler (int type, *RecordHandler handler) : void│
│ +RegisterPlayback (int type, *RecordPlayback playback) : void│
│ +SetMode(int mode) : void                                │
│ +SetTime(int time) : void                                │
│ +SetTarget(int id) : void                                │
└──────────────────────────────────────────────────────────┘
```

Figure 6.4

Recorder manager class diagram.

6. Debugging AI with Instant In-Game Scrubbing

Starting with one of the most critical internal tasks within the recorder manager is the correct allocation and deallocation of recorder packets and frames. Internally, the manager uses the memory buffer to server as a circular buffer where the oldest recorded frames are discarded to allow new frames to be recorded. Initialization of the manager begins with allocating a contiguous memory block to become the memory which the buffer internally manages. Registration of both record handlers and playback handlers soon follows before the manager begins recording game object data.

The game engine's overall management and update ticking of the recorder system are handled by a single instance of a recorder manager. The recorder manager's update function is called after the end of the game simulation loop to ensure that all processing of game objects has been completed before record handlers process each game object. As the recorder manager processes each game object, the game object is first classified based on object type, and the corresponding record handler is used for determining the proper amount of memory to request from the buffer. Once memory has been allocated, the recorder manager passes both the allocated memory and game object directly to the record hander for serialization. After a packet of information is serialized, the manager will correctly fix up each packet pointer as well as assigning the frame's starting pointer to the first packet of recorded information.

Once all packet data within a recorder frame are serialized, the manager will update the corresponding next and previous frame pointers of the current first frame of recorder data to attach the newly recorded frame of data to the doubly linked list. The new frame of data now becomes the first frame of data for the manager to use when playback is requested.

Additional information is stored within the manager to allow quick access to both the most recent recorded frame of data as well as the oldest recorded frame of data for scrubbing as well as updating the doubly linked list when frames are deallocated and new frames are allocated. During recorder playback, the current frame of data being replayed is stored separately to allow for quick resuming of in-game scrubbing as well as selectively stepping forward and backward.

6.4.2 Memory Management

Since the recorder continuously runs in the background working within a fixed memory budget, whenever the memory buffer is unable to allocate a requested amount of memory, the recorder manager will continuously deallocate the oldest recorded frame until enough free memory is available to accommodate the new allocation request. Continuously deallocating the oldest recorded frames and replacing those frames with new frame data achieve minimal memory fragmentation within the memory buffer, causing the buffer to act as a circular buffer, even though only contiguous memory is used.

Figure 6.5 shows the state of memory as frames are continuously added to the buffer until the amount of free memory remaining would not be sufficient for an additional frame of recorder data. In this case, Figure 6.6 shows how the memory buffer handles the deallocation of the first frame of stored data, Frame 1, being immediately replaced with Frame 3's data. Acting as a circular buffer, the only portions of unable memory with this setup will be between the last recorded frame and the first recorded frame as well as some portion of unusable memory at the tail end of the memory buffer's allotted memory.

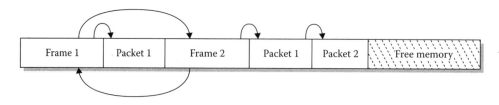

Figure 6.5

Contiguous memory layout of recorder frames and frame packets.

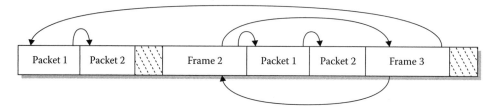

Figure 6.6

Memory buffer with minimal unusable memory and fragmentation.

6.5 Frame Playback

In order to play back recorded frames, a few considerations need to be made to prevent affecting the game simulation itself. Since restoring recorded data such as position and orientation will act directly on a game object's current state, the recorder must wait till the end of recording the latest frame's packet data before pausing the game simulation and overwriting game object data. Inversely before the recorder exits playback mode, the last recorded frame data must be reapplied to each game object to leave every game object in the same condition before playback mode was enabled.

When playback mode is requested to the recorder manager, the simulation pauses without any other work being necessary from the recorder unless an external source has requested the recorder to jump back in time to a specific timestamp. In this case when traversing frame data based on a timestamp, the recorder will start with the latest recorded frame data and work backward within the linked list of data to find the frame either matching the exact requested timestamp, the first timestamp immediately before the requested time, or the oldest remaining timestamp within the linked list.

Scrubbing forward and backward in time works on a completely different principle than the game world's time. Scrubbing can either occur stepping a single frame of data forward or backward or can replay data at the exact same rate as the original recording. When scrubbing in real time, the recorder's update loop will maintain a delta time since scrubbing was requested and continuously move backward or forward replaying frame data based solely on the accrued delta time of each frame's data. Managing time delta based on the original recording rate allows for frames of data to be replayed regardless of the game's delta time, which may differ from the actual delta time between each frame of recorder data.

6.5.1 Controlling Recorder Playback

Once in playback mode, overwriting the standard controller scheme with a custom controller scheme provides the necessary flexibility to manipulate playback. In particular, at least two speeds of operation for fast forwarding and rewinding are crucial for interacting with playback. Being able to play back data at a normal game simulation rate allows for fine tuning animation work while stepping the recorder one frame at a time is typically necessary for debugging decision-making logic. Since behavior selection is typically determined on a specific frame of simulation, all relevant recorded debug primitives are typically only drawn during a single frame of recording. In addition, the controller scheme is used for selectively targeting which game object's debug primitives are rendered during playback, which helps narrow debugging of any specific game object.

6.6 Debugging AI

AI in previous Treyarch titles used a recorder system extensively for animation, decision-making, and steering debugging. To debug animation playback and selection, an AI's entire animation tree was recorded with each of the AI's animation contribution, rate, normalized time, and selection criteria available. Scrubbing back and forth in time was pivotal for debugging animation pops, incorrect animation blends, and incorrect animation selection.

Debugging decision-making with the recorder allowed for recording an AI's entire behavior tree in game, which displayed which branches within the tree were currently executing as well as where within other possible decision branches, execution terminated prematurely. Whenever an AI exhibited an incorrect behavior or lacked selecting the correct behavior, it was trivial to immediately drop into recorder playback; scrub backward in time, and immediately understand which branch of the behavior tree did not execute as expected.

Debugging steering-related bugs with the recorder typically involved understanding and addressing undesired velocity oscillations or incorrect animation selections, which caused AI to run into each other or other obstacles. Rendering both the velocity, steering contributions, as well as projected animation translation of an AI frame by frame visually, quickly narrowed down incorrect AI settings, incorrectly authored animations, and malicious scripting overriding normal AI movement behavior.

6.6.1 Synchronizing External AI Tools

In addition to in-game debugging with the recorder, external AI tools tapped directly into the recorder's current timestamp. Using a custom message bus system, the recorder would broadcast what current timestamp was being scrubbed, which allowed other tools to synchronize playback of externally stored information with the recorder's visual playback. Utilizing the same message bus, the recorder could also be controlled externally through other tools to enter playback mode and jump to specific timestamps. In addition, a new type of assert was added to the engine called a recorder assert, which would pause the game simulation and set the camera immediately to a particular game object notifying all other external tools to synchronize with the targeted game object through the recorder.

6.7 Conclusion

Debugging the root cause of any AI bug can be a challenge; let alone during development where the state of the world is constantly fluctuating and new additions, modifications, and removals are occurring simultaneously. Although the use of a recorder is not a panacea and cannot stop bugs from being added, the ability to debug directly in production levels without the need to reproduce the issue in a test map once seen by the user is an incredibly powerful tool that saves countless man hours. No logging of debug information or text output can even begin to compare with the immediateness of being able to visualize every frame of game simulation both backward and forward in time. Past and present development of AI at Treyarch now uses a recorder as a central tool around which other tools and processes are created, and the benefits of such a system are still being discovered.

References

Dickinson, P. 2001. Instant replay: Building a game engine with reproducible behavior. *Gamasutra.* http://www.gamasutra.com/view/feature/131466/instant_replay_building_ a_game_.php

Llopis, N. 2008. Back to the future. *Game Developer Magazine.* http://gamesfromwithin.com/ back-to-the-future-part-1,http://gamesfromwithin.com/back-to-the-future-part-2 (accessed June 11, 2016).

7

But, It Worked on My Machine! How to Build Robust AI for Your Game

Sergio Ocio Barriales

7.1 Introduction

Every AI programmer has been through this stage at some point in their careers: you are young, full of energy, and keen to prove to everyone that you can make great things happen—and that you can do it fast! You finish your feature, test it on your map, and now it is in the game. Job done. Or is it?

Effective testing tries to ensure our AI meets design requirements and reacts and handles unforeseen situations properly. Experience helps you identify common pitfalls and errors. Seasoned AI developers can identify these and work with sets and categories of tests that try to catch problems, making their systems more robust. In this chapter, we show some of these strategies, analyze different scenarios, and provide tricks to help AI engineers approach AI testing with some inside knowledge.

7.2 Presenting Our Example

Debugging can be a very abstract topic, so, in order to make this chapter easier to read, we will present an example problem and use it to illustrate the different tests we can perform during the creation of an AI character. Let us use a sniper archetype, an enemy with increased accuracy when using their sniper rifle, which comes equipped with a scope and a laser sight. The sniper also carries a side pistol for close encounters. This role can be found in many action games, and they generally show similar behaviors. Our snipers will have three main states, *precombat*, *combat*, and *search*, as depicted in Figure 7.1.

Snipers can go into combat if they spot the enemy. Once there, they can go to search if the target is lost and, potentially, return to combat if the enemy is redetected. Snipers cannot go back to precombat after leaving this state.

7.2.1 Precombat

During precombat, our snipers will patrol between *n* points, stopping at each of them. There they sweep the area with their rifle. In this state, the sniper is completely unaware of the presence of any enemy.

7.2.2 Combat

When snipers are in combat, they have two options, depending on range to the enemy. At long distances, snipers will use their rifle to target and take down their enemy. In close quarters, snipers will revert to a side pistol and act like any other regular AI archetype in a cover shooter game.

7.2.3 Search

If the sniper loses line-of-sight to the enemy during combat, the sniper will go into the search state. In the search state, the sniper first confirms that the enemy is not at their last known position. During search, the sniper can sweep areas with his or her rifle and/or check the immediate region on foot if the enemy was last spotted nearby.

7.3 Basic Functionality Tests

After we implement a first version of our sniper, the first thing we have to verify is that the archetype works as described in the different design documents we have been working from. Please note that in a real-world scenario, we would not implement the whole enemy AI before we start testing it, but instead follow an iterative process. The tests described in this chapter—especially the basic functionality tests—should be applied to smaller parts as we develop our full feature. When we confirm that the sniper works as intended, our

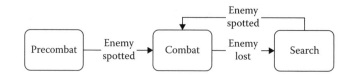

Figure 7.1

Base FSM that will control our AI behavior.

next job is to try and break the character in every possible way. This is the hardest part of testing an AI character, as every simple change can have unforeseen repercussions in other systems.

In the following sections, we will focus on the different parts that make up our AI agent, such as perception, reactions, and navigation, and will show some potential tests that are relevant for each case. While we will use the sniper to illustrate the process, our goal is to provide readers with enough information so they can identify similar problems on their own AI characters, and we can help them focus their testing efforts in areas that experience has shown us need special care. So let us get down to business!

7.4 Perception Stress Tests

When we talk about perception, we refer to all the systems that make the AI aware of its surroundings, and particularly those that allow it to detect other entities, such as the player. Traditionally, this includes the vision and hearing of the AI character, but it could potentially involve other senses, depending on the type of game and/or AI we are working on (e.g., smell tracking for dogs).

Let us focus on the vision system. For this, our sniper probably uses a few cones or boxes around their head that help them determine what enemies can be seen. As part of our basic functionality testing, we should have already checked that the player—or any other enemy—can indeed be detected, but we want to edge-case test this.

The sniper has two perception modes, depending on the weapon it is using: sniper rifle and side pistol, so we have to test them separately.

7.4.1 Rifle Perception Testing

Our sniper rifle has a laser sight, which is very common in games with this type of enemies. The laser is normally used as a way to telegraph both that a sniper is in the area and what the sniper is currently looking at.

What is the length of this laser? In the real world, design will probably have decided this for us, so let us say it is 60 m. The sniper is looking around an area through his or her sights, and we decide to pop right in front of its laser at 59 m. But … nothing happens. Why?

The most common answer to this problem is that our vision range does not match the expectations set by the laser. Should we increase this range for the sniper? The problem is shown in Figure 7.2.

The danger of extending the vision cone is that we will not be only extending its length, but also its width, if we want to maintain the same FOV. This, of course, will depend on the actual implementation of our vision system, but let us assume that we use vision cones for simplicity. This vision range problem raises some more questions. For example, if the sniper is looking through his or her rifle's sight, should he or she actually be able to focus on things that are on the periphery of its cone?

After further testing and discussions with design, we could decide to modify the vision of the sniper and have a shorter cone and a box that surrounds the laser, as shown in Figure 7.3, and our problems seem to have gone away.

We could do some additional testing to make sure all the possible target distances work as expected, and we should also check that the sniper will not detect enemies that are not inside the areas defined by its vision model.

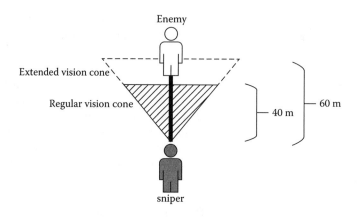

Figure 7.2

If the sniper's laser range is longer than their vision range, the enemy will not be detected.

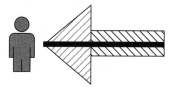

Figure 7.3

Upgraded vision model for the sniper.

7.4.2 Pistol Perception Testing

The sniper can be in a *regular guard* mode when using its pistol, so we retest regular perception. Everything looks ok, but suddenly we notice that the sniper detects things that are very far away. Why? Well, the answer in this case is that the new vision model we introduced to fix the perception problems we had with the rifle should not be used if the sniper is not looking through the rifle! We make the change, and everything looks good now. Perception works!

7.5 Reaction Stress Tests

A good AI character should be able to react to multiple different stimuli in plausible ways. Not reacting or playing a wrong reaction can break the immersion of the player very easily. Reaction tests look mainly for realization problems, that is, reactions that do not look good or that break the believability of our AI character. Here we focus on trying to break the AI reactions. Let us look at some reaction types in more detail.

7.5.1 Spotting the Enemy

The AI should be able to detect the enemy in any state, and we checked this by applying the tests presented in the previous section. What we are trying to double check now is that the sniper

7. But, It Worked on My Machine! How to Build Robust AI for Your Game

plays an appropriate reaction behavior (e.g., barks and/or animations) when the detection happens. For this, we should try to test every possible combination of sniper state (i.e., sniper rifle equipped vs. pistol equipped) over a few distance ranges (e.g., long, medium, and short distance). At long/medium distances, most of our reactions will probably work pretty well: the AI will play a reaction animation and some barks, and a transition will happen. At short distances though, things start getting more interesting.

The first thing we have to test is if our animations make sense at close quarters. We probably should not play the same animation when the AI sees the enemy at 40 m, right in front of the AI, or if the enemy just bumped into the AI. A *surprise* behavior, probably a more exaggerated animation, should be used in the latter cases. Another potential problem is that the sniper could be showing slow reaction times when the rifle is equipped—as per our design, the sniper uses its pistol when in close proximity. Switching weapons after the reaction is complete can look robotic and will be slower, so the best solution probably involves adding some special case animations that bake the weapon swap into the reaction.

7.5.2   Shooting at the AI

We should also test that the AI is reacting when it is shot at. We need to check that the AI will always react to this—although the reaction can be subtler in full combat. We should also check that our different animations look believable depending on what weapon was used to hit the AI, how hard it was hit, what body part was affected, and so on. The system for these reactions can be more or less complex depending on the game.

7.5.3   Reacting to Nondamage Events

If we do not shoot directly at the AI, but start doing things such as shooting at the ground nearby, whistling or throwing a rock, our sniper needs to react properly to all these different stimuli. Depending on the type of event and how aggressive it is (e.g., loud gun bullet whiz vs. a light switch turned off), the sniper should react in different ways. The objective of our tests is making sure that the reactions follow the design and that they make sense. Some of the tests we could try are:

- Is the AI able to react to two events in a row?
- What if those events are of the same type? Are we playing the same reaction over and over? In this case, we may want to add some antiexploit code perhaps to escalate the AI reaction and potentially for transition into a different state.
- Can the AI handle a second event while it is still reacting to a previous one?
- Will the AI finish the current reaction before reacting to the second stimulus? Does this look broken?
- If the second event is of a lower priority (e.g., rock throw vs. bullet impact), it should probably ignore the second event.
- If, contrariwise, the second event is of a higher priority, is this new event handled right away?

- Is it realistic for the AI to be able to react to a second event while reacting to the first one?
- Is the AI reacting appropriately based on the distance to the event? For example, the sniper should probably look more agitated if it hears a gunshot right behind it than if the sound comes from 50 m away.

7.6 Targeting Stress Tests

Now that we have double checked that our AI can detect enemies and react to whatever they do, it is time to make sure it can handle being attacked by multiple targets or from different, unexpected directions properly. Depending on the game and the implementation, AIs can use the actual position of the enemy to select their behaviors, or they can keep a last known position (LKP) (Champandard 2009). LKP gets updated by the individual AI perception system or by perception shared with a group or squad of AIs. To illustrate these tests better, we will say our AI uses an LKP. We will not enter into details about how an LKP system works, and we will simplify some aspects for our examples.

With our tests, we want to validate two things: first, we need to know the LKP is being set appropriately when the player is detected and updated as necessary. Second, we need to know the LKP is propagated to other AIs at the right time.

7.6.1 LKP-Updating Tests

When the sniper detects an enemy, it will react and then go into combat, setting an LKP and updating it as long as line-of-sight remains unbroken. The best way to test that the LKP is being created or updated to a new position after a big event happens (such as the enemy being spotted by the AI) is teleporting an enemy to random positions around the AI and shooting a loud gun in the air (or using any other event that causes a transition into combat, based on the game's design): when an LKP is set, we move that enemy to another position, trigger the event again, and continue doing this for a few seconds, making sure the LKP is being updated accordingly.

To test the above in a normal gameplay scenario, we should probably make the enemy invincible, create an LKP, and start circling around an AI. It is possible that the AI can lose us during this process, which would indicate a problem. In real life, if someone is running in circles around ourselves, we will probably notice it—so should our AI! This loss can be caused by an LKP update that is too tightly coupled to the vision system. In order to fix this, we could add some time buffering so that vision has to be broken for a few seconds before the enemy is considered as lost. We could also consider the AI is actually seeing the enemy if the vision tests fail, but the enemy was visible before, and the AI can still ray-cast to them, which means they have not been able to occlude their position. We probably need a combination of both systems for best results.

We should also make sure that any detection HUD our game uses works as intended. Such systems communicate to players that they are in the process of being spotted, that they are fully detected, or that the AI has just lost them. Changes in the AI targeting code need to be cross-tested against the HUD as well.

7.6.2 LKP Propagation Tests

Stealth mechanics are becoming more important in mainstream action games, and thus everything that is related to perception, reaction, and player position communication

7. But, It Worked on My Machine! How to Build Robust AI for Your Game

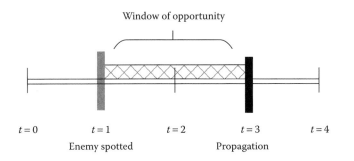

Figure 7.4

A window of opportunity allows enemies to deal with their AI spotters before the LKP is propagated.

should be thoroughly tested. LKP propagation is the typical system an individual AI uses to communicate to other AIs in an area or level that there is a threat, and where this threat is located. We need to double check that propagation is actually happening, but we also have to ensure LKPs will not get propagated during a reaction. The goal of this delay is to give the enemy a window of opportunity to eliminate the potential problem (e.g., by killing the detector) before their position is compromised after the detection, as shown in Figure 7.4.

7.7 Unreachability Stress Tests

Once LKPs are being set and updated correctly, we have to go a step forward in our tests and start checking how the AI behaves if the enemy was spotted in a location the AI cannot reach. We also need to check how the AI behaves if the enemy was spotted in a location the AI cannot see. What we are looking for is, at the very least, a believable behavior.

If the AI can see an unreachable enemy, we want the AI to move to a good position that still gives it line-of-sight on the enemy, and try to shoot from there. With this in mind, our first set of tests should be able to answer these questions:

- Is the AI stuck if the LKP is unreachable?
- Does the AI go into combat if it is shot at from an unreachable location?
- Is the AI staying in combat if the LKP is visible but unreachable?

The AI should also look good if the unreachable position is not visible. In this case, we probably want the AI to hold its position and get ready to defend itself from enemies trying to take advantage of the situation. After making sure the AI is not stuck in this situation either, we could perform some extra tests, such as:

- Is the AI aiming through walls directly at the LKP? We should avoid this, and systems like the Tactical Environment Awareness System (Walsh 2015) could help us decide what locations the AIs should be targeting.
- Is the AI aiming at a sensible target?

- Is the AI stuck in perpetual combat if the enemy is never redetected and the LKP stays unreachable and invisible? This is a question that needs to be answered by game design, but we probably want to time out in the LKP that allow our AI to recover from this situation.
- If there is a position the AI could move to gain LOS on the enemy, is the AI moving to it?

7.8 Navigation Stress Tests

An AI character in a cover shooter action game normally spends all its life doing one of the two things: playing animations and navigating from point to point. Bad navigation can suspend immersion quickly, so spending some extra time making sure it looks nice and debugged will pay off.

Going back to the sniper example, our design says that, in precombat, the sniper patrols from point A to B stops at the destination and does a sweep between a set of points associated to this vantage point. So let us go and follow a sniper and see what it does.

The sniper is at point A, finishes scanning and starts moving toward point B, walking with its rifle in its hands. Our two-hand walk cycles are probably tuned for smaller weapons—again, depending on the game and our animation budget—so the way the sniper moves could look a bit cartoony. An option to fix this is having the sniper stow the rifle before moving to a new point and either moving with pistol in hand or unarmed. Our job is to find the best-looking results with the tools and resources we have at hand.

Another thing to test is navigation during combat. We have a few candidates for buggy or undesirable scenarios here:

- Can the AI run and take cover properly with the currently equipped weapon?
- Can the AI cancel a move if the enemy moves and gets in the way?
- When/how do we detect this?
- Does the AI choose a new destination and never stop moving? Does it just stop in place and hold position? Does it play some sort of reaction animation before deciding to move to a new point?
- If the AI navigates near an enemy, will the AI look at the enemy?
- Should it strafe looking at the enemy? Should it aim at the enemy?
- Is the AI moving at the appropriate speed?
- Is the AI using traversals? (e.g., ladders, or being able to jump over gaps or obstacles)
- If there are two doors to enter a room, and there is another AI using one of the doors already, does the AI under test choose the other door?
- Can the AI open doors in its path?
- What does the AI do if it ends up outside the limits of the navigation mesh?
- If the game has different levels of detail, is the AI navigation properly on low LOD?

We should also try to do reaction testing when the AI is navigating to try and see if we can break it. Focusing on transition points is probably the best way to do this. For example:

- If the AI is entering a cover position and we expose the cover, how does it react? Is the behavior to enter the cover broken?
- If the AI is using a traversal in precombat and we shoot a single shot at it, does the traversal animation end? Does the AI fall and end up off-navmesh?

7.9 Weapon-Handling Stress Tests

When our AI can use multiple weapons and switch between them at any point, just as our sniper does between rifle and pistol, we need to make sure swapping weapons is not broken. Particularly, we want to try and avoid ending up with an improperly unarmed AI. Let us go back to our sniper. We made some changes in the previous section to allow it to navigate without a gun in precombat, so now we have three possible scenarios: the sniper is holding a rifle, the sniper is using a pistol, and the sniper is unarmed.

The simplest tests are just to check basic functionality, that is, make sure weapon transitions work as expected when the AI is not disrupted. However, the most interesting ones require trying to break the weapon swaps. For our particular example, we would like to test the following:

- The sniper is about to move from point A to B in precombat, so it starts stowing the rifle. If an enemy shoots it midway through the animation: does the AI play the hit reaction? Does it drop the rifle? Does it stow it at all? Do we let the animation finish?
- If the sniper does not have a weapon and gets shot, does it equip a weapon after reacting? Which one? Also, as we mentioned before, we should probably have reaction animations that bake in the equipping of a weapon to make reactions snappier.
- If the sniper has just reached point B and starts grabbing its rifle, what does it do if it gets shot?
- If the sniper detects an enemy nearby and starts stowing the rifle in order to draw its pistol and the enemy shoots the AI, what happens?
- Consider when the sniper gives up after the enemy runs away in combat. The AI tries to go into search, putting its pistol away and trying to equip the rifle. What does the AI do if it gets shot in the middle of the process?

Other interesting tests have to do with weapon reloading. The main questions we want to answer in this case are, if the AI gets shot in the middle of a reload:

- Is the animation played completely? Is the animation interrupted?
- Is the weapon reloaded at all?

7.10 Exotic Elements Stress Tests

Some of the different systems that we use to build our characters can be shared between different archetypes or reused among different types of characters with some minor modifications or tweaks. However, other parts are inheritably specific to certain characters, like, for example, the sniper rifle. These are the exotic elements that define what makes our character different from others, and thus we need to put extra work in making sure they work well and look polished. Defining these tests in advance can be difficult, due to the uniqueness of some of these components but the main goal, as it has been the trend in this chapter, is testing and making sure the feature cannot be broken.

As an example, for the sniper rifle's laser, we probably would like to test the following:

- Is the laser coming out the right location on the weapon?
- Is the laser following the weapon when it moves? Is the laser moving independently from the weapon?
- If it is, is the deviation noticeable?
- Is there a reason why the laser is allowed to move independently?
- Does the laser look good in every situation? For example, what should we do with the laser when the sniper is stowing the weapon? Should it be turned off? Same question for the sniper playing a reaction to a big hit—is the movement of the laser acceptable?

7.11 Group and Timing Stress Tests

At this point, our AI should be robust, fun, and believable when it operates as an individual unit. But what happens if we start using our character in conjunction with other characters of the same and/or different types? Tests that we could want to perform are:

- If a group of AIs receive an event, are all of them reacting to the event in perfect synchrony? We may want to add some small, random delays to the reactions to smooth things.
- Are different types of AI working well together? Is there any type that is breaking behaviors for others? For example, our sniper can see from longer distances if the enemy is still at the LKP, potentially put the other AIs in the level into search before they have been able to get past their reaction behaviors. We may want to control these interactions if we consider they are affecting the game negatively. For example, in the case of the ultrafast LKP validation sniper, we can prevent snipers from validating LKPs if there is any other nonsniper unit in the level that can reach the enemy position.

7.12 Conclusion

Building good character AI requires going the extra mile. Making sure our characters follow the design of the game is the first step, but long hours of work tweaking and testing should follow our initial implementation. Having a good eye to find problems or knowing how to polish and take features to the next level is an important skill that every AI developer should have, and it is a skill we all keep improving with time and practice, discussions, and advice.

Readers may have noticed all the tests presented in this chapter follow some progression. We start by testing if things are correct if left undisturbed, and increasingly generate problems and poke the AI in different ways to check how the system handles these interruptions: How does the AI react when it is interrupted? Like, for example, the AI getting shot at while it is swapping weapons. What happens if we ask it to do two different things at the same time? For instance, when the AI is reacting to a small event and receives a second one. Alongside, we continuously are on the lookout for unintended consequences—such as snipers detecting players at extended range after we modify their vision boxes—and always ensuring that every system, even if it is not directly connected to our change, is still functioning as expected.

It is our hope that readers have understood the problem of testing character AI thoroughly and that the techniques and examples presented in this chapter have served as a starting point to approach the testing challenges they may face in their own work.

References

Champandard, A. J. Visualizing the player's Last Known Position in Splinter Cell Conviction. http://aigamedev.com/insider/discussion/last-known-position/(accessed May 15, 2016).

Walsh, M. 2015. Modelling perception and awareness in Tom Clancy's Splinter Cell Blacklist. In *Game AI Pro 2: Collected Wisdom of Game AI Professionals*, ed. S. Rabin. Boca Raton, FL: A K Peters/CRC Press, p. 313.

SECTION II
Architecture

8

Modular AI

Kevin Dill and Christopher Dragert

8.1 Introduction

Repetition is everywhere in AI. The same patterns, the same fragments of code, the same chunks of data, the same subdecisions get used over and over again in decision after decision after decision. As a general rule, when we as software engineers see repetition we try to encapsulate it: put it in a procedure, put it in a class, or build some abstraction so that there is only a single instance of that repeated pattern. This encapsulation can now be reused rather than rewriting it for each new use-case. We see this approach throughout software engineering: in procedures, in classes, in design patterns, in C++ templates and macros, and in data-driven design—to name just a few examples.

Reducing repetition has numerous advantages. It decreases the executable size. It decreases the number of opportunities to introduce a bug, and increases the number of ways in which the code is tested. It avoids the situation where you fix a bug or make an improvement in one place but not others. It saves time during implementation, allowing you to write new code rather than rewriting something that already exists. It allows you to build robust, feature-rich abstractions that can perform complex operations which would take too much time to implement if you were only going to use them once. Beyond all of these incremental advantages, however, it also offers something fundamental. It allows you to take a chunk of code in all of its nitty-gritty, detail-oriented glory, and wrap it up into a human-level concept that can be reused and repurposed throughout your project.

It allows you to work closer to the level of granularity at which you naturally think, and at which your designers naturally think, rather than at the level which is natural to the machine. It changes, for example:

```
d = sqrt(pow((a.x - b.x), 2) + pow((a.y - b.y), 2));
```

into:

```
d = Distance(a, b);
```

The challenge with AI, however, is that while there are often aspects of a decision that are similar to other decisions, there are also invariably aspects that are quite different. The AI might measure the distance between two objects both to determine whether to shoot at something and to determine where to eat lunch, but the objects that are evaluated and the way that distance is used in the larger decision is certain to be different (unless you are building a nonplayer character (NPC) that likes to shoot at restaurants and eat its enemies). As a result, while the distance function itself is a standard part of most math libraries, there is a much larger body of code involved in distance-based decisions that is more difficult to encapsulate and reuse.

Modular AI is fundamentally about this transition. It is about enabling you to rapidly specify decision-making logic by plugging together modular components that represent human-level concepts. It is about building up a collection of these modular components, where each component is implemented once but used over and over, throughout the AI for your current game, and on into the AI for your next game and the game after that. It is about enabling you to spend most of your time thinking about human-sized concepts, to build up from individual concepts (e.g., distance, line of sight, moving, firing a weapon) to larger behaviors (taking cover, selecting and engaging a target) to entire performances (ranged weapon combat), and then to reuse those pieces, with appropriate customization, elsewhere. It is an approach that will allow you to create your decision-making logic more quickly, change it more easily, and reuse it more broadly, all while working more reliably and generating fewer bugs because the underlying code is being used more heavily and thus tested more robustly, and also because new capabilities added for one situation immediately become available for use elsewhere as part of the reusable component they improved.

This chapter will first discuss the theoretical underpinnings of modular AI and relate them to broadly accepted concepts from software engineering, and then describe in detail the Game AI Architecture (GAIA). GAIA is a modular architecture, developed at Lockheed Martin Rotary and Mission Systems, that has been used to drive behavior across a number of very different projects in a number of very different game and simulation engines, including (but not limited to) both educational games and training simulations. Its roots go back to work on animal AI at Blue Fang Games, on boss AI for an action game at Mad Doc Software, and on ambient human AI at Rockstar Games.

8.1.1 Working with this Chapter

This chapter goes into great depth, and different readers might be interested in different aspects of the discussion. If your primary interest is in the big ideas behind modular AI and how the modular pieces work together, your focus should be on Sections 8.2, 8.5, and 8.6. If you are interested in an approach that you can take away right now and use in an existing architecture, without starting over from scratch, then you should consider implementing just considerations (Sections 8.5.1 and 8.6). Finally, if you are interested in a full architecture that can be reused across many projects, across many game engines, and which allows you to rapidly configure your AI in a modular way, then the full chapter is for you!

8.2 Theoretical Underpinnings

Modular AI, and modular approaches in general, seek to raise the level of abstraction of development. Rather than focus on algorithms and code, a good modular solution leads to a focus on AI behaviors and how they fit together, abstracting away the implementation details. The question is how this can be done safely and correctly, while still giving designers and developers the fine-grained control needed to elicit the intended behaviors.

Success in modular AI development is driven by the same principles found in good software development: encapsulation, polymorphism, loose coupling, clear operational semantics, and management of complexity. Each of these familiar concepts gains new meaning in a modular context.

Modules themselves encapsulate a unit of AI functionality. Good modules follow the "Goldilocks Rule": not too big, not too small, but sized just right. Large modules that include multiple capabilities inhibit reuse—what if only part of the functionality is needed for a new AI? Modules that are too small do not do enough to raise the level of abstraction. The goal is to capture AI functionality at the same level that a designer uses to reason about NPCs in your game. Then, the development problem shifts to selecting and integrating the behaviors and capabilities needed for a new NPC, rather than implementing those capabilities from scratch, which is a highly appropriate level of abstraction.

Using modules in this fashion requires that module reuse to be safe. For this, module encapsulation must be strictly enforced. Preventing spaghetti interactions between modules ensures that each module can run correctly in isolation. This is essential for reuse—even subtle dependencies between modules quickly become problematic.

Encapsulation leads naturally to the creation of a module interface. Much like an API, a module interface describes exactly how to interact with that module. It shows the inputs that it can accept, the outputs that it provides, and details the parameters that are exposed for customization of module behavior when applied to a specific AI. With an explicit interface, handling dependencies between behaviors becomes a much simpler problem of connecting the inputs and outputs needed to properly express the behavior. Since each module is properly encapsulated, the results of adding and removing new modules become predictable.

Polymorphism arises as a result of this loose coupling. Imagine a module tasked with fleeing from an enemy. As a bite-sized module, it could perform the checks and tests needed to find an appropriate flee destination, and then send off a move output. The module that receives this output no longer matters. One AI can use a certain type of move module, while a different AI can use another. The exact type of move module should not matter much. Complicating factors, like "is my NPC on a bicycle," or "is she on a horse," and so on, can all be handled by the move module, or by other submodules. This keeps each module cleanly focused on a single functional purpose while ensuring that similar behaviors are not repeated across modules.

8.3 GAIA Overview

GAIA is a modular, extensible, reusable toolset for specifying procedural decision-making logic (i.e., AI behavior). GAIA emphasizes the role of the game designer in creating decision-making logic, while still allowing the resulting behavior to be flexible and responsive to the moment-to-moment situation in the application.

Taking those points more slowly, GAIA is:

- A library of tools that can be used to specify procedural decision-making logic (or "AI behavior").
- Focused on providing *authorial control*. In other words, the goal of GAIA is not to create a true artificial intelligence that can decide what to do on its own, but rather to provide a human author with the tools to specify decisions that will deliver the intended experience while still remaining flexible enough to handle varied and unexpected situations.
- *Modular*, meaning that behavior is typically constructed by plugging together pre-defined components. Experience has shown that this approach greatly improves the speed with which behavior can be specified and iterated on.
- *Extensible*, making it easy to add new components to the library, or to change the behavior of an existing component.
- *Reusable*, meaning that GAIA has been designed from the ground up with reuse in mind. This includes reuse of both code and data, and reuse within the current project, across future projects, and even across different game engines.

GAIA is data driven: behavior is specified in XML files and then loaded by the code at runtime. This chapter will generally refer to the XML as the *configuration* or the *data* and the C++ as the *implementation* or the *code*. For simplicity, this chapter will also use the term *NPC* to denote GAIA-controlled entities, *PC* to denote player-controlled entities, and *character* to denote entities that may be either NPCs or PCs.

8.3.1 GAIA Control Flow

GAIA makes decisions by working its way down a tree of decision makers (*reasoners*) that is in many ways similar to Damian Isla's original vision of a Behavior Tree (BT) (Isla 2005). As in a BT, different reasoners can use different approaches to decision-making, which gives the architecture a flexibility that is not possible in more homogenous hierarchical approaches (e.g., hierarchical finite-state machines, teleoreactive programming, hierarchical task network planners, etc.).

Each reasoner picks from among its *options*. The options contain *considerations*, which are used by the reasoner to decide which option to pick, and *actions*, which are executed if the option is selected. Actions can be *concrete*, meaning that they represent things that the controlled character should actually do (e.g., move, shoot, speak a line of dialog, cower in fear, etc.), or *abstract*, meaning that they contain more decision-making logic.

The most common abstract action is the AIAction_Subreasoner, which contains another reasoner (with its own options, considerations, and actions). Subreasoner actions are the mechanism GAIA uses to create its hierarchical structure. When an option that contains a subreasoner is selected, that subreasoner will start evaluating its own options and select one to execute. That option may contain concrete actions or may, in turn, contain yet another subreasoner action.

Options can also contain more than one action, which allows them to have multiple concrete actions, subreasoners, or a combination of both, all operating in parallel.

8.3.2 GAIA Implementation Concepts

Reasoners, options, considerations, and actions are all examples of *conceptual abstractions*. Conceptual abstractions are the basic types of objects that make up a modular AI. Each conceptual abstraction has an *interface* that defines it, and a set of *modular components* (or just *components*) that implement that interface. As discussed above, there are multiple different types of reasoners, for example, but all of the reasoners—that is, all of the modular components that implement the reasoner conceptual abstraction—share the same interface. Thus the surrounding code does not need to know what types of components it has. The reasoner, for example, does not need to know what particular types of considerations are being used to evaluate an option, or how those considerations are configured—it only needs to know how to work with the consideration interface in order to get the evaluation that it needs. This is the key idea behind modular AI: identify the basic parts of the AI (*conceptual abstractions*), declare an interface for each abstraction, and then define reusable *modular components* that implement that interface.

Modular components form the core of modular AI reuse—each type of component is implemented once but used many times. To make this work, each type of component needs to know how to load itself from the configuration, so that all of the parameters that define the functionality of a particular instance of a modular component can be defined in data.

Continuing with the distance example from the introduction, GAIA makes distance evaluations reusable by providing the Distance consideration. The configuration of a particular Distance consideration specifies the positions to measure the distance between, as well as how that distance should be evaluated (Should it prefer closer? Farther? Does it have to be within a particular range?). For example, a sniper selecting a target to shoot at might use a Distance consideration to evaluate each potential target. This consideration might be configured to only allow the sniper to shoot at targets that are more than 50 m and less than 500 m away, with a preference for closer targets. This consideration could then be combined with other considerations that measure whether the prospective target is friend or enemy, how much cover the target has, whether it is a high-value target (such as an officer), and so on. What is more, the consideration does not work in isolation—it makes use of other conceptual abstractions in its configuration. For instance, the two positions are specified using *targets*, and the way the distance should be combined with other considerations is specified using a *weight function*. Targets and weight functions are two of the other conceptual abstractions in GAIA.

One advantage of this approach is that it is highly extensible. As development progresses and you discover new factors that should be weighed into a decision, you can create new types of considerations to evaluate those factors and simply drop them in. Because they share the same interface as all the other considerations, nothing else needs to change. Not only does this make iterating on the AI behavior much faster, it also decreases the chance that you will introduce a bug (because all changes are localized to the consideration being added, which can be tested in isolation). Consequently, it is safer to make more aggressive changes later in the development cycle, allowing you to really polish the AI late in development once gameplay has been hammered out and QA is giving real feedback on what you have built.

This ability to rapidly specify and then easily reuse common functionality greatly reduces the amount of time it takes to specify behavior, generally paying back the cost of implementation within weeks. We have used modular AI with great success on several projects where there were only a few months to implement the entire AI—including one game whose AI was implemented in less than 4 months that went on to sell millions of copies.

8.3.3 An Example Character: The Sniper

Throughout this chapter, we will use as our example a sniper character that is based on, but not identical to, a character that was built for a military application. Broadly speaking, the sniper should wait until there are enemies in its kill zone (which happens to be an outdoor marketplace), and then take a shot every minute or two as long as there are still enemies in the marketplace to engage, but only if (a) it is not under attack and (b) it has a clear line of retreat. If it is under attack then it tries to retreat, but if its line of retreat has been blocked then it will start actively fighting back, engaging targets as rapidly as it can (whether they are in the kill zone or not). The overall structure for this configuration is shown in Figure 8.1.

At the top level of its decision hierarchy, our sniper has only four options to choose between: snipe at a target in the kill zone, retreat, fight back when engaged, or hide and wait until one of the other options is available. The decision between these options is fairly cut-and-dried, so a fairly simple reasoner should work. GAIA includes a `RuleBased` reasoner that works much like a selection node in a BT—that is, it simply evaluates its options in the order in which they were specified and takes the first one that is valid given the current situation. In this case, a `RuleBased` reasoner could be set up as follows:

- If the sniper is under fire and its line of retreat is clear, retreat.
- If the sniper is under fire, fight back.

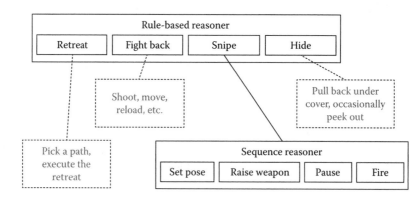

Figure 8.1

Overall structure for a sniper AI. Aspects of the AI that are not fully defined are shown with dotted lines.

- If the sniper's line of retreat is clear, there is a valid target in the kill zone, and a minute or two has elapsed since the sniper's last shot, snipe.
- Hide.

None of those options are likely to contain concrete actions. Retreat, for example, will require the AI to pick a route, move along that route, watch for enemies, react to enemies along the way, and so forth. Fight back requires the AI to pick targets, pick positions to fight from, aim and fire its weapon, reload, and so on. Hide requires it to pull back out of sight and then periodically peer out as if checking whether targets have become available. Thus, once the top-level reasoner has selected an option (such as Snipe), that option's subreasoner will evaluate its own options. In Figure 8.1, we see that the Snipe option, for example, uses a `Sequence` reasoner to step through the process of taking a shot by first getting into the appropriate pose (e.g., the "prone" pose), then raising its weapon, pausing (to simulate aiming), and finally firing.

8.4 GAIA Infrastructure

Before delving into the different conceptual abstractions and modular components, it is helpful to have an understanding of the surrounding infrastructure. This section provides an overview of the major singletons, data stores, and other objects which, while not themselves modular, support evaluation of and communication between the modular components.

8.4.1 The `AIString` Class

Strings are tremendously useful, but they also take up an unreasonable amount of space and are slow to compare. Many solutions to this problem exist; GAIA's is to use the djb2 hash function (http://www.cse.yorku.ca/~oz/hash.html) to generate a 64 bit hash for the strings and then to keep a global string table that contains all of the raw strings (as `std::strings`). This lets GAIA do constant time comparisons and store copies of strings in 64 bits. It also lets GAIA downcase the string when it is hashed, so that comparisons are case insensitive (which makes them much more designer friendly). On the other hand, it has an up-front performance cost and makes a permanent copy of every string used (whether the string itself is temporary or not), so GAIA still uses `char*` and `std::string` in places where the `AIString` does not make sense (such as debug output).

Of note, no hash function is a guarantee. If you do take this approach, it is a very good idea to have an assert that checks for hash collisions; simply look in the string table each time you hash a string and ensuring that the stored string is the same as the one you just hashed.

8.4.2 Factories

GAIA uses factories to instantiate all of the modular objects that make up the AI. In other words, the portion of a configuration that defines a consideration, for example, will be contained within a single XML node. GAIA creates the actual C++ consideration object by passing that XML node (along with some supporting information, like a pointer to the NPC that this configuration will control) to the `AIConsiderationFactory`, which instantiates and initializes an object of the appropriate type. GAIA's factory system was the topic of an earlier chapter in this book, so we will not repeat the details here (Dill 2016).

8.4.3 The `AIDataStore` Base Class

Data stores are `AIString`-indexed hash tables that can store data of any type. GAIA uses them as the basis for its blackboards and also all of its different types of entities. As a result, individual modular components can store, share, and retrieve information to and from the blackboards and/or entities without the rest of the AI having to know what is stored or even what type the information is. This allows data to be placed in the configuration that will be used by the game engine if an action is executed, for instance, or even for the game engine to pass data through to itself. Of course, it also allows AI components to share data with one another—we will see an example of this in the sniper configuration, below.

There are many ways to implement this sort of hash table, and GAIA's is not particularly special, so we will skip the implementation details. It is worth mentioning, however, that since the data stores are in essence of global memory, they run the risk of name collisions (that is, two different sets of components both trying to store data using the same name). With that said, experience has shown that as long as you have a reasonably descriptive naming convention, this is not normally a problem. Nevertheless, GAIA does have asserts in place to warn if the type of data stored is not the expected type. This will not catch every possible name collision, but it should catch a lot of them.

GAIA currently has two types of blackboards and three types of entities, described as follows.

8.4.3.1 The `AIBlackboard_Global` Data Store

The game has a single *global blackboard*, which can be used as a central repository for information that should be available to every AI component, regardless of what character that component belongs to or what side that character is on.

8.4.3.2 The `AIBlackboard_Brain` Data Store

Every AI-controlled character also has a blackboard built into its brain. The *brain blackboard* allows the components that make up that character's AI to communicate among themselves.

8.4.3.3 The `AIActor` Data Store

Every NPC is represented by an *actor*. The game stores all of the information that the AI will need about the character (e.g., its position, orientation, available weapons, etc.), and AI components can look that information up as needed. The actor also contains an `AIBrain`, which contains the top-level reasoner and all of the decision-making logic for that character.

On some projects, actors are used to represent every character, whether AI controlled or not. In these cases, actors that are not AI controlled may not have a brain or, if they switch back and forth between AI and player control, they will have a brain but it will be disabled when the AI is not in control.

8.4.3.4 The `AIContact` Data Store

As hinted above, there are two ways to keep track of what an NPC knows about the other characters in the game. The first is to use actors to represent every character and give the AI components in each NPC's brain direct access to the actors for other characters.

This works, but it either means that all NPCs will have perfect information, or that every AI component has to properly check whether they should know about a particular piece of information or not. Furthermore, even if the AI components make these checks, it still means that everything that they know is correct. This makes it much more difficult to, for example, allow the AI to know that an enemy exists but have an incorrect belief about its location.

The alternative is to have each NPC create a *contact* for every other character that it knows about, and store its knowledge of that NPC on the contact. Thus the contacts represent what the NPC knows about other characters in the game, whether that knowledge is correct or not. For example, imagine an RPG where the player steals a uniform in order to sneak past hostile guards. The guards would each have a contact that stores their knowledge of the player, and if the guards are fooled then that contact would list the player as being on their side even though he or she is actually an enemy. This allows each NPC to have its own beliefs about the characters that it is aware of, but it also means that the AI has to store a lot of redundant copies of the information for each character.

There is no single right answer here, which is why GAIA supports both approaches—the best one is the one that best supports the needs of the individual project. Using actors to represent all characters is simpler and more efficient when there is little uncertainty in the environment (or the behavior of the characters is not greatly affected by it), while using contacts is better when imperfect situational awareness plays an important role in the behavior of the NPCs.

8.4.3.5 The AIThreat Data Store

Threats represent things that an NPC knows about and should consider reacting to. They can include enemy characters (whether represented as actors or contacts), but may also include more abstract things such as recent explosions, or locations where bullets have impacted. This enables characters to react to the impact of a sniper's shot even if they do not actually know about the shooter, or to break out of cover based on where rounds are impacting rather than where they are being fired from, for example. Like contacts, threats are not used by every project, and are stored on the brain blackboard.

8.4.4 Singletons

Singletons provide managers that are globally accessible. You can access a singleton from anywhere in the codebase by simply calling the static Get() function for that class. You can also replace the default implementation of any singleton with a project-specific version (which must be a subclass) by calling Set().

8.4.4.1 The AIManager Singleton

The *AI manager* is responsible for storing all of the actors. It also has an Update() function that the game should call every tick in order to tick the actors, and thus their brains.

8.4.4.2 The AISpecificationManager and AIGlobalManager Singletons

As we have said, GAIA is data driven. All of the decision-making for an NPC is stored in its configuration, in XML. The *specification manager* is responsible for loading, parsing, and storing all of the configurations. Then, when the game creates an NPC's brain, it specifies the name of the configuration that character should use.

Duplication can happen in data as well as in code. GAIA partially addresses this by allowing configurations to include *globals*, which are component specifications that can be reused within a configuration or across all configurations. The globals are stored by the *global manager*. Globals were discussed in the earlier chapter on factories (Dill 2016).

8.4.4.3 The `AIOutputManager` Singleton

Good debug output is critical to AI development. GAIA has the usual mix of log messages, warnings, errors, and asserts, along with "status text," which describes the current decision (and is suitable for, for example, displaying in-engine next to the NPC in question). The *output manager* is responsible for handling all of those messages, routing them to the right places, enabling/disabling them, and so forth.

8.4.4.4 The `AITimeManager` Singleton

Different game engines (and different games) handle in-game time in different ways. The *time manager* has a single function (`GetTime()`), and is used throughout the AI to implement things like cooldowns and maximum durations. The built-in implementation just gets system time from the CPU, but most projects implement their own time manager that provides in-game time instead.

8.4.4.5 The `AIBlackboard_Global` Singleton

As described above, the global blackboard is a shared memory space that can be used to pass information between the game and the AI, and/or between AI components. It is a singleton so that it will be globally accessible, and also so that projects can implement their own version which is more tightly coupled with the data being shared from the game engine if they wish.

8.4.4.6 The `AIRandomManager` Singleton

Random numbers are central to many games, both inside and outside of the AI. The *random manager* contains functions for getting random values. The default implementation uses the dual-LCG approach described by Jacopin elsewhere in this volume (Jacopin 2016), but as with other singletons individual projects can replace this with a custom implementation that uses some different RNG implementation if they so desire. For example, we have a unit test project whose RNG always returns 0, making it much easier to write deterministic tests.

8.5 Modular AI: Conceptual Abstractions and Modular Components

Conceptual abstractions define the base class types that the architecture supports. In other words, these abstractions define the interfaces that the rest of GAIA will use. A modular component is the counterpart, with each component providing a concrete implementation for a conceptual abstraction. This approach, where objects interact through well-defined interfaces, allows GAIA to provide an environment that supports loosely coupled modular composition untethered from specific implementations. The developer is free to think about types of abstractions that will produce desired behaviors, and then configure the implementation by reusing and customizing existing modular components, or by creating new components as necessary. This section will describe the major conceptual abstractions used by GAIA, provide examples of their use, and give their interfaces.

8.5.1 Considerations

Considerations are the single most useful conceptual abstraction. If you are uncertain about building a full modular AI, or are just looking for a single trick that you can use to improve your existing architecture, they are the place to start.

Considerations are used to represent each of the different factors that might be weighed together to make a decision. At the core, each type of consideration provides a way to evaluate the suitability of an action with respect to the factor being considered. Listing 8.1 shows the consideration interface in full.

Listing 8.1. The consideration interface.

```
class AIConsiderationBase
{
public:
    // Load the configuration.
    virtual bool Init(const AICreationData& cd) = 0;

    // Called once per decision cycle, allows the
    // consideration to evaluate the situation and determine
    // what to return.
    virtual void Calculate() = 0;

    // These are GAIA's weight values. They return the
    // results computed by Calculate().
    virtual float GetAddend() const;
    virtual float GetMultiplier() const;
    virtual float GetRank() const;

    // Certain considerations need to know if/when they are
    // selected or deselected.
    virtual void Select()   {}
    virtual void Deselect() {}
};
```

To understand how these work in action, let's take a look at the sniper's decision to snipe at an enemy. It will only select this option if:

- The line of retreat is clear.
- There is a target in the kill zone.
- It has been "a minute or two" since the last time the sniper took a shot.

Building the configuration for this option requires three considerations: one for each of the bullet items above. Each one is a modular component that implements the consideration interface.

First, an `EntityExists` consideration is used to check whether there are any enemies in the area that the sniper will retreat through. The `EntityExists` consideration goes through all of the contacts (or all of the actors, or all of the threats, depending on how

---

it is configured) to see whether there is at least one which meets some set of constraints. In this case, the constraints are that the entity must be an enemy and that it must be inside the area that the sniper plans to escape through. That area is defined using a region, which is another conceptual abstraction (described below). This first consideration vetoes the option (i.e., does not allow it to be picked) if there is an enemy blocking the line of retreat, otherwise it allows the option to execute (but the other considerations may still veto it).

Next, the sniper needs to pick a contact to shoot at, and for this a second `EntityExists` consideration is used. The contact must be an enemy and must be in the kill zone. Other constraints can easily be added—for example, the sniper could be configured to prefer contacts that are closer, those that have less cover, and/or those that are high-value targets (such as officers). The consideration is configured to use a picker (discussed in a later section) to select the best target and store it on the brain's blackboard. If the option is selected then the Fire action will retrieve the selected target from the blackboard, rather than going through the process of selecting it all over again. As with the escape route, this consideration will veto the option if no target is found, otherwise it has no effect.

Finally, an `ExecutionHistory` consideration is used to check how long it has been since the sniper last fired a shot. This consideration picks a random delay between 60 and 120 seconds, and vetoes the option if the time since the last shot is less than that delay. Each time the option is selected (i.e., each time the reasoner picks this option and starts executing it) the consideration picks a new delay to use for the next shot.

Considerations are the single most powerful conceptual abstraction, and can be used with or without the other ideas described in this chapter. They are straightforward to implement (the only slightly tricky part is deciding how to combine them together—that topic is discussed in detail later in this chapter), but all by themselves allow you to greatly reduce duplication and increase code reuse. Once you have them, configuring a decision becomes a simple matter of enumerating the options and specifying the considerations for each option. Specifying a consideration is not much more complex than writing a single function call in code—it typically takes anywhere from a few seconds to a minute or two—but each consideration represents dozens, or often even hundreds of lines of code. From time to time you will need to add a new consideration, or add new capabilities to one that exists—but you only need to do that once for each consideration, and then you can use it again and again throughout your AI.

As considerations are heavily reused, they also allow you to take the time to add nuance to the decision-making that might be difficult to incorporate otherwise. `EntityExists` is a good example of how complex—and powerful—considerations can become, but even a very simple consideration like `ExecutionHistory` can make decisions based on how long an option has been executing, how long since it last ran, or whether it has ever run at all. This allows us to implement things like cooldowns, goal inertia (a.k.a. hysteresis), repeat penalties, and one-time bonuses with a single consideration (these concepts were discussed in detail in our previous work [Dill 2006]). It can also support a wide range of evaluation functions that drive decision-making based on that elapsed time—for example, by comparing to a random value (as we do in this example) or applying a response curve (as described in Lewis's chapter on utility function selection and in Mark's book on Behavioral Mathematics [Lewis 2016, Mark 2009]). Having a single consideration that does all of that means you can reuse it in seconds, rather than spending minutes or even hours reimplementing it. It also means that when you reuse it, you can be confident that it will work because it has already been heavily tested and thus is unlikely to contain a bug.

One issue not discussed above is how the reasoners actually go about combining considerations in order to evaluate each option. This is a big topic so we will bypass it for now (we devote an entire section to it below) and simply say that considerations return a set of *weight values* which are combined to guide the reasoner's decisions.

8.5.2 Weight Functions

While considerations do a lot to reduce duplication in your code base, there is still a lot of repetition between different types of considerations. Consequently, many of the remaining conceptual abstractions were created in order to allow us to encapsulate duplicate code within the considerations themselves. The first of these is the *weight function*.

Many different types of considerations calculate a floating point value, and then convert that single float into a set of weight values. The weight function abstraction is responsible for making that conversion. For example, the Distance consideration calculates the distance between two positions, and then uses a weight function to convert that floating point value into a set of weight values. Some games might use a Health consideration, which does the same thing with the NPC's health (or an enemy's health, for that matter). Other games might use an Ammo consideration. The ExecutionHistory consideration that we used on the sniper is another example. It actually has three weight functions: one to use when the option is selected, one to use if it has never been selected, and one to use if it was previously selected but is not selected right now.

Of course, not all considerations produce a floating point value. The EntityExists consideration, for example, produces a Boolean: TRUE if it found an entity, FALSE if it did not. Different instances of the EntityExists consideration might return different weight values for TRUE or FALSE, however. In the sniper example, one EntityExists consideration vetoes the option when an entity was found (the one that checks line of retreat) while the other vetoes the option if one is not found (the one that picks a target to shoot at). This is done by changing the configuration of the weight function that each one uses. Other considerations might also produce Boolean values—for instance, some games might have a LineOfSight consideration that is TRUE if there is line of sight between two characters, FALSE if there is not.

There are a number of different ways that we could convert from an input value to a set of weight values. For floating point numbers, we might apply a response curve (the BasicCurve weight function), or we might divide the possible input values into sections and return a different set of weight values for each section (e.g., veto the Snipe option if the range to the enemy is less than 50 m or more than 300 m, but not if it is in between—the FloatSequence weight function), or we might simply treat it as a Boolean (the Boolean weight function). We might even ignore the input values entirely and always return a fixed result (the Constant weight function)—this is often done with the ExecutionHistory consideration to ensure that a particular option is only ever selected once or that it gets a fixed bonus if it has never been selected, for example.

The consideration should not have to know which technique is used, so we use a conceptual abstraction in which the conversion is done using a consistent interface and the different approaches are implemented as modular components (the BasicCurve, FloatSequence, Boolean, or Constant weight functions, for example). The interface for this conceptual abstraction is given in Listing 8.2.

Listing 8.2. The weight function interface.

```
class AIWeightFunctionBase
{
public:
    // Load the configuration.
    virtual bool Init(const AICreationData& cd) = 0;

    // Weight functions can deliver a result based on the
    // input of a bool, int, float, or string. By default
    // int does whatever float does, while the others all
    // throw an assert if not defined in the subclass.
    virtual const AIWeightValues& CalcBool(bool b);
    virtual const AIWeightValues& CalcInt(int i);
    virtual const AIWeightValues& CalcFloat(float f);
    virtual const AIWeightValues& CalcString(AIString s);

    // Some functions need to know when the associated option
    // is selected/deselected (for example, to pick new
    // random values).
    virtual void Select()   {}
    virtual void Deselect() {}
};
```

Coming back to the sniper example, both of the `EntityExists` considerations would use a `Boolean` weight function. The `Boolean` weight function is configured with two sets of weight values: one to return if the input value is TRUE, the other if it is FALSE. In these two cases, one set of weight values would be configured to veto the option (the TRUE value for the escape route check, the FALSE value for the target selection), while the other set of weight values would be configured to have no effect on the final decision.

The `ExecutionHistory` consideration is a bit more interesting. It has three weight functions: one to use when the option is executing (which evaluates the amount of time since the option was selected), one to use if the option has never been selected (which evaluates the amount of time since the game was loaded), and one to use if the option has been selected in the past but currently is not selected (which evaluates the amount of time since it last stopped executing). In this instance, when the option is selected (i.e., when the sniper is in the process of taking a shot) we use a `Constant` weight function that is configured to have no effect. We also configure the weight function for when option has never been selected in the same way—the sniper is allowed to take its first shot as soon as it has a target. The third weight function (which is used if the option is not currently selected but has been executed in the past) uses a `FloatSequence` weight function to check whether the input value is greater than our cooldown or not, and returns the appropriate result. This weight function is also configured to randomize the cooldown each time the option is selected.

8.5.3 Reasoners

As discussed in previous sections, *reasoners* implement the conceptual abstraction that is responsible for making decisions. The configuration of each reasoner component will specify the type of reasoner, and also what the reasoner's options are. Each option can contain a set of considerations and a set of actions. The considerations are used by the reasoner to evaluate each option and decide which one to select, and the actions specify what should happen when the associated option is selected. The interface for this abstraction is given in Listing 8.3.

Listing 8.3. The reasoner interface.

```
class AIReasonerBase
{
public:
    // Load the configuration.
    virtual bool Init(const AICreationData& cd);

    // Used by the picker to add/remove options
    void AddOption(AIOptionBase& option);
    void Clear();

    // Enable/Disable the reasoner. Called when containing
    // action is selected or deselected, or when brain is
    // enabled/disabled.
    void Enable();
    void Disable();
    bool IsEnabled() const;

    // Sense, Think, and Act.
    // NOTE: Subclasses should not overload this. Instead,
    // they should overload Think() (ideally they shouldn't
    // have to do anything to Sense() or Act()).
    void Update();

    // Get the current selected option, if any. Used by the
    // picker.
    AIOptionBase* GetSelectedOption();

    // Most reasoners are considered to be done if they don't
    // have a selected option, either because they failed to
    // pick one or because they have no options.
    virtual bool IsDone();

protected:
    void Sense();
    virtual void Think();
    void Act();
};
```

GAIA currently provides four different modular reasoner components:

- The Sequence reasoner, which performs its options in the order that they are listed in the configuration (much like a sequence node in a BT). Unlike the other types of reasoners, the sequence reasoner always executes each of its options, so it ignores any considerations that may have been placed on them.
- The RuleBased reasoner, which uses the considerations on each option to determine whether the option is valid (i.e., whether it should be executed, given the current situation). Each tick, this reasoner goes down its list of options in the order that they are specified in the configuration and selects the first one that is valid. This is essentially the same approach as that of a selector node in many BT implementations.

- The FSM reasoner, which allows us to implement a finite-state machine. For this reasoner, each option contains a list of *transitions*, rather than having considerations. Each transition specifies a set of considerations (which determines whether the transition should be taken), as well as the option (i.e., the state) which should be selected if the transition does fire. The reasoner uses a picker (described in Section 8.7, below) to pick from among the transitions.
- The DualUtility reasoner, which is GAIA's utility-based reasoner. The dual utility reasoner calculates two floating point values: the *rank* and the *weight*. It then uses these two values, along with the random number generator, to select an option. Dual utility reasoning is discussed in our previous work (Dill 2015, Dill et al. 2012) and also in Section 8.6.2.

Of course, a modular architecture does not need to be limited to only these approaches to decision-making. For example, we have often considered implementing a Goal-Oriented Action Planner (GOAP) reasoner (for those cases when we want to search for sequences of actions that meet some goal). Like the FSM reasoner, this would require a bit of clever thinking but should be quite possible to fit into GAIA by implementing a new type of reasoner component.

8.5.4 Actions

Actions are the output of the reasoner—they are responsible for sending commands back to the game, making changes to the blackboard, or whatever else it is that the reasoner has decided to do. Their interface is given in Listing 8.4.

Listing 8.4. The action interface.

```
class AIActionBase
{
public:
    // Load the configuration.
    virtual bool Init(const AICreationData& cd) = 0;

    // Called when the action starts/stops execution.
    virtual void Select()    {}
    virtual void Deselect() {}

    // Called every frame while the action is selected.
    virtual void Update()    {}

    // Check whether this action is finished executing. Some
    // actions (such as a looping animation) are never done,
    // but others (such as moving to a position) can be
    // completed.
    virtual bool IsDone()    { return true; }
};
```

As discussed above, actions can either be abstract or concrete. Abstract actions are actions which exist to guide the decision-making process, like the subreasoner action. Other abstract actions include the Pause and SetVariable actions. The Pause action delays a specified amount of time before marking itself as complete. It is commonly used in the Sequence reasoner, to control the timing of the concrete actions. The SetVariable action is used to set a variable on a data store (most often the brain's blackboard).

Concrete actions, by their very nature, cannot be implemented as part of the GAIA library. They contain the game-specific code that is used to make NPCs do things. Common concrete actions include things like Move, PlayAnimation, PlaySound, FireWeapon, and so on. Our factory system handles the task of allowing the developer to inject game-specific code into the AI (Dill 2016).

8.5.5 Targets

Targets provide an abstract way for component configurations to specify positions and/or entities. For example, the Distance consideration measures the distance between two positions. In order to make this consideration reusable, GAIA needs some way to specify, in the configuration, what those two positions should be. Perhaps one is the position of the NPC and the other is the player. Perhaps one is an enemy and the other is an objective that the NPC has been assigned to protect (in a "capture the flag" style game, for instance). Ideally, the distance consideration should not have to know how the points it is measuring between are calculated—it should just have some mechanism to get the two positions, and then it can perform the calculation from there. Similarly, the LineOfSight consideration needs to know what positions or entities to check line of sight between, the Move action needs to know where to move to, the FireWeapon action needs to know what to shoot at, and so on.

GAIA's solution to this is the *target* conceptual abstraction, whose interface is shown in Listing 8.5. Targets provide a position and/or an entity for other components to use. For example, the Self target returns the actor and position for the NPC that the AI controls. The ByName target looks up a character by name (either from the actors or the contacts, depending on how it is configured).

Listing 8.5. The target interface.

```
class AITargetBase
{
public:
    // Load the configuration.
    virtual bool Init(const AICreationData& cd) = 0;

    // Get the target's position. If the target has an
    // entity, it should generally be that entity's
    // position.
    virtual const AIVectorBase* GetPosition() const = 0;

    // Not all types of targets have entities. If this one
    // does, get it. NOTE: It's possible for HasEntity() to
    // return true (i.e. this type of target has an entity)
    // but GetEntity() to return NULL (i.e. the entity that
    // this target represents doesn't currently exist). In
    // that case, HasEntity() should return true, but
    // IsValid() should return false.
    virtual AIEntityInfo* GetEntity() const { return NULL; }
    virtual bool HasEntity() const          { return false; }
```

(Continued)

```
    // Checks whether the target is valid. For instance, a
    // target that tracks a particular contact by name might
    // become invalid if we don't have contact with that
    // name. Most target types are always valid.
    virtual bool IsValid() const            { return true; }
};
```

All targets can provide a position, but some do not provide an entity. For example, the Position target returns a fixed (x, y, z) position (which is specified in the target's configuration), but does not return an entity. The person writing the configuration should be aware of this and make sure not to use a target that does not provide an entity in situations where an entity is needed, but GAIA also has checks in place to ensure that this is the case. In practice this is really never an issue—it simply would not make sense to use a Position target in a situation where an entity is needed, so why would a developer ever do that?

As with all conceptual abstractions, some types of targets can be implemented in GAIA, while others need to be implemented by the game. For example, some games might add a Player target which returns the contact (or actor) for the PC. For other games (such as multiplayer games, or games where the player is not embodied in the world) this type of target would make no sense.

8.5.6 Regions

Regions are similar to targets, except that instead of specifying a single (x, y, z) position in space, they specify a larger area. They are commonly used for things like triggers and spawn areas, although they have a myriad of other uses. The sniper configuration, for example, would use them to specify both the kill zone (the area it should fire into) and the line of retreat (the area it plans to move through in order to get away).

Regions are a conceptual abstraction because it is useful to supply the AI designer with a variety of ways to specify them. Implementations might include a circular region (specified as a center position—or a target—and a radius), a parallelogram region (specified as a base position and two vectors to give the length and angle of the sides), and a polygon region (specified as a sequence of vertices). Similarly, some games will be perfectly happy with simple 2D regions, while others will need to specify an area in all three dimensions. The interface for this abstraction is given in Listing 8.6.

Listing 8.6. The region interface.

```
class AIRegionBase
{
public:
    // Load the configuration.
    virtual bool Init(const AICreationData& cd) = 0;

    // Test if a specified position is within the region
    virtual bool IsInRegion(const AIVector& pos) const = 0;
```
(Continued)

```
    // Set the outVal parameter to a random position within
    // the region
    // NOTE: IT MAY BE POSSIBLE FOR THIS TO FAIL on some
    // types of regions. It returns success.
    virtual bool GetRandomPos(AIVector& outVal) const = 0;
};
```

8.5.7 Other Conceptual Abstractions

Conceptual abstractions provide a powerful mechanism that allows us to encapsulate and reuse code which otherwise would have to be duplicated. The abstractions discussed above are the most commonly used (and most interesting), but GAIA includes a few others, including:

- Sensors, which provide one mechanism to pass data into the AI (though most projects simply write to the data stores directly).
- Execution filters, which can control how often reasoners and/or sensors tick.
- Entity filters, which are an alternative to pickers for selecting an entity that meets some set of constraints.
- Data elements, which encapsulate the things stored in data stores.
- Vectors, which abstract away the implementation details of how a particular game or simulation represents positions (it turns out that not every project uses (x, y, z)).

Furthermore, as GAIA continues to improve, from time to time new conceptual abstractions are found and added (vectors are the most recent example of this). GAIA includes a system of macros and templatized classes that allow us to create most of the infrastructure for each conceptual abstraction, including both their factory and the storage for any global configurations, by calling a single macro and passing in the name of the abstraction (Dill 2016).

8.6 Combining Considerations

Considerations are the single most important type of modular component. They are, in many ways, the key decomposition around which GAIA revolves. In general terms, they are the bite-sized pieces out of which decision-making logic is built. They represent concepts like the distance between two targets, the amount of health a target has left, or how long it is been since a particular option was last selected. Reasoners use the considerations to evaluate each option and select the one that they will execute—but how should reasoners combine the outputs of their considerations?

Over the years we have tried a number of different solutions to this problem. Some were quite simple, others were more complex. This chapter will present one from each end of the spectrum: a very simple Boolean approach that was used for a trigger system in an experimental educational game (Dill and Graham 2016, Dill et al. 2015) and a more complex utility-based approach that combines three values to perform the option's evaluation (Dill 2015, Dill et al. 2012). While the latter approach might initially seem too hard to work with, experience has shown that it is both extremely flexible and, once the basic conventions are understood, straightforward to use for both simple and complex decisions.

8.6.1 Simple Boolean Considerations

The simplest way to combine considerations is to treat them as Booleans. Each option is given a single consideration, which either returns TRUE (the option can be selected) or FALSE (it cannot). Logical operations such as AND, OR, and NOT can be treated as regular considerations, except that they contain one or more child considerations and return the combined evaluation of their children. Thus an option's single consideration will often be an AND or an OR which contains a list of additional considerations (some of which may, themselves, be Boolean operations).

This approach was used for the trigger system in *The Mars Game*, which was an experimental educational game, set on Mars, that taught topics drawn from ninth and tenth grade math and programming. An example of a *Mars Game* trigger is shown in Listing 8.7 (specified in YAML). This particular trigger waits 15 seconds after the start of the level, and then plays a line of dialog that gives a hint about how to solve a particular challenge in the game, and also writes a value on the blackboard indicating that the hint has been played. However, it only plays the hint if:

- The hint has not already been played during a previous level (according to that value on the blackboard).
- The player has not already started executing a Blockly program on their rover.
- The player's rover is facing either south or west (i.e., 180° or 270°), since the hint describes how to handle the situation where you start out facing the wrong way.

Listing 8.7. Trigger a hint.

```
playHint_2_9_tricky:
  triggerCondition:
  - and:
    - delay:                      # Wait 15 seconds after the
      - 15                        #   start of the level.
    - not:
      - readBlackboard:           # Check the blackboard and
        - thisOneIsTrickyHint     #   only play it once.
    - not:                        # Don't play it if the player
      - isBlocklyExecuting:       #   has already started their
        - rover                   #   program.
    - or:
      - hasHeading:               # Only play it if the rover
        - rover                   #   is facing south or west.
        - 180
      - hasHeading:
        - rover
        - 270
  actions:
  - playSound:                    # Play the hint dialog.
    - ALVO37_Rover
  - writeToBlackboard:            # Update the blackboard so
    - thisOneIsTrickyHint         #   that it won't play again.
```

This approach has the obvious advantage of great simplicity. Most developers—even game designers—are comfortable with Boolean logic, so it is not only straightforward to implement but also straightforward to use. It works quite well for things like trigger systems and rule-based reasoners that make decisions about each option in isolation, without ever needing to compare two options together to decide which is best. It suffers greatly, however, if there is ever a case where you do want to make more nuanced decisions—and those cases often pop up late in a project, when the designer (or QA, or the publisher, or the company owner) comes to you to say "what it does is mostly great, but in this one situation I would like it to…"

With that in mind, most projects will be best served by an approach that allows Boolean decisions to be specified in a simple way, but also supports complex comparisons when and where they are needed—which brings us to dual utility considerations.

8.6.2 Dual Utility Considerations

Dual utility considerations are the approach used by GAIA. Each consideration returns three values: an *addend*, a *multiplier*, and a *rank*. These three values are then combined to create the overall *weight* and *rank* of the option, which are the two utility values that give this approach its name.

8.6.2.1 Calculating Weight and Rank

Taking those steps one at a time, the first thing that happens is that the addends and multipliers are combined into an overall weight for the option (W_O). This is done by first adding all of the addends together, and then multiplying the result by all of the multipliers.

$$W_O = \left(\sum_{i=1}^{n} A_i \right) \cdot \left(\prod_{i=1}^{n} M_i \right) \tag{8.1}$$

Next, the option's overall rank (R_O) is calculated. This is done by taking the max of the ranks of the considerations.

$$R_O = \text{Max}_{i=1}^{n} \left(R_i \right) \tag{8.2}$$

There are other formulas that could be used to calculate weight and rank, and GAIA does support some alternatives (more on this in a later section), but the vast majority of the time these two formulas are the ones that we use.

8.6.2.2 Selecting an Option

Once the weight and rank have been calculated, the reasoner needs to use them to select an option. Exactly how this is done depends on the type of the reasoner, but all are based on the dual utility reasoner.

The idea behind dual utility reasoning is that the AI will use the rank to divide the options into categories, and then use weight-based random to pick from among the options in the highest ranked category. In reality, there are actually four steps to accomplish this:

1. Eliminate any options that have $W_O \leq 0$. They cannot be selected in step 4 and will make step 2 more complicated, so it is best to eliminate them up front.

2. Find the highest *rank* from among the options that remain, and eliminate any option with a rank lower than that. This step ensures that only options from the highest ranked category are considered.

3. Find the highest *weight* from among the options that remain, and eliminate options whose weight is "much less than" that weight. "Much less than" is defined as a percentage that is specified in the reasoner's configuration—and in many cases the reasoner is configured to skip this step entirely. This step makes it possible to ensure that the weight-based random will not pick a very low weight option when much better options exist, because doing so often looks stupid—the option was technically possible, but not very sensible given the other choices available.

4. Use weight-based random to select from among the options that remain.

A couple things are worth calling out. First, notice step 1. Any option can be eliminated simply by setting its weight to 0, no matter what the weights and ranks of the other options are. What is more, looking back at Equation 8.1, any consideration can force the weight of an option to 0 (i.e., *veto* it) by returning a multiplier of 0, no matter what the values on the other considerations. Anything times 0 is 0. This provides a straightforward way to treat dual utility options as if they had purely Boolean considerations when we want to. We say that an option is *valid* (which is to say that it is selectable) if it has $W_O > 0$ and *invalid* if it does not. The rule-based reasoner works by checking its options in order, and selecting the first valid one, regardless of rank.

8.6.2.3 Configuring Dual Utility Considerations

The key to implementing dual utility considerations is to provide default values that ensure that even though the system is capable of considerable complexity, the complexity is hidden when configuring a consideration unless and until it is needed. This section will discuss the default values, naming conventions, and other tricks that GAIA uses to accomplish this. Along the way, it will give examples that might be used by our sniper AI to pick a target.

In GAIA, the most basic way to specify weight values is to simply specify the `addend`, `multiplier`, and/or `rank` as attributes in the XML. Any of the three values that are not specified will be set to a default value that has no effect (i.e., an `addend` of 0, a `multiplier` of 1, and a `rank` of `-FLT_MAX`, which is the smallest possible floating point value). Thus the developer who is configuring the AI only needs to specify the values that he or she wants to change.

As an example, a good sniper should prefer to shoot at officers. In order to implement this, the game can place a Boolean "IsOfficer" value on each contact (remember that contacts are data stores, so we can store any value that we want there). This value would be true if the NPC believes that contact to be an officer (whether or not the belief is true), false otherwise. Then, in the configuration, we use a `BooleanVariable` consideration to look up this value from the `PickerEntity` target (the picker entity is the entity that we are considering picking). The consideration uses a `Boolean` weight function to set the multiplier to 10 if the value is true, otherwise it does nothing (i.e., returns default values). Assuming that there are about 10 enlisted enemies (each with a weight of roughly 1) per officer (with a weight of roughly 10) this means that, all other things being equal, the sniper will shoot at an officer about half of the time. This consideration's configuration is shown in Listing 8.8.

Listing 8.8. A consideration that prefers to pick officers.

```
<Consideration Type="BooleanVariable"
               Variable="IsOfficer"
               DataStore="Target">
  <DataStoreTarget Type="PickerEntity"/>
  <WeightFunction Type="Boolean">
    <TrueWeights Multiplier="10"/>
  </WeightFunction>
</Consideration>
```

In some cases, a consideration wants to prevent its option from being selected no matter what the other considerations say. For example, when the sniper is picking its target we might want to ensure that it only shoots at entities that it thinks are enemies. This could be implemented by storing the "Side" of each contact as an AIString, with possible values of "Friendly," "Enemy," or "Civilian." If the "Side" is not "Enemy," then the sniper should not select this target no matter where it is or whether it is an officer or not. This could be configured by specifying a multiplier of 0, but configurations should be more explicit and easier to read. With this in mind, rather than specifying an addend, multiplier, and rank, weights can specify a Boolean veto attribute. If veto is true then, under the covers, the multiplier will be set to 0. If it is false, then the default values will be used for all three weight values.

The resulting consideration for the sniper would look like Listing 8.9. This consideration is much like the one in Listing 8.8, except that it looks up a string variable rather than a Boolean one, and passes the result into a String weight function. The string weight function tries to match the string against each of its entries. If the string does not match any of the entries, then it returns the default values. In this case, that means that if the string is "Enemy," then the consideration will have no effect (because when veto is false it returns the default values), otherwise it will set the multiplier to 0 (because veto is TRUE) and thus make the option invalid.

Listing 8.9. A consideration that vetoes everything other than enemies.

```
<Consideration Type="StringVariable"
               Variable="Side"
               DataStore="Target">
  <DataStoreTarget Type="PickerEntity"/>
  <WeightFunction Type="String">
    <Entries>
      <String Value="Enemy" Veto="False"/>
    </Entries>
    <Default Veto="True"/>
  </WeightFunction>
</Consideration>
```

As an aside, the considerations in Listings 8.8 and 8.9 do a nice job of showing exactly why modular AI is so powerful. These considerations evaluate the value from a variable on a data store. It could be any variable on any data store. In this particular case the data store is specified using a target (rather than being, say, the NPC's actor or the brain's blackboard), which again could be any type of target that specifies an entity. Once the consideration has looked up the value for the variable, it passes that value to a weight function to be converted into weight values. Without the ideas of considerations, and data stores, and weight functions, we would have to write a specialized chunk of code for each of these checks that is only used inside of the sniper's target selection, and is duplicated anywhere else that a Boolean data store variable is used. Furthermore, that code would be dozens of lines of C++ code, not a handful of lines of XML. Most importantly, though, the values being specified in the XML are for the most part the sorts of human concepts that we would use when describing the logic to a coworker or friend. What should the AI evaluate? The target that it is considering shooting (the `PickerEntity` target). How should it evaluate that target? By checking whether it is an enemy, and whether it is an officer. What should it do with this evaluation? Only shoot at enemies, and pick out the enemy officers about half the time.

There is one other detail to configuring considerations that has not been discussed yet. In order to be selected, every option needs to have a weight that is greater than 0, but the default addend for all of the considerations is 0. If we do not have at least one consideration with an addend greater than 0 then the overall weight is guaranteed to be 0 for the same reason it is when we set the multiplier to 0—anything times 0 is 0. Furthermore, we would like the default weight for all options to be something reasonable, like 1.

We address this problem with the `Tuning` consideration, which is a consideration that simply returns a specified `addend`, `multiplier`, and `rank`, and which has a default `addend` of 1. The option's configuration can (and often does) specify a `Tuning` consideration, but if it does not then a default `Tuning` consideration with an addend of 1 will automatically be added.

8.6.2.4 Changing Combination Techniques at Runtime

Up until now, we have said that the option owns the considerations, and is responsible for combining them together for the reasoners. This is actually slightly inaccurate. The option has an `AIConsiderationSet`, which in turn contains the considerations. The consideration set is responsible for combining its considerations and returning the overall weight and rank, and it can also return the combined addend and multiplier for its considerations without multiplying them into an overall weight. Its interface is shown in Listing 8.10. This distinction is important, because it means that we can place flags on the consideration set to specify that the considerations in that particular set should be combined with different rules. What is more, there is a special type of consideration that contains another consideration set (called the `AIConsideration_ConsiderationSet`). This makes it possible to have different rules for some of the considerations on an option than for the others.

The most commonly used alternate approaches for combining considerations are ones that apply different Boolean operations to the weights. By default, if any consideration vetoes an option (i.e., returns a multiplier of 0) then that option will not be selected. This is in essence of a conjunction (i.e., a logical AND)—all of the considerations have to be "true" (i.e., have multiplier greater than 0) in order for the option to be "true" (i.e., valid). In some cases, rather than an AND, we want a logical OR—that is, we want the option to be valid as long as at least one consideration does not have a multiplier of 0. This is implemented by having the consideration set ignore any consideration with a multiplier less than or equal to 0, unless every consideration has a multiplier that is less than or equal to 0. Similarly, NOT is implemented by having the consideration replace any multiplier that is less than or equal to 0 with 1, and any multiplier that is greater than 0 with 0.

```
class AIConsiderationSet
{
public:
    bool Init(const AICreationData& cd);

    // Evaluate all of the considerations and calculate the
    // overall addend, multiplier, weight, and rank.
    void Calculate();

    // Sets the best rank and weight currently under
    // consideration. These don't change the calculated
    // values, but they will change the values returned by
    // GetRank() and GetWeight().
    void SetScreeningWeight(float bestWeight);
    void SetScreeningRank(float bestRank);

    // Get the rank and weight. GetWeight() returns 0 if
    // the screening rank or screening weight checks fail.
    float GetWeight() const;
    float GetRank() const;

    // Get the raw values, unscreened.
    float GetAddend() const;
    float GetMultiplier() const;
    float GetWeightUnscreened() const;
    float GetRankUnscreened() const;
};
```

GAIA also supports different approaches for combining the ranks: rather than taking the max, it can take the min or add all of the considerations' ranks together to get the overall rank. All of these changes are configured just like everything else—which is to say that there is an attribute that tells the consideration set which calculation method to use, and the defaults (when the attribute is not specified) are to use the standard approaches.

More techniques for configuring dual utility considerations and for working with utility in general can be found in Dill (2006), Dill et al. (2012), Lewis (2016), and Mark (2009).

8.7 Pickers

The last topic that we will cover in this chapter is *pickers*. Pickers use a reasoner to go through a list of things (typically either the list of contacts, actors, or threats, but it could also be the list of transitions on an FSM option) and select the best one for some purpose (e.g., the best one to talk to, the best on to shoot at, the best one to use for cover, etc.). There are slight differences between the picker used by the EntityExists consideration (which picks an entity) and the one used by an FSM reasoner (which picks a transition), but the core ideas are the same; in the interests of brevity, we will focus on picking entities.

While most reasoners have all of their options defined in their configuration, a picker's reasoner has to pick from among choices that are determined at runtime. For example, we might use a picker to look through our contacts to pick something to shoot at, or to look through our threats to pick one to react to, or to look through nearby cover positions to pick one to use (although the game would have to extend GAIA with support for cover positions to do this last one). The `EntityExists` considerations in our sniper example use pickers to pick something to shoot at, and also to check for an entity that is blocking its line of retreat. The first picker should use a dual utility reasoner, because it wants to pick the best entity. The second one might use a rule-based reasoner, because it just needs to know whether such an entity exists or not.

Picker options are created on-the-fly by taking all of the entities in some category (for instance all of the actors, or all of the contacts, or all of the threats), and creating an option for each one. Each of these options is given the same considerations, which are specified in the configuration. The considerations can access the entity that they are responsible for evaluating by using the `PickerEntity` target. For example, the picker that is used to pick a sniper's target might have considerations that check things like the distance to the target, whether it is in the kill zone, how much cover it has, whether it is an enemy, whether it is an officer, and so forth. The picker that checks line of retreat would simply check whether each entity is an enemy, and whether it is in the region that defines the escape route.

Putting everything together, a simple option for the sniper that considers taking a shot might look like Listing 8.11. This option uses an `EntityExists` consideration to pick a target, and then stores the selected target in the `SnipeTarget` variable on the brain's blackboard. The picker has two considerations—one to check that the target is an enemy, and the other to check that it is between 50 m and 300 m away. It uses a `Boolean` weight function to veto the option if a target is not found. If a target is found, it uses the `Fire` action to take a shot. In reality, we would probably want to add more considerations to the picker (to make target selection more intelligent), but the key ideas are shown here.

Listing 8.11. An option for the sniper, which picks a target and shoots at it.

```
<Option Type="ConsiderationAndAction">
  <Considerations>
    <!-- Look through the contacts, pick a target, store it
         on the brain's blackboard as SnipeTarget. -->
    <Consideration Type="EntityExists"
                   Location="Contacts"
                   Variable="SnipeTarget">

      <Picker>
        <!-- This picker uses a dual utility reasoner because
             it wants to pick the *best* target. A picker
             that just wants to check whether any entity
             meets some set of constraints (like the one for
             checking line of retreat) would likely use a
             rule-based reasoner instead. -->
        <Reasoner Type="DualUtility"/>
```

(Continued)

```xml
            <Considerations>
               <!-- Only targets between 50m and 300m away -->
               <Consideration Type="Distance">
                  <FromTarget Type="Self"/>
                  <ToTarget Type="PickerEntity"/>
                  <WeightFunction Type="FloatSequence">
                     <Entries>
                        <Entry Exact="50" Veto="true"/>
                        <Entry Exact="300" Veto="false"/>
                     </Entries>
                     <Default Veto="true"/>
                  </WeightFunction>
               </Consideration>

               <!-- Only enemies -->
               <Consideration Type="StringVariable"
                              Variable="Side"
                              DataStore="Target">
                  <DataStoreTarget Type="PickerEntity"/>
                  <WeightFunction Type="String">
                     <Entries>
                        <String Value="Enemy" Veto="False"/>
                     </Entries>
                     <Default Veto="True"/>
                  </WeightFunction>
               </Consideration>

               <!-- Other considerations (like the one to prefer
                       officers, or one to check that the target is
                       in the kill zone) could be added here. -->

            </Considerations>
         </Picker>

         <!-- Use a default Boolean weight function - that is,
                 veto if a target is not found -->
         <WeightFunction Type="Boolean"/>
      </Consideration>

      <!-- The considerations to check line of retreat and time
              since the last shot would go here. -->
      ...

   </Considerations>

   <Actions>
      <!-- Fire at the target the picker picked -->
      <Action Type="Fire">
         <Target Type="DataElement_EntityList"
                 Variable="SnipeTarget"/>
      </Action>
   </Actions>
</Option>
```

8.8 Conclusion

Modular AI is an approach to AI specification that draws heavily on principles from software engineering to dramatically reduce code duplication and increase reuse. It allows the developer to rapidly specify decision-making logic by plugging together modular components that represent human-level concepts, rather than by implementing code in C++. Because these components are implemented once and then widely reused, they become both more robust (i.e., more heavily tested) and more feature laden (i.e., capable of more subtle nuance) than would be feasible if each component were only ever used once. What's more, because most of the work consists of invoking code that has already been written, AI specification can be done much, much faster than would otherwise be possible. Modular AI has been used with success on several projects that were only a couple months long, including one game that sold over 5,000,000 copies in which we implemented all of the boss AI, from scratch (including implementing the architecture), in less than 4 months.

This chapter presented a full modular architecture (GAIA), which uses a variety of different types of modular components. Of all of those conceptual abstractions, considerations are by far the most powerful. For those who are constrained to work within an existing architecture, it is very possible to get much of the benefit of modular AI even within an existing architecture, simply by implementing considerations and allowing them to drive your evaluation functions. We took this approach on another best-selling game with great success.

References

Dill, K. 2006. Prioritizing actions in a goal based RTS AI. In *AI Game Programming Wisdom 3*, ed. S. Rabin. Boston, MA: Charles River Media, pp. 321–330.

Dill, K. 2015. Dual utility reasoning. In *Game AI Pro 2*, ed. S. Rabin. Boca Raton, FL: CRC Press, pp. 23–26.

Dill, K. 2016. Six factory system tricks for extensibility and library reuse. In *Game AI Pro 3*, ed. S. Rabin. Boca Raton, FL: CRC Press, pp. 49–62.

Dill, K., B. Freeman, S. Frazier, and J. Benito. 2015. Mars game: Creating and evaluating an engaging educational game. *Proceedings of the 2015 Interservice/Industry Training, Simulation & Education Conference*, December 2015, Orlando, FL.

Dill, K. and R. Graham. 2016. Quick and dirty: 2 lightweight AI architectures. *Game Developer's Conference*, March 2016, San Francisco, CA.

Dill, K., E.R. Pursel, P. Garrity, and G. Fragomeni. 2012. Design patterns for the configuration of utility-based AI. *Proceedings of the 2012 Interservice/Industry Training, Simulation & Education Conference*, December 2012, Orlando, FL.

Isla, D. 2005. Handling complexity in Halo 2 AI. http://www.gamasutra.com/view/feature/130663/gdc_2005_proceeding_handling_.php (accessed June 26, 2016).

Jacopin, É. 2016. Vintage random number generators. In *Game AI Pro 3*, ed. S. Rabin. Boca Raton, FL: CRC Press, pp. 471–478.

Lewis, M. 2016. Choosing effective utility-based considerations. In *Game AI Pro 3*, ed. S. Rabin. Boca Raton, FL: CRC Press, pp. 167–178.

Mark, D. 2009. *Behavioral Mathematics for Game AI*. Boston, MA: Charles River Media.

9

Overcoming Pitfalls in Behavior Tree Design

Anthony Francis

9.1 Introduction

Unless you have been living under a rock, or are new to the game industry, you have probably heard of behavior trees (Isla 2005, Champandard and Dunstan 2012). Behavior trees are an architecture for controlling NPCs based on a hierarchical graph of tasks, where each task is either an atomic, a simple behavior an agent can directly perform, or a composite, a behavior performed by a lower level behavior tree of arbitrary complexity. As they provide a cleaner decomposition of behavior than alternatives such as hierarchical finite-state machines—and because of the many good reports from people who have successfully used them—behavior trees are increasingly used to allow large software teams to collaborate on complex agent behaviors, not just in games but in the robotics industry. But there are a few key choices in their implementation, which can either make them much harder to architect than they need to be—or much more flexible, easy to extend, and easy to reuse.

I found this out the hard way. By a weird trick of fate, I have implemented behavior trees five times, including three systems in Lisp similar to the architecture that later got the name behavior trees as part of the *Halo 2* AI, and more recently two behavior tree implementations in C++ for robots at Google. Along the way, I have learned some of the things to NOT do when creating a behavior tree—including needlessly multiplying core primitives, inventing a whole programming language for control, and jumping the gun on routing all communication through "proper" channels like a blackboard—and I have developed specific recommendations on how to create a system which avoids these pitfalls, especially if licensing or interoperability concerns prevent you from building on existing commercial or open-source solutions.

9.2 What Makes Behavior Trees Work

Ideas like behavior trees were around long before *Halo*. Hierarchical decompositions of behavior into tasks were pioneered in particular by reactive action packages, or RAPs (Firby 1987): high-level RAPs get decomposed into low-level RAPs, ultimately bottoming out in leaf skills used to directly control real and simulated robots (Bonasso et al. 1997). My TaskStorm architecture is even closer to modern behavior trees, integrating hierarchical task decomposition directly into a blackboard system encapsulating the agent state, enabling cognitive operations to be time sliced with each other over the course of behavior (Francis 2000).

Although these systems are *functionally* similar to behavior trees, the key insight that Damian Isla added is a software design focus on simplifying the code needed to generate behaviors (Isla 2005). Isla argues that four key features made it possible to create the *Halo 2* AI and its successors at large scales: customizability, explicitness, hackability, and variability. Behavior trees are customizable because behaviors are decomposed into smaller components, which can be individually changed or parameterized; they are explicit because the things that an agent does can be represented as distinct behavior nodes, and the whole behavior as a graph; they are hackable because the radical decomposition of behaviors makes it easy to replace nodes with custom versions, and they allow variability because the control algorithms themselves are represented as nodes.

In my experience, it is easy to get lost building functionality that you think you will need and in the process lose sight of this simplification focus. A system which functionally breaks behaviors into atomic behaviors orchestrated by trees of composite behaviors may act like a behavior tree, but it will not be customizable or hackable if behaviors are too tightly coupled, nor will it be explicit or variable if the nodes are too large. What is worse, architectural constraints to enforce these features can become a cure worse than the disease, making the overall system harder to maintain. Although some of these problems are unavoidable, other pitfalls are easy enough to avoid if we are careful about how we design our behavior trees.

9.3 Pitfalls in Behavior Tree Design

A behavior tree runs as a decision-making component within a larger structure—a game engine, a robot operating system, or a cognitive architecture—and it is tempting to design something that serves all the needs of the parent system. But software components work better when they have clearly defined responsibilities and clear separation of concerns, and making your behavior tree too much can, perversely, leave you with something that does too little. Three of these pitfalls are

1. Adding too many kinds of classes to the decision architecture of your behavior tree.
2. Building a complete programming language into your behavior tree before you need it.
3. Forcing all communication to route through the blackboard as a point of principle, rather than when required by the needs of the application at hand.

If you are on a large project and have a clear specification for (or experience with) what you need, (2) and (3) may not apply to you; but if you are on a smaller or novel project, simpler structures may work for you.

9.3.1   Pitfall #1: Creating Too Many Organizing Classes

Occam's Razor gets reduced to "Keep It Simple, Stupid," but originally stated, translated more like "Do not multiply entities needlessly"—which is more on point for understanding a pitfall of behavior tree architecture: creating a separate architectural category for every kind of thing that your system needs to do. This, perversely makes it harder to develop the features you need.

For example, in addition to atomic behaviors that perform actions and composite behaviors which orchestrate them, your characters may need low-level "skills" that directly manipulate your animation system or your robot controllers, or high-level "modules" that manage the resources provided by your game engine or your robot operating system. But it is probably a mistake to have a separate architectural category for each of these—that is root classes for Behaviors, Composites, Skills, and Modules. Behavior trees already provide low-level and high-level constructs, and with the addition of an external memory store, their decision-making power is Turing-complete. So why not just use behaviors?

Many of the prehistoric behavior tree-like systems, described earlier, made distinctions between concepts like skills, tasks, task networks, or modules—and created classes or modules to implement each. This approach got the job done, and maybe was a fine way to do things in the bad old days of Lisp hacking—but this multiplication of entities introduces pitfalls in modern C++ development, which often depends on having smaller numbers of classes to enable quicker refactoring.

For example, one behavior tree we developed for an internal Google robotics project had both `Modules`, which talked to the robot operating system via `Contexts`, and `Tasks` that made up the behavior tree themselves, which communicated to agents indirectly through thin wrappers called `AgentHandles` that hid the underlying communication protocols. But as the architecture of the system evolved, every simple refactoring affected both trees of classes—`Modules` and `Tasks`—and more complex new functionalities affecting things like the blackboard system had to be developed for and woven into both since their features were not quite in parity.

The converse of creating too many kinds of organizing abstractions is to use just one: tasks. We have yet to be burned by thinking of everything we can do in a behavior tree as creating a new kind of task. Performing an atomic action? A task. Grouping several actions? Another kind of task. Accessing system resources? A task. Running an entire behavior tree script? Yet another kind of task. We ultimately adopted a mantra "It's Tasks, All the Way Down."

When we ported this behavior tree to a new robotic platform, everything became a task. Well, technically, not everything—resources from the robot operating system were provided uniformly by `ExecutionContext`, but all classes responsible for behaviors—Modules, things like the old `AgentHandles`, and scripts—were implemented as children of a single task, the `SchedulableTask`, shown in Listing 9.1; this class provides an interface for a single decision-making step, given a particular `ExecutionContext`.

Forcing all these different types into a single model did not hurt us; on the contrary, the result was that our new behavior tree became a system with a single responsibility—decision-making—whose API had just two points of external contact: the `ExecutionContext`

```
class SchedulableTask {
 public:
  SchedulableTask(
    const string& name,
    ExecutionContext* execution_context);
  virtual ~SchedulableTask() = default;
  virtual TaskStatus Step();
  // More member functions relevant to our use case ...

 private:
  string name_;
  ExecutionContext* execution_context_;
  TaskStatus status_;
};
```

provided at the top or custom code in leaf tasks at the bottom. This simpler design enabled us to build out functionality in weeks where the old system had taken us months.

9.3.2 Pitfall #2: Implementing a Language Too Soon

A behavior tree is a decision-making system, which means that the behavior nodes that make up the tree need two separate properties: a node needs both the ability to run a behavior and to decide whether to run it. This raises the question of whether the behavior tree system itself should implement a condition language.

You can do a lot with a little; even very simple decision-making structures are Turing-complete: you can perform virtually any computation with just NANDs or NORs. Therefore, you can implement sophisticated control behaviors with very few node types. Tests can be implemented by atomic actions that simply succeed or fail; if–thens can be implemented by composites like Selectors that execute the first nonfailing action, and blocks of code can be implemented by Sequences that execute all their nonfailing actions or Parallel nodes, which allow multiple actions to be executed concurrently (Champandard and Dunstan 2012).

But implementing complicated behaviors out of very simple components, Tinkertoy-style, can lead to a lot of boilerplate—so it is tempting to add more control constructs. A Decorator task that wraps other tasks enables the creation of Not that inverts the significance of failures; a subclass of a Sequence can create an And task that succeeds only if all its tasks succeed, and so on, and so on. Soon you find yourself developing a whole programming language, which enables you to parsimoniously represent character logic.

Perhaps surprisingly for a "pitfalls" section, I am not recommending that you do not implement a whole programming language (how is that for a double negative); if your behavior tree gets a lot of usage, you probably do want to implement a language. But I have implemented these kinds of languages in two different ways: driving from the top–down from language concerns and driving from the bottom up based on an understanding of the problem domain, and the latter is a much more effective strategy.

There are an enormous number of possible language constructs—`Not`, `And`, `Or`, `If-Then-Else`, `Cond`, `Loop`, `For`, `While`, `Repeat-Until`, `Progn`, `Parallel`, `Any`, `All`, `Try-Catch-Except`—one or more of which you may have fallen in love with when learning your favorite programming language (which may not be the C++ you are forced to program in). The logic for most of these constructs is very clear, so it is easy to build up a large library for any possible need.

The problem is, much of this logic is better implemented using just standard behavior tree nodes—Actions, Decorators, Sequences, Parallels, and Selectors. (I challenge you to find a meaningful difference between a Selector and a Cond). The best case scenario is that you end up with a node with a nonstandard name. A worse scenario is that you code functionality you do not need. The actual worst-case scenario is that you end up with duplicated logic between very similar nodes that you actually need but now have trouble maintaining as your API evolves.

A better approach is to begin with the standard set of behavior tree nodes—Actions, Decorators, Sequences, Parallels, and Selectors—and to push these as far as you can for your problem domain. If you are implementing it yourself, each behavior tree will have slightly different semantics for task execution, failure and success, and logical tests. Once you understand what patterns you need for your problem domain, you can then expand out your language—often by specializing an existing construct for a new need. This will result in less duplicated, easier to maintain code—and a library of constructs driven by what is useful for your game.

This is easy to see for structural features like object containment; for example, if the SchedulableTask has GetChildren and AddChild to manage its children, these should be overridden differently in atomic leaf tasks with no children and in composite tasks which have children. For almost all of the different kinds of containers in our use case, one high-level class, the ContainerTask shown in Listing 9.2, suffices to handle all these implementation details.

Listing 9.2. Expanding SchedulableTask to support ContainerTask.

```
// Expanded SchedulableTask definition ...
class SchedulableTask {
 public:
  // ... previously declared member functions
  virtual std::vector<SchedulableTask*> GetChildren() = 0;
  virtual bool AddChild(std::unique_ptr<SchedulableTask> child) = 0;
  ...

// ContainerTask definition ...
class ContainerTask : public SchedulableTask {
 public:
  ContainerTask(
    const string& name,
    ExecutionContext* execution_context);
  ~ContainerTask() override = default;

  std::vector<SchedulableTask*> GetChildren() override;
  bool AddChild(
      std::unique_ptr<SchedulableTask> child) override;

 private:
  std::vector<std::unique_ptr<SchedulableTask>> children_;
};
```

This is bread and butter class design, so I will assume you have no trouble carrying forth the implementation of this class, or of its counterpart, the AtomicTask. Virtually every composite task we have inherits from ContainerTask; the only departures we have from this pattern are certain kinds of queues that do not inherit from a vector.

But we have an even better opportunity for reuse in the area of behavior. Rather than simply implementing each task's Step member function separately, we should decompose the Step member function and expose the innards of the stepping API to subclasses through the class's protected interface, shown in Listing 9.3.

Listing 9.3. Implementing stepping.

```
// Expanded SchedulableTask definition ...
class SchedulableTask {
 public:
  // ... previously defined member functions
  virtual TaskStatus Step();
  virtual bool IsFailure() const;
  virtual bool IsTerminated() const;
  virtual TaskStatus GetStatus() const;
  // More member functions for our use case ...

 protected:
  virtual TaskStatus PerformAction() = 0;
  virtual void SetStatus(TaskStatus status);
  // More member functions for our use case …
  ...

// Expanded SchedulableTask implementation ...
TaskStatus SchedulableTask::Step() {
  if (!IsTerminated()) {
     SetStatus(PerformAction());
  }
  return GetStatus();
}
```

Using these protected member functions, the Step member function is implemented in SchedulableTask in a way which looks almost trivial. But by defining this (and similar member functions) near the top of the tree, we define the execution model for tasks, so all that we really need to know about a task is how it differs from the norm. The ContainerTask we have already shown just holds tasks; it does not have execution semantics. But at the very next level of the tree appear tasks like ParallelTask or SequenceTask, which do override these protected methods, as shown in Listing 9.4.

The meat of an actual SequenceTask can be fairly simple, encoded in its PerformAction member function. But we did more than just implementing this member function; we exposed some of its innards in the protected API as well, including HandleChildFailure and AdvanceToNextChild.

9. Overcoming Pitfalls in Behavior Tree Design

Listing 9.4. Implementing stepping in `SequenceTask`.

```cpp
// SequenceTask definition ...
class SequenceTask : public ContainerTask {
 public:
  SequenceTask(string name,
               ExecutionContext* execution_context);
  ~SequenceTask() override = default;

 protected:
  uint current_task_;
  TaskStatus PerformAction() override;
  virtual bool AdvanceToNextChild();
  virtual TaskStatus HandleChildFailure(
      TaskStatus child_status);
  // More member functions related to our use case ...
};

// SequenceTask implementation ...
TaskStatus SequenceTask::PerformAction() {
  if (GetStatus() == WAITING) {
      SetStatus(STEPPING);
      current_task_ = 0;
  }

  TaskStatus child_status{STEPPING};
  auto child = GetCurrentChild();
  if (child != nullptr) {
    // Step the child unless it has stopped.
    if (!child->IsTerminated()) {
      child->Step();
        }

    // Now check for and handle completed children.
    if (child->IsTerminated()) {
      if (child->IsFailure()) {
        // Propagate child failure up
        child_status = child->GetStatus();
      } else {
        // Move to next task
        AdvanceToNextChild();
      }
    }
  }

  // Now check for and handle failed children.
  if (IsStatusFailure(child_status)) {
    SetStatus(HandleChildFailure(child_status));
  } else if (current_task_ >= GetChildren().size()) {
    SetStatus(SUCCESS);
  }
  // Propagate status up the API.
  return GetStatus();
}
```

(Continued)

```
bool SequenceTask::AdvanceToNextChild() {
  // Advance until we run out of children.
  current_task_++;
  return HasCurrentChild();
}

TaskStatus SequenceTask::HandleChildFailure(
    TaskStatus child_status) {
  // Propagate failure up to parent.
  return child_status;
}
```

We chose to do so by looking at the actual decision-making use cases of our robot application, where we wanted finer-grained control on how the tasks responded to various circumstances without making the actual SequenceTask very complicated.

For example, we wanted a TryTask which tried tasks in sequence but did not fail itself if a child failed. By exposing AdvanceToNextChild and HandleChildFailure in the protected API, we were able to write a TryTask with (essentially) half a page of code, shown in Listing 9.5.

Listing 9.5. Implementing a TryTask—essentially, the whole thing.

```
// try_task.h
// Header includes omitted ...
class TryTask : public SequenceTask {
 public:
  TryTask(const string& name,
          ExecutionContext* execution_context);
  ~TryTask() override = default;
 protected:
  TaskStatus HandleChildFailure(TaskStatus_) override;
};

// try_task.cc
// More header includes omitted ...
TaskStatus TryTask::HandleChildFailure(TaskStatus _) {
  // Ignore failures, continue until we are done.
  return AdvanceToNextChild() ? STEPPING : SUCCESS;
}
```

The only member function we needed to override was HandleChildFailure, and that override itself was very simple. This made developing and testing this class easy; we could rely on the containment and stepping logic of the parent class, and focus our testing on HandleChildFailure and its impact on, well, child failure.

This design breaks behavior tree down based on a class hierarchy with overridable member functions. In C++, this can be less efficient than carefully written code specialized to the use case at hand. The chapter on the Behavior Tree Starter Kit in the first volume of *Game AI Pro* describes a series of these tradeoffs, which you could consider in more detail (Champandard and Dunstan 2012).

For our use case, this explicit breakdown of behavior was appropriate for a robot whose top-level decision-making cycle needed to run no more than 30 hertz. This may not necessarily work for a game that needs to optimize every cycle, but we were able to run a behavior tree step for a simple benchmark at 60 million hertz on a not too beefy computer. So you may want to begin with a clean breakdown, which is easily extensible and return to optimize it later as your benchmarks, profiling, and the needs of your game demand.

9.3.3 Pitfall #3: Routing Everything through the Blackboard

Previously, BT-like systems were designed to break cognitive tasks apart into small parts (Francis 2000), so the thinking that the system did could be interleaved with the system's memory retrieval processes; for that memory retrieval to work, virtually all the data that the system manipulated needed to be exposed in the system's blackboard. A robot control system where multiple independent processes communicate, like ROS (ROS.org 2016), has similar constraints, and the first version of Google's robotics behavior tree supported close interaction between the system blackboard and the behavior tree. Although not a required part of the system, this enabled us to specify a behavior tree and its data at the same time.

Similar concerns operate in games with characters that need sensory models, like stealth games (and many other modern shooters), but it is probably a mistake to tie the overall behavior tree logic too closely to the logic of the blackboard—and even more of a mistake during prototyping to make simple tasks dependent on a blackboard for communication. Coding all tasks to use a system blackboard or sensory manager, while providing many advantages as systems grow larger and more complicated, is much more complex than using native language features for communication—and is often less reliable, unless you are enough of a C++ template wizard to create a fully typesafe blackboard (and if so, more power to you).

In the prototyping phase, doing things "right" this way can actually interfere with exploring the design space of your behavior trees and perfecting their logic. For our first behavior tree, the blackboard and the behavior tree were designed together to complement each other. Unfortunately, this meant a change to the API of one affected the other—particularly in how the hierarchy of tasks referred to the hierarchy of the blackboard, and vice versa. On at least two separate occasions, a lower level API change led to a month or more work rewiring the tasks and the blackboard so that all the data were available to the right tasks.

The alternative is to strongly decouple the behavior tree from the blackboard. The same behavior tree logic should work with a complicated hierarchical blackboard with a rich knowledge representation—or with a simple C++ plain old data structure (POD), or even with no explicit blackboard at all, and communication performed ad hoc between cooperating tasks. Using ad-hoc communication can make it more difficult to build a full data-driven behavior tree, but for many problems, it is sufficient. For example, one machine learning system that successfully learned better-than-human behavior trees for controlling an unmanned aerial vehicle used a C++ POD containing only a handful of values as its "blackboard."

When we reimplemented our behavior tree for a new robot platform, we temporarily abandoned the blackboard in favor of ad-hoc communication, which had two benefits. First: we were able to complete and test the logic of the blackboard to a very high degree; second, when we made the decision to abandon a low-level API, only two leaf tasks needed to be changed. We still have a use case for the old blackboard in the new behavior tree—but the clean separation of concerns from the old blackboard means we have a behavior tree which is reliable, well tested—and can work with a variety of communication mechanisms.

I cannot as cleanly show you this difference between these two approaches using just code—the old blackboard is a lot of code, and the new communications mechanisms are peculiar to their use case—but if your behavior tree is properly architected, you should be able to use the same core decision logic in both a small toy example whose "blackboard" is a C++ POD and whose decisions are made by C++ lambdas and a full system that has a distributed blackboard and a complete behavior tree condition system that is purely data driven.

9.4 Conclusion

I have slogged through creating many, many behavior trees and BT-likes, and it is really easy to get bogged down. But the pattern I am outlining above is simple: figure out what you need to do, don't jump the gun on building too much of it until you have a good idea of what you need, and refine your abstractions until the complexity is squirreled away in a few files and the leaves of your functionality are *dead bone simple*. This approach can be applied everywhere, and when you do, it can radically improve your development experience.

I could preach about how test-driven development and continuous integration made this easier, or how refactoring tools help (and what to do when you cannot use them; sed, awk, and shell scripting are your friends). But the major point I want to make is that behavior trees can be surprisingly complicated—and yet surprisingly regular in structure—and it is very important to look carefully at the places you are repeating work and to aggressively seek ways to eliminate them using judicious use of class hierarchies.

Our first shot at creating a behavior tree had too many concepts, too much repeated code, and too much boilerplate. Through the process of reducing the number of entities, looking at the needs of our application domain, and *corralling* complexity into carefully chosen superclasses and support files, we not only radically reduced the amount of similar code we had to maintain, but the actual code we needed often collapsed to a single page—or occasionally a single line. When you have done that, and you can benchmark your system to show it is still efficient, you have done your job architecting your behavior tree right.

References

Bonasso, R. P., Firby, R. J., Gat, E., Kortenkamp, D., Miller, D. P., and Slack, M. G. 1997. Experiences with an architecture for intelligent, reactive agents. *Journal of Experimental & Theoretical Artificial Intelligence* 9(2–3):237–256.

Champandard, A., and Dunstan, P. 2012. The behavior tree starter kit. In *Game AI Pro*, ed. S. Rabin. Boca Raton, FL: CRC Press, pp. 73–95.

Firby, R. J. 1987. An investigation into reactive planning in complex domains. *AAAI* 87:202–206.

Francis, A. G. 2000. Context-sensitive asynchronous memory. PhD diss. Georgia Institute of Technology. Available online http://dresan.com/research/publications/thesis.pdf (accessed June 8, 2016).

Isla, D. 2005. Handling complexity in the Halo 2 AI. *2005 Game Developer's Conference.* Available online http://www.gamasutra.com/view/feature/130663/gdc_2005_proceeding_handling_.php (accessed June 8, 2016).

ROS.org. 2016. Powering the world's robots. Available online http://www.ros.org (accessed June 8, 2016).

10

From Behavior to Animation

A Reactive AI Architecture for Networked First-Person Shooter Games

Sumeet Jakatdar

10.1 Introduction

First-person shooters (FPS) are a very specific and popular genre of video games. Many of the general AI principles and techniques are applicable for FPS AI, but they need to be modified to cater to the needs of fast-paced action. The challenge lies in selecting, modifying, and combining algorithms together efficiently, so that AIs can react quickly to player actions. For an AAA FPS game with strict deadlines, the AI system needs to be ready early in the development cycle, allowing content creators to start using it. The system also needs to be simple to use, data driven, and flexible enough to be able to support creating a variety of AI archetypes. The system also needs to support networked gameplay without needing any extra effort from design and animation teams.

This chapter will provide a high-level and simple overview of an AI system that could be used for a networked FPS game. We will look into modifications to well-known AI algorithms such as behavior trees (BTs) and animation state machines (ASMs), which were made to suit specific needs of the game. We will discuss ways to keep the BT simple but still reactive to high-priority events by introducing a concept called *interrupts*. Furthermore, we will touch upon animation layers that are designed to handle aiming and shooting animations independent of the BT. Here, we will discuss modifications to traditional ASMs to help network animations, allowing cooperative or competitive gameplay across the internet.

We will also look into a Blackboard system to solve behavior and animation selection problems. Here we will introduce techniques that will help keep the Blackboard attributes up-to-date by using a *function-based* approach.

Whenever applicable, we will provide pseudocode and real examples to better explain the concepts presented. Many of you probably know these techniques individually. Hopefully, by reading this chapter, you will get an idea of how they can work together for networked FPS games.

10.2 Client-Server Engine and AI System

We will assume that our game engine is built using a client-server paradigm, where the server is authoritative in nature. This means that server dictates the position, orientation, and gameplay logic for all game entities.

From time to time, the client receives a *network snapshot* from the server for all of the entities. While processing this snapshot, each entity's position and orientation will be corrected to match the server. The frequency of these snapshots depend upon the network bandwidth and CPU performance requirements of the game. Between network snapshots, the client interpolates entities for smoother 60 fps gameplay. It is important to keep the size of the network snapshots (measured in bits) small to support hundreds of entities and to avoid packet fragmentation. The upper limit for network snapshots is usually referred to as the *maximum transmission unit* (MTU), and the recommended size is approximately 1200–1500 bytes for Ethernet connections. To be able to achieve the smallest possible MTU, we will look for opportunities to infer logic on the client side by sending across minimalistic information about entities.

The AI system is just one part of this engine. In addition, the server is responsible for handling many other systems, such as controller logic, player animation, physics, navigation, and scripting. Similarly, the client is responsible for handling effects, sounds, and most importantly rendering.

Figure 10.1 shows a high-level overview of the system and important AI modules in the engine. The BTs are responsible for choosing behavior using the knowledge stored in the Blackboard (a shared space for communication). The ASM is responsible for selecting animations and managing the animation pose of the AI. The client-side ASM has the same responsibilities as the server, but the implementation is slightly different from the server, as it does not make any decisions but merely follows the server. We will explore the details of the ASM further in this chapter.

At first, we will concentrate on the AI system on the server side. After we are done with the server, we will move on to the client side. We will finish by looking at the networking layer between the server and client AI systems. The pseudocode provided in this chapter will look very similar to C, but it should be fairly easy to translate these concepts in an object-oriented coding environment.

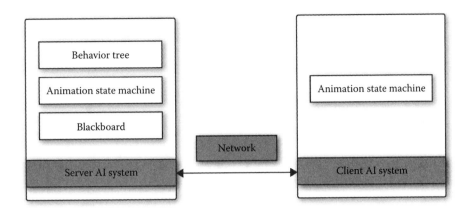

Figure 10.1

Client-server engine and AI system.

10.3 The AI Agent

Before moving on to create various AI modules, we will define the `AIAgent` structure that lies at the core of our AI system, as shown in Listing 10.1. All three of our AI modules will be contained within this structure. Both server and client will have their own representation of the `AIAgent`.

Listing 10.1. Defining `AIAgent`.

```
struct AIAgent
{
    // Blackboard
    // Behavior Tree
    // Animation State Machine
    // ...
};
```

10.4 The Blackboard

The Blackboard holds key information about the AI agent, which can be manipulated and queried by other AI modules for choosing behaviors, animations, and so on. In some cases, the Blackboard is also used as a communication layer between modules.

Our implementation of the Blackboard will support three different types of variables; strings, floats, and integers. We will call them *value-based* variables. We will also support a special variable, referred in this chapter as *function-based*.

10.4.1 Value-Based Variables (Strings, Integers, and Floats)

Table 10.1 creates four Blackboard variables for the human soldier archetype. From the first three Blackboard variables, we can infer that the human soldier is currently *standing*.

Table 10.1 Sample Blackboard for the Human Soldier Archetype

Variable	Type	Current_value	Update_function
Weapon	string	rifle_longrange	null
Number_of_bullets	int	50	null
Stance	string	stand	null
Angle_to_player	float		getangletoplayer

He or she is holding a weapon, a *long range rifle* with *50 bullets* in its magazine. There is no specific range, or possible set of values associated with these variables. So, for example, the number of bullets can be negative, which might be illogical. In such cases, it is the responsibility of other AI logic to handle that situation gracefully. However, adding support for ranges or enums should be fairly straightforward and is recommended in a final implementation.

10.4.2 Function-Based Variables

The first three Blackboard variables in Table 10.1 will be modified by external systems. For these variables, the Blackboard can be considered as some form of storage. But sometimes, we need the Blackboard to execute logic to calculate the latest value of a given variable. This is the purpose of the `update _ function`.

When a human soldier needs to turn and face the player, it will query the Blackboard to get the latest value of the `angle_to_player`. In this case, the Blackboard will execute the `getangletoplayer` function and return the latest yaw value. We call these types of variables *function-based*, as a function is executed when they are requested.

10.4.3 Implementation of the Blackboard

Let us look at some implementation details for our Blackboard. Listing 10.2 shows the implementation for `BlackboardValue`, which will essentially hold only one of the three types of values: a string, float, or integer. We have also created an enum to indicate the type of Blackboard variable and use it in the `BlackboardVariable` structure. Remember, the `update_function` is only defined and used for *function-based* Blackboard variables.

Listing 10.2. Definition of `BlackboardVariable` and `BlackboardValue`.

```
struct BlackboardValue
{
    union
    {
        const char* stringValue;
        int intValue;
        float floatValue;
    };
};
```

(Continued)

10. From Behavior to Animation

```
enum BlackboardVariableType
{
    BLACKBOARD_INT,
    BLACKBOARD_FLOAT,
    BLACKBOARD_STRING,
};
typedef BlackboardValue
    (*BlackboardUpdateFunction)(AIAgent *agent);

struct BlackboardVariable
{
    const char* name;
    BlackboardValue value;
    BlackboardVariableType type;
    BlackboardUpdateFunction updateFunction;
};
```

The Blackboard, in Listing 10.3, is essentially a collection of many Blackboard Variable structures stored as a fixed-size array. We also add numVariables to easily keep track of the actual number of variables in use. Finally, a Blackboard is added to the AIAgent definition. When an AI agent spawns, a script is responsible for populating and assigning default values to the AI agent's blackboard.

Listing 10.3. Setting up the Blackboard for the AIAgent.

```
struct Blackboard
{
    BlackboardVariable variables[MAX_BLACKBOARD_VARIABLES];
    int numVariables;
};

struct AIAgent
{
    // AI agent's blackboard
    Blackboard blackboard; }
```

Listing 10.4 shows an example of creating one of the Blackboard variables for a human soldier.

Listing 10.4. BlackboardVariable example for human soldier.

```
BlackboardValue value;
Value.name = "weapon";
value.stringValue = "rifle_longrange";
value.type = BLACKBOARD_STRING;
value.updateFunction = null;
```

10.5 The Behavior Tree

At the core of an AI agent's behaviors is a way to select various actions. A BT consists of many of these actions arranged in a tree format and inherently provides priority in its hierarchy. Every action will have prerequisite conditions, which are needed to be satisfied for that action to be chosen. If you need to get familiar with the basics of BTs, please refer to chapters in earlier *AI Game Pro* and *AI Game Programming Wisdom* books (Isla 2005, Champandard 2008, Champandard and Dunstan 2013). You can also refer to the many online articles available at *AiGameDev.com* (AiGameDev 2015) and *Gamasutra.com*. Here, we will focus on some specific modifications to known BT paradigms.

Our AI agent is going to have many behaviors. Every behavior will consist of one or more actions. However, it is important to understand that only one action will be active at a given time. For example, the human soldier behavior for suppressing the enemy can be composed of two actions; first the *throwing grenade* action and then the *charging toward the player* action. We will design the BTs with this consideration in mind.

10.5.1 Creating a Behavior Tree for the AI Agent

We will start by defining a `BehaviorTree`, and then look at the `BehaviorTreeNode` definition.

Listing 10.5. Setting up `BehaviorTree` for `AIAgent`.

```
struct BehaviorTree
{
    const char* name;
    BehaviorTreeNode nodes[MAX_BT_NODES];
    int numNodes;
};

struct AIAgent
{
    // AI agent's own blackboard
    Blackboard blackboard;
    // pointer to behavior tree definition
    const BehaviorTree *behaviorTree;
    //...
}
```

As seen in Listing 10.5, the `BehaviorTree` itself is just a fixed-size array of `BehaviorTreeNode` nodes. This size depends upon the complexity of various AI agent's behaviors, but generally it is a good idea to keep the size under 1000 nodes. If the tree gets bigger than this, then it might be worth looking at the granularity of condition nodes and finding opportunities to consolidate them.

We add one more variable, `numNodes`, to easily keep track of number of nodes used in a `BehaviorTree`. Another important assumption made here is that the "root node" will always appear first, at the 0th index of the nodes array. Each BT also has a unique name, which is used only for debugging purposes.

You would have noticed that there is only one definition for nodes, `BehaviorTreeNode`. In the next section, we will explore how it is used for supporting different types of nodes.

We saw earlier that, every AI agent stores its own copy of the Blackboard, but this is not the case with a BT. At runtime, only one, nonmodifiable copy will reside in memory for a given BT definition. Every AI agent who uses this BT will store a pointer to this definition and refer to it time and again to choose an action.

10.5.2 Behavior Tree Nodes

Now that we have represented the BT in the `BehaviorTree` structure, let us move on to representing actual BT nodes, as shown in Listing 10.6.

Listing 10.6. Implementing Behavior Tree nodes.

```
enum BTNodeType
{
    BT_NODE_ACTION,             // action
    BT_NODE_CONDITION,          // condition
    BT_NODE_PARALLEL,           // parallel
    BT_NODE_SEQUENCE,           // sequence
    BT_NODE_SELECTOR,           // selector
    //...
};

enum BTNodeResult
{
    BT_SUCCESS,
    BT_FAILURE,
    BT_RUNNNING,
    //...
};

typedef BTNodeResult (*BTFunction)
    (AIAgent *agent, int nodeIndex);

struct BehaviorTreeNode
{
    const char* name;
    // type of the node
    BTNodeType type;
    // parent node index
    int parentNodeIndex;
    // children nodes
    int childrenNodeIndices[MAX_BT_CHILDREN_NODES];
    int numChildrenNodes;

    // condition node attributes
    BTFunction condition;
    // action node attributes
    BTFunction onActionStart;
    BTFunction onActionUpdate;
    BTFunction onActionTerminate;
};
```

We start by specifying the types of BT nodes we want to support using the `BTNodeType` enum. Typically, a BT supports conditions, actions, parallels, selectors, and sequences. You can add support for additional nodes, but the core idea of the implementation remains the same.

As we have only one definition for all of the nodes, the type will be used to figure out how the node is processed during the BT evaluation.

The child and parent relationship of a `BehaviorTreeNode` is defined by storing `parentNodeIndex` and an array of `childrenNodeIndices`. This setup is going to make it easy to traverse up and down the tree. It is possible that certain types of nodes are not allowed to have any children at all. In our implementation, the leaf nodes, action, and conditions are not allowed to have children. If we need to have a condition to be successful before executing further, then we can just use the sequence node with that condition as its first child. Similarly, two actions can be put together under one sequence if one action needs to follow another action, only if the first one was successful. This approach helps keep the tree simple and readable, and we always know to reevaluate the tree from the root if an action fails.

Actions and conditions can only be part of a composite node in our BT, which guarantees that there will not be any logical issues with our tree. Allowing conditions to have children adds ambiguity about the nature of that node. Unless we add more attributes to the condition, it will be difficult to decide if the condition node needs to be treated as a sequence or a parallel. We rather choose to do it in more elegant way by using the composite nodes.

Only the composite node types such as selectors, parallels, and sequences are allowed to have children. So, if we need to create a behavior consisting of one condition and one action, then it would be represented using a sequence or a parallel node. Listing 10.7 shows an example of a sequence node for a human soldier.

Listing 10.7. Turn behavior for a human soldier.

```
{
    "name": "turnBehavior",
    "type": "sequence",
    "children":
    [
        {
            "type": "condition",
            "name": "turnCondition",
            "condition": "isPlayerBehind"
        },
        {
            "type": "action",
            "name": "turnAction",
            "onActionStart": "sayDialogue"
        }
    ]
}
```

It is worth mentioning that there is only one parent for a node in our implementation. We will validate all these requirements while populating BTs at runtime.

Just knowing the relationship between BT nodes is not enough. We need to be able to associate some logic to nodes, so that we can execute that logic and find out the result. This is where `BTFunction` comes in handy. To start with, we only need functions for two types of nodes: conditions and actions. For action nodes in particular, we need three functions: `onActionStart, OnActionUpdate,` and `onActionTerminate.`

These functions can be used to execute additional gameplay logic when an action is active. If any one of these functions returns BT _ FAILURE, then we will have to reevaluate the tree.

To explain this a little better, we go back to the human soldier example again. Let us say that one of the behaviors for our human is a *Turn Behavior*. If the player is behind, our agent will turn to face the player and say a line of dialogue while turning. For this behavior, we will need three nodes in our BT. Listing 10.7 shows a raw behavior tree asset that we will use to populate the human soldier's BT at runtime. Many of you might recognize the JSON format. If you plan to write your own tools to create and edit BT, then a format like JSON is worth considering as there are many available parsers and editors available which might save you time.

The isPlayerBehind condition will make use of the Blackboard variable angle _ to _ player to decide if the player is behind. If the condition is successful, then the sequence will continue and select turnAction and call the sayDialogue function once, as the action starts.

10.5.3 Handling Parallel Conditions

The only node in our BT that will last for a longer period of time is the action node. In our case, an action will continue while the corresponding animation state is active. We will look into animation states a little later in this chapter.

For some actions, it is important that all of the prerequisite conditions remain valid for the duration of the action and not just at the start. We will achieve this by using parallel nodes. Let us say our human soldier has another behavior called *Relaxed Behavior*. He or she continues to remain relaxed until he or she sees a threat and then switches to another behavior. So, when he or she is relaxing, we need a way to continue to make sure that there is no threat.

In Listing 10.8, notice that the relaxedBehavior node is a parallel node. This node will act exactly the same as a sequence node while evaluating the tree to find an action.

Listing 10.8. Relaxed behavior for a human soldier using parallel nodes.

```
{
    "name": "relaxedBehavior",
    "type": "parallel",
    "children":
    [
        {
            "type": "condition",
            "name": "checkThreat",
            "condition": "noThreatInSight"
        },
        {
            "type": "action",
            "name": "relaxedAction"
        }
    ]
}
```

Although, once the `relaxedAction` is chosen and started, the parallel node will be used to populate all of the conditions that are needed to remain valid throughout this behavior.

In a full-blown BT, there will be many parallel nodes active for a given action. We will need a way to store all active parallel nodes for every AI agent independently, so we can execute them every frame and make sure that they are valid to continue executing the current action.

Listing 10.9 extends the `AIAgent` definition to support active parallel nodes. Once the action is chosen by the BT, then the `PopulateActiveParallelNodes` function will be called to generate the list of all parallel nodes that were executed on the way to the current action nodes. This is achieved by traversing back up the tree, all the way to the root node. We make use of `parentNodeIndex` to quickly traverse back up the tree. While updating the action, the BT logic will go through all the active parallel nodes and process their children condition nodes. If any of those conditions are invalid, then the action is

Listing 10.9. Extending `AIAgent` to support parallel conditions.

```
struct AIAgent
{
    // AI agent's own blackboard
    Blackboard blackboard;
    // pointer to behavior tree definition
    const BehaviorTree *behaviorTree;
    // active parallel conditions
    int   activeNodes[MAX_ACTIVE_PARALLELS];
    int   numActiveNodes;

    //...
}

void PopulateActiveParallelNodes
    (AIAgent *agent, int actionNodeIndex)
{

    const BehaviorTreeNode* btNode
        = &agent->behaviorTree->nodes[actionNodeIndex];
    agent->numActiveNodes = 0;

    while(btNode->index != 0)
    {
        int parentNodeIndex = btNode->parentNodeIndex;
        btNode
            = &agent->behaviorTree->nodes[parentNodeIndex];

        if(btNode->type == BT_NODE_PARALLEL)
        {
            agent->activeNodes[agent->numActiveNodes]
                                        = btNode->index;
            agent->numActiveNodes++;
        }
    }
}
```

considered to be invalid. At this time, the BT will be reevaluated from root node to find a new, more suitable action.

This approach helps to create an extremely efficient BT, as we do not evaluate the complete tree every frame. It also keeps the reactiveness of the tree intact. However, extra care has to be taken while designing the tree, so that all the possible conditions are accounted for. This is a tradeoff that we could live with, as efficiency is very important.

Sequence nodes can be handled in very similar fashion with a small implementation difference. There is no need to store any active sequences, as we are only interested in advancing the immediate parent sequence when an action is complete.

10.5.4 Handling Interruption Events in the Behavior Tree

After implementing the behavior tree architecture, we still have one more problem to deal with. We need a way to forcefully reevaluate the tree for certain key events, which can happen any time. In the case of a human soldier, *damage* is a high-priority event. Most of the time, we want humans to immediately react to *damage*.

To ensure that the AI will always react to *damage,* we found ourselves duplicating the same parallel condition for most of our actions. This approach works, but it is not ideal as it makes the tree unnecessarily complex. To handle this problem, we will introduce a new concept called interrupts.

Interrupts are basically events that will force the behavior tree logic to immediately invalidate the current action and initiate a full reevaluation of the tree. Interrupts themselves know nothing about AI behaviors in the tree at all. They usually last only until the next update of the BT.

When an interrupt occurs, the full reevaluation update should lead us to an action that was meant to be chosen when this interrupt is present and other conditions are met. Hence, some condition nodes need to have additional parameters so that they will only be valid during an interrupt. To achieve this, we need to add another attribute to the condition nodes, as shown in Listing 10.10.

Listing 10.10. Adding support for interrupts to `BehaviorTreeNode`.

```
struct BehaviorTreeNode
{
    //...
    // only used by condition nodes
    const char* interrupt;
};
```

The `interrupt` attribute is optional and only used by condition nodes. However, if it is specified for a condition node, then that node will only be evaluated when the specified interrupt event is being processed.

This simple modification helps reduce the complexity of the tree greatly. This approach works well when there are only handful of interrupt events associated with the behavior tree. It is possible that interrupt events are not mutually exclusive and may occur on the same frame. This problem can be solved by having a predefined priority list of interrupt events and only processing the highest interrupt event on that list.

A good optimization is to ignore an interrupt if none of the nodes in a BT refer to it. For this to work, you can populate a separate list of referenced interrupts while creating the tree at runtime.

10.6 Animation State Machine

Now that we have a system to choose an action, it is time to figure out how our AI agent will be animated. Let us look at two basic types of animations we need to support for our AI agents in our ASM.

A *full-body* animation forms the base pose of the AI. In most cases, an AI agent needs to only play one *full-body* animation. This is not a limitation of the animation system but rather a choice we made to keep things simple. Then comes the *additive* animation type, which modifies the base pose. Contrary to the *full-body* animation, an AI agent can play multiple additive animations at a time. In fact, we will make use of *additive* animations to allow our agents to aim and shoot at the player. Let us start with the problem of selecting animations.

10.6.1 Animation Tables

The most important job of the ASM is to select animations, and it does so by using Animation Tables (ATs).

ATs can be thought of as a simple database of all possible animations, given a set of pre-defined conditions. These conditions are nothing but Blackboard values we defined earlier in our system. In our ASM, every animation state will have one or more ATs associated with it.

Table 10.2 shows one of the ATs for our human soldier. We will use this table to find one *full-body* animation when the human soldier is in an idle animation state. There are two types of columns for ATs. One is an *input column*, and another is *output column*. *Input columns* are helpful to form a query of Blackboard variable values. This query is then used to find a *first fitting row* by matching the value of each variable against that row. Once a row is found, the AT will return the corresponding entry in its animation column.

For example, if a human soldier is `crouching` and holding a `shotgun` in his hands, then the AT will end up choosing the `shotgun _ crouch _ idle` animation by selecting row number 1. It is that simple!

You might have noticed the "–" symbol in Table 10.2. This dash signifies that the value of that Blackboard variable can be ignored while evaluating that row. This is very useful, as we can always have a fallback row, which will make sure that we always find an animation to play. In this example, the fifth row is a fallback row. We also have an explicit column for *row numbers*. This column is actually not stored as part of the ATs, but it is there to explain another concept later in this chapter (so for now, let us ignore it).

Table 10.2 Sample "Idle" Animation Table for Human Soldier

Row	Stance	Weapon	Animation
0	stand	shotgun	shotgun_stand_idle
1	crouch	shotgun	shotgun_crouch_idle
2	–	shotgun	shotgun_prone_idle
3	prone	–	prone_idle
4	crouch	–	crouch_idle
5	–	–	stand_idle

Table 10.3 Aim Table for the Human Soldier

Row	Weapon	anim_aim_left	anim_aim_right	anim_aim_up	anim_aim_down
0	shotgun	shotgun_aim_left	shotgun_aim_right	shotgun_aim_up	shotgun_aim_down
1	–	rifle_aim_left	rifle_aim_right	rifle_aim_up	rifle_aim_down

As shown in Table 10.3, ATs can have multiple *input* and *output columns*. In fact, we use this to return more than one animation for the aiming and shooting of *additive* animations. In the case of the *Aim Table*, the AT will return *left*, *right*, *up*, and *down* animations. It will be the responsibility of ASM to figure out the blend weights for these animations to achieve the desired aiming pose.

Let us look at how we can implement ATs in our AI system, as shown in Listing 10.11.

Listing 10.11. Animation Table column and row definitions.

```
enum AnimationTableColumType
{
    AT_COLUMN_INPUT,
    AT_COLUMN_OUTPUT
};

struct AnimationTableColumn
{
    const char* blackboardVariableName;
    BlackboardValue expectedValue;
    AnimationTableColumType type;
};

struct AnimationTableRow
{
    AnimationTableColumn columns[MAX_COLUMNS_PER_ROW];
    int numColumnsInUse;
};

struct AnimationTable
{
    const char* name;
    AnimationTableRow rows[MAX_ROWS_PER_TABLE];
    int numRowsInUse;
};
```

Essentially, `AnimationTableColumn` stores a Blackboard variable name that it refers to and an `expectedValue` of that variable to compare against. We can easily look up the type of Blackboard variable in the `blackboard` array in our `AIAgent` definition. In the final implementation however, it is ideal to use hashes to avoid string comparisons. The structure `AnimationTableRow` is a collection of columns, and finally `AnimationTable` is a collection of rows.

Depending on the number of AI agents alive, the amount of queries can be a performance concern. To help improve performance, we can also implement a caching mechanism for the results.

10.6.2 Animation States

As mentioned earlier, every animation state is responsible for finding and applying one *full-body* animation. If it cannot find one, then there is a bug that needs to be fixed.

Depending on the state, we also need *additive* animations to modify the base pose. *Additive* animations are optional and may not be used by every animation state. In this chapter, we will assume that there are only two possible *additive* animations per animation state. One for aiming and another for the shooting animation.

To achieve this, we will need to refer to three different ATs in our animation state, as shown in Listing 10.12.

Listing 10.12. `Animation State` definition.

```
struct AnimationState
{
    const char* name;
    const AnimationTable *fullBodyTable;
    const AnimationTable *aimTable;
    const AnimationTable *shootTable;
};
```

10.6.3 Choosing the Animation State for an AI Agent

For a given action, we need to choose an animation state. We could infer the animation state by using the Blackboard variables alone, but this approach is complex and potentially unreliable. However, this approach is successfully used in many other games, and it does work very well. Keeping up with the theme of simplicity, we opt for another, rather easy solution. In our system, the BT action is responsible for choosing the corresponding animation state.

As shown in Listing 10.13, we added an animation state index to the `BehaviorTreeNode` definition. When an action is selected by the BT, a corresponding animation state will be requested by the BT and then immediately processed by the ASM.

Listing 10.13. Animation state for the current BT action.

```
struct BehaviorTreeNode
{
    // ...
    // used by action nodes to request animation state
    int animationStateIndex;
};
```

10.6.4 Managing Animations with the ASM

Given an animation state, we are now equipped to find animations. Although, once they are found, we will need to apply those animations to our agent. In the case of aiming with the given aim animations, we would need to calculate blend weights based on the direction to the player. In the case of shooting, we would need a way to select one of the animations based on the weapon agent is holding. We will achieve this by adding three functions to our ASM definition. These functions will query the ATs when the animation state is changed. They will also manage blend weights for the selected animations based on specific gameplay logic.

Listing 10.14. Definition of the ASM.

```
typedef void(*ATFunction)(AIAgent *agent, AnimationTable* table);

struct AnimationStateMachine
{
    AnimationState states[MAX_ANIMATION_STATES];
    int numAnimationStatesInUse;

    ATFunction fullBodyAnimUpdate;
    ATFunction aimAnimUpdate;
    ATFunction shootAnimUpdate;
};
```

As shown in Listing 10.14, we have created an `AnimationStateMachine`, which is essentially a collection of many animation states. We have also added three functions for managing animations for all three different animation tables.

Listing 10.15. Storing current animations and Animation State for an `AIAgent`.

```
struct AIAgent
{
    //...
    AnimationStateMachine *animationStateMachine;

    int currentStateIndex;
    int currentFullBodyRowIndex;
    int currentAimRowIndex;
    int currentShootRowIndex;
    //...
};
```

Finally, in Listing 10.15, we add a reference to the ASM. Additionally, we store the indices of the current rows we got our animations from in `currentStateIndex`. This will come in handy when we look at networking AI animations later in this chapter.

10.6.5 Transitions

It is trivial to add the concept of a transition to our ASM. Transitions are very similar to the animation states, except they are not requested specifically by a BT action. They are chosen by the ASM while transitioning from one animation state to a state requested by the BT. The BT itself is unaware of transitions and leaves this responsibility to the ASM completely. The transition can have their own *full-body*, *additive* layers, and related ATs. While searching for an animation in an AT for a transition, it is acceptable if no fitting animation is found. In that case, the ASM will just blend animations from the previous to next state directly. This helps the animation team, as they only add transition animations where they fit and rely on animation blending in other cases.

10.6.6 Aiming and Shooting

While designing the ASM in the earlier section, we gave the responsibility of managing the aiming and shooting logic to the ASM. In our case, using the logic in `ATFunction`, the ASM will decide to aim and shoot independent of the BT action based on the existence of tables and their respective functions. This is where our FPS version of the ASM is slightly different from traditional state machines.

This method helps to keep our BT simpler, as it will not have to worry about managing shooting and aiming. The BT can still influence animation selection for aiming and shooting by changing Blackboard variables. We can also disable the aiming and shooting logic completely if needed. In the case of an FPS game, whenever possible, the AI agents shoot the players, or choose to perform melee combat at a close range. This solution solves the problem in the ASM instead of the BT, making it easier for the BT to handle high-level logic.

In some games, shooting needs to be controlled as a behavior in the BT. In such cases, this approach may not be suitable as it does not give fine-grain control over shooting using behaviors. One suggestion is to split the shooting and aiming logic into another, lightweight state machine. Then this state machine can be controlled independently by adding more attributes and logic to the BT actions.

10.6.7 Animation Alias Tables

So far, whenever we referred to an animation in an AT, we were actually referring to an Animation Alias. An AT is purely a one-to-many mapping, responsible for choosing one of the many variations of a given animation. This simple table empowers animators to create a lot of animation variety by truly staying independent of AI logic and behaviors. Table 10.4 shows an example of an AAT for a human soldier.

We complete our `AIAgent` definition by adding a reference to an `AnimationAlias Table` in Listing 10.16.

At runtime, we can allow switching between different AATs. In fact, we can use them to change the AI's look and feel in order to make them more interesting. For example, when a human soldier is shot, we can switch to another AAT with wounded animations. This is achieved by using one default AAT and another override AAT, as seen in Listing 10.16.

Table 10.4 Example of Animation Alias Table for a Human Soldier

animation_alias	variation 0	variation1	variation2
rifle_idle	rifle_idle_lookaround	rifle_idle_smoke	rifle_idle_checkgun

Listing 10.16. Adding Animation Alias Tables (AATs) to an `AIAgent`.

```
struct AIAgent
{
    //...
    AnimationAliasTable *aliasTableDefault;
    AnimationAliasTable *aliasTableOverride;
    //...
};
```

We also allow multiple active layers of tables and search for animations starting with the `aliasTableOverride` table first. If no override animation is found, then we will fall back to the `aliasTableDefault` table. This allows creating smaller batches of animation variations.

It is important to validate all of the animations within one `AnimationAlias` to ensure that they are compatible with one another. Some of the validations include animation length, animation event markers, and most importantly positions of certain key bones relative to the root bone.

10.7 Networking AI

Players connect to the game as clients, and all of the systems we have created so far work only on the server side. At this point, we need to add a network component to our AI system to see the AI in action on the client. As mentioned earlier, we will assume that an entity's position and orientation are already parts of the general network layer. In the AI system, we are more concerned about animations as no generic animation networking layer exists in the engine otherwise.

To be able to achieve this, we will need to send across enough information to the client so that it can replicate the animation pose of the AI. This is where the ASM and ATs come in very handy, as the definitions for both are available on the client as well.

Table 10.5 lists the minimized `AIAgent` data that are sent over to the client, which is used to choose the same animations as the server. First is `currentStateIndex`, which allows the client to use the same animation state as the server. Now, the client can refer to the same AT tables as the server though the selection animation state, but it does not have any ability to choose animations yet.

On the server, ATs choose animations using a query of Blackboard variables. Unfortunately, there is no Blackboard available on the client, as our server handles all the decision-making authoritatively. If we could somehow tell the client the row number in the table, then we can look up the animation directly without needing a Blackboard at all. This is exactly why we send over row indices for all three ATs to the client: *full-body*, *additive* aim, and shoot.

With this setup, it is guaranteed that the client will always choose the same animations as the server. We need to run the same `ATFunction` on the client to be able to apply the chosen animations in the same way as server. Mostly, the server and client versions of `ATFunction` are very similar to each other in this case.

Using the row indices, we are merely choosing animation aliases and not actual animations. It is critically important that both server and client choose the same animation variation for a given animation alias. If this does not work properly, then the server and client may generate a different animation pose which can result in bugs. Let us take an example of a player

Table 10.5 Animation State Machine Data Sent Over the Network to the Client AI System

Data	Number of Bits
currentstateindex	8 bits (up to 256 states)
currentfullbodyrowindex	7 bits (up to 128 rows)
currentaimrowindex	4 bits (up to 16 rows)
currentshootrowindex	4 bits (up to 16 rows)

shooting and damaging the AI. The bullet collision will be performed on the server using the animation pose on the server. If the animation chosen is different on the client as compared to server, then sometimes players might see that they are clearly hitting the AI on client, but in fact, on the server they are not. We will have to make sure that this never happens.

We could send an extra couple of bits for animations to solve this problem, but a more optimal solution is using a deterministic random seed, which results in the same variation on both ends.

10.8 Conclusion

Presented in this chapter is a basic AI system which supports a variety of behaviors, animations, and networked gameplay. There are many more aspects to this system that we could not discuss in this chapter, but hopefully you now have a solid idea of the foundation that can be extended to match your own needs.

Let us quickly recap what we covered in this chapter. We started with laying down the design and technical requirements and then moved on to implement a Blackboard system. In addition to basic *value-based* variables, the Blackboard supported *function-based* variables to calculate up-to-date values. We used BTs as our behavior selection algorithm and also looked at how parallel conditions can be implemented to incorporate reactivity without complete evaluation of the tree every frame. We also introduced *interrupts* to handle some common high-priority events.

Then we moved on to Animation Tables, which are smart animation databases capable of selecting animations based on Blackboard variables. We also added support for selecting more than one animation and used it for shooting and aiming animations. Next up was the ASM, which made use of Animation Tables to network AI animations. Finally, we created an `AIAgent` definition that keeps track of all these systems for every AI in the game. At this time, we considered our basic AI system complete and ready for prime time.

Although there are a myriad of AI architectures and techniques available, it is important to choose appropriate ones by keeping simplicity and flexibility of a system in mind, at least in the early stages of development. Once you choose the right architecture, you can always add more paradigms to your system as you go. Usually the best approach is to start with proven, simple AI techniques and mold them to your needs in order to get something working quickly. Then you can iterate based on feedback from the team and the changing needs of the game.

References

Champandard, A. J. 2008. Getting started with decision making and control systems. In *AI Game Programming Wisdom*, ed. S. Rabin. Boston, MA: Course Technology, Vol. 4. pp. 257–263.

Champandard, A. J. and Dunstan P. 2013. The behavior tree starter kit. In *Game AI Pro: Collected Wisdom of Game AI Professionals*, ed. S. Rabin. Boca Raton, FL: A K Peters/ CRC Press.

Champandard, A. J. 2015. Behavior Trees for Next-Gen Game AI AiGameDev.com. 2015. http://www.aigamedev.com/.

Isla, D. 2005. Handling complexity in Halo 2 AI. In *Proceedings of the Game Developers Conference (GDC)*, San Francisco, CA.

11

A Character Decision-Making System for *FINAL FANTASY XV* by Combining Behavior Trees and State Machines

Youichiro Miyake, Youji Shirakami, Kazuya Shimokawa,
Kousuke Namiki, Tomoki Komatsu, Joudan Tatsuhiro,
Prasert Prasertvithyakarn, and Takanori Yokoyama

11.1 Introduction

Behavior trees and state machines were originally separate techniques—each with their own positive and negative points. The intent behind behavior trees is to make a series of character behaviors, whereas the intent behind finite-state machines (FSMs) is to make a stable cycle of character actions (Miyake 2015a, Miyake 2015b). For *FINAL FANTASY XV* shown in Figure 11.1, we have developed a new decision-making system that combines behavior trees and state machines into a single structure using the LUMINOUS STUDIO (SQUARE ENIX's game engine). This system has both the flexibility of behavior trees and the strict control of state machines as well as giving scalability to the development of a character decision-making system (Figure 11.2). This new decision-making system, which we call the AI Graph, extends the node formalism to enable sharing nodes between FSMs and behavior trees, provides advanced techniques for code reuse using trays that organize code reuse and behavior blackboards, and also provides many features for integrating with detailed low-level character behavior (Miyake 2016a).

Level designers can make a multilayered decision-making system for each character by using a visual node graph tool called the AI Graph. For example, for the first step, a level designer makes a top-layer state machine with several states by setting and connecting state machine nodes. Then the level designer can make a new state machine as a substate of one or more of the top-level states, or the designer can also make a new behavior tree inside any of the top-level states. Furthermore, the level designer can then make new state machines or behavior trees inside each subsequent substates. In this way, the level designer can make a hierarchical structure of state machines and behavior trees by simply editing nodes on the tool.

Each layer of the AI Graph also has a blackboard system by which the designer can register variables used in the game. By connecting the blackboards of separate nodes, the different layers can share and use these variables.

Figure 11.1

FINAL FANTASY XV screenshot.

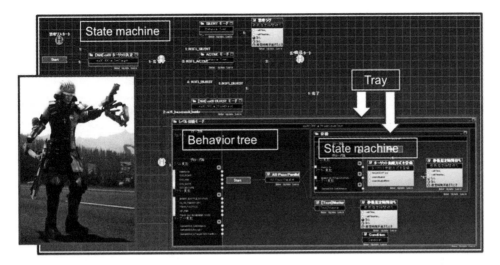

Figure 11.2

AI Graph image.

The AI Graph system has a real-time debug system that connects to and communicates with the game's run-time. Active nodes are highlighted on the decision graph tool as they are executed. During development, this makes finding any problems in the decision graph much easier. AI Graph maintains scalability, variation, and diversity in character AI design through the course of development because of its data-driven approach. In this chapter, we will explain the AI Graph structure, operation principle, and examples from *FINAL FANTASY XV*.

FINAL FANTASY XV is an RPG game in which a player travels in a large open world with three buddies while they fight with monsters and enemies in real time (Figure 11.1). All characters have intelligence to make their decisions by themselves. Also for the player character, AI supports the player character's behaviors.

11.2 AI Graph Structure and Operation Principles

AI Graph is a node-based graph system in which it is possible to make a hierarchical structure with a GUI-based node graph tool. The tool works both offline and while the game is running.

By using the AI Graph tool, a user can make a state machine or behavior tree for each layer (Figure 11.3). To make the next layer, a user can select one node and make a state machine or behavior tree in it. In this way, AI Graph makes a hierarchical nested structure. As requirements change, the hierarchical nested structure allows developers to make as many layers as they want. Finally, the AI Graph generates the data to be executed by the AI program.

The hierarchy executes in the following manner. When a node in the state machine or behavior tree contains another layer, it immediately executes that next layer. The process continues executing nodes until it cannot go to a deeper layer. It then returns to a higher layer after finishing a lower layer.

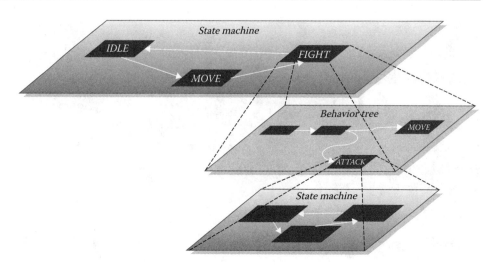

Figure 11.3

AI Graph model.

When a state machine's transition happens in an upper layer, the state currently executing lower layers must be finished. In this case, after all processing of lower layers has finished, the transition occurs. (See Section 11.5.3 for dealing with interruptions.)

11.3 AI Graph Tool

AI Graph tool is one part of the SQUARE ENIX game engine used to make a character's AI. It has three regions (Figure 11.4). The center of the screen is a field to build a state machine and behavior tree graph by connecting nodes. The left vertically long window

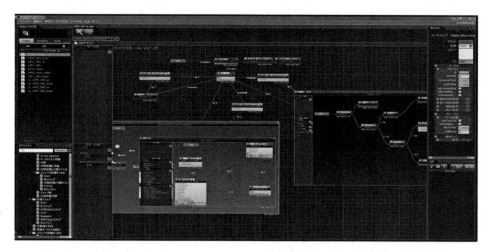

Figure 11.4

AI Graph tool screenshot.

11. A Character Decision-Making System for *FINAL FANTASY XV*

shows variables and nodes that are already made and can be reused. The right vertically long window shows properties for customizing a node and is called the property window. A node can be connected with another node by an arc. In a state machine, a node denotes a state, and an arc indicates transition of the state. In a behavior tree, a node denotes a behavior or operator of the behavior tree, and an arc is used to express the behavior tree structure.

A tray is used to enclose a state machine or a behavior tree. This enables a user to move one entire state machine or behavior tree by moving the tray, and it is also easy to see the layered architecture through the tray hierarchy.

11.4 Implementation Techniques of the AI Graph Node

In the AI Graph, all nodes are reused. For example, a node that can be used in a state machine can also be used in a behavior tree. But ordinarily, the execution method of state machines and behavior trees is different. To make it possible for an AI node to be executed in both a state machine and behavior tree, each AI Graph node has four methods:

1. Start process (when a node is called)
2. Update process (when a node is executed)
3. Finalizing process (when a node is terminated)
4. A condition to signal termination

For both a behavior tree and state machine, the start process, the finalizing process, and the update process are necessary to begin to execute, finalize, and execute a node. The difference between them is what causes stopping a node. For a behavior tree, a node terminates itself by judging an internal terminate condition, whereas a state machine node is terminated by an external transition condition. Thus if a node has these four components, it can be executed in both behavior trees and state machines.

11.5 AI Graph Features

The following describes features of the AI Graph.

11.5.1 The Blackboard within the AI Graph

Variables can be shared via a blackboard consisting of two types (Figure 11.5). One is a local blackboard, which belongs to a tray. Variables of a local blackboard can be shared only in that local blackboard. The other is the global blackboard. Variables of the global blackboard can be shared with the game and all characters' individual AIs. In the AI Graph tool, both blackboards are shown on the left side. In Figure 11.5, you can see there are several variables listed. In the tool, two connected blackboards can share variables.

These variables are used to describe the properties of a node, the transition conditions of a state machine, and so on. For example, the global variable "IS_IN_CAMERA" means whether an actor is in camera or not, and this variable can be used to describe a transition condition inside a state machine contained in a tray.

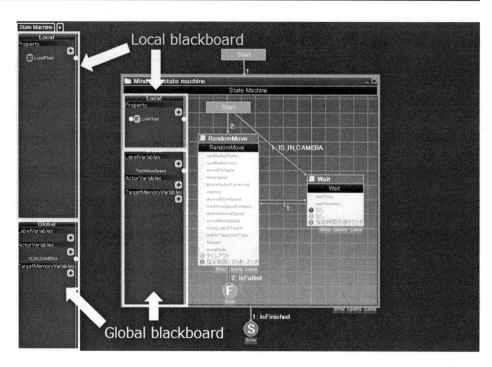

Local blackboard

Global blackboard

Figure 11.5

Blackboard architecture.

11.5.2 Parallel Thinking within the AI Graph

For some situations, a character must think about two things at a time. The AI Graph allows a character to have two concurrent thinking processes, and it is better to make two simple graphs rather than one big complex graph (Figure 11.6).

For example, one thinking process is a simple state machine to set a character behavior, and the other is a simple state to cause the character to look at a target that suddenly appears. The one state machine begins from a "START" node, and the other state machine begins from "PSTART" node.

The two state machines are executed concurrently. So the character can look around and search for a new target while it keeps attacking. Further, a behavior tree can execute two processes by a parallel node. For example, one behavior is to decide on a target and the other is to approach and attack.

11.5.3 Interrupting the Thinking Process

Often, a character will need to interrupt its current execution and execute another specific action. An interrupt node interrupts a process in the AI Graph when an interrupting condition is satisfied, and it executes the node linked to the interrupt node. For example, when a new game mission starts, monsters must rush to a player. After rushing toward a

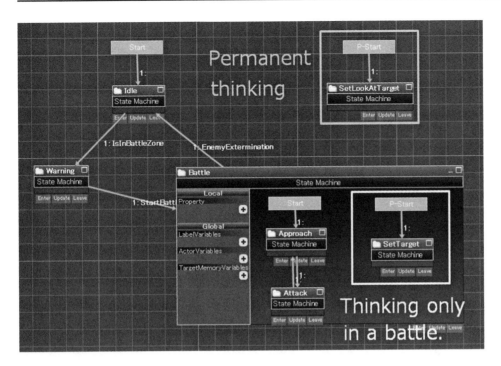

Figure 11.6

Parallel thinking.

player's position, they begin their original thinking process. In this case, two AI Graphs are prepared. One AI Graph includes an interrupt node (Figure 11.7). It causes the current tray to stop and the other tray process to start when the transition condition connected to the interrupt node is satisfied. And after the tray process finishes, the process returns to the original process.

11.5.4 Data and Overrides

An AI Graph can be saved as an asset file. If an AI Graph is fundamental for a character, it is repeatedly called and used. But an AI Graph often requires changes, because it needs to be specialized for each character. For example, when a state machine is saved as an asset file, a user might change a state of the state machine to customize the behavior. In this case, a function to change a node is called an "override," much like in C++.

In *FINAL FANTASY XV*, there are many different types of monsters. For all monsters, the top layer is set through a common template, but their fighting states are different. Therefore, the fighting state is overridden for each monster. Furthermore, a monster's AI Graph can be created by overriding the graph repeatedly from the common logic to monster battle logic (Figure 11.8). In this way, overriding methods make the AI Graph development easier and more effective.

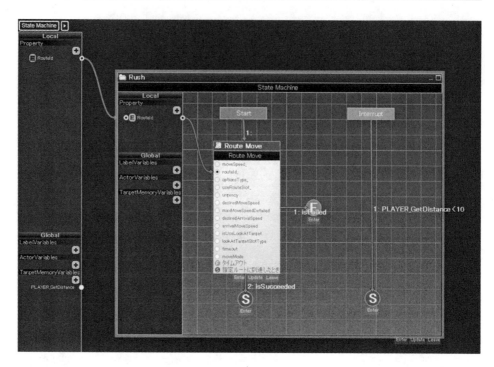

Figure 11.7

Interrupting an AI Graph.

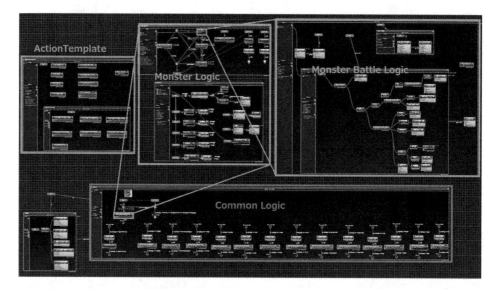

Figure 11.8

Overriding a monster's AI Graph.

11. A Character Decision-Making System for *FINAL FANTASY XV*

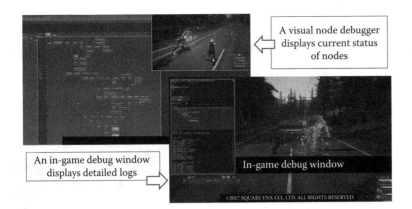

A visual node debugger displays current status of nodes

An in-game debug window displays detailed logs

In-game debug window

Figure 11.9

Visual node debugger (a) and in-game debug window (b).

11.6 Debugging with the AI Graph

For AI development, fast iteration is one of the most important features to keep the AI improving until the end of development. As such, a user should be able to reload an AI Graph without compiling when they want to make a change. In our AI Graph Editor, an AI Graph can be compiled in the Editor independently from other systems' code. This is an example of a data-driven system.

There are two debug windows (Figure 11.9). While a game program runs, an AI Graph keeps a connection with the program. This is called the visual node debugger. In this debugger, the active node currently being executed is highlighted in green. This enables a user to trace the active node in real time.

The other debug window is in a game window. The window displays detailed logs that are generated from a character's AI Graph and AI Graph variables.

11.7 Extracting Animation Parameters through Simulation

In the early stages of development, some monsters' attacks could not reach a player because the attack distance was not large enough. Our solution was to simulate a monster's attack motion, measuring and storing the exact attack distance for each move.

During development, many spheres were distributed around a monster to find the orbit of the monster's attack motion (Figure 11.10). If the motion hits a sphere, the sphere is marked. All marked spheres show the orbit region of the monster's motion. Then the region can be approximated by simple solid figures such as a sphere and sector, and parameters such as the attack distance and attack angles are extracted. These parameters are assigned to an attack node of the AI Graph as the attack parameters. When the node is executed, these new parameters are used when a monster attacks a player.

Manually adjusting AI parameters would have taken too much time during development. This method of analyzing the motion through simulation adjusts the AI parameters automatically and reduces development time.

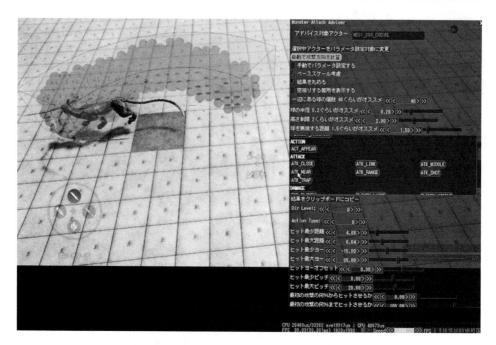

Figure 11.10

Attack motion analysis in simulation.

11.8 Cooperation of Characters via "Meta-AI"

Our meta-AI (more commonly called an AI Director) is an AI that monitors the game and dynamically changes the situation by giving characters orders (Miyake 2016b).

In *FINAL FANTASY XV*, the meta-AI arranges battle sequences. It monitors a battle situation and each character's behavior. When a player or the buddies get into danger, the meta-AI will select one of the buddies who is most appropriate to help (e.g., the nearest buddy who is not attacking). The meta-AI gives the selected character an order to go help the character in danger (Figure 11.11). Buddies' decision-making always depends on the AI Graph. But when a buddy receives an order from the meta-AI, it must stop its AI Graph and obey the meta-AI's order.

In a battle, the meta-AI can give four kinds of orders as follows:

1. Save a player or a buddy in danger.
2. When a player is surrounded by enemies, allow a player to escape.
3. Follow an escaping player.
4. Obey the team tactics.

By using these orders, a meta-AI can tighten a battle flow and can control a player's tension and relaxation.

11. A Character Decision-Making System for *FINAL FANTASY XV*

Figure 11.11

Meta-AI gives an order to save a player to a buddy.

11.9 Sensors

A monster's visual sensors consist of two fan-shaped regions (Figure 11.12). One is a wide fan-shaped region, and the other is a narrow fan-shaped region to detect enemies more precisely. When enemies are in these regions, they will be assigned to a target list.

Figure 11.12

Monster sensor system consisting of two fan-shaped regions.

There is a node to select a target in the AI Graph. In this node, a user can select a targeting mode which is a way to select one target from a target list. Such a target mode can be customized by parameters such as min distance, max distance, min angle, max angle, and priority setting. A priority setting is the parameter type used to decide an enemy's priority in a target list.

11.10 Rule-Based AI System and the AI Graph

For some monsters, a rule-based system and AI Graph are combined. For these monsters, an AI Graph for the top layer is fixed. But there is an independent rule-based system, which includes many rules. It always checks which rule can be fired. Then it selects one of the rules, which calls a corresponding AI Graph template. This is a very simple system with the benefit that one rule condition perfectly corresponds to a single AI Graph to be executed. Although the degree of freedom is partly limited, simplicity of data and the ease of maintenance are clear benefits in our case.

11.11 Body State Machine and the AI Graph

In our game, a character system consists of three layers: an AI layer, a body layer, and an animation layer. These three modules send messages to each other and share variables via blackboards. The AI Graph does not directly initiate animation data. The AI Graph sends a message to the animation layer via a body layer, which consists of a state machine. Especially for shooting and damage behavior, the AI Graph calls the special control nodes within the body layer.

This three-layered architecture separates the roles to control a character, separating concerns between intelligence and animation. It also avoids increasing the size of an AI Graph (Figure 11.13).

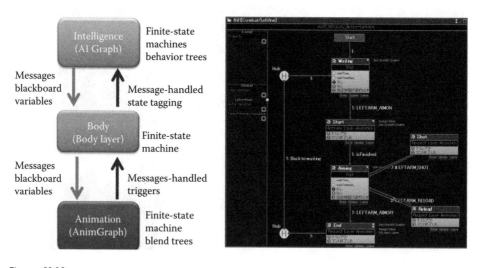

Figure 11.13

Three-layered character system.

A body layer represents a character's body as a node of a state machine. For example, a character's body state is expressed as running, jumping, or climbing a ladder.

A body layer has two roles:

1. Restricting character's actions, a body state can prohibit some actions in this state. For example, while a character is climbing a ladder, it cannot shoot using its hands.
2. Informing a change of body state to the AI layer. Sometimes a character body takes a reactive action to external force or damage. When a reactive action happens, only the body layer knows the information. Then it must send the information by a message to the AI layer. The AI layer will use it for decision-making.

11.12 Conclusion

As game environments and rules become more complex, a character is required to behave more smoothly and intelligently. When development for a next-gen AI began, we realized that it was critical to improve our AI tools. After many discussions within the team, the idea to combine state machines and behavior trees was agreed upon. This allows our developers to leverage both techniques in a nested hierarchical node structure, enabling a very flexible architecture. We called this tool the AI Graph Editor, and it was critical to completing *FINAL FANTASY XV*, which was released in 2016. Additional videos for each technical topic are available in PDF form (Shirakami et al. 2015).

All figures ©2016 SQUARE ENIX CO., LTD. All Rights Reserved. Main character design by TETSUYA NOMURA. All other trademarks are the property of their respective owners.

References

Miyake, Y., 2016a. A multilayered model for artificial intelligence of game characters as agent architecture, in *Mathematical Progress in Expressive Image Synthesis III, Volume 24 of the series Mathematics for Industry*, pp. 57–60. http://link.springer.com/chapter/10.1007/978-981-10-1076-7_7.

Miyake, Y., 2016b. Current status of applying artificial intelligence in digital games, in *Handbook of Digital Games and Entertainment Technologies*, Springer, 2016, http://link.springer.com/referenceworkentry/10.1007/978-981-4560-52-8_70-1.

Miyake, Y., 2015a. Current status of applying artificial intelligence for digital games, *The Japanese Society of Artificial Intelligence*, 30(1), 45–64. doi:10.1007/978-981-4560-52-8_70-1.

Miyake, Y., 2015b. AI techniques for contemporary digital games, *SA '15: SIGGRAPH Asia 2015 Courses*, November 2015, http://dl.acm.org/citation.cfm?id=2818164.

Shirakami, Y., 2015. Miyake, Y., Namiki, K., and Yokoyama, T., Character Decision Making System for FINAL FANTASY XV -EPISODE DUSCAE-, CEDEC 2015, In SQUARE ENIX PUBLICATIAONS, http://www.jp.square-enix.com/tech/publications.html, http://www.jp.square-enix.com/tech/library/pdf/2015cedec_FFXV_AI_English_part1.pdf, http://www.jp.square-enix.com/tech/library/pdf/2015cedec_FFXV_AI_English_part2.pdf

12

A Reusable, Light-Weight Finite-State Machine

David "Rez" Graham

12.1 Introduction

Finite-state machines are an architectural structure used to encapsulate the behavior of discrete states within a system and are commonly used in games for AI, animation, managing game states, and a variety of other tasks (Fu 2004).

For example, consider a guard character that can walk to different waypoints. When he or she sees the player, he or she starts shooting. The guard can be in one of the two states: patrol or attack. It is easy to expand on this behavior by adding more states or tweaking existing ones.

State machines are great for composing behaviors because each state can be parameterized and reused for multiple different characters. For example, you could have a state for attacking the player with each type of enemy determining the attack animations to run, how close they need to be, and so on. The biggest advantage of state machines is that they offer a lot of flexibility while still being extremely simple to implement and maintain. Due to this simplicity, this architecture is best suited for games with smaller AI needs.

Going back to the guard example, one common place for parameterization is the vision cone for the guard. How close does the player have to be before the guard sees him or her?

You could have different kinds of guards with different capabilities. For instance, an elite guard may have a bigger vision cone than a regular guard.

One decision you need to make when building a state machine is how to organize the states and where to put the transition logic. This chapter will discuss how to use transition objects to create encapsulated, reusable objects for managing transitions. This allows designers to compose the overall behavior of an enemy by selecting the appropriate states, choosing transitions for those states, and setting the necessary parameters.

The biggest difference between a traditional state machine and the one presented in this chapter is that this state machine can monitor and change states as necessary. In a traditional state machine, state changes come externally.

The techniques in this chapter were used in the platformer game *Drawn to Life: The Next Chapter* for the Wii, developed by Planet Moon Studios, to handle all of the enemy AI.

12.2 Finite-State Machine Architecture

The driver of the state machine is the `StateMachine` class. This class is owned by the intelligent `GameObject` and manages the behaviors for that object. It owns a list of every possible state the object can be in as well as a pointer to the current state the object is in right now.

The state machine is updated periodically (either every frame or on a cadence that makes sense from a performance point of view) and has an interface for setting the state. The states owned by the state machine are handled with a `State` base class. There are virtual functions for handling the entering and exiting of states, as well as a function to be called on periodic updates. All of the concrete states used by the system will inherit from this class and will override the appropriate methods.

The third major component of this architecture is the `StateTransition` class, which is also owned by the state machine. This class has a `ToTransition()` virtual function that returns a Boolean for whether or not the transition should occur. Much like states, every possible transition in the game is a subclass of `StateTransition`. Figure 12.1 shows a diagram of this architecture.

The states owned by the state machine are handled with a `State` base class, shown in Listing 12.1.

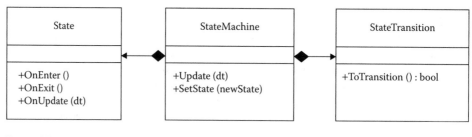

Figure 12.1

State machine architecture.

Listing 12.1. Base class for a single state.

```
class State
{
    GameObject* m_pOwner;

public:
    State(GameObject* pOwner)
        : m_pOwner(pOwner)
    { }
    virtual ~State() { }
    virtual void OnEnter() { }
    virtual void OnExit() { }
    virtual void OnUpdate(float deltaTime) { }

protected:
    GameObject* GetOwner() const { return m_pOwner; }
};
```

It is important to note that state instances live for the entire lifetime of the state machine, so it is important for OnEnter() or OnExit() to handle resetting the state.

12.3 State Transitions

The key to this architecture lies in the transition objects and the way that the state machine is updated. Every possible state inside the state machine is linked to a sorted list of transition/state pairs. Listing 12.2 shows a partial definition for the StateMachine class to illustrate this data structure.

Listing 12.2. StateMachine class.

```
class StateMachine
{
    typedef pair<Transition*, State*> TransitionStatePair;
    typedef vector<TransitionStatePair> Transitions;
    typedef map<State*, Transitions> TransitionMap;

    TransitionMap m_transitions;

    State* m_pCurrState;

public:
    void Update(float deltaTime);
};
```

The variable m_transitions holds the network of transitions for this state machine and defines how the game object will move from state to state. These are typically read from data and built at initialization time, which we will address later in this chapter.

During every update, the state machine checks to see if there are any transitions for this state. If there are, it walks through the list of those transitions and checks to see if it is time to move to another state. If it is, the transition occurs. Listing 12.3 shows the code for this update.

Having no transitions for a state is perfectly valid. For instance, you might not want to allow an enemy to transition out of the death state, or you might have a state that you want to be permanent until some outside force causes the state to manually change via a call to `StateMachine::SetState()`.

Listing 12.3. State machine update.

```
void StateMachine::Update(float deltaTime)
{
    // find the set of transitions for the current state
    auto it = m_transitions.find(m_pCurrState);
    if (it != m_transitions.end())
    {
        // loop through every transition for this state
        for (TransitionStatePair& transPair : it->second)
        {
            // check for transition
            if (transPair.first->ToTransition())
            {
                SetState(transPair.second);
                break;
            }
        }
    }

    // update the current state
    if (m_pCurrState)
        m_pCurrState->Update(deltaTime);
}
```

Using this technique, the states are completely decoupled from each other. Ideally, only the state machine cares about the states, and it never has to know which specific state a character is in.

The transition class itself is trivial and defined in Listing 12.4.

Listing 12.4. Transition class.

```
class Transition
{
    GameObject* m_pOwner;

public:
    Transition(GameObject* pOwner)
        :m_pOwner(pOwner)
    { }

    virtual bool ToTransition() const = 0;
};
```

Each `Transition` holds a reference to the owning game object and declares a pure virtual `ToTransition()` function, which is overridden in the subclass.

States will often need the ability to end naturally and transition into another state. A good example of this is a state that handles pathing to a location. It will naturally end once the game object reaches its destination and needs to move to another state.

One way of doing this is to define a transition that asks if the current state is finished. If it is, the transition occurs and moves to the new state. This keeps all the transition logic in the same place (the transition map) while still allowing natural transitions.

12.4 Hierarchies of State Machines and Metastates

One way to expand this state machine system is to add hierarchy to state machines through metastates. A metastate is a state that contains its own state machine, which has multiple internal states. The simplest way to manage this is by having a special `MetaState` subclass that internally has its own state machine. It would be tuned just like any other state machine and could reuse any existing states.

To illustrate this concept, let us go back to the guard example from the beginning of the chapter where we had a guard that could patrol and attack. Both of these are metastates. The patrol metastate has a transition that tests to see if the player is within the guard's vision cone. The attack metastate has a transition that tests to see if the player is outside of a large radius, which is when we consider the guard to have lost the player. So far, there is nothing special or different. As far as the root system is concerned, there are two states with simple transitions.

Inside of the attack metastate, there are two states. The initial state is an alert state that plays an alert animation. It transitions to the shoot state after a few seconds as long as the player remains in the vision cone. The shoot state will transition back to alert if the player steps out of the vision cone.

The important thing to note is that every active state machine is getting its update, which means that any state can transition at any moment. If the attack state suddenly transitions to the patrol state, it will immediately end whatever state the attack metastate was in. This allows you to treat that entire branch as self-contained.

The addition of metastates adds more complexity but also allows considerably more flexibility. You can create a metastate tree as deep as you wish. One interesting side effect with this kind of system is that it can make going from initial prototype to final implementation a little easier. For example, when implementing the above guard character, the attack and patrol states could start as regular states just to test the concepts and see how they feel in game. Once the character was locked in with animation and a full design, those states could be broken into metastates to manage the low-level nuts and bolts of the AI.

Although you do get a considerable amount of flexibility with a hierarchical approach, it is often not needed. For *Drawn to Life*, we did not find this complexity necessary at all.

12.5 Data-Driving the State Machine

One of the most important things to get right is how to drive this whole system from designer-authored data. Specific implementations are beyond the scope of this chapter and would not be useful since every project will have different needs. The original code on *Drawn to Life* used Lua tables for data. Similar solutions have been implemented in

Unity using C#, which used Unity's inspector and C# reflection for the data. These state machines and transition maps have also been built using XML.

Regardless of which solution you choose, there are several considerations for how to organize this data. The most important is to allow your states and transitions to be parameterized from data. Ideally, you should only have a handful of generic states and transitions, each of which can deliver different behaviors based on those parameters.

For example, consider the AI of a shopkeeper who needs to tend their shop. He or she might wipe down the counter, sweep the floor, tend to shelf of goods, or wait patiently at the shop counter. These all may seem different, but they really are not. At their core, each one paths to a specific target and runs an animation. That is it.

You could take this even further and have this generic state send an optional event to the target. This would allow you to reuse the same state for things like opening windows, restocking inventory, or even striking someone by sending a damage event. This same state could optionally change the internal state of the NPC, so our shopkeeper could eat when hungry. While eating, their hunger needs are fulfilled.

This is the power of data-driving this system. Designers will come up with dozens (or hundreds) of more cases for the simple state described above. Listing 12.5 shows an example of a data-driven `RunAnimationState`.

Listing 12.5. Generic state for running an animation.

```
class RunAnimationState : public State
{
    AnimationId m_animToRun;

public:
    RunAnimationState(GameObject* pOwner)
        :State(pOwner)
    { }

    // Function to load the state definition from XML, JSON,
    // or some other data system. This will fill all the
    // internal data members for this state.
    virtual bool LoadStateDef(StateDef* pStateDef)override;

    virtual void OnEnter() override
    {
        GetOwner()->RunAnimation(m_animToRun);
    }
};
```

12.6 Performance and Memory Improvements

The performance and memory footprint of this system can definitely be improved, and in this section, we will discuss a few of these improvements.

The simplest performance improvement is to time-slice the state machine update by limiting how often the state machine is updated, and how many game objects can update in a single frame. This can be done with an update list where every state machine is put into a list, and the game only allows a certain amount of time to be dedicated to the AI updates. As long as the transition map stays static during a frame, there is no reason you could not time-slice in the middle of an update either.

Another performance improvement would be to remove state updates entirely and make the whole thing event driven. This is a bit trickier to implement, but it is worth it if the performance of this system is a huge concern. In this version, states have no `OnUpdate()` function, only an `OnEnter()` and `OnExit()`. `OnEnter()` will spin up a task if necessary and will wait for a notification of completion. For example, say you have a `GoToObject` state. The `OnEnter()` function would tell the pathing system to find a path and then do nothing until the path was complete.

This system works well if many of your states do not require an update, or you can easily fit it within an existing system. At the very least, it can help eliminate a few virtual function calls.

On the memory side of things, one big issue is that the state machine class proposed above can be very wasteful if it exists on multiple game objects. For example, say you have a dozen orc enemies, and they all have the same behavior. All twelve of those orcs would be duplicating a lot of data.

One solution here is to split `StateMachine` into two different classes, one for handling the static data that never change at run-time and the other to handle the volatile data that does. The class with the volatile data is given a reference to the static data class. This would not even require a change to the interface. This is effectively the Flyweight design pattern (Freeman-Hargis 2006).

The specific choices of what data to pull out of the run-time class will depend on your game. For example, on *Drawn to Life* the transition maps never changed during run-time, so pulling those into a data class would be perfectly fine.

Along these same lines, you could pull out all of the run-time data from each state instance and store it in a state blackboard. States would be parameterized through this blackboard, allowing you to have only a single instance for each state in your system. Transitions could work the same way; all run-time data would exist on a blackboard for that character so only one instance would be required per class.

12.7 Conclusion

This chapter has only touched on the surface of this kind of architecture. It is very simple and light-weight, yet flexible enough to allow a considerable amount of power and control. This architecture can be applied directly to your AI needs, but there are a few takeaways that can apply to any architecture.

The power of the transition objects to decouple the states from one another comes from a common programming design pattern called the strategy pattern (Gamma et al. 1997). The basic idea is to wrap up an algorithm into a self-contained class so that several such algorithms can be composed at run-time to change behavior. It is very good for data-driven systems since these objects can be instantiated with a factory and composed into a data structure (the transition map in our case) to determine the final behavior. You can even change these at run-time, significantly altering behavior by swapping a few objects.

This system can also be used in conjunction with other systems. For example, you might have a `UtilityTransition` class that scores its target state to see if it is something the character wants to do. You could have a decision tree as your transition logic, using states only to manage their actions.

Either way, hopefully you see the power and flexibility of this kind of architecture.

References

Gamma, E., R. Helm, R. Johnson, and J. Vlissides. 1997. *Design Patters: Elements of Reusable Object-Oriented Software.* Upper Saddle River, NJ: Addison-Wesley.

Freeman-Hargis, J. 2006. Using STL and patterns for game AI. In *AI Game Programming Wisdom 3*, ed. S. Rabin. Newton, MA: Charles River Media, pp. 13–28.

Fu, D. and Houlette, R. 2004. The ultimate guide to FSMs in games. In *AI Game Programming Wisdom 2*, ed. S. Rabin. Newton, MA: Charles River Media, pp. 283–302.

Choosing Effective Utility-Based Considerations

Mike Lewis

13.1 Introduction

Theatrical actors are (perhaps stereotypically) known for asking the pointed question, "What's my motivation?" AI designers and implementers often must ask the same thing on behalf of their digital creations. In fact, entire systems of AI architecture center on that very idea: why would a creature or NPC do some specific action at a given moment in time?

In particular, *utility theory* offers a powerful and compelling model for game AI (Graham 2014). In a nutshell, available decisions are scored using some mathematical formulas, and the agent selects a course of action from among the best-scoring options. There are several available models for utility-based architectures described in existing literature and lectures (Dill 2015, Mark 2013).

Interestingly, most of the resources available until now have focused on the architectural side. The specifics of building decision-making systems are often left as a proverbial exercise to the reader, often with vague allusions to "game-specific" details.

Throughout the next several pages, we will explore some of those specific details, taking a tour of some of the decisions available to NPCs in *Guild Wars 2: Heart of Thorns*. Each decision will be broken down into the *considerations* that affect whether or not the decision is considered optimal at any given point in time. From there, we will look at the rationale for choosing each specific consideration. We will conclude with a series of general-purpose tips that can be applied to consideration selection in any utility-based architecture.

13.2 Architecture

The *Heart of Thorns* AI implementation is modeled on the Infinite Axis Utility System (Mark 2013). A major guiding principle of the design is that the AI should be data driven as much as possible. This allows for maximum flexibility and configurability, while simultaneously easing the load on engineers and empowering the design team (Lewis and Mark 2015).

To this end, AI characters are allotted a certain selection of *decisions*—actions which the AI can take at various points in time. Different archetypes or "species" of character may have very different sets of available decisions. Each possible action for a given AI agent is mapped to a decision score evaluator, or DSE. During a think cycle, each DSE for an agent is scored, and the best-scoring option determines the action the AI takes for that think cycle.

The scoring of a DSE consists of accumulating all the scores of the considerations assigned to that DSE. Each consideration is essentially a raw numeric input, normalized to the interval [0, 1]. This score is processed through a *response curve*, which remaps the original number to a final score, again normalized. These scores are then multiplied together to obtain the overall score of the DSE itself.

Suppose a DSE has two considerations: distance to target and health of the target. Health can be a simple fraction, abstracting away the detail of "hit points" or other mechanics that describe the healthiness of the target. Distance can be normalized by providing "bookends"—so, for example, a distance of 100 m might be "maximum," and 0 m might be "minimum." The normalization process will take any distance between 0 and 100 m and map it onto a score of 0–1. Any distance above the maximum automatically scores 1.

The next step is to process these raw numbers via the response curves. In this case, imagine that closer targets are more appealing than distant ones. Given a target at 25 m, the "raw" consideration score would be $25/100 = 0.25$. Passed through a suitable function, however, 25 m might score as, say, 0.95. This remapped score allows the designer fine-grained control over the relative importance of each consideration. As the setup of the response curve (as well as the choice of input that is fed into it) is entirely data driven, there is no engineering burden for modifying the preferences of an AI character.

A key trait of this design is that any consideration can disqualify an entire decision from being selected simply by scoring zero. As soon as a consideration drops the decision score to zero, the system stops processing further considerations and early-outs, moving on to the next decision. This makes it trivial to encode rules for when a decision is absolutely not supposed to be used. Additionally, it allows AI designers to optimize the decision evaluation process itself, since cheaper considerations can be ordered first and early-out to avoid processing more expensive ones.

Given these building blocks, the real art of building a character's AI lies in selecting considerations and pairing them with appropriate response curves. To properly explore the nuances of this process, let us take a closer look at some DSEs used in *Heart of Thorns*.

13.3 Tactical Movement

A considerable portion of the combat-related work that went into *Heart of Thorns* focused on the moment-to-moment, "tactical" positioning and maneuvering of individual NPCs. Many characters have an archetypical "style" or "flavor" that they represent, and the choices driving the movement of those characters on the battlefield have a substantial impact on how well the designer's intent is actually conveyed during gameplay.

However, there are also common and widely used sorts of movement—the type of things that basically every reasonably intelligent character is expected to do during a fight. A perfect example of such a common movement is "Evade Dangerous Areas." This DSE examines the environment for magical spells, mechanical traps, and other hazards created by players as well as hostile NPCs. If the AI character is too close to such a danger zone, they will rapidly exit the area, often playing a specific "dodge" animation and momentarily avoiding any incoming attacks.

13.3.1 Evade Dangerous Areas

The DSE for this action is relatively simple but highly instructive. There are only six considerations used. The first two are binary on/off switches that prevent the action from being chosen in the middle of another decision, or if the character has been prevented from moving by, say, a rooting spell. Virtually all DSEs use basic switches like these to help ensure that the AI does not do something ridiculous, like trying to move while frozen in place.

It would of course be possible to hard-code these switches into *every* DSE—and indeed there are a small number of other control factors which are hardwired into the engine. However, we chose to simply prepopulate newly created DSEs with a few commonly required switches. The more hard-coded logic that gets added, the more brittle the system becomes when exceptions are desired. Inevitably, someone will think of a good use case for bypassing those switches. When that day comes, it is beneficial to be able to simply omit a consideration versus having to add *more* hard-coded logic for bypassing the *first* bit of hard-coded logic.

Moving on, the third consideration on the Evade Dangerous Areas DSE is the real workhorse. This consideration uses an *infinite-resolution influence map* to detect nearby dangerous activities and locales (Lewis 2015). The influence map is populated every few frames with data on all potential hazards. Creating more hazards in a particular location results in a higher score for that area.

The input from this consideration is mapped through a response curve that effectively amplifies the perceived danger of moderately dangerous areas, while simultaneously squelching the perceived danger of unimportant hazards. The goal of this is to ensure that characters on the fringes of a hazard will still get out of the way, whereas characters will stay put if they are *near* a hazard but not *inside* its effective radius. The graph of the response curve is shown in Figure 13.1.

Coming in fourth and fifth are a pair of considerations designed to break cycles of repetitive behavior. They are termed *runtime* and *cooldown*, respectively. Runtime's job is to guarantee that the decision will stop being chosen after a certain number of repetitions. In this case, a response curve is used to drop the score of the consideration (and therefore

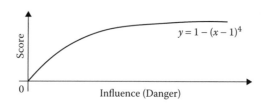

Figure 13.1

Response curve for influence map filtering on Evade Dangerous Areas.

the decision as a whole) to zero after a short time. This ensures that, even if the decision is otherwise valid, it will not be chosen too many times back-to-back. This mechanism is extremely useful for avoiding edge cases where the character constantly evades and becomes impossible to hit.

Cooldown is a standard timer that forces the decision to score zero (or nearly zero) until a given delay has elapsed. This is useful for avoiding strobing between two otherwise competing decisions and also helps ensure that a single decision is not selected too frequently. The response curve on cooldowns returns very small scores until near the end of the cooldown period, at which time the score spikes back up to its full potential (subject, of course, to the other considerations on the decision). Graphs of the standardized runtime and cooldown response curves can be seen in Figure 13.2.

The final consideration for Evade Dangerous Areas is based on the health value of the character itself. It simply dials back the score of the DSE if the character has plenty of health to absorb the damage of whatever hazard it may be standing in. This mechanism lends a bit of flavor and personality to the AI characters, since they will become willing to withstand some pain in order to, say, land a blow on an enemy player. Moreover, the same characters will become more conservative as they take damage and lose health.

13.3.2 Close to Melee when Invisible

Much like its Evade Dangerous Areas counterpart, Close to Melee When Invisible is a DSE that attempts to move a character into a more advantageous position on the battlefield. However, it is much less widely applicable; only a few characters can be invisible at all, and not all of them want to get *closer* to their enemies when they are hidden from view.

As before, the DSE begins with two switch considerations that prevent the decision from activating for immobilized or otherwise occupied characters. The third consideration

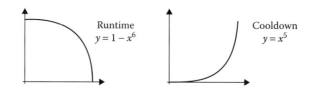

Figure 13.2

Runtime and cooldown response curves.

simply queries the game rules to see if the character is presently invisible to its target. It, too, is a binary on/off switch, rendering the decision unavailable if the AI is not in fact invisible.

Where things get interesting is the fourth consideration. This factors in the distance between the AI and its target, and elects to move closer to the target *if and only if* it can reach the target before regaining visibility. (In truth this is a constant time value, but the time was deliberately chosen to attain this effect. More complex queries may be warranted if the design rules are more sophisticated, but this was sufficient for our purposes.) The approximation for this is handled quite easily by a single response curve, which tapers off at the extreme long-range end.

The next consideration is again based on health, making the decision score lower if the AI does not have enough health to justify a sneaky attack maneuver. Finally, there is a runtime limitation of a few seconds to avoid traveling extreme distances while invisible—something which could be confusing and frustrating to players.

Overall, the effect of these considerations is striking. AI characters might engage in relatively standard combat behavior for a time, then suddenly cloak themselves and vanish from sight. As the bewildered player tries to figure out where his or her foe disappeared to, the AI is making a mad dash toward the player. Once within striking distance, the AI reappears and delivers a surprise volley of damage to the unsuspecting target.

During prototyping on *Heart of Thorns*, this behavior (among others) was used to illustrate the power of carefully chosen considerations. A stealthy predator, an assassin, and even a cheeky thief could all use the basic pattern constructed here to great effect. Such predefined patterns proved so handy during implementation that over one hundred of them were made and used in the final game. The *a la carte* power of the architecture allowed designers to mix and match ready-made behaviors and preference patterns into new creatures in a mere handful of minutes (Lewis and Mark 2015).

13.4 Skill Selection

In addition to tactical movement, characters in *Heart of Thorns* have access to an array of "skills"—abilities that are typically combat focused, aiming to deal damage to enemy targets or reinforce allies. Selection of considerations for these skills is worth exploring in its own right, since the various types of offensive and defensive abilities often require specially tailored scoring to be effective.

For the sake of increased modularity and ease of reuse, skill-related DSEs can be assigned to premade sets of considerations. This allows related skills to reuse the same decision scoring logic across the game. In addition to making the AI more discoverable and recognizable to the player, this dramatically cuts down on the number of custom-tuned DSEs that must be created during the design process.

13.4.1 Charge Attacks

The skill DSE for a basic rushing or charging attack begins with two familiar faces: considerations to avoid using the attack in the middle of another activity and while unable to move. The third consideration looks at the distance to the target. This particular consideration carries a special response curve, which scores higher for targets at moderate range; it does not make sense to burn a rush attack skill on a target which is already within easy striking distance, for example. By the same token, it makes no sense to use the charge if the actual attack will not reach the target at all.

An interesting new consideration on this DSE examines the influence map to see if there are already a reasonable number of allies in the area of the target. This is designed to ensure that players are not overwhelmed by enemy characters. A player already fighting two opponents should not need to worry about a third suddenly charging in and piling on. This is a fantastic example of a design constraint that can be easily expressed using utility AI and supporting modular AI information systems.

The next consideration simply prefers the attack to be used when the character's health is at least moderately high. It does not usually look good to charge into a horde of enemies when near death, so this consideration helps maintain some sensibility in the character's behavior. Of course, a more reckless, even suicidal type of enemy might find that the opposite is true—deploying an attack into a nearby group of enemies at low health may be just the thing for that character. This is trivial to accomplish by tweaking the response curve on the health consideration.

Another new consideration is the *relative direction* check. This is tuned for charge attacks in such a way as to prefer to charge at targets that are mostly in front of the AI. By imposing this limitation, we avoid ugly animation snaps and directional flip-flopping. The AI will not choose to charge at something behind itself, because that looks bad and typically does not make as much sense to the observing player.

Bringing up the rear is a simple line-of-sight consideration. This is another on/off switch that avoids deploying the charge attack at something that cannot be directly reached. Of course due to the limited nature of line-of-sight, it is possible for the AI to "see" a target but not be able to navigate to it on the navmesh. In *Heart of Thorns*, we mostly ignored this restriction, because of processing power limitations—it was too expensive to compute paths to all targets all the time, and the edge cases where it made a visible difference were mercifully rare.

13.4.2 Side and Rear Attacks

As a variant on the usual frontal assault style of combat, some characters in *Heart of Thorns* prefer to be a little sneakier, attacking primarily when their target is facing away from them. For melee attacks, this is handled largely by a single skill DSE. Remember that the same DSE can be used for many different skills, allowing designers to create consistent mechanics without duplicated data.

The flanking/backstab attack DSE is similar to most others in that it starts with an early-out switch to prevent the skill from being used if another action is already running for that AI character. However, unlike DSEs that involve movement, this one does not turn off for immobilized characters. This is a great example of why hard-coding the rules can be a net negative; instead of having to wire in some logic to allow this particular skill DSE to activate on rooted AIs, we simply omit the consideration that would otherwise turn it off.

As such, the second consideration on this DSE checks to make sure that the target is facing away from the AI character. This is done by checking the normalized facing direction of the target and taking the dot product of that vector by the normalized vector from the target to the AI. The closer this dot product is to 1, the closer the target is to pointing directly at the AI character. Therefore, the response curve for this consideration simply tapers off as the dot product's value reaches 1. The net result is that the character will score targets facing perpendicularly (or completely away) more highly.

The next consideration limits the DSE to avoid making flanking attacks when the character is badly wounded. Accomplishing this with a response curve is trivial: simply keep the curve value high until some arbitrary health value threshold, then drop off quickly as health continues to decline to zero.

Following the health check, there are three prioritization considerations that are used to help determine which targets are most eligible for the attack. All other things being equal, the DSE will prefer closer targets, weaker (lower health) targets, and targets that are in the AI's cone of vision.

Checking for closer targets is as simple as looking at the distance to a prospective target and scoring lower as the distance increases. By contrast, the enemy health check uses a gradual tapering effect to *diminish* the priority of full-health targets but not *zero* it.

For prioritizing targets in front of the AI (or, roughly speaking, in its vision cone), there is again a directional check. This time, however, the check looks at the AI's facing direction and compares it to the offset vector pointing toward the target. As a result, the score will drop off toward zero the more the character is looking *away* from the target.

Finally, the DSE finishes off with a simple line-of-sight check, which operates much the same as the one used for charge attacks and other skills. The order of this is actually significant, since the raycast used for the check is fairly expensive; if we can early-out from the DSE before having to do an actual check here, so much the better. This sort of optimization is a large part of what made the *Heart of Thorns* AI sufficiently performant.

13.5 Guiding Principles

On a general level, the considerations we have seen can be broken down into three basic categories. There are those which are mandatory for a decision to function at all; those which distinguish the decision from other, similar behavioral patterns; and those which mostly affect balance and the "feel" of the AI.

Mandatory considerations are the easiest to select from the toolbox. The commonly used switches and toggles enumerated earlier are all mandatory—things like "don't interrupt a running action" or "don't move when immobilized." When building a utility-based AI, it is immensely helpful to know what considerations absolutely must be in place in order for the logic to operate correctly.

Many of these rules can be hard-coded into the game rather than data driven; however, as remarked upon before, it is often beneficial *not* to hard-code mandatory considerations on the chance that someone will want to bypass or circumvent them as part of a design.

Distinguishing one behavioral pattern from another is typically a matter of tapping into game rules. For *Heart of Thorns*, there are numerous status flags ("buffs") that can be applied to a given character. As we saw with the Close to Melee When Invisible example, a consideration that looks at these buffs or status flags can go a long way.

Balance and "feel" considerations are probably the trickiest to get right. Selecting a response curve can be difficult. Within the *Heart of Thorns* architecture, it is common place to use runtime and cooldown considerations to control the timing and repetition of decisions. All of these considerations use standardized response curves to simplify the design process.

As a matter of fact, the vast majority of the response curves used in the game are chosen from a small palette of preset curves. Permitting arbitrary curves is immensely powerful but has the substantial drawback of being intimidating and possibly even unintuitive. When using an architecture that permits this sort of configurability, it is worth hiding it behind an "advanced mode" and favoring preset curves for the majority of use cases.

13.5.1 Selecting Consideration Inputs

Before reaching the point of building a response curve (or other general scoring function), it is important to gather a list of the input factors that might contribute to making a particular decision.

Some generic inputs that are broadly applicable to most AI simulations include distance (both straight-line and pathfinding distance can be useful), time, relative direction/heading, line-of-sight, and so on. These are nearly universal concepts that can be applied to most decisions in some way. Moreover, they are conceptually portable between game applications and even into nongame AI usage.

More game-specific ideas may include things like health, mobility, special status effects, relative proximity of other characters, and so on. Feeding these sorts of considerations with game data is typically straightforward and can yield remarkable results. An especially useful approach is to adapt the data from other game systems via a translation layer that converts game rules into consideration inputs. Coupled with parameters on the considerations themselves, this layer helps keep the AI data-driven and flexible without requiring huge amounts of code for each unique type of character.

As one example of pulling data from the game itself, *Heart of Thorns* uses influence maps heavily, as noted earlier. There are several common queries that extract useful AI decision-making data from those influence maps. The presence or absence of allies and enemies can be obtained individually or even combined to yield a metric that estimates how much conflict is present at a given location (Mark 2015). Environmental hazards and artificial danger zones (spells, traps, etc.) are also represented in the influence map.

When building a DSE, it is important to consider all the relevant inputs so that the character will ultimately make the "right" decisions. Some inputs may also need further parameterization, such as distance ranges, time limits, which in-game status effects to query, and so on. Although the options may seem overwhelming at first, it helps to do a little bit of applied role-play.

Suppose the character is a thief who wishes to stealthily approach targets and pickpocket them, avoiding overt combat as much as possible. Put yourself in the character's shoes, so to speak, and think about *why* you would (or would not!) want to decide to do a particular action. Distill these reasons into concrete metrics. Deciding to approach a mark should probably be based on considering things like the perceived value of the target, relative distance, whether they are facing away from the thief, and so on.

Once a variety of input factors have been identified, it is time to score the decision based on the relative importance of each factor. This is where finely tuned scoring functions come in—in the case of *Heart of Thorns*, we used response curves.

13.5.2 Constructing Response Curves

Even if most response curves used by the engine are presets, it can be very helpful to follow a few simple guidelines for choosing which curve makes the most sense. To that end, there are essentially three characteristics of the curve to consider.

An *increasing* curve tends toward higher y-values as the x-value increases, while *decreasing* curves do the exact opposite. This can be thought of as whether the curve climbs or dips as it moves to the right on a graph. Increasing curves make a decision *more relevant* toward the upper end of the input range, whereas decreasing curves will make the same decision *less relevant*.

Once the overall direction of a curve is established, the next characteristic is whether the curve is *monotonic* or not. An increasing curve is monotonic if it never "turns around" and begins decreasing instead. Recall that we only care about the response curve's behavior in the domain $[0, 1]$ and the range $[0, 1]$—that is, the square from the origin to $(1, 1)$ on the coordinate plane. Therefore, many simple monomial functions (for example) can be considered monotonic *on the relevant interval* even though they are strictly speaking not monotonic in the domain of the reals.

Monotonicity is important because it greatly simplifies the process of understanding how a consideration's score works. Most response curves in *Heart of Thorns* are monotonic, although it is occasionally useful to use nonmonotonic curves to get specific effects. A great example is keeping an enemy at arm's length. Using a distance consideration and an upside-down U-shaped response curve, we can make a character approach its enemy only if the enemy is not already too close or too far away.

The last characteristic to consider is the curve's *endpoints*. The endpoints of the curve are simply the function's values at $x = 0$ and $x = 1$. These points describe the score of the consideration at the minimum and maximum of the input range, respectively. For monotonic curves, these will also correspond to the minimum and maximum scores of the consideration. An increasing, monotonic curve will score its minimum value at $x = 0$ and its maximum at $x = 1$. By contrast, a decreasing monotonic curve will score its maximum at 0 and its minimum at 1.

Selection of response curves can make or break a utility-based AI. Broadly speaking, the scoring function (whether using a response curve or a more general function) is the heart and soul of how the AI will decide to do one thing versus another. A simple checklist can be invaluable for choosing an appropriate scoring function.

The first key question is to determine what input is being scored. For each input type, decide on bookends for the input—a clamped range that controls what input value carries a significance of 0, and what input value translates to 1 on the x-axis.

Given a well-defined range of input to work with, the next key component is the slope of the curve. Does the importance of making this decision *increase* as the input nears 1, or does it *decrease* instead? For a thief considering the perceived wealth of a target, an increasing curve makes sense. The same thief thinking about the distance to a target will probably favor a decreasing curve for that consideration—the farther away a mark is, the more danger is involved in reaching them, and therefore the less opportune that target will be.

Monotonicity is generally preferable for a response curve unless some specific behavior is needed. Think carefully about whether there should be an artificial "high point" or "low point" to the consideration's score *in between* the input extremes of 0 and 1. Configure this peak or valley such that it corresponds to the appropriate input value.

Finally, it is important to plan out the endpoints of the scoring curve. As noted earlier, these correspond to the consideration's score at the low and high ends of the input range. Endpoints have a strong influence on the decision's overall score when the inputs are at extremes. Should the score drop to zero when an input reaches minimum/maximum? Or should it simply *deprioritize* the decision instead of invalidating it altogether?

Most of the time, it is simplest to have a minimum/maximum input correspond to a consideration score of 1. In other words, if a consideration is in a perfect situation, it should yield a perfect score—subject of course to the scores of other considerations for the same decision. The primary exception is when considering the interplay of multiple decisions with similar considerations. However, there are many factors to take into account for this scenario.

13.5.3 Interleaving Decision Scores

A commonly referenced strength of utility-based systems is their organic, fluid nature. As scores rise and fall in the heat of the moment, the AI will always pick something sensible from the list of options—even if it is just doing *something, anything* rather than stand still. In practice, this is a powerful tool for ensuring robust behavior, but it can also be a double-edged blade.

Done carefully, interleaving decision scores can produce interesting effects. For example, creating a *sequence* of decisions is as simple as setting up cooldowns, and then having each subsequent decision weighted slightly lower than the prior action. As successive actions are chosen by the AI, they will enter cooldown, leaving the AI to choose the next best thing—which, by construction, is the next action in the sequence.

One scenario where decisions can clash is when the considerations and response curves happen to generate very similar scores for different decisions. Even if the absolute best-scoring decision is always selected (highly recommended), the two may oscillate or ping-pong as their respective scores rise and fall. There are a few ways to combat this: give a "commitment bonus" (small score boost factor) to the last-chosen decision, increasing the odds of it being chosen again; add weights to each decision so that their total score could be, say, 3 or 4 instead of just 1; and make judicious use of runtime and cooldown considerations.

Unfortunately, all of these methods (useful as they are) share a single common drawback. In effect, they do not eliminate the possibility of two decisions oscillating—they simply shift *where* the scores will land when the oscillation happens. It could be that those scores land far enough away from the problem zone that the oscillation is irrelevant or easily dominated by other scores in the mix. But it can also happen that scores will continue to compete in harder and harder to recognize ways.

The simplest fix to this issue is to add another consideration to one of the decisions. Although it may be counterintuitive, this will add more variation to the overall scoring process, increasing the chances that the competing decision will consistently win (or lose)—thereby eliminating the oscillation.

However, there may be situations where design constraints simply do not allow for any other consideration to "make sense." This is readily encountered when working with highly specialized set pieces and other similar sorts of AI characters. If another suitable consideration cannot be found, the next best thing is to adjust the involved response curves to minimize the zone of oscillation.

Although most of the time there is a closed-form, analytical solution to the problem, it is often not worth the effort to solve the equations on paper. Instead, it is much more effective to build a tool that allows AI developers to manipulate the various inputs for a consideration using simple sliders. Providing a visual mechanism for experimenting with considerations (and, by extension, multiple competing decisions) can radically improve the accessibility and discoverability of any utility-based AI system.

13.6 Choosing Effective Considerations

We can use the rules discussed thus far as a starting point for defining how considerations should factor into making a decision in a utility-based AI model. But even before the selection and tuning of scoring functions (such as response curves), it can be tricky to determine which specific inputs should be used at all.

Broadly speaking, answering this question requires getting into the mind of the AI agent itself, and thinking in terms of what would motivate (or deter) that agent with regards to the particular decision being modeled. Many inputs—like distance, speed, relative directions, health, and so on—are fairly easy to take into account. But what about the case where a decision is nuanced, complex, possibly expensive to evaluate, and hard to capture in a single equation?

Recall the example from earlier with the invisible character trying to get into melee range of a target before its invisibility wears off. This could be done by modeling the duration of invisibility explicitly in the model, measuring the relative velocities of the invisible agent and the target, and so on. However, we preferred a simple and elegant *proxy variable*, which is just a time constant.

In practice, the difference between the explicit, detailed model of "before invisibility wears off" and the simplified proxy time is visible only extremely rarely. When the differences *are* visible, the player herself actually offers the best solution to explaining away the problem. Players will, in general, be eager to add their own narrative reasons for why AI does what it does. As a result, there will almost always be a tiny story in the player's mind about what happens when the time constant is too short or too long.

We can extrapolate from this example to general-purpose consideration design. Always be on the lookout for situations where a complex or hard-to-capture metric can be substituted for a proxy variable. Moreover, keep in mind that the best proxy may not even be the same kind of metric.

The first question to ask is "why would I do (or not do) this action?" Once a list of potential motivations is amassed, the next order of business is to look for what data are available (or can be readily made available) that best match those abstract motivations. Look for proxy variables that can capture multiple considerations at a time, such as modular influence map combinations (Mark 2015). Lastly, consider the relative importance of each input and design a suitable scoring function or response curve.

13.7 Conclusion

Utility theory offers a compelling model for building AI agents. Yet even with a robust architecture for utility-based AI in hand, it is not always immediately apparent how to actually create good decision-making and behavior. Seeking to address this, we explored some of the specifics of how decision modeling was done for *Guild Wars 2: Heart of Thorns* and a set of general principles that should hopefully carry forward to any project using utility-based AI.

References

Dill, K. 2015. Dual-utility reasoning. In *Game AI Pro Vol. 2*, ed. S. Rabin. Boca Raton, FL: CRC Press, pp. 23–26.

Graham, R. 2014. An introduction to utility theory. In *Game AI Pro Vol. 1*, ed. S. Rabin. Boca Raton, FL: CRC Press, pp. 113–126.

Lewis, M. 2015. Escaping the grid: Infinite-resolution influence mapping. In *Game AI Pro Vol. 2*, ed. S. Rabin. Boca Raton, FL: CRC Press, pp. 327–342.

Lewis, M. and Mark, D. 2015. Building a better centaur: AI at massive scale. *Lecture, Game Developers Conference 2015*. http://gdcvault.com/play/1021848/Building-a-Better-Centaur-AI (accessed May 24, 2016).

Mark, D. 2013. Architecture tricks: Managing behaviors in time, space, and depth. *Lecture, Game Developers Conference 2013*. http://www.gdcvault.com/play/1018040/Architecture-Tricks-Managing-Behaviors-in (accessed May 9, 2016).

Mark, D. 2015. Modular tactical influence maps. In *Game AI Pro Vol. 2*, ed. S. Rabin. Boca Raton, FL: CRC Press, pp. 343–364.

13. Choosing Effective Utility-Based Considerations

14

Combining Scripted Behavior with Game Tree Search for Stronger, More Robust Game AI

Nicolas A. Barriga, Marius Stanescu, and Michael Buro

14.1 Introduction

Fully scripted game AI systems are usually predictable and, due to statically defined behavior, susceptible to poor decision-making when facing unexpected opponent actions. In games with a small number of possible actions, like chess or checkers, a successful approach to overcome these issues is to use look-ahead search, that is, simulating the effects of action sequences and choosing those that maximize the agent's utility. In this chapter, we present an approach that adapts this process to complex video games, reducing action choices by means of scripts that expose choice points to look-ahead search. In this way, the game author maintains control over the range of possible AI behaviors and enables the system to better evaluate the consequences of its actions, resulting in smarter behavior.

The framework we introduce requires scripts that are able to play a full game. For example, a script for playing an RTS game will control workers to gather resources and construct buildings, train more workers and combat units, build base expansions, and attack the enemy. Some details, such as which combat units to build and where or when to expand, might be very dependent on the situation and difficult to commit to in advance. These choices are better left open when defining the strategy, to be decided by a search algorithm which can dynamically pick the most favorable action.

In this chapter, we chose to represent the scripts as decision trees because of the natural formulation of choice points as decision nodes. However, our approach is not limited to decision trees. Other types of scripted AI systems such as finite-state machines and behavior trees can be used instead by exposing transitions and selector nodes, respectively.

14.2 Scripts

For our purposes, we define a script as a function that takes a game state and returns actions to perform now. The method used to generate actions is unimportant: it could be a rule-based player hand coded with expert knowledge, or a machine learning or search-based agent, and etc. The only requirement is that it must be able to generate actions for any legal game state.

As an example, consider a *rush*, a common type of strategy in RTS games that tries to build as many combat units as fast as possible in an effort to destroy the opponent's base before he or she has the time to build suitable defenses. A wide range of these aggressive attacks are possible. At one extreme, the fastest attack can be executed using workers, which usually deal very little damage and barely have any armor. Alternatively, the attack can be delayed until more powerful units are trained.

14.2.1 Adding Choices

Figure 14.1 shows a decision tree representing a script that first gathers resources, builds some defensive buildings, expands to a second base, trains an army, and finally attacks the enemy. This decision tree is executed at every frame to decide what actions to issue. In a normal scripted strategy, there would be several hardcoded constants: the number of defensive buildings to build before expanding, the size of the army, and when to attack. However, the script could expose these decisions as choice points, and let a search algorithm explore them to decide the best course of action.

When writing a script, we must make some potentially hard choices. Will the AI expand to a new base after training a certain number of workers or will it wait until the current bases' resources are depleted? Regardless of the decision, it will be hardcoded in the script, according to a set of static rules about the state of the game. Discovering predictable patterns in the way the AI acts might be frustrating for all but beginner players. Whether the behavior implemented is sensible or not in the given situation, they will quickly learn to exploit it, and the game will likely lose some of its replay value in the process.

As script writers, we would like to be able to leave some choices open, such as which units to rush with. But the script also needs to deal with any and all possible events happening during the strategy execution. The base might be attacked before it is ready to launch its own attack, or maybe the base is undefended while our infantry units are out looking for the enemy. Should they continue in hope of destroying their base before they raze ours? Or should they come back to defend? What if when we arrive to the enemies' base, we realize we do not have the strength to defeat them? Should we push on nonetheless? Some, or all, of these decisions are best left open, so that they can be explored and the most appropriate choice can be taken during the game.

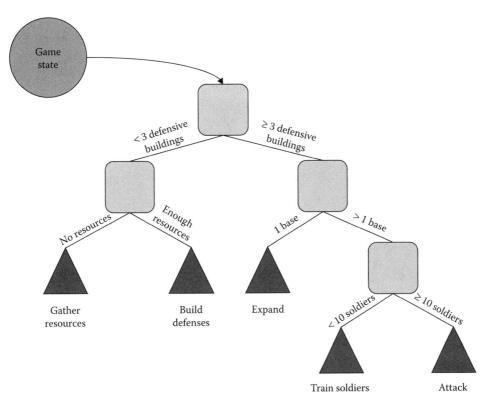

Figure 14.1

Decision tree representing script choices.

The number of choice points exposed can be a configurable parameter with an impact on the strength and speed of the system. Fewer options will produce a faster but more predictable AI, suitable for beginner players, while increasing their number will lead to a harder challenge at the cost of increased computational work.

14.3 Adding Search

So far we have presented a flexible way to write AI scripts that include choice points in which multiple different actions can be taken. However, we have not mentioned how those decisions are made. Commonly, they would be hardcoded as a behavior or decision tree. But there are other techniques that can produce stronger AI systems without relying as heavily on expert knowledge: machine learning (ML) and look-ahead search.

An ML-based agent relies on a function that takes the current game state as input and produces a decision for each choice in the script. The parameters of that function would then be optimized either by supervised learning methods on a set of game traces, or by reinforcement learning, letting the agent play itself. However, once the parameters are learned, the model acts like a static rule-based system and might become predictable. If the system is allowed to keep learning after the game has shipped, then there are no guarantees on how it will evolve, possibly leading to unwanted behavior.

The second approach, look-ahead search, involves executing action sequences and evaluating their outcomes. Both methods can work well. It is possible to have an unbeatable ML player if the features and training data are good enough and a perfect search-based player if we explore the full search space. In practice, neither requirement is easy to meet: good representations are hard to design, and time constraints prevent covering the search space in most games. Good practical results are often achieved by combining both approaches (Silver et al. 2016).

14.3.1 Look-Ahead Search

To use look-ahead search, we need to be able to execute a script for a given timespan, look at the resulting state, and then go back to the original state to try other action choices. This has to happen without performing any actions in the actual game, and it has to be several orders of magnitude faster than the real game's speed because we want (a) to look-ahead as far as possible into the future, to the end of the game if feasible and (b) to try as many choice combinations as possible before committing to one.

This means we need to be able to either save the current game state, copy it to a new state object, execute scripts on the copy, and then reload the original, or execute and undo the actions on the original game state. The latter approach is common in AI systems for board games, because it is usually faster to apply and undo a move than to copy a game state. In RTS games, however, keeping track of several thousand complex actions and undoing them might prove difficult, so copying the state is preferable.

When performing look-ahead, we need to issue actions for the opponents as well. Which scripts to use will depend on our knowledge about them. If we can reasonably predict the strategy they will use, we could simulate their behavior as accurately as possible and come up with a best response—a strategy that exploits our knowledge of the enemy. For example, if we know that particular opponents always rush on small maps, then we will only explore options in the choice points that apply to rushes to simulate their behavior, while fixing the other choices. If the script has a choice point with options (a) rush; (b) expand; and (c) build defenses, and a second choice point with the type of combat units to build, we would fix option (a) for the first choice point and let the search explore all options for the second choice point. At the same time, we will try all the possible choices for ourselves to let the search algorithm decide the best counter strategy.

However, the more imprecise our opponent model is, the riskier it is to play a best response strategy. Likewise, if we play against an unknown player, the safest route is to try as many choices for the opponent as for ourselves. The aim is to find an equilibrium strategy that does not necessarily exploit the opponent's weaknesses, but cannot be easily exploited either.

14.3.2 State Evaluation

Forwarding the state using different choices is only useful if we can evaluate the merit of the resulting states. We need to decide which of those states is more desirable from the point of view of the player performing the search. In other words, we need to evaluate those states, assign each a numerical value, and use it to compare them. In zero-sum games, it is sufficient to consider symmetric evaluation functions `eval(state, player)` that return positive values for the winning player and negative values for the losing player with

`eval(state, p1) == -eval(state, p2)`.

The most common approach to state evaluation in RTS games is to use a linear function that adds a set of values that are multiplied by a weight. The values usually represent simple features, such as the number of units of each type a player has, with different weights reflecting their estimated worth. Weights can be either hand-tuned or learned from records of past games using logistic regression or similar methods. An example of a popular metric in RTS games is lifetime damage, or LTD (Kovarsky and Buro 2005), which tries to estimate the amount of damage a unit could deal to the enemy during its lifetime. Another feature could be the cost of building a unit, which takes advantage of the game balancing already performed by the game designers. Costlier units are highly likely to be more useful, thus the player that has a higher total unit cost has a better chance of winning. The chapter *Combat Outcome Prediction for RTS Games* (Stanescu et al. 2017) in this book describes a state-of-the-art evaluation method that takes into account combat unit types and their health.

A somewhat different state evaluation method involves Monte Carlo simulations. Instead of invoking a static function, one could have a pair of fast scripts, either deterministic or randomized, play out the remainder of the game, and assign a positive score to the winning player. The rationale behind this method is that, even if the scripts are not of high quality, as both players are using the same policy, it is likely that whoever wins more simulations is the one who was ahead in the first place.

If running a simulation until the end of the game is not feasible, a hybrid method can be used that performs a limited playout for a predetermined amount of frames and then calls the evaluation function. Evaluation functions are usually more accurate closer to the end of a game, when the game outcome is easier to predict. Therefore, moving the application of the evaluation function to the end of the playout often results in a more accurate assessment of the value of the game state.

14.3.3 Minimax Search

So far we have considered the problem of looking ahead using different action choices in our scripts and evaluating the resulting states, but the fact that the opponent also has choices has to be taken into account. Lacking accurate opponent models, we have to make some assumptions about their actions. For simplicity, we will assume that the opponents use the same scripts and evaluate states the same way we do.

To select a move, we consider all possible script actions in the current state. For each, we examine all possible opponent replies and continue recursively until reaching a predefined depth or the end of the game. The evaluation function is then used to estimate the value of the resulting states, and the move which maximizes the player-to-move's score is selected. This algorithm is called Negamax (CPW 2016b)—a variant of the minimax algorithm—because in zero-sum games, the move that maximizes one player's score is also the one that minimizes the other player's score. The move that maximizes the negated child score is selected and assigned to the parent state, and the recursion unrolls, as shown in Figure 14.2. Listing 14.1 shows a basic implementation returning the value of the current game state. Returning the best move as well is an easy addition.

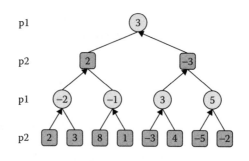

Figure 14.2

Negamax search example.

Listing 14.1. Negamax implementation in Python.

```python
def negaMax(state, depth, player):
  if depth == 0 or terminal(state):
    return evaluate(state, player)
  max = -float('inf')
  for move in state.legal_moves(player):
    childState = state.apply(move)
    score = -negaMax(childState, depth-1, opponent(player))
    if score > max:
      max = score
  return max

#example call
#state: current game state
#depth: maximum search depth
#player: player to move
value = negaMax(state, depth, player)
```

A modification is needed for the minimax algorithm to work in our scripted AI. The moves in an RTS game are simultaneous, so they need to be serialized to fit the game tree search framework. Randomizing the player to move or alternating in a p1-p2-p2-p1 fashion are common choices to mitigate a possible player bias (Churchill et al. 2012). The resulting algorithm is shown in Listing 14.2.

In Listings 14.1 and 14.2, Negamax takes as an input the height of the search tree to build, and being a depth-first algorithm, it only returns a solution when the tree has been fully searched. However, if the computation time is limited, we need an *anytime* algorithm that can be stopped at any point and returns a reasonable answer. The solution is to search a shallow depth, 2 in our case, and then iteratively deepen the search by two levels until time runs out. At first it might look like a waste of resources, because the shallower levels of the tree are searched repeatedly, but if we add a *transposition table*, the information from previous iterations can be reused.

In this chapter, we use the Negamax version of the minimax algorithm for simplicity. In practice, we would use AlphaBeta search (CPW 2016a), an efficient version of minimax that prunes significant parts of the search tree, while still finding the optimal solution.

---

14. Combining Scripted Behavior with Game Tree Search for Stronger, More Robust Game AI

AlphaBeta is more efficient when the best actions are examined first, and accordingly, there exist several move-ordering techniques, such as using *hash moves* or *killer moves*, which make use of the information in the transposition table (CPW 2016c).

Listing 14.2. Simultaneous Moves Negamax.

```
def SMNegaMax(state, depth, previousMove=None):
  player = playerToMove(depth)
  if depth == 0 or terminal(state):
    return evaluate(state, player)
  max = -float('inf')
  for move in state.legal_moves(player):
    if previousMove == None:
      score = -SMNegaMax(state, depth-1, move)
    else
      childState = state.apply(previousMove, move)
      score = -SMNegaMax(childState, depth-1)
    if score > max:
      max = score
  return max

#Example call
#state: current game state
#depth: maximum search depth, has to be even
value = SMNegaMax(state, depth)
```

Another class of algorithms that can be used to explore the search tree is Monte Carlo Tree Search (MCTS) (Sturtevant 2015). Instead of sequentially analyzing sibling nodes, MCTS randomly samples them. A sampling policy like UCT (Kocsis and Szepesvári 2006) balances exploration and exploitation to grow the tree asymmetrically, concentrating on the more promising subtrees.

14.4 Final Considerations

So far, we have introduced scripts with choice points, a state evaluation function, and a search algorithm that uses look-ahead to decide which choices to take. Once the search produces an answer in the form of decisions at every choice point applicable in the current game state, it can be executed in the game. Given enough time, whenever the AI system needs to issue actions, it would start the search procedure, obtain an answer and execute it. However, in practice, actions have to be issued in almost every frame, with only a few milliseconds available per frame, so this can be impractical. Fortunately, as the scripts can play entire games, a previous answer can be used as a standing plan for multiple frames. The search can be restarted, and the process split across multiple frames until an answer is reached, while in the meantime, the standing plan is being executed. At that point, the new solution becomes the standing plan. The search can be started again, either immediately, or once we find the opponent is acting inconsistently with the results of our search.

Experiments using *StarCraft: Brood War* have shown good results (Barriga et al. 2015). A script with a single choice point that selects a particular type of rush was tested against state-of-the-art *StarCraft* bots. The resulting agent was more robust than any of the individual strategies on its own and was able to defeat more opponents.

One topic we have not touched on is fog-of-war. The described framework assumes it has access to the complete game state at the beginning of the search. If your particular game does not have perfect information, there are several choices. The easiest one is to let the AI cheat, by giving it full game state access. However, players might become suspicious of the unfair advantage if the AI system keeps correctly "guessing" and countering their surprise tactics. A better option is to implement an inference system. For instance, a particle filter can be used to estimate the positions of previously seen units (Weber et al. 2011), and Bayesian models have been used to recognize and predict opponent plans (Synnaeve and Bessière 2011).

14.5 Conclusion

In this chapter, we have presented a search framework that combines scripted behavior and look-ahead search. By using scripts, it allows game designers to keep control over the range of behaviors the AI system can perform, whereas the adversarial look-ahead search enables it to better evaluate action outcomes, making it a stronger and more believable enemy.

The decision tree structure of the scripts ensures that only the choice combinations that make sense for a particular game state will be explored. This reduces the search effort considerably, and because scripts can play entire games, we can use the previous plan for as long as it takes to produce an updated one.

Finally, based on promising experimental results on RTS games, we expect this new search framework to perform well in any game for which scripted AI systems can be built.

References

Barriga, N.A., Stanescu, M. and Buro, M. 2015. Puppet search: Enhancing scripted behavior by look-ahead search with applications to real-time strategy games. *Proceedings of the Eleventh Annual AAAI Conference on Artificial Intelligence and Interactive Digital Entertainment* November 14–18, 2015. Santa Cruz, CA.

Chess Programming Wiki. 2016a. Alpha-beta. http://chessprogramming.wikispaces.com/Alpha-Beta (accessed February 8, 2017).

Chess Programming Wiki. 2016b. Minimax. http://chessprogramming.wikispaces.com/Minimax (accessed February 8, 2017).

Chess Programming Wiki. 2016c. Transposition table. http://chessprogramming.wikispaces.com/Transposition+Table (accessed February 8, 2017).

Churchill, D., Saffidine, A. and Buro, M. 2012. Fast heuristic search for RTS game combat scenarios. *Proceedings of the Eighth Artificial Intelligence and Interactive Digital Entertainment Conference*, October 8–12, 2012. Stanford, CA.

Kocsis, L. and Szepesvári, C. 2006. Bandit based Monte-Carlo planning. *17th European Conference on Machine Learning*, September 18–22, 2006. Berlin, Germany.

Kovarsky, A. and Buro, M. 2005. Heuristic search applied to abstract combat games. *Proceedings of the Eighteenth Canadian Conference on Artificial Intelligence*, May 9–11, 2005. Victoria, Canada.

Silver, D., Huang, A., Maddison, C.J., Guez, A., Sifre, L., Van Den Driessche, G., Schrittwieser, J., Antonoglou, I., Panneershelvam, V., Lanctot, M. and Dieleman, S. 2016. Mastering the game of Go with deep neural networks and tree search. *Nature*, 529, 484–489.

Stanescu, M., Barriga, N.A. and Buro, M. 2017. Combat outcome prediction for RTS games. In *Game AI Pro 3: Collected Wisdom of Game AI Professionals*, ed. Rabin, S., Boca Raton, FL: CRC Press.

Sturtevant, N.R. 2015. Monte Carlo tree search and related algorithms for games. In *Game AI Pro 2: Collected Wisdom of Game AI Professionals*, ed. S. Rabin. Boca Raton, FL: CRC Press, pp. 265–281.

Synnaeve, G. and Bessière, P. 2011. A Bayesian model for plan recognition in RTS games applied to StarCraft. *Proceedings of the Seventh Artificial Intelligence and Interactive Digital Entertainment Conference*, October 10–14, 2011. Stanford, CA.

Weber, B.G., Mateas, M. and Jhala, A. 2011. A particle model for state estimation in real-time strategy games. *Proceedings of the Seventh Annual AAAI Conference on Artificial Intelligence and Interactive Digital Entertainment*, October 10–14, 2011. Stanford, CA.

SECTION III
Movement and Pathfinding

15
Steering against Complex Vehicles in *Assassin's Creed Syndicate*

Eric Martel

15.1 Introduction

The different worlds in which videogames exist are becoming more and more complex with each passing day. One of the principal reasons NPCs appear intelligent is their ability to properly understand their environments and adjust their behaviors accordingly. On *Assassin's Creed Syndicate*, part of the mandate for the AI team was to support horse-drawn carriages at every level for the NPCs. For this reason, we adapted the NPCs' steering behaviors to navigate around a convex hull representing the vehicles instead of using a traditional radius-based avoidance. We succeeded in building general-purpose object avoidance behavior for virtually any obstacle shape.

A real-time JavaScript implementation of this material is available at http://steering.ericmartel.com should you wish to experiment with the solution as you progress throughout the article.

15.2 Challenges and Initial Approaches

Most object avoidance steering behaviors are implemented by avoiding circles or ellipses (Reynolds 1999, Buckland 2005). In our case, the vehicles were elongated to such an extent that even by building the tightest possible ellipse encompassing the entire bounding box of the vehicle, we ended up with unrealistic paths from our NPC agents. They would venture far away from the sides of the vehicle despite having a straight clear path to their destination. We wanted NPCs to be able to walk right next to a vehicle like a person in real life would. Note that the solution provided here was only for the navigation of humanoids. Steering behaviors for the vehicles themselves are handled differently and will not be described here.

15.2.1 Navigation Mesh Patching

From the very beginning, we decided that the NPCs should reject a path request if it is physically impossible for them to pass when a vehicle is blocking their way. This implies that, in these situations, changes needed to be made to the navigation mesh. Considering that many vehicles can stop at the same time, each forcing the navigation mesh to be recomputed, we decided to time slice the process. In other words, several frames might be required before the pathfinder properly handles all the stopping vehicles. To avoid having NPCs run against them, a signal system is used to turn on the vehicle in the obstacle avoidance system as soon as it moves and then turn it off as soon as the navigation mesh underneath it is updated. Unfortunately, the steering technique described here will not identify situations where vehicles will completely block a path. The algorithms could be adapted, if required, to test the intersection with the navigation mesh outside edges.

15.2.2 Obstacle Avoidance

Classical obstacle avoidance provides an agent with a lateral pushing force and a braking force, allowing the agent to reorient itself and clear obstacles without bumping into them, as shown in Figure 15.1. Given circular or even spherical obstacles, this is pretty straightforward.

15.2.3 Representation Comparison

Starting off with our existing technology, we experimented with various representations. The first implementation used a circle-based avoidance, increasing the diameter of the circle to encompass the entire vehicle. Although this worked, it did not look realistic enough; agents would walk far away from the sides of a vehicle to avoid it, as is shown in Figure 15.2.

To mitigate the wide avoidance paths, we considered modifying the circular obstacles into ellipses. Ellipses are slightly more complicated to use for obstacle avoidance, as their orientation needs to be taken into account when calculating the lateral push and the breaking factor. Unfortunately, as seen in Figure 15.3, even without implementing them, we knew we would not get the kind of results needed, as the sides were still too wide. Another solution had to be created.

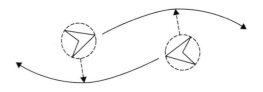

Figure 15.1

Circle-based obstacle avoidance between two agents.

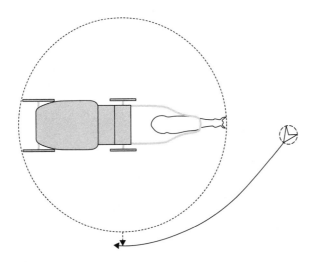

Figure 15.2

Circle-based representation of an elongated obstacle.

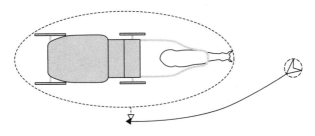

Figure 15.3

Ellipse-based representation of an elongated obstacle.

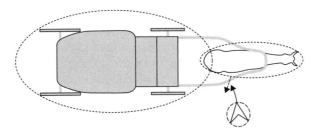

Figure 15.4

Multiple ellipses representing an elongated obstacle.

We considered representing each portion of the vehicle as an ellipse, as it would allow us to represent our collision volumes more accurately. The problem with this representation, as depicted in Figure 15.4, is that by using multiple ellipses, a nook is created between the horse and the carriage. Without handling multiple obstacles at the same time, one risks having the agent oscillate between both parts and then get stuck in the middle.

15.3 Convex Hull Generation

The best representation of the vehicle we could conceive was a convex hull, as it could wrap around all of the subparts of the vehicle without creating any concave sections. This would allow the NPC to steer against the horse-drawn carriage as if it were a single uniform obstacle.

Our obstacles are made out of multiple rigid bodies, each representing a subpart of the vehicle. Some carriages have two horses, others a single one, and after firefights or accidents, a carriage can be left with no horse at all.

15.3.1 Rigid Body Simplification

In order to reduce the number of elements in our data structures, we simplified the representation of our rigid bodies to 2D object-oriented bounding boxes (OOBB). Since our NPCs are not able to fly, we could forgo the complexity of 3D avoidance. By flattening down the 3D OOBB encompassing the rigid bodies provided by our physics engine, we managed to have an accurate representation of our vehicle from top view. In the following examples, we have omitted adding yaw or roll to the subparts (Figure 15.5).

When computing circle-based avoidance, it is easy to simply add the radius of the agent to the repulsion vector, thus making sure it clears the obstacle completely. In our case, we simply grew the shapes of our OOBB of half the width of the characters, making sure that any position outside that shape could accommodate an NPC without resulting in a collision. From that point on, NPCs are navigating as a single point against the expanded geometry of the vehicles.

15.3.2 Cases to Solve

We identified three main situations that need to be handled, pictured in Figure 15.6, ordered from most to least frequent. The most interesting case is the one where shapes are partially overlapping (Figure 15.6a). The algorithm to solve this case is provided in Section 15.3.4.

Two shapes are disconnected when all of the vertices of the first shape are explored finding that none of its edge segments intersect with the second shape, and that none of the vertices of either shape lie inside the other. When shapes are disconnected, we decided to simply merge the two closest edges. In our example from Figure 15.6b, the edges "AD" and "BC" would be removed. Starting from the first vertex of the bottom shape, we iterate on the shape until we reach vertex "A," then switch shape from vertex "B." The process continues until we reach vertex "C" at which point we go back to the initial shape from "D." The operation is complete once we loop back to the first vertex. As long as our vertices are kept in clockwise order, performing this operation remains trivial.

A case that we did not tackle in our implementation is demonstrated in Figure 15.7, where the shapes loop, creating two contours. Given the shape of our entities, this is simply

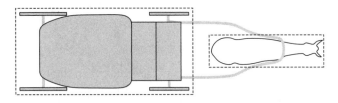

Figure 15.5

Object-oriented bounding boxes representing the obstacle subparts.

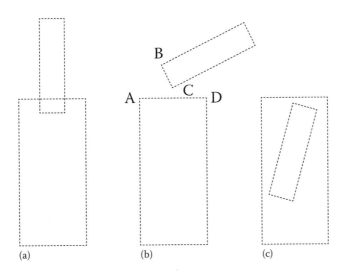

(a)   (b)   (c)

Figure 15.6

The various cases that need to be supported when joining shapes, from left to right:
(a) partial overlap, (b) disconnection, and (c) complete overlap.

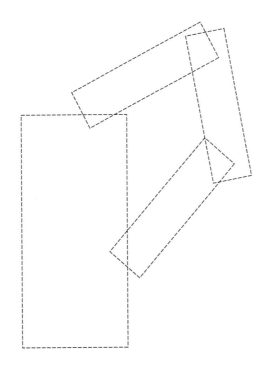

Figure 15.7

Additional case. When enough subparts are present or when the subparts themselves are
concave polygons, multiple contours have to be handled.

not required. It would be easy to adapt the algorithm to support multiple contours with a single convex hull built around the outer contour.

15.3.3 Building the Contour

Before diving into the construction of the contour, the following algorithms were chosen in order to keep things simple, understandable, and to make most of the intermediate data Vuseful. There might be specialized algorithms that are more efficient in your case, feel free to replace them.

First, let us take a look at a useful function, as shown in Listing 15.1, that will be used on multiple occasions in the code. This method simply moves an index left or right of a current value, while wrapping around when either ends of the list are reached. This will allow us to avoid having to include modulo operations everywhere in the code. Although adding `listSize` to `currentValue` might look atypical at first, it allows us to handle negative increment values which in turn make it possible to iterate left and right in the list.

Listing 15.1. Pseudocode to handle index movement in a circular list of items.

```
uint circularIncr(uint currentValue,
                  int  increment,
                  uint listSize)
{
    return (currentValue + listSize + increment) % listSize;
}
```

What follows next is an example of how the algorithm merges and constructs intersecting shapes. As pictured in Figure 15.8, we start from a vertex outside of the second shape, and we iterate in a clockwise fashion as long as we are not intersecting with any edge of the second shape. When finding an intersection, we simply insert the intersection point and swap both shapes as we are now exploring the second shape looking for intersections until we loop around.

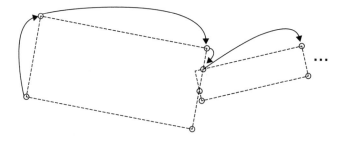

Figure 15.8

Algorithm for intersecting shapes. Merging the shapes by iterating over them, creating vertices on intersections.

The code in Listing 15.2 merges shapes one at a time. Instead of handling the complexity of merging *n* shapes at the same time, shapes are added to a contour that grows with every subpart added.

Listing 15.2. Pseudocode to merge shapes into a contour.

```
currVtx = newShapeToAdd;
altVtx = existingContour;

firstOutsideIndex = firstOutsideVtx(currVtx, altVtx);
nextVtx = currVtx[firstOutsideIndex];
nextIdx = circularIncr(firstOutsideIndex, 1, currVtx.size());

mergedContour.push(nextVtx);

while(!looped)

{
    intersections = collectIntersections(nextVtx,
                                         currVtx[nextIdx],
                                         altVtx);
    if(intersections.empty())
    {
        nextVtx = currVtx[nextIdx];
        nextIdx = circularIncr(nextIdx, 1, currVtx.size());
    }
    else
    {
        intersectionIdx =
            findClosest(nextVtx, intersections);
        nextVtx = intersections[intersectionIdx];
        // since we're clockwise, the intersection can store
        // the next vertex id
        nextIdx = intersections[intersectionIdx].endIdx;

        swap(currVtx, altVtx);
    }
    if(mergedContour[0].equalsWithEpsilon(nextVtx))
        looped = true;
    else
        mergedContour.push(nextVtx);
}
```

For the full source code, please visit the article's website listed in Section 15.1. Consider that `firstOutsideVtx` could fail if all the vertices of `currVtx` are inside `altVtx` as seen in Figure 15.6c. If the while loop completes and `mergedContour` is the same size as `currVtx`, either no intersections happened or all the vertices of `currVtx` are inside `altVtx`, which is easy to test.

15.3.4 Expanding the Convex Hull

At this point, we now have a list of vertices ordered clockwise that might, or might not, represent the convex hull. For the polygon to represent a convex hull, all of its interior angles need to be lower or equal to 180°. If an angle is greater than 180, it is easily solved by removing the vertex and letting its two neighbors connect to one another. Removing it from the array corrects this because of the use of ordered list of vertices. Listing 15.3 describes how this can be accomplished with a few lines of code by using the Z value of the cross product to determine on which side the angle is heading. It is important to always step back one vertex after the removal operation, as there is no guarantee that the newly created angle is not greater than 180° as well.

Listing 15.3. Pseudocode to create a convex hull out of a contour.

```
convexHull = contour.copy();
for(index = convexHull.size(); index >= 0; --index)
{
    leftIndex = circularIncr (index, -1, convexHull.size());
    rightIndex = circularIncr (index, 1, convexHull.size());

    goingLeft = convexHull[leftIndex] - convexHull[index];
    goingRight = convexHull[rightIndex] - convexHull[index];

    if(zCross(goingLeft, goingRight) < 0)
    {
        convexHull.removeAtIndex(index);
        index = min(convexHull.size() - 1, index + 1);
    }
}
```

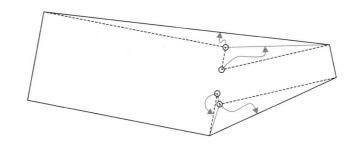

Figure 15.9

Removing vertices that make the polygon concave.

As can be seen in Figure 15.9, it is as if we are folding out the pointy ends of the polygon until we end up with a convex hull.

15.4 Obstacle Avoidance

Now that the geometry is constructed, we can go about shaping the NPCs' behavior around it. This implies that we must first find out if our current position or our destination is inside the convex hull. Any position between the vehicle's OOBB and the convex hull is actually a walkable area. If neither position is located inside the convex hull, we must then check if there is a potential collision between the NPC and the obstacle.

15. Steering against Complex Vehicles in *Assassin's Creed Syndicate*

15.4.1 Obstacle Detection

Most steering behavior systems use a feeler system to detect potential incoming obstacles. In our case, to accelerate and parallelize the system, we utilize axis-aligned bounding boxes that are sent to the physics system. The physics system then matches pairs that are intersecting and allows us to easily know, from the gameplay code, which other entities to test for avoidance.

Once we know we have a potential collision, we can determine if either the start or end positions are inside the convex hull. Using a method similar to Listing 15.4, that is by counting the number of intersections between a segment starting at the tested position and ending at an arbitrary position outside of the polygon and with the polygon itself, we can determine whether or not we are located outside of the shape. An odd number of intersections signals that the position is inside. Otherwise it is outside, as our segment went in and out of the shape an even number of times.

Listing 15.4. Pseudocode to validate if a position is inside an arbitrary polygon.

```
// add small offset
testedXValue = findMaxXValue(vertices) + 5;

intersections = collectIntersections(point.x,

                              point.y,
                              testedXValue,
                              point.y,
                              vertices);

return intersections.size() % 2;
```

For an example of `collectIntersections` or how to check for intersections between segments, feel free to refer to the website listed in the introduction.

15.4.2 Movement around the Convex Hull

When we know that both our current position and destination are outside of the convex hull, a simple intersection check using a segment between both of these positions and the convex hull can confirm whether or not the NPCs are clearing the shape. Having expanded the shape by the radius of the agent guarantees us that if there is no intersection; the NPC is free to go in straight line and will not collide with the obstacle. If the agents have different radii, it is also possible to simply offset the intersection check by the radius of the agent, either on its right or left vector, depending on the relative side of the obstacle.

If an intersection is detected, the NPC must avoid the obstacle. Depending on the relative velocities, you might want to control on which side the avoidance occurs. For the purpose of demonstration, we define that our objective is to minimize the angle between our avoidance vector and our current intended heading.

From the intersection detection, we can extract the vertex information from both ends of the segment with which we intersect. As the vertices are in clockwise order, we know that we can explore their neighbors by decreasing the index of the start vertex to go on

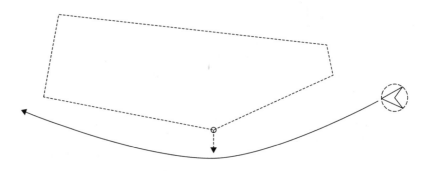

Figure 15.10

Obstacle avoidance when both the start and end points are outside of the obstacle.

the right, and increase the index of the end vertex to go on the left. We are looking for the furthest vertex to which we can draw a straight line without intersecting with the other segments of the convex hull, which also minimizes the angle difference with the intended direction. In Figure 15.10, the end vertex of the intersected segment happened to be the best vertex matching this criterion, as its next neighbor would cause an intersection with the convex hull, and the exploration on the right leads to a greater angle difference.

15.4.3 Movement into the Convex Hull

In the game, NPCs are able to interact with vehicles even while in movement. For this reason, it can happen that their interaction point lies inside the convex hull. In this case, two situations can occur: either the segment between the character and its destination intersects with the contour, or it does not. The convex hull being only a virtual shell around the vehicle does not prevent the agent from going through it, so if no intersection is found with the contour, the NPC can simply walk in straight line to its destination, as shown in Figure 15.11.

The real challenge when an intersection is detected is to find the right direction to send the NPC, since if it walks around the obstacle, it will eventually clear the contour and enter the convex hull. A solution for this problem is to find the edge of the convex hull that is closest to the destination. Doing this, we have two vertices that represent an entry point to the convex hull. By reusing part of the solution in Section 15.4.2, we iterate over the convex hull from our initial intersection toward the two vertices we found earlier. We are trying to find the closest vertex to us that minimizes the distance between it and one of the two vertices without

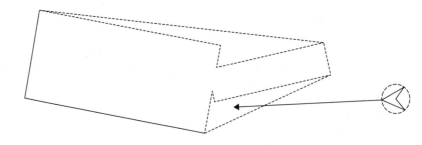

Figure 15.11

Obstacle avoidance when the destination is inside the convex hull.

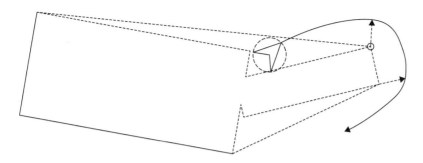

Figure 15.12

Obstacle avoidance when the agent is inside the convex hull.

intersecting with the contour. This distance can be calculated by summing the length of the edges of the convex hull as we are moving in either direction. As we progress, the edge of the convex hull that connects with space where the destination lies will be reached.

At this point, we know the destination is in a polygon, and we are about to enter it. Unfortunately, it is possible that the shape between the contour and the convex hull is a concave polygon. No trivial solution is available, but two well-known options are available to you. Either the NPC "hugs the walls" of the contour by following its neighbor edge until it gets a straight line between itself and the destination or the space is triangulated allowing the algorithm to perform a local path planning request, which will be described in Section 15.5.1.

15.4.4 Movement Out of the Convex Hull

When the agent lies inside the hull, we can deduce the way to exit the shape by reversing the operations of those proposed in Section 15.4.3. We first make the NPC navigate out of the polygon representing the difference between the contour and the convex hull. Once outside, the methods described in Sections 15.4.2 and 15.4.3 should be applied, as the destination will either be inside or outside of the convex hull (Figure 15.12).

15.5 Pushing It Further

The following suggestions are not required to make steering against arbitrary shapes work, but it could improve the quality of your results.

15.5.1 Triangulation from Convex Hull Data

When taking a closer look at Figure 15.9, one might notice that as we removed the vertices, we were actually adding triangles to the contour to push it outward and create the convex hull. As pictured in Figure 15.13, a simple adjustment to the algorithm can push the triangle data as the vertices are popped in order to create a simple local navigation mesh. Local path planning can be used to guide the obstacle avoidance going in and out, generate optimal paths, and simplify the logic required when positions are inside the convex hull.

15.5.2 Velocity Prediction

Given that the state of these obstacles are volatile, we did not spend the time to model the velocity of the subparts of the vehicle but only the obstacle's velocity. If you were to model

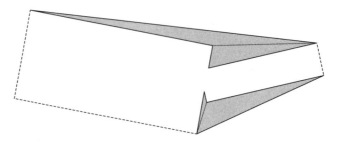

Figure 15.13

Adapting the convex hull generation algorithm to produce a navigation mesh inside the convex hull.

a giant robotic space snake, then allowing NPCs to predict where the tail will be ahead of time may be required, but it comes at the expense of computing the position of the sub-parts in advance.

In most cases, mimicking what humans would do gives the best results. In the case of our game, an agent crossing a moving vehicle will often try to go behind it. Modeling whether the agent is going roughly in the same direction, in opposite direction, or in a perpendicular direction will allow you to give more diversity in which vertex from the convex hull you want to target and how much you want to modulate the braking factor.

15.6 Conclusion

Converting obstacles' shapes to a convex hull really improved the quality of the navigation of our NPCs around them. This solution is also generic enough to be applied to any rigid body, from vehicles to destructible environments. Performance wise, by lazily evaluating the shape of the rigid body and caching the results for all surrounding characters, we managed to get the best of both worlds.

References

Buckland, M. 2005. *Programming Game AI by Example*. Plano, TX: Wordware Publishing.
Reynolds, C. W. 1999. Steering behaviors for autonomous characters, in *The Proceedings of Game Developers Conference 1999*, San Jose, CA. San Francisco, CA: Miller Freeman Game Group, pp. 763–782.

16

Predictive Animation Control Using Simulations and Fitted Models

Ingimar Hólm Guðmundsson, Hendrik Skubch,
Fabien Gravot, and Youichiro Miyake

16.1 Introduction

In the move toward more believable realism in games, animation and AI continue to play an important role. For *FINAL FANTASY XV's* diverse world, one of the challenges was the large amount of different types of characters and monsters. The need for a well-informed steering solution and total freedom for each team to implement animation state graphs that suited their needs called for an unconventional solution to the problem of accurate steering and path following. Our solution treats the game as a black-box system, learning the character's movement parameters to later build an independent motion model that informs steering. In the following sections, the steps taken to fulfill this aim are described, along with the unexpected side effects that came from simulating almost every character type in the *FINAL FANTASY XV.*

16.2 Getting Actors to Hit Their Marks

Games share one thing in common with theatre and cinema: actors must hit their marks. When the AI has no control over the actor's root motion, this problem quickly devolves from interpolating along a curve into begging the animators to stop changing the stop animations and blends. This can affect various aspects of gameplay such as in-engine cut-scenes as well as physical combat, where game actors will overstep their mark or worse, never reach it and the cut-scene will not progress.

Although this simple example is not the only challenge in steering actors, it is a good one to start with as it will highlight all the moving parts in the actor's update as it approaches its mark. In a typical game engine (Gregory 2009), the update order is something like:

Begin frame $\Rightarrow$ AI $\Rightarrow$ Steering $\Rightarrow$ Animation $\Rightarrow$ Physics $\Rightarrow$ End frame.

In each frame, we want to approach our goal and not fall off the mesh or bump into collision unless absolutely necessary. In the first frame, AI will decide that it wants to go to a specific goal point $\vec{p}$ and does the necessary pathfinding and informs steering of the path. Steering will have some model of the actor's motion capabilities, such as

- Min speed, v_{min}
- Max speed, v_{max}
- Acceleration, a

When steering starts to accelerate with its desired velocity vector along the path, animation will receive information about the desired velocity and will trigger an animation clip to play (using its internal representation of locomotion), and physics will ensure that the character does not pass through walls or the floor. In this setup, animation receives only two inputs from AI, the speed and the desired direction; it then outputs a transform to reflect the character motion. In some games, this might be the end of it; the transform is applied to the actor, and it reaches his or her target and everyone is happy. Now let us break down all the different ways this might break, and the actor will not reach his or her goal.

1. *Animation is lying just a tiny bit to steering*: In some cases, there could be a variant in one of the animation clips that might have a different acceleration or even exceed the min/max speeds.
2. *Other parts of the game interfere*: For either a single character or a range of characters, it may have been discovered that the animations needed some slight nudge here or there, and a brave programmer took it upon himself to add bespoke code that slightly modifies the movement.
3. *The environment is too restrictive*: For very sharp turns, an actor running at the AI's desired velocity will not necessarily know that it needs to slow down or else it will slam into a wall or fall off a ledge instead of smoothly following his or her path.
4. *The character's playback rate and/or size are being dynamically modified in the runtime*: It is clear that an actor that has been scaled up to double its size will have also doubled its speed, which if unchecked will wreak havoc when the actor tries to follow its path.

Each and every one of these problems can be addressed with a number of solutions, one being motion graphs (Ciupinski 2013). In the case of *FINAL FANTASY XV*, the solution was to assume that all the errors exist at all times and apply a form of machine learning to model the motion capabilities of actors, therefore solving all the problems with a single approach.

16. Predictive Animation Control Using Simulations and Fitted Models

16.3 Simulations to the Rescue

Our desire is to be able to construct an arbitrarily complex motion model that steering can use to accurately control actors at any given desired velocity or angle, moving an actor to the goal without ever accidentally leaving the navigation mesh. This means running simulations and, from the observed motion, building a set of parameters that approximate the actor's motion *accurately enough*. As described in Section 16.2, our update loop was something as shown in Figure 16.1.

In an update loop that is only built for offline simulations, we no longer need any AI or steering, as we want to control the actor in a different way. Furthermore, we are no longer interested in using the output from the actor to inform our future velocity; we only measure it. The new loop can be seen in Figure 16.2.

In this simulation loop, we replace the AI with a simulation controller that drives the movement space exploration. This is perfectly reasonable, as we are not interested in path-finding or avoidance, only the velocity we feed to the animation and the effect it has on the actor.

16.3.1 Simulation Controller

The simulation controller is the piece of the update that manages the exploration of the motion range. As each game has a different way to initialize its actors, the only aim for the simulation controller is to interfere as little as possible with the *normal* way of spawning, initializing, and updating an actor.

There are a couple of requirements though

- We must ensure that the actor is of unit-scale size and playback rate.
- We must spawn the actor close to the origin and move it back when it strays too far, as floating point precision issues may affect the measurements.

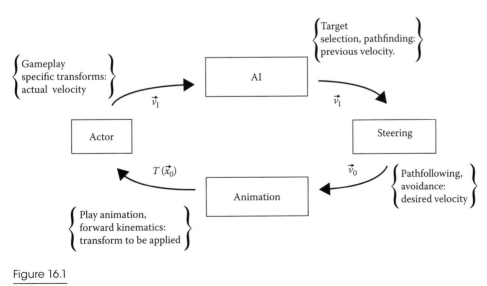

Figure 16.1

A typical game loop.

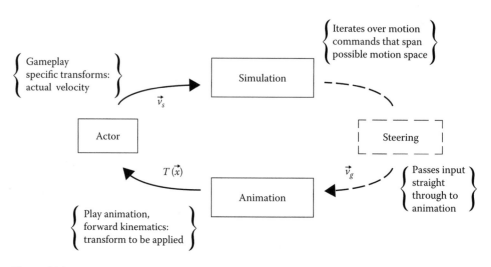

Figure 16.2

The simulation loop.

We expect the game to provide rough estimates of each actor's motion capabilities, such as its approximate minimum and maximum speed. This range will form the basis of the motion range to explore.

Once the actor has been initialized, a series of movement commands are issued to the actor. It is recommended that the actor be given a deterministic set of movement commands and that each command perform some sampling, so some measure of variance can be calculated, as well as noise can be filtered out in the analysis stages. Having a deterministic set of movement commands helps greatly in catching rare bugs, for example, a float overflow in the animation system.

Each simulation command C_s is a point on an interpolation over a range, such as $(v,\theta)_n \rightarrow (0,\theta)_n$, signifying the exploration of the motion from speed v to stopping, over n intervals between v and 0 with a constant facing θ. The set of simulation commands might differ slightly depending on the animation capabilities of the game, but generally, quantities such as speed, turn motion, and so on should be explored.

A command C_s is considered finished once the measurement has reached a stable output. For example, starting at speed v and wanting to reach speed v_g, the command is considered complete once the measured output v_s is stable.

16.3.2 Measurement Output

At the end of every command, the observed motion parameters are logged. Below the quantities measured are described with an attached notation set in Table 16.1.

We declare the rotational speed to be $\partial\theta/\partial t = \dot{\theta}$ for time t. The raw measurements are therefore a set of trajectories where each data point T_i on the trajectory is defined as the tuple:

$$T_i = \left(t, \vec{p}, \theta_s, \dot{\theta}_s, v_s\right)$$

16. Predictive Animation Control Using Simulations and Fitted Models

Table 16.1 Measurement Variables and Notation

Name	Notation	Description
Goal speed	v_g	The speed at which the actor should travel
Simulated speed	v_s	The speed that the actor actually traveled at
Desired angle	θ_g	The direction to which the actor should travel
Simulated angle	θ_s	The direction in which the actor traveled

with $\vec{p}$ as the position on the trajectory. From the trajectories T_i, other quantities can then be derived, such as variance of speed and rotation, distance travelled, and so on.

16.4 Building an Accurate Movement Model

Once the measurement phase is complete, the construction of the movement model that accurately describes the actor begins. The following sections will address different parts of an actor's motion and will give a rough overview of how the model parameters are formed.

16.4.1 Speed

The first constraint to determine is the speed range of an actor, as it will go on to inform the rest of the model construction. Our goal is to find the largest speed range in which the error between the goal speed v_g and the stable simulated speed v_s will not exceed a given minimum error. We determine the valid speed range using only data points where the actor is moving straight forward, that is, with $\dot{\theta}=0$ and at a stable speed $\dot{v}=0$. Figure 16.3 depicts the stable speeds obtained from fixed input speeds in these data (for a dog character). The error in this graph is the deviation between the resulting speed and the goal

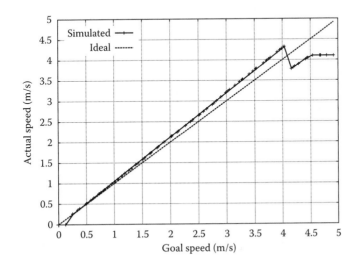

Figure 16.3

Speed measurements.

speed $\varepsilon = |v_g - v_s| / v_s$. We look for the largest interval of speeds in which ε does not exceed a fixed bound. Minimum and maximum speed then simply equate to the bounds of this interval.

If no speed range can be determined in this way, or if the speed range is significantly smaller than expected, the simulation is marked as a failure and no model is extracted, such as in Figure 16.3 where a drop in v_g occurs at around 4 m/s.

16.4.2 Stopping

Given the real speed range of the actor, the next part of the motion model can be constructed. As was mentioned in the introduction, stopping on the mark can be a difficult problem both in the real world as in the virtual one. We analyze trajectories where the actor moves at a stable speed in a straight line and stops due to receiving a goal speed of zero.

Since at runtime, we need to answer questions such as when to issue a stopping signal such that an actor will come to a halt at a predetermined goal position; we cast these data as a function of distance mapping onto velocity. In other words, given an available distance d, the function maps to the velocity at which the actor would take exactly a distance of d in order to come to a complete halt. Figure 16.4 shows an example of this curve. It clearly shows data points generated from different stopping animations, that is, stop-from-walking and stop-from-running. After manually analyzing a varied set of characters, we concluded that most data behaved in a piece-wise linear fashion, as shown in Figure 16.4.

16.4.3 Deceleration

Generalizing from stopping, we arrive at deceleration. Having accurate information about how long it takes to decelerate a given amount of speed allows the actors to fluidly decelerate before taking a turn and to confidently accelerate again afterward.

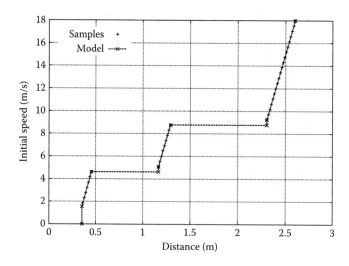

Figure 16.4

Stopping measurements.

16. Predictive Animation Control Using Simulations and Fitted Models

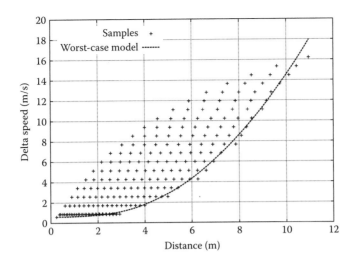

Figure 16.5

Deceleration measurements.

Figure 16.5 shows a typical result when recording the distance necessary to decelerate by a certain delta speed. Note the large spread for medium delta speeds. This is because the actual relationship depends on the absolute speed, not just the relative speed. The faster an actor travels, the larger a distance is necessary to decelerate by 1 m/s.

Instead of representing the full 3D relationship, we opted to project the data into 2D and use a worst-case estimate:

$$\Delta v(d) = ad^2 + bd + c\sqrt{d} \qquad (16.1)$$

With only three parameters, this is a very compact representation that is easily regressed by using sequential least squares programming. The increase in fidelity when using a 3D representation was deemed too small to warrant the additional memory investment necessary.

16.4.4 Overshoot

Overshoot is a measurement for how much space a character requires to turn. More specifically, it is the distance between the trajectory that a character would follow if it would follow the control input perfectly and the actual trajectory measured after a change in direction has been completed. Figure 16.6 shows the measured distance between ideal and performed trajectory.

This overshoot distance can be represented as a function of velocity and angle.

Figure 16.7 shows the overshoot of a monster in *FINAL FANTASY XV*. We represent these data as a velocity function over distance and turn angle. The approximation is done as a set of piece-wise linear functions, uniformly distributed over angles between 0° and 180°.

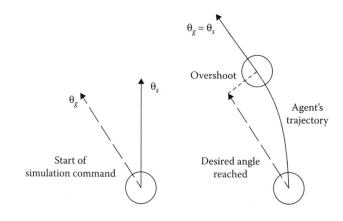

Figure 16.6

Overshoot definition.

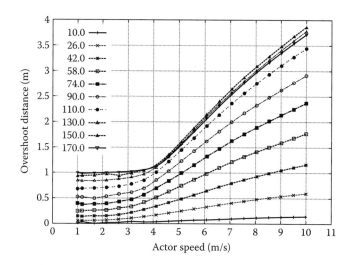

Figure 16.7

Actor speed versus overshoot distance.

16.4.5 Rotation Radius

We record the rotation radius of a character as a function of speed by letting the character run in a circle at a constant linear speed, as shown in Figure 16.8. Thus, we measure the character's rotational speed. We represent the rotation radius as a piece-wise linear function of speed. Thereby, we assume a constant maximum rotation speed for large proportions of the speed range. At runtime, this information is used to interrupt a movement command early and avoid characters getting stuck on a circular path around their goal position.

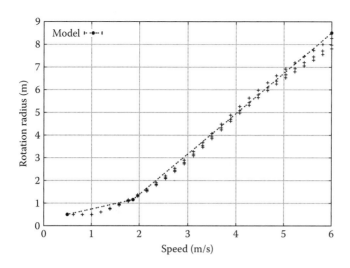

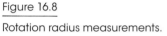

Figure 16.8

Rotation radius measurements.

16.5 Runtime

The extracted motion model is made available to inform steering decisions at runtime.

First and foremost, minimal and maximal speeds are used to limit the range of selectable speeds. The remainder of the data is used to improve control precision. Steering control and animation form a loop in which steering commands are sent to animation, which changes the physical state of the agent, which in turn is observed by steering.

The deceleration function informs the runtime of how much space is needed to achieve a certain negative Δv. Consequently, it is used to calculate the current control speed given a future goal speed. For example, if an agent is supposed to move at 2 m/s at a distance of 3 m, its current speed is capped by the deceleration function to 4 m/s for example. This is used in all cases where a future goal speed is anticipated, such as when charging for an attack and thus arriving with a certain speed at a target or following a path with a tight turn.

Collision avoidance, however, asserts the necessity to stop within a certain distance. The special case of stopping is handled by a stopping function. Deceleration is typically achieved by a combination of a blend and changes to the playback speed. In contrast, stopping typically is achieved by a separate animation altogether. Playing this animation does not fit the simple deceleration model we introduced in Section 16.4.3.

Whenever an agent is required to stop within a certain distance, be it in order to hit its mark, or avoid a collision, an upper limit for the control velocity is looked up in the stopping function. In addition, whenever the current physical velocity of the agent exceeds this limit, the control velocity is immediately pulled down to zero, thereby triggering a transition to a stopping animation. In order to avoid accidentally triggering this stopping maneuver due to noisy velocity measurements, the maximum control velocity is actually capped at 95% of this limit.

The overshoot function is used to calculate the maximum speed while taking a turn and when anticipating a future turn in a path currently followed. In addition, for characters without a turn-in-place animation, such as some larger monsters, it is also used to judge whether to turn left or right when aligning with a path. In case of an anticipated turn, an upper bound of future speed is simply a look up using the sine of the anticipated turn angle; the resulting velocity then serves as an input for the deceleration function to obtain an upper bound for the control speed as described above. In *FINAL FANTASY XV*, path information is imperfect, meaning that a path may only be part of the surrounding free space. Moreover, the path does not take moving obstacles into account. Thus, for immediate turns, both due to path following and due to collision avoidance, the available distance as given by collision avoidance sampling is used to look up a limit to the control speed in the overshoot function.

Finally, the rotation function is used to avoid circling around a target indefinitely by increasing the arrival radius, given an actor's current physical velocity and angle to its target.

16.6 Pipeline

All of this work can be wrapped up in a nice little continuous integration loop, as can be seen in Figure 16.9, containing the following steps:

1. Create a valid movement model for steering.
2. Provide the developers a view for an actor's movement model for the whole period of development.
3. Alert the developer when there is a problematic movement model that needs addressing.

Due to the fact that the simulation of an actor takes more time than to build the animation data per actor, the pipeline structure tries to reduce the lag as much as possible by running constantly. The choice of the next actor to simulate is made by a simple

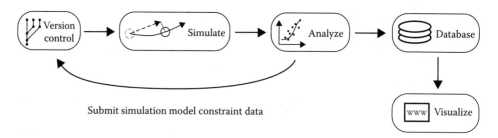

Submit simulation model constraint data

Figure 16.9

Continuous simulation pipeline.

16. Predictive Animation Control Using Simulations and Fitted Models

heuristic of the time since last simulation and whether the actor has been just added to the repository. Failures are logged to a database, and stakeholders are automatically notified.

16.7 Scaling Up

There are two scale issues to take into account when building the simulation pipeline.

16.7.1 Size and Playback

A game might want to scale the size of actors and expect the motion constraint model to still apply. Similarly, the animation playback rate might vary on a frame-to-frame basis. Both factors must be applied to the motion model and, depending on the different parts in the model, both size and/or time scales must be applied. As an example, the deceleration function (Equation 16.1 in Section 16.4.3) with respect to size scaling u and playback rate scale p becomes:

$$\Delta v(d, u, p) = p \left(\frac{ad^2}{u} + bd + c\sqrt{ud} \right)$$

The rest of the overall model is either multiplied by u, p, or both.

16.7.2 Content

When the need arises to scale up the number of entities via the use of prefabs, the simulation pipeline does not suffer as much from the time delay between authoring data and exporting constraints. However, there is still a possibility that the prefabs have an element in either some part of their unique-data setup or in code that will differentiate their motion, and there is no easy way to test this without simulating all users of the prefab and doing a similarity test between the results.

16.8 Benefits

The biggest benefit of this methodology is how well it scales to differences in characters and changes to the data and code throughout the development cycle. Precision is also increased with this methodology. As an example, the stopping distance is normally the distance of some "to-stop" animation plus whatever may be done to the animation in the runtime. This overall distance can be hard to parameterize at the authoring time, but the simulation can easily extract the worst case from the observed movement.

Issues, such as a nonmonotonic speed function, can be easily identified from a graph, instead of through loading the game. This is seen in an example of a *FINAL FANTASY XV* cat speed graph found in Figure 16.10.

When comparing the speed graphs of cats (Figure 16.10) and dogs (Figure 16.3), it is clear from the simulated data that cats are indeed more independent than dogs with respect to speed, at least in *FINAL FANTASY XV*.

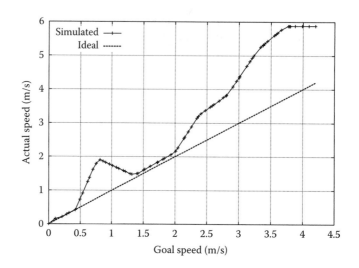

Figure 16.10

Speed measurements of a cat.

16.9 Conclusion

We have presented a way of significantly decoupling dependencies between AI and animation. This approach treats animation as the dominant party in this relationship of motion and shows a way of gaining benefit from such an approach.

Although significant work was invested in setting up and maintaining the pipeline, the work needed to identify and fix issues has dramatically decreased. Typically, it amounts to analyzing graphs on a web server and determining from there what the fault is. Common bugs include the gait being exported from the raw animation, so the actor does not have a fixed acceleration or a genuine code bug that has been introduced, which can be found by looking at the graphs by date and revision to determine what revision introduced the code bug.

Overall, the usage of simulations to improve steering control of an animation-driven agent has proved to be a success. It is not particularly expensive at runtime, as the models are mostly sets of piece wise linear functions and one nonlinear function. Furthermore, scaling of size, playback rate, or both are easily supported.

References

Ciupinski, J. 2013. Animation-driven locomotion with locomotion planning. In *Game AI Pro: Collected Wisdom of Game AI Professionals*, ed. S. Rabin. Natick, MA: A. K. Peters, Ltd, pp. 325–334.

Gregory, J. 2009. *Game Engine Architecture*. Wellesley, MA: A. K. Peters, Ltd.

16. Predictive Animation Control Using Simulations and Fitted Models

Fast Cars, Big City
The AI of Driver San Francisco

Chris Jenner and Sergio Ocio Barriales

17.1 Introduction

Driver San Francisco was an open-world driving game set in a fictionalized version of the city of San Francisco. The game's version of the city was very large, and in some areas had very dense traffic.

The player was given different missions that involved navigating through traffic at high speeds interacting with other mission-critical NPC vehicles, which also had to move quickly through the traffic. NPC vehicles might be chasing another vehicle, evading a vehicle, racing around a set course or trying to get to a particular point in the city. Also, at any point, the player could switch vehicles and start controlling any other car in the city; when this happened, it was the job of the AI to take over control of the player's vehicle, continue driving, and try to achieve the player's mission objective.

An important part of the game design was to produce dramatic, cinematic car chase sequences. Due to this, the AI-controlled vehicles as well as the player vehicle were often the centers of attention, being closely watched by the game camera. To create the most impressive visuals, it was a requirement that the AI code could control a vehicle simulated by the same system that was used for the player vehicle. We were not allowed to cheat by giving the AI vehicles more power or tighter grip between the tires and the road.

We also had to perform at a level that was similar to the best human players, so the cars had to be capable of coming close to the limits of friction when cornering, without pushing too far and skidding out of control.

The game was designed to run at 60 frames per second. This put a significant restriction on the amount of work we could do in any single frame. For this reason, the AI system was designed to be asynchronous and multithreaded. Individual tasks to update the state of a particular AI were designed to run independently and to update the state of the AI when the task was finished. Even if the task was finished after several frames, the AI would be able to continue intelligently while waiting for the result.

Planning a path for the AI vehicles in this environment posed several problems:

- The vehicles' main interactions were with other vehicles, so the path planning had to deal with moving obstacles. This meant that we had to look ahead in time as well as space and plan to find gaps in traffic that would exist at the time we got to them.
- Valid paths for vehicles must take into account parameters of the physical vehicle simulation, such as acceleration, turn rates, and tire grip if they are to be feasible for a vehicle to drive.

Classical path planning algorithms such as A* work well for static environments of limited dimension, but trying to search through a state space including time, velocity, and orientation would be impractical.

In this chapter, we present the path planning solution *Driver San Francisco* used: a three-tier path optimization approach that provided locally optimal paths. The three stages of the process—route finding, mid-level path planning, and low-level path optimization—will be detailed in the subsequent sections.

17.2 Active Life AI

Driver San Francisco had two distinct types of AI to control his or her vehicles: *Civilian Traffic AI* and *Active Life AI*. Civilian vehicles were part of a deterministic traffic system that simply moved vehicles around a set of looping splines throughout the city. Each spline had been defined to ensure that it did not interact with any other spline. Each civilian vehicle would follow a point around the spline, knowing that there was no chance of colliding with other civilian vehicles. Nontraffic vehicles were controlled by the more complex Active Life AI system. These vehicles perform much more complex actions than simply blending in with traffic, such as racing, chasing, or escaping from other vehicles. The Active Life AI system performed much more complex path generation.

Driver San Francisco's most important gameplay mechanic, *shift*, allowed players to switch cars at any point. When the player activated *shift*, the vehicle the player left was taken over by an Active Life AI, which would start running the appropriate behavior to replace the player. For example, if the player *shifted* out of a cop car chasing a suspect, the AI would give a "chase target" behavior to the cop car, which would continue what the player was doing before the switch. If the player had been driving a civilian vehicle with no particular objective, the AI would select the closest free slot on the traffic splines and try to rejoin traffic; as soon as this happened, the driver was downgraded to a regular civilian vehicle.

17.2.1 Vehicle Paths

As any car could transition from civilian to Active Life and vice-versa at any moment, it was important to keep an unified system to define what vehicles were trying to do, so each one owned a *vehicle path*. These paths represented the predicted movement of the vehicle for the next couple of seconds, and the AI system was constantly updating them—actually, path updating happened approximately every second. Paths were updated appending new segments at their end before they were completely used. So, from the vehicle's perspective, the path was continuous. Updating paths this way allowed us to run costly calculations in parallel over multiple frames. Even the player's vehicle had a path!

The way vehicle paths were generated depended on the system that was controlling them. For player vehicles, physics and dead reckoning generated this path; traffic splines generated paths for civilians. For Active Life AIs, we used different levels of detail, based on range to the AI. We had three levels of detail (LODs):

- AIs using the lowest level of detail generated their paths using only their route information. A route, as we will talk about later, is a list of roads that can take us from point A to B. These roads are defined as splines, and these splines are connected by junction pieces. Routes were basically very long splines. Low-LOD vehicle paths were a portion of the route's spline with an offset to simulate that they were driving in a certain lane on the road.
- The next level of detail used mid-level paths to generate vehicle paths. A mid-level path is a first approximation of a good path for a vehicle. It uses the route information plus some extra details, such as lane information (we prefer maintaining our current lane if possible), some rough dynamic obstacle avoidance, and some speed limit data. Mid-level path generation is described in detail in a subsequent section.
- Finally, the highest level of detail was used for vehicles around the player that were in camera and needed to be fully simulated and as polished as possible. They used the full three-tier path generation (route finding, mid-level path planning, and low-level path optimization).

The vehicle paths also supported another significant optimization in the game's simulation code. The large number of vehicles being simulated in the world at any one time would be very costly in terms of physics and vehicle handling. For this reason, there was a system of simulation level of detail acting at the same time as, but independently of the AI LOD. When vehicles were close to the player, they would be fully simulated by the physics and handling system, and they would follow their paths using the AI path-following system to calculate driving input into the handling system. When vehicles were distant from the player, they could be removed from the physics engine and vehicle-handling code, and simply placed at the position defined by their path for that particular time.

17.2.2 Driver Personalities

In the game, AIs had different goals, but also different driving styles or *personalities*. AIs had a set of different traits that defined their characters. Some examples of these traits were:

- Likeliness to drive in the oncoming traffic.
- Likeliness to drive on sidewalks.
- Preferred driving speed.
- How desirable highways, alleyways, or dirt roads were?
- How strongly hitting other vehicles should be avoided?

Personality traits affected every stage of the path planning, as we will see in later sections.

17.3 Road Network

Our virtual San Francisco was, in the eyes of the AI, a network of interconnected roads. For each of these roads, the game exposed the following information, as shown in Figure 17.1:

- A spline that represents the road.
- Each road had a start and an end extremity. For each extremity, we had:
- A list of roads that were connected to the extremity.
- Cross-section information: This defines the number of lanes at the extremity, as well as the width and the type of each of these lanes.

In the example, our road has two directions. We call the lanes that travel from the *start* to the *end* extremity as "with traffic" lanes, and the ones traveling in the opposite direction are called "oncoming." The example road presents two "with traffic" and two "oncoming" lanes; it also has a sidewalk on the oncoming side (the left-most lane on the cross section) and a sidewalk on the right side of the road that disappears at the end of the spline.

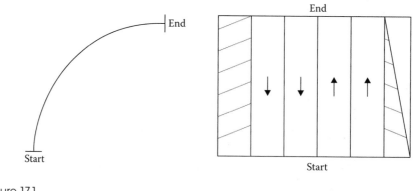

Figure 17.1

An example road spline with its cross section information.

17.4 Route Finding

The path generation process for Active Life AIs started by selecting the roads that these vehicles would use to reach their destination. The goal was to generate a list of connected roads, a *route*, which allowed cars to drive to their destination. For this, we used the connectivity information in the road network.

Depending on the goal or behavior of a vehicle, we used one of the following two methods to generate a route:

- A traditional A* search on the road network was used when we knew what our destination road was.
- A dynamic, adaptive route generator was used by the AI when its objective was to get away from a pursuer. For more details on this system, readers can refer to Ocio (2012).

Due to the size of the map and the strict performance requirements the AI systems had to meet (*Driver San Francisco* runs at 60 FPS on Xbox 360, PS3 and PC), we split the map in three different areas, which are connected by bridges, and used a hierarchical A* solution. If two points, A and B, were in different areas, we would first find a path to the closest bridge that connected both areas, and then find a path from the bridge to position B on the second area.

The path planning system itself imposed extra requirements. For instance, we always needed to have "enough road length" ahead of our vehicle, so sometimes an artificial node was appended at the end of the route. This was very often the case when an AI was following another vehicle, and both cars were pretty close to each other. This extra road allowed vehicles to predict where they should be moving to next and helped them maintain their speed. This will be explained in the following sections. During a high-speed chase, approaching junctions required a constant reevaluation of the intentions of the vehicle being chased. The goal was to predict which way the chased car was trying to go. We achieved this by making use of our simplified physics model that provided us with a good estimation of what a car was capable of doing based on its current state and capabilities. Figure 17.2 depicts the problem.

Route finding was also affected by the personality of the driver. The cost of exploring nodes varied based on the specific traits of the AI, and this could produce very different results. For example, civilian-like drivers could follow longer but safer routes to try and avoid a dirt road, whereas a racer would not care. Finally, AIs would, in some situations, try to avoid specific roads. For instance, a getaway driver would try to not use roads with cops.

17.5 Mid-Level Path Planning

Driver San Francisco's path planning solution did not look for optimal paths, as a more traditional A*-based approach would normally do. Instead, we were trying to generate locally optimal paths by optimizing some promising coarser options that we called *mid-level paths*. Mid-level path planning was the second stage of our three-tier process that happened after a route had been calculated.

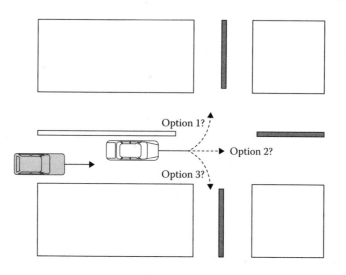

Figure 17.2

When chasing another vehicle, our AIs needed to decide which road the chased car was going to take at every intersection.

The route was defined in terms of the splines describing the center lines of the roads we wanted to follow, but it contained no information about which road lane we should drive down. The mid-level path allowed us to specify where on the road the vehicle should drive. The mid-level path was generated by searching for a path between a set of possible path nodes spread out in a grid over the road in front of the vehicle. The search space began at the current position of the vehicle and extended forward down the road far enough that the path would be valid for several seconds. The search space would typically be about 100 m in length. We placed sets of nodes at regular intervals over this part of the spline. With regard to width, one node was placed in each traffic lane. We show an example search space in Figure 17.3.

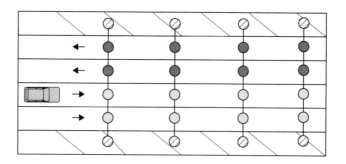

Figure 17.3

Node sets placed every few meters along the roads in the route constitute our search space for the midlevel path planning.

17. Fast Cars, Big City

Once the search space was defined, we generated all the possible paths from the vehicle to each node on the last set, scoring them, and then selecting the five best options, which became the seeds for the optimizer. Evaluating a path meant giving each node used a numeric value; the final cost would be the sum of all the individual values. The game used costs for paths, which meant the higher the number, the less ideal the path was. The criteria used to generate these costs were:

- Nodes near dynamic obstacles (i.e., other vehicles) were given some penalty; if the obstacle was static (e.g., a building), the node could not be used.
- We always preferred driving in a straight line, so part of the score came from the angle difference between the vehicle's facing vector and the path segment.
- Depending on the driver AI's personality, some nodes could be more favorable. For example, a car trying to obey traffic rules will receive big penalties from driving on sidewalks or in the oncoming lane, whereas a reckless driver would not differentiate between lane types.

Figure 17.4 shows a couple of example mid-level paths and their costs.

In the example, the cost calculation has been simplified for this chapter, but the essence of the process remains. Moving in a straight line costs 1 unit and switching lanes costs 2 units. Driving close to another car costs an additional point, so does driving in the oncoming lane. With these rules, we calculated a cost of 5 for the first path and 11 for the second one.

Although in Figure 17.4, we treated other vehicles as static when we calculated the cost of driving next to an obstacle, in the real game, these calculations were made taking into account current vehicle speeds and predicting the positions of the obstacles (by accessing their *vehicle paths*). So path 2 could potentially have been scored even higher in a couple of locations. For example, the first node, which got a cost of 4, could have produced a bigger cost if the car driving in the opposite direction was moving. Path 1 could have even just been a completely straight line, if the vehicles we are trying to avoid in the example were moving fast enough, so they were not real obstacles for our AI!

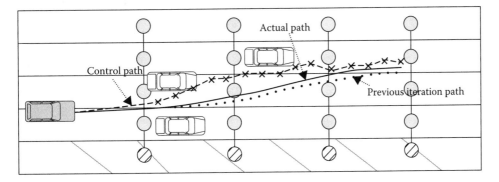

Figure 17.4

Two possible midlevel paths found for the given search space; path 1 has a lower cost, so it would be the preferred option.

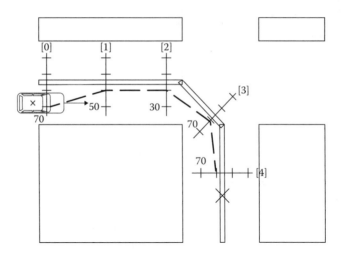

Figure 17.5

Midlevel paths contained information about the maximum speed the vehicle could travel at each of their nodes.

Another piece of information we could get out of mid-level was speed information and, particularly, speed limitations, or how fast a corner can be taken without overshooting. Starting from the last node set backward, we calculated the maximum speed at certain nodes based on the angle that the path turned through at that node. This speed was then propagated backward down the path based on the maximum acceleration/deceleration, so the path contained some information the vehicle could use to start slowing down before taking a corner. Figure 17.5 shows an example mid-level path with speed limits.

In the example, calculations would start at node set 4. The maximum speed at that node is the maximum desired speed for our vehicle (let us use 70 mph for this). Traveling from node 3 to node 4 is almost a straight line, so the vehicle can travel at maximum speed. However, moving from node 2 will require a sharp turn. Let us say that, by using the actual capabilities of our car, we determined the maximum speed at that point should be 30 mph. Now, we need to propagate this backward, so node 1 knows the maximum speed at the next node set is 30. Based on how fast our vehicle can decelerate, the new speed at node 1 is 50 mph. We do the same thing for the very first node, and we have our speeds calculated. Path speeds also took part in the path cost calculation; we tried to favor those paths that took us to the last set of nodes faster than others.

17.6 Low-Level Path Optimizer

Mid-level paths represented a reasonable approximation of a path that could be driven by a vehicle, but this was not good enough for our needs. Although the velocity of the path has been calculated with an idea of the capabilities of the vehicle, the turns have no representation of the momentum of the vehicle or the limits of friction at the wheels. These problems are resolved by the low-level path optimizer.

The low-level optimizer uses a simplified model of the physics of the vehicle, controlled by an AI path-following module, to refine the path provided by the mid-level into a form that a vehicle could actually drive. When the constraints on the motion of the vehicle are applied to the mid-level path, it is likely to reduce the quality of the path—perhaps the vehicle will hit other cars or skid out of control on a tight corner. These problems are fixed by an iterative path optimization process.

To choose a good path, it was necessary to have a method of identifying the quality of a particular path. This was done by creating a scoring system for paths that could take a trajectory through the world and assign it a single score representing the desirability of the path. Good paths should move through the world making forward progress toward our goal as close as possible to a desired speed while avoiding collisions with other objects. The aim of the optimization process is to find a path with the best possible score.

The environment through which the vehicles were moving is complex, with both static and dynamic obstacles to avoid, and a range of different target locations that could be considered to be making progress toward a final goal. To simplify the work of the optimizer, the environment is initially processed into a single data structure representing where we want the vehicle to move. This structure is a potential field, in which every location in the area around the vehicle is assigned a "potential" value. Low-potential areas are where we want the vehicle to be, and high-potential areas are where we want the vehicle to move from. Good paths can then be found by following the gradient of the potential field downward toward our goal.

The various different systems that came together to form the low-level path optimizer are described in the following sections.

17.6.1 Search Area

Before the optimizer could start generating paths, it needed to prepare data to use during its calculations. The first piece of data we prepared was a small chunk of the world where the path planning process would take place, the *search area*.

A rectangle was used to delimit the search area. This rectangle was wide enough to encompass the widest road in the network, and it was long enough to allow the vehicle to travel at full speed for a couple of seconds (remember mid-level paths were generated for this length). The area was almost centered on the AI vehicle, but not quite; while the car was indeed centered horizontally, it was placed about ¼ along the rectangle's length. Also, the area was not axis aligned. Instead, we would use the vehicle's route to select a position in the future and align the rectangle toward this point. Figure 17.6 shows an example rectangle.

After the rectangle was positioned, we detected the edges of the roads and used them to calculate inaccessible areas. Vehicles in *Driver San Francisco* were only able to drive on roads and some special *open areas*, designer-placed zones attached to a road spline that we wanted to consider as a drivable area. Likewise, we had *closed* areas or zones that we wanted to block, such as a static obstacle. Figure 17.7 shows the previous search zone, now annotated with some example areas.

In this example, the lower left building was cut by an open area, and a road separator (closed area) was added to the first road in the route.

The search area was used to define the limits within which we calculated a potential field, where the potential of a particular area represents the desirability of that location for our AI.

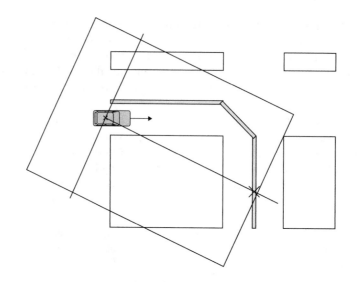

Figure 17.6

The search area is a rectangular zone that encompasses the surroundings of the AI vehicle.

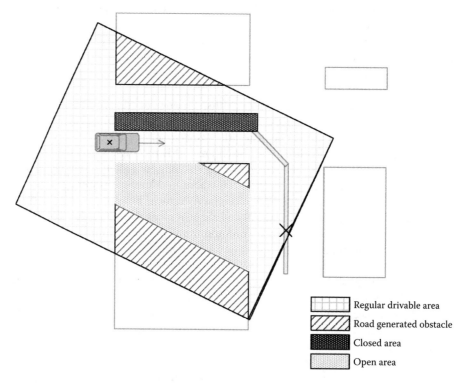

	Regular drivable area
	Road generated obstacle
	Closed area
	Open area

Figure 17.7

The search area's static obstacles were calculated from the road information and from some special areas placed by designers on the map to open or close certain zones.

Movements through the potential field toward our target should always result in a lowering of the potential value. Areas that were inaccessible because of static or dynamic obstacles needed to have high potential values. As the path planning algorithm was trying to find a path that was valid for several seconds into the future, and other vehicles could move a significant distance during the time that the path was valid, it was important that we could represent the movement of obstacles within the potential field. For this reason, we calculated both a static potential field and a dynamic potential field. By querying the static potential field for a particular location, querying the dynamic potential field at the same location for a particular time, and then summing the results, we could find the potential for a location at a particular time. Similarly, we could find the potential gradient at a location at a particular time by summing the potential gradient value from both fields.

17.6.2 Static Potential Field

With the search area defined, the next data calculated were a static potential field. This was used to help us define how movement should flow—in what direction while avoiding obstacles. It worked almost as water flowing down a river. This potential field was created using the fast marching method (Sethian 1996). The search area triangle was split into a grid, so we could do discrete calculations. We set a row of goal positions at the end part of the search area rectangle and calculated the values for each cell in the grid.

For the algorithm, we needed to define the propagation speed at each cell, and this came mainly from the type of lane below the cell's center position and the personality of the AI driver. For a civilian driver, for example, a cell on the oncoming late should be costlier to use, which means the gradient of the field on those cells will be pointing away from them. Figure 17.8 shows what the field's gradient would look like in our example.

In this example, we set two goal cells for the potential field. With a civilian personality, oncoming lanes should normally be avoided, and sidewalks should be avoided at all costs. This produced a nice gradient that helps navigate toward the goals. If we dropped a ball on any cell and move it following the arrows, we will end up at the objective cell.

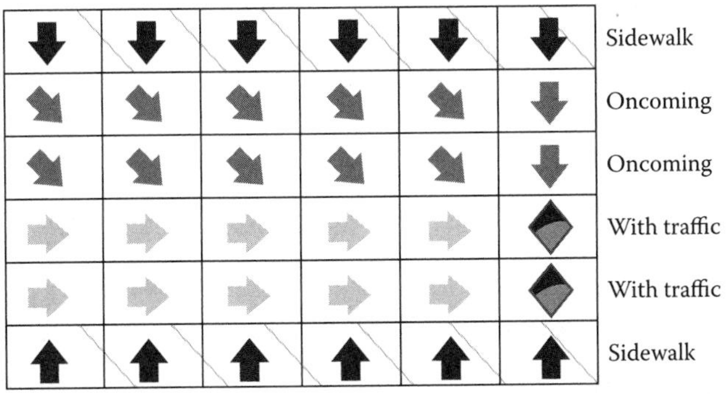

Figure 17.8

The search area was split into cells, and a potential field was generated to show how movement should flow to avoid static obstacles.

17.6.3 Dynamic Potential Field

AIs in *Driver San Francisco* had to deal with static obstacles but mostly with dynamic, moving ones. Although the static potential field was necessary to avoid walls, we needed a way to produce some extra forces to avoid surrounding vehicles. The approach taken in *Driver San Francisco* was to apply these forces as an extra layer on top of the static field.

The dynamic potential field could be queried at any point for any particular time. If we visualized it overtime, we were able to see forces produced around vehicles, pushing things out of the obstacle. Clusters of vehicles could produce gaps between them or forces to go around the whole cluster, depending on how far apart the different vehicles were. Figure 17.9 shows an example.

17.6.4 Simple Physics Model

The vehicle motion in the game was modeled using a complex physics engine with 3D motion, and collisions between dynamics and with the world. Vehicle dynamics were calculated using a wheel collision system and modeling of the suspension extension, which gave information about tire contacts with the world feeding into a model of tire friction. The wheels were powered by a model of a vehicle drive train applying a torque to the wheels.

This model was computationally expensive, but we needed to get some information about what constraints this model applied to the motion of the vehicle into our path planning algorithm, in order to create paths that the vehicle was capable of driving.

The fundamental aspects of vehicle behavior come from the torque applied by the engine and the tire forces on road, and this part of the vehicle simulation can be calculated relatively quickly. We implemented a simple 2D physics simulation for a single vehicle, driven by the same inputs as the game vehicle. This simulation shared the engine and drive-train model and the tire friction calculations from our main game vehicle-handling code but made simplifying assumptions about how the orientation of the vehicle changed as it was driving. Parameters of the handling model were used to ensure the simulation of vehicle was as close to the full game simulation as possible. The results of collisions were not modeled accurately; this was not a significant problem as the aim of the optimization process was to avoid collisions, so any paths that lead to collisions were likely to be rejected by the optimization process.

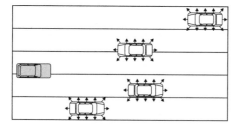 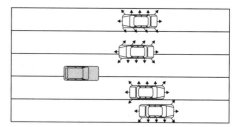

Figure 17.9

The dynamic potential field dealt with moving obstacles, generating forces around them so they could be avoided.

17.6.5 AI Path Following

To control the vehicle in the simple physics simulation, a simple AI path-following module was used. This module was exactly the same as the AI that was used to follow paths in the real game. The AI was fed with information about the current dynamic state of the vehicle and details of the path it was expected to follow. The module calculated controller input based on these data that were sent to the vehicle simulation. The action of the AI in any frame is based on the desired position and orientation of the vehicle, as defined in the path it is following, at a time in the future.

Internally, the AI used a simple finite-state machine to define the type of maneuver that was being attempted. Each state had some heuristics that allowed the control values to be calculated based on the differences between the current heading and velocity and the target position and orientation of the vehicle.

17.6.6 Simulating and Scoring a Path

The physics simulation and AI code could be used together to simulate the progress of a vehicle following a path. The physics simulation could be initialized with the current dynamic state of the vehicle, and then it could be stepped forward in time using the AI module to generate control inputs designed to follow a particular control path.

The output of this simulation was the position and orientation of the vehicle at each step of the simulation. We will refer to this series of position/orientation pairs as an actual path for a vehicle. This path generated for a particular control path is the trajectory we would expect the vehicle to follow if the control path was used to control the full game simulation representation of the vehicle. It is worth noting that we expect the actual path to deviate from the control path to some extent, but that the deviation should be small if the control path represents a reasonable path for the vehicle to take, given its handling capabilities.

The score for a particular control path is calculated by considering the actual path that the vehicle follows when given that control path. The total score is calculated by summing a score for the movement of the vehicle at each step of the physics simulation. In our case, we chose to assign low scores for desirable motion and high scores for undesirable motion, which leads to us trying to select the path that has the lowest total score. The main aim of the scoring system was to promote paths that moved toward our goal positions, avoided collisions, and kept the speed of the vehicle close to a desired speed. To promote these aims, the score for a particular frame of movement was calculated by summing three different terms:

- Term 1 was calculated from the direction of the movement vector of the vehicle over that frame, compared with the gradient of the potential field at the vehicle's location and the time of the frame. The value of the dot product between the two vectors was scaled and offset to add a penalty to movements that went toward higher potential.
- Term 2 was calculated by considering the current speed of the vehicle and the desired speed. The absolute value of any difference between the two was added to the score.
- Term 3 was calculated based on collisions. If the physics engine had found any collisions for the vehicle on that frame, a large penalty was added to the score.

The three terms were scaled by factors we arrived at empirically to give the best results.

17.6.7 Optimizing a Path

A single mid-level path can be converted to a path that is suitable for the capabilities of the vehicle that has to drive it. Initially, the mid-level path is converted into control path by sampling points from it at regular time intervals, corresponding to the frame times for the simplified vehicle simulation. This control path is then scored by passing it through the simplified simulation system as described in Section 17.6.6, which generates an actual path for the vehicle. This is shown in Figure 17.10.

This actual path can then be compared with the potential field and used to generate an optimized control path that we expect to have a lower score. First, the actual path is converted to a control path by using the positions of the vehicle at each frame to represent the positions in the control path. These positions are then adjusted based on the gradient of the potential field at those points. This process will push the path away from areas of high potential—that is, obstacles and parts of the world where we would prefer the vehicle not to drive. Figure 17.11 shows the results of this first iteration of the optimization process.

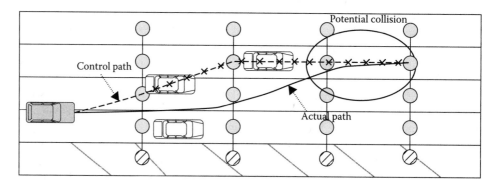

Figure 17.10

The first control path is created from the midlevel path we used as a seed and can still present problems, such as potential collisions.

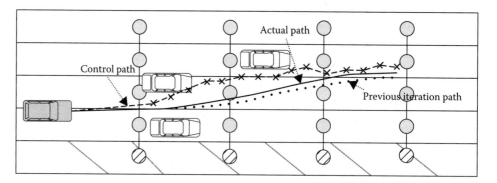

Figure 17.11

Vehicle positions along the first actual path are modified by the potential field; we use this as our second control path, which generates an optimized version of the original actual path.

This optimized control path is then ready for evaluation by the scoring algorithm and can be optimized again in an iterative process while the score continues to decline. The paths that we are dealing with only last for a few seconds, and over that time, the motion of the vehicle is initially dominated by its momentum. The control input can only have a limited effect on the trajectory of the vehicle through the world. Due to this, we found that three or four iterations of the optimization loop were enough to approach a local minimum in scoring for a particular mid-level path starting point.

17.6.8 Selecting the Best Path

The optimization process begins with a set of five potential paths from the mid-level planner and ends up with a single best path that is well suited to the capabilities of the vehicle that is expected to follow the path. Each mid-level path was optimized in turn, iterating until it reached a local minimum of score. The path that leads to the lowest score overall is selected as the final path and returned to the vehicle to be used for the next few seconds.

17.7 Conclusion

Driver San Francisco's AI used state-of-the-art driving AI techniques that allowed the game to run a simulation with thousands of vehicles that could navigate the game's version of the city with a very high level of quality, as our path generation and following used the same physics model as any player-driven vehicle. The system was composed of multiple levels of detail, each of which updated vehicle paths only when required to do so. This allowed the updates to be spread asynchronously across many threads and many frames, meaning the game could run smoothly at 60 FPS. Path optimization allowed the system to deal efficiently with a world composed of highly dynamic obstacles, a world which would have been too costly to analyse using more traditional A*-based searching.

References

Ocio, S. 2012. Adapting AI behaviors to players in driver San Francisco: Hinted-execution behavior trees. In *Proceedings of the Eighth AAAI Conference on Artificial Intelligence and Interactive Digital Entertainment (AIIDE 12)*, October 10–12, 2012, Stanford, CA.

Sethian, J. A. 1996. A fast marching level set method for monotonically advancing fronts. *Proceedings of the National Academy of Sciences* 93(4), 1591–1595.

18
A Unified Theory of Locomotion

Graham Pentheny

18.1 Introduction

AI character movement in games is a complex problem with many disparate solutions. Character movement techniques must account for many considerations and constraints. Different movement solutions for games address different aspects of the problem, necessitating a combination of complementary solutions for robust character movement. Often, combining multiple movement systems results in complex, intricate, and brittle logic that is both difficult to debug and reuse.

The unified theory of locomotion is a common language by which all movement systems can be defined. Common systems such as velocity obstacle collision avoidance, steering behaviors, and PID controllers can be viewed as specific applications of this theory, with their own individual strengths. Viewing movement systems in this way can help solve many issues faced in aggregating multiple movement systems together. The unified theory of locomotion is a common language for movement that can provide a basis for improving AI movement systems to be more robust to design changes, debugging, and experimentation.

18.2 Unified Theory of Locomotion

Character movement in games can be viewed as a series of steps, each answering a different question about the desired behavior. First and most fundamentally, the character must have a goal location. This is often determined by domain-specific high-level reasoning. Once a destination is established, the character must figure out the best way to move through the world to the destination. Path-planning algorithms are designed to solve this problem, breaking a larger positional goal into a series of shorter subgoals. Next, the character must determine what dynamic obstacles, if any, exist that would prevent them from getting to their next subgoal. These obstacles must be avoided, while maintaining a course toward the character's current subgoal. Finally, the character must move itself through the world, holding as close as possible to an ideal velocity.

The unified theory of locomotion breaks down movement solutions into the component values of motion that they influence and the type of influence they impart on each value. Movement systems are categorized as affecting one or more of the character's position, velocity, or acceleration values. Additionally, each system is categorized as either restricting or directing each value they influence. In this way, we can describe systems with terms like "velocity restrictor" and "acceleration director."

Systems that are defined as a value restrictor remove allowed values from the possible range of outputs. For example, a velocity restrictor generates a set of velocity vectors that the agent is not allowed to follow. A value director, conversely, determines a specific desired value for a movement attribute. Steering behaviors, for example, are generally "velocity directors," each outputting a single, ideal velocity value. By categorizing behaviors by the attributes they affect, and whether they direct or restrict them, we can easily compare two or more movement systems objectively.

18.3 Positional Restrictors and Directors

The simplest influencer on a character's movement is the environment that they move within. A simplified representation of the walkable area is usually generated in the form of a navmesh (Tozour 2004). A navmesh dictates which areas the character is able to move in and thus restricts the positions that a character can have in an environment. Because it is narrowing the infinite domain of positional values to a small subset, it is considered a "positional restrictor."

Conversely, path planning takes a goal location and directs the movement of a character though the environment toward that goal. Path planning determines a sequence of positional subgoals, defining the ideal movement direction and position of the character. Because it provides a specific position, or sequence of positions, it is considered a "positional director."

18.4 Velocity Restrictors and Directors

Reciprocal velocity obstacles (RVO) (van den Berg et al. 2011) are a common approach to local collision avoidance. This technique avoids localized collisions with obstacles and other characters by disallowing velocities that would result in a collision with another character or obstacle. As velocity obstacle approaches directly limit the allowed velocity values, velocity obstacles are an ideal example of a "velocity restrictor."

PID controllers (Melder and Tomlinson 2014) are a signal feedback control mechanism that is often used to control character velocity in games. PID controllers modify a character's velocity incrementally, attempting to smoothly match it to a goal velocity. Often, a character's ideal velocity will be computed as their fastest move speed along the direction of the path to their goal. PID controllers augment the character's velocity incrementally to match this ideal computed velocity. As PID controllers output a single velocity that respects the current set of velocity restrictions, PID controllers are considered a type of "velocity director."

18.5 Cascading Value Dependencies

An important aspect of the unified theory of locomotion is the relationship between restrictors and directors across physical values. Effects on lower level movement attributes indirectly affect higher level derived values. For example, positional restrictors also indirectly affect the velocities that the character is allowed to follow. Velocities that move the character into a disallowed position should also be disallowed. In a similar way, velocity restrictors also indirectly affect the domain of allowed accelerations.

The opposite, however, does not hold true. Velocity value restrictions should not affect the positions a character can reach. For example, certain types of characters may not be able to move backward very quickly. Although this characteristic imparts a restriction on the set of allowed velocities, it does not affect the positions where the character is allowed to be. Additionally, a character might have certain restrictions on the magnitude that it is capable of accelerating in a given direction. This should not affect what velocities the character is able to reach, just the steps necessary to achieve their desired velocity. This assertion, however, does not hold if the character is only able to accelerate in a single direction. This is a rare case that would necessitate special consideration and will not be addressed.

18.6 Combining Movement Systems

Often, combining multiple movement systems is difficult because each system is designed and tested in isolation. Combining multiple systems is greatly simplified by applying the unified theory of locomotion as a context for viewing movement systems. In this context, combining multiple systems simply consists of separately combining the restrictions and directions that each system imparts on each movement value. For example, context steering (Fray 2015) generates a map of velocity values and weights the benefit of each according to a set of rules. RVO performs a similar action, restricting sets of velocities that would result in a collision with an obstacle. As RVO and context steering are both velocity restrictors, we can compute the union of their velocity domain restrictions to combine their effects. This combination reaps the benefits of both systems; however, it simplifies them to a single result.

18.7 Value Arbitration and Combination

Combining multiple movement systems necessitates combining the restrictions and directions that each system imparts on each physical value. Combining restrictors simply involves generating the union of the sets of restrictions they impart on a physical value.

The process of combining value directors, however, is more involved. It consists of combining individually computed physical values, while respecting the limitations imparted by the restrictors. The director combination process can be broken down into two steps: high-level arbitration between directors and low-level combination of the resulting values.

High-level director arbitration determines which director techniques are combined to drive a character. High-level arbitration observes the character, its position, and its relationship to the other characters and the environment and makes a judgment about which value directors should affect the character and with what precedence. For example, a character with many neighbors might prefer a collision avoidance director over a formation-following director, as avoiding collisions is considered more important than maintaining formation. High-level arbitration is a subtle, domain-specific process that has a significant impact on the resulting character behavior. Designing an arbitration system involves understanding the behavioral considerations of a character, and how different systems address those considerations.

Low-level combinators are systems that combine the results of multiple value directors. Different techniques exist for combining value directors, and like high-level arbitrators, designing effective combinators involves understanding the problem domain and the character's desired behavior. A common low-level combinator approach is to prioritize each value director and combine their resulting values in priority order until a threshold of total influence is met. This ensures that important behaviors are more impactful on character behavior than others. This straightforward approach is often utilized successfully in the context of steering behaviors (Reynolds 1987).

In addition to prioritized summation, value directors can additionally be weighted, artificially amplifying their output. The result of each director is scaled by a specific, corresponding value before being combined. This approach gives control over how sensitive a specific system should be on a character and can be used to create unique movement styles or personalities.

18.8 Conclusion

The unified theory of locomotion provides a context for viewing and reasoning about character movement. It provides a common language that can describe the behavior of different movement systems. Each system can be broken down into either directing or restricting one of the physical movement values of a character. These directors and restrictors on low-level movement values also indirectly affect derived values.

Applying the unified theory of locomotion helps simplify and direct the combination of multiple movement systems. Value restrictors are combined by taking the logical union of their results, while combining directors are broken into high-level arbitration and low-level combination. High-level arbitration determines which value directors affect a character and in what precedence. Low-level combination aggregates the resulting values in a way that prioritizes more important behaviors while giving AI designers the ability to control the characteristics of a character's movement behavior.

References

Fray, A. 2015. Context steering: Behavior-driven steering at the macro scale. In *Game AI Pro 2*, ed. S. Rabin. Boca Raton, FL: CRC Media, pp. 173–181.

Melder, N., and S. Tomlinson. 2014. Racing vehicle control systems using PID controllers. In *Game AI Pro*, ed. S. Rabin. Boca Raton, FL: CRC Media, pp. 491–500.

Reynolds, C. 1987. Flocks, herds and schools: A distributed behavioral model. *International Conference and Exhibition on Computer Graphics and Interactive Techniques*, Anaheim, CA: Association for Computing Machinery, pp. 25–34.

Tozour, P. 2004. Search space representations. In *AI Game Programming Wisdom 2*, ed. S. Rabin. Hingham, MA: Charles River Media, pp. 85–102.

van den Berg, J., S. J. Guy, M. Lin, and D. Manocha. 2011. Reciprocal n-body collision avoidance. *Springer Tracts in Advanced Robotics*, 70: 3–19.

19

RVO and ORCA

How They Really Work

Ben Sunshine-Hill

19.1 Introduction

The reciprocal velocity obstacles (RVO) algorithm and its descendants, such as hybrid reciprocal velocity obstacles (HRVO) and optimal reciprocal collision avoidance (ORCA), have in recent years become the standard for collision avoidance in video games. That is a remarkable achievement: Game AI does not readily adopt new techniques so quickly or broadly, particularly ones pulled straight from academic literature. But RVO addresses a problem that previously had no broadly acceptable solution. Moreover, it is easy to understand (because of its simple geometric reasoning), easy to learn (because its creators eschewed the traditional opaqueness of academic writing, and wrote about it clearly and well), and easy to implement (because those same creators made reference source code available for free). Velocity obstacle methods, at least for the moment, are the deserving rulers of the kingdom of collision avoidance.

Which is why it is a little ironic that very few people actually understand how VO methods work. Not how the papers and tutorials and videos describe them as working, but how they *really* work. It's a lot weirder, more complicated, and cooler than you suppose.

There are four stages to really *getting* RVO:

1. Understanding the assumptions that RVO makes, and the guarantees it provides.
2. Realizing that those assumptions and those guarantees are, in practice, constantly violated.
3. Figuring out why, then, RVO still seems to work.
4. Tweaking it to work even better.

In the remainder of this chapter, we will take you through these stages. Our goal is not to present you with a perfect collision avoidance system but to walk you through the nuances of VO methods and to help you iteratively develop a collision avoidance system that works well for your game. First, though, a brief history of RVO, and VO methods in general. We promise it's important.

19.2 History

The velocity obstacle method originally targeted mobile robots—that is to say, real physical robots in the real world, moving around without hitting each other. Compared to previous approaches to robot steering, velocity obstacles were intended to be:

- Decentralized, with each robot making its own decisions rather than all robots being slaved to a central controller.
- Independent, with decisions based solely on each robot's observation of other robots' positions and velocities.

These features are not of much use to game developers, but they are important to understanding the strengths and weaknesses of VO methods. VO agents do not explicitly communicate or coordinate with each other. Cooperation between them is an emergent effect of their observations, decisions, and actions over time. VO methods spare us the morass that is multiagent planning, focusing on the behavior of individual agents. But the lack of coordination means that agents can make mistakes when predicting what other agents are going to do, thus failing to cooperate properly.

The original VO method was hilariously prone to such failures, with two agents almost guaranteed to start oscillating back and forth when they encountered each other, as in Figure 19.1. Each expected the other to be a mindless blob traveling at a constant velocity, and each was repeatedly surprised when the other instead changed direction and ruined its plan.

19.2.1 Introducing RVO

Those oscillations motivated the design of RVO (van den Berg et al. 2008). The idea was to come up with a decision process for the agent, which assumed that the other agent was *also* using that decision process. Each agent would move only halfway out of the way of a collision, anticipating that the other agent would do its part as well by moving halfway in the other direction. The paper proved that this would eliminate incorrect predictions, and set agents on optimal noncolliding paths in a single step once they came into view. This is shown in Figure 19.2.

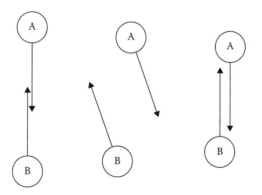

Figure 19.1

The original velocity obstacles method causes oscillation between two agents attempting to avoid each other.

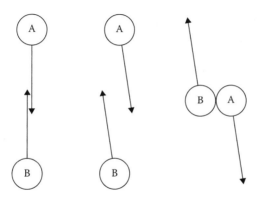

Figure 19.2

The reciprocal velocity obstacles resolve an upcoming collision between two agents in a single frame, putting them on optimal noncolliding trajectories.

19.3 Examining RVO's Guarantees

The proof of collision-free movement only holds for a world containing two agents (and no obstacles). With only two agents, each one is free to choose the perfect reciprocating velocity, without having to also dodge something else. Moreover, with nothing else in the world, each agent can assume that the current velocity of the other agent is also their preferred velocity.

Let us throw a third agent into the mix and see what happens in Figure 19.3. A and B are moving south side-by-side, when they see C coming toward them. A dodges a bit west, assuming that C will dodge a bit east. B dodges a bit east, assuming that C will dodge a bit west. Obviously C cannot do both of these. In fact it does neither, instead dodging west in order to pass to the west of both A and B. (It would be equally valid for C to dodge east instead, but let's say it breaks ties by going west.)

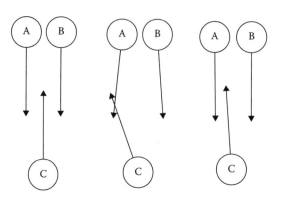

Figure 19.3

Three RVO agents attempting to resolve an upcoming collision.

All three agents are unhappy now. A and C are on a collision course, having both dodged west. B is not going to hit anything, but it has dodged for no good reason, straying from its preferred velocity. For C, it makes the most sense to move to a nearly northward trajectory; its deviation back east, it thinks, will be reciprocated by A deviating west, and even after B's reciprocation will graze by B. A decides to return to a due south trajectory, which it likes doing better and which it expects C to reciprocate by going even further west than he or she was already. B also returns to due south, reasoning that C is going so far west now that B does not have to worry about a collision.

In short, after two frames, we are back to the original problem. The oscillation that RVO solved for two agents still occurs for three. RVO, in other words, is not guaranteed to avoid collisions in situations such as the above because of an inconsistent view of possible velocities and preferred velocities between agents.

Except… it does avoid collisions. Set up that situation in a real RVO implementation, and C will get past A and B just fine. We have seen that the noncollision guarantee does not hold here, so what is really going on?

Well, after two frames, we aren't *really* back to the original problem. Over the two frames, A and B have moved slightly apart from each other. C has moved slightly west and is now traveling slightly west of north. In future frames, these displacements become more pronounced affecting later decisions. While there is a great deal of "flickering" going on with the velocities initially, the three eventually manage to cooperate.

In fact, you could argue that that's what *real* cooperation should look like, with each agent not only guessing each other's plans but reacting when those guesses don't work out. Eventually the three make simultaneous decisions that are entirely compatible, and then they stick to them until they are safely past.

So reciprocation—perfect avoidance through perfect prediction—has failed. Has RVO, then, gained us anything over original VO? As it turns out, yes. Run the scenario with VO avoidance, and the three will oscillate for much longer. It is easy to construct scenarios where RVO will avoid collisions and VO will not. There's something more to RVO, beyond the possibility of getting it right the first time.

In Figure 19.4, let's look at a scenario where A is going south toward B. But, let's also say that B is malfunctioning, and at a standstill rather than performing proper avoidance.

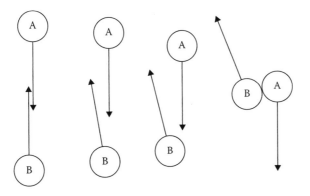

Figure 19.4

An RVO agent steers around a malfunctioning agent.

This is a perfect scenario for A to be using VO, and you might expect RVO to fail entirely, expecting a reciprocation that never comes. Surprisingly, though, RVO still works pretty well! On the first frame, A only dodges half as much as it should... but on the second frame, seeing that a collision is still imminent, dodges half of the remaining half... and then a half of that on the third frame... and so on, asymptotically avoiding the collision. (More or less.) A really *expected* B to dodge, but when it did not, A could deal with that too.

The magic in RVO, then, is that it strikes a balance between eager collision avoidance and a cagey wait-and-see attitude. An RVO agent faced with a collision dodges *some*, but not all, of the way. It is less likely than VO to dodge too much, overshooting the optimal velocity and requiring corrections. Moreover, if it has dodged too little, it's still set up to make up the difference on future frames. This magic is not unique to RVO: so-called *gradient methods*, such as the gradient descent algorithm for finding minima of functions, and similar techniques, use a multiplier to avoid overshooting the goal.

19.4 States, Solutions, and Sidedness

The goal of any gradient method is to converge to a locally optimal state, where no further improvements can be made. For collision avoidance, that generally looks like agents on trajectories which *just* squeeze past each other. Any closer and they would collide; any further and they would be wasting time.

RVO isn't exactly a gradient method, though. In a normal gradient method, you have as many steps as you want to converge onto an optimum; you are only limited by processing time. But in standard VO methods, after every iteration, the agents move along their chosen velocities. So while the "state" of an RVO simulation is the momentary positions and velocities of all agents, the "solution" is the full trajectories of the agents over time.

There is a more obvious—and, in my opinion, more useful—way to think about the "solution" to an avoidance problem, though: Sidedness. Two agents heading toward each other can each dodge left or each can dodge right; either way is a potential solution. If the two are not on perfect head-on trajectories, one may be a better solution, in the sense that they will get to their goals sooner; but both are *stable*: Once on one of those trajectories, they will not change their minds unless the situation changes.

There are three closely related ways to define sidedness. All involve the point of closest approach. Consider two agents whose trajectories are currently bringing them closer together. Determine the time at which A and B are predicted to be closest together (allowing penetration between them), and compute the vector from A's center to B's center.

The first notion of sidedness is an absolute one: If that vector is (say) eastward, then A is projected to pass to the west of B, and B is projected to pass to the east of A. Sidedness computed in this way is always symmetric between A's calculations and B's calculations.

The second notion is relative to current velocity: If the closest approach vector winds left of A's velocity relative to B, then A is projected to pass B on the left, and similarly if the vector winds right, A is projected to pass B on the right. This calculation is likewise symmetric: Both will project passing left, or both will project passing right.

The third notion is relative to A's desired velocity, wound against the closest approach vector. This formulation most closely aligns with our intuitive sense of "passing side." However, it can be inconsistent between A and B in situations where their current velocities diverge from their desired velocities. As a result, "sidedness" as a tool for coordination generally uses one of the first two formulations.

19.5 ORCA

The ORCA algorithm (van den Berg et al. 2011), which succeeded the original RVO algorithm (the reference library implementing ORCA is called RVO2) had this sidedness concept as its central insight. ORCA was less concerned with stability, though, and more concerned with optimality. Looking back at the three-agent avoidance scenario in Figure 19.3, a central problem was the agents' inconsistent intentions regarding passing sides. If one agent plans to pass on the left, and the other intends to pass on the right, a collision is inevitable. Since ORCA maintained the independent, decentralized design of other VO methods, it was not possible to centrally settle on a set of passing sides. Instead, ORCA forces agents to maintain their current passing sides. Two agents that are not on an *exact* collision course have consistently defined passing sides, even if they do not have enough separation in their trajectories to avoid the collision. ORCA picks trajectories that maintain those passing sides while expanding the separation to prevent the collision.

An implicit assumption behind ORCA is that the "original" passing sides, as of whenever the agents first encountered each other, just so happen to be reasonable ones. Remarkably, this assumption is usually true, particularly in situations without static obstacles. When ORCA's solver succeeds, it reliably produces reasonably optimal trajectories, and it absolutely eliminates velocity flicker from inconsistent passing sides.

The problem is that ORCA's solver often does not succeed. Although the set of illegal velocities generated by one RVO agent is an infinite cone (ruling out a significant percentage of potential velocities), the set of illegal velocities generated by one ORCA agent is an infinite half-space (ruling out about half of them). It is easy for a small number of nearby agents to completely rule out all velocities. In fact, the three-agent problem from Figure 19.3 does that. C is passing A on the right and B on the left; A's obstacle prohibits it from going left, B's obstacle prohibits it from going right, and both prohibit it from going straight, or even from stopping or going backward. ORCA satisfies this by linearly relaxing all constraints. This produces a velocity that maximizes the minimum passing distance.

Like RVO's partial dodging, ORCA's constraint relaxation has the effect of resolving complex avoidance scenarios over several frames. Although A must resort to a "least-worst" solution, B and C have legal velocities that have the effect of making more room for A. In fact, ORCA resolves this scenario in a single frame, as A's "least-worst" velocity is actually due north. More generally, when two rows of agents heading in different directions encounter each other, ORCA has the effect of expanding the rows, starting with the outer ranks. RVO does this too, but ORCA prohibits the middle ranks from taking extreme dodging action while it is happening, thereby leading to cleaner and more optimal solutions by maintaining the original set of passing sides.

19.6 Cornering

ORCA exhibits a more serious problem in real-world scenarios. In most articles on VO methods, there is an assumption that each agent has a preferred direction of travel, either constant or directly toward a fixed goal point. But in most game situations, the direction of travel is generated by following a path toward a goal, which winds around corners.

VO methods can adapt to occasional changes in heading without much issue. But while rounding a corner, an agent's preferred direction of travel will change every frame. This violates the assumption mentioned earlier that each agent's velocity from the previous frame is their preferred velocity for the current frame. RVO agents can exhibit unusual trajectories when rounding corners or when reacting to a nearby agent rounding a corner, that is, there is a characteristic "snap" turn as the agents change their passing sides.

But ORCA does not allow that snap. As mentioned earlier, the original passing sides are generally a good approximation of ideal passing sides, but that is not the case for cornering. ORCA agents at corners will often travel far, far from their desired trajectories to maintain passing sides, or simply become stuck at the corner, unwilling to cross paths and unable to make progress otherwise (as shown in Figure 19.5). This behavior is sometimes

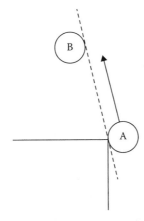

Figure 19.5

ORCA agent A is unable to continue turning around the corner without violating the sidedness constraint against B.

acceptable when all agents are traveling toward the same goal, as the front agents can still make progress but in general leads to frequent deadlocks.

19.7 Gradient Methods Revisited

What we want from collision avoidance is for agents to find a consistent set of passing sides quickly, and ideally for that solution not to be *too* far from the optimum. When the situation changes—when a new agent arrives, or when existing agents change their minds about which way to go—we would like the system to adapt and find a new solution quickly, and for that new solution to look as much like the old one as possible. The key to that is weights.

19.7.1 Modifying Weights

In the original RVO paper, agents can be "weighted" with respect to each other—one agent can dodge by a larger or smaller percentage of the total required dodge than the other, as long as the two weights add up to 1 and the agents agree on what those weights are. But if we view RVO as a gradient method, as opposed to an instant, perfect collision solver, then it is clear that nothing forces that constraint. For instance, you could set both weights to 0.1, making agents slowly move out of each other's way over many frames, but reliably settling into a stable configuration. Or you could set both weights to 0.9, causing agents to dodge sharply and exhibit the reciprocal oscillations that RVO was designed to avoid. (In fact, original-recipe VOs are simply a special case of RVO, with all weights set to 1.)

As mentioned, RVO is not quite a gradient method, because agents move after each iteration. In addition, if an upcoming collision has not yet been resolved, it just got a bit closer, and the problem just got a bit harder. If two agents are on a collision course, and the weights between them sum to anything less than 1.0, then their decisions each frame are guaranteed *not* to fully resolve the collision, and eventually they are guaranteed to veer off sharply and collide. If an algorithm can be said to "panic," that's what it looks like when an algorithm panics.

Low weights have their advantages, though. They tend to result in better solutions in the sidedness sense, particularly with large numbers of agents. But we need a way to cope with their tendency to fail asymptotically.

19.7.2 Substepping

Recall that as an algorithm for robot control, RVO relies on a cycle of steering, moving, and observing. One robot cannot react to another until that other robot has actually turned and started moving in another direction. But we have the benefit of knowing all agents' velocities immediately after each steering step, even without moving the agents. We can use this knowledge to cheat, running multiple iterations of RVO between each movement step. The velocity outputs of one RVO substep become the velocity inputs of the next substep, and the positions remain unchanged.

This has a number of advantages. When groups of agents come upon each other, there is likely to be a number of frames of velocity flicker, as in the earlier example. Substepping allows that flicker to die down before velocities are presented to the animation system, giving the illusion that all agents made consistent choices the first time around.

Substepping also gives you more flexibility with your weights. Weightings that sum to less than 1.0 failed to resolve collisions, but they were good at finding the seeds of efficient solutions. During a step consisting of many substeps, you can start the weights low to smoothly hint toward an efficient solution, then ramp the weights up to 0.5 to fully settle into that solution along noncolliding trajectories.

If you're familiar with stochastic optimization methods, you may find that sort of schedule, moving from the conservative to the abrupt, to be counterintuitive and backward. The goal here, though, is to converge reliably to a constraint-satisfying local optimum, rather than to converge reliably to the global optimum while maintaining constraints.

19.7.3 Time Horizons

ORCA's cornering problem (getting stuck rather than changing passing side) is one example of a larger class of problems exhibited by VO methods when the assumption of constant preferred velocity is violated. Another, simpler form can be demonstrated with a single VO agent traveling north toward a goal point with a wall behind it. All northward velocities are blocked by the wall's static velocity obstacle, so the agent can never reach the goal.

The original RVO reference library does not exhibit this problem, because it diverges from the paper and ignores collisions with static obstacles if they are further than the maximum stopping distance of the agent. Other RVO implementations address the problem by defining a maximum time-to-collision (TTC) beyond which projected collisions are ignored, causing the agent to slow as it approaches the obstacle, keeping its TTC above the threshold. The first approach assumes that the future policy is to come to a stop; the second approach assumes that the trajectory past the maximum TTC is too unpredictable to take into account. Both approaches are reasonable, but both are fairly arbitrary and can lead to collisions when agents end up squeezed between static obstacles and other agents.

In both cornering and approaching a goal in front of a wall, the basic issue is that agents are attempting to avoid a collision at a point that they would never reach. The cornering agent would veer off before getting to the collision point; the goal-approaching agent would stop first.

A more formal approach, then, would be to calculate the time at which the agent planned to stop at their goal, or to turn a corner, and to avoid collisions that would occur later than that time. The time horizon is specific to a given velocity candidate.

Time horizons are a little tricky to apply to cornering, because the agent does not plan to *disappear* after that but merely to turn a little bit. An agent currently rounding a corner has a time horizon approaching zero, yet should not ignore collisions entirely. Instead, one can construct a plane, perpendicular to the agent's postcornering direction, which the agent never plans to cross. Collisions past that plane can safely be discarded, as shown in Figure 19.6.

This is not a perfect solution, as agents still fail to consider collisions that *will* occur *after* cornering. And it is not necessarily true that an agent will never cross their cornering plane: On occasion they may do so to avoid a collision right next to the corner. A better solution would involve predicting collisions along a space defined by the agent's path, rather than world space. But because each agent has its own path, doing this in a way which would ensure proper reciprocation is, as far as we know, intractable in the general case.

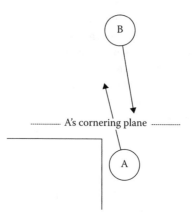

Figure 19.6

While A and B are on a colliding trajectory, the collision can be ignored as it would occur after A turns the corner.

19.8 Progress and Penalties

Original VO methods treated the duty to avoid collisions as absolute. Making progress in their preferred directions was a secondary concern, only coming into play when choosing among a set of noncolliding and therefore valid trajectories. But as we have seen, avoiding far-off collisions is not always necessary or reasonable: Between the current step and the projected collision, a lot can happen, particularly when many agents are involved.

The RVO algorithm softens VO constraints, treating projected collisions as only one aspect when "scoring" a velocity candidate, making it a utility method. (ORCA does not soften its constraints in the same way: Its constraint relaxation is to produce at least one admissible velocity, not to allow colliding velocities when noncolliding velocities are available.) The base utility of a velocity candidate is calculated as the distance between the preferred velocity and the velocity candidate. Predicted collisions are treated as penalty terms reducing the utility of a velocity candidate, with the penalty term increasing as the collision becomes more imminent. If a velocity candidate is predicted to result in multiple collisions, the soonest collision can be used to determine the penalty, or each collision can generate a separate penalty term; the latter approach tends to push agents away from crowds decreasing congestion.

An additive formulation like this is motivated by practicality, not theory: It makes no guarantees of collision avoidance and increases the number of user-specified parameters, making tuning more difficult. Nevertheless, in practice, it is more effective than "absolute" VO methods at clearing congestion, as it discounts distant collisions, making it more reactive to closer ones.

19.8.1 Putting Sidedness Back In

The additive formulation does not automatically maintain sidedness (though substepping with low weights helps). However, nothing is stopping us from adding it as an additional penalty term. Simply calculate, for each velocity candidate, how many agents it changes the sidedness of; then add a penalty for each. Sidedness-change penalty terms should be scaled similarly to collision penalty terms; since they sometimes need to be applied to agents without projected collisions, though, the time to closest approach can be used instead of the TTC.

19.8.2 Progress and Energy Minimization

In the additive formulation above, the base utility of a velocity candidate is calculated as the distance from preferred velocity. This is not the only option: Another is rate of progress. In this formulation, the main metric is how fast an agent is making progress toward their goal, computed as the dot product of the velocity candidate with the unit-length preferred direction of travel. Compared to the distance metric, rate of progress encourages sideways dodging over slowing and tends to get agents to their goals sooner.

Rate of progress is an unrealistic utility from the point of view of actual human behavior. Consider that when moving from place to place, humans have the option of sprinting, yet generally move at a walking speed. Biomechanics researchers have explained this as a tendency toward energy minimization: A normal walking gait allows a human to reach their goal with the minimum expenditure of energy by maximizing the ratio of speed to power output. A rough approximation to the energy wasted by traveling at a nonpreferred velocity may be calculated as the squared distance between the preferred velocity (at preferred speed) and the velocity candidate; the squared term differentiates it from RVO's approach. Agents using this utility calculation exhibit human-like trajectories, often slowing slightly to avoid a collision rather than turning left or right.

19.9 Putting It All Together: How to Develop a Practical Collision Avoidance System

Having a thorough knowledge of all the nuances and decisions and parameters involved in a VO-based collision avoidance system does not automatically give you the ability to make a perfect one. We are convinced that there is no perfect collision avoidance system, only one that works well with your scenarios, your needs, and your animation system. Developing such a system, like developing game systems in general, is an iterative process. There is a few important things you can do to increase the effectiveness of the process:

- Build up a library of collision avoidance scenarios, covering a variety of situations that your system will need to deal with. These should include all the factors you are likely to encounter in your game: static obstacles, cornering, multiple groups of agents, and so on. As you encounter problems with your system, make new scenarios that you can use to reproduce the problems, and test whether changes to your system have resolved them.
- Build up a library of collision avoidance algorithms too! As you make changes— either to the basic algorithms in use or the values you use for their parameters— keep the old algorithms around, not merely in source control but in active code. This will allow you to assess how well your iterative changes have improved collision avoidance quality, and it will allow you to test multiple approaches to resolving particular problems. Often later tweaks to a system will render earlier tweaks unnecessary, and keeping earlier versions around can help you recognize this and remove them, keeping your system as simple as possible.

- Put together a framework to automatically test each collision avoidance algorithm against each collision avoidance scenario. This isn't quite as easy as it sounds: It is difficult to formulate criteria to determine whether a particular algorithm "passes" a particular test. As a first pass, you can simply check whether an algorithm succeeds in eventually bringing all agents to their goals without collisions along the way. You can compare two algorithms to determine which one gets agents to their goals sooner, but keep in mind that a difference of a few fractions of a second is not significant in a game scenario. It is important not to test collision avoidance in isolation: If your collision avoidance feeds into your animation system, rather than directly controlling agent positions, then you have to make your animation system part of the test rig in order to ensure accurate results. An automated testing rig is primarily useful for quickly checking for significant regressions in one or more test scenarios. It can also be used to quickly determine the optimal values for a set of control parameters.
- Don't rely too heavily on your automated testing rig without doing frequent eyes-on testing of the results it is producing. Some collision avoidance algorithms can exhibit artifacts, which do not significantly impact the objective optimality of the results but which nevertheless look unrealistic to the player; velocity flicker is a prime example. You can try to come up with tests for this, but there's no substitute for subjective evaluation.

19.10 Conclusion

Much of the popularity of VO methods can be traced to the ease of understanding them as prohibited shapes in velocity space. RVO in particular is seductively elegant in sharing the burden of collision avoidance between agents. But the success in practice of VO methods—particularly RVO—depends on subtler factors, and treating RVO as a purely geometric method makes it more difficult to leverage and maximize the effectiveness of these factors. So it is important to view VO methods through multiple lenses: As geometric solvers, as gradient methods, and as utility methods. There is nothing simple about this holistic approach, but collision avoidance is not a simple problem. Understanding both the nuances of the problem space and the complexity of the solution space is the key to developing a system that works for you.

References

van den Berg, J., Guy, S. J., Lin, M., and Manocha, D. 2011. Reciprocal n-body collision avoidance. In *Robotics Research*. Berlin, Germany: Springer, pp. 3–19.
van den Berg, J., Lin, M., and Manocha, D. 2008. Reciprocal velocity obstacles for real-time multi-agent navigation. *Proceedings of the IEEE International Conference on Robotics and Automation (ICRA)*, 2008. http://gamma.cs.unc.edu/RVO/icra2008.pdf.

20

Optimization for Smooth Paths

Mark Langerak

20.1 Introduction

Path planning for games and robotics applications typically consists of finding the straight-line shortest path through the environment connecting the start and goal position. However, the straight-line shortest path usually contains abrupt, nonsmooth changes in direction at path apex points, which lead to unnatural agent movement in the path-following phase. Conversely, a smooth path that is free of such sharp kinks greatly improves the realism of agent steering and animation, especially at the path start and goal positions, where the path can be made to align with the agent facing direction.

Generating a smooth path through an environment can be challenging because there are multiple competing constraints of total path length, path curvature, and static obstacle avoidance that must all be satisfied simultaneously. This chapter describes an approach that uses convex optimization to construct a smooth path that optimally balances all these competing constraints. The resulting algorithm is efficient, surprisingly simple, free of special cases, and easily parallelizable. In addition, the techniques used in this chapter serve as an introduction to convex optimization, which has many uses in fields as diverse as AI, computer vision, and image analysis. A source code implementation can be found on the book's website (http://www.gameaipro.com).

20.2 Overview

The corridor map method introduced by Geraerts and Overmars, 2007 is used to construct an initial, nonoptimal path through the static obstacles in the environment. In the

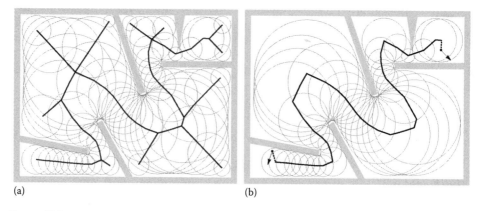

(a)   (b)

Figure 20.1

The corridor map (a) and a path between two points in the corridor map (b).

corridor map method, free space is represented by a graph where the vertices have associated disks. The centers of the disks coincide with the vertex 2D position, and the disk radius is equal to the maximum clearance around that vertex. The disks at neighboring graph vertices overlap, and the union of the disks then represents all of navigable space. See the leftside of Figure 20.1 for an example environment with some static obstacles in light gray and the corresponding corridor map graph.

The corridor map method might be a lesser known representation than the familiar methods of a graph defined over a navigation mesh or over a grid. However, it has several useful properties that make it an excellent choice for the path smoothing algorithm described in this chapter. For one, its graph is compact and low density, so path-planning queries are efficient. Moreover, the corridor map representation makes it straightforward to constrain a path within the bounds of free space, which is crucial for the implementation of the path smoothing algorithm to ensure it does not result in a path that collides with static obstacles.

The rightside of Figure 20.1 shows the result of an A* query on the corridor map graph, which gives the minimal subgraph that connects the vertex whose center is nearest to the start position to the vertex whose center is nearest to the goal. The arrows in the figure denote the agent facing direction at the start position and the desired facing direction at the goal position. The subgraph is prepended and appended with the start and goal positions to construct the initial path connecting the start and the goal. Note that this initial path is highly nonoptimal for the purpose of agent path following since it has greatest clearance from the static obstacles, which implies that its total length is much longer than the shortest straight-line path.

Starting from this initial nonoptimal path state, the iterative algorithm described in this chapter evolves the path over multiple steps by successively moving the waypoints closer to an optimal configuration, that is, the path that satisfies all the competing constraints of smoothness, shortest total length, alignment with the start/goal direction and collision-free agent movement. The result is shown in the left of Figure 20.2.

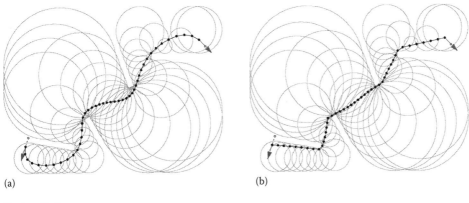

(a)   (b)

Figure 20.2

A smooth (a) and a straight-line path (b).

20.2.1 Definitions

In this section, we will define the mathematical notation used along with a few preliminary definitions. Vectors and scalars are denoted by lowercase letters. Where necessary, vectors use x, y superscripts to refer to the individual elements:

$$a = \begin{pmatrix} a^x \\ a^y \end{pmatrix}$$

The vector dot product is denoted by angle brackets:

$$\langle a, b \rangle = a^x b^x + a^y b^y$$

The definition for the length of a vector uses double vertical bars:

$$\|v\|_2 = \sqrt{\langle v, v \rangle}$$

(The number 2 subscript on the double bars makes it explicit that the vector length is the L^2 norm of a vector.)

A vector space is a rather abstract mathematical construct. In the general sense, it consists of a set, that is, some collection of elements, along with corresponding operators acting on that set. For the path smoothing problem, we need two specific vector space definitions, one for scalar quantities and one for 2D vector quantities. These vector spaces are denoted by uppercase letters U and V, respectively:

$$U = \mathbb{R}^n$$
$$V = \mathbb{R}^{2n}$$

The vector spaces U and V are arrays of length n, with vector space U an array of real (floating point) scalars, and V an array of 2D vectors. Individual elements of a vector space are referenced by an index subscript:

$$a \in V: \ a_i$$

In this particular example, a is an array of 2D vectors, and a_i is the 2D vector at index i in that array. Vector space operators like multiplication, addition, and so on, are defined in the obvious way as the corresponding pair-wise operator over the individual elements. The dot product of vector space V is defined as:

$$a, b \in V: \ \langle a, b \rangle_V = \sum_{i=1}^{n} \langle a_i, b_i \rangle$$

That is, the vector space dot product is the sum of the pair-wise dot products of the 2D vector elements. (The V subscript on the angle brackets distinguishes the vector space dot product from the vector dot product.)

For vector space V, we will make use of the norms:

$$v \in V: \ \|v\|_{V,1} = \sum_{i=1}^{n} \|v_i\|_2$$

$$v \in V: \ \|v\|_{V,2} = \sqrt{\sum_{i=1}^{n} \left(\|v_i\|_2 \right)^2}$$

$$v \in V: \ \|v\|_{V,\infty} = \max_{i=1}^{n} \|v_i\|_2$$

(The V subscript is added to make the distinction between vector and vector space norms clear.) Each of these three vector space norms are constructed similarly: they consist of an inner L^2 norm over the 2D vector elements, followed by an outer L^1, L^2, or L^∞ norm over the resulting scalars, respectively. In the case of the vector space L^2 norm, the outer norm is basically the usual definition of vector length, in this case a vector of length n. The vector space L^1 and L^∞ norms are generalizations of the familiar L^2 norm. The vector space L^1 norm is analogous to the Manhattan distance of a vector, and the L^∞ norm is the so-called max norm, which is simply the absolute max element.

An indicator function is a convenience function for testing set membership. It gives 0 if the element is in the set, otherwise it gives ∞ if the element is not in the set:

$$I_S(x) = \begin{cases} 0 & x \in S \\ \infty & x \notin S \end{cases}$$

The differencing operators give the vector offset between adjacent elements in V:

$$v \in V: \delta^+ (v)_i = \begin{cases} (v_{i+1} - v_i)/h & i < n \\ 0 & i = n \end{cases}$$

$$v \in V: \delta^- (v)_i = \begin{cases} v_i/h & i = 1 \\ (v_i - v_{i-1})/h & 1 < i < n \\ -v_{i-1}/h & i = n \end{cases}$$

$$v \in V: \delta^s (v) = -\delta^+ (v) + \delta^- (v)$$

20. Optimization for Smooth Paths

The forward differencing operator δ^+ gives the offset from the 2D vector at index i to the next vector at index $i+1$. The boundary condition at index $i=n$ is needed because then there is no "next" vector, and there the offset is set to 0. Similarly, the backward differencing operator δ^- gives the offset from the vector at index i to the previous vector at index $i-1$, with boundary conditions at $i=1$ and $i=n$ to ensure that δ^+ and δ^- are adjoint. The sum-differencing operator δ^s is the vector addition of the vector offsets δ^+ and δ^-. The scalar h is a normalization constant to enforce scale invariance. It depends on the scale of the 2D coordinate space used, and its value should be set to the average distance between neighboring graph vertices.

20.3 Path Smoothing Energy Function

An optimization problem consists of two parts: an energy (aka cost) function and an optimization algorithm for minimizing that energy function. In this section, we will define the energy function; in the following sections, we will derive the optimization algorithm.

The path smoothing energy function gives a score to a particular configuration of the path waypoints. This score is a positive number, where large values mean the path is "bad," and small values mean the path is "good." The goal then is to find the path configuration for which the energy function is minimal. The choice of energy function is crucial. Since it effectively will be evaluated many times in the execution of the optimization algorithm, it needs to be simple and fast, while still accurately assigning high energy to nonsmooth paths and low energy to smooth paths.

As described in the introduction section, the fundamental goal of the path smoothing problem is to find the optimal balance between path smoothness and total path length under the constraint that the resulting path must be collision free. Intuitively, expressing this goal as an energy function leads to a sum of three terms: a term that penalizes (i.e., assigns high energy) to waypoints where the path has sharp kinks, a term that penalizes greater total path length, and a term that enforces the collision-free constraint. In addition, the energy function should include a scaling factor to enable a user-controlled tradeoff between overall path smoothness and total path length. The energy function for the path smoothing problem is then as follows:

$$w \in U, v \in V: \quad E(v) = \frac{1}{2}\left(\left\|w\delta^s(v)\right\|_{V,2}\right)^2 + \left\|\delta^+(v)\right\|_{V,2} + I_C(v)$$

$$C = \left\{v, c \in V, r \in U : \left\|(v-c)/r\right\|_{V,\infty} \le 1\right\}$$

(20.1)

Here, v are the path waypoint positions, and w are per waypoint weights. Set C represents the maximal clearance disk at each waypoint, where c are the disk centers, and r are the radii. (Note that this path smoothing energy function is convex, so there are no local minima that can trap the optimization in a nonoptimal state, and the algorithm is therefore guaranteed to converge on a globally minimal energy.)

The first term in the energy function gives a high score to nonsmooth paths by penalizing waypoints where the path locally deviates from a straight line. See Figure 20.3 for a visual representation, where the offsets δ^s, δ^+, and δ^- for waypoint 3 are drawn with arrows. The dark arrow shows offset vector δ^s, and it can be seen from the left and

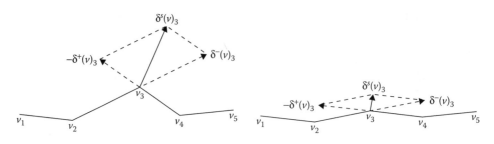

Figure 20.3

A visual representation of the model.

the right Figure 20.3 that its length is relative to how much waypoint v_3 deviates from the straight line connecting v_2 and v_4. The offset vector δ^s length is squared to penalize sharp kinks progressively more than shallow ones, which forces the optimization algorithm to spread out sharp kinks over adjacent waypoints, leading to an overall smoother path.

The second term in the energy function gives a higher score to greater total path length by summing the lengths of the δ^+ vectors. It effectively forces path waypoints to be closer together, resulting in a path that has a shorter total length and which is thus more similar to the straight-line shortest path connecting the start and goal.

Set C acts as a constraint on the optimization problem to ensure the path is collision free. Due to the max norm in the definition, the indicator function I_C gives infinity when one or more waypoints are outside their corresponding maximal clearance disk, otherwise it gives zero. A path that has waypoints that are outside their corresponding maximal clearance disk will have infinite energy therefore, and thus can obviously never be the minimal energy state path.

The required agent facing directions at the start and goal positions are handled by extending the path at both ends with a dummy additional waypoint, which are shown by the small circles in Figure 20.2. The position of the additional waypoints is determined by subtracting or adding the facing direction vector to the start and goal positions. These dummy additional waypoints as well as the path start and goal position are assigned a zero radius clearance disk. This constrains the start/goal positions from shifting around during optimization and similarly prevents the start/goal-facing direction from changing during optimization.

The per waypoint weights w allow a user-controlled tradeoff between path smoothness and overall path length, where lower weights favor short paths and higher weights favor smooth paths. In the limit, when all the weights are set to zero, the energy function only penalizes total path length, and then the path optimization will result in the shortest straight-line path as shown in the right of Figure 20.2. In practice, the weights near the start and goal are boosted to improve alignment of the path with the required agent facing direction. This is done using a bathtub-shaped power curve:

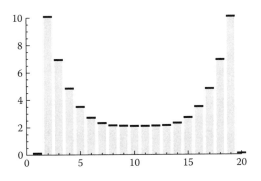

Figure 20.4

A waypoint weight curve.

$$w_i = \begin{cases} w_m + \left(w_s - w_m\right)\left(\dfrac{-2\left(i-2\right)}{n-3}+1\right)^4 & 2 \leq i \leq \dfrac{n}{2} \\[4mm] w_m + \left(w_e - w_m\right)\left(\dfrac{2\left(i-2\right)}{n-3}-1\right)^4 & \dfrac{n}{2} < i \leq n-1 \\[4mm] 0 & \text{otherwise} \end{cases}$$

The scalars w_s and w_e are the values of the weight for the start and goal position waypoints, respectively. The end position weights taper off with a power curve to weight w_m at the middle of the path. Index $i=1$ and $i=n$ are the dummy waypoints for the agent facing direction, and there the weights are zero. Figure 20.4 shows a plot for an example weight curve with $w_s = w_e = 10$, $w_m = 2$, and $n = 20$.

20.4 Optimization Algorithm

Minimizing the energy function (Equation 20.1) is a challenging optimization problem due to the discontinuous derivative of the vector space norms and the hard constraints imposed by the maximal clearance disks. In this context, the path smoothing problem is similar to optimization problems found in many computer vision applications, which likewise consist of discontinuous derivatives and have hard constraints. Recent advances in the field have resulted in simple and efficient algorithms that can effectively tackle such optimization tasks; in particular, the Chambolle–Pock preconditioned primal-dual algorithm described in Chambolle and Pock 2011, and Pock and Chambolle 2011 has proven very effective in computer vision applications due to its simple formulation and fast convergence. Furthermore, it generalizes and extends several prior known optimization algorithms such as preconditioned ADMM and Douglas–Rachford splitting, leading to a very general and flexible algorithm.

The algorithm requires that the optimization problem has a specific form, given by:

$$\min_{v \in V}\left\{E_p\left(v\right) = F\left(K \cdot v\right) + G\left(v\right)\right\} \tag{20.2}$$

That is, it minimizes some variable v for some energy function E_p, which itself consists of a sum of two (convex) functions F and G. The parameter to function F is the product of a matrix K and variable v. The purpose of matrix K is to encode all the operations on v that depend on adjacent elements. This results in a F and G function that are simple, which is necessary to make the implementation of the algorithm feasible. In addition, matrix K is used to compute a bound on the step sizes, which ensures the algorithm is stable.

The optimization problem defined by Equation 20.2 is rather abstract and completely generic. To make the algorithm concrete, the path smoothing energy function (Equation 20.1) is adapted to the form of Equation 20.2 in multiple steps. First, we define the functions F_1, F_2, and G to represent the three terms in the path smoothing energy function:

$$F_1(v) = \frac{1}{2} \left(\|v\|_{V,2} \right)^2, \quad F_2(v) = \|v\|_{V,2}, \quad G(v) = I_C(v)$$

In the path smoothing energy function (Equation 20.1), the operators $w\delta^s$ and δ^+ act on adjacent elements in v, so these are the operators that must be encoded as matrix K. As an intermediate step, we first define the two submatrices $K_1 = w\delta^s$ and $K_2 = \delta^+$. We can then state the equivalence:

$$K_1 \cdot v = w\delta^s(v), \quad K_2 \cdot v = \delta^+(v)$$

Substituting these as the parameters to functions F_1 and F_2 results in:

$$F_1(K_1 \cdot v) = \frac{1}{2} \left(\left\| w\delta^s(v) \right\|_{V,2} \right)^2, \quad F_2(K_2 \cdot v) = \left\| \delta^+(v) \right\|_{V,2}$$

which leads to the minimization problem:

$$\min_{v \in V} \left\{ E_p(v) = F_1(K_1 \cdot v) + F_2(K_2 \cdot v) + G(v) \right\}$$

This is already largely similar to the form of Equation 20.2, but instead of one matrix K and one function F, we have two matrices K_1 and K_2, and two functions F_1 and F_2. By "stacking" these matrices and functions, we can combine them into a single definition to make the path smoothing problem compatible with Equation 20.2:

$$K = \begin{pmatrix} K_1 \\ K_2 \end{pmatrix}, \quad F(K \cdot v) = \begin{pmatrix} F_1(K_1 \cdot v) \\ F_2(K_2 \cdot v) \end{pmatrix}$$

Next, matrix K is defined to complete the derivation of the path smoothing problem. For the matrix-vector product $K \cdot v$, it is necessary to first "flatten" v into a column vector $\left(v_1^x, v_1^y, v_2^x, v_2^y, \cdots, v_n^x, v_n^y \right)^T$. Then K is a $4n \times 2n$-dimensional matrix where rows 1 to $2n$ encode the $w\delta^s$ operator, and rows $2n+1$ to $4n$ encode δ^+. See Figure 20.5 for an example with $n=4$. From Figure 20.5, it is easy to see that applying $K \cdot v$ is the same operation as $w\delta^s(v)$ and $\delta^+(v)$.

Note that in practice, the definition of matrix K is only needed to analyze the optimization algorithm mathematically; it is not used in the final implementation. The matrix

$$
\begin{pmatrix}
\dfrac{2\omega_1}{h} & 0 & -\dfrac{\omega_1}{h} & 0 & 0 & 0 & 0 & 0 \\[4pt]
0 & \dfrac{2\omega_1}{h} & 0 & -\dfrac{\omega_1}{h} & 0 & 0 & 0 & 0 \\[4pt]
-\dfrac{\omega_2}{h} & 0 & \dfrac{2\omega_2}{h} & 0 & -\dfrac{\omega_2}{h} & 0 & 0 & 0 \\[4pt]
0 & -\dfrac{\omega_2}{h} & 0 & \dfrac{2\omega_2}{h} & 0 & -\dfrac{\omega_2}{h} & 0 & 0 \\[4pt]
0 & 0 & -\dfrac{\omega_3}{h} & 0 & \dfrac{2\omega_3}{h} & 0 & -\dfrac{\omega_3}{h} & 0 \\[4pt]
0 & 0 & 0 & -\dfrac{\omega_3}{h} & 0 & \dfrac{2\omega_3}{h} & 0 & -\dfrac{\omega_3}{h} \\[4pt]
0 & 0 & 0 & 0 & -\dfrac{\omega_4}{h} & 0 & 0 & 0 \\[4pt]
0 & 0 & 0 & 0 & 0 & -\dfrac{\omega_4}{h} & 0 & 0 \\[4pt]
-\dfrac{1}{h} & 0 & \dfrac{1}{h} & 0 & 0 & 0 & 0 & 0 \\[4pt]
0 & -\dfrac{1}{h} & 0 & \dfrac{1}{h} & 0 & 0 & 0 & 0 \\[4pt]
0 & 0 & -\dfrac{1}{h} & 0 & \dfrac{1}{h} & 0 & 0 & 0 \\[4pt]
0 & 0 & 0 & -\dfrac{1}{h} & 0 & \dfrac{1}{h} & 0 & 0 \\[4pt]
0 & 0 & 0 & 0 & -\dfrac{1}{h} & 0 & \dfrac{1}{h} & 0 \\[4pt]
0 & 0 & 0 & 0 & 0 & -\dfrac{1}{h} & 0 & \dfrac{1}{h} \\[4pt]
0 & 0 & 0 & 0 & 0 & 0 & 0 & 0 \\[4pt]
0 & 0 & 0 & 0 & 0 & 0 & 0 & 0
\end{pmatrix}
\begin{pmatrix}
v_1^x \\ v_1^y \\ v_2^x \\ v_2^y \\ v_3^x \\ v_3^y \\ v_4^x \\ v_4^y
\end{pmatrix}
=
\begin{pmatrix}
\omega_1\delta^s(v)_1^x \\
\omega_1\delta^s(v)_1^y \\
\omega_2\delta^s(v)_2^x \\
\omega_2\delta^s(v)_2^y \\
\omega_3\delta^s(v)_3^x \\
\omega_3\delta^s(v)_3^y \\
\omega_4\delta^s(v)_4^x \\
\omega_4\delta^s(v)_4^y \\
\delta^+(v)_1^x \\
\delta^+(v)_1^y \\
\delta^+(v)_2^x \\
\delta^+(v)_2^y \\
\delta^+(v)_3^x \\
\delta^+(v)_3^y \\
\delta^+(v)_4^x \\
\delta^+(v)_4^y
\end{pmatrix}
$$

Figure 20.5

Matrix K for $n = 4$.

is very large and sparse, so it is obviously much more efficient to simply use the operators $w\delta^s$ and δ^+ in the implementation instead of the actual matrix-vector product $K \cdot v$.

Instead of solving the minimization problem (Equation 20.2) directly, the Chambolle–Pock algorithm solves the related min–max problem:

$$\min_{v \in V} \max_{p \in V} \left\{ E_{pd}(v) = \langle K \cdot v, p \rangle_V + G(v) - F^*(p) \right\} \tag{20.3}$$

The optimization problems Equations 20.2 and 20.3 are equivalent: minimizing Equation 20.2 or solving the min–max problem (Equation 20.3) will result in the same v. The original optimization problem (Equation 20.2) is called the "primal," and Equation 20.3 is called the "primal-dual" problem. Similarly, v is referred to as the primal variable, and the additional variable p is called the dual variable.

The concept of duality and the meaning of the star superscript on F^* are explained further in the next section, but at first glance it may seem that Equation 20.3 is a more complicated problem to solve than Equation 20.2, as there is an additional variable p, and we are now dealing with a coupled min–max problem instead of a pure minimization. However, the additional variable enables the algorithm, on each iteration, to handle p separately while holding v constant and to handle v separately while holding p constant. This results in two smaller subproblems, so the system as a whole is simpler.

In the case of the path smoothing problem, we have two functions F_1 and F_2, so we need one more dual variable q, resulting in the min–max problem:

$$\min_{v \in V} \max_{p,q \in V} \left\{ E_{pd}(v) = \left\langle K \cdot v, \begin{pmatrix} p \\ q \end{pmatrix} \right\rangle_V + G(v) - F_1^*(p) - F_2^*(q) \right\}$$

Note that, similar to what was done to combine matrices K_1 and K_2, the variables p and q are stacked to combine them into a single definition $(p,q)^T$.

20.4.1 Legendre-Fenchel Transform

The Legendre–Fenchel (LF) transform takes a function f and puts in a different form. The transformed function is denoted with a star superscript, f^*, and is referred to as the dual of the original function f. Using the dual of a function can make certain kinds of analysis or operations much more efficient. For example, the well-known Fourier transform takes a time domain signal and transforms (dualizes) it into a frequency domain signal, where convolution and frequency analysis are much more efficient. In the case of the LF transform, the dualization takes the form of a maximization:

$$f^*(k) = \max_{x \in \mathbb{R}^n} \{ \langle k, x \rangle - f(x) \} \tag{20.4}$$

The LF transform has an interesting geometric interpretation, which is unfortunately out of scope for this chapter. For more information, see Touchette 2005, which gives an excellent explanation of the LF transform. Here we will restrict ourselves to simply deriving the LF transform for the functions F_1 and F_2 by means of the definition given by Equation 20.4.

20.4.1.1 Legendre-Fenchel Transform of F_1

Substituting the definition of F_1 for f in Equation 20.4 results in:

$$p \in V: \quad F_1^*(p) = \max_{x \in V} \left\{ \langle p, x \rangle_V - \frac{1}{2} \langle x, x \rangle_V \right\} \tag{20.5}$$

The maximum occurs where the derivative w.r.t. x is 0:

$$\frac{\partial}{\partial x} \left(\langle p, x \rangle_V - \frac{1}{2} \langle x, x \rangle_V \right) = 0 \Rightarrow p - x = 0$$

So the maximum of F_1 is found where $x = p$. Substituting this back into Equation 20.5 gives:

$$F_1^*(p) = \frac{1}{2} \langle p, p \rangle_V$$

20.4.1.2 Legendre-Fenchel Transform of F_2

Substituting the definition of F_2 for f in Equation 20.4 gives:

$$q \in V: \quad F_2^*(q) = \max_{x \in V} \left\{ \langle q, x \rangle_V - \|x\|_{V,2} \right\} \tag{20.6}$$

The $\langle q,x\rangle_V$ term can be (loosely) seen as the geometric dot product of q and x. This is maximized when q and x are "geometrically coincident," that is, they are a scalar multiple of each other. When q and x are coincident, then by the definition of the dot product $\langle q,x\rangle_V = \|q\|_{V,2}\|x\|_{V,2}$ holds. Substituting this back into Equation 20.6 gives:

$$F_2^*(q) = \max_{x\in V}\left\{\|q\|_{V,2}\|x\|_{V,2} - \|x\|_{V,2}\right\}$$

This makes it obvious that when $\|q\|_{V,2}\leq 1$, the maximum that can be attained for Equation 20.6 is 0; otherwise when $\|q\|_{V,2} > 1$, the maximum goes to ∞. This is conveniently expressed as the indicator function of an additional set Q:

$$F_2^*(q) = I_Q(q), \quad Q = \left\{q\in V : \|q\|_{V,2}\leq 1\right\}$$

20.4.2 Proximity Operator

In the previous section, we derived the dual functions F_1^* and F_2^*. Before we can define the path smoothing algorithm, we also need to derive the so-called proximity operator for functions F_1^*, F_2^*, and G. The proximity operator bounds a function from below with a quadratic in order to smooth out discontinuities in the derivative. This ensures the optimization converges on the minimum without getting trapped in an oscillation around the minimum. See Figure 20.6 for a simple example where the solid line is the original function with a discontinuous derivative, and the dotted lines are quadratic relaxations of that function. The general definition of the proximity operator is given by the minimization:

$$prox_{f,\tau}(x) = \operatorname*{argmin}_{y\in\mathbb{R}^n}\left\{f(y) + \frac{1}{2\tau}\left(\|y-x\|_2\right)^2\right\} \tag{20.7}$$

where the parameter τ controls the amount of relaxation due to the quadratic.

20.4.2.1 Proximity Operator of F_1^*

Substituting F_1^* into Equation 20.7 gives:

$$p\in V: \quad prox_{F_1^*,\sigma}(p)_i = \operatorname*{argmin}_{y\in\mathbb{R}^2}\left\{\frac{\langle y,y\rangle}{2} + \frac{1}{2\sigma}\left(\|y-p_i\|_2\right)^2\right\}$$

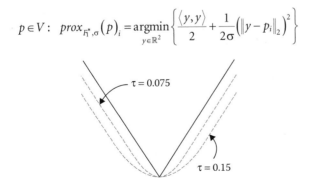

$\tau = 0.075$

$\tau = 0.15$

Figure 20.6

Quadratic relaxation.

Note that the proximity operator F_1^* is point-wise separable, meaning that it can be defined in terms of the individual elements p_i. The point-wise separation is possible due to the fact that the operations that depend on adjacent elements of v are encoded in matrix K, and as a consequence, there similarly is no mutual dependence between adjacent elements of p here. This simplifies the derivation of the proximity operator greatly. (In fact, without point-wise separation, the derivation of the proximity operator would not be feasible.) The minimum occurs where the derivative w.r.t. y is 0:

$$\frac{\partial}{\partial y}\left(\frac{\langle y, y \rangle}{2} - \frac{1}{2\sigma}\langle y - p_i, y - p_i \rangle\right) = 0 \Rightarrow y + \frac{y - p_i}{\sigma} = 0$$

Solving this equation for y results in:

$$p \in V: \quad prox_{F_1^*, \sigma}(p)_i = \frac{p_i}{1 + \sigma}$$

20.4.2.2 Proximity Operator of F_2^*

Substituting F_2^* into Equation 20.7 gives:

$$q \in V: \quad prox_{F_2^*, \mu}(q) = \underset{y \in V}{\mathrm{argmin}}\left\{I_Q(y) + \frac{1}{2\mu}\left(\|y - q\|_{V,2}\right)^2\right\}$$

The indicator function I_Q completely dominates the minimization—it is 0 when $y \in Q$, otherwise it is ∞ in which case the minimum does not exist. So to attain a minimum, y must be member of Q. Hence, the solution to the proximity operator for F_2^* consists of finding the nearest y to q that is also a member of Q (in convex optimization terms, this is called "projecting" y onto Q.) If y is in Q, this is simply y itself; otherwise y is divided by its L^2 norm, so it satisfies $\|q\|_{V,2} \le 1$. Thus:

$$q \in V: \quad prox_{F_2^*, \mu}(q) = \frac{q}{\max\left(1, \|q\|_{V,2}\right)}$$

20.4.2.3 Proximity Operator of G

Substituting G into Equation 20.7 gives:

$$v \in V: \quad prox_{G, \tau}(v) = \underset{y \in V}{\mathrm{arg\,min}}\left\{I_C(y) + \frac{1}{2\tau}\left(\|y - v\|_{V,2}\right)^2\right\}$$

Similar to the proximity operator of F_2^* above, here the indicator function I_C dominates the minimization, and so the solution consists of finding the nearest y that is in C. The problem is point-wise separable, and the solution is given as the point inside the maximal clearance disk with center c_i and radius r_i that is nearest to v_i:

$$v \in V: \quad prox_{G, \tau}(v)_i = c_i + (v_i - c_i)\frac{r_i}{\max\left(r_i, \|v_i - c_i\|_2\right)}$$

20.4.3 The Chambolle–Pock Primal-Dual Algorithm for Path Smoothing

The general preconditioned Chambolle–Pock algorithm consists of the following steps:

$$p^{k+1} = prox_{F^*,\Sigma}\left(p^k + \Sigma \cdot K \cdot \hat{v}^k\right)$$

$$v^{k+1} = prox_{G,T}\left(v^k - T \cdot K^T \cdot p^{k+1}\right) \tag{20.8}$$

$$\hat{v}^{k+1} = 2v^{k+1} - v^k$$

These are the calculations for a single iteration of the algorithm, where the superscripts k and $k+1$ refer to the value of the corresponding variable at the current iteration k and the next iteration $k+1$. The implementation of the algorithm repeats the steps (Equation 20.8) multiple times, with successive iterations bringing the values of the variables closer to the optimal solution. In practice, the algorithm runs for some predetermined, fixed number of iterations that brings the state of variable v sufficiently close to the optimal value. Prior to the first iteration $k=0$, the variables are initialized as $p^0 = q^0 = 0$ and $v^0 = \hat{v}^0 = c$. The diagonal matrices Σ and T are the step sizes for the algorithm, which are defined below.

The general algorithm (Equation 20.8) is adapted to the path smoothing problem by substituting the definitions given in the previous sections: the differencing operators $w\delta^s$ and δ^+ are substituted for K, P is substituted with the stacked variable $(p,q)^T$, and $prox_{F^*,\Sigma}$ is substituted with $prox_{F_1^*,\sigma}$ and $prox_{F_2^*,\mu}$. Then the final remaining use of matrix K is eliminated by expanding the product:

$$K^T \cdot \binom{p}{q}^{k+1} \Rightarrow w\delta^s\left(p^{k+1}\right) - \delta^-\left(q^{k+1}\right)$$

This results in the path smoothing algorithm:

$$p^{k+1} = prox_{F_1^*,\sigma}\left(p^k + \sigma w\delta^s\left(\hat{v}^k\right)\right)$$

$$q^{k+1} = prox_{F_2^*,\mu}\left(q^k + \mu\delta^+\left(\hat{v}^k\right)\right)$$

$$v^{k+1} = prox_{G,\tau}\left(v^k - \tau\left(w\delta^s\left(p^{k+1}\right) - \delta^-\left(q^{k+1}\right)\right)\right)$$

$$\hat{v}^{k+1} = 2v^{k+1} - v^k$$

By substituting K and K^T with their corresponding differencing operators, the step size matrices Σ and T are no longer applicable. Instead, the step sizes are now represented by the vectors $\sigma, \mu, \tau \in U$, which are the diagonal elements of matrices Σ and T. As proven in Pock and Chambolle 2011, deriving the step-size parameters σ, μ, τ as sums of the rows and columns of matrix K leads to a convergent algorithm:

$$\sigma_i = \frac{1}{\beta \sum_{j=1}^{2n} K_{1_{i,j}}{}^\alpha}, \quad \mu_i = \frac{1}{\beta \sum_{j=1}^{2n} K_{2_{i,j}}{}^\alpha}, \quad \tau_i = \frac{\beta}{\sum_{j=1}^{4n} K_{j,i}{}^{2-\alpha}}$$

Expanding the summation gives:

$$\sigma_i = \frac{h^\alpha}{\left(2+2^\alpha\right)\beta\,w_i^{\,\alpha}}, \quad \mu_i = \frac{h^\alpha}{2\beta}, \quad \tau_i = \frac{\beta\,h^{2-\alpha}}{2+w_{i-1}^{\,2-\alpha}+\left(2w_i\right)^{2-\alpha}+w_{i+1}^{\,2-\alpha}} \tag{20.9}$$

(Note that μ_i is a constant for all i.) The scalar constants $0<\alpha<2$ and $\beta>0$ balance the step sizes to either larger values for σ,μ or larger values for τ. This causes the algorithm to make correspondingly larger steps in either variable p,q or variable v on each iteration, which affects the overall rate of convergence of the algorithm. Well-chosen values for α,β are critical to ensure an optimal rate of convergence. Unfortunately, optimal values for these constants depend on the particular waypoint weights used and the average waypoint separation distance h, so no general best value can be given, and they need to be found by experimentation. Note that the Equations 20.9 are valid only for $2<i<n-1$, that is, they omit the special cases for the step size at $i=1$ and $i=n$. They are omitted because in practice, the algorithm only needs to calculate elements $2<i<n-1$ for p, q, v and $\hat{v}$ on each iteration. This is a consequence of extending the path at either end with two dummy additional waypoints for the agent facing direction. Since these additional waypoints are assigned a zero radius clearance disk, their position remains fixed on each iteration. Their contribution to the path energy is therefore constant and does not need to be calculated. Restricting the algorithm implementation to elements $2<i<n-1$ eliminates all special cases for the boundary conditions of operator δ^s, δ^+, δ^-, and the step sizes.

The leftside of Figure 20.7 shows the state of the path as it evolves over 100 iterations of the algorithm. Empirically, the state rapidly converges to a smooth path after only a few initial iterations. Subsequent iterations then pull the waypoints closer together and impose a uniform distribution of waypoints over the length of the path. The rightside of Figure 20.7 is a plot of the value of the energy function (Equation 20.1) at each iteration, which shows that the energy decreases (however not necessarily monotonically) on successive iterations.

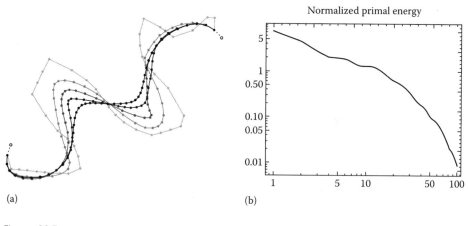

(a) (b)

Figure 20.7

(a) Path evolution and (b) energy plot.

20.5 Conclusion

In this chapter, we have given a detailed description of an algorithm for path smoothing using iterative minimization. As can be seen from the source code provided with this chapter on the book's website (http://www.gameaipro.com), the implementation only requires a few lines of C++ code. The computation at each iteration consists of simple linear operations, making the method very efficient overall. Moreover, since information exchange for neighboring waypoints only occurs after each iteration, the algorithm inner loops that update the primal and dual variables are essentially entirely data parallel, which makes the algorithm ideally suited to a GPGPU implementation.

Finally, note that this chapter describes just one particular application of the Chambolle–Pock algorithm. However, the algorithm itself is very general and can be adapted to solve a wide variety of optimization problems. The main hurdle in adapting it to new applications is deriving a suitable model, along with its associated Legendre–Fenchel transform(s) and proximity operators. Depending on the problem, this may be more or less challenging. However, once a suitable model is found, the resulting code is invariably simple and efficient.

References

Chambolle, A. and T. Pock. 2011. A first-order primal-dual algorithm for convex problems with applications to imaging. *Journal of Mathematical Imaging and Vision*, 40(1), 120–145.

Geraerts, R. and M. Overmars. 2007. The corridor map method: A general framework for real-time high-quality path planning. *Computer Animation and Virtual Worlds*, 18, 107–119.

Pock, T. and A. Chambolle. 2011. Diagonal preconditioning for first order primal-dual algorithms in convex optimization. *IEEE International Conference on Computer Vision (ICCV)*, Washington, DC, pp. 1762–1769.

Touchette, H. 2005. Legendre-Fenchel transforms in a nutshell. School of Mathematical Sciences, Queen Mary, University of London. http://www.physics.sun.ac.za/~htouchette/archive/notes/lfth2.pdf (accessed May 26, 2016).

21

3D Flight Navigation Using Sparse Voxel Octrees

Daniel Brewer

21.1 Introduction

Navigating two-dimensional spaces is something we are quite familiar with in the game AI field. Regular grids, corridor maps, and navigation meshes (navmeshes) are all very well known and documented problem spaces. However, navigating in full three-dimensional environments where the agents are not constrained to the ground is quite a challenging problem space and is compounded when having to deal with very large, sparsely populated volumes that have clusters of dense, complex regions.

A Sparse Voxel Octree (SVO) is a spatial structure used in graphics rendering, particularly ray-tracing. This structure is optimized for handling large, sparsely populated regions. This chapter will cover how we adapted SVOs for use in 3D flight navigation in *Warframe*, discuss modifications to the A* search algorithm to work on this adaptive grid representation and go into the details of tuning the heuristic to speed up the search by sacrificing optimality.

21.2 Alternative Techniques

Before covering how to use SVOs to represent flight navigation, we will briefly cover a few other alternatives.

A simple approach is to use a connected waypoint graph. Bounding volumes of free space can be manually placed by the level designer. Clear paths between volumes can be marked up as connections in the graph. These annotations work well in small areas or to simply provide occasional extra flight shortcuts above normal ground navigation. But, waypoint graphs in 3D have the same problems as in 2D space. There are a limited number of connections between volumes, which results in unnatural flight-paths as agents deviate to go back to a specific connection. Another limitation of this approach is that the graphs are typically made by hand and are therefore static and cannot easily adapt to changes in the level.

Alternatively, it is possible to extend navmeshes to be used for flight path planning. A series of navmeshes can be created at various heights above the ground. Special flight-links can be used to connect these meshes to allow flying avatars to path up or down through the multiple layers of NavMesh. This technique can work well in confined spaces such as indoors or for creatures restricted to hovering near the ground. In very large volumes, such as a 2 km by 2 km by 2 km cube in an asteroid field, it becomes impossible to decide how many layers of NavMesh will be required to cover the volume adequately.

Regular grids are another option, though the sheer size of the search space is a major drawback. A 3D regular grid covering the aforementioned 2 km cube at 2 m resolution would require a billion grid locations!

Given the issues mentioned with each approach, an adaptive representation of the volume is required. More detail is needed in the dense, cluttered regions and wide the open regions should occupy as little memory as possible. Ideally, this representation can be constructed quickly and dynamically at runtime in order to handle dynamic levels where the collision geometry is not known ahead of time.

21.3 Sparse Voxel Octrees

SVOs are a popular graphics structure used for lighting and ray-tracing. Since they are essentially an octree, they facilitate fast position lookups, as you hierarchically split the volume into eight partitions at each level of the tree. The data structure contains neighbor connectivity information instead of just parent–child links to speed up traversal through the tree for ray-tracing. We can repurpose this connectivity information for path planning. There are several techniques for constructing SVOs, some of which boast interactive frame-rate performance by optimizing and parallelizing the construction algorithm (Schwarz and Seidel 2010). These optimizations are beyond the scope of this chapter, however you can refer to their paper for further information.

One big difference between a typical octree data structure and an SVO is the way the data are stored in memory. In an SVO, the data for each level of the tree are usually compacted together and stored in Morton Code order in memory. The Morton order is a z-shaped space-filling curve that maps three-dimensional coordinates into a one-dimensional sequence (Morton 1966, Haverkort and Freek van Walderveen 2008). It does this by interleaving the bits from each coordinate. For instance, the 2D x/y coordinate (0,3) is represented in binary as (00,11) and encoded as 1010. This method has the advantageous property of keeping neighbors within a quadtree or octree locally coherent. Figure 21.1 shows how Morton Codes fill 2D and 3D space. Storing the nodes in Morton order flattens the entire three-dimensional octree into a linear, one-dimensional array.

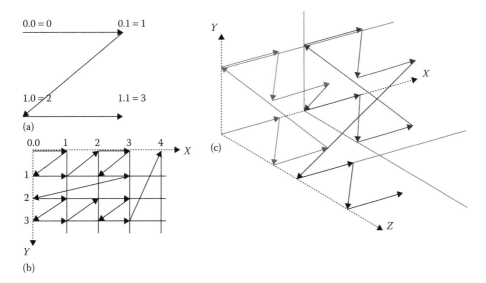

Figure 21.1

Diagrams showing 2D Morton Order (a, b). Note how the two-dimensional coordinates are mapped onto a single-dimensional sequence, shown by the line with arrows. 3D coordinates are mapped onto a single-dimensional sequence of Morton Codes in a similar fashion (c).

Figure 21.2 provides a high-level illustration of how the data in the SVO are arranged. Nodes from each level of the octree are stored in their own array, shown in the upper right of the figure, and the leaf nodes are stored in a separate array of 64-bit values. Following are the details of what is stored each node, and how the leaf nodes differ from other nodes in the SVO.

Each node in the tree requires a position so we know where it is in space. It also needs a link to its lower resolution parent node and a link to the first, higher resolution, child node. All nodes, except leaf nodes, will always have eight children. Since these children are stored contiguously in Morton Code order, we only need a link to the first child, and we can simply offset 0–7 to go to individual child nodes. Additionally, to help in traversal through the tree, each node contains six links to its neighbors through each of its faces.

Leaf nodes are handled differently. Since we are only concerned with collision or free space, our voxel data require only a single bit to store its state. The overhead of storing links with each voxel would be too costly. We can however use a small, compact $4 \times 4 \times 4$ voxel grid for each leaf; this fits nicely into 64 bits.

When dealing with massive environments, every bit of memory is important. Using pointers for links will mean that the data size will vary drastically between 32 bit and 64 bit operating systems. In order to control memory usage, offsets into arrays are used for the links instead of pointers. Links are a general purpose way of referencing both an arbitrary node in the octree and an arbitrary voxel. They are used both within the octree and in the A* search. So, links need to be able to go up and down layers of the octree, not only between neighbors on the same layer. Additionally, the voxels in our leaf nodes are really

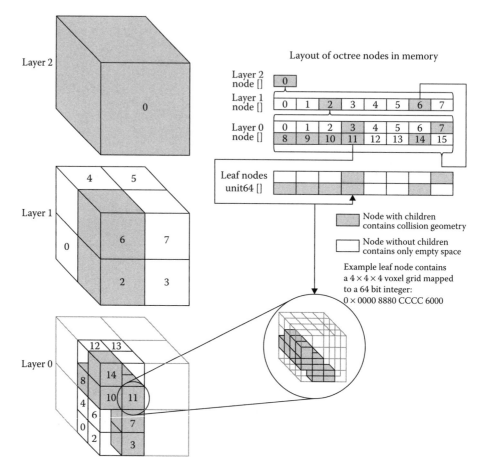

Figure 21.2

Simple illustration of the arrangement of the nodes in a Sparse Voxel Octree. Each occupied node in a layer has eight children in the layer below it. The bottom-most layer maps directly onto the leaf node array. The leaf nodes, however, are not Octree nodes but simply a 64-bit integer representing a 4 × 4 × 4 voxel grid.

compound nodes representing 64 different locations, which we call subnodes. We pack our links into 32 bit integers as follows:

> 4 bits—layer index 0 to 15
> 22 bits—node index 0 to 4,194,303
> 6 bit—subnode index 0 to 63 (only used for indexing voxels inside leaf nodes)

21.4 Creating the SVO

We based our construction of the SVO on the article mentioned in the previous section (Schwarz and Seidel 2010). The tree is constructed from the bottom up, one layer at a time. This is different from the typical octree construction that splits parent nodes from the top down until arriving at the desired resolution of the child node. Doing it one layer at a time keeps each layer coherent in memory and also allows for parallelization to speed up the construction.

The first step is to determine how many leaf nodes are required. To do this, rasterize the collision geometry at a low resolution. If the final resolution is 2 m per voxel, then the leaf nodes in the SVO will be $4 \times 2 = 8$ m cubes. The parent of a leaf node will always have to be split; this means having two leaf nodes next to each other in each direction. The low-resolution rasterization can therefore be performed at a 16 m resolution, which is effectively layer 1 in the octree, where the leaves are in layer 0. Instead of rasterizing into a voxel grid, we simply keep a sorted list of unique Morton Codes of the solid voxels.

Once complete, the number of leaf nodes required can be calculated by counting the number of unique Morton Codes from the low resolution (layer 1) rasterize step. Eight leaf nodes (at layer 0) are required for each Morton Code. Their 3D coordinates can be calculated from the Morton Codes, and the memory for the nodes can be allocated and initialized in a single contiguous block.

The octree structure can now be built up from the lowest to the highest level. Bitwise operations can be used to modify nodes at the current level to get the Morton Code for the parent level. The parent–child links between layers are filled in on the way up; afterward the neighbor links are filled in while traversing back down.

If a node has no neighbor at the same level, then the neighbor link is set to that node's higher level parent's neighbor. This ensures that each node always has a link to a neighbor through each of its faces. Figure 21.3 illustrates how the neighbor links are set up.

Finally, rasterization is performed at the desired resolution into the leaf nodes. Note that unlike a traditional octree, the term leaf node only refers to the occupied, highest resolution nodes in the octree, that is, layer 0 nodes. The SVO only requires leaf nodes where collision geometry exists. A higher layer node that does not contain any collision geometry will not have any child nodes. These nodes are referred to as childless nodes

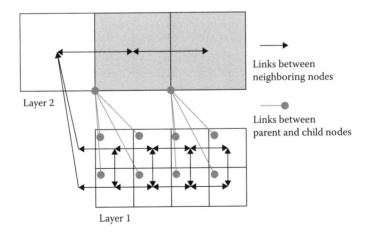

Links between neighboring nodes

Links between parent and child nodes

Figure 21.3

Neighbor links in the Sparse Voxel Octree connect to neighbors of the same layer, and if there is no neighbor in the same layer, the neighbor links point to the parent's neighbor.

instead of leaf nodes in traditional octrees. Taking the example SVO in Figure 21.2, node 0 in layer 1 is a childless node and contains only empty space and can be freely traversed. Node 6 in layer 1 however, does have children: layer 0, nodes 8–15. Most leaf nodes, such as node 11 in layer 0, will be partially blocked and have some solid and some empty voxels.

Some leaf nodes will be completely free of collision geometry, such as node 0 in layer 0. The data payload for a leaf is only a 64-bit integer, and an empty leaf will contain the value 0. These nodes can be considered padding for memory alignment. The speed advantage of not culling them outweighs the small additional memory cost. As explained below, during pathfinding, any leaf node with a value of 0 can be skipped over, as it is open space, and any node with a value of −1, or 0xFFFFFFFFFFFFFFFF, will be fully blocked and need not be explored.

21.5 Pathfinding through a SVO

The SVO is now a connected graph representing the free space that agents can traverse. A graph search algorithm can be used to find paths through this space. We initially chose to implement the standard A* search.

The first step is to look up the locations of the start and end points for the desired path and push the start node onto the open list. Next, pop the best node off the open list and mark it as visited. Expand this node by getting the neighboring nodes, scoring them with the A* f-cost, distance traveled plus the estimate of the distance to goal, and then push them onto the open list. This continues until the end point is reached.

Looking up positions is the same in an SVO as in a standard octree. Start at the top of the tree and test whether the point is inside the axis-aligned box of each child. Once the child containing the point has been identified, we repeat the test one layer deeper down the octree. Since octrees subdivide the volume by eight at each layer of the tree, this procedure is very fast. If we arrive at a childless node, then the point is inside a large volume of empty space. If we arrive at a leaf node, then we can calculate which voxel within the leaf contains the point. We refer to this as the subnode index, and it ranges from 0 to 63 as it indexes a specific bit in the 64-bit voxel grid. In either case, a link can be used to represent this location.

To explore nodes in the SVO graph, we simply consult the neighbor links. Referring back to Figure 21.2, layer 1 node 4 has neighbor links to layer 1 node 0, layer 1 node 5, and layer 1 node 6. It is not a problem if a node has a link to a higher level node (e.g., layer 1 linking to layer 2), as this means the search is moving into a larger open space. The search can freely jump between layers of the SVO as necessary.

A minor complication comes when moving from a low-resolution level to a neighbor that has higher resolution children, such as going from layer 1 node 4 to layer 1 node 6 in Figure 21.2. This is solved by pushing the low-resolution node (i.e., layer 1 node 6) to the open list when first encountered. When this node is popped off, instead of processing it as normal, we find the higher resolution children that are neighbors of the previous node and score and push those onto the open list. In our Figure 21.2 example, these new nodes would be layer 0 nodes 8, 9, 12, and 13. The search loop then proceeds as normal. Figure 21.4 shows a 2D example of the order of exploration of nodes jumping from higher level layers through lower level nodes and back up to higher level nodes again.

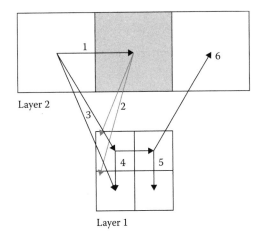

Figure 21.4

Node expansion during A* search. To expand a node that has higher resolution children, add the children neighboring the previous node to the open list and expand each of them in turn through the usual search loop.

Another complication to the search arises when we reach a leaf node. The voxel grid representing each leaf is a 64-bit integer. If this value is 0, it means the leaf node is a empty space, and it is treated like any other node in the tree. If the value is 0xFFFFFFFFFFFFFFFF, or −1, it means the leaf is entirely solid and will block all movement. This node is then marked closed, and the search will continue through the rest of the open nodes. Any other value means the leaf node contains some open space and some solid collision.

Each voxel can be treated as a separate node in the search graph. However, there are no explicit links in these tiny $4 \times 4 \times 4$ voxel grids. Neighbors are calculated implicitly between voxels based on the 3D coordinates within the voxel grid. To avoid confusion between voxels and octree nodes, voxels inside leaf nodes are referred to by the subnode index, which is simply the 6-bit index into the 64-bit integer representing the voxel in the $4 \times 4 \times 4$ grid. Once we reach edge of the tiny voxel grid, the search continues to the neighbor of the leaf node containing the grid.

21.6 Complications and Optimizations

It is easy to forget how big the 3D search space can get. Adding visualizations and statistics to the search will show how much space A* is actually searching. The results can be significantly larger than anticipated (Brewer 2015). The adaptive grid nature of the octree certainly helps the search jump over large tracts of open space. However, the plain A* search is designed to find the optimal path and will often get bogged down exploring all the tiny nodes in the densely populated regions instead of circling around them through larger nodes. Figure 21.5 shows a simple form of this "leap-ahead-and-back-fill" problem.

It is possible to tweak the distances by using center of faces of the cubes instead of node centers and to use Manhattan distance instead of Euclidian distance. This tends to

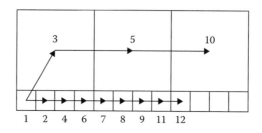

Figure 21.5

Vanilla A* search does not take advantage of exploring larger nodes and instead goes back to explore all the small nodes on a more direct route to the goal.

only help in simple cases and does not provide as much benefit in more complex maps. It is important to experiment on your own maps to see which is better for your specific situation.

Another optimization is to bias the A* toward a greedier search by weighting the score more toward the estimation than the distance traveled. This is not an uncommon A* optimization in games (Rabin and Sturtevant 2013) and adjusts the search to prefer exploring nodes it thinks are closer to the goal. This greedy approach does help significantly, however the search can still push through lots of tiny nodes instead of taking advantage of the larger, open ones.

The heuristic can further be adjusted with a node size compensation factor. In this approach, both the cost and estimation values are adjusted depending on the size of the node. Different compensation amounts are used for each component. The goal is to make it cheaper to go through large nodes and more expensive to go through small ones. This helps dramatically, but one final adjustment is to use a unit cost for distance traveled instead of Euclidian distance. This means that no matter how big the node is, traveling through it has the same cost. This effectively biases the search even more toward exploring through large nodes.

Using a greedy search and node size compensation are always at least an order of magnitude better than straight A* and using unit node costs helps the search use the larger nodes and more often than not, gets an extra order of magnitude speed boost. The resulting path is not an optimal path. Agents will prefer to stay to open-space regions and will tend to avoid dense clusters of collision geometry, unless it is necessary to navigate into them.

The next problem that still hurts the optimized heuristic is an expected A* issue that gets exacerbated in 3D. This is the wave-front exploration pattern as A* tries to search around an obstacle. In 2D, when A* hits a line obstacle, it spreads out to either side in order to try find a way around. In 3D when the search hits an obstacle, it has to explore up and down as well as left and right. This can result in an expanding cone of explored nodes, spreading out behind the surface until a way around is found.

JPS (Harabor and Grastien 2011) is one approach to overcome the A* wave-front expansion shortfall. It should be possible to extend our 3D search in the same way. We attempted this approach and found a great reduction in the number of nodes expanded during the search, however the time taken for the search was actually an order of magnitude slower than the tweaked heuristic A*. Our initial implementation of 3D JPS was admittedly quite naive and unoptimized, however JPS still visits a lot of nodes in 2D while finding the jump points, and in 3D, this becomes an $O(n^3)$ flood fill instead of $O(n^2)$. This optimization was not pursued further, though a form of jump point expansion may prove to be a useful optimization. Caution must be taken to ensure that it does in fact improve performance instead of hindering it. See (Sturtevant and Rabin 2016) for more discussion of these issues.

Another obvious optimization would be to use a hierarchical search. Since we already have a hierarchical graph structure, this does seem like an obvious choice. This approach would find a path at the lowest resolution and then refine the higher detail levels until a suitably detailed path has been found. However, doing this would require the search to know whether it can traverse from each face to every other face of each node at every level of the tree. Care needs to be taken, so this extra information does not end up bloating memory usage substantially. This is still an option worthy of future exploration, as it may substantially help the search performance.

21.7 Conclusion

As video game environments become more complex and detailed, players are becoming more demanding of new gameplay experiences. Using octrees for 3D navigation is not a particularly novel idea, however if you have never faced this problem, it can be a daunting problem space with many unforeseen traps. The advice provided in this chapter should provide you with a good starting direction.

If you do not take anything else away from this chapter, be sure to add visualizations and statistical reports to your algorithms to fully understand how they are functioning and ensure they are functioning as intended.

References

Brewer, D. 2015. Getting off the NavMesh: Navigating in Fully 3D Environments. GDC 2015. San Francisco, CA: AAAI Press. Slides http://www.gdcvault.com/play/1022017/Getting-off-the-NavMesh-Navigating, Video http://www.gdcvault.com/play/1022016/Getting-off-the-NavMesh-Navigating.

Harabor, D., and Grastien, A. 2011. Online graph pruning for pathfinding on grid maps. In *Proceedings of the 25th National Conference on Artificial Intelligence (AAAI)*. San Francisco, CA. https://users.cecs.anu.edu.au/~dharabor/data/papers/harabor-grastien-aaai11.pdf.

Haverkort, H., and van Walderveen, F. 2008. Space-filling curves for spatial data structures. TU Eindhoven. http://http://www.win.tue.nl/~hermanh/stack/dagstuhl08-talk.pdf.

Morton, G. M. 1966. *A Computer Oriented Geodetic Data Base and a New Technique in File Sequencing. Technical Report*. Ottawa, Canada: IBM Ltd.

Rabin, S., and Sturtevant, N. R. 2013. Pathfinding architecture optimizations. In *Game AI Pro*, ed. S. Rabin. Boca Raton, FL: CRC Press, pp. 241–252. http://www.gameaipro.com/GameAIPro/GameAIPro_Chapter17_Pathfinding_Architecture_Optimizations.pdf.

Schwarz, M., and Seidel, H. P. 2010. Fast Parallel Surface and Solid Voxelization on GPUs. *ACM Transactions on Graphics, 29, 6 (Proceedings of SIGGRAPH Asia 2010), Article 179*. New York, NY: ACM. http://research.michael-schwarz.com/publ/files/vox-siga10.pdf.

Sturtevant, N. R., and Rabin, S. 2016. Canonical orderings on grids. In *International Joint Conference on Artificial Intelligence*. New York: IJCAI, pp. 683–689. http://web.cs.du.edu/~sturtevant/papers/SturtevantRabin16.pdf.

Faster A* with Goal Bounding

Steve Rabin and Nathan R. Sturtevant

22.1 Introduction

Goal bounding is a pathfinding optimization technique that can speed up A* by roughly eight times on a grid (Rabin and Sturtevant 2016), however, it is applicable to any graph search space, including waypoint graphs or navmeshes (navigation meshes). Goal bounding is not a search algorithm itself, but rather a method to *prune* the search space, thus radically reducing the number of nodes that need to be considered to find the goal. This is accomplished by preprocessing the search space offline and using the precomputed data to avoid exploring many nodes that do not lead to the goal.

This chapter will introduce the goal-bounding concept, walk through the runtime code, and then show the necessary preprocessing steps. We will then discuss experimental data that shows the effective speed-up to a standard A* implementation.

22.1.1 Goal-Bounding Constraints

Goal bounding has three constraints that limit whether it is appropriate to use in your game:

1. *Map constraint:* The map must be static and cannot change during gameplay. Nodes and edges cannot be added or deleted.

2. *Memory constraint:* For each node in the map, there is a requirement of four values per node edge in memory during runtime. Grid nodes have eight edges, and navmesh nodes have three edges. Typically, each value is 2 bytes.
3. *Precomputation constraint:* The precomputation is $O(n^2)$ in the number of nodes. This is a costly computation and can take from 5 minutes to several hours per map. This is performed offline before the game ships.

The most important constraint is that your game maps must be static. That is to say that the nodes and edges in your search space must not change during gameplay, and the cost to go from one node to another must also not change. The reason is that connection data must be precomputed. Changing a single node, edge, or cost would invalidate all of the precomputed data. Because the precomputed data takes so long to create, it is not feasible to dynamically rerun the computation if the map changes.

The other primary constraint is that goal bounding requires extra memory at runtime for the precomputed data. For every node, there has to be four values per edge leading to another node. On a grid, each node has eight edges (or connections) to other nodes, so the necessary data for a grid search space are 32 values per node. On a navmesh, typically each poly node has three edges, so the necessary data for a navmesh search space are 12 values per poly node. Typically, these values will need to be 2 bytes each, but for smaller maps, 1 byte each might suffice (e.g., a grid map with a height and width less than 256).

Lastly, a minor constraint is that each map must be precomputed offline, which takes time. The precomputation algorithm is $O(n^2)$ in the number of total nodes on the map. For example, a very large 1000×1000 grid map would have 1 million nodes, requiring $1,000,000^2$ or 1 trillion operations during precomputation for that map. Depending on the map size, this can take between 5 minutes and several hours per map. It is computationally demanding enough that you could not precompute the data at runtime. However, there are optimizations to Dijkstra for uniform cost grids, such as Canonical Dijkstra that can make this computation much faster (Sturtevant and Rabin 2017).

Fortunately, there are many things that are not constraints for goal bounding. For example, the following aspects are very flexible:

1. Goal-bounding works on *any* graph search space, including grids, waypoint graphs, quadtrees, octrees, and navmeshes, as long as the points in these graphs are associated with coordinates in space.
2. Goal bounding can be applied to *any* search algorithm (A*, Dijkstra, JPS+, etc.). Typically, A* is best for games, but goal bounding can work with Dijkstra and works extremely well with JPS+ (a variant of A* only for uniform cost grids).
3. The map can have nonuniform costs between nodes, meaning the cost to go from one node to another node can vary as long as it does not change during the game. Some algorithms like JPS+ have restrictions such that they only work on uniform cost grids, where the cost between grid squares must be consistent.

22.2 Concept

The name *goal bounding* comes from the core concept. For each edge adjacent to a node, we precompute a bounding box (4 values) that contains all goals that can be optimally reached by exploring this edge. At runtime, we only explore this node's edge if the goal of the search lies in the bounding box. Reread those last two sentences again, because this is the entire runtime algorithm.

In Figure 22.1, consider the node marked with a circle. The gray nodes in the left map can all be reached *optimally* by exploring the left edge of the circle node (we will discuss later how this is computed). The gray *bounding box* in the right map contains all of the gray nodes from the left map and represents what needs to be precomputed (4 values that define a bounding box: left, right, top, and bottom). This precomputed bounding box is stored in the left edge of the circle node. At runtime, if we are at the circle node and considering exploring the left edge, we would check to see if the goal lies in the bounding box. If it does, we explore this edge as is normally done in the A* algorithm. If the goal does not lie in the bounding box, we skip this edge (the edge is pruned from the search).

Goal bounding can be similarly applied to navmeshes. Consider the black node in the navmesh in Figure 22.2. The dark gray nodes can be reached optimally through the bottom right edge of the black node. Figure 22.3 shows a bounding box around these nodes. This is the identical concept as shown on the grid in Figure 22.1.

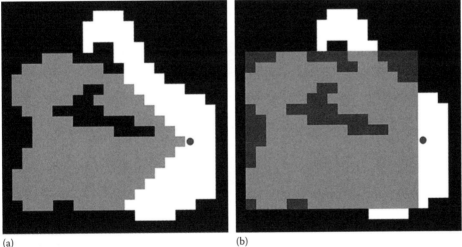

(a)   (b)

Figure 22.1

The map in (a) shows all of the nodes (in gray) that can be reached optimally by exploring the left edge of the circle node. The map in (b) shows a bounding box of the nodes in the left image. This bounding box is stored in the left edge of the circle node.

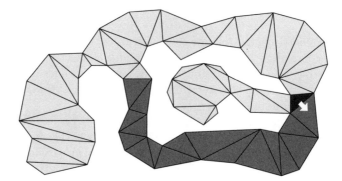

Figure 22.2

Nodes marked in dark gray can be reached optimally from exploring the bottom right edge of the black node. All other nodes in the map can only be reached optimally by exploring either the top edge or the left edge of the black node.

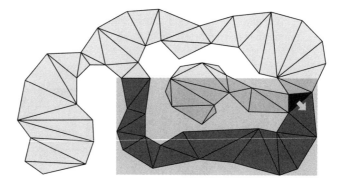

Figure 22.3

The bounding box containing all nodes that can be reached optimally from the bottom right edge of the black node. In goal bounding, this bounding box is stored in the bottom right edge of the black node.

22.3 Runtime

For A* with goal bounding to work, it is assumed that every node edge has a precomputed bounding box containing all nodes that can be reached optimally through that edge. With this data, the only addition to the runtime is a simple check, as shown in bold in Listing 22.1.

The goal-bounding check in Listing 22.1 tests whether we really want to explore a neighboring node, through the parent node's edge. If the check succeeds (the goal of the search is within the bounding box), then the search algorithm proceeds as normal through this edge. If the check fails, the edge is *pruned* by simply skipping it. This has the dramatic effect of not exploring that edge *and all of the subsequent edges*, thus pruning huge swaths of the search space. This accounts for goal bounding's dramatic speed improvement

Listing 22.1. A* algorithm with the goal bounding check added (in bold).

```
procedure AStarSearch(start, goal)
{
    Push (start, openlist)
    while (openlist is not empty)
    {
        n = PopLowestCost(openlist)

        if (n is goal)
            return success

        foreach (neighbor d in n)
        {
            if (WithinBoundingBox(n, d, goal))
            {
                // Process d in the standard A* manner
            }
        }

        Push (n, closedlist)
    }
    return failure
}
```

(Rabin and Sturtevant 2016). Note that this goal-bounding check can be inserted into any search algorithm at the point the algorithm is considering a neighboring node.

22.4 Precomputation

Precomputation consists of computing a bounding box for every edge of every node. If we can design an algorithm that computes this information for a single node, then it is just a matter of iterating that algorithm over every node in the map. In fact, the problem is *embarrassingly parallel* in which we can kick off one thread per node in the map, since each node's bounding boxes are independent of all other node's bounding boxes. With enough cores running the threads, the precomputation time can be greatly minimized.

To compute the bounding boxes for all edges of a single node, we need to use a slightly enhanced Dijkstra search algorithm. Recall that Dijkstra is the same as A*, but the heuristic cost is zero. This causes the search to spread out evenly, in cost, away from the starting point. For our purposes, we will start the Dijkstra search at our single node and give it no destination, causing it to search all nodes in the map, as if it was performing a floodfill.

Using Dijkstra to floodfill, the map has the effect of marking every node with the *optimal* "next step" to optimally get back to the start node. This next step is simply the parent pointer that is recorded during the search. However, the crucial piece of information that we really want to know for a given node is not the next step to take, but which starting node edge was required to eventually get to that node. Think of every node in the map as being marked with the starting node's edge that is on the optimal path back to the starting node, as shown in Figure 22.4.

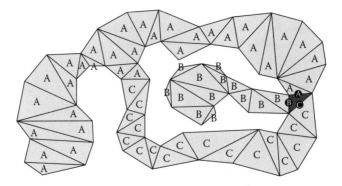

Figure 22.4

The result of a Dijkstra floodfill starting from the black node. Each node during the Dijkstra search is marked with the starting edge on the optimal path back to the starting node.

In a Dijkstra search, this starting node edge is normally not recorded, but now we need to store this information. Every node's data structure needs to contain a new value representing this starting node edge. During the Dijkstra search, when the neighbors of a node are explored, the starting node edge is passed down to the neighboring nodes as they are placed on the open list. This transfers the starting node edge information from node to node during the search.

Once the Dijkstra floodfill has completed, every node is marked with a starting node edge. In the case of Figure 22.4, each node is marked with either an A, B, or C. The final task is to iterate through all nodes in the map and build up the bounding boxes that contain each starting node edge, as shown in Figure 22.5. Once complete, each bounding box (4 values representing left, right, top, and bottom) is stored on the appropriate starting node's edge. This is the data that are used during runtime to prune the search during the goal-bounding check.

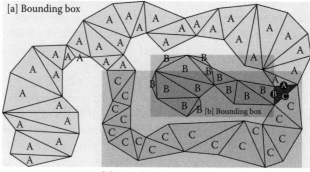

Figure 22.5

All nodes are iterated through to determine each bounding box for each starting edge.

22. Faster A* with Goal Bounding

22.5 Empirical Results

In order to evaluate the effectiveness of goal bounding, we applied the algorithm to a similar setup as the Grid-Based Path Planning Competition (Sturtevant 2014), a competition that has run since 2012 for the purpose of comparing different approaches to grid-based path planning. All experiments were performed on maps from the GPPC competition and the Moving AI map repository (Sturtevant 2012). This includes maps from *StarCraft*, *Warcraft III*, and *Dragon Age*. We ran our code on a 2.4 GHz Intel Xeon E5620 with 12 GB of RAM.

Table 22.1 shows the comparison between a highly optimized A* solution, the same A* solution with goal bounding, JPS+, and JPS+ with goal bounding. The A* solution with goal bounding was 8.2 times faster than A* by itself. The JPS+ solution with goal bounding was 7.2 times faster than JPS+.

22.5.1 Applying Goal Bounding to JPS+

As shown in Table 22.1, JPS+ is an algorithm that can dramatically speed up pathfinding compared with A*, however it only works on uniform cost grids (where the cost between nodes must be consistent). JPS+ is a variant of A* that achieves its speed from pruning nodes from the search space, similar to goal bounding. However, JPS+ and goal bounding work in complementary ways so that combined effect is to speed up pathfinding by ~1500 times over A*. Although it is outside the scope of this chapter to explain JPS+ with goal bounding, there are two good resources if you wish to implement it (Rabin 2015, Rabin and Sturtevant 2016).

22.6 Similarities to Previous Algorithms

At its core, goal bounding is an *approximation* of the Floyd–Warshall all-pairs shortest paths algorithm. In Floyd–Warshall, the path between every single pair of nodes is precomputed and stored in a look-up table. Using Floyd–Warshall at runtime, no search algorithm is run, because the optimal path is simply looked up. This requires an enormous amount of data, which is $O(n^2)$ in the number of nodes. This amount of data is impractical for most games. For example, a *StarCraft* map of roughly 1000×1000 nodes would require about four terabytes.

As goal bounding is an approximation of Floyd–Warshall, it does not require nearly as much data. However, as mentioned previously in Section 22.1.1, it does require 32 values per node on a grid search space and 12 values per node on a navmesh search space (assuming triangular nodes). A *StarCraft* map of roughly 1000×1000 nodes would

Table 22.1 Comparison of Search Algorithm Speeds

Algorithm	Time (ms)	A* Factor
A*	15.492	1.0
A* with goal bounding	1.888	8.2
JPS+	0.072	215.2
JPS+ with goal bounding	0.010	1549.2

require about 60 MB of goal bounding data. Luckily, modern games using a navmesh might only have about 4000 total nodes for a level, which would require less than 100 KB of goal-bounding data.

The goal-bounding algorithm was first introduced as an optimization to Dijkstra on road networks in 2005 and at the time was called geometric containers (Wagner et al. 2005). In 2014, Rabin independently reinvented geometric containers for use with A* and JPS+, introducing it as goal bounding to a GDC audience (Rabin 2015). Due to this history, it would be appropriate to refer to the algorithm as either geometric containers (Wagner et al. 2005), goal bounding (Rabin 2015), or simply as bounding boxes (Rabin and Sturtevant 2016).

22.7 Conclusion

For games that meet the constraints, goal bounding can speed up pathfinding dramatically—by nearly an order of magnitude. Not only can goal bounding be applied to any search algorithm on any type of search space, it can also be applied with other optimizations, such as hierarchical pathfinding, overestimating the heuristic, or open list optimizations (Rabin and Sturtevant 2013).

References

Rabin, S. 2015. JPS+ now with Goal Bounding: Over 1000 × Faster than A*, GDC 2015. http://www.gameaipro.com/Rabin_AISummitGDC2015_JPSPlusGoalBounding.zip (accessed February 12, 2017).

Rabin, S., and Sturtevant, N. R. 2013. Pathfinding optimizations. In *Game AI Pro*, ed. S. Rabin. Boca Raton, FL: CRC Press.

Rabin, S., and Sturtevant, N. R. 2016. Combining Bounding Boxes and JPS to Prune Grid Pathfinding, *AAAI'16 Proceedings of the Thirtieth AAAI Conference on Artificial Intelligence*. Phoenix, AZ: AAAI.

Sturtevant, N. R. 2012. Benchmarks for grid-based pathfinding. *Transactions on Computational Intelligence and AI in Games*, 4(2), 144–148.

Sturtevant, N. R. 2014. The grid-based path-planning competition. *AI Magazine*, 35(3), 66–68.

Sturtevant, N. R., and Rabin, S. 2017. Faster Dijkstra search on uniform cost grids. In *Game AI Pro 3*, ed. S. Rabin. Boca Raton, FL: CRC Press.

Wagner, D., Willhalm, T., and Zaroliagis, C. D. 2005. Geometric containers for efficient shortest-path computation. *ACM Journal of Experimental Algorithmics*, 10.

Faster Dijkstra Search on Uniform Cost Grids

Nathan R. Sturtevant and Steve Rabin

23.1 Introduction

Dijkstra search is commonly used for single-source shortest path computations, which can provide valuable information about distances between states for many purposes in games, such as heuristics (Rabin and Sturtevant 2013), influence maps, or other analysis. In this chapter, we describe how we borrowed recent ideas from Jump Point Search (JPS) (Harabor and Grastien 2011) to significantly speed up Dijkstra search on uniform cost grids. We call this new algorithm Canonical Dijkstra. Although the algorithm has been described before (Sturtevant and Rabin 2016), this chapter provides more detail and examples of how the algorithms work in practice. This is just one example of how the ideas of JPS can be applied more broadly; we hope this will become a valuable part of your library of approaches. Note that the chapter does assume that the reader is familiar with how A* works.

23.2 Decomposing Jump Point Search

As Canonical Dijkstra builds on the ideas of JPS, we will describe the key ideas from JPS first. JPS has been described elsewhere in this book series (Rabin and Silva 2015). We describe it here in a slightly different manner (following Sturtevant and Rabin 2016) that will greatly simplify our presentation of Canonical Dijkstra.

23.2.1 Canonical Ordering of Paths

One of the problems with search on grids is that there are many duplicate paths between states. While A* will find these duplicates and avoid putting duplicates on the open list, it is costly to do so, because we still generate all of these states during the search and must look them up to detect that they are duplicates. It would be better if we could never generate the duplicates in the first place.

We can do this in two steps. In the first step, we generate a basic canonical ordering. A canonical ordering is a way of choosing which optimal path we prefer among all possible optimal paths. In Figure 23.1, we show a small map that has three possible optimal paths between the start and the goal. We define the canonical path as the path that has all diagonal moves before cardinal moves. It is more efficient to only generate the canonical path(s) and never generate any other paths.

We can generate states according to the canonical ordering directly (without comparing optimal paths) by limiting the successors of each state according to the parent. If the current state was reached by a diagonal action, then we allow three legal moves from the child: (1) the same diagonal action that was used to reach the state and (2 and 3) the two cardinal components of the same diagonal action. If a cardinal action (N/S/E/W) was used to reach a state, the only legal move is to move in the same direction. In the canonical ordering, we always take diagonal actions before cardinal actions, so once a cardinal action is part of a path, all remaining actions must also be cardinal actions.

We illustrate this in part (a) on the left of Figure 23.2, where the start state is marked with an "S" and lines label the canonical paths. Each state that is reached is reached optimally by a single path, and no duplicates will be generated. But, we also notice that not all states in the map are reached. In particular, there are obstacles that block some canonical paths. Luckily, we can fix this problem when generating the canonical ordering.

Suppose the search is currently moving north. Normally the search would continue north until an obstacle was reached and then would stop. But now, we need to do one additional check. If the search passes on obstacle to the east, which then ends, it knows that the basic canonical ordering will not reach this state. So, we need to reset the canonical ordering to allow it to reach states that are blocked by obstacles. We illustrate this in part (b) on the right of Figure 23.2. The black dots are the places where the canonical ordering was restarted (once again allowing diagonal moves) after passing obstacles. These dots are called *jump points*.

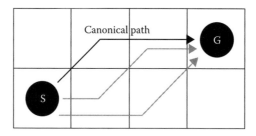

Figure 23.1

The canonical path (top) has diagonal actions before cardinal actions, unlike the noncanonical paths (in gray).

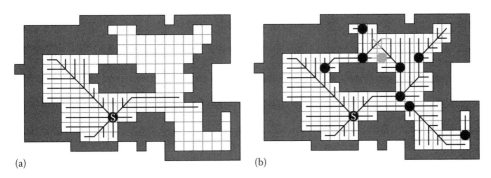

Figure 23.2

(a) The basic canonical ordering starting from the state marked S. (b) The full canonical ordering, including jump points (black circles).

Using jump points guarantees that every state in the map will be reached. While the number of duplicate paths is greatly reduced, because we only generate successors along the black lines, there still can be duplicates such as the one jump point in gray. This jump point can be reached from two different directions. Search is needed to resolve the optimal path lengths in this region of the map.

23.2.2 JPS and Canonical Orderings

We can now describe JPS in terms of the canonical ordering. The basic version of JPS does no preprocessing on the map before search. At runtime, it starts at the start state and generates a basic canonical ordering. All states visited when generating the canonical ordering are immediately discarded with the exception of jump points and the goal state, which are placed in the open list. It then chooses the best state from the open list to expand next. If this state is the goal, it terminates. Otherwise, it generates the canonical ordering from this new state, putting any new jump points or the goal into the open list. This process continues until the goal is found. It is possible that a jump point can be reached from two different directions, which is why jump points need to be placed in the open list. This ensures that a jump point is not expanded until it is reached with the optimal path.

JPS can be seen as searching on an abstract graph defined by the jump points and the goal in the graph. These are the only states that are put into the open list. But, because it has not preprocessed the map, it still has to scan the map to find the jump points and the goal. Scanning the map is far faster than putting all of these states into the open list, so JPS is usually faster than a regular A* search. Note, however, that JPS might scan more of the map than is necessary. So, in large, wide open spaces JPS can have a significant overhead. Given this understanding of JPS, we can now describe Canonical Dijkstra.

23.3 Canonical Dijkstra

Canonical Dijkstra is, in many ways, similar to JPS. It uses the canonical ordering to generate states and searches over jump points. But, while JPS only puts jump points and the goal into the open and closed lists, Canonical Dijkstra needs to record the distance to every state in the state space in the closed list. Thus, Canonical Dijkstra must write the g-cost of every state that it visits (not just the jump points) into the closed list. This is where Canonical Dijkstra saves over a regular Dijkstra search—Dijkstra's algorithm would put all of these states into the open list before expanding them and writing their costs to the closed list. Canonical Dijkstra writes these values directly to the closed list.

We show the first step of Canonical Dijkstra in Figure 23.3, but now we label the g-cost of each state as it is filled in by the search. In this example, diagonals have cost 1.5. To begin (part (a) on the left), the start is in open with cost 0.0. When the start state is expanded (part (b) on the right), the canonical ordering is generated, and the g-cost of every state visited is filled in a single step. Three jump points are reached, which are added to the open list; these states are marked with circles. This process continues until all states are reached by the search.

The most interesting step is shown in Figure 23.4. Here we see what happens when the search reaches the same state from different directions. The next state to be expanded

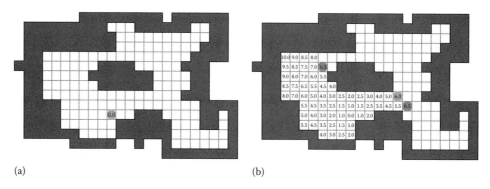

(a)   (b)

Figure 23.3

The first step of Canonical Dijkstra. Initially, (a) the start state is in the open list with cost 0. After the first expansion step, (b) the canonical ordering is followed until jump points are reached, and all visited states are labeled with their g-costs.

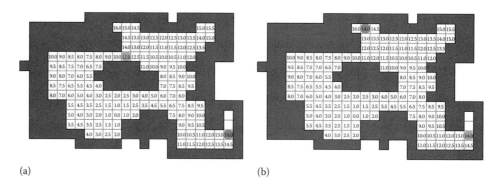

(a)   (b)

Figure 23.4

(a) In this step, Canonical Dijkstra expands the state at the top, finding a shorter path to several states nearby that have already been visited. (b) The search also finds a state that was not previously a jump point, but when reached from the new path is now a jump point.

(part (a) on the left) has cost 11.0 and is found at the top of the map. This state can reach its N, NE, and E neighbors with shorter path cost than they were previously reached. So, the g-costs are updated (part (b) on the right) after the node is expanded. One of these states (with g-cost 14.0 in the top side of the figure) was not previously a jump point. But, when reached from this direction, this state is a jump point. So, the state must be removed from the closed list and put onto the open list for further expansion.

Pseudocode for the Canonical Dijkstra algorithm can be found in Listing 23.1. The main procedure is a best-first search that repeatedly removes the best state from the open list. The canonical ordering code is the meat of the algorithm. While generating the canonical ordering, it keeps track of the current g-cost. As long as the canonical ordering finds a shorter cost path to a given state, the g-costs for that state are written directly into the closed list. When the canonical ordering generates a state with equal or larger g-cost than the copy in the open list, the process stops. When the canonical ordering finds a jump point, it adds that jump point to the open list. Since there is no goal, we do not have to check for the goal.

Listing 23.1. Canonical Dijkstra pseudocode.

```
CanonicalDijkstra(start)
{
    initialize all states to be in closed with cost ∞
    place start in open with cost 0
    while (open not empty)
        remove best from open
        CanonicalOrdering(best, parent of best, 0)
}

CanonicalOrdering(child, parent, cost)
{
    if (child in closed)
        if (cost of child in closed > cost)
            update cost of child in closed
        else
            return
    if (child is jump point)
        if on closed, remove from closed
        update parent // for canonical ordering
        add child to open with cost
    else if (action from parent to child is diagonal d)
        next = Apply(d, child)
        CanonicalOrdering(next, child, cost + diagonal)
        next = Apply(first cardinal in d, child)
        CanonicalOrdering(next, child, cost + cardinal)
        next = Apply(second cardinal in d, child)
        CanonicalOrdering(next, child, cost + cardinal)
    else if (action from parent to child is cardinal c)
        next = Apply(c, child)
        CanonicalOrdering(next, child, cost + cardinal)
}
```

23.3.1 Performance

The performance of Canonical Dijkstra depends on the type of map used. In random maps, there are many jump points, so the savings are lesser than on maps with larger open areas, where many g-costs can be written very quickly, bypassing the open list. We found 2.5× speedup on random maps and a 4.0× speedup on maps from *StarCraft*. These savings were independent of whether the base implementation was standard or high performance.

23.4 Conclusion

This chapter shows that JPS is using a canonical ordering to avoid duplicates during search. It borrows the idea of the canonical ordering to build an improved version of Dijkstra search that can perform single-source shortest path computations more efficiently by avoiding putting too many states into the open list.

References

Harabor, D. and Grastien, A. 2011. Online graph pruning for pathfinding on grid maps. In *Proceedings of the Twenty-Fifth {AAAI} Conference on Artificial Intelligence*. San Francisco, CA, pp. 1114–1119.

Rabin, S. and Sturtevant, N. R. 2013. Pathfinding architecture optimizations. In *Game AI Pro*, ed S. Rabin. Boca Raton, FL: CRC Press, pp. 241–252. http://www.gameaipro.com/GameAIPro/GameAIPro_Chapter17_Pathfinding_Architecture_Optimizations.pdf.

Rabin, S. and Silva, F. 2015. JPS+: An extreme A* speed optimization for static uniform cost grids. In *Game AI Pro 2*, ed. S. Rabin. Boca Raton, FL: CRC Press, pp. 131–143.

Sturtevant, N. R. and Rabin, S. 2016. Canonical Orderings on Grids, *International Joint Conference on Artificial Intelligence (IJCAI)*, pp. 683–689. http://web.cs.du.edu/~sturtevant/papers/SturtevantRabin16.pdf.

SECTION IV
Tactics and Strategy

24
Being Where It Counts
Telling Paragon *Bots Where to Go*

Mieszko Zieliński

24.1 Introduction

From an AI point of view, multiplayer online battle arena (MOBA) games have two distinct layers: the tactical layer, which is responsible for the individual behavior of the AI-controlled players (aka "bots"), and the strategic layer, which is responsible for the broader, team-level, strategic decision-making. The goal of the tactical layer is to handle moment-to-moment combat in a fashion that will not break the players' suspension of disbelief. Although this is visually appealing, it has a relatively small impact on the game's outcome (assuming a certain level of skill among the players). The strategic layer, on the other hand, has a much more important goal of providing the bots with their strategic, long-term goals. It is responsible for knowing where the enemies are, deducing what the opponent's next strategic step might be, and determining which defensive structures are in danger, which enemy structures to attack, who should attack them, and so on. This is the part of the AI that can win or lose the game and that can keep players engaged over the course of the entire match.

Paragon is the latest MOBA from Epic Games. This chapter will describe the approach taken while developing the first version of the strategic layer for *Paragon's* bots. It is a simple solution that can be applied to a wide range of games, but despite its simplicity, it has achieved powerful results.

24.2 Problem Description

From a strategic point of view, being in the right place at the right time is the key to success in a MOBA. Assuming that all players are more or less on the same skill level, the only way to win an encounter is to have an advantage in numbers or the element of surprise. You need to be able to concentrate your forces to attack or defend in the right places, at the right times, without leaving an opening that the enemy can exploit. Both are extremely difficult to achieve if every bot thinks for itself. This is not an AI-specific problem—in Player versus Player (PvP) games, the teams using voice communication have an enormous advantage over the teams that do not.

Any kind of cooperation is better than no cooperation. The simplest form of cooperation is "going together." If two teammates head down the same map route, they will help each other even if only by accident, splitting the danger in two, doubling the firepower. From this point of view, it should be enough, at least initially, to just make sure bots are where they are needed. If there are three enemy heroes attacking a bot team's tower and only one bot is defending it, for example, then the obvious course of action is to get some teammates over to boost the defense. Merely having bots show up in such a scenario is enough to create an illusion of cooperation—anything achieved on top of that is a bonus.

Before the systems described in this chapter were implemented, the *Paragon* bots already had their individual behaviors in place. They had a basic understanding of how their abilities should be used. They could use healing potions when low on health points. They had reasonable target selection policies. They also knew to run for their lives when in mortal danger. Although the bots' behavior was perceived as correct, the absence of cooperation between the bots lacked the strategy necessary to compete against humans.

In summary, the problem can be formulated in simple terms as *making sure bots go where they are needed*. Once they arrive, the tactical layer can take over and do the rest.

24.3 The Graph

The very first thing needed when deciding where to go is a knowledge of the places that one can go. Experienced human players have it easy: they look at the mini-map and get information about all important places at a glance. They see where their teammates are, where the minions are going, which towers are still alive, and so on. Tracking minions, the lesser AI-controller soldiers, is especially important since players need minions to be able to attack enemy towers. The AI needs the same information, but those data need to be somehow gathered or generated, which is done using specialized AI subsystems.

Every MOBA game map has a similar structure: There are two team bases at far ends of the map, and there are defensive structures (called *towers* in *Paragon*), which are arranged into chains, forming *lanes*. There is usually more than one lane, and in between the lanes, there is a *jungle* that hides additional interesting places. In *Paragon*, those include *experience (XP) wells* and *jungle creeps' camps*. XP wells are places where teams can place *harvesters* to extract and store XP. The stored XP needs to be retrieved on a regular basis by a player hero because harvesters have limited capacity. Jungle creeps' camps are places where heroes can kill neutral inhabitants of the jungle for experience and buffs (temporary stat improvements).

The strategic AI needs to know about all such places—both the towers and the contents of the jungle—because every one of them has some strategic significance and can become an objective for the AI. Using information regarding the important places on the map, we can build a graph for the AI to use as the game-world's abstraction. Since nodes represent potential objectives, we call it the *Objective Graph*.

Let us take a step back from *Paragon* for a second. Our approach for generating a graph from relevant locations on the map does not depend on *Paragon's* specifics and can be easily applied to nearly any game that deals with spatial reasoning. The algorithm will be described in the following subsections.

24.3.1 Nodes

Every important location (such as a tower or XP well in *Paragon*) should have a corresponding graph node. Nodes are packed nicely in an array. Every node has an index, a pointer to the related structure on the map, a location (which is polled from said structure), and some additional cached properties. Examples of these properties include the structure type, which team currently owns it, and in which lane (if any) the node lies.

In addition to structures, places of strategic importance like vantage points, spawn locations, good places for an ambush, and so on, are all good candidates for graph nodes. In short, any location that bots might be interested in for strategic reasons should be represented as a node in the graph.

24.3.2 Edges

The edges in the graph represent the game-world connections between the locations symbolized by nodes. A connection is created between two game-world locations if there is an AI navigable path between them. Building edge information can be done in two steps. The first step is to generate all possible connections so that every node has information about every other reachable node. A game-world pathfinding query from every node to every other node is performed; if the path is found, the path's length is stored on the edge. This information is referred to as the edge's *cost*. Connections need to be tested both ways because path-length information is going to be used in a meaningful way later, and for nontrivial maps, A-to-B and B-to-A paths will sometimes have different lengths.

In most games, there are no isolated locations. Given enough time, a player can reach every location on a map from any other location—otherwise, why include that location in the game at all? With that in mind, the resulting graph is a *complete digraph*, which means it has an edge between every pair of nodes in the graph. This graph may sound expensive to create, but for our maps, it took less than three seconds. In any case, the computation is done offline when the game is created, so the cost does not impact the player's experience.

The second step of the edge-building process is to prune unnecessary connections. By unnecessary, we mean edges that, when replaced with a combination of other edges, still sum up to a similar cost (within some configurable tolerance). Listing 24.1 describes the algorithm with pseudocode.

The `EdgeCostOffset` variable defines the tolerance that we allow in the combined cost of the edges that are replacing a single edge and is designer-configurable, which gives the map maker a degree of control over the edge generation process. The offset value should be ideally configurable for each map, as the values that work well on one map may

```
Graph::PruneEdges(InNodes, InOutEdges)
{
  SortEdgesByCostDescending(InOutEdges)
  for Edge in InOutEdges:
    for Node in (InNodes - {Edge.Start, Edge.End}):
      if Edge.Cost >= InOutEdges[Edge.StartNode][Node].Cost
        + InOutEdges[Node][Edge.EndNode].Cost
        + EdgeCostOffset:
          Edge.IsPruned = true
          break
}
```

not be as good on another. Having a way to force connections (i.e., shield them from pruning), as well as a way to manually prune edges, can come in handy as well.

Note that in the algorithm presented, pruned edges are not being removed, just marked as pruned. This is an important point. As described in Section 24.4, in some cases, it is advantageous to use the pruned edges, whereas in others, it is not.

24.3.3 Closest Graph Node Lookup Grid

There is one more piece of information that we incorporate as part of the graph building process—a *closest graph node lookup grid*. This is a coarse grid covering the whole map that stores calculated information regarding the closest nodes. Since this information is calculated offline, in the editor or as part of some build process, it is not limited to simple-and-fast distance checks. Instead, full-featured path-length testing can be used to maximize the quality of the data stored. For every grid cell, an arbitrary location is picked (center is arbitrary enough), and paths are found to every node in the graph. Then a note is taken of the node closest in terms of path length. Optionally, the specific path-length value can be stored as well; there are a plenty of ways to prove that this kind of information is useful.

Note that the grid's resolution is arbitrary, but it has consequences—the smaller the cells, the higher the resolution of data, but it will take more time to build that information (a lesser problem), and it will take up more memory (a potential deal breaker).

24.4 Enemy Presence

One type of data that would be beneficial to associate with graph nodes, which is available only at runtime, is *enemy presence* or *influence* (Dill 2015). On the strategic level, where the graph lives, it does not really matter which hero is where exactly, or how many minions are left alive from which wave (minions move in waves). The relevant information is what the "combat potential" is or how "in danger" a given area is.

A simple runtime update step can be performed on the graph periodically. There should already be a way to query other game systems for information regarding the location and state of all heroes and all minion waves. This information can be used to build influence information with the algorithm shown in Listing 24.2.

Listing 24.2. Influence calculations.

```
Graph::UpdateInfluence(InAllHeroes, InAllMinionWaves)
{
  ResetInfluenceInformation()

  for Hero in InAllHeroes:
    Node = LookupClosestGraphNode(Hero.Location)
    Influence = CalculateHeroInfluence(Hero, 0)
    Node.ApplyInfluence(Influence)
    for Edge in Node.Edges:
      Influence = CalculateHeroInfluence(Hero, Edge.Cost)
      Edge.End.ApplyInfluence(Hero.Team, Influence)

  for Wave in InMinionWaves:
    Node = LookupClosestGraphNode(Wave.CenterLocation)
    Influence = CalculateWaveInfluence(Wave, 0)
    Node.ApplyInfluence(Influence)
    for Edge in Node.Edges:
      if Edge.EndNode.LaneID != Wave.LaneID:
        continue
      Influence = CalculateWaveInfluence(Wave, Edge.Cost)
      Edge.End.ApplyInfluence(Wave.Team, Influence)
}
```

Note that `LookupClosestGraphNode` takes advantage of the closest graph node lookup grid described in the previous section.

In essence, what the code in Listing 24.2 is doing is calculating the influence score for every relevant source and distributing it across the graph. This is one of the places where information from pruned graph edges is being used. `Cost` information is relevant regardless of whether an edge is pruned or not, and here it is being used as a reliable indication of game map distance.

Minions' influence is limited to lane nodes because minions are restricted to a specific lane. Minion influence should not seep through the jungle to another lane, since that would result in misinformation—minions are not allowed to change lanes.

24.5 Putting the Graph to Use

By now, it should be clear that the graph described in previous sections is the top level of a *hierarchical navigation graph*. It has nodes corresponding to actual locations in the game world. It has connections corresponding to paths in the game world. This means any path calculated in the graph can be translated into a regular navigation path in the game world.

Using the information regarding dangers on the map, strategically smart paths can be found. Pathfinding can be configured to find paths serving multiple purposes, like paths that avoid an enemy, paths that go through enemy-dense areas, paths that stick to lanes as much as possible, and so on. With this ability, there are a large number of possibilities for an AI programmer to explore.

Regular A* search (Buckland 2004) can be used to find paths along unpruned edges of the graph. Using unpruned edges promotes bots moving between interesting locations. The resulting paths are sequences of nodes that the AI should visit to reach its goals. If we do not want the AI to visit "interesting locations," then we can skip this or better yet apply a heuristic to the search which forces it to avoid "bad" nodes (such as those with high enemy influence). This ensures that we pick a smart path, and the graph node is small enough that the use of a heuristic will not make our searches overly expensive.

The bot's path-following code uses a graph path to generate consecutive navigation paths. When a bot following a graph path reaches a graph node on the path, it then searches a regular path to the next node on the path, repeating the process until the last node is reached. This saves us some path-finding performance cost, since finding a series of short paths is cheaper than finding one long path. Building the full path ahead of time would be a waste: the bot usually will not even utilize the whole hierarchical path. Often, it will get distracted by petty things like enemies or death.

24.6 The Objectives

Every node in the graph has some strategic importance. They might be places to attack, or to defend, or places where a bot can go to gather XP or wait in an ambush, for example. Thus, every node of the graph can have some kind of objective associated with it.

A *Bot Objective* in *Paragon* is a type of behavior modifier. When a bot is assigned to an objective, the objective tells it where to go and what to do when it gets there. An objective is usually associated with a structure on the game map and, by extension, with a node in the objective graph. An objective knows how to deal with the structure: for example, defend it, attack it, or stand on it to get XP. It also knows which agents would be best suited to deal with the structure and how many agents are required. An objective can also influence how agents are scored.

Not all objectives are equally important. An objective's priority is based on a number of factors. These include the objective's type (for example, defending is more important than attacking) and its location (e.g., defending the base is more important than defending a tower somewhere down the lane). It is also related to the structure's health and enemy presence in the area. The enemy presence is read directly from the Objective Graph, using the influence information described in Section 24.4.

There are also objective-specific factors influencing the objective's priority. The "experience well" objective is an interesting example in this regard. The longer an XP harvester is waiting at full capacity, the more XP potential gets wasted and the more important it is to retrieve XP from it. On the other hand, the higher the level of heroes on the team, the less important it is to acquire that XP.

24.6.1 Where do Objectives Come From

Every type of objective has its own generator, and all generators create instances of objectives before the match starts. These objectives then register themselves with their respective graph nodes, as well as with any game system they need notifications from. For example, a defend objective would register to be notified when its tower gets destroyed, and an XP harvesting objective would register to be notified when the XP harvester on a particular well is full. In all cases, these objectives register with the *AI Commander*.

24.7 The AI Commander

The AI Commander is responsible for assigning objectives to bots based on all the information described above. Objective assignment is done as a response to events in the game world. Each team is processed separately, and human-only teams get skipped altogether. The pool of available objectives is also separate for each team, which is pretty intuitive—bots should not know whether the other team is planning to attack a given tower that would be cheating! However, some of the objectives do care about aspects of the other team's actions or state. For example, the "experience well" objective has two modes—it is "regular" when the well is unoccupied, or owned by the objective's team, and it switches to "offensive" when the enemy team takes possession of the well by placing its own harvester on it. This kind of knowledge gathering is encapsulated inside each specific objective's logic.

The objective assignment process can be split into multiple steps. As a first step, each team's objectives have a chance to update their own state. Every objective can be in either a "Dormant" or "Available" state. It is up to each objective's internal logic to determine which state it is in. If an objective is dormant, then it is skipped by the AI Commander during the objective assignment process. As part of the update, objective priorities are calculated as well. As previously mentioned, the objective's priority is based on multiple factors, and every objective can also specify how much a given factor influences its score. For example, "experience well" objectives are not concerned with enemy influence, while tower defense objectives treat it very seriously. Once every objective is updated and scored, all the available objectives are sorted by priority.

In step two, each available objective filters and scores all of the teammates, and stores the results for use in step three. Filtering gives objectives a chance to exclude unfit agents on a case-by-case basis. For example, a special ability is required to place a harvester on an experience well, so that objective excludes heroes who do not have that ability. Agent scoring is described in greater detail in Section 24.7.1. It would actually be more efficient to do the scoring and filtering as part of step three, but splitting the process this way makes it easier to explain.

The third step of the objectives assignment process is responsible for assigning agents to objectives. We do this by iterating over the following loop until all agents have been assigned:

1. Find the highest priority objective.
2. Allow that objective to pick a minimum set of resources (e.g., a single Brawler, or a Support and Caster pair).
3. Reduce the priority of that objective according to the amount of resources it took. The amount of priority reduction per agent assigned is in relation to all active objectives' max priority. It means that with every agent assigned, an objective will lose MaxPriority/TeamSize priority.

One potential tweak some adopters might want to consider is to use different limits to how many resources an objective is allowed to take. Allowing only the minimum amount will result in carrying out as many objectives as possible, but for some games, it would make more sense to focus all the power on just one or two objectives.

It is important to note that the result of this process depends heavily on how the objectives' priority is calculated and on how the individual objectives calculate their agent scores. Tweaking those two elements is necessary for good results.

24.7.1 Agent Scoring

There are two ways the agents' scoring can be performed by an objective. One is fully custom scoring, where the objective is the only scoring authority and calculates the scores itself. The other way, the default method, allows an objective to specify a hero role preference (Support, Tank, Caster, etc., as a single hero can have multiple roles). The preference is expressed as a set of multipliers for every role, and the score is based on the best role that the agent has. For example, if a hero is a Tank and a Brawler, and the objective has 0.1 preference for Tanks but 0.3 for Brawlers, then that given hero's score will be 0.3.

Regardless of the method, the agents' scores are calculated per objective. This makes it easier to tweak the results of the whole objective assignment process since potential mistakes in agent scoring will be localized within individual objectives and will have limited effect on which objectives are being carried out.

Distance (or travel time, if you have agents that move at different speeds) is another component of agent score. It usually makes most sense to assign a medium-scoring agent that is close to an objective rather than picking the highest scoring one that is on the other side of the map. Calculating a reliable distance-based portion of the score is really fast, since that information is already available within the Objective Graph; it already knows the path cost for every node pair in the graph! The path distance is retrieved from the graph and multiplied by a factor supplied by the objective.

Using one fun trick, a distance to the objective can be calculated even for dead heroes. To do this, we have to use travel time (that is, how long will it take the unit to travel to the objective) rather than distance. We then treat dead heroes as standing in their team's base but needing an additional X seconds (X being the time left to respawn) to arrive at the destination. This way, if one additional agent is needed to defend the base, then from two similarly adequate bots, the one that respawns in 10 seconds will be picked over the one that would need 20 seconds to get there.

24.7.2 Humans

The AI Commander treats human players in mixed human-bot teams just like other agents. The objective assignment code makes no exception for human agents. An assumption is made that the AI Commander will pick a reasonable objective for every agent, including players. If so, a player can be expected to carry out the assigned objective without being directly controlled by the game AI. Moreover, the on-screen team communication system can be used to request players to do something specific, like "defend left" or "group up!" (just like human players can do in regular PvP games). In any case, both the game and AI Commander are flexible in this regard, so even if an agent does not fulfill its role, the game will not break, and adjustments will be made during the next objective assigning iteration.

An interesting possible extension should be pointed out here. Since human players can use team communication, we could include messages from them as hints and temporarily increase the priority of the objectives associated with received messages. We cannot have human players control which objectives the AI Commander picks directly, since that would have a potential of ruining the experience by sending the AI to all the wrong places, but we can use it to influence the decisions in a weaker way.

24.7.3 Opportunistic Objectives

When a bot carries out an objective, it usually involves following an objective graph path. The path-finding algorithm can be configured to prefer graph nodes containing unassigned objectives. Then as a bot progresses through the graph path on every node, a check can be done to see if there is an unassigned objective that said bot can carry out. The objective gets a chance to specify if it is interested in being assigned this way. For some objective types, it simply does not make sense to be picked up "on the way." Good opportunistic objectives should be easy and quick to carry out, for example, gathering XP from wells or destroying a jungle creeps' camp.

24.8 Future Work

The ideas described in this chapter have a lot more potential uses. The Objective Graph is a convenient abstraction of the map, and more data can be associated with every node. Below are some examples.

24.8.1 Probabilistic "Presence" Propagation

As of this writing, the *Paragon* AI Commander has perfect knowledge of all heroes' locations. Human players only know about enemy heroes that they have seen themselves or that have been sighted by the team. Although this is not completely fair, it helps compensate for other shortcomings (such as not being able to synchronize ability usage with their teammates).

It would be possible to build a probabilistic net of locations of all heroes based on the objective graph. If an enemy hero is visible to any of the team's heroes or minions, the graph node closest to the enemy's location gets annotated with information that the given hero is at that node with probability of 1. If a hero is not visible, then that hero's last known location is used; based on the time of last sighting, propagate information to all neighbors of the last known location node. The probability of a hero being at any other graph node is proportional to the distance (read directly from the graph nodes) and the time passed; it may also be influenced by the knowledge of currently hot locations on the map and where a hero could be interested in being. An information diffusion step could also be added to the process. This whole idea is a variation of Occupancy Maps (Isla 2006).

24.8.2 Map Evaluation

One of the few reliable use cases of neural networks (NNs) in game AI is data classification. It is possible to imagine a NN that would take the "world state" as input and generate a sort of "quality" or "desirability" value as output. Having a map abstraction such as a graph already at hand makes converting the world state into a vector of values into a relatively straightforward process. Data from games played online by human players can be used to construct a training set. Grabbing graph snapshots at regular intervals and associating them with the final result of the match would be a good start. Once trained, the net could be used to help the AI Commander to evaluate current game's state and guide high-level strategy, such as by hinting whether the current world state requires a more defensive or a more offensive stance.

24.9 Conclusion

As proven by our internal user experience tests, the introduction of a strategy layer to the *Paragon* bot AI greatly improved players' experiences. The game did not instantly become harder, because no behavioral changes have been made to the bots' individual behaviors, but users did notice the game being more interesting. Bots started showing signs of a deeper strategic understanding of the game: filling in for fallen comrades, switching lanes, attacking enemy harvesters, and even *ganking* (which is MOBA-speak for *ambushing*), although the latter behavior was entirely emergent. The system telling the bots where to go was simple but competent. Players will generate their own explanations for what is going on in the game as long as the AI is doing its job well enough!

A graph representation, due to its discrete nature, is an easy way to represent complex data like a level filled with gameplay. Pathfinding over long distances is a breeze. Estimating enemy danger at a node location is a simple lookup operation (provided regular influence updates are performed). Last but not least, the Objective Graph gives spatial context to the otherwise abstract concept of objectives. This is just a start; there is so much more that could be done with a graph abstraction of the game map. There is no (good) excuse not to give it a try and build one of your own!

References

Buckland, M. 2004. *Programming Game AI by Example.* Jones & Bartlett Learning.

Dill, K. 2015. Spatial reasoning for strategic decision making. In *Game AI Pro 2: Collected Wisdom of AI Professionals*, ed. S. Rabin. Boca Raton, FL: A. K. Peters/CRC Press.

Isla, D. 2006. Probabilistic target tracking and search using occupancy maps. In *AI Game Programming Wisdom 3*, ed. S. Rabin. Hingham, MA: Charles River Media, pp. 379–388.

Combat Outcome Prediction for Real-Time Strategy Games

Marius Stanescu, Nicolas A. Barriga, and Michael Buro

25.1 Introduction

Smart decision-making at the tactical level is important for AI agents to perform well in real-time strategy (RTS) games, in which winning battles is crucial. Although human players can decide when and how to attack based on their experience, it is challenging for AI agents to estimate combat outcomes accurately. Prediction by running simulations is a popular method, but it uses significant computational resources and needs explicit opponent modeling in order to adjust to different opponents.

This chapter describes an outcome evaluation model based on Lanchester's attrition laws, which were introduced in Lanchester's seminal book *Aircraft in Warfare: The Dawn of the Fourth Arm* in 1916 (Lanchester 1916). The original model has several limitations that we have addressed in order to extend it to RTS games (Stanescu et al. 2015). Our new model takes into account that armies can be comprised of different unit types, and that troops can enter battles with any fraction of their maximum health. The model parameters can easily be estimated from past recorded battles using logistic regression. Predicting combat outcomes with this method is accurate, and orders of magnitude are faster than running combat simulations. Furthermore, the learning process does not require expert knowledge about the game or extra coding effort in case of future unit changes (e.g., game patches).

25.2 The Engagement Decision

Suppose you command 20 knights and 40 swordsmen and just scouted an enemy army of 60 bowmen and 40 spearmen. Is this a fight you can win, or should you avoid the battle and request reinforcements? This is called the *engagement decision* (Wetzel 2008).

25.2.1 Scripted Behavior

Scripted behavior is a common choice for making such decisions, due to the ease of implementation and very fast execution. Scripts can be tailored to any game or situation. For example, *always attack* is a common policy for RPG or FPS games—for example, guards charging as soon as they spot the player. More complex strategy games require more complicated scripts: attack closest, prioritize wounded, attack if enemy does not have cavalry, attack if we have more troops than the enemy, or retreat otherwise. AI agents should be able to deal with all possible scenarios encountered, some of which might not be foreseen by the AI designer. Moreover, covering a very wide range of scenarios requires a significant amount of development effort.

There is a distinction we need to make. Scripts are mostly used to make decisions, while in this chapter we focus on estimating the outcome of a battle. In RTS games, this prediction is arguably the most important factor for making decisions, and here we focus on providing accurate information to the AI agent. We are not concerned with making a decision based on this prediction. Is losing 80% of the initial army too costly a victory? Should we retreat and potentially let the enemy capture our castle? We leave these decisions to a higher level AI and focus on providing accurate and useful combat outcome predictions. Examples about how these estimations can improve decision-making can be found in Bakkes and Spronck (2008) and Barriga et al. (2017).

25.2.2 Simulations

One choice that bypasses the need for extensive game knowledge and coding effort is to simulate the battle multiple times, without actually attacking in the game, and to record the outcomes. If from 100 mock battles we win 73, we can estimate that the chance of winning the engagement is close to 73%. For this method to work, we need the combat engine to allow the AI system to simulate battles. Moreover, it can be difficult to emulate enemy player behaviors, and simulating exhaustively all possibilities is often too costly.

Technically, simulations do not directly predict the winner but provide information about potential states of the world after a set of actions. Performing a playout for a limited number of simulation frames is faster, but because there will often not be a clear winner, we need a way of evaluating our chances of winning the battle from the resulting game state. Evaluation (or scoring) functions are commonly employed by look-ahead algorithms, which forward the current state using different choices and then need to numerically compare the results. Even if we do not use a search algorithm, or partial simulations, an evaluation function can be called on the current state and help us make a decision based on the predicted combat outcome. However, accurately predicting the result of a battle is often a difficult task.

The possibility of equal (or nearly equal armies) fighting with the winner seeing the battle through with a surprisingly large remaining force is one of the interesting aspects of strategic, war simulation-based games. Let us consider two identical forces of 1000 men each; the Red force is divided into two units of 500 men, which serially engage the single (1000 men) Blue force. Most linear scoring functions, or a casual gamer, would identify this engagement as a slight win for the undivided Blue army, severely underestimating the "concentration of power" axiom of war. A more experienced armchair general would never make such a foolish attack, and according to the Quadratic Lanchester model (introduced below), the Blue force completely destroys the Red army with only moderate loss (i.e., 30%) to itself.

25.3 Lanchester's Attrition Models

The original Lanchester equations represent simplified combat models: each side has identical soldiers and a fixed strength (i.e., there are no reinforcements), which governs the proportion of enemy soldiers killed. Range, terrain, movement, and all other factors that might influence the fight are either abstracted within the parameters or ignored entirely. Fights continue until the complete destruction of one force, and as such the following equations are only valid until one of the army sizes is reduced to 0. The general form of the attrition differential equations is:

$$\frac{dA}{dt} = -\beta A^{2-n} B \ \text{ and } \ \frac{dB}{dt} = -\alpha B^{2-n} A \tag{25.1}$$

where:

t denotes time

A, B are force strengths (number of units) of the two armies assumed to be functions of time

By removing time as a variable, the pair of differential equations can be combined into $\alpha(A^n - A_0^n) = \beta(B^n - B_0^n)$.

Parameters α and β are attrition rate coefficients representing how fast a soldier in one army can kill a soldier in the other. The equation is easier to understand if one thinks of β as the relative strength of soldiers in army B; it influences how fast army A is reduced. The exponent n is called the *attrition order* and represents the advantage of a higher rate of target acquisition. It applies to the size of the forces involved in combat but not to the fighting effectiveness of the forces which is modeled by attrition coefficients α and β. The higher the attrition order, the faster any advantage an army might have in combat effectiveness is overcome by numeric superiority.

For example, choosing $n=1$ leads to $\alpha(A - A_0) = \beta(B - B_0)$, which is known as Lanchester's *Linear Law*. This equation models situations in which one soldier can only fight a single soldier at a time. If one side has more soldiers, some of them will not always be fighting as they wait for an opportunity to attack. In this setting, the casualties suffered by both sides are proportional to the number of fighters and the attrition rates. If $\alpha = \beta$, then the above example of splitting a force into two and fighting the enemy sequentially will have the same outcome as without splitting: a draw. This was originally called Lanchester's Law of Ancient Warfare, because it is a good model for battles fought with melee weapons (such as spears or swords, which were the common choices of Greek or Roman soldiers).

Choosing $n = 2$ results in the *Square Law*, which is also known as Lanchester's Law of Modern Warfare. It is intended to apply to ranged combat, as it quantifies the value of the relative advantage of having a larger army. However, the Squared Law has nothing to do with range—what is really important is the rate of acquiring new targets. Having ranged weapons generally lets soldiers engage targets as fast as they can shoot, but with a sword or a pike, one would have to first locate a target and then move to engage it. In our experiments for RTS games that have a mix of melee and ranged units, we found attrition order values somewhere in between working best. For our particular game—*StarCraft Broodwar*—it was close to 1.56.

The state solution for the general law can be rewritten as $\alpha A^n - \beta B^n = \alpha A_0^n - \beta B_0^n = k$. Constant k depends only on the initial army sizes A_0 and B_0. Hence, if $k > 0$ or equivalently $\alpha A_0^n > \beta B_0^n$, then player A wins. If we denote the final army sizes with A_f and B_f and assume player B lost, then $B_f = 0$ and $\alpha A_0^n - \beta B_0^n = \alpha A_f^n - 0$, and we can predict the remaining victorious army size A_f. We just need to choose appropriate values α and β that reflect the strength of the two armies, a task we will focus on in the next section.

25.4 Lanchester Model Parameters

In RTS games, it is often the case that both armies are composed of various units, with different capabilities. To model these heterogeneous army compositions, we need to replace the army effectiveness with an average value

$$\alpha_{avg} = \frac{\sum_{j=1}^{A} \alpha_j}{A} \tag{25.2}$$

where:
   α_j is the effectiveness of a single unit
   A is the total number of units

We can see that predicting battle outcomes will require strength estimates for each unit involved. In the next subsections, we describe how these parameters can be either manually created or learned.

25.4.1 Choosing Strength Values

The quickest and easiest way of approximating strength is to pick a single attribute that you feel is representative. For instance, we can pick $\alpha_i = \text{level}_i$ if we think that a level k dragon is k times as strong as a level 1 footman. Or maybe a dragon is much stronger, and if we choose $\alpha_i = 5^{\text{level}_i}$ instead, then it would be equivalent to 5^k footmen.

More generally, we can combine any number of attributes. For example, the cost of producing or training a unit is very likely to reflect unit strength. In addition, if we would like to take into account that injured units are less effective, we could add the current and maximum health points to our formula:

$$\alpha_i = \frac{\text{Cost}(i)\,\text{HP}(i)}{\text{MaxHP}(i)} \tag{25.3}$$

This estimate may work well, but using more attributes such as attack or defense values, damage, armor, or movement speed could improve prediction quality, still. We can create a function that takes all these attributes as parameters and outputs a single value. However, this requires a significant understanding of the game, and, moreover, it will take a designer a fair amount of time to write down and tune such an equation.

Rather than using a formula based on attack, health, and so on, it is easier to pick some artificial values: for instance, the dragon may be worth 100 points and a footman may worth just one point. We have complete control over the relative combat values, and we can easily express if we feel that a knight is five times stronger than a footman. The disadvantage is that we might guess wrong, and thus we still have to playtest and tune these values. Moreover, with any change in the game, we need to manually revise all the values.

25.4.2 Learning Strength Values

So far, we have discussed choosing unit strength values for our combat predictor via two methods. First, we could produce and use a simple formula based on one or more relevant attributes such as unit level, cost, health, and so on. Second, we could directly pick a value for each unit type based mainly on our intuition and understanding of the game. Both methods rely heavily on the designer's experience and on extensive playtesting for tuning. To reduce this effort, we can try to automatically learn these values by analyzing human game replays or, alternatively, letting a few AI systems play against each other.

Although playtesting might ensure that AI agents play well versus the game designers, it does not guarantee that the agents will also play well against other unpredictable players. However, we can adapt the AI to any specific player by learning a unique set of unit strength values taking into account only games played by this player. For example, the game client can generate a new set of AI parameters before every new game, based on a number of recent battles. Automatically learning the strength values will require less designer effort and provide better experiences for the players.

The learning process can potentially be complex, depending on the machine learning tools to be used. However even a simple approach, such as logistic regression, can work very well, and it has the advantage of being easy to implement. We will outline the basic steps for this process here.

First, we need a dataset consisting of as many battles as possible. Some learning techniques can provide good results after as few as 10 battles (Stanescu et al. 2013), but for logistic regression, we recommend using at least a few hundred. If a player has only fought a few battles, we can augment his dataset with a random set of battles from other players. These will be slowly replaced by "real" data as our player fights more battles. This way the parameter estimates will be more stable, and the more the player plays, the better we can estimate the outcome of his or her battles.

An example dataset is shown in Table 25.1. Each row corresponds to one battle, and we will now describe what each column represents. If we are playing a game with only two types of soldiers, armed with spears or bows, we need to learn two parameters for each player: w_{spear} and w_{bow}. To maintain sensitivity to unit injuries, we use $\alpha_j = w_{spear}HP(j)$ or $\alpha_j = w_{bow}HP(j)$, depending on unit type. The total value of army A can then be expressed as:

$$L(A) = \alpha_{avg}A^n = A^{n-1}\sum_{j=1}^{A}\alpha_j = A^{n-1}\sum_{j=1}^{A}w_jHP(j)$$

$$= A^{n-1}(w_{spear}HP_s + w_{bow}HP_b)$$

(25.4)

HP_s is the sum of the health points of all of player A's spearmen. After learning all w parameters, the combat outcome can be estimated by subtracting $L(A) - L(B)$. For simplicity, in Table 25.1, we assume each soldier's health is a number between 0 and 1.

25.4.3 Learning with Logistic Regression

As a brief reminder, logistic regression uses a linear combination of variables. The result is squashed through the logistic function F, restricting the output to $(0,1)$, which can be interpreted as the probability of the first player winning.

$$y = a_0 + a_1X_1 + a_2X_2 + \cdots \qquad F(y) = \frac{1}{1+e^{-y}}$$

(25.5)

For example, if $y=0$, then $F=0.5$ which is a draw. If $y>0$, then the first player has the advantage. For ease of implementation, we can process the previous table in such a way that each column is associated with one parameter to learn, and the last column contains the battle outcomes (Table 25.2). Let us assume that both players are equally adept at controlling spearmen, but bowmen require more skill to use efficiently and their strength value could differ when controlled by the two players:

$$y = L(A) - L(B)$$

$$= w_{spear}\left(A^{n-1}HP_{sA} - B^{n-1}HP_{sB}\right) + w_{bowA}\left(A^{n-1}HP_{bA}\right) - w_{bowB}\left(B^{n-1}HP_{bB}\right)$$

(25.6)

This table can be easily used to fit a logistic regression model in your coding language of choice. For instance, using Python's *pandas* library, this can be done in as few as five lines of code.

Table 25.1 Example Dataset Needed for Learning Strength Values

Battle	HP$_s$ for A	HP$_b$ for A	A	HP$_s$ for B	HP$_b$ for B	B	Winner
1	3.80	0.95	5	4.20	0.00	6	A
2	10.00	1.00	11	7.00	3.00	10	B
...	...	...	...	...	...	...	...

Table 25.2 Processed Dataset (All But Last Column Correspond to Parameters to be Learned)

$A^{n-1}HP_{sA} - B^{n-1}HP_{sB}$	$A^{n-1}HP_{bA}$	$-(B^{n-1}HP_{bB})$	Winner
...	...	...	...

25.5 Experiments

We have used the proposed Lanchester model but with a slightly more complex learning algorithm in UAlbertaBot, a *StarCraft* open-source bot for which detailed documentation is available online (UAlbertaBot 2016). The bot runs combat simulations to decide if it should attack the opponent with the currently available units if a win is predicted or retreat otherwise. We replaced the simulation call in this decision procedure with a Lanchester model-based prediction.

Three tournaments were run. First, our bot ran one simulation with each side using an *attack closest* policy. Second, it used the Lanchester model described here with static strength values for each unit based on its damage per frame and current health: $\alpha_i = \text{DMG}(i)\text{HP}(i)$. For the last tournament, a set of strength values was learned for each of 6 match-ups from the first 500 battles of the second tournament. In each tournament, 200 matches were played against 6 top bots from the 2014 AIIDE *StarCraft* AI tournament. The results—winning percentages for different versions of our bot—are shown in Table 25.3. On average, the learned parameters perform better than both static values and simulations, but be warned that learning without any additional hand checks might lead to unexpected behavior such as the match against Bot2 where the win rate actually drops by 3%.

Our bot's strategy is very simple: it only trains basic melee units and tries to rush the opponent and keep the pressure up. This is why we did not expect very large improvements from using Lanchester models, as the only decision they affect is whether to attack or to retreat. More often than not this translates into waiting for an extra unit, attacking with one unit less, and better retreat triggers. Although this makes all the difference in some games, using this accurate prediction model to choose the army composition, for example, could lead to much bigger improvements.

25.6 Conclusions

In this chapter, we have described an approach to automatically generate an effective combat outcome predictor that can be used in war simulation strategy games. Its parameters can be static, fixed by the designer, or learned from past battles. The choice of training data provided to the algorithm ensures adaptability to specific opponents or maps. For example,

Table 25.3 Our Bot's Winning % Using Different Methods for Combat Outcome Prediction

	Bot1	Bot2	Bot3	Bot4	Bot5	Bot6	Average
Simulations	60.0	79.0	84.0	65.5	19.5	57.0	60.8
Static	64.5	**81.0**	80.5	69.0	22.0	66.5	63.9
Learned	**69.5**	78.0	**86.0**	**93.0**	**23.5**	**68.0**	**69.7**

learning only from siege battles will provide a good estimator for attacking or defending castles, but it will be less precise for fighting in large unobstructed areas where cavalry might prove more useful than, say, artillery. Using a portfolio of estimators is an option worth considering.

Adaptive game AI can use our model to evaluate newly generated behaviors or to rank high-level game plans according to their chances of military success. As the model parameters can be learned from past scenarios, the evaluation will be more objective and stable to unforeseen circumstances when compared to functions created manually by a game designer. Moreover, learning can be controlled through the selection of training data, and it is very easy to generate map- or player-dependent parameters. For example, one set of parameters can be used for all naval battles, and another set can be used for siege battles against the elves. However for good results, we advise acquiring as many battles as possible, preferably tens or hundreds.

Other use cases for accurate combat prediction models worth considering include game balancing and testing. For example, if a certain unit type is scarcely being used, it can help us decide if we should boost one of its attributes or reduce its cost as an extra incentive for players to use it.

References

Bakkes, S. and Spronck, P., 2008. Automatically generating score functions for strategy games. In *Game AI Programming Wisdom 4*, ed. S. Rabin. Hingham, MA: Charles River Media, pp. 647–658.

Barriga, N., Stanescu, M., and Buro, M., 2017. Combining scripted behavior with game tree search for stronger, more robust game AI. In *Game AI Pro 3: Collected Wisdom of Game AI Professionals*, ed. S. Rabin. Boca Raton, FL: CRC Press.

Lanchester, F.W., 1916. *Aircraft in Warfare: The Dawn of the Fourth Arm*. London: Constable limited.

Stanescu, M., Hernandez, S.P., Erickson, G., Greiner, R., and Buro, M., 2013. October. Predicting army combat outcomes in StarCraft. In *Ninth Annual AAAI Conference on Artificial Intelligence and Interactive Digital Entertainment (AIIDE)*, October 14–18, 2013. Boston, MA.

Stanescu, M., Barriga, N., and Buro, M., 2015, September. Using Lanchester attrition laws for combat prediction in StarCraft. In *Eleventh AIIDE Conference*, November 14–18, 2015. Santa Cruz, CA.

UAlbertaBot github repository, maintained by David Churchill., 2016. https://github.com/davechurchill/ualbertabot.

Wetzel, B., 2008. The engagement decision. In *Game AI Programming Wisdom 4*, ed. S. Rabin. Boston, MA: Charles River Media, pp. 443–454.

26

Guide to Effective Auto-Generated Spatial Queries

Eric Johnson

26.1 Introduction

Intelligent position selection for agents—that is, analyzing the environment to find the best location for a given behavior—has evolved rapidly as spatial query systems such as CryENGINE's Tactical Point System and Unreal Engine 4's Environment Query System have matured. Once limited to evaluating static, preplaced markers for behaviors such as finding cover or sniping posts, dynamic generation gives us the ability to represent a much wider and more sophisticated range of concepts. The ability to generate points at runtime allows us to sample the environment at arbitrary granularity, adapting to changes in dynamic or destructible environments. In addition, when used to generate a short-term direction rather than a final destination, we can represent complex movement behaviors such as roundabout approaches, evenly encircling a target with teammates, or even artificial life algorithms such as Craig Reynold's boids (Reynolds 1987), all while navigating arbitrary terrain.

Originally developed as a generalized, data-driven solution for selecting pregenerated points in the environment, Crysis 2's Tactical Point System (TPS) is now freely available to the public as part of CryENGINE, while Bulletstorm's Environmental Tactical Querying system is now integrated into Unreal Engine 4 as the Environment Query System (EQS), making these techniques accessible to a massive audience (Jack 2013, Zielinsky 2013). As game environments grow increasingly complex, other studios are also adopting this approach with implementations like the Point Query System in *FINAL FANTASY XV* and the SQL-based SpatialDB in MASA LIFE (Shirakami et al. 2015, Mars 2014).

Designing effective queries is the key to maximizing the quality of agent position selection while dramatically reducing the amount of work required to implement and tune these behaviors. Done well, you can consolidate the majority of a game's position selection logic into a library of queries run on a spatial query system, rather than managing a collection of disparate and independent algorithms. However, the functionality of these systems has become increasingly sophisticated as they gain wider adoption, presenting developers with more possibilities than ever before. This introduces new challenges to use the array of tools and techniques at our disposal effectively.

In this chapter, we present a selection of tricks and techniques that you can integrate into your agent's queries to ultimately deliver higher quality, more believable behavior. Each component of a spatial query is covered, from sample generation to failure resistance, to improve the effectiveness of spatial queries in your project.

26.2 Overview

In modern implementations, a single spatial query generally consists of the following components:

- *Sample points*: Locations in the world which we want to evaluate in order to determine their suitability for a particular movement task.
- *Generator*: Creates the initial set of sample points in the environment. For example, one type of generator might create a 100 m 2D grid of points along the floor of the level, whereas another might create a ring of points at a radius of 10 m.
- *Generator origin*: The location around which we want to run the generator—for example, the center of the grid or ring of points that are created. Most often, the generator origin is either the agent itself or some target that it is interacting with.
- *Test*: Measures the *value* of a sample point, or defines an *acceptance condition* for it. For example, the sample's distance from the agent can be a measure of value, while its visibility to the agent's target can serve as an acceptance condition.
- *Test subject*: A location, object, or list of locations/objects that serve as the subject of comparison for a test. For example, a distance test might compare each sample point's location against the querying agent, its destination, the set of nearby enemies, recently discovered traps, etc.

To get an idea how these components work together, consider a scenario in which we need to implement a typical approach-and-surround behavior for a group of melee enemies (Figure 26.1). Our goal is to get them into attack range quickly while at the same time fanning out in a circle around the player. To accomplish this, we might begin by using a *ring generator*, using the player as the *generator origin* to create a set of *sample points* in range of our target. Next, by using a series of *tests* measuring the distance from each sample point to the player, the agent, and the agent's teammates (as *test subjects*), we can combine their

Figure 26.1

Four enemies using spatial queries to approach and surround the player.

value to find positions that get the agent closer to the player from its current location while avoiding areas occupied by teammates. A visibility test from each point to the player, used as an *acceptance condition*, can additionally discard destinations where the agent would be unable to see the player. Finally, the location with the highest total score across all tests is returned as the query result.

The remainder of this chapter assumes a basic familiarity with publicly available query system implementations such as TPS and EQS. For a more in-depth explanation of how an environment query is structured and executed, please refer to Chapters 26 and 33 of *Game AI Pro* (Jack 2013, Zielinsky 2013).

26.3 Generating Sample Points

The first step in selecting a useful destination for an agent is to generate a set of potentially viable locations to evaluate. When using pregenerated points this is trivial; we typically collect all marker objects in a given range and move on to the ranking phase. For dynamically-generated points, things are more complex as the generation method itself can heavily impact the quality of the final result.

26.3.1 Generation on the Navigation Mesh

The simplest method of dynamically generating a set of sample points is to create a localized 2D grid on the surface of the agent's environment. Although it is possible to use collision raycasts against level geometry to map out the level floor, this is not only computationally expensive, but the generated points may not be reachable by the agent (e.g., if they lie on a steep slope or narrow corridor). By sampling along the surface of the navigation mesh instead of the actual level geometry, we can both reduce generation cost and ensure that the sample position is reachable by the agent.

However, the overhead of finding the navmesh surface for a large number of sample points can still be significant. To be practical at runtime, we can further minimize generation cost by localizing our projection test to a limited set of navmesh polygons that match as closely as possible the area to be sampled by the generator. The caveat is that there are multiple valid techniques we can use to define this subset, and the one we choose can significantly affect the outcome of the query. For example, two common approaches are either to gather the set of navmesh polygons within a bounding box centered on the query origin, or to gather the navmesh polygons within a given path distance of the query origin, and then to generate points only on those polygons. The bounding box approach is straightforward to implement, but can generate positions that, measured by path distance, are distant or even unreachable (Figure 26.2a). For behaviors such as finding ranged attack locations, this can be a good fit. Using path distance on the other hand ensures that the origin is reachable from all positions, but ignores locations that are spatially indirect, even if they are physically close (Figure 26.2b). Thus the bounding box approach may work better for behaviors that only require line-of-sight (such as ranged attacks), whereas the path distance method is preferable for behaviors dependent on spatial distance, such as following or surrounding.

Other options exist as well. For instance, we can merge both techniques, relaxing the path distance requirement to find reachable points within a given radius even when the path to that location is long and indirect. For example, given a radius r, we can gather all navmesh polygons within some multiple of that radius (say, $2r$). Then, during generation, we can eliminate sample points with a linear distance greater than r, giving us better coverage over an area while still ensuring a path to the generator origin.

After we have selected the most appropriate method for gathering navmesh polygons, we have a few different methods for generating samples that will impact the effectiveness of our final query:

1. *One-to-one mapping*: Some common navigation libraries, such as Recast/Detour, provide functionality to find the nearest point on the navmesh, given a point and bounding box. We can thus run a search over the gathered polygons at each (x, y) position on the grid, with some reasonably large z value, to verify that a point lies on the section of the navmesh gathered in the previous step. Although efficient, a weakness of this technique is that if your environment has vertically overlapping areas, such as a multi-floored building or bridges, only one level will be discovered (Figure 26.2c).

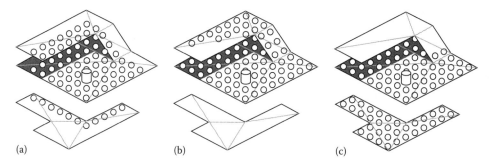

(a) (b) (c)

Figure 26.2

(a) Navigation mesh-based sample generation restricted by bounding box distance. (b) Sample generation restricted by path distance. (c) Sample generation restricted to a one-to-one mapping from the original grid coordinates to the nearest location on the navmesh.

26. Guide to Effective Auto-Generated Spatial Queries

2. *One-to-many mapping*: A second technique is to use a vertical navigation ray-cast over the gathered polygons at each (x, y) position, generating multiple hits along the z axis whenever we pass through a gathered navmesh polygon. Here, we trade efficiency for accuracy, handling multi-level terrain at the cost of some performance.

26.3.2 Generation Structure

Grids are not the only way to arrange our generated sample points. A custom generator can produce items along walls, arranged in rings, hexes, along waypoint graphs, inside Voronoi cells, or countless other configurations depending on the situation. This decision is important; a poor layout can introduce bias into your query, causing agents to cluster around or avoid certain locations. For tests that are intended to create a smooth scoring gradient, such as distance from a target, it is immediately noticeable when this distribution becomes uneven as agents will begin to approach targets only from specific directions, or settle into locations at specific intervals from the target.

For example, consider a query that wishes to find a location that is as close to an agent's target as possible, while leaving a 3 m buffer zone around the target. With a grid-based approach, we can first generate a set of sample points around the target, discard those closer than 3 m away, and rank the rest based on their distance from the target. Unfortunately, this exposes a problem, as illustrated in Figure 26.3. Depending on the desired radius, the closest points to the target invariably lie either on the diagonal or cardinal directions. As a result, agents not only cluster around four points, they may also approach the target at an unnatural angle to do so—that is, instead of moving directly toward the target to a point that is 3 m away, they will veer to one side or the other to get to one of the "optimal" points found by the search. In addition, selecting a grid layout for a circular query is intensely inefficient; a large portion of the sample points will either be too close (and thus

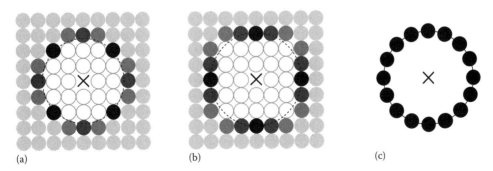

(a) (b) (c)

Figure 26.3

(a, b) Examples of diagonal and cardinal distance bias introduced by range tests over grid-generated points. (c) Elimination of distance bias by using a ring generator. Darker circles indicate higher priority positions. Empty circles indicate points that were generated but discarded, whereas light circles indicate positions that were ranked but have no possibility of being used.

immediately discarded by the distance test) or too far (and thus will never be selected, because a closer valid point exists).

In this instance, we can replace the grid generator with a ring generator, eliminating distance bias by guaranteeing that all points closest to the target are the same distance from the target. In addition, we gain an efficiency boost, as we need only generate a fraction of the sample points to perform the same test.

In our projects, this category of query was by far the most common. By changing approach/surround queries to use ring generators, agents selected more natural destinations, and the improved efficiency allowed us to enhance these queries with more complex sets of tests.

26.4 Testing Techniques and Test Subjects

Tests are the building blocks that allow complex reasoning about the environment, and are thus the most crucial components of a query system. Although projects invariably require some domain-specific tests, knowing how to combine and reuse simple, generic tests to produce complex results is the key to rapid development. For example, by only mixing and matching the two most versatile tests in a query system's toolkit, distance and dot product, we can support a surprisingly wide range of tasks beyond the common but simple "move within X meters of target Y" or "find the closest cover point between myself and the target" behaviors. Section 26.8 provides several practical examples of queries built with these two tests.

26.4.1 Single versus Multiple Test Subjects

Some query systems, such as EQS, allow a test to be run against multiple reference locations. By preparing specific concepts such as "all nearby allies," "all nearby hostiles," or "all agent destinations," we can add tests to our queries to improve the final result.

For example, a minimum distance test (Section 26.4.3) weighted against both ally locations and ally destinations can prevent agents from attempting to move not only into currently occupied locations, but also into locations that *will be occupied in the near future*. For agents that do not require advanced coordinated tactical movement, this single powerful addition can eliminate most location contention without the need to implement specific countermeasures such as point reservation systems.

26.4.2 Distance Test Scoring

When performing a test against multiple test subjects, we have a choice to make: What score do we keep? For example, is it better to record the shortest distance or the average? As shown in Figure 26.4, each can be used to express a different concept. Minimum distance helps us create local attraction or avoidance around the test subjects; this allows us to keep our distance from any area of the map occupied by a test subject. Conversely, average distance gives us the centroid of the subjects, useful for enforcing team cohesion by prioritizing samples within a specific distance from the centroid.

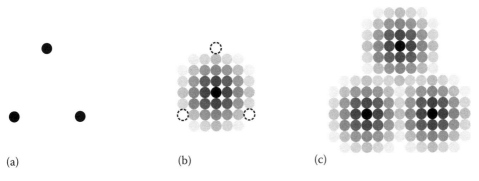

(a)   (b)   (c)

Figure 26.4

(a) Multiple targets used as the context of a distance test. (b) Score using average distance from targets. (c) Score using minimum distance from targets.

26.4.3 Dot Product Test Techniques

Within our project, this test is the most frequently used after the distance test, and these two as a pair have been used to express more movement concepts than all other tests combined. The dot product test measures the angle between two directions, allowing us to, for example, prioritize sample points in front of or behind an agent. By choosing our test subjects carefully, we can handle virtually any direction-related weighting by stacking dot product tests. Some examples:

- Testing the vector from the agent to a sample point against the agent's orientation allows us to prioritize locations in front of (or behind) the agent.
- Similarly, testing points against the agent's right vector instead of its orientation (forward vector) lets us prioritize locations to its right or left.
- We can use one of the tests above to prioritize a heading in front of, behind, to the left or to the right of the agent. However, using both together will prioritize the area where they overlap, allowing us to represent a diagonal heading instead.
- Testing against the world forward and right vectors, instead of the agent's, can give us prioritization along cardinal or ordinal directions.
- Using a target as the test subject, rather than the agent, gives us the ability to position ourselves in a specific direction relative to that target—for instance, to stand in front of an NPC vendor, to attack an armored enemy from behind, or to walk alongside the player in formation.
- For even more flexibility, we can accept an optional orientation offset in the dot product test itself: By applying a user-defined angle to the set of forward vectors above, we can prioritize points in any direction, not just the cardinal and ordinals.
- By defining both directions as vectors between two subjects, rather than the orientation of the subjects themselves, we can go even further:
- Comparing the vector from the agent to a sample point against the vector from the sample point to an agent's target prioritizes locations between the agent and the target. This provides us with locations that get us closer to the target from our current position, ranked by the directness of that approach.

- By using a sine scoring function (Section 26.5.1) over the same vectors, we prioritize locations where the dot product value approaches zero, generating destinations ranked by *indirectness*. While still approaching the target, these locations allow us to do so in a curved, flanking manner.
- Flipping the direction of the first vector (i.e., using the vector from a sample point to the agent instead of the agent to a sample point) reverses the prioritization, providing retreat suggestions ranked by directness away from the target (Figure 26.5).

We can even apply these concepts beyond actors in the scene. For example, ranking sample points based on the dot product of the vector from the camera to a sample point against the camera's orientation provides us with locations near the center of the screen (though potentially obstructed). Used with a minimum threshold and low weight, this can provide encouragement for buddy AI characters or other agents we want the player to see as much as possible.

26.4.4 Subject Floor Position

In action games where the player can fly, jump, or climb walls, an agent's target can easily become separated from the navmesh. When used as a generator origin, this results in the entire query failing, as there is no navmesh at the origin location to generate sample points around. On our project, we used two techniques to resolve this issue:

1. We provided a "Target Floor" test subject to supplement Target (the default). This modified version projected the agent's position down to the navmesh floor, if present.
2. We provided a "Closest Navmesh Point to Target" test subject, which scanned the immediate area when the target was off mesh.

Both of these techniques allowed agents to find a suitable location to approach the player when jumping or performing off-mesh traversal. For ground-based enemies, this solution was robust enough to become the default test subject used for engaging the player.

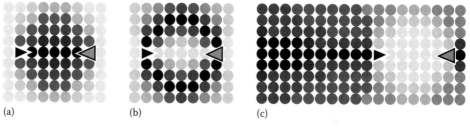

(a) (b) (c)

Figure 26.5

(a) Approach locations prioritized by directness. (b) Approach locations prioritized by indirectness. (c) Retreat locations prioritized by directness.

26. Guide to Effective Auto-Generated Spatial Queries

26.5 Test Scoring Functions

Once all sample points have been scored, they must be normalized and ranked. Most commonly, we use this value as-is, inverting the priority when needed with a negative test weight. However, as the final post-processing stage in a test's evaluation, we can pass the normalized score of each sample point to a scoring function to transform its value. Doing so allows us to increase or decrease the influence of certain samples, adding precision to our test's intent, or transforming the concept it measures entirely.

- *Linear scoring* (Figure 26.6a) is the backbone of most tests, returning the value of normalized test scores exactly as they were passed in.
- *Square scoring* (Figure 26.6b) strongly deemphasizes all but the highest ranked samples in the test. Useful when we want emphasis to drop off rapidly.
- *Square root scoring* (Figure 26.6c) does the opposite; overemphasizing all but the lowest-ranked samples in the test.
- *Sine scoring* (Figure 26.6d) differs from other methods, in that it emphasizes mid-range values, and de-emphasizes both the highest- and lowest-ranked sample points.
- Where scoring functions describe the *rate* at which emphasis should change, a test's weight determines the *direction* of change. When a test's weight is negative, an increase in score is replaced with a corresponding decrease, inverting the scoring curve (Figure 26.6b and e, c and f).

Queries typically require several tests to express a useful concept. In these cases, the highest ranked location will almost always represent a compromise between multiple competing goals. The role of scoring equations is to allow each test to define how tolerant it is of suboptimal locations, and how quickly that tolerance changes. In conjunction with the test weight, this lets us define how that compromise should be met.

For example, if we want an agent that steps away from others as its personal space is encroached, how should we express its level of discomfort? We might approximate it using

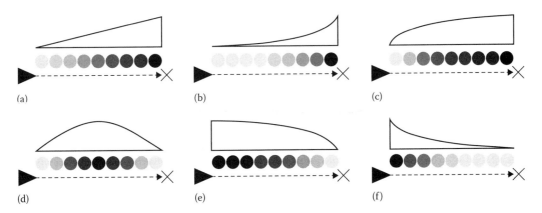

Figure 26.6

Normalized result of a distance test from sample points to an agent's target, after applying linear (a), square (b), square root (c), sine (d) scoring functions. Response curves become inverted when a negative scoring weight is used, as shown in (b) and (e), and (c) and (f), respectively. Darker shades indicate better locations.

two tests: A distance test against our current location, expressing our desire to move as little as possible, and a second distance test, negatively weighted against other actors in the scene, expressing our desire to move as far away from them as possible. The balance of these two tests determines when the agent will react. For example, if we use square scoring with a negative weight on the second test (Figure 26.6e), in general other actors will have little effect on the agent's evaluation of its current location, but when approached extremely closely its desire to stay in its current location will be outweighed by its desire to avoid others and it will try to find a slightly less crowded position. Alternatively, if we instead use square root scoring with a negative weight (Figure 26.6f) then even the influence of distant actors will quickly become overwhelming, creating a nervous agent with a strong desire to keep far away from anyone in the area.

The advantage to expressing satisfaction with scoring functions is that it allows us to produce a dynamic, natural response that is not easily expressed by the hard edges of an acceptance condition. If, instead of measuring satisfaction, we simply invalidated all locations within 2 m of another actor, our agent's response becomes predictable and artificial. However, by defining a level of comfort for all sample points in the test, our response can change along with the environment. For example, when entering a quiet subway car the agent in our scoring equation example will naturally maintain a polite distance from other passengers, but will gradually permit that distance to shrink as it becomes packed at rush hour, continuously adjusting its reaction as the environment becomes more or less crowded.

26.5.1 Sine Scoring Techniques

Although square, square root, and other monotonic scoring functions can be used to tune test results by compressing or expanding the range of suitable positions, sine scoring gives us an opportunity to use existing tests in altogether new ways. For example, applied to a distance test with a minimum and maximum range, we can define a specific ideal radius to approach a target—the average of the two ranges—while still accepting positions closer or further from the target, but with reduced priority.

When applied to the dot product, we have even more options:

- When used against the agent's orientation, we can express preference for positions to both the left and right, or both forward and behind with a negative weight.
- If we use the absolute value of the dot product with an agent's orientation, this produces the same result. However, when both are combined, we can now represent preference for either the cardinal or intermediate directions.
- As described in Section 26.4.3, applied to the dot product *(Agent→Sample Point)· (Sample Point→Target)*, we can create a circle between the agent and the target, representing a roundabout approach.

There are many other instances where the most interesting samples are those that lie in the mid-range of a test's scoring function; sine scoring is the key to discovering them!

26.6 Continuous versus Sequential Updates

Most queries are designed to be executed once, at the start of a behavior, to provide the agent with a suitable destination for its current goal (Figure 26.7a). To adapt to changing world conditions, such as a cover point becoming exposed, it is common to periodically run a validation test on the agent's destination while en route, but for efficiency we typically do not execute another full query until after we have arrived. In some cases, however, it is worth the expense to update continuously, periodically reexecuting the original query without waiting to arrive, and thus generating new recommendations as world conditions change (Figure 26.7b). Not only does this allow us to react more dynamically, it opens the door to new types of query-based behaviors that previously could only be expressed in code. Common concepts like surrounding, orbiting, zig-zag approaches and random walks can all be expressed as a single, repeatedly executed query without any programming required.

26.6.1 Continuous Query-Based Behaviors

By periodically rerunning the same query, providing frequent updates to the agent's destination, we can create the illusion of sophisticated navigation or decision-making. For example, as shown in Figure 26.8, by generating a ring of points on the navigation mesh around the agent's target, then simply prioritizing samples a few meters away as well as those in front of our current position, an agent will begin to circle-strafe around the target, avoiding obstacles as it moves and even reversing direction when it becomes stuck.

Traditional positioning can be enhanced by this technique as well. For example, when approaching a target as part of a group, not only can we maintain ideal distance from the target as it moves, but by negatively weighting the area around the agent's teammates the group can dynamically reposition themselves in relation to each other, creating a natural and responsive surround behavior (Figure 26.9).

26.6.2 Continuous Querying versus Destination Validation

While promising, there are caveats to this method. Compared to destination validation, continuous querying is responsive and can produce high-quality results, but is also

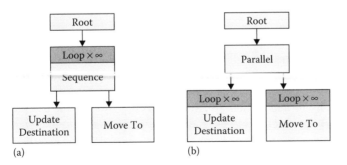

Figure 26.7

Behavior tree implementation of a sequential query-based behavior (a) versus a continuous query-based behavior (b).

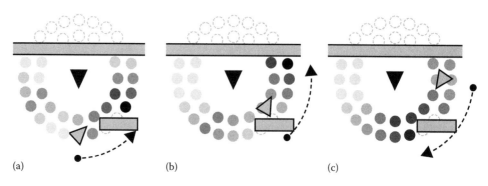

(a) (b) (c)

Figure 26.8

Orbiting a target with a continuously updated query (a). As positions in front of the agent become increasingly unsuitable, positions behind the agent gradually gain utility (b), ultimately causing the agent to automatically reverse direction when it can no longer proceed (c).

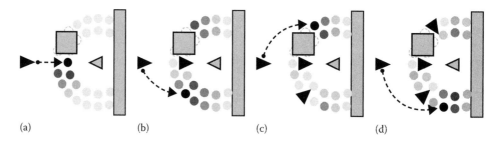

(a) (b) (c) (d)

Figure 26.9

A group of agents approach and surround a target in sequence. In this example, agents prefer locations that are near the target, as well as along the vector between the agent and the target (a), but negatively weight locations near other agents to prevent clustering (b, c, and d). This produces an organic surround behavior that maintains formation continuously as the target moves, and adapts naturally as the number of agents increases or decreases.

computationally expensive. If too many agents in the scene are issuing too many queries, you can easily burn through your AI's CPU budget. It is also more challenging to avoid degenerate behavior: agents becoming stuck in local minima, oscillating between destinations unnaturally, or moving in a stop-and-go fashion by selecting destinations too close to their current position. Nevertheless, the benefits can be substantial and are well worth consideration.

26.7 Reducing Query Failure

Using the techniques thus far, we have been able to reason about the ideal layout for generated points, apply tests on single or multiple subjects, and adjust their scoring based on our needs. In theory, this should be enough to produce high-quality results from a spatial

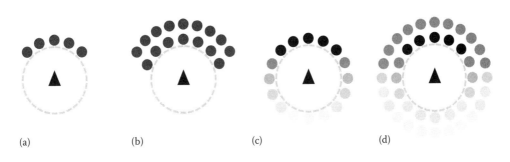

Figure 26.10

Reducing query failure of a strict, brittle query (a) by increasing robustness (b), permissiveness (c), or both (d). Whenever possible, strategies (c) and (d) will return the same result as the original query.

query system for most position selection tasks. However, in practice we rarely are so lucky. For example, the player may be in a narrow corridor, causing all samples in our flanking query to fail, or they may be facing a wall, making a dramatic surround from the front impossible. A query is useless if it never works and, unfortunately, it is common to design one that fails too easily in unexpected circumstances like these. Fortunately, by making some simple adjustments, a brittle query can be adapted to provide graceful degradation of position quality in unfavorable conditions. In this section, we show how a query can be modified to give the AI the ability to execute a behavior in a wider range of conditions while still returning the ideal result when possible, making them resilient to the complexities of a modern game environment (Figure 26.10).

26.7.1 Increasing Permissiveness

The first action we can take to make a brittle query more failure-resistant is to make it more *permissive*. That is, we can relax our success conditions so that we have more sample points that can serve as a destination, but use tests to give them a lower final rank so that they are only selected when the ideal conditions are unavailable. In Figure 26.10, we have an example query that attempts to find an attack position in front of the agent's target. If it is acceptable to attack from behind, but not preferred, we can add additional sample points around the target, but weight them with a dot product test so that the samples behind the target receive a low rank. Done this way, agents will still approach the player from the front, unless it is impossible due to the player's location (near the edge of a cliff, facing a wall, etc.).

26.7.2 Increasing Robustness

The next action we can take is to make the query more *robust*. In this case, we relax our concept of the ideal case entirely, providing a larger pool of sample points to draw from under ideal circumstances. For example, our query may specify a position 5 m away and up to 30° from the front of the target, but in reality it may be the case that it will actually work fine at any distance between 5 and 8 m away, and up to 45° in front of the target. Figure 26.10 also shows an example of this solution.

26.7.3 Fallback Queries

Some query systems, such as EQS, provide multiple query *options*, or strategies, that can be defined as part of a single query. These can be thought of as fallback queries, providing alternative location suggestions to consider if the initial query fails. Thus if the initial option has no usable samples, subsequent ones are executed in order until one succeeds. Only when all options fail does the query itself fail. Clever use of fallback queries can also create opportunities for optimizing high-quality behavior: By defining a narrow initial sample set, we can run more expensive tests in the primary option that would normally be cost prohibitive, such as collision raycasts. In the fallback query, with a wider range of sample points, we can remove these tests to find a more mediocre, but still acceptable, location.

26.7.4 Preserving Quality

Taking advantage of these techniques, we can adapt our queries to be both permissive and robust, while still returning the same results as the initial query when possible. In Figure 26.9, the result of the rightmost query can be achieved in two ways:

1. Combine permissive and robust testing strategies: Pair a dot product gradient ranking with a larger valid sample area, then further add a distance test to weight the closest points higher. This layering results in the original set of points receiving the highest rank whenever they are available.
2. Define the leftmost query as the initial query strategy; if this fails, execute a fallback query that combines the permissive and robust testing strategies. This has the benefit of only incurring additional cost when ideal conditions are unavailable, at the expense of a higher overall cost of running both queries in suboptimal conditions.

26.8 Example Behaviors

In this section, we provide a handful of the many behaviors possible using only the most basic tests and the continuous movement behavior tree in Figure 26.7. For each behavior listed below, the only difference in the agent's AI is the query itself.

26.8.1 Directed Random Walk

By selecting a random item from the set of sample points, instead of the one that has the highest rank, we can add variety and unpredictability to a query-based behavior. For example, the classic NPC random walk (moving a short distance in an arbitrary direction, stopping briefly between moves) can be represented as a query by generating a filled circle of points up to a specified radius, ranking them by sine-scored distance to define an ideal move distance, and finally selecting randomly among the top 25% highest ranked points. By adding a dot product test to favor the agent's current direction, we eliminate harsh turns and unnatural oscillations, creating an agent that takes a long winding path through its environment. Finally, a minimum distance test weighted against other agents keeps agents evenly distributed and avoids collisions in crowded environments. By including our current position in the set of generated points, an agent that is boxed in can choose not to move until a reasonable location becomes available (Table 26.1).

Table 26.1 Directed Random Walk: Moves Relatively Forward, Avoiding Others

Weight	Type	Parameters	Scoring
N/A	Ring generator	0–8 m around agent	
1	Distance	Relative to agent	Sine
1	Dot	(Agent→Sample)· (Agent rotation)	Sigmoid
1	Minimum distance	Relative to other agents	Linear, 2–10 m range

26.8.2 Stay on Camera

If we want to position agents where they can be seen by the player, we can use the location and orientation of the camera to prioritize sample points based on their distance from the center of the screen. A camera frustum test can be approximated with a dot product, using a lower clamp to define the angle of a view cone. A negatively weighted distance test relative to the agent ensures the agent moves as little as possible to stay in view. Optionally, adding a raycast test between each point and the camera will eliminate points in front of the camera but hidden behind other objects or scenery, improving behavior quality at the cost of performance (Table 26.2).

26.8.3 Orbit

To walk or run in a circle around a target, we generate a ring of points within the minimum and maximum acceptable radius, then use a set of tests that when combined generate forward movement around the ring. The first, a sine-scored distance test around the agent, defines an ideal movement distance a few meters away from its current position; far enough that we should not arrive before reexecuting the query, but close enough to ensure small, smooth adjustments in heading. Next, a dot product test prioritizes items in the direction that the agent is currently heading, which encourages stable forward movement along the ring (clockwise or counter-clockwise). A second sine-ranked dot product test prioritizes points on the tangent line from the agent to the ring. This serves two purposes: It directs the agent to approach the ring along the tangent line (rather than head on, then turning 90° to begin orbiting), and it strongly prioritizes items directly in front of and behind the agent, allowing the agent to reverse direction when blocked while further stabilizing forward movement. Finally, clamped minimum distance tests around the positions and current destinations of other agents provide local avoidance (Table 26.3).

Table 26.2 Stay on Camera: Agent Attempts to Stay on Screen While Moving as Little as Possible

Weight	Type	Parameters	Scoring
N/A	Grid generator	20 m around agent	
−1	Distance	Relative to agent	Linear
1	Dot	(Camera→Sample)· (Camera rotation)	Linear, 0.85–1.0 range

Table 26.3 Orbit: Moves in a Circle around a Target Avoiding Others

Weight	Type	Parameters	Scoring
N/A	Ring generator	5–9 m around target	
8	Distance	Relative to agent	Sine, 0–6 m range
4	Dot	(Agent→Sample) (Agent→Destination)	Linear
2	Dot	(Agent→Sample)·(Agent→Target)	Sine
1	Minimum distance	Relative to other agents	Sigmoid, 0–5 m range
1	Minimum distance	Relative to other agent destinations	Sigmoid, 0–5 m range

Note: If forward movement is obstructed by the environment or other agents, the agent will turn around and continue orbiting in the opposite direction.

26.8.4 Boids

Spatial queries can even represent artificial life simulations. Craig Reynold's historic boids program, simulating the flocking behavior of birds, produces complex, emergent group behavior from an unexpectedly simple set of rules (Reynolds 1987). By implementing these rules using spatial query tests, we can recreate the original boids simulation as a continuous query behavior. In the original SIGGRAPH paper, individual boid movement was produced by combining the influence of three separate rules:

- Separation, to avoid crowding
- Alignment, to coordinate the flock direction
- Cohesion, to prevent the flock from dispersing

Within a query, separation can be represented as a minimum distance test against other agents, alignment as a dot product test against the average heading of the group, and cohesion as a distance test against the group centroid. By tuning the weights and ranges of these tests, we can adjust the emergent properties of the behavior (Table 26.4).

Table 26.4 Boids: Simulates Boid Flocking Behavior

Weight	Type	Parameters	Scoring
N/A	Ring generator	1–20 m around agent	
1.2	Minimum distance	Relative to other agents	Linear, 0–4 m range
0.5	Dot	(Agent→Sample)· (Average rotation of other agents)	Linear
−1	Distance	Relative to other agents	Linear

Note: Simulates boid flocking behavior using minimum distance, dot product, and average distance tests to represent separation, alignment, and cohesion respectively.

26.9 Conclusion

Once a novel alternative to traditional techniques, over the past five years spatial query systems have evolved into indispensable tools for AI development. Now commonplace and supported by multiple widely used game engines, integrating spatial query systems into your AI is more practical than ever, providing faster iteration time and higher quality position selection in dynamic and complex environments. By understanding the strengths and weaknesses of each component of a query, we can improve query quality and flexibility over a wider range of environmental conditions. Single queries, executed continuously, can even express traditionally code-driven movement behaviors, making query systems an increasingly versatile tool, able to single-handedly support most, if not all, destination selection in a project.

References

Jack, M. 2013. Tactical position selection: An architecture and query language. In *Game AI Pro*, ed. S. Rabin. New York: CRC Press, pp. 337–359.

Mars, C. 2014. Environmentally conscious AI: Improving spatial analysis and reasoning. *GDC 2014*, San Francisco, http://www.gdcvault.com/play/1018038/Spaces-in-the-Sandbox-Tactical.

Reynolds, C. W. 1987. Flocks, herds, and schools: A distributed behavioral model. *Computer Graphics*, 21(4) (SIGGRAPH '87 Conference Proceedings), 25–34.

Shirakami, Y., Miyake, Y., Namiki, K. 2015. The decision making Systems for Character AI in Final Fantasy XV -EPISODE DUSCAE-. *CEDEC 2015*, Yokohama, http://cedec.cesa.or.jp/2015/session/ENG/5953.html.

Zielinski, M. 2013. Asking the environment smart questions. In *Game AI Pro*, ed. S. Rabin. Boca Raton, FL: CRC Press, pp. 423–431.

The Role of Time in Spatio-Temporal Reasoning

Three Examples from Tower Defense

Baylor Wetzel and Kyle Anderson

27.1 Introduction

In Akira Kurosawa's film *Seven Samurai*, a small group of defenders are hired to defend a small village from an invading army of bandits. Vastly outnumbered, their survival depended on mastering their environment. Humans are good at spatio-temporal reasoning. Understanding how objects flow through space over time is how we know whether we can cross the street when there's a car coming. It is also how samurai know where to place ambushes when defending a village.

Spatio-temporal reasoning is an important part of many decisions (in and out of games). It is how armies know where to place gun nests, prisons know where to place cameras, firemen know where to place firebreaks, cities know where to place highways, and malls know where to place stores. Much has been written about the spatial aspect of spatio-temporal reasoning. Identifying choke points, flanks, and avenues of approach is an important part of video game AI, and at this point is fairly well understood. Far less has been written about time. Consequently, this chapter will focus specifically on the temporal aspect of spatio-temporal reasoning.

Temporal strategies are harder to visualize than spatial ones and, we believe, best explained by working through examples. Like Kurosawa's *Seven Samurai*, this chapter will focus on protecting a location from incoming enemies by identifying the best place to deploy our limited defenses. Defending a location is a common scenario in games that include any amount of strategic planning, such as tower defense games, strategy games, and "hold out until help arrives" missions in first-person shooters or action games. We will look at three examples. The first can be solved without directly thinking about time, whereas the second cannot be solved. The third shows how changing one's focus from space to time can produce new solutions.

27.2 Defend the Village

To keep our focus on the temporal part of spatio-temporal reasoning, our examples will use a tower defense game. This gives us difficult problems to solve but abstracts out the details not relevant to the topic.

For those unfamiliar with tower defense games, the genre grew out of real-time strategy games, with many players realizing they enjoyed designing the defenses around their base more than they liked attacking other players. The player is given a location to protect and one or more paths to that location. The player cannot directly attack the enemies (generically referred to as *creeps*) that will come down the path. Instead, they are given a set of objects (generically referred to as *towers*) that attack any enemy in range. Specifics vary by game—in some games the towers are soldiers with fast rifles or slow rocket launchers, in other games the towers are pits of acid, wizards with fire, or monkeys with darts. But what is always the same is that the gameplay revolves around placing towers strategically, in such a way that they prevent the enemies from getting past them.

Our examples come from *GopherTD*, a game we built to study how humans play strategy games. It is based on the popular tower defense game *Vector TD*. These are the details relevant to this chapter:

- There are 28 enemies (creeps) divided into two lines of 14 creeps each.
- Each line of creeps follows a fixed path through the map. Normally the two lines move side-by-side.
- Creeps move at a constant, fixed speed unless slowed by a slowing tower.
- Towers have a fixed rate of fire, do not run out of ammo, and never miss.
- There are several types of towers. To keep things simple, our examples will use only two types:
  - Attack towers attack the closest creep in range, staying on them until the creep dies or moves out of range, after which it moves to whichever creep is closest at that time. A creep must be hit multiple times before it is stopped.
  - Slowing towers attack the closest creep. Attacked creeps move at half speed for two seconds.
- The score is the number of creeps prevented from reaching the exit.

Figure 27.1 shows three examples of *GopherTD* levels.

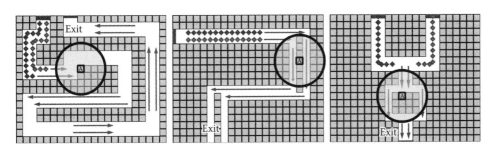

Figure 27.1

Maps from *GopherTD*. Creeps are shown at the entrance. Their goal is to make it to the spot marked Exit, representing the location you are trying to protect. The player's goal is to stop them by placing defenses (towers) along the path. Arrows show the direction the creeps move. A tower can be placed on any gray square. Circles show the range of the attack tower located at the cell marked A.

27.3 Example 1: U-Turns and the Maximum Usable Range Strategy

Our first example, while simple, illustrates some important concepts we should understand before tackling more complex problems.

27.3.1 The Problem

Consider the leftmost map in Figure 27.1. If you had only one attack tower, where should you place it? Figure 27.2 shows five options, each representing a different type of spatial structure—a hallway, corner, U-turn, double-sided wall, and an interior corner. Which is the best position and why?

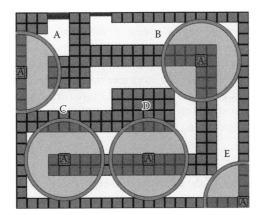

Figure 27.2

An attack tower placed at five different types of positions. (A) A wall. (B) A corner. (C) A U-turn. (D) A wall. The tower overlooks two hallways. (E) An interior corner.

We wanted to design an AI that thought like a human so we began by studying humans. We asked 59 people, a mixture of gamers and nongamers, where they would put the tower (among other things [Wetzel 2014]). The answer was nearly unanimous: C, the U-turn (only one person disagreed, choosing D, the hallway).

What makes the U-turn a better position than the others? People answered in different ways. Some said that it covers three hallways, whereas B and D only covered two and A and E covered one. Some said C covered everything positions such as D did plus more. Others said that C simply looked like it covered more area. Unsurprisingly, given how good humans are at visual estimation, they were correct: position C has a usable range of 30 (i.e., there are 30 path tiles the creeps move across that are inside the tower's range) as opposed to 29 at B, 26 at D, 16 at A, and 8 at E.

27.3.2 Discussion: Space-Time Equivalence

Each of the above explanations means essentially the same thing: maximize the tower's usable range, meaning place the tower where it covers the largest number of tiles that the creeps will walk over. We call this the *Maximum Usable Range* strategy and it is a common and obvious strategy.

Words say a lot about our thinking process. If you look at the reasons given for selecting position C you should notice that the language is almost entirely spatial. If this does not seem surprising, it might be because you believe the problem is a spatial problem. It is not. The goal is nonspatial: maximize the score, with one point earned for each creep destroyed. The action is spatial: place the tower on the map. The effectiveness of the action is temporal: since the tower fires at a fixed rate of speed doing a fixed amount of damage per shot, maximizing the tower's effectiveness means maximizing the amount of time it spends firing. Since the tower only fires when creeps are in range (a spatial property), maximizing the tower's effectiveness means maximizing the amount of time there are creeps in the tower's range.

As with many terrain reasoning problems, the problem is a mixture of spatio-temporal reasoning and nonspatio-temporal goals. Why, then, do people treat it like a spatial problem? One reason is that is easier for people to think about space than time. A large part of the human brain is dedicated to understanding space, something that is not true for time. If a spatio-temporal problem can be converted to a spatial one, it can leverage that hardware.

Two other reasons why people convert spatio-temporal problems to spatial ones are that it works well and that it makes sense. In many cases, space and time are proportional and linearly correlated. In this case, the more area inside a tower's range, the longer it takes the creeps to move through it and therefore the more time creeps are in range and the more time the tower has to fire at them. Increasing a tower's usable range (space) increases the amount of time it spends firing (time).

27.3.3 Discussion: Strategies and Affordances

We wrote AIs to solve each of the maps mentioned in this chapter. The best AIs perform as well as the best human players we studied (which is perhaps unsurprising given that we based them on those players). All of the AIs work in the same way: they are given a set of affordance-keyed strategies and query our Spatial Affordance Query System for places to apply their strategies. We will give examples later but first we need to define how we use the terms "affordance" and "strategy."

An *affordance* is something that affords (allows) an action. More importantly, it suggests an action. The classic example is a door handle (Norman 1988). A plate on a door says (to most people) "push me," whereas a handle says "pull me." In our example, the U-turn was an affordance that said (to most people) "place your tower here." Alternately, for those who measured usable range directly rather than using the U-turn as a proxy for maximum usable range, usable range is an affordance. There are many types of affordances. In the case of U-turns, the affordance is spatial geometry, whereas in the case of usable range, it is a variable to be maximized.

It is important to point out that affordances are contextually defined—whether something is an affordance depends on a number of things including one's goal, capabilities, and other relevant factors. In our example, several things must be true for position C to be a U-turn. First, the creeps must move all the way around it. If the creeps came from two different directions and met in the middle, as they do in the rightmost map in Figure 27.1, the space might still be shaped like a U-turn but it does not afford the expected behavior of creeps moving around the U-turn. Second, C is only a U-turn if the attack tower's range is large enough to cover all three sides. If the tower's range were significantly wider, position D would also be a U-turn, whereas if it were taller, position B would be a U-turn (i.e., it would cover the U-turn that is down and to the left). Third, we only notice the U-turn because the action it affords is relevant to our Maximum Usable Range strategy. If we had different goals, the U-turn might stop affording us actions we care about. The important point for the AI developer is this: You cannot identify an affordance without knowing how you intend to use it. In this example, you not only need to know the map geography, you need to know the path the creeps take and the range of the tower to be placed.

In our experience, a *strategy* tends to be a simple action designed to achieve a single, concrete goal. Strategies exploit or otherwise rely upon an affordance. A player only considers using a U-turn strategy when the map contains U-turn affordances (i.e., areas that can be used as a U-turn by the strategy). Likewise, a player that does not know the U-turn strategy does not notice the afforded U-turns on the map.

Strategies are, in our view, small things. Most problems require the use of multiple strategies, which we refer to alternately as *strategy sets* or a person's *play-* or *problem solving-style*. In this example, where we only have one tower and wish to place it at the spot where it has the most usable range, a single strategy is sufficient. We will see more complicated playstyles in the next examples.

The implementation for the maximum usable range agent is given in Listing 27.1. It is only a few lines: Define the strategy then ask the solver to solve it. Defining a placement strategy involves specifying a *PlacementDecision*, which consists of three parts: *placement object*, *placement relationship*, and *anchor* (Wetzel 2014). For this AI, the strategy is to place the tower (placement object) on a spot that has the maximal (placement relationship) value for the relative property `PhysicalPathCellsInRange` (anchor). Relative properties can vary in magnitude (e.g., usable range), whereas an absolute property does not (e.g., a location either is or is not a corner). The relative property used by this AI is usable range, which it wants to maximize. The anchor could be a spatial feature but more often it is an affordance, as it is here. Other examples of strategies include placing an attack tower's range (placement object) so that it overlaps (placement relationship) another tower's range (anchor) or placing a slowing tower so that the exit to its range

Listing 27.1. The Maximum Usable Range agent.

```
Solution AI::getSolution(MapModel map)
{
    SolutionRequest request = new SolutionRequest(map);
    GroupToPlace group = new GroupToPlace();
    request.groups. Add(group);
    group.towers. Add(new AttackTower());
    Strategy strategy =
        new PlaceTowerOnRelativePropertyStrategy(
            MapPropertyOrdinal. PhysicalPathCellsInRange,
            StrategyOperator. Maximum));
    group.placementStrategies. Add(strategy);
    return Solver.getSolution(request);
}
```

(placement object) is in front of (placement relationship) the start to an attack tower's range (anchor) (Wetzel 2014).

The solver code (Listing 27.2) is equally simple: Find the affordances on the map and execute the strategy for each affordance. In this case, the AI asked the solver to place

Listing 27.2. The Solver creates a solution (list of tower placements) by instantiating the strategy for each group of towers. In practice, this means identifying affordances on the map and matching towers to those using each tower's strategy, which is a `PlacementDecision` specifying the affordance to use.

```
static Solution Solver::getSolution(SolutionRequest request)
{
  Solution solution = new Solution();
  solution.map = MapAnalyzer.getMapAnalysis(request.map);
  foreach (GroupToPlace group in request.groups)
  {
    foreach (Tower t in group.towers)
    {
      foreach (Strategy s in group.strategies)
      {
        List<GridPoint> candidates = s.getPositions(t, map);
        if (candidates. Count > 0)
        {
          GridPoint p = group.tieBreaker.get(candidates);
          solution.add(t, p);
          break;
        }
      }
    }
  }
  return solution;
}
```

27. The Role of Time in Spatio-Temporal Reasoning

one attack tower with the strategy "place the tower at the position where it gets the most usable range." The solver asks the MapAnalyzer for all the affordances on the given map for the specified tower (getMapAnalysis), compares the strategies to the affordances and places the tower on the best match (i.e., where the tower's usable range is maximized) then returns where the highest usable range for an attack tower is on the given map and returns a list of positions and the tower to place on each.

For this code to work a few things have to be true. You must be able to explicitly define your strategies (in Listing 27.1, the Maximum Usable Range strategy is an instantiation of the more general PlaceTowerOnRelativePropertyStrategy). Second, you must be able to define your affordances. Third, strategies need to be keyed to affordances, or at least, the computer needs to know how to apply a strategy given an affordance (in this case, the tower is placed on the spot where the affordance is detected). Fourth, you need to be able to identify the affordances on the map. We do this through our Spatial Affordance Query System, SAQS. Although the AI and solver code are quite short, SAQS is not and is therefore outside of the scope of this chapter. We believe, however, that by walking through examples, it will be clear how to identify the ones you need.

27.4 Example 2: Spatial Symmetry and the Differential Slowing Strategy

It is often enough to convert a spatio-temporal problem to a spatial one and solve that, but not always. In this example, we consider a situation where we need to think explicitly about time.

27.4.1 The Problem

The map in Figure 27.3 has an interesting property: It is essentially featureless. It has no switchbacks or U-turns or any usable spatial features. The only positions where a tower could reach the creeps on both paths are on the thin strip of wall between the two. The positions on the wall are all essentially identical, with a usable range of 14, less than half that on the U-turn in Example 1 and not nearly enough to stop the invading creeps.

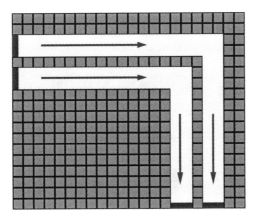

Figure 27.3

The map no left turns.

27.4.2 Discussion: Temporal Asymmetry and the Path Gap Affordance

In Example 1 we said that, although these problems were temporal, not spatial, it did not matter because space is often a good proxy for time. This is a problem where that is not true.

The spatial geometry is mirrored across the diagonal axis. This makes the map symmetric, but only spatially. When it comes to time, the map is strongly asymmetric. We can measure this by measuring where an object is at a given point in time. Pick a position along the path and consider which line of creeps will reach it first. Before the corner, the answer is neither, both lines will arrive at the same time. After the corner, however, the creeps on the inside (lower, left) path will reach a given position before those on the outer one. That is because the outer path is longer, taking longer to go around the corner (Figure 27.4).

We use the term *path gap* to refer to the difference between when a group on one path reaches a position versus when a group on a second path reaches it. Once you know the concept exists, it is easy to see and you will see path gap on every map where you are trying to solve a similar problem (an affordance only exists when it is relevant to one of your goals; if you do not have that goal, the concept stops making sense). If the concept suggests an action, a strategy to exploit it, then it is an affordance. Path gap is certainly an affordance.

We said earlier that our goal is to maximize the amount of time a tower spends firing, which we do by maximizing the amount of time that creeps are in range. Note that this does not refer to the amount of time that a single creep is in range, it is the amount of time that any creep is in range. With that in mind, consider Figure 27.4. A tower placed on the top half of the map will be active for the amount of time it takes a line of creeps to move through it. It does not matter which line since both move through at the same time. A line of creeps is 14 creeps long so the tower is active for as long as it takes for 14 creeps to move through it.

Now consider the same tower placed on the lower part of the map. The outer path is six tiles longer so the second line of creeps does not reach the tower until six tiles worth of creeps has already entered its range. The tower is therefore active for the amount of time it takes the first line of creeps to move through the tower's range, as in the positions along the top of the map, plus the time it takes for the last six tiles worth of creeps from the second line to move through. If we say that a creep is one tile wide, the tower's active

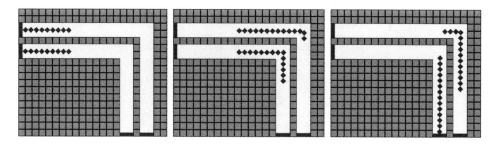

Figure 27.4

As they round the corner, the creeps on the outer path fall behind.

27. The Role of Time in Spatio-Temporal Reasoning

time on the bottom part of the map grows from the amount of time it takes 14 creeps to move through to the amount of time it takes 20 creeps to move through. The physical space in range did not change but the amount of time the tower spends firing did; the map is spatially symmetric but temporally asymmetric and the positions on it are spatially equivalent but temporally different. We have grown time without growing space. We call this the *Exploit Path Gap* strategy.

27.4.3 Discussion: Forcing Affordances and the Differential Slowing Strategy

Path Gap is a spatial affordance in the sense that it is based on the length of a path. As such, it can only be used on maps where the geometry supports it. The key idea, however, is not the length of the paths, it is the difference between when two groups arrive at a location. That gap in arrival times is an affordance we can exploit. Once we know this is valuable property, we not only become more sensitive to other features that can create it, we can consider ways to create it ourselves, even on maps where the geometry does not support it.

In Section 27.2 we mentioned that there are two types of towers, attack and slowing. We did not use the slowing towers in Example 1 because it did not affect the strategy we used (maximizing usable range) or the way we thought about space. Here, where we want to exploit the difference in arrival times, slowing towers give us an interesting option. We could use the slowing towers to slow the creeps while they are in the attack tower's range, a good and straightforward strategy, but we can do better.

In the *Differential Slowing* strategy, slowing towers are placed where they only slow one group, causing it to fall behind the other and effectively creating a path gap. Using our slowing towers, we can slow one line of creeps and not the other, thus causing one group to fall behind the other. In this example, we can combine Differential Slowing with the Exploit Path Gap strategy to create a much larger gap (obviously, both strategies should target the same group).In practice, using both Exploit Path Gap, which exploits a temporal affordance caused by a spatial feature, and Differential Slowing, which creates a temporal affordance, fully separates the two groups, causing them to go through the tower's range at different times (Figure 27.5). This doubles the amount of time the tower spends firing.

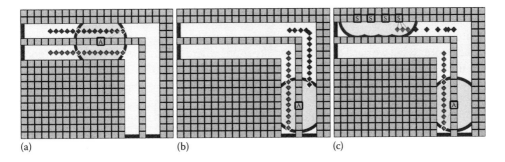

Figure 27.5

Three strategies. (a) *Maximum Usable Range,* tower placed before the corner. (b) *Exploit Path Gap.* (c) *Differential Slowing.*

27.4.4 Implementing the Differential Slowing Strategy

In our study, once players recognized the path gap affordance and figured out the Differential Slowing strategy, they seemed to have little trouble successfully applying it, even on maps they previously struggled on. In contrast, this was the most difficult AI for us to implement. Because of that, we feel it is valuable to spend a little time explaining how we did it.

SAQS keeps an influence map of each affordance it tracks. These maps can be used as filters or weighted and combined. The resulting map is a desirability map. Our AI uses a solver which picks the highest value spot on a desirability map.

For the differential slowing AI we need to combine a few strategies. The attack tower's placement depends on three affordances: usable range, path gap and coverage balance (a ratio of how much of the tower's usable range covers one path versus another; if the spot with the best usable range does not allow the tower to attack both paths, the enemies approaching from the second path will get through). The desirability map is a weighted combination of these three. The slowing towers want to maximize their usable range but only on positions that are *single path overwatch* positions. A single path overwatch is a position that affords the tower the ability to attack one path but not another. The map of single path overwatch positions is a filter. The solver only applies the maximum usable range strategy to those positions returned by the single path overwatch filter.

Creeps must be separated before they are attacked; there is no point in slowing them after they have passed the tower. To achieve this, the map must be divided into two zones, the slowing zone and the kill zone, and the slowing zone must be placed before the kill zone *temporally* (i.e., we do not care where on the map it happens spatially but the creeps must pass through it before they enter the kill zone). In order to determine where *before* is, we need a way to measure the flow of creeps over time through the space. We used a *path* feature (not affordance; the path does not directly or immediately suggest an action and it is an invariant feature of the map rather than being dependent on our goals) with the property *step number*, which is simply how many steps it is from the start of the path.

Dividing the map into zones is not as easy as it might sound. At its most basic we just need a split point—slowing towers go before this point, attack towers after—but determining that split point is not straight forward. The slowing towers want the path-specific single path overwatch positions with the highest usable range. The offense tower wants the position with the highest (weighted) combination of path gap, coverage balance and usable range. If we are lucky, the best kill zone positions are "later" than the best slowing zone positions but we need to handle the situations where they are not. If the best kill zone position is at the start of the map (which it is not here but is on many other maps), you either have to abandon the strategy or pick an inferior kill zone—but not too inferior, or the strategy is not worth it.

To determine whether the strategy makes sense, let us set some minimum requirements (values were chosen after a few iterations of play testing). A slowing zone must have at least four single path overwatch positions (again, overwatching the desired path) with a 45% or greater usable range ration (i.e., at least 45% of the tower's range covers the desired path). The kill zone must have at least one position of some value, say four path gap, 70% usable range ratio, and 60% coverage balance.

We generate a set of candidate split points by using a sliding space-time window. Start at the beginning of time and space (the path start) and move along it, scoring the adjacent positions. In practice, we grab the path of interest, start at the first position on it and ask SAQS for all positions within a slowing tower's range of it. Those that match we store on a map and the count of matches we store on the path. We then move to the next step on the path and repeat. The same process is done for the kill zone but moving backward through time (i.e., start at the end of the path).

Once the sliding window maps are built you can find the split points for the slowing and kill zones where the strategy's minimum needs are met. If the borders cross, the strategy is not going to work and the AI picks a different one (the recognition of affordances on the map triggers strategies that the AI knows; if multiple strategies activate, each can be tested to see which are the most effective). Once found, there are three regions: the minimum areas for the slowing and kill zones, and the unclaimed area between them. Our AI places attack towers first since the quality of attack tower positions often vary greatly, whereas all of the slowing zone positions are guaranteed to let a tower slow one group and not the other. The attack tower placement evaluates positions in the combined kill zone and unclaimed area. Once the towers are placed, the rest of the area is added to the slowing zone and the differential slowing towers are placed.

27.5 Example 3: Quantifying Space-Time and the Attack Window Separation Strategy

Our goal (maximize the amount of time a tower spends firing) is temporal and our action (place an object on a map) is spatial. If space and time are linearly correlated, we can measure everything spatially knowing that when we increase space we also increase time. If space and time can be manipulated independently, as they were with Differential Slowing, we need a way to measure time and a way to convert between space and time. In this section we consider such a metric, as well as its implications for the original U-turn example.

27.5.1 AL: A Metric for Measuring Space-Time

Our work uses a unified space-time metric called *al* (for agent length). It represents the amount of time it takes an agent (in this case, the creep) to cross their body length. It allows us to measure items both spatially and temporally and convert between the two.

We are going to work several examples so we need to set some values:

- A creep is 1 tile wide
- A creep can move 1 tile per second
- An attack tower fires 10 times a second

These are not the exact values from the game but they make the math easier to follow. For the same reason, we are also going to pretend in these examples that all values are whole numbers.

Let us start with a simple example. Suppose we say that a tower has an active time of 6al. We can convert this to a spatial measure and say that the path through the tower's range is six tiles long. We can convert this to a temporal measure and say that the tower is active for six seconds. We can convert this to a nonspatio-temporal measure and say that it fires 60 times and does 60x damage, where x is the amount of damage per shot. If the tower covers four path tiles at a second position, its size at that position is 4al, it will be active for four seconds and fire 40 times doing 40x damage. Placed at the first position, the tower does 50% more damage.

In this case, time and space are linearly correlated and we can find the best spot by just maximizing space, meaning we get no value from the al metric. To see where this is not true, we need to talk about attack windows.

27.5.2 Attack Windows: Spatial and Temporal, Unified and Separated, Agent and Group

In the previous example we said "If the tower covers four path tiles at a second position, *its* size is 4al." We did not say what "it" was. *It* refers to the tower's attack window. An attack window is the opportunity an object has to attack. There are several ways to measure them. A *spatial attack window* is a contiguous block of space where the tower can attack. In Figure 27.2, the tower on the U-turn (C) has one large spatial attack window, whereas the tower in the hallway (D) has two small spatial attack windows. A *temporal attack window* is the period of time the tower has to attack. A tower will have as many temporal attack windows as spatial ones under two conditions. First, the group only crosses through the space once. If a tower has one spatial attack window but a group passes through it multiple times, it is the same as if it had multiple attack windows since the tower gets to attack on multiple occasions. If a group crosses the same space multiple times, the number of temporal windows can be larger than the number of spatial windows. Second, if a tower has two spatial attack windows but a group can be in both at the same time, it is a single temporal window—since, from the tower's point of view, there is no pause between attacks, it is all the same time period. If the group is long enough or the spatial attack windows close enough that a group can be in both at once, the tower can have fewer temporal attack windows than spatial ones. Whether temporal windows are unified or separated is important, as will be shown in the next section.

An attack window's *temporal agent size* is the temporal size of the window for a single agent, meaning it is the amount of time it takes one creep to make it through the attack window. Its *temporal group size* is the size of the window for a group of agents moving through it. This is the one to pay attention to as it is not necessarily correlated with space. The reason for this is that, from a functional perspective (e.g., from the perspective of a tower attacking), groups do not move through time the way individuals do.

Finally, a tower's *active time* is the amount of time the tower spends firing. This is equivalent to the combined temporal group size of all attack windows.

A tower can have multiple temporal group attack windows. The size of each window is the amount of time it takes a group to move through the space. This is equivalent to the time it takes the first member of the group to make it through, the time it takes the last member of the group to make it through and the difference between the first creep exits the range and the last one enters. The time it takes for the first creep to make it through the range plus the time it takes for the last creep to enter the range is just the line length so the temporal group size is:

```
temporalGroupSize = lineLength + temporalAgentSize - 1
```

(the −1 is to avoid counting the last creep twice).

It is worth noting that a tower will fire for as long as there is a creep in range. It does not matter how many there are; the tower does not fire faster with ten enemies than with two. For this reason, the density of enemies does not matter. If two lines of enemies pass through a tower's range at different times, the tower gets two opportunities to attack, but if two lines move through at the same time, the tower only gets one. In the first example we talked about usable range. This turns out to be unimportant. What matters is the path length through the window. To use an example from a different genre, imagine you are in a first-person shooter and have the option of camping over an alleyway or in front of a bank of windows. In the alleyway you can see an enemy running the length of the alley, which takes five seconds. In front of the building you can see five windows. There are five people inside, all of whom cross in front of the window at the exact same, spending one second—the same second—in their respective windows. Even if both positions look over the same amount of space, the amount of time you have to attack (five seconds in the alley, one in front of the windows) is different.

27.5.3 The U-Turn Problem, Revisited

Let us revisit the question asked in Example 1—what is the best position to place an attack tower in Figure 27.2. 58 of 59 people we studied said position C, the U-turn. An attack tower at C has one spatial and one temporal attack window. Its usable range is 30, the length of the inner path is 13 and the outer path 16. Since the temporal agent size is the time it takes one creep to follow the path through the tower, the temporal agent size is the same as the longest path, 16al. There are 28 creeps in two lines of 14. The outer line of creeps takes a longer path, with each corner adding 2 tiles, causing the last four creeps of the outer line to still be in range once the inner line has left (see Figure 27.6). The line length is therefore 18. The data are summarized in Table 27.1. The temporal group size of the U-turn at position C is:

```
temporalGroupSize = lineLength + temporalAgentSize - 1
temporalGroupSize = 18al + 16al - 1al = 33al.
```

An attack tower placed on the U-Turn has an active time of 33al, meaning it has 33 seconds to fire 330 shots to stop 28 creeps.

One of 59 players chose position D, an unremarkable position in a hallway that overlooks two halls. It has two spatial attack windows. They are far enough apart that no creep will still be in the first when the first creeps enters the second. As with the U-turn, because the outer line of creeps passes two corners before entering the second attack window, the line length changes from 14 in the first window to 18 in the second. The data are summarized in Table 27.1. The size of the temporal group attack windows are:

```
Hall AW1 TGS = 14al + 7al - 1al = 20al
Hall AW2 TGS = 18al + 6al - 1al = 23al
Combined Hall TGS          = 43al
```

An attack tower placed in the hallway far enough away from the U-turn that the attack windows are independent (which we call the *Attack Window Separation* strategy) has an active time of 43al, meaning it has 43 seconds to fire 430 shots to stop 28 creeps.

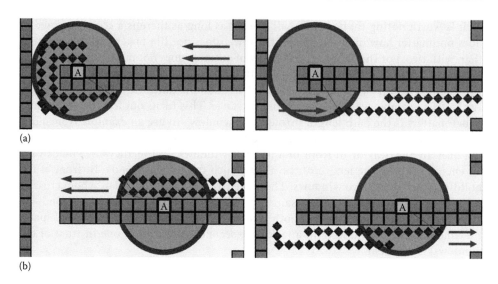

(a)

(b)

Figure 27.6

Two lines of agents moving through across a U-turn. (a) Creeps moving through the range of a tower covering a U-turn. (b) Moving through the range of a tower covering a hallway.

Table 27.1 Spatial data for positions in Figure 27.2

	(C) U-Turn	(D) Hallway
Usable range	30 tiles	26 tiles
Path length	13 inside	AW1: 7 inside/6 outside
	16 outside	AW2: 6 inside/4 outside
AW agent size	16al	AW1: 7al
		AW2: 6al
Line length	18al	AW1: 14al
		AW2: 18al

In most respects, the U-turn is a better position. An attack tower placed there has 15% more usable range, a 23% longer path, a 23% larger attack window temporal agent size (+23%) and 12% longer average line length (+12%). Despite this, the same tower placed in the hallway will active for 30% longer (43 seconds vs. 33) and do 30% more damage.

27.5.4 Attack Window Decay

Because it has a 30% larger combined temporal attack window, it is tempting to say that a hallway tower it is 30% better than a U-turn tower. It is not. In the game, an attack tower placed on the U-turn stops 14 creeps, whereas the same tower in the hall stops 20, 43% more. If the tower only fires 30% more often and therefore only does 30% more damage, why does it achieve a 43% higher score?

We said that the attack window temporal agent size is the amount of time it takes for one agent to walk through a tower's range and is the amount of time the tower has to attack

27. The Role of Time in Spatio-Temporal Reasoning

the agent, which can also be phrased as the amount of time the agent is in danger. We need to amend that a little.

The U-turn in the last example had an attack window temporal agent size of 16, meaning it took an agent 16al to move through it and the tower had 16al of space-time to attack it. Suppose the tower kills the agent in 2al. If the enemies are back to back, a second enemy came into range 1al later and has moved another 1al along the path. During this time the tower has been busy with the first enemy, meaning the second enemy has not been attacked or hurt yet. By the time the tower is free to attack it, the second enemy only has 15al it needs to cross, and the tower only has 15al to attack him or her. The temporal attack window has shrunk. By the time the tower stops the second enemy, the third enemy is 2al into the region and the tower only has 14al left to stop him or her. Assuming enough enemies relative to window size and how quickly the tower can dispatch enemies, the tower eventually runs out of time to destroy enemies and can only wound them, which in many applications, from stopping zombies to damaging incoming tanks, earns you no points since the agent still makes it to the area you are defending and is able to do damage.

When an agent is holding a tower's attention, he or she is buffering for the other agents, keeping them from taking damage—in many games, when players do this it is referred to as "tanking." Once the tower finishes with the agent it must play catch up. Since the tower has a fixed rate of fire, catching up is impossible as long as there are enemies in range.

How does a tower catch up? It needs time. It needs to process the queue it has before starting on new work—which it can do if the attack window is divided into parts and it can process each one independently. This is exactly what happens when the tower is placed in the hallway and exactly what goes wrong when it is on the U-turn. It is also why we said earlier that two spatially independent attack windows are a single temporal attack window if enemies can enter the second attack window while the tower is busy with enemies in the first one—the tower does not have a chance to catch up and the temporal attack window continues to decay. The tower needs a breather so that the attack window size can reset.

As a note, we call the strategy we are using here *Attack Window Separation*, and the affordance that triggers it is, of course, *attack window separation*, a numeric measure of the distance between the end of one spatial attack and the start of the next (as before, you need to know how time flows through space, which for us meant path step number). If you know how long the enemy line length is, you could ask the SAQS for all positions where the attack window separation is enough to temporally decouple the windows. As with differential slowing, you can use slowing towers placed between the attack windows to stretch the length as necessary, creating attack window separation affordances that enable an attack window separation strategy on maps where it was not possible before. Because implementing this has no new ideas that were not covered in the previous sections Differential Slowing, we will not walk through the implementation here. We do hope, however, that this and the earlier examples let you appreciate the value of a good spatial affordance query system.

27.6 Conclusion

We know we live in a world of objects moving through space over time and to deal with it we need to do spatio-temporal reasoning, but much of what we do is actually spatial reasoning, allowing space to be a proxy for time. Often our thoughts are spatial, our reasoning is spatial, our strategies are spatial, and the affordances we recognize are spatial. This is not a bad thing and we can often perform quite well this way, but if we can bring ourselves to focus on time—to recognize temporal affordances and craft temporal strategies—we can sometimes do much better.

References

Norman, D. 1988. *The Design of Everyday Things*, New York.
Wetzel, B. 2014. Representation and reasoning for complex spatio-temporal problems: From humans to software agents. PhD diss., University of Minnesota.

28

Pitfalls and Solutions When Using Monte Carlo Tree Search for Strategy and Tactical Games

Gijs-Jan Roelofs

28.1 Introduction

The biggest challenge when building AI for modern strategy games is dealing with their complexity. Utility- or expert-based techniques provide good bang for their buck in the sense that they get the AI to a reasonable, even decent level of play quickly. Problems start to arise, however, when an AI programmer is faced with situations that are not straight-forward or too time-consuming to encode in heuristics. Or when he or she is faced with above average gamers who demand a good opponent and are quick to find any exploits in an AI.

Search techniques seem like an interesting solution to provide adaptable and more dynamic AI. Traditional search techniques, like minimax, iterate over all possible moves, evaluate each resulting state, and then return the best move found. This approach does not work in strategy games because there are simply too many moves to explore.

MCTS (*Monte Carlo Tree Search*) is a new and increasingly popular technique that has shown it is capable of dealing with more complex games. This chapter outlines solutions to common pitfalls when using MCTS and shows how to adapt the algorithm to work with strategy games.

An example of one such pitfall is that implementations of search techniques in game AI tend to work by limiting the search to a subset of moves deemed interesting. This approach can lead to an AI that can easily be exploited because it literally does not see the pruned moves coming. Techniques outlined within this chapter will give MCTS the opportunity to discover these moves while still ensuring a good base level of play in those worst-case situations where it does not find them.

Throughout the chapter we showcase how these techniques were implemented using two vastly different strategy games: *Berlin*, an online Risk-like game in which the player commands hundreds of units in an effort to capture all regions, and *Xenonauts 2*, a tactical game akin to *X-Com* developed by Goldhawk Interactive in which the player commands a squad of 12 soldiers. In *Berlin*, the introduction of the core techniques outlined in this chapter led to a 73% win and a 15% draw rate over the best hierarchical AI based implementation (utility-based driven by behavior tree adjusted weights). The actual gameplay shown by MCTS was adaptive to new player strategies without requiring any input or rebalancing (Roelofs 2015).

This chapter delves into details which assume a basic understanding of MCTS. Those unfamiliar with this technique should start by reading the introduction provided in *Game AI Pro 2* (Sturtevant 2015). For this chapter, we use the most common and battle tested variant of MCTS: *UCT* (*Upper Confidence Bounds Applied to Trees*) (Chaslot 2010).

To ease understanding, the sections of this chapter are grouped into two categories: design principles and implementation tricks. The design principles outline general principles which need to be adapted to each game to which they are applied, and require full understanding to apply correctly. Implementation tricks are general ways to improve any MCTS implementation.

In the next section, we give an overview of the problem. The sections beyond that are structured according to the four major phases of MCTS (shown in Figure 28.1): *Selection*, *Expansion*, *Simulation*, and *Backpropagation*.

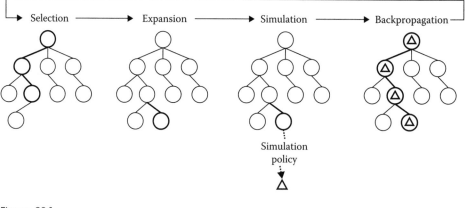

Figure 28.1

The *Monte Carlo Tree Search* algorithm.

28.2 The Problem

The strength of MCTS lies in its ability to cope with large, complex problems in which the long-term ramifications of a move are generally more important than its short-term effects. In other words, in problems where the actual effects only become apparent after executing long sequences of moves, that is, a *deep* search space. It excels in areas where alternative techniques, such as minimax, given ample depth (6–12 ply) still do not return useful strategies.

In general, performance for search techniques starts to falter when the number of choices possible per level of the tree starts to increase, that is, a *wide* search space. Although MCTS tends to cope better with this than many other techniques, increasing the width is still the quickest way to drastically reduce performance (Roelofs 2015).

For strategy games, one common problem is when a single move for a player can be broken down into several actions (e.g., many orders to individual units). If each of these actions affects the outcome of the sequence as a whole, we need to examine all possible combinations of them, resulting in search spaces of often insurmountable width and subsequently, size (Churchill and Buro 2015, Roelofs 2015).

For example, in *Xenonauts 2* a unit can move to upwards of 50 different locations and select between 4 different weapons to attack 1 of 16 different targets, not to mention additional unit abilities. Even after pruning those locations, weapons, and targets which are not interesting we are still left with about 12 options per unit. Given 16 different units, this results in 12^{16} different combinations of actions to search through per turn. No amount of calculation time will ensure that the search returns with good results if we try to look at all combinations of actions.

Luckily, more often than not these actions do not influence each other that much, or if they do, there are specific actions which have large ramifications and thus stand out. Often, the AI programmer might not know which particular action would work well, but he or she has an understanding that certain types of actions have the potential to perform far better than others. This is better explained with some concrete examples:

In *Xenonauts 2*, some units had the ability to mind control an enemy unit. This ability tended to have a far bigger effect on the outcome of a mission than other actions. By creating a heuristic function based on the worth (objectives or worth of the units to the player) and potential for the AI (weapons, abilities, and position) we were quickly able to get the AI to function at a decent level of play. However, throughout development we kept discovering that the AI missed crucial moves which were extremely situational and nightmarish to encode through heuristics. Moves which were the result of combinations of abilities or weaknesses on units in both the player and AI squad, objectives which invalidated or revalidated certain tactics, or moves which resulted in wins further in the future through sacrifice of units.

In *Berlin*, an example of such an action would be the capture of a region that would not be deemed valuable using common heuristics, but would provide a crucial vector of attack in subsequent turns giving the AI an advantage in the long run.

These are actions that if done correctly would have given the player pause but if done incorrectly would be glaring mistakes. In short, actions that are not easily found through the use of heuristics or for which the actual effects several turns from now need to be simulated to see their actual worth. The essence of the solution we propose is to enable

MCTS to discover and subsequently exploit these actions—that is, actions that have a large impact on the overall outcome of a move—in an effort to exploit those moves that contain them.

Before delving into the details and actual approach, we reiterate and define the key terms used throughout the chapter:

- *Move*: A sequence of independent actions constituting a full player turn.
- For example: All units have received orders for the turn.
- *Action*: An independent part of a move.
- For example: The orders to be sent to a single unit, attack enemy X, or move to location A.
- *Action set*: All of the possible values for a particular action.
- For example: A unit can attack {X, Y, or Z}, move to {A, B, or C}, or use special ability {J, K, or L}.

28.3 Expansion

This section outlines how to restructure the search such that MCTS will be able to identify good actions and subsequently use exploitation to ensure it can spend more time on moves that contain them and less on moves that do not. The key to this is to first expand into those actions which we expect to perform well. This provides good early estimates that later help the exploitation process of MCTS. Which actions we expand into can be specified through heuristics, learned using entropy learning or by restructuring the expansion such that MCTS learns it during search (Roelofs 2015). Furthermore, splitting up the move also allows us to prune actions or options in an action set which are not of interest, or simply select without search those for which we know a good solution exists through heuristics.

28.3.1 Restructuring Your Search Space (Design Principle)

By default, at each expansion step MCTS expands into all possible moves from the current node. The problem with this type of expansion is that there is no transfer of information between moves at the same level. MCTS simply cannot exploit information gained from one move to prefer one over another and needs to inspect each move individually.

By dividing the move into actions we can enable MCTS to understand that move B, which is a minor variation of a good move A that it explored earlier, might be a good move as well. Instead of expanding over all possible moves at each expansion step, we select a specific action within the current move and expand into the actions defined in its action set. We can further enhance performance by carefully pruning or ordering the action set of an action before the start of the search, or during it based on the actions already explored in the current move. To distinguish from the default expansion strategy, we term *hierarchical expansion* as expanding into actions as opposed to moves.

In *Xenonauts 2*, we carved up a move into the orders per unit, each action being a single order assigned to a unit. Each unit could have multiple orders assigned to it until a move consisted of actions in which it had spent all of its time units or was put on overwatch. The reasoning behind this was that often the outcome of a mission could be swayed by the actions of a single unit, and thus the selection between individual actions was crucial.

This was helped by the fact that we limited the search to those units in engagement with the player and let overall positioning of nonengaging squads be done by simple heuristics.

In *Berlin*, the move was carved up into a single action per region, in which we decided how soldiers would attack or reinforce adjacent regions. The reasoning behind this was that we only needed to hone in on the decisions of specific regions. Looking at the soldier level would result an in excessive increase in size of the search space.

Figure 28.2 gives a graphical example of hierarchical expansion given three action sets, each with two actions ({A, B}, {C, D}, {E, F}). In this example, as the search starts MCTS will explore the actions *A* or *B* and subsequently all moves which contain those actions. As it becomes apparent that one action results in significantly better results, it will avoid the other action, and subsequently all moves that contain it. The core idea being that if action *A* or *B* is truly better than the other, it will show through the simulations, regardless of which move it was played in.

Herein lies the drawback of this approach. If we start with an action set which has no apparent good move, or if a good move happens further down the line, we may lose crucial calculation time. MCTS will keep switching between the nodes as it is unapparent which sequence of actions is good, and the quality of the result suffers. Another issue is that this technique works only when the search space starts becoming large. If it is not, we are simply wasting time by adding in extra nodes and splitting the tree. As a general rule, once we start dealing with games in which a single move can be broken down into actions, and a combinatorial number of moves exist, the technique can be applied (Roelofs 2015).

28.3.2 Expansion Order of Actions (Design Principle)

The key understanding in all this is that we stimulate MCTS to exploit the value found for an action, and thus avoid those moves which do not contain any interesting actions.

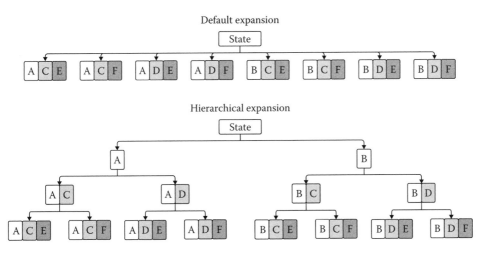

Figure 28.2

Hierarchical expansion for three action sets, each with two actions, resulting in one level for normal expansion, and three levels for hierarchical. (*Note:* As MCTS is a best-first search algorithm, more interesting lines of the tree will be explored in favor of others. The above figure of a balanced tree is to illustrate how expansion happens in a fully explored tree.)

If we can ensure that action sets with apparent good choices are explored first, MCTS will quickly converge and exploit the moves which contain them, avoiding large swathes of uninteresting search space. This basic understanding is why the algorithm performs well while we are counterintuitively increasing the number of nodes in the tree. This approach also has the added benefit of ensuring that most time is spent on those actions which are important as they are simply considered first.

Per example, in *Xenonauts 2* we first expand into orders for enemy units nearer to the player under the assumption that they would provide good opportunities of attack. The action set itself was ordered to prefer attack and ability actions, followed by movement. This ensured that the algorithm was unlikely to miss any crucial attacks on player units. The AI played stronger, and players were quick to label the AI as "stupid" if it missed obvious strong ways to attack thus necessitating the focus on attacks.

In *Berlin* we expanded into regions closer to enemy regions first, under the assumption that crucial troop movement would occur there.

Even if the value of an action is not apparent it is often relatively intuitive to provide an ordering on which actions to explore first. From our earlier example: We might not know the heuristic value of the mind control ability, but we know it tends to be more valuable than any other action. Even if it is not effective in the current situation it allows us to exclude those moves that do not contain it.

To test the overall strength of a given ordering, or find out an ordering if no heuristic is known, we can use two alternative strategies to provide one:

1. *Entropy-based*: The *entropy* of an action set represents the ease with which MCTS can make a decision between the actions in it. If the entropy is low, and thus all values are nearly equal to each other, MCTS will often find it hard to converge on a specific action. If the entropy is high, values of actions differ wildly and MCTS will be quicker to converge. We can simply calculate the entropy of an action set by using the ratio of the number of times MCTS has visited an action compared to its parent as $P(x)$ in *Shannon Entropy*: $-\sum_{i=1}^{n} P(x_i) \log P(x_i)$

2. This technique is mostly used to either discover an ordering we can use as a heuristic or to check whether the heuristic ordering you have defined is good enough.

3. *Dynamic ordering*: Normally, we select a specific ordering to the actions at the start of the search, and which action is expanded is determined by the layer of the tree we are in. Looking at Figure 28.2 we can see that we first expand into $\{A, B\}$, followed by $\{C, D\}$ and finally $\{E, F\}$. If we select a random action set to expand into for *each expansion of an action*, we essentially allow MCTS to exploit the ordering itself during the search. To better explain this concept using Figure 28.2: After action A we could expand into $\{E, F\}$; after action B we could expand into $\{C, D\}$. This strategy works best if actions are truly without sequence. It works because if an action set truly has an important choice, the search will gravitate toward where this action set exists nearest to the root. This strategy tends to give far better results than just choosing an arbitrary ordering as there we can have the bad luck that the action sets with interesting choices exist too deep in the tree, with the search never reaching them (Roelofs 2015).

28.3.3 Dealing with Partial Results (Design Principle)

Using default expansion, only complete moves are explored in MCTS. The end result of a search is simply the best node at the root of the tree: a move that can be applied immediately. However, if we split up the move, the actions at the root are just part of the answer. We need to reconstruct the complete action by iteratively applying the *final node selection* strategy up the tree gathering the resulting actions and reconstructing the move.

When using the above approach, MCTS will not always be able to return a move if the actions in the tree are not sufficient to create a complete move. We used two different strategies to complete a so-called partial move, in order of performance:

1. *Estimated values*: During the backpropagation phase of MCTS, maintain an average value of the actions used in the playout. When completing a partial move, we simply select the action that scored the best on average through all playouts. This technique worked well when the playout itself was guided by heuristics as well, or even better, a portfolio of heuristics. The actions which returned then would always be at least actions we approved by heuristics, but evaluated in context. This would allow us to reclaim information lost due to MCTS switching between branches of actions.
2. *Heuristics*: Apply the strategies used in the playouts to complete the action, assuming they are using heuristics. This tends to lead to better performance than just randomly completing the action as we can then ensure at least a base level of play.

28.3.4 Pruning Action Sets (Design Principle)

The key concept is that we only explore those actions in MCTS which we think actually need exploration. If a solution is apparent for a certain action set, then there is no reason to add these to the search. By pruning those action sets from expansion all together and letting them be resolved through heuristics we can improve on the quality of the search as it can spend more time on action sets which actually require it.

For example, in *Xenonauts* any unit far away from the area of conflict would either just go to the nearest applicable cover, or move toward the conflict if so requested by any unit in it. We do not need to explore the actions of these units as the choice is rather apparent.

For *Berlin* we determined that regions some distance away from the front should move their units toward the front, as this was the decision returned often by the search.

When applying MCTS to multiplayer games with more than two players, this concept can be applied by only focusing on the strongest player. At expansion into the moves of other players, simply determine the strongest opponent and ignore moves from others (Schadd and Winands 2011).

28.3.5 Iterator-Based Expansion (Implementation)

The default implementation of the expansion phase is to create all actions, adding them as child actions as shown in Figure 28.1. However, if there are many possible moves this tends to be quite wasteful as MCTS might decide that the parent action is no longer interesting after a single iteration. By using an *iterator pattern* and only adding a single action per expansion we can avoid a lot of resource waste resulting in a significant performance boost.

The order in which actions are created by this pattern affects the performance of the algorithm. If the sequence is always the same, the first actions returned will be explored far more often in the overall search. When the first action returned is a badly performing action the node will be undervalued in its first iteration and it might take the algorithm a while before revisiting it, if at all. Returning a random ordering of actions, or providing the best actions according to some heuristic first thus tends to improve the quality of the result.

28.4 Simulation

Complexity rears its ugly head again in the simulation phase of MCTS. In the following sections we will explore how judiciously applying heuristics to guide the playout can increase its value and how abstracting over the simulation can lead to more and better iterations, and thus a better result.

28.4.1 Better Information (Design Principle)

For strategy games the traditional approach, in which we simulate the move chosen by the search by playing random moves until the game ends, tends to give little useful information. Due to the enormous size of the search space, playing random moves rarely gives any interesting results or represents good play. Using heuristic-based strategies tends to increase performance of the algorithm as the information provided by a single playout increases. However, this does come at an expense: It will ensure that certain actions are overlooked in the simulation and that the AI works with partial information. This in turn can result in exploitable behavior as the AI becomes blind to certain actions, or even lower performance if the AI misses crucial actions.

Heuristics strategies can further decrease performance if they are expensive to compute. Increasing the time in simulation reduces the number of iterations of MCTS, in turn reducing performance. On the other hand, heuristic strategies can actually speed up the simulation by ensuring that a game ends quickly in the simulation phase. A game played randomly can take quite a lot longer before it ends as opposed to a game played with a valid strategy.

The best of both worlds is to use a mixed strategy approach, often called an epsilon-greedy playout, resulting in far stronger play than a pure random or heuristic strategy. This can be achieved by constructing a weighted portfolio of strategies to use in the playout, including the default random playout, and selecting an action from this portfolio (Roelofs 2015).

28.4.2 Abstract Your Simulation (Design Principle)

Most often the simulation phase uses the actual game rules as they are readily available and correct. However due to the fact that by their very nature strategy games tend to be complex problems, it is advisable to use an abstraction in the simulation phase. Instead of actually calculating the results of sending your units and simulating the full conflict using game logic, build an abstraction of the conflict and define a function that given a setup quickly calculates whether the conflict is a loss or victory. The key to this approach is that the actions explored within the tree are still legal moves in your game.

In *Xenonauts* using the actual game logic was infeasible as it was tied to too many systems outside the AI and performance-wise was never intended to be used in simulations. We therefore created a model in which soldiers were represented solely by their computed strength (based on their health, inventory, and abilities), and position (to calculate cover and LOS). The outcome of confrontations then became a simple computation that could be iterated over much more quickly. Actions executed during the expansion and selection phases, and thus not in simulation, would be executed using actual logic to ensure they would be correct. The moment the search entered simulation, the current values of the state would be transferred to the constructed model.

28.5 Backpropagation

Game AI programmers have ample experience in constructing evaluation functions in order to enact specific behavior on a character. Modeling an evaluation function for a search technique has some minor, albeit very important, distinctions. The primary difference is that how we structure our evaluation function influences not only the results found (and thus the behavior of the character), but also influences the *behavior of the search* as it executes.

MCTS has a poor track record for tactical decision-making. More accurately, it struggles with problems that have a very narrow path of victory or success. The game Tic Tac Toe is a prime example of this: Making a single mistake will lead to a loss. A simple evaluation function that returns –1 for losses and that returns +1 for wins will take quite a while to converge on the proper set of moves. However, if we severely punish the AI for losses with –100, MCTS displays a very paranoid behavior in which it will only select nodes that give the enemy no chance of a win. The end result is a search that converges to the correct move far sooner.

Adjusting the evaluation function in this way causes MCTS to quickly move away from nodes that lead to negative reinforcement, or alternatively make it so that it is eager to explore nodes that have not encountered any losses.

Proper evaluation functions, such as evaluating the margin of victory, that give continuous values are preferred. However, these functions run the risk of diluting which actions are better from the perspective of the algorithm. We would rather have that the search explores one action deeper than keep switching between two actions of similar value. Changing the range of your function to make the differences in actions more apparent often leads to better results.

28.6 Selection

The goal of the selection phase is to determine the "best" node according to some strategy, often *UCT*. The optimization in this section is based on the fact that only a single node per layer gets its value updated during backpropagation. Also, as MCTS starts to converge, most nodes do not, or barely, change their position in this order. So, instead of repeatedly recomputing the rank of each node during selection, an optimized variation of insertion sort can be used to cache the rank of each node and store which node should be selected next. This becomes particularly important when the number of moves or actions increases. A code example of this is provided in Listing 28.1. In a single thread environment, or in *playout* parallelization, this solution will be sufficient. If a *root* parallelization technique is chosen, the update of this order should be moved to the backpropagation phase, in order to more easily lock the node in question (Chaslot et al. 2008).

Listing 28.1 also showcases an often overlooked requirement: The *selection* phase of MCTS should ensure that all child nodes have received some minimum number of visits T (often $T = 20$) before actively selecting the best child. This ensures that the value of the node is somewhat reliable, and not just the result of a single lucky playout.

Listing 28.1. Returns the next node to visit, after all children have been visited a minimum number of times.

```
public Node selectNextNode(Node node, int minVisits)
{
    Array<TreeSearchNode> children = node.getChildren();
    int childrenNo = children.size;
    int minVisitsOnParent = minVisits * childrenNo;

    // If the parent node hasn't been visited a minimum
    // number of times, select the next appropriate child.
    if(minVisitsOnParent > node.visits) {
        return children.get(node.visits % childrenNo);
    }
    else if(minVisitsOnParent == node.visits) {
        // Sort all children once, the sorted state
        // which we'll keep updated afterwards with
        // minimal effort
        children.sort(nodeComparator);
    }
    else {
        // The first child is always the one updated;
        // so it is the only node we need to sort to
        // a new location.
        Node frontChild = children.first();

        // Determine its new location, often very near
        // to it's previous location.
        int i = 1;
        for ( ; i < children.size; i++){
            if(frontChild.score >= children.get(i).score)
                break;
        }

        i--;

        // Move everyone by one, and set the child
        // at its newest index.
        if(i > 0) {
            if(i == 1) {
```

(Continued)

28. Pitfalls and Solutions When Using Monte Carlo Tree Search for Strategy and Tactical Games

```
                        // Special case where we optimize for
                        // when we are just better than the
                        // second item. (often)
                        Object[] items = children.items;
                        items[0] = items[1];
                        items[1] = frontChild;
                }
                else {
                        Object[] items = children.items;
                        System.arraycopy(items, 1, items, 0, i);
                        items[i] = frontChild;
                }
        }
        else {
                return frontChild;
        }
    }

return children.first();
}
```

28.7 Conclusion

This chapter introduced new insights and optimizations to tackle large and complex problems using MCTS. Any reader implementing MCTS is recommended to skim through the sections marked as implementation to find optimizations to the algorithm that can be used in any situation.

The main technique explored to deal with complexity is to break up a move into smaller actions, and provide these in order of apparent importance such that the strengths of MCTS may be used to explore and exploit the search space, judicially applying heuristics to various aspects of the algorithm to make it feasible.

Readers interested in the details of hierarchical expansion and concrete results on the comparison of the various techniques outlined in this chapter are referred to (Roelofs 2015), where a complete analysis is presented using the game of *Berlin*.

References

Chaslot, G. Monte-Carlo Tree Search. Maastricht University, 2010.

Chaslot, G. M. J.-B., M. H. M. Winands, and H. J. van den Herik. Parallel Monte-Carlo Tree Search. In *Computers and Games*, eds. H. Jaap van den Herik, X. Xu, Z. Ma, and M. H. M. Winands. Berlin, Germany: Springer, pp. 60–71, 2008.

Churchill, D., and M. Buro. 2015. Hierarchical Portfolio Search: Prismata's Robust AI Architecture for Games with Large Search Spaces. *Proceedings of the Artificial Intelligence in Interactive Digital Entertainment Conference.* University of California, Santa Cruz, 2015.

Roelofs, G. Action space representation in combinatorial multi-armed bandits. Maastricht University, 2015.

Schadd, M. P. D., and M. H. M. Winands. Best reply search for multiplayer games. *IEEE Transactions on Computational Intelligence and AI in Games* 3(1): 57–66, 2011

Sturtevant, N. R. Monte Carlo tree search and related algorithms for games. In *Game AI Pro 2: Collected Wisdom of Game AI Professionals*, ed. S. Rabin. Boca Raton, FL: CRC Press, 2015, pp. 265–281.

Petri Nets and AI Arbitration

Sergio Ocio Barriales

29.1 Introduction

A Petri net is an abstract, formal model of information flow in systems, particularly in those in which events can occur concurrently and where some form of synchronization or ordering is required.

In a video game, there are a variety of situations that require some sort of coordination or arbitration to decide what a group of agents should be doing and make sure their actions do not invalidate their peers'. Deciding who gets to use a special resource (e.g., a mounted gun) or how roles are selected in a combat scenario are examples of problems Petri nets can help resolve. Also, since these nets are represented as graphs and, at a first glance, can look similar to FSMs, they are easy for AI developers who are familiar with that approach to understand.

In this chapter, we will talk about Petri nets and how they can be used for arbitration in multiagent scenarios.

29.2 Petri Net Basics

Petri nets are a graphical and mathematical modeling language used to describe how information flows in a distributed system. They were developed by Carl Adam Petri in 1962 (Petri 1962). A Petri net is a graph built using two different types of nodes: *places* and *transitions*. Places are connected to transitions via directed *arcs* and vice versa, but nodes of the same type can never be connected directly. A *place* represents a condition and a *transition* is a gate between places. There is a fourth element involved, a *token*. Tokens are found inside places, and a single place can hold multiple tokens; when a token is present in a place, it means that the condition associated with that place is met.

In a Petri net, execution is controlled by the position and movement of the tokens. For example, in Figure 29.1a we have a single token in $p1$, which means that this node is the only one that is currently active.

Transitions have a number of preconditions, or input places. A token in an input place is interpreted to mean that the precondition is true. Transitions are fired when they are enabled; a transition is enabled when it has tokens in each of its input places. For example, in Figure 29.1a, $t1$ is enabled and can fire. Figure 29.1b shows the state of the net after the first transition is triggered. When a transition fires, it consumes the tokens in its input places and generates a new token for each of its output places. This new state—also known as a *marking*—of the net enables $t2$; $t3$ is not yet enabled, since it is missing a token in $p3$. The execution continues in Figure 29.1c. Finally, $t3$ is enabled, since both $p3$ and $p4$ have tokens. The net keeps running and $p5$ receives a token, as shown in Figure 29.1d.

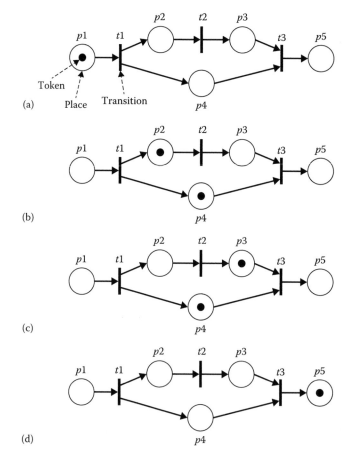

Figure 29.1

An example Petri net with five places and three transitions.

Running a Petri net becomes more complicated if multiple transitions are connected to a single place. In this case, the evolution of the network is no longer deterministic; if we have one token in the place, every transition will be enabled. If we fire any of the transitions, the token will be consumed, invalidating the remaining, previously enabled transitions. In this case, we say the transitions are *in conflict*. Depending on which one we choose to trigger, we will have different resulting markings, as shown in Figure 29.2.

Arcs can be labeled with the number of tokens a transition requires in a particular input place before it can be enabled. After the transition fires, it will consume that number of tokens from the input place. Likewise, a transition can generate multiple tokens if the arc to the output place shows the label. This is depicted in Figure 29.3.

We can also have transitions without any input place—*source* transitions—that are unconditionally enabled and whose sole purpose is generating tokens, and transitions with no output place—*sink* transitions—that only consume tokens.

This section has only presented a few examples and key concepts, but a vast amount of work has been done with Petri nets over the past 50 years. Many resources are available on them; the articles by Peterson (Peterson 1977) and by Murata (Murata 1989) are good places to start.

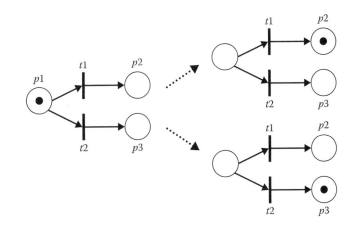

Figure 29.2

Both *t1* and *t2* are enabled in this markings; if either fires, the other will be invalidated.

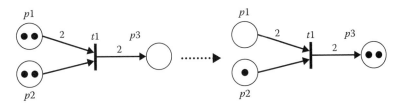

Figure 29.3

Transitions can consume and generate multiple tokens as required.

29.3 An Example Arbitration Scenario

Now that we know the basics, let us discuss how we can use Petri nets to coordinate multiple characters in a setup where they must utilize a finite number of nonshareable resources (i.e., resources that can only be used by a single agent) to accomplish their goal. To do so, we will choose an example and analyze how we would model it with Petri nets.

Let us depict a scenario where a group of agents that were unaware of enemy presence are suddenly attacked by the player. After an initial reaction, the agents must decide how to deal with the attacker. A quick analysis of the surroundings reveals there is a mounted gun nearby, and the AI decides controlling that weapon is the key, but only one character can use the special weapon at a time. So how do we decide who goes first?

One option is to use a first-in, first-out solution, so the first agent that gets updated by the system selects and locks the gun, whereas the others select other actions. However, this could lead to the AI that is farthest from the weapon being chosen, making the characters look stupid and inefficient. We could also modify this approach and have each AI ask the rest of the group "is there anyone closer than me to the gun?" and skip the assignment until the closest agent is updated and selected. This method generates a better looking result, but the behaviors and decision-making logic of our agents gets polluted by these interagent communication requirements.

Trying to resolve every potential scenario by having individual behaviors take into account every other possible AI and their desires and intentions can be problematic. Having a higher level AI entity—that we will call *arbiter*—help agents resolve these resource management disputes can help simplify the system. It is the arbiter's job to track and manage resources and assign them to the appropriate actors.

Going back to our example, a Petri net controls the arbiter. For simplicity, we will just focus on assigning the mounted gun, and will not model how other points are chosen for the NPCs, so the net will just queue AI agents' requests and put them on hold until the special weapon is available. In a more complete solution, our agents would not really directly know about the mounted gun—they would be running a behavior that would try to use the best possible point to attack the enemy, and this point would be returned by the arbiter. Agents would not be reserving this point directly, but just registering to be assigned the best possible one.

Initially, this net's marking is as shown in Figure 29.4a, a single token in the "gun available" place, which indicates nobody has requested using the gun and thus it is still unused. When the agents in the group start reacting to discovering the enemy, they register with the system. For each registered actor, we get a new in the "ready to assign" place. Once the "n" agents in the group are registered, the "start assignment" transition is enabled and run, getting our "n" tokens transferred to the "ready to use gun" place. This is shown in Figure 29.4b and c.

In order for the "assign gun" transition to run, we need the gun to be available and at least one actor to be ready to use it. When both conditions are met, the transition runs some logic to select the best agent to fill the role—based on factors such as proximity to the gun, archetype and capabilities (e.g., an AI agent with better accuracy would be preferred)—and a token will be transferred to "gun busy," while the "gun available" and one of the tokens "ready to use" are consumed. We show this in Figure 29.4d.

If at any point the agent manning the gun is incapacitated, the "agent incapacitated" transition will trigger, moving the token to "gun available," as shown in Figure 29.4e. As long as we have other agents to reassign, the process will continue, just as depicted in Figure 29.4f.

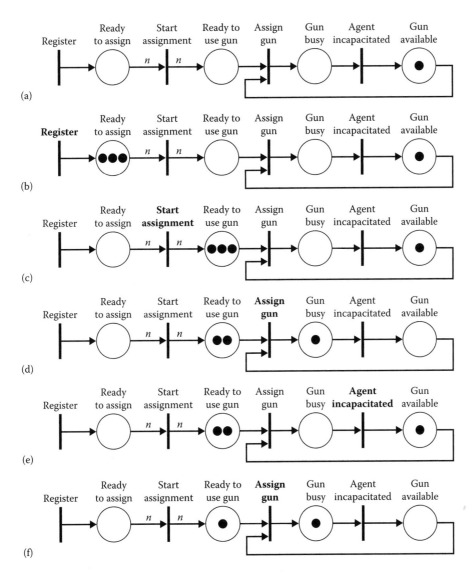

Figure 29.4

The arbiter runs a simple Petri net that controls the status of the mounted gun, allowing other agents to register and get their turn as the weapon becomes available.

29.4 Conclusion

Petri nets are powerful tools that offer a simple way to describe processes where actions need to be synchronized or depend on one another. They have been applied to a broad set of problems, from manufacturing to chemistry and beyond.

In this chapter, we have presented the basics of what the Petri net model offers and how to apply them to model resource arbitration for multiagent scenarios. By using a Petri net, we can separate group coordination to use shared resources from individual behaviors, leaving the high-level decision-making and agent synchronization in the hands of the net. This greatly simplifies the complexity of our single agent behaviors.

References

Murata, T. 1989. Petri nets: Properties, analysis and applications. *Proceedings of the IEEE*, 77(4), 541.

Peterson, J. L. 1977. Petri nets. *ACM Computing Surveys (CSUR)*, 9(3), 223–252.

Petri, C. A. 1962. *Kommunikation mit Automaten*. Bonn, Germany: Institut für Instrumentelle Mathematik, Schriften des IIM Nr. 2, 1962, Second Edition, New York: Griffiss Air Force Base, Technical Report RADC-TR-65-377, Vol. 1, 1966, Suppl. 1, English translation.

Hierarchical Portfolio Search in *Prismata*

David Churchill and Michael Buro

30.1 Introduction

Many unique challenges are faced when trying to write an AI system for a modern online strategy game. Players can control groups of tens or even hundreds of units, each with their own unique properties and strategies, making for a gigantic number of possible actions to consider at any given state of the game. Even state-of-the-art search algorithms such as Monte Carlo Tree Search (MCTS) are unable to cope with such large action spaces, as they typically require the exploration of all possible actions from a given state in a search tree. In addition to the difficulty of dealing with large state and action spaces, other design features must be considered such as varying difficulty settings, robustness to game changes, and single player replay value.

In this chapter we will discuss the AI system designed for *Prismata*, the online strategy game developed by Lunarch Studios. For the *Prismata* AI, a new algorithm called Hierarchical Portfolio Search (HPS) was created which reduces the action space for complex strategy games, which helps deal with all of the challenges listed above. This results in a powerful search-based system capable of producing intelligent actions while using a modular design which is robust to changes in game properties.

30.2 AI Design Goals

In addition to creating an intelligent AI system for strategy games, other design decisions should also be considered in order to ensure an enjoyable user experience. When designing *Prismata*, the following design goals were laid out for the AI system:

- *New player tutorial*: Strategy games often have complex rules, many different unit types, and a variety of scenarios that the player must adjust to. All of this leads to a steep learning curve. Our primary goal with the *Prismata* AI was to aid new players as they learned to play the game, so that they would eventually become ready to face other players on the online ladder. This required the creation of several different difficulty settings so that players could continue to be challenged from beginner all the way up to expert play.
- *Single player replay value*: Single player missions in video games are sometimes designed as rule-based sequences of events that players must navigate to achieve some goal. In *Prismata*, that goal is to destroy all of the enemy units, which can become quite boring if the AI does the same thing every time it encounters similar situations. Our goal was to build a dynamic AI system capable of using a variety of strategies so that it does not employ the exact same tactics each time.
- *Robust to change*: Unlike games in the past which were finalized, shipped, and forgotten about, modern online strategy games are subject to constant design and balance changes. Due to their competitive nature, designers often tweak unit properties and game rules as players find strategies that are too powerful, too weak, or simply not fun to play against. We required an AI system that is able to cope with these changes and not rely on handcrafted solutions that rely on specific unit properties which would be costly to update and maintain as units continue to change.
- *Intuitive/modular design*: Often times when creating a game, the behavior of the AI system, although intelligent, may not fit with the designer's views of how the AI should act. By designing the AI in such a way that its structure is modular and intuitive, designers are better able to understand the capabilities of the AI system and thus can more easily make suggestions on how behaviors should be modified. This leads to a much smoother overall design process than if the AI system was simply viewed as a magic black box by designers.

30.3 *Prismata* Gameplay Overview

Before diving into the details of the AI system, we need to understand the characteristics of the game it is playing. Here we will briefly describe the high-level game rules for *Prismata*.

Prismata is a two-player online strategy game, best described as a hybrid between a real-time strategy (RTS) game and a collectible card game. Players take turns building resources, using unit abilities, purchasing new units, and attempting to destroy the units of their opponents. Unlike many strategy/card games, there is no hidden information in *Prismata*—no hands of cards or decks to draw from. Units that players control are globally visible and players can purchase additional units from a shared pool of available units which changes randomly at the start of each game (similar to the board game Dominion [Vaccarino 2009]). The rules of *Prismata* are also deterministic, meaning that there is no possible way for the AI to cheat by magically drawing the right card from the top of the deck, or by getting some good "luck" when most needed. In game theoretic terms, this makes *Prismata* a two-player, perfect information, zero-sum, alternating move game. This means that the AI does not need any move history in order to pick its next move—it can act strictly on the visible game state at any time.

Due to these properties, the *Prismata* AI was designed as a module that is separate from the rest of the game engine, accepts a current game state as input, and as output produces an ordered sequence of actions for the current player to perform. This architecture also gives the developer an option of where to run the AI calculations—a game state could be sent over a network to be calculated (if the game is being run on a platform with limited computational power), or run locally on a user's hardware (as they are in *Prismata*).

30.4 Hierarchical Portfolio Search

The algorithm that was used to form the basis of the *Prismata* AI is hierarchical portfolio search (Churchill and Buro 2015). HPS was designed to make decisions in games with extremely large state and action spaces, such as strategy games. It is an extension of the portfolio greedy search algorithm, which is a hill climbing algorithm that has been used to guide combat in RTS games (Churchill and Buro 2013). The main idea behind these "portfolio-based" search systems is to reduce the branching factor of the game tree by using a portfolio of algorithms to generate a much smaller, yet hopefully intelligent set of actions. These algorithms can range from simple hand-coded heuristics to complex search algorithms. This method is useful in games where a player's decision space can be decomposed into many individual actions. For example, in an RTS game in which a player controls an army of units, or in a card game where a player can play a sequence of cards. These decompositions are typically done *tactically*, so that each grouping in the portfolio contains similar actions, such as attacking, defending, and so on.

HPS is a bottom-up, two-level hierarchical search system which was originally inspired by historical military command structures. The bottom layer consists of the portfolio of algorithms described above, which generate multiple suggestions for each tactical area of the game. At the top layer, all possible combinations of those actions sequences generated by the portfolio are then iterated over by a high-level game tree search technique (such as alpha–beta or MCTS) which makes the final decision on which action sequence to perform. While this method will not produce the truly optimal move on a given turn it does quite well (as we will show in Section 30.5). Furthermore, the original problem may have contained so many action possibilities that deciding among them was intractable.

30.4.1 Components of HPS

HPS consists of several individual components that are used to form the search system. We define these components as follows:

- **State** s containing all relevant game information
- **Move** m = <a_1, a_2, ..., a_k>, a sequence of Actions a_i
- **Player** function p [m = p(s)]

- Takes as input a State s
- Performs the Move decision logic
- Returns Move m generated by p at state s
- **Game** function g [s' = g(s, p_1, p_2)]
  - Takes as input state s and Player functions p_1, p_2
  - Performs game rules/logic
  - Implements Moves generated by p_1, p_2 until game is over
  - Returns resulting game State s'

These components are the same as those needed for most AI systems which work on abstract games.

In order to fully implement HPS, we will need to define two more key components. The first is a *Partial Player* function. This function is similar to a Player function, but instead of computing a complete turn Move for a player in the game, it computes a partial move associated with a tactical decomposition. For example, in a RTS game if a player controls multiple types of units, a Partial Player may compute moves for only a specific type of unit, or for units on a specific part of the map.

- **Partial Player** function pp [m = pp(s)]
  - Takes as input State s
  - Performs decision logic for a subset of the turn
  - Returns partial Move m to perform at state S

The final component of HPS is the portfolio itself, which is simply a collection of Partial Player functions:

- **Portfolio** P = <pp_1, pp_2, ..., pp_n>

The internal structure of the portfolio will depend on the type of game being played, however it is most useful if the Partial Players are grouped by tactical category or game phase. Iterating over all moves produced by combinations of Partial Players in the portfolio is done by the GenerateChildren procedure in Listing 30.1. Once we have created a portfolio, we can then apply any high-level game tree search algorithm to search over all legal move combinations produced by the portfolio.

30.4.2 Portfolio Creation

An important factor in the success of HPS is the creation of the Portfolio itself, since only actions generated by partial players within the portfolio will be considered by the top-level search. Two factors are important when designing the portfolio: The tactical decomposition used to partition the portfolio and the variety of Partial Players contained within each partition.

In Table 30.1, we can see an example tactical decomposition for the portfolio of partial players in *Prismata*, which is broken down by game phase. The Defense is the "blocking" phase of the game, and contains partial players that decide in which order to assign blocking units. The ability phase involves players using the abilities of units to do things such as gather resources or attack the opponent. The buy phase involves purchasing additional

Table 30.1 A Sample Portfolio Used in *Prismata*

Defense	Ability	Buy	Breach
Min cost loss	Attack all	Buy attack	Breach cost
Save attackers	Leave block	Buy defense	Breach attack
	Do not attack	Buy econ	

Note: Organized by tactical game phase.

units to grow the player's army. Finally, the breach phase involves assigning damage to enemy units in order to kill them. Each of these partial players only compute actions which are legal in that phase of the game—so in order to generate a sequence of actions which comprises the entire turn we must concatenate actions produced by one of the Partial Players from each phase.

This "game phase" decomposition works well for games that can be broken down temporally, however not all games have such abstract notions. Depending on the game you are writing AI for, your decomposition may be different. For example, in a RTS game setting categories may involve different types of units, or a geometric decomposition of units placed in different locations of the map. In strategy card games these categories could be separated by different mechanics such as card drawing, card vs. card combat, or spell casting. It is vital that you include a wide variety of tactical Partial Players so that the high-level search algorithm is able to search a wide strategy space, hopefully finding an overall strong move for the turn.

30.4.3 State Evaluation

Even with the aid of an action space reducing method such as HPS, games that go on for many turns produce very large game trees which we cannot hope to search to completion. We therefore must employ a heuristic evaluation on the game states at leaf nodes in the search. Evaluation functions vary dramatically from game to game, and usually depend on some domain-specific knowledge. For example, early heuristic evaluations for Chess involved assigning points to pieces, such as 1 point for a Pawn and 9 points for a Queen, with a simple player sum difference used as the state evaluation.

These formula-based evaluations have had some success, but they are outperformed by a method known as *symmetric game playout* (Churchill and Buro 2015). The concept behind a symmetric game playout is to assign a simple deterministic rule-based policy to both players in the game, and then play the game out to the end using that policy. Even if the policy is not optimal, the idea is that if both players are following the same policy then the winner of the game is likely to have had an advantage at the original evaluated state. The Game function is used to perform this playout for evaluation in HPS. We can see a full example of the HPS system using Negamax as the top-level search in Listing 30.1.

30.4.4 HPS Algorithm

Now that we have discussed all of the components of HPS, we can see a sample implementation of HPS in Listing 30.1, which uses the Negamax algorithm as the high-level search algorithm. Negamax is used here for brevity, but could be replaced by any high-level search algorithm or learning technique (such as MCTS, alpha–beta, or evolutionary

```
procedure HPS(State s, Portfolio p)
    return NegaMax(s, p, maxDepth)

procedure GenerateChildren(State s, Portfolio p)
    m[] = empty set
    for all move phases f in s
        m[f] = empty set
        for PartialPlayers pp in p[f]
            m[f].add(pp(s))
    moves[] = crossProduct(m[f]: move phase f)
    return ApplyMovesToState(moves, s)

procedure NegaMax(State s, Portfolio p, Depth d)
    if (d == 0) or s.isTerminal()
        Player e = playout player for evaluation
        return Game(s, e, e).eval()
    children[] = GenerateChildren(s, p)
    bestVal = -infty
    for all c in children
        val = -NegaMax(c, p, d-1)
        bestVal = max(bestVal, val)
    return bestVal
```

algorithms). The core idea of HPS is not in the specific high-level search algorithm that you use choose, but rather in limiting the large action space that is passed in to the search by first generating a reasonable-sized set of candidate moves to consider.

30.4.5 Creating Multiple Difficulty Settings

In most games, it is desirable to have multiple difficulty settings for the AI that players can choose from so that they can learn the game rules and face an opponent of appropriate skill. One of the strengths of HPS is the ease with which different difficulty settings can be created simply by modifying the Partial Players contained in the portfolio, or by modifying the parameters of the high-level search. There are many difficulty settings in *Prismata*, which were all created in this way, they are as follows:

- *Master Bot*: Uses a Portfolio of 12 Partial Players and does a 3000 ms MCTS search within HPS, chosen as a balance between search strength and player wait time
- *Expert Bot*: Uses the same Portfolio as Master Bot, with a 2-ply Alpha–Beta search, typical execution times are under 100 ms.
- *Medium Bot*: Picks a random move from Master Bot's Portfolio
- *Easy Bot*: Same as Medium, but with weaker defensive purchasing
- *Pacifist Bot*: Same as Medium, but never attacks
- *Random Bot*: All actions taken are randomly

An experiment was performed, which played 10,000 games between each difficulty setting pairing, the results of which can be seen in Table 30.2. The final column shows

Table 30.2 Results of 10,000 Rounds of Round Robin between Each Difficulty Setting

	UCT100	AB100	Expert	Medium	Easy	Random	AVG
UCT100	—	52.1	67.3	96.4	99.7	99.9	83.1
AB100	47.9	—	68.0	94.7	99.5	99.9	82.0
Expert	32.7	32.0	—	90.7	98.9	99.8	70.8
Medium	3.6	5.3	9.3	—	85.9	97.4	40.3
Easy	0.3	0.5	1.1	14.1	—	86.3	20.5
Random	0.1	0.1	0.2	2.6	13.7	—	3.3

Note: Score = win% + (draw%/2) for row difficulty versus column difficulty. UCT100 and AB100 refer to UCT (MCTS with UCB-1 action selection) and Alpha–Beta each with 100 ms think times. Pacifist Bot was omitted, since it is designed not to attack and therefore cannot win.

the average scores of each difficulty setting (100 meaning unbeatable, 0 meaning never wins), from which we can see that the difficulty settings perform in line with their intuitive descriptions. The modular design of HPS allowed us to make slight changes to the portfolio and search settings to create multiple difficulty settings, which satisfied our design goals of creating both a new player tutorial for beginners, and strong opponents for expert players.

30.5 Evaluation of HPS Playing Strength

To test the strength of the AI system in *Prismata* in an unbiased fashion, an experiment was run in which the AI secretly played against human players on the ranked *Prismata* ladder. *Prismata's* main competitive form of play is the "Ranked" play mode, where players queue for games and are auto-matched with players of similar ranking. Player skill is determined via a ranking system that starts at Tier 1 and progresses by winning games up until Tier 10. Once players reach Tier 10, they then ranked using a numerical system similar to those used in chess.

To test against humans, a custom build of the client was created in which the AI queued for a ranked play match, played the game against whichever human it matched against, and then requeued once the match was finished. The AI system was given randomized clicking timers in order to minimize the chances that the human players would suspect that they were playing against an AI. The AI used was the hardest difficulty setting, "Master Bot," which used MCTS as its top-level search with a think time of 3 seconds. After 48 hours and just over 200 games played, the AI had achieved a rank of Tier 6 with 48% progression toward Tier 7, and stayed at that rank for several hours. This placed the AI's skill level within the top 25% of human players on the *Prismata* rank ladder, the distribution of which can be seen in Figure 30.1.

Since this experiment was performed, many improvements have been made to the AI, such as improved tactical decision-making in the blocking and breaching phase, an improved playout player, and fixing some obvious blunders that the bot made in its attack phase. Master Bot is estimated to now be at Tier 8 skill level, which is stronger than all but the top 10%–15% of human players.

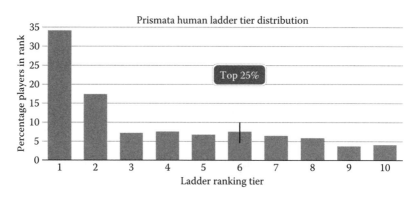

Figure 30.1

Distribution of player rankings in "Ranked" play mode in *Prismata*. After 48 hours of testing, Master Bot had achieved a rank of Tier 6 with 48% progress toward Rank 7, which placed its skill level in the top 25% of human players.

30.6 Conclusion

In this chapter, we have introduced HPS, a new algorithm which was designed to make strong decisions in games with large state and action spaces. HPS has been in use for over two years as the basis of the *Prismata* AI system, with nearly a million games played versus human opponents. Because of its modular design, search-based decision-making, and intuitive architecture, it has been robust to over 20 game balance patches, producing intelligent actions even with major changes to many of units in *Prismata*.

The search-based nature of the AI has yielded a system which has high replay value, in which the bot will have different styles of play depending on the given state of the game. Creating different difficulty settings using HPS was merely a matter of changing the algorithms in the underlying portfolio, which resulted in a total of seven different difficulties—from pacifist punching bag to the clever Master Bot. These difficulty settings have proved to be a valuable tool for teaching players the rules of the game as they progress to new skill levels. The hardest difficulty of the *Prismata* AI, Master Bot, was played in secret on the human ranked ladder and achieved a skill within the top 25% of human players, showing that HPS is capable of producing strong moves in a real-world competitive video game.

References

Churchill, D., Buro, M. 2013. Portfolio greedy search and simulation for large-scale combat in starcraft. *CIG*, Niagara Falls, ON, Canada, 2013.

Churchill, D., Buro, M. 2015. Hierarchical portfolio search: Prismata's robust AI architecture for games with large search spaces. *AIIDE*, Santa Cruz, CA, 2015.

Vaccarino, D. X. 2009. Dominion. Rio Grande Games.

SECTION V
Character Behavior

31

Behavior Decision System
Dragon Age Inquisition's *Utility Scoring Architecture*

Sebastian Hanlon and Cody Watts

31.1 Introduction

The real-time combat sequences of *Dragon Age: Inquisition* (*DA:I*) pit the player-controlled Inquisitor in a fight to the death against shambling undead, fearsome demons, and—of course—towering dragons. It is a tough job, but the Inquisitor is not alone; fighting alongside his or her are three AI-controlled allies—fellow members of the Inquisition such as The Iron Bull, a towering, axe-swinging mercenary, Varric Tethras, a smooth-talking dwarf, and Dorian Pavus, a charming and quick-witted mage.

In *Dragon Age*, combat is driven by "abilities." A typical combatant will have anywhere from 2 to 20 abilities at their disposal, ranging from the simple ("hit your foe with the weapon you are holding") to the elaborate ("call down a rain of fire upon your enemies"). Each ability has an associated cost expressed in terms of a depletable resource called "mana" or "stamina." Because mana/stamina is limited, abilities also have an implicit opportunity cost—the mana/stamina consumed by one ability will inevitably preclude the use of future abilities. This creates a challenging problem for human players and AI characters alike: When faced with limited resources, a plurality of choices, and a constantly changing game state, how can a combatant quickly identify the course of action which will yield the greatest possible benefit? For *DA:I*, we created a utility-based AI system called the Behavior Decision System (BDS) to answer this question and to handle the complex decision-making which combatants must perform. In this chapter, we will describe the principles and architecture of the BDS, providing you with the necessary information to implement a similar system and extend it to meet the needs of your own game.

31.2 The Behavior Decision System

The architecture of the BDS is based upon the following assumptions:

1. At any given time, there is a finite set of actions which an AI character can perform.
2. An AI character can only perform one action at a time.
3. Actions have differing utility values; some actions are more useful than others.
4. It is possible to quantify the utility of every action.

When taken together, these assumptions naturally suggest a simple greedy algorithm to determine an AI character's best course of action: Start by identifying the set of actions which it can legally take. Then, evaluate each action and assign it a score based on its utility. After each action has been evaluated, the action with the highest score is the action which should be taken (Graham 2014).

There are two major challenges to this approach. First, how can an AI character enumerate all the actions which it can perform? Second, how can an AI character qualify the utility of an action? Before an AI character can answer these questions, we must first impart it with knowledge—knowledge about itself and the world in which it lives.

Consider, for example, a simple action such as "drinking a health potion." Most human players know that it is useful to drink a health potion when their health is low. Unfortunately, AI characters do not intuitively understand concepts like life, death, health, and healing potions. They do not know that being alive is "good" and being dead is "bad." They do not understand that drinking a health potion at low health is good, but drinking a health potion at full health is wasteful. And they do not understand that health potions are consumable objects, and that one cannot drink a health potion unless one owns a health potion.

At its most basic level, the BDS is a framework which allows gameplay designers to impart knowledge to AI characters. Specifically, the BDS exists to provider answers to the following questions: Which actions can an AI character perform? Under what circumstances can they perform those actions? How should those actions be prioritized relative to each other? And finally: How can those actions actually be performed?

31.3 Enumerating Potential Actions

There are more than 60 abilities in *DA:I*, but many of these abilities can be used in different ways to achieve different purposes. For example the "Charging Bull" ability allows a warrior to charge directly into combat, damaging and knocking-aside any enemy who stands in his or her way. This is its intended, obvious purpose. However, this same ability can also be used as a way for an injured warrior to quickly retreat from combat. Though the underlying ability is the same, the motivation for the ability is completely different. Therefore, when enumerating potential actions, it is not sufficient to simply count the number of abilities at a character's disposal—we must also include the various ways in which those abilities can be performed. In order to distinguish between the various ways an ability can be used, we defined a data structure called a "behavior snippet."

Behavior snippets are the fundamental unit on which the BDS operates. Each snippet contains the information an AI character requires to evaluate and execute an ability in a particular way. In a sense, a snippet represents a fragment of knowledge—and throughout the game knowledge can be granted to characters by "registering" a snippet with to a character via the BDS. For example, a piece of weaponry may have one or more behavior snippets attached which tell AI characters how to use the weapon. When an AI character equips the weapon, these snippets will be registered to the character through the BDS. Similarly, when the weapon is unequipped, the snippets will be unregistered from that character.

Behavior snippets make it simple for the BDS to enumerate the list of actions available to a character; one merely needs to look at the set of registered snippets. The most complex AI characters in *DA:I* have over 50 behavior snippets registered simultaneously, though an average AI character will have 10–20 registered snippets.

31.4 Evaluating Behaviors

A behavior snippet contains the information an AI character requires to evaluate and execute an ability in a particular way—but what exactly does this mean? As stated previously, the BDS is based upon the assumption that it is possible to quantify the utility of every action. In order for this assumption to hold, each behavior snippet must contain within it a method to quantify the utility of the action it represents. There are many possible ways to quantify utility, but for *DA:I*, we chose to represent utility using a modified behavior tree which we call an "evaluation tree."

31.4.1 Calculating Utility

In the broadest possible terms, the purpose of an evaluation tree is simply to produce a score value for its associated behavior snippet. These scores can then be used as a basis for comparing two behavior snippets against each other in order to rank their relative utility. Score values are assigned via "scoring nodes" embedded within the evaluation tree itself. When the tree begins executing from its root node, it starts with a score of zero. As the tree progresses from one node to the next, any scoring nodes it executes will add their value to the tree's total score.

Evaluation trees are evaluated "in context"—that is to say, the nodes within the tree have access to information such as the AI character who is performing the evaluation. This allows for the creation of evaluation trees which produce different scores depending on the context in which they are evaluated (Merrill 2014). For example, Figure 31.1 shows an evaluation tree which will return a score of 5 if the evaluating character's health is less than 50%, and a score of 0 otherwise.

When constructing our scoring system, we considered various schemes for automatic normalization or scaling of scoring values. Ultimately, we chose to use (and recommend using) a designer-facing scoring convention to provide a framework for how actions

Figure 31.1

This evaluation tree returns different scores based on the health of the evaluating character.

Table 31.1 Scoring Framework Used in *Dragon Age: Inquisition*

Action Type	Point Values	Description
Basic	10	Preferable to doing nothing, and if multiple options are available, they are equivalent to each other.
Offensive	20–40	As a class, always preferable to basic actions, and compared against each other with 20 points of "urgency dynamic range" for prioritizing based on situational influences.
Support	25–45	As a class, preferable to offensive actions with the same level of "urgency," as they are either preparatory and should be used before engaging offensively, or used in reaction to emerging bad situations.
Reaction	50–70	All actions in this class have evaluation trees that respond to specific and immediate execution criteria (typically responding to an imminent threat to the AI character); if these criteria are present these actions should be executed in priority over any other (and otherwise valid) choices.

should be scored relative to each other. Note that these rules are guidance for content creators and have no explicit representation in game data. Table 31.1 shows an example of a scoring convention.

It is the responsibility of the designer constructing the evaluation trees for each snippet to conditionally allocate score so that the tree will produce a value within the appropriate dynamic range. In *DA:I*, each class of action uses a different set of scoring logic assets, built to return score values within the appropriate range. For example, the evaluation tree for a "Support" action starts by granting a baseline 25 points and conditionally adds contextual score up to a maximum of 45.

31.4.2 Target Selection

Most abilities in *DA:I* require a target to function. For example, an AI character cannot simply "cast Immolate"—they must cast Immolate *on* a specific foe. The chosen target of an ability can greatly affect the outcome (i.e., the utility value) of executing that ability. Consider: Casting Immolate on a target who is weak against fire will deal significant damage, whereas casting it on a target who is fire-immune will do nothing but waste mana. For that reason, target selection is a necessary part of the evaluation step; to accurately represent the value of an action, we must consider all the potential targets of that action, and then select the target which provides the greatest utility value. Therefore, in the BDS framework, evaluation trees return not only a score, but a target too.

The contextual nature of evaluation trees allows us to add target selection logic by introducing a "target selector" node. This node iterates over a list of designer-specified

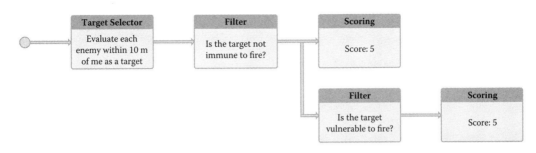

Figure 31.2

This evaluation tree specifically targets hostiles who are not immune to fire. Targets who are vulnerable to fire are scored higher than those who are not.

targets, and evaluates and assigns a score to each of them separately. Figure 31.2 shows an evaluation tree which makes use of the target selector node.

The target selector node maintains its own temporary evaluation state and record table, and executes according to the following algorithm:

1. Record the evaluation context's current score value as the "initial score."
2. For each targetable specified by the iterator data:
   a. Reset the context's score value to the initial score.
   b. Set the context's "behavior target iterator" slot to the current targetable.
   c. Evaluate the child node.
   d. If the child node returns true, record the context's current score value for the iterator's current targetable.
3. If at least one targetable has been recorded with an evaluation score:
   a. Set the context's Behavior Target slot to the targetable with the highest score.
   b. Set the context's score value to the score associated with that targetable.
   c. Return true.
4. If no targetables were recorded with an evaluation score, return false.

In this way, multiple targets are compared and only the target that generates the highest score for each snippet is associated with that snippet in the main BDS evaluation table.

31.4.3 Comparing Snippets

As part of the AI character's update, the evaluation tree for each registered behavior snippet is run, and the score & target produced by that tree is stored along with the snippet in a summary table. When all of the evaluation trees have been run, the snippet with the highest recorded score is selected to be executed. This cycle is typically repeated on every AI update pass, but can be performed as often as appropriate. Listing 31.1 contains a pseudocode implementation of this evaluation step.

It is not strictly necessary to retain any of the per-snippet evaluation results beyond the scope of the evaluation step; the execution step requires only a reference to the highest priority snippet and the selected targetable. In practice, though, we found that retaining the evaluation results in a debug-viewable table provides great insights when debugging and iterating on AI behavior.

Listing 31.1. Pseudocode for evaluating registered behavior snippets.

```
struct SnippetEvaluation
{
    BehaviorSnippet snippet;
    Boolean result;
    Integer score;
    Character target;
};

// This function evaluates registered behaviors
// and returns the one with the highest utility.
Optional<SnippetEvaluation> EvaluateSnippets()
{
    list<SnippetEvaluation> evaluatedSnippets;
    for (BehaviorSnippet snippet: registeredBehaviors)
    {
        SnippetEvaluation evaluation = snippet.evaluate();
        if (evaluation.result == true)
            evaluatedSnippets.push(evaluation);
    }

    sortByDescendingScore(evaluatedSnippets);
    if (evaluatedSnippets.empty() == false)
        return evaluatedSnippets.first();
    else
        return None;
}
```

31.5 Execution Step

Having identified the highest scoring snippet, and a target for its associated ability, the final step is to execute that snippet. Just as each snippet contains an evaluation tree to show how the behavior should be evaluated, it also contains a behavior tree (termed the "execution tree") to show how the behavior should be executed. The execution tree is responsible for including any preparation or positioning required before performing the animation and game logic for the effective part of the action: the "active execution" of the action.

Like evaluation trees, execution trees have access to contextual information when being executed. Specifically, the BDS exposes information about the target which was selected during the evaluation step and the ability that the snippet is associated with. In order to simplify our execution trees, we defined a task node called "Execute Ability" which simply triggers the AI character to use the contextually-specified ability against the contextually-specified target. Figure 31.3 shows a typical "move-into-range-and-strike" execution tree.

Storing information about the ability and the target in the context (rather than explicitly referencing them in the execution tree) allows execution trees to remain generic, thus enabling their reuse across several different snippets. For example, the execution tree shown in Figure 31.3 could be applied to a punching attack, a stabbing attack, or a biting attack—just as long as the behavior occurs at melee range.

The execution tree belonging to the behavior snippet selected during the previous BDS evaluation pass will be executed once every AI update pass until the "Execute Ability"

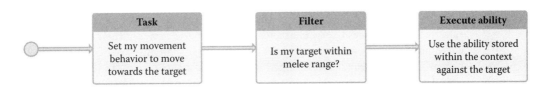

Figure 31.3

This execution tree handles moving to achieve range and line-of-sight before executing a ranged attack and stopping movement.

node is fired, signaling that the execution of the behavior is complete. However, even while an AI character is executing a particular snippet, it is still desirable for the BDS to continue performing the evaluation step. Reevaluating in this way allows AI characters to execute new snippets in response to changing circumstances rather than mindlessly carrying out a previously selected snippet which has since become suboptimal. In fact, the contract between evaluation and execution logic is that the evaluation tree is responsible for identifying and guarding against any conditions which would make it impossible to fulfill the directives contained within the execution tree. In circumstances where an execution tree has become impossible to complete (e.g., if the target of the execution dies before the ability can be used) then reevaluation ensures that the now-invalid snippet will be replaced with a valid one. Having said that, once an AI character triggers the "Execute Ability" node, it is reasonable to suspend AI updates until the ability finishes executing; this minimizes wasted AI decisions that cannot be fulfilled while the character is occupied.

31.6 Movement and Passive Behaviors

Although the BDS was originally designed to prioritize, prepare, and execute discrete actions, in the course of developing *DA:I*, we discovered that the BDS evaluation-execution framework is also useful for regulating ongoing or "passive" behaviors.

For example, in *DA:I* if the player's AI-controlled allies have nothing else to do, they will simply follow the player, wherever he or she goes. This was incorporated into the BDS by registering a snippet whose evaluation tree simply returned a constant score lower than any action (e.g., a score of 0 in the context of the scoring system in Table 31.1) and whose execution tree does nothing but trigger the "follow the leader" movement behavior. This snippet is automatically invoked by the BDS when it becomes the character's highest priority (i.e., when no other snippets with scores of greater than 0 are viable.)

Further application of this approach allows us to use the BDS to choose between contextually appropriate movement behaviors by conditionalizing scoring logic just as we do for combat abilities. *DA:I* uses this approach to apply variations on the follower behavior if the party is in combat, or if the player has commanded a party member to remain at a certain location; these evaluate conditionally to higher priorities than the basic party movement while still yielding to active actions.

It can also be useful to create behavior snippets which conditionally exhibit extremely high priorities, as this will suppress the execution of any other actions that might otherwise be viable. *DA:I* uses this method on characters who are expected to remain within a certain "tethered" area. For these characters, we created a behavior snippet whose execution tree simply forces the AI character to return to the center of their assigned area. The corresponding evaluation tree returns a score higher than any other combat ability—but only when the character is positioned outside their assigned area. In this way, we ensure that if an AI character strays too far from their assigned position, they will always disengage from their current target and return home rather than allowing themselves to be drawn further and further away.

31.7 Modularity and Opportunities for Reuse

Through its use of behavior snippets, the BDS emphasizes a modular approach to AI design. A modular approach offers several benefits. When debugging, it allows developers to easily isolate the evaluation logic for a specific behavior, or to compare an AI character's relative priorities by examining the results of the evaluation step.

The modular design also allows behaviors to easily be shared or moved between AI characters and archetypes. *DA:I* leverages this functionality to allow human players to customize their AI-controlled party members. Throughout the game, the player can add, remove and modify AI characters' equipment and abilities. By tying behavior snippets to equipment and ability assets, and by following a consistent scoring system (as described in Section 31.4.1) we can ensure that AI characters will be able to make effective use of the equipment and abilities at their command—regardless of what those may be.

Although the desire for modularity was initially driven by the requirements of our AI-controlled allies, the benefits extend to hostile AI characters too. During the development of our hostile creature factions, we found that an ability or behavior which was developed for a specific AI character type could be easily shared with others, assuming that the relevant assets (e.g., animations and visual effects) also available for the new characters.

In order to support the modular design of the BDS, it is important to implement the evaluation and execution tree data structures so that they can be authored once and reused across multiple behavior snippets. In developing *DA:I*, we found that most behavior snippets could be implemented using a small pool of frequently-reused tree assets, whereas only a small number of complex actions required specific evaluation or execution logic. Modular decomposition and content-reuse can be promoted even further by separating commonly-recurring subtrees into standalone tree assets which can then be referenced from other trees. Consolidating scoring logic in this fashion can help reduce the ongoing maintenance cost of implementing a standardized scoring system.

31.8 Conclusion

In this chapter, we have presented the Behavior Decision System: a simple but powerful framework developed to support AI decision-making. At the core of the BDS are "behavior snippets"—data structures which encapsulate the information required to both evaluate and execute a discrete action. Snippets are both evaluated and executed using behavior trees; "evaluation trees" are modified behavior trees, which return both a utility score and a target, whereas execution trees contain the necessary instructions to carry out the action.

At runtime, behavior snippets can be registered to AI characters via the BDS, with each registered snippet representing a single action that the character can perform. By evaluating these snippets as part of the character's update loop and regularly executing the snippet which yields the greatest utility score, the BDS produces patterns of behavior which are directed, purposeful, and reactive.

Acknowledgments

The authors would like to thank Darren Ward who implemented the behavior tree system on which the BDS is based, along with Jenny Lee and Chris Dalton who adapted Darren's system to the Frostbite engine.

References

Graham, D. 2014. An introduction to utility theory. In *Game AI Pro: Collected Wisdom of Game AI Professionals*, ed. S. Rabin. Boca Raton, FL: CRC Press, pp. 113–126.

Merrill, B. 2014. Building utility decisions into your existing behavior tree. In *Game AI Pro: Collected Wisdom of Game AI Professionals*, ed. S. Rabin. Boca Raton, FL: CRC Press, pp. 127–136.

32

Paragon Bots
A Bag of Tricks

Mieszko Zieliński

32.1 Introduction

Paragon is a MOBA-type game developed by Epic Games, built with Unreal Engine 4 (UE4). Relatively late in the project a decision was made to add AI-controlled players (a.k.a. bots) into the game. Limited time and human resources, and the fact that crucial game systems had already been built around human players, meant there was no time to waste. Redoing human-player-centric elements was out of the question, so the only way left to go was to cut corners and use every applicable trick we could come up with. This chapter will describe some of the extensions we made to the vanilla UE4 AI systems as well as some of the simple systems tailored specifically for *Paragon* player bots. In the end, we added a few enhancements to our basic behavior tree implementation, came up with a few useful MOBA-specific spatial representations, integrated all of those with our mature spatial decision-making system, the environment query system (EQS), and added a few other tricks. The results exceeded our expectations!

32.2 Terms Primer

There are a number of terms in this chapter that might be unknown to the reader, so we will explain them here.

In *Paragon*, players control heroes. A *hero* is a character on a team that can use *abilities* to debuff or deal damage to enemy characters and structures, or to buff his or hers own teammates. Buffing means improving capabilities (like regeneration, movement or attack speed, and so on) whereas debuffing has an opposite effect. Abilities use up hero's *energy*, which is a limited resource. Abilities also use up time, in a sense, since they are gated by cooldowns. Some abilities are always active, whereas others require explicit activation. The goal of the game is to destroy the enemy's base, while protecting your own team's base. Defending access to the base are *towers* which teams can use to stop or slow advancing enemies. The towers are chained into paths called *lanes*. A lane is what *minions* use to move from one team's base to the other's. Minions are simple creatures that fight for their team, and they are spawned in *waves* at constant intervals.

There is more to the game than that; there is jungle between lanes, inhabited by jungle creeps (neutral creatures that heroes kill for experience and temporary buffs), where *experience wells* can be found. There is the hero and ability leveling up, and cards that provide both passive and active abilities, and much more. However, this chapter will focus only on how bots wrapped their heads around game elements described in the previous paragraph.

32.3 Extremely Parameterized Behavior Trees

An experienced AI developer might be surprised that all *Paragon* bots use the same behavior tree. With the time and resources constraints we were under, we could not afford to develop separate trees for every hero, or even every hero type. This resulted in a specific approach: The master behavior tree defines the generic structure, specifying the high-level order of behaviors, but details of behavior execution (like which ability to use, which spatial query to perform, and so on) are parameterized so that runtime values are polled from the AI agent when needed.

32.3.1 Vanilla UE4 Behavior Trees

Before we get into details of how Vanilla UE4 Behavior Trees (BTs) were used and expanded in *Paragon*, here is a quick overview. Since BTs have been in AI programmers' toolkit for years (Isla 2005) the description will be limited to what the UE4 implementation adds to the concept.

UE4 BTs are an event-driven approach to generic BTs. Once a leaf node representing a task is picked the tree will not reevaluate until the task is finished or conditions change. Execution conditions are implemented in the form of *decorator* nodes (Champandard 2007). When its condition changes, a decorator node may abort lower priority behaviors or its own subtree, depending on the setup.

The UE4 BT representation is closely tied to UE4's Blackboard (BB). In UE4, the blackboard is an AI's default generic information storage. It takes the form of a simple key-value pair store. It is flexible (it can store practically any type of information) and has a lot of convenient built-in features. Blackboards are dynamic in nature and are populated by data at runtime. BB entries are the easiest way to parameterize behavior tree nodes; it makes it possible for a BT node requiring some parameters to read the values from a blackboard entry indicated by a named key. BT decorator nodes can register with BB to observe specific entries and react to stored value changes in an event-driven fashion. BB entries are also used to parametrize BT nodes. One example of parametrized BT nodes is the *MoveTo* node, which gets the move goal location from a blackboard entry.

Our BT implementation has one more auxiliary node type—the *service* node. It is a type of node that is attached to a regular node (composite or leaf) and is "active" as long as its parent node is part of the active tree branch. A service node gets notification on being activated and deactivated, and has an option to tick at an arbitrary rate.

32.3.2 Environment Querying System

In UE4, the EQS is the AI's spatial querying solution and is mentioned here since it is mostly used by the BTs to generate and use runtime spatial information. EQS is used for tasks such as AI positioning and target selection (Zielinski 2013). EQS' queries are built in the UE4 editor, using a dedicated tool, and are stored as reusable templates. The vanilla UE4 BT supplies a task node and a service node for running EQS queries and storing the results in the blackboard.

For *Paragon*, we made changes to the EQS so that it would be possible to point at a query template we want to use by specifying a key in the blackboard. The query templates themselves are regular UE4 UObjects, so no work on the blackboard side was required. The only thing that needed to be done was to extend the BT task that issues environmental queries to be able to use query templates indicated by blackboard values. We then used this new feature to implement different positioning queries for melee and ranged heroes; melee heroes want to be very close to enemies when attacking, whereas ranged ones (usually) want to be at their abilities' range while keeping their distance so that the enemy does not get too close.

32.3.3 Blackboard Extension

Allowing the blackboard to store a new type is as simple as implementing a dedicated BB key type. For *Paragon* we added a dedicated key type for storing an *ability handle*, a value that uniquely identifies an ability the given hero could perform. With the new blackboard key type, we gained an easy way to configure BT nodes to use abilities picked for different purposes. Section 32.4 describes the way abilities are picked.

32.3.4 Behavior Moods

It is easy to think about the behavior tree as the final consumer of AI knowledge. The BT takes the data and decides on the best behavior, based on that knowledge. We do, however, have additional subsystems that need information regarding what is going on in the BT. It is not really about what the BT is doing specifically, just what its current "mood" is. We need to know if the bot is running away, attacking characters, attacking towers, and so on.

The current mood is set through a dedicated service node. The mood information is then used by some of the native code that is doing derived work, like setting AI agent's focus or deciding which movement-related abilities are allowed.

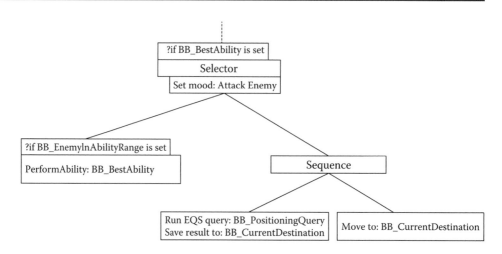

Figure 32.1

Example behavior tree branch controlling use of offensive abilities.

An example of how the described extensions and features mix together is shown in Figure 32.1. Names prefixed with BB indicate blackboard entries.

32.4 Ability Picker and Bot Ability Usage Markup

Deciding which ability to use in a given context, against a given target, is not a trivial task. The decision depends on multiple factors, like the target type, what we want to do to it, how much energy we have available at the moment, and which abilities are on cooldown. In addition, many abilities have multiple different effects. For example, there are abilities that damage or slow enemies, but they may also heal friendly heroes.

Abilities in *Paragon* are defined in UE4's Blueprint visual scripting language. This gives designers great flexibility in terms of how exactly each ability executes its behavior. Although this is great for content creator iteration and expressing creativity, it makes it practically impossible to extract the ability's usage information automatically. Besides, raw information about an ability is not enough to figure out how and when it makes sense to use it. To address that, we came up with a family of tags that designers used to mark up every ability an AI is supposed to use. We called those *bot ability usage* tags; examples are shown in Table 32.1.

Table 32.1 Examples of Bot Ability Usage Tags

BotAbilityUsage.Target.Hero	Use given ability to target heroes.
BotAbilityUsage.Effect.Damage	Given ability will damage the target.
BotAbilityUsage.Effect.Buff.Shield	Given ability will give the target a shield.
BotAbilityUsage.Mobility.Evade	Given ability can be used to evade enemy attack.

32.4.1 Ability Cached Data

When a bot-controlled hero is granted an ability, we digest the ability's blueprint to extract information useful for the AI. We store the results in the bot's *Ability Cached Data*, putting a lot of care into making sure the data representation is efficient. Ability usage tags get digested and represented internally as a set of flags. Other information stored includes the ability's range, type, damage, energy use, cooldown length, and so on. It also caches timestamps indicating when the given ability's cooldown will be over and when AI will have enough energy to cast the given ability. Every active ability available to a bot-controlled hero has its representation in the ability cache. Ability cached data is the key to the Ability Picker's efficiency.

32.4.2 Ability Picker

The *Ability Picker* is a simple yet surprisingly powerful service that is responsible for picking the right ability from a set of given abilities, given a certain target. The way the Ability Picker does that is extremely simple—actually, all the magic is already contained in the way the data is digested and stored as *ability cached data*. All the Ability Picker does is iterate through the list of abilities usable at a given point in time and checks if it matches the desired effect and target type. The returned ability is the one of "best cost" among the ones applicable. "Best cost" can have different meanings depending on the target type. When targeting minions, we prefer cheaper abilities, whereas we save the more expensive ones to target the heroes. Needless to say this scoring approach leaves a lot of room for improvement.

The core Ability Picker algorithm is extremely straightforward and is presented in pseudocode in Listing 32.1.

Listing 32.1. Ability Picker's core algorithm.

```
FindAbilityForTarget(AIAgent, InTargetData, InDesiredEffects)
{
    BestAbility = null;

    for Ability in AIAgent.AllAbilities:
        if Ability.IsValidTarget(InTargetData)
            && (Ability.DesiredEffects & InDesiredEffects)
            && (Ability.CooldownEndTimestamp < CurrentTime)
            && (Ability.EnoughEnergyTimestamp < CurrentTime):
            Score = Ability.RequiredEnergy;
            if IsBetterScore(InTargetData, Score, BestScore):
                BestScore = Score;
                BestAbility = Ability;

    return BestAbility;
}
```

`AllAbilities` is an array containing ability cached data of every ability available to the bot. The `IfValidTarget` function checks if a given target is of an appropriate type (Hero, Minion, Tower), if it is of a valid team, and if the target's *spatial density* (described below) is high enough. `IsBetterScore`, as mentioned above, prefers lower scores for minions and higher scores for heroes, so that we go cheap while fighting minions and wait to unload on heroes.

32.4.3 Target's Spatial Density

Some abilities are tagged by designers as usable against minions, but it makes sense to use them only if there is more than one minion in the area. This applies to *Area-of-Effect* abilities (AoE), which affect multiple targets in a specified area rather than a single target. Using such an ability on a single minion is simply a waste of energy and time.

To be able to efficiently test if a given target is "alone," we find *Spatial Density* for every target we pass to the Ability Picker. Target density is calculated as part of influence map calculations, which is described later in this chapter, so getting this information at runtime is a matter of a simple lookup operation.

32.4.4 Debugging

Having one system to control all ability selection had an added benefit of being easier to debug. It was very easy to add optional, verbose logging that once enabled would describe which abilities were discarded during the selection process, and why. The logged information combined with the spatial and temporal context we get out of the box with UE4's Visual Log allowed us to quickly solve many ability selection problems—which usually turned out to be bugs in ability markup. You can never trust those darn humans!

A handy trick that proved invaluable during bots' ability execution testing was adding a console command used at game runtime to override ability selection to always pick the specified ability. Thanks to the centralized approach we were able to implement it by plugging a piece of debugging logic into Ability Picker's `FindAbilityForTarget` function that would always pick the specified ability.

32.5 One-Step Influence Map

The influence map is a concept well known in game AI; it has been around for many years (Tozour 2001). It is a very simple concept, easy to grasp, straightforward to set up, but produces great, useful data from the very simple information it is being fed. The idea is based on a notion that units exert a "spatial influence" on their environment, proportional to their strength, health, combat readiness, or anything else that decays with distance. The influence map is a superposition of all those influences and can be used to guide AI decisions.

Normally, building an influence map involves every agent going through two steps. First is to apply the agent's influence at the agent's current location. This usually is the place where the agent has the highest influence (although there are other possibilities [Dill 2015]). The second step is influence propagation. We take the given agent's influence and propagate it to all neighboring areas, and then to areas neighboring those areas, and so on. The agent's influence distributed this way is a function of distance—the further from the source, the weaker the influence is.

Influence propagation can be a very expensive operation; depending on the influence map representation and resolution (although there are algorithms supplying infinite-resolution influence maps [Lewis 2015]). Also, it gets even more expensive the more influence sources we consider. Due to the constraints on processing for *Paragon* servers, the naive approach was not chosen.

There are multiple ways to represent an influence map. Performance is very important to *Paragon* bots, so we went for a very simple structure to represent influence on our maps. Since there is no gameplay-relevant navigable space overlaps on the vertical axis, we were able to represent the map with a simple 2D cell grid, with every cell representing a fixed-size square of the map. The size of the square used was a compromise between getting high-resolution data and not taking too much memory to store the map or using too much CPU when calculating influence updates. After some experimentation, we settled on using cells of 5×5 m which was a good compromise between memory requirements (320 kB for the whole map) and tactical movement precision. In addition, we have auxiliary information associated with every cell where we store influence source's counters that are used in multiple ways. More on that later.

We cannot simply ignore the fact that different enemies have different range and strength properties, that would affect the influence map naturally with influence propagation. In lieu of actual influence propagation, we apply influence of some agents to map cells in a certain radius rather than just in the one cell where the agent is currently present. We used zero radius for every minion (even the ranged ones) and for heroes we used every given hero's primary ability range. One could argue that applying influence in a radius rather than a point is almost the same as influence propagation, but there is a substantial performance gain when applying the influence to every cell in a radius compared to propagating it to consecutive neighbors, especially if the propagation would care about cell-to-cell connectivity. Applying influence to all cells in a radius does have a side effect of ignoring obstacles that would normally block influence, but due to the dynamics of *Paragon* matches and the way *Paragon* maps are built, this effect is negligible.

The main way we wanted to use the influence map was to determine bot positioning in combat. Depending on the hero type and situation, we might want a bot to keep away from enemies (the default case for ranged heroes), or on the contrary, keep close to enemies (the default for melee heroes). We can also use "friendly influence" as an indication of safer locations, or the opposite, to help bots spread out to avoid being easy AoE attack targets. It turns out that influence propagation is not really required for the described use cases because the influence range, defined as heroes' effective range, is already embedded into influence map data. Propagated data would give us some knowledge regarding how the tactical situation may change, but in *Paragon* it changes all the time, so we went for a cheaper solution over the one that would produce only subtly better results. Influence propagation can also be faked to a degree by deliberately extending the radius used for every hero. The extension can even be derived from runtime information, like current speed, amount of health, energy, and so on, because we build the influence map from scratch on a regular basis.

As will be discussed below, the influence map integrates with EQS to impact spatial processes like positioning, target selection, and so on.

32.5.1 Other Influence Sources

Other game actor types can also alter the influence map. Let us first consider towers (defensive structures described in Section 32.2). All characters entering an enemy tower's attack range are in serious danger, since towers pack a serious punch, even to high-level heroes. However, influence information is being used only by hero bots, and heroes are safe inside enemy tower range as long as the hero is accompanied by minions—minions are the primary target for towers. For this reason, we include a given tower's influence information in the map building only if the tower has no minions to attack; otherwise the bot does not care about the tower danger (or in fact, even know about it!).

One thing worth mentioning here is that since towers are static structures we do not need to recalculate which influence map cells will be affected every frame. Instead, we gather all the influenced cells at the start of the match and then just reuse that cached information whenever we rebuild the influence map.

One other influence source we consider during influence map building is AoE attacks. Some of those attacks persist long enough for it to make sense to include them in influence calculations. Having that information in the influence map makes it easy to "see" the danger of going into such an area! We do not annotate the influence map with short-lasting AoE attacks since the AI would not have a chance to react to them anyway—those attacks last just long enough to deal damage and there is practically no chance to avoid them once they are cast.

32.5.2 Information Use

As stated previously, the main use of the influence information is for bot positioning. This information is easily included in the rest of positioning logic by adding another test type expanding our spatial querying system (EQS). Thanks to EQS test mechanics, a single test that is simply reading influence information from specified locations in the world can be used to both score and filter locations a bot would consider as potential movement goals. Incorporating this one simple test into all bots' positioning queries allowed us to get really good results quickly. Thanks to this change, bots gained the power to avoid entering enemy towers' fire or running into groups of enemies and to pick locations close to friends, and so on.

Recall the auxiliary information associated with every cell of the map. That information is not strictly part of the influence map, but it is gathered as part of influence map building. The auxiliary information includes a list of agents influencing each cell. We use this information to improve the performance of minions' perception by effectively reducing the number of targets they consider for regular line-of-sight tests. Querying the influence map for enemy minions or heroes in a given area boils down to a simple lookup operation.

One last bit of influence-derived data is something we called *target density*. It is a simple per-cell counter of enemies of a given type (minion or hero), and we use that to determine if a given target is "alone" or if we would potentially hit some other targets when attacking the specific considered target. This is the information that hints to the Ability Picker whether using an AoE ability on a given target would be a waste of *energy* or not.

This kind of creative data reuse was necessary due to our time restrictions. We spent time building a system, so then we had to squeeze as much from it as possible.

32.6 Lane Space

A question we often had to answer was "how far bot X is from Y in terms of the lane it is on," where Y could be an enemy tower, a hero, a minion wave, or just an arbitrary location in the world. We did not really care about actual 3D distance, just about "how far along

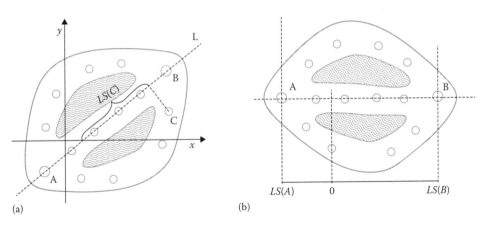

(a)

(b)

Figure 32.2

(a) A traditional MOBA map. (b) Map transformed to align with one of the axes.

the lane" things were. This is extremely easy to answer if lanes are straight lines, but that is not quite the case in *Paragon*… unless we straighten them out!

Figure 32.2a depicts a regular MOBA map, where A and B mark locations of both teams' bases. There are three lanes, with left and right lanes being not at all straight. This is where the concept of *Lane Space* comes in. Transforming a 3D world location into the lane space is a matter of projecting it to the line defined by $\overline{AB}$ segment. See Figure 32.2b for an illustration of this transformation.

Introducing lane space made it easy to add a new type of EQS test for scoring or filtering based on relative distance to the combat line on a given lane. We used it for example to make ranged bots prefer locations 10 meters behind the minions.

32.6.1 Lane Progress

A natural extension of the lane space is the idea of *Lane Progress*. It is a metric defined as a location's lane space distance from A or B, normalized by $|\overline{AB}|$ (distance from A to B). Lane progress is calculated in relation to a given team's base, so for example for team A lane progress value of base A location would be 0, and base B location would be 1. For team B it is the other way around; in fact, for every team A's lane progress value of x, the value for team B will be equal to $(1 - x)$.

32.6.2 Front-Line Manager

It is important in a MOBA for heroes to understand positioning in a lane based on areas of danger and safety. In combat, the ranged heroes prefer staying a bit behind the minion line, whereas melee heroes should be at the front-line, where the brawling takes place.

To allow the bots to behave like real humans do, we created the Front-Line Manager. Its sole purpose is to track all the minions left alive, along with all the remaining towers, and calculate where the lane's combat is. The Front-Line Manager is being fed information regarding minions by the influence map manager during influence map building. Based on that information and on the current state of a given team's towers on every lane, the Front-Line Manager is calculating the *front-line* on every lane for both teams. The exact front-line value is expressed in terms of lane progress.

Similarly, to the influence map information, we incorporate front-line information into the positioning logic by implementing another EQS test that measures locations' distance to the front-line.

One other place the front-line information is relevant is during enemy selection. We want to avoid bots chasing enemy heroes too deep into the enemy territory, so the distance from the front-line contributes to target scoring. Again, this is done with a dedicated EQS test.

32.7 Other Tricks

Cutting corners was crucial due to time constraints, so there is a fair amount of other, smaller tricks we used. Those are usually simple temporary solutions that either work well enough so that players would not notice, or are placeholders for solutions that will come in the future.

The first one worth mentioning is *perfect aim*. The ranged hero bots aim exactly at their target's location. This is not strictly speaking cheating, since experienced players do not have a problem doing the same. And it is not even as deadly as it sounds, since most ranged abilities used physical projectiles (meaning the hits are not instant) and some of them have ballistic properties (meaning they obey gravity). It is not a problem to add a slight aim angle deviation; *Paragon*'s easy-difficulty bots actually do that, it is just that the "perfect aim" helps revision-one bots to bridge the skill gap to human players. Besides, there are so many things humans have brain-hardware support for (especially visual processing), why should bots give up one of the few things bots are born with!

Another simple trick we used was to address a complaint we got from people playing in mixed human-bot teams. The problem was that as soon as the game started, all the bots were taking off to race down the lanes. It was suggested that bots should wait a bit, for example until minion waves started spawning. Since that would be a one-time behavior, considering it as a part of regular AI reasoning would be a waste of performance. Good old *scripted behavior* came to the rescue. We came up with a very simple idea (and implementation) of a one-time behavior that is triggered at the beginning of the match. It makes bots wait for minions to spawn and then *flow* down the lanes until they've seen an enemy, or reached the middle of the map, at which point bots simply switch over to the default behavior. *Flowing* down the lane involves using *Paragon*'s custom navigation flow-field, which makes movement fully pathfinding-free, and thus a lot cheaper than regular AI navigation. Once we had scripted behavior support, it came in useful in testing as well.

32.8 Conclusion

I feel that working on game AI is an art of using what is available and coming up with simple solutions to usually not-so-simple problems. In the chapter we've shown how this approach has been applied to work done on *Paragon* bots. Reusing and extending your AI systems is especially crucial when working under heavy time pressure, so investing effort ahead of time to make those systems flexible will pay off in the future. Using a single behavior tree for all bots in *Paragon* would not be possible otherwise. When it comes to solving game-specific problems, it is usually best to come up with a simple solution that isolates the problem and hides the complexity from the rest of AI code by supplying some easy-to-comprehend abstraction. The Ability Picker and Front-Line Manager are great examples of this. The "Keep It Simple" rule is always worth following!

References

Champandard, A., Behavior trees for Next-Gen AI, *Game Developers Conference Europe*, Cologne, Germany, 2007.

Dill, K., Spatial reasoning for strategic decision making. In *Game AI Pro 2: Collected Wisdom of AI Professionals*, ed. S. Rabin. Boca Raton, FL: A. K. Peters/CRC Press, 2015.

Isla, D., Handling complexity in the Halo 2 AI, *Game Developers Conference*, San Francisco, CA, 2005.

Lewis, M., Escaping the grid: Infinite-resolution influence mapping. In *Game AI Pro 2: Collected Wisdom of AI Professionals*, ed. S. Rabin. Boca Raton, FL: A. K. Peters/CRC Press, 2015.

Tozour, P., Influence mapping. In *Game Programming Gems 2*, ed. M. Deloura. Hingham, MA: Charles River Media, 2001.

Zielinski, M., Asking the environment smart questions. In *Game AI Pro: Collected Wisdom of AI Professionals*, ed. S. Rabin. Boca Raton, FL: A. K. Peters/CRC Press, 2013.

33

Using Your Combat AI Accuracy to Balance Difficulty

Sergio Ocio Barriales

33.1 Introduction

In a video game, tweaking combat difficulty can be a daunting task. This is particularly true when we talk about scenarios with multiple AI agents shooting at the player at the same time. In such situations, unexpected damage spikes can occur, which can make difficulty balancing harder. This chapter will show how to avoid them without compromising the player experience and while still giving designers lots of affordances for balancing.

There are a few different ways to deal with this problem. We could adjust the damage AI weapons do; we could add some heuristics that dynamically modify damage values based on things such as the time elapsed since the player was last hit or the number of AIs that are simultaneously targeting the player; or we could have AIs be less accurate and only really hit the player once every few shots.

The latter will be our focus for this chapter: Playing with AIs' accuracy to achieve better control over the amount of damage the player can receive each frame. This is a complicated and interesting topic, with two main parts:

1. What algorithm is used to decide when it is time to hit the player? How many agents can hit the player simultaneously?
2. How can we make our AIs not look ridiculous or unrealistic when they are purposely missing or holding off their shots?

33.2 Damage Dynamics

In an action game, difficulty level is usually related to how likely the player is to die during a game, or to the amount of experience required to progress through the experience (Suddaby 2013). Depending on the design of the game the way we control this can change. For example, in a first-person shooter we can decide to make enemies more aggressive, carry more powerful weapons, or simply spawn a higher enemy count; or, in a survival game, we could reduce the ammunition a player will find scattered through the world.

Adjusting how challenging a video game experience should be is normally a long and costly process in which different teams collaborate to improve the final player experience (Aponte et al. 2009). Programmers will expose new parameters for designers to tweak, enemy placement will change, levels will continue evolving and things will be tested over and over until the game is released ... and beyond!

Let us focus on the average cover shooter game. Normally, in these games, a few enemies will take covered positions that give them line-of-sight on the player. AIs will move around the level to try and find better firing locations if their positions are compromised or if they lose line-of-sight on their target, and they will unload their clips at the player, taking breaks for weapon reloading to add some variety to their behaviors. Combat will usually continue until (a) every AI is killed, (b) the player is killed, or (c) the target is not detected anymore.

In a scenario like this, one of the easiest ways to control difficulty, providing we keep enemy count constant, would be playing with damage dynamics, that is, adjusting the amount of damage inflicted by the AI when the player is hit (Boutros 2008). This is not a complex method in terms of the programming involved, but it requires lots of tweaking by designers.

Although this is a good strategy, it also has its problems. For instance, we could still face the problem of multiple AIs potentially shooting and hitting the player at the same time. This is solvable, for example, by tracking the total damage the target has received each frame and adjust incoming damage accordingly (e.g., not damaging the target anymore after a certain threshold has been hit), but this could lead to other believability problems; though solvable, the focus of this chapter is on a different type of solution, that we will talk about in the subsequent sections.

33.3 Token Systems

One way to address the one-hit kill syndrome is to have AIs take turns when attacking the player. This is commonly achieved by using a logical token that gets passed around the different agents involved in combat. Tokens can control different behaviors, but they basically fulfill the same purpose no matter what the action is: Only the AIs that hold a token will be able to execute the behavior. For example, we could decide that only AIs with a token can fire their weapons. If we have, let us say, just one token for the whole game, this means one, and only one, AI will be able to shoot at any given point in time. When the shooting is done, the token holder will release it, and another agent will take a turn.

The problem is that since only one AI is allowed to use its weapon at a time this could yield potentially unbelievable behaviors, such as AIs being at perfect spots to shoot and hit the player but not even trying to do so because they are clearly waiting for their turn.

33.4 Dynamic Accuracy Control

Our goal is to control the difficulty of our game and offer players a fairer, less chaotic game. Token systems will help us achieve that, but we can still make some improvements to offer a more polished experience.

Let us change the rules we used in the previous section. Tokens will not gate the shooting behavior anymore; instead, AIs can freely enter any of the shooting behaviors, but shots can only actually hit the player if the shooter has a token; any other shot will deliberately miss the player and hit some location around him or her.

Token distribution is controlled by a global timer that tracks how long has passed since the last hit. But, how long should the delay between hits be? Players will understand agents are not so accurate if, for example, they are far from their targets. In that case, having a long delay between hits is not a problem. But missing shots can affect the believability of our AI if the target is clearly visible and in range. To try and have the best of both worlds—predictability over the damage the target is going to take and a believable behavior, we need to use a variable, dynamic delay between hits.

33.4.1 Calculating the Final Delay

To define this delay, we will start from a base value, and define a few rules that will generate multipliers for our base value, increasing or decreasing the final time between shots. The final delay will be calculated as:

$$\text{delay} = \text{delay}_{\text{base}} * \prod_{i=0}^{n} \text{rule}_i$$

Where rule_i is a floating-point value resulting of running one of our rules.

In this section we will simplify things and say that we are fighting a single AI agent— we will show how to deal with multiple agents in the next section. With this in mind, let us define a few rules and show what the delay would look like in a couple of different scenarios.

33.4.2 Rules and Multipliers

Our first rule is distance. We want players to feel more pressure if they are closer to the AI, so we will allow our agents to hit players more frequently the closer they are to their targets. For our example, we will say that any distance greater than 15 m will not affect the delay, and that anything closer than 5 m will halve the time. Figure 33.1 shows the function we will use to generate our multiplier based on distance.

For our second multiplier, we will check the current stance of the player. In this case, we will keep the base delay if the player is standing (i.e., the multiplier is 1), but double it

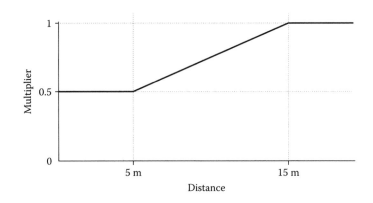

Figure 33.1

Our distance rule will generate a multiplier that will make the delay smaller the closer the player is to the AI.

if they are crouching, making the player feel safer. Likewise, we will use another rule that will double the delay if the player is in a valid cover position.

The current facing direction of the player is also an interesting factor. In this case, we can use it to be fairer and more forgiving with players if they are looking away from the AI, doubling the delay if the angle difference between the facing vector and the vector that goes from the player to the AI is greater than 170 degrees, and leaving the delay unchanged otherwise. Similarly, we can use the velocity of the player to check if they are trying to run away from the AI or toward our agents. Based on the angle between the velocity vector and, again, the vector that goes from the player to the AI, we will calculate a multiplier such as shown in Figure 33.2.

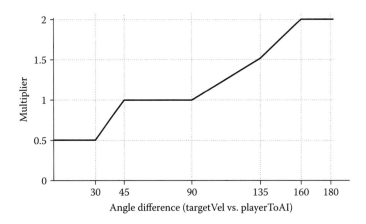

Figure 33.2

For our rule that takes into account target velocity, we have used a more complex curve to define how the multiplier is calculated.

For our example, this rule will halve the delay if the angle is lower than 30°, maintain it unchanged between 45° and 90° and make if longer the closer we get to 180° (we are actually capping it at 160°).

Finally, we could use other rules and multipliers, such as a rule based on the weapon the AI is wielding, but, for simplicity, we will not study these in this chapter.

33.4.3 Dynamic Delay Calculation Examples

With our rules defined, let us say our base delay is 0.5 s and define a first scenario in which the player is hiding, crouching behind cover 30 m away from the AI. With these constrains, we have:

- The distance multiplier is 1, since we are well over the 20 m cap.
- The stance of the player generates a multiplier of 2.
- Because the player is behind cover, we have another multiplier of 2. Also, since we are in cover, we will ignore the rest of the rules, as they are not applicable in this case (e.g. there is no player velocity, and we can consider the player facing is not relevant).

The final delay is $0.5 * (1*2*2) = 2$ s.

We will define a second scenario in which the player is out in the open, running toward the AI, 10 m away. Our rules would be yielding the following results:

- Based on distance, we have a multiplier of 0.75.
- The player is standing, which results in a multiplier of 1, and not behind cover, so that is another 1 for that rule.
- The player is looking at the AI and running toward it. Let us say that, in this case, both facing and velocity vectors are the same—they could be different if, for instance, the player was strafing—and the angle difference is very close to 0 degrees. This will generate a multiplier of 1 based on facing and the target velocity rule will calculate a 0.5 multiplier.

The delay for the second scenario is $0.5 * (0.75 * 1 * 1 * 1 * 0.5) = 0.1875$ s.

The dynamic delay will handle what the player is doing and increase—by allowing the AI to hit the player more frequently—or decrease difficulty accordingly. This system avoids multiple hits occurring on the same frame and can be tweaked by designers to balance the game in a way that is reactive to players' actions.

33.5 Dealing with Multiple AIs and Different Archetypes

In the previous section, we studied how our solution would work if we are dealing with a single enemy. However, this is normally not the case. Enemies will most likely be spawned in groups, and we can, as well, face different enemy types (archetypes). In this case, the algorithm remains very similar: We still use a single timer and we need to update its duration properly. The main difference is that, in the case of a single AI, all the calculations were made by applying our rules to that agent; when multiple AIs are present, we need to choose which should receive the token, and calculate the duration of the delay for that particular agent.

33.5.1 Selecting the Most Relevant Agent

Calculating which AI should get the token involves looking at a few different variables. Some of these are as follows:

- *Distance to the player:* The closer an agent is to the target the more options it has to receive a token.
- *Target exposure:* Depending on the position of the AI agent, the player can be more or less exposed to the attacks of the AI. For example, a cover position can be valid against a particular agent, but the same position can be completely exposed to an AI agent that is standing directly behind the player. The latter agent would have a better chance of obtaining the token.
- *Archetype:* The tougher the type of enemy, the easier it is for it to get the token.
- If an agent is currently under attack, it is more likely that it will receive the token.
- *Token assignment history:* Agents that have not received a token in a long time may have a higher chance of receiving the token soon.

A weighted sum will be used to combine these factors, generating a score for each actor. The actor with the highest score will be chosen as the most relevant agent. The weights we use can vary depending on the type of experience we want to offer. For example, if we had an enemy with a special weapon that generates some effect on the player that is really important for our game, we could use a very high weight for the archetype factor while using lower values for other ones. That way we would almost be guaranteeing that the special enemy will be the one hitting the player.

33.5.2 Dealing with Changes

Rechecking who is the most relevant agent every frame, we solve problems that are inherently common in action games, such as what happens if an AI reaches a better position, if the player keeps moving, or if an AI gets killed. Let us analyze a couple of scenarios.

In the first one, we have two agents, *A* and *B*. *A* is selected as the most relevant agent and the delay is 1s. The player runs toward *B* and starts shooting at it. The algorithm determines *B* is more relevant now since it is under attack and changes the selection. Also, because the player is running directly toward it, the facing and target velocity rules decide the delay should be shorter, so it is recalculated as 0.75 s. Time passes and the timer expires based on the new delay, so *B* hits the player, who turns around trying to retreat after being hit. *A* becomes the new selected AI and the delay goes back to 1 s. A second later, *A* hits the player.

For the second scenario, we have three agents—two regular soldiers (*A* and *B*) and a heavy soldier (*C*). *C* has just hit the player and now *A* is the most relevant AI. The delay for *A* is 2 s. After 1.5 s, *A* is killed. The algorithm determines *C* is, again, the most relevant AI, since it is in a better position than *B* and it is wielding a more powerful weapon. *C* is also a heavy, and the system calculates the delay is now 0.75 s. Since it has already been 1.5 s since the last hit, *C* gets a token immediately and the player is hit.

33.6 Improving Believability

If we want players to enjoy our game and our AI, we need to prevent breaking the suspension of disbelief (Woelfer 2016). In our case, this means hiding the processes that are happening behind the scenes—our damage control system—from players, so they are not distracted by the fact that the AI is being generous and missing shots on purpose to make the game more fun.

With this in mind, we have to take two points into consideration:

1. Although we normally communicate to the player he or she is being hit by using some HUD or VFX on the screen, we would completely lose that information if the player is not actually being hit.
2. Since most of the shots are going to miss the target, we need to make players not notice this fact.

33.6.1 Conveying Urgency

An important part of every game is that players understand the different situations they face and know how to identify and read the messaging the game provides about its systems and/or the state of the world.

If we stop hitting the player, we still need to produce a feeling of "being under pressure" when he or she is being targeted by an AI, in order to maintain engagement. We will mainly do this through sound effects and visual effects. For the former, 3D positioned sounds can help players pinpoint where shots are coming from, and also that some of them are missing the target; for visuals, we will use tracers and some VFX, like sparks or other particle effects.

33.6.2 Choosing Interesting Random Targets

If we want to make things interesting and good looking—so we can divert attention from the fact that the AI's accuracy is not very good—we need to ensure bullet hits will be seen by players and that they will clearly convey the player is under attack (Lidén 2003). This applies both to single shot weapons and automatic or semi-automatic ones; for the latter types, we could either calculate an interesting target for each bullet in the burst or, potentially, generate a single target and add some randomization around it or some special patterns, such as straight lines that the recoil of the weapon may be generating, to create better effects. The objective to keep in mind is that we are trying to polish the looks of things!

Let us refine the idea of picking random locations around the target, and ask ourselves: Are all these missed shots going to be noticed by the player? The answer is probably not. If we are just aiming at a random position in a circle around the target, as we show in Figure 33.3, the only thing players are going to notice for most of the shots is their tracers.

Instead, what we want is to make our "accuracy problems" an interesting situation from the visual standpoint, so what we should try to do is hit things surrounding the player to generate sparks, dust… in a nutshell, destruction. We still want to randomize our shots and fire the occasional one that does not hit anything, but we should try and minimize them.

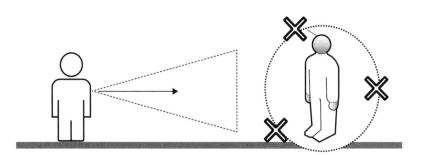

Figure 33.3

An AI that is consciously missing shots could target random positions around the enemy.

So, how do we choose better targets? In the average cover shooter, we will find that almost all scenarios fall in one of these three categories: Target is behind full cover, target is behind half cover, and target is out in the open. Let us analyze each of these individually.

33.6.2.1 Target Behind Full Cover

We call "full cover" anything that occludes the full height of the target. These are normally door sides, columns, pillars, and so on. Peeking out can only be done left and/or right, depending on which sides of the cover gives the user of the cover line-of-sight on its target. Figure 33.4 depicts this type of location.

If the target is behind full cover, we have two options. First, we can aim at positions near the ground next to the peek-out side of the cover; this are most likely going to be noticed by the player, since they are hitting the area he or she would have to use to leave the cover. Alternatively, we could also hit the cover directly, especially when the player is completely peeking out, as these hits are going to remind the player he or she can be hit at any point.

33.6.2.2 Target Behind Half Cover

A "half cover" is that which only occludes half of the height of the user, requiring him or her to crouch behind it to be fully protected. In this case, peeking out can also be done standing up and looking above the cover. Figure 33.5 shows this scenario.

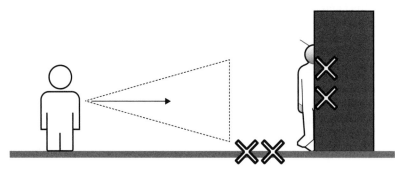

Figure 33.4

The AI's target is behind full cover, so we can target both the ground next to the cover and the cover itself.

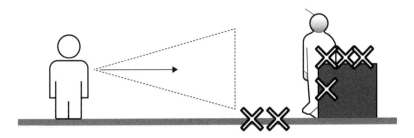

Figure 33.5

The AI's target is behind half cover, so we can target the ground next to the cover, the top of the cover and its side.

If the target is behind half cover, our options are similar to the ones we had in a full-cover situation. However, now we have an extra targetable area: the top of the cover. Most of our missed shots should aim at this zone, since they are closer to the eyes of the target, and thus, more likely to be seen.

33.6.2.3 Target Out in the Open

If our target is out in the open, the position we should choose is not as clear, and it depends on what the player is trying to do. For example, if the player is stationary, we could potentially shoot at the ground in front of the player, if this area is within camera view. But normally players will be moving around, so our best bet will be trying to whiz tracers right past the player's face at eye level.

33.6.3 Targeting Destructible Objects

Although we have presented some tricks to help choose the best random targets we can try to hit when we do not have the shooting token, we can always tag certain objects in the scene that are destructible and use them to create more spectacular and cinematic moments.

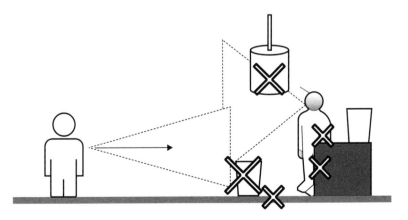

Figure 33.6

Destructible objects that are within the player's FOV should be targeted when our AI agents miss shots.

It is important to note that the destructibles we choose to target should also be in generally the same area as the player, if we want things to remain credible. Moreover, we should only target these special items if the player is going to see it, since these objects are limited in number and we should not waste the opportunity to use them. Figure 33.6 shows an area with destructible objects.

33.7 Conclusion

In this chapter, we have talked about different options to help make damage throughput more predictable, making it easier for designers to balance the game. But we also showed that, in order for our AI to look smart and believable, we need to control how the AI is going to deal with its targeting decisions.

Game AI is an art of smoke and mirrors—everything is permitted as long as we create a spectacular and fun experience. Tricks like playing with our AIs' accuracy can be used to control difficulty, and can help designers create better and more enjoyable games. It is our hope that readers can make use of these, or similar, techniques to keep improving what AI has to offer.

References

Aponte, M., Levieux, G., and Natkin, S. 2009. Scaling the level of difficulty in single player video games. In *Entertainment Computing–ICEC 2009*, eds. S. Natkin and J. Dupire. Berlin, Germany: Springer, 2009, pp. 24–35.

Boutros, D. Difficulty is difficult: Designing for hard modes in games. http://www.gamasutra.com/view/feature/3787/difficulty_is_difficult_designing_.php (accessed April 29, 2016).

Lidén, L. 2003. Artificial stupidity: The art of intentional mistakes. In *AI Game Programming Wisdom 2*, ed. S. Rabin. Rockland, MA: Charles River Media Inc.

Suddaby, P. Hard mode: Good difficulty versus bad difficulty. http://gamedevelopment.tutsplus.com/articles/hard-mode-good-difficulty-versus-bad-difficulty--gamedev-3596 (accessed May 9, 2016).

Woelfer, A. Suspension of disbelief|game studies. Video game close up. https://www.youtube.com/watch?v=Y2v3cOFNmLI (accessed May 9, 2016).

1000 NPCs at 60 FPS

Robert Zubek

34.1 Introduction

In this chapter we look at the AI used to implement characters in the game *Project Highrise* by SomaSim, a skyscraper construction management sim where players build, lease out, and manage a series of highrise buildings.

The AI goal in this simulation game was to implement a "living building," simulating the everyday lives of hundreds of inhabitants of the player's skyscraper, their daily lives and routines. As described in more detail in the next section, we gave ourselves a benchmark goal to hit: In order to meet gameplay needs, up to 1000 NPCs should be able to live in the player's building simultaneously, without dropping below 60 FPS on commodity hardware.

This chapter will describe how we approached the AI implementation that achieves this goal. We will first look at the game itself to illustrate the motivations and constraints behind the AI problem, then in the subsequent section, we will describe two action selection mechanisms we implemented (and why we settled on using just one of them), and following that, a performant system for actually executing these actions.

34.1.1 About the Game

Let us quickly introduce the game itself, as shown in Figure 34.1. The player's job in *Project Highrise* is to invest in the construction of highrise buildings, and then manage them successfully: Get tenants to move in, keep them happy, make sure everybody gets what

Figure 34.1

Screenshot from early game in *Project Highrise*.

they need, and pays rent on time. As in management simulation games of this type, the game board is populated by an ever-increasing variety and number of units, such as offices and restaurants renting space in the building, and characters going in and out of those units, going to work, getting lunch, coming home at night, and so on.

We will not go into further details on the gameplay or the economic simulation in the game, since they are beyond the scope of this chapter, except to point out that they all introduced a common goal: We needed the building to feel alive, to be filled with computer characters whose daily comings and goings would fill the building with irresistible bustle. In addition to the aesthetic feel of that, the NPCs' economic activity drives the economy of the building, which provides the main challenge for the player, so we needed the NPCs to be simulated on an ongoing basis instead of being simply instanced into view and then culled.

We gave ourselves a concrete performance goal: The game needed to be able to simulate and display 1000 NPCs, running at 60 FPS on a reasonably recent desktop-grade personal computer. Furthermore, there was a resource challenge: We were a tiny team, and we knew that during most of the development, we would only have one developer on staff whose job would involve not just AI, but also building *the entire rest of the game* as well. So we needed an AI system that was very fast to build, required very little ongoing maintenance once built—and primarily, helped us reach our performance goal.

Early on we decided to keep things very simple, and to split our character AI into two parts, with *action selection* driving decision-making, and separate *action performance module* acting on those orders.

34.2 Action Selection

Action selection is a fundamental decision process in character AI: What should I be doing at the given point in time? During the game's development, we actually tried two different implementations of action selection: first, a propositional planner, and second, a much simpler time-based scheduler of daily routine scripts.

The goal was to reproduce everyday human behavior: Office workers coming in to work in the morning, maybe taking a lunch break, and working at their desk most of the time until it is time to go home; apartment dwellers coming home in the evening and puttering about until bedtime; maintenance and janitorial crews doing their nightly work, whereas everybody else is sound asleep, and so on.

We did not have to worry too much about animation fidelity as the characters were just 2D sprites. Rather, our focus was on overall character behavior, because the actions of your residents and workers directly drive the in-game economy. For example, your food court restaurants need those office workers taking their lunch breaks so they can turn a profit, and you in turn depend on those restaurants paying rent, so you can recoup your investment. Character behavior is central to the economy core loop.

34.2.1 First System: A Propositional Planner

The planning system was our first stab at action selection for NPCs. This happened early in preproduction, and at that point we did not yet know how much "smarts" we would need or want from our characters, but we knew flexibility was crucial. Since the game simulates people with fairly simple goals, it made sense to use a planner to try to string together sequences of actions to achieve them.

We had some concerns about the runtime performance of a planner vis-à-vis the performance goal, so we decided to implement it using a *propositional planner*, due to its potential for very efficient implementation. A detailed description of such a planner is beyond the scope of this short chapter, but we can describe it briefly at a high level. By a propositional planner, we mean one whose pre- and postconditions come from a finite set of grounded propositions, instead of being expressed as predicates. For example, a planning rule in a propositional planner might look like this (using "~" for negation):

```
Rule: Preconditions:  at-home & is-hungry
      Action:         go-to-restaurant
      Postconditions: ~at-home & at-restaurant
```

Compare this with a rule that uses predicate logic, which is more common in planners descended from STRIPS (Fikes and Nilsson 1971):

```
Rule: Preconditions:  (at-location X) &
                      (desired-location Y) & ~(equal X Y)
      Action:         (go-to Y)
      Postconditions: (at-location Y) & ~(at-location X)
```

Predicate rules are more compact than propositional ones—they let us describe relationships between entire families of entities.* At the same time, this expressiveness is

---

* Of course one can also convert predicate rules into propositional rules by doing Cartesian products of the predicates and all the possible values for their free variables, at the cost of exploding the set of propositions.

expensive: The planner has to find not just the right sequence of actions to reach the goal, but also the right set of value bindings for all those free variables.

Propositional rules allow some interesting optimizations, however. Since all propositions are known at compile time, pre- and postcondition can be represented as simple bit vectors—then during planning, the process of checking preconditions and applying postconditions reduces down to very fast bitwise operations. Another benefit is easy plan caching: It is easy to annotate each propositional plan with a bitmask that describes world states in which this plan could be reused, so that it can be cached and reapplied verbatim in the future. At the same time, propositional rules also have a clear shortcoming: they lack the expressiveness of predicate logic, and require more propositions and rules, which complicates the decision of when it makes sense to use them.

Once implemented, the planner's performance exceeded expectations. Although this was early in production and we did not have a full set of NPCs defined yet, we knew intuitively that search space fan-out was not going to be a big issue.* Even so, plan caching was immediately useful: with the relatively small number of NPC types living fairly stereotyped lives, only a handful of distinct plans actually got created and then cached, so the planner only had to run that many times during the course of the game.

We ended up switching away from planning for a reason unrelated to performance, as discussed next. But even so, our takeaways were that (1) we had a positive experience with planning as a way to prototype AI behavior and explore the design space and (2) there are good ways to make it performant enough for use in games (e.g., using propositional planning, or compact GOAP planners such as presented in [Jacopin 2015]).

34.2.2 Second System: Daily Scripts

In the process of implementing character AI, our understanding of our own design changed. We realized that we wanted to have our NPCs live very stereotyped, routinized lives—they should be pretty predictable, because there were too many of them in the building for the player to care about them in detail. We also wanted a lot of designer control over our peoples' daily routines, to enhance the fiction of the game: so that worker and resident behavior would match the socio-economic status of their workplace or apartment, but at the same time, have a lot of variety and quirks for "flavor."

In the end, we realized that *by employing planning, we were working on the wrong level of abstraction.* We were authoring individual planning steps and trying to figure out how to turn them turn into the right behaviors at runtime—but what we actually wanted to do, was to author peoples' *entire daily routines* at a high level, so that we could have strong authorial control over when things happened and how they varied. We needed to author content not on the level of "how am I going to react to this situation," but on the order of "what does my workday look like today, and tomorrow, and the day after tomorrow."

The representation of behavior in terms of *routines* certainly has a rich history in AI. Some of the anthropologically-oriented research (e.g., Schank and Abelson 1977, Suchman 1987), makes a compelling case that our everyday human interactions are

---

* We saw this later re-affirmed by Jacopin in his empirical studies of planning in games (Conway 2015): in many games, NPC planning tends to result in numerous short plans, and relatively small search spaces.

indeed highly routinized: that given standard situations, people learn (or figure out) what to do and when, without having to rederive it from first principles, and these stereotyped routines drive their behavior.

Once we realized we were modeling behavior at the wrong level of abstraction, the solution was clear: we decided to abandon planning altogether, and reimplement NPC behavior as libraries of *stereotyped scripts*, which were descriptions of routine activities such as going to the office, going to a sit-down restaurant and sitting down to eat, processing a repair request from a tenant, and so on. Scripts would then be bundled together into various *daily schedules*, with very simple logic for picking the right script based on current conditions, such as the time of day and the contents of a simple "working memory" (e.g., info on where the NPC wants to go, where its current job is, where its current home is, and so on). Below is an example definition of a daily script, for someone who works long hours at the office:

```
name "schedule-office.7"
blocks [
    { from 8 to 20 tasks [ go-work-at-workstation ] }
    { from 20 to 8 tasks [ go-stay-offsite ] }
]
oneshots [
    { at 8 prob 1 tasks [ go-get-coffee ] }
    { at 12 prob 1 tasks [ go-get-lunch ] }
    { at 15 prob 0.5 tasks [ go-get-coffee ] }
    { at 17.5 prob 0.25 tasks [ go-visit-retail ] }
    { at 20 prob 0.5 tasks [ go-get-dinner ] }
    { at 20 prob 0.25 tasks [ go-get-drink ] }
]
```

This definition is split into two sections. In the `blocks` section, we see that they work from 8 am to 8 pm at their assigned work station (e.g., their desk), and otherwise spend time at home. Those *continuous* scripts such as `go-work-at-workstation` are performed as simple looping activity, repetitive but with tunable variations. Then the `oneshots` section specifies individual *one-shot* scripts that might or might not take place, depending on the probability modifier prob, and each script itself will have additional logic to decide what to do (e.g., `go-get-coffee` might start up and cause the NPC to go buy a cup of coffee, thus spending money in your building, but if there are no cafes in the building it will abort and cause the NPC to complain). Finally, all of these scripts bottom out in sequences of individual actions, as described in the next section.

This knowledge representation is simple compared to our previous planning approach, but it was a positive trade-off. Interestingly enough, early in preproduction we had also attempted a more complex internal personality models for NPCs, which included physiological state such as hunger or tiredness, but over time we removed all of this detail. The reasons were two-fold: (1) internal state acted as "hidden information" that made it difficult for both the designer and the player to understand why an individual is behaving in a certain way and (2) when multiplied by dozens or hundreds of NPCs, this made for many frustrating moments of trying to understand when entire populations behaved unexpectedly.

Our main take-away was that *the utility of detailed NPC representation is inversely proportional to the number of NPCs the player has to manage*. When the number of simulated people is small, players appreciate them being complex. However, as the number gets larger, this does not scale. Having to understand and manage them in detail becomes a burden for both the player and the designer, so it is better to increase the level of abstraction as the number of NPCs increases, and limit the complexity that the player has to deal with.

34.3 Action Performance

Both of our action selection systems—the planner, and the script scheduler—produced sequences of actions that needed to be performed by the NPC. In this section we will look at the flip side of this coin: action performance. We will also talk about two simplifications that enabled efficient implementation: open-loop action performance, and domain-specific representation for pathfinding.

34.3.1 Action Queues and Open-Loop Action Performance

Many NPC AI systems are *closed-loop feedback systems*—they monitor the world while actions are performed, and adjust behavior appropriately, primarily so that they can handle failures intelligently. This comes at a price, however: checking the world has a nonzero computational cost (based on the frequency of updates, the fidelity of the sensory model, etc.), as does deciding whether to act on this new information. Some architectures like *subsumption* (Brooks 1986) or *teleoreactive trees* (Nilsson 1994) accept constant resensing and recomputation as the cost of doing business—while various *behavior tree* implementations, for example, differ greatly in whether the individual nodes revalidate themselves in teleoreactive fashion or cache their activation for extended periods of time.

In our system we take this to a stark extreme: we run action performance almost entirely *open-loop,* without trying to monitor and fix up our behavior based on changes in the world. The main AI setup looks something like this:

1. Action selection picks a script (e.g., *go to work*), and combines it with the NPC's working memory (e.g., *I work at office #243*) to produce a sequence of simple actions: *go into the lobby, wait for elevator, take elevator, walk into office #243, sit down at my desk, etc.*

2. Actions get dropped into an *action queue* and executed in linear order. This is detailed in (Zubek 2010), but anyone who has played The Sims or classic base-building real-time strategy games will be immediately familiar with how this works at runtime.

3. Each action can optionally monitor for custom failure conditions. For example, a navigation action will fail if a path to the destination cannot be found.

4. If a failure is detected, the queue is flushed immediately, and optionally a fallback script may be queued up instead (e.g., *turn to the camera, play displeased animation, and complain about the conditions in this building*).

5. Once the queue is empty, the system runs action selection all over again, which picks the next set of actions and refills the queue.

In effect the system only evaluates the world when it has nothing to do, and once a course of action is decided, it runs open-loop until it either succeeds or gets interrupted.

These sequences of actions also end up being rather short—for example, a script for going to a restaurant and eating might produce a dozen individual actions, altogether taking about an hour of game time (or: less than a minute of real time) to execute.

This works only thanks to the mostly benign nature of this game world: it is usually okay to run open-loop without paying too much attention to the world. If something unexpected does happen, action selection is so inexpensive that we can just abandon the previous activity and start over. So the brief take-away is that, for game designs that allow it, inexpensive action selection enables a whole host of other simplifications, such as skipping proper failure handling in favor of just starting all over again.

34.3.2 Pathfinding over a Simplified Model

The second optimization had to do with pathfinding. The game takes place on what is essentially a 2D grid—a cut-away side view of a building, which can be, say, 100+ stories tall and several hundred grid cells wide, depending on the scenario. A naive implementation of A* pathfinding on the raw grid representation quickly turned out to be insufficient when hundreds of NPCs tried to navigate the grid at the same time.

Naturally, we reformulated pathfinding to be hierarchical to reduce search space. However, instead of using a generic clustering approach such as for example, HPA* (Botea et al. 2004), we used our domain knowledge to produce a specialized compact representation, which made it easier to support the player making ongoing changes to the path graph (as they built, altered or expanded their highrise). In short: based on the game's design, the pathable space divided up into distinct *floor plates*, which were contiguous sequences of tiles on the same floor, such that the character could do a straight-line movement inside a floor plate. Additionally, each floor plate was connected with those above or below it via stairs, escalators, or elevators, together known as *connectors*. Floor plates and connectors became nodes and edges in our high-level graph, respectively, and movement inside each floor plate became simple straight-line approach.

This search space reduction was significant: for an example of a dense building 100 stories tall by 150 tiles wide with four elevator shafts, we reduced the space from 15,000 grid cells to only 100 graph nodes with 400 edges between them. At this point, the data model was sufficiently small to keep running A*, and additional tweaks to the heuristic function prevented the open set from fanning out unnecessarily.

I should also add that we considered alternatives such as JPS and JPS+ over the raw grid, but found them to be an uneasy fit given that the player would be altering the grid space all the time. In particular, JPS (Harabor and Grastien 2012) effectively builds up a compact representation as needed, in order to simplify its search, but as the player keeps changing the game board it would have to keep redoing it over and over again—which seems less optimal than just keeping the source data model compact to begin with. Additionally, JPS+ (Rabin 2015) gains a performance advantage from preprocessing the search space, but this is an expensive step that is not intended to be reapplied repetitively while the game is running.

In the end, although we considered more complex approaches than A*, they became unnecessary once we realized how to *optimize the search space instead of optimizing the algorithm*. We used our domain knowledge to reduce the data model so drastically that the choice of algorithm no longer mattered, and it was a very positive development. Many areas of AI involve search, and model reduction is a classic technique for making it more tractable.

34.4 Conclusions

Drastic simplifications of character AI allowed us to reach our goal of 1000 NPCs at 60 FPS, while keeping development costs down. It was a good example of the power of a super-specialized AI implementation which, although not generalizable to more complex behaviors or more hostile environments, was an excellent fit to the problem at hand, and carried no extra computational (or authoring) burden beyond the minimum required.

This might be an interesting example of the benefits of tailoring one's AI implementation to fit the problem at hand, instead of relying on more general middleware. Although general solutions have their place, it is amazing what can be achieved by cutting complexity mercilessly until there is nothing left to cut.

References

Botea A., Mueller M., Schaeffer J. 2004. Near optimal hierarchical path-finding. *Journal of Game Development,* 1(1), 7–28.

Brooks, R. 1986. A robust layered control system for a mobile robot. *IEEE Journal of Robotics and Automation,* RA-2(1), 14–23.

Conway, C., Higley, P., Jacopin, E. 2015. Goal-oriented action planning: Ten years old and no fear! *Game Developers Conference 2015,* San Francisco, CA.

Fikes, R. E., Nilsson, N. J. 1971. STRIPS: A new approach to the application of theorem proving to problem solving. *Artificial Intelligence,* 2(3–4), 189–208.

Jacopin, E. 2015. Optimizing practical planning of game AI. In S. Rabin (ed.), *Game AI Pro 2,* CRC Press, Boca Raton, FL.

Harabor, D., Grastien A. 2012. The JPS pathfinding system. In *Proceedings of the Annual Symposium on Combinatorial Search (SoCS),* Niagara Falls, Ontario, Canada.

Nilsson, N. 1994. Teleo-reactive programs for agent control. *Journal of Artificial Intelligence Research,* 1, 139–158.

Rabin, S. 2015. JPS+: Over 100x faster than A*. *Game Developers Conference 2015,* San Francisco, CA.

Schank, R., Abelson, R. 1977. *Scripts, Plans, Goals, and Understanding.* Lawrence Erlbaum Associates, Hillsdale, NJ.

Suchman, L. 1987. *Plans and Situated Actions.* Cambridge University Press, Cambridge.

Zubek, R. 2010. Needs-based AI. In A. Lake (ed.), *Game Programming Gems 8,* Cengage Learning, Florence, KY.

35

Ambient Interactions

Improving Believability by Leveraging Rule-Based AI

Hendrik Skubch

35.1 Introduction

It is a hot day in the city of Lestallum. An old man rests comfortably on a bench. Shaded by the nearby palm trees, he reads the local newspaper. A passing tourist takes a break from sightseeing and joins him. Wiping sweat from his forehead, he glances at the newspaper. With a puzzled look in his face, he poses a question to the old man. A brief conversation ensues.

This small scene is one of many that contributes to the realism and vibrancy of a city scenario. Although it is irrelevant for the main plot of a game or for its game play, we value the added immersion. *FINAL FANTASY XV* emphasizes the idea of a journey through a diverse landscape featuring different cultures. In order to bring that world to life and convey different cultures, it is not enough to just place NPCs in the environment. Instead, these NPCs need to interact with the environment and with each other.

This goal leads to two requirements; first, a way to mark up the environment with sufficient information to motivate AI decision-making, and second, a way to express how multiple characters can react to this information. Classical AI scripting methodologies in games such as state machines or behavior trees focus on the actions of individuals. Expressing causal and temporal relationships between the actions of different actors is difficult at best.

We present an interaction-centric approach in which interactions are described using STRIPS-like rules. A type of smart object, called *Smart Locations*, use the resulting scripts to control the actions of multiple NPCs. In contrast to planning, symbolic effects are not used to reason about future world states, but instead are used to coordinate the actions of multiple participants by updating a common knowledge representation in the form of a blackboard and reactively applying rules based on that structure. Thereby coordination becomes the focus of the language and is expressible in a straightforward manner. Moreover, the resulting rule-based scripts are highly adaptive to different situations. For example, in the city scene mentioned above, if there was no old man, the tourist might still sit down to rest. Alternatively, if the old man was joined by a friend, the tourist might have walked by due to lack of space.

35.2 From Smart Objects to Smart Locations

The concept of smart objects was originally conceived for The Sims (Forbus 2002). Smart objects are inanimate objects in a scene that carry information about how they can be used by an agent. For example, a chair may carry the information that it can be used to sit on. It even provides the necessary animation data for doing so. In a sense, by emphasizing objects instead of agents, smart objects reverse the idea of traditional agent-based AI, thereby decoupling the AI from the data necessary to interact with an asset. This allows for new objects to be added to a scene and become usable by the AI without modifications to the AI itself.

More recently, the concept of smart objects has evolved into that of smart zones by de Sevin et al. (2015). Smart zones abstract away from concrete objects and add the idea of roles that NPCs can fulfill, thereby facilitating multiple NPCs interacting with the environment in order to create a richer scene.

In a similar way, smart locations abstract away from concrete objects, as shown in Figure 35.1. They are invisible objects that refer to multiple concrete objects. For example, a single smart location may refer to two chairs and a table. This allows it not only to inform agents about the existence and usability of individual objects, but also to capture relationships between them, such as furniture grouping. Although smart zones use timeline-based scripts with synchronization points to drive the behavior of NPCs, we use a more expressive scripting language based on declarative scripting rules. Furthermore, we add an additional abstraction layer between the location object embedded in the world and the static script object. These script objects may contain additional data necessary for its execution, such as animations. The resulting decoupling allows for scripts to be exchanged, whereas the smart locations stay in place. But smart locations do not just contain information; they essentially govern the usage of the objects they refer to. To that end, they emit signals to agents in the vicinity. These signals can range from mere notifications to commands, depending on the type of emitter. In *FINAL FANTASY XV*, we use four different kinds of emitters:

- *Notification emitter*: These emitters merely inform agents about the existence of the smart location, the objects it knows about, and a set of ontologically grounded tags. Notification emitters are mainly used to inform the more autonomous characters, such as the player's buddies.

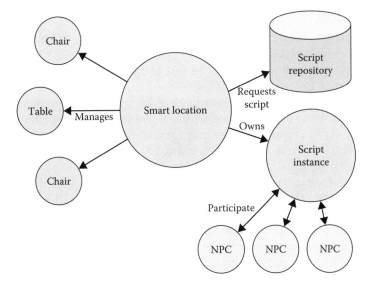

Figure 35.1

Smart locations manage static props and dynamic script instances.

- *Script emitter*: This is the most frequently used emitter type. Based on the number and type of NPCs in the vicinity, this emitter performs a role allocation and initiates the execution of a script. We will elaborate on this process in the following sections.
- *Spawn emitter*: Scripts that require three or more specific characters occur rarely when using just NPCs that pass by the location. This has already been noted by Blondeau during the development of *Assassin's Creed Unity* (Blondeau 2015). Spawn emitters fill this gap by spawning a set of NPCs at points specified by designers. This is also used to place NPCs at otherwise unreachable locations, such as balconies.
- *Player emitter*: Finally, the player emitter communicates with the player by means of interaction icons, which, when reacted to, will initiate a script. The player themselves joins this script as an NPC. Player input is fed to the script's blackboard, allowing designers to script short interactive scenes in a dynamic fashion without changing methodology.

35.3 Expressing Interactive Acts

We express interactions in the form of rule-based scripts. Rules are drawn from STRIPS (Fikes and Nilsson 1971), but instead of being used for planning, they form a declarative scripting language, where rules operate over a special kind of blackboard, a tuple space. Tuple spaces were originally devised as a way to coordinate data access in distributed systems (Carriero et al. 1994). The combination of both methodologies allows agents to exchange information by executing rules on the same tuple space. In the following, we briefly introduce STRIPS and tuple spaces as the two foundations of interaction scripts.

35.3.1 Foundation: STRIPS

Stanford Research Institute Problem Solver, or STRIPS, was one of the first automated planning systems. Here, we refer to the language of that system. In STRIPS, an action is described by a precondition that must be true in order for the action to be executable, and the positive and negative effects it has on the world. Positive effects add facts to the world, whereas negative effects remove them. Note that, although the original formulation of STRIPS is based on pure propositional logic, we use a first-order notation here and in the remainder of this chapter. Since we only consider finite domains under closed-world assumption, this is nothing more than syntactic sugar, as all formulas can be compiled into propositional logic.

Consider a classic example from academia, called the Blocks-world. In this world, a robot is tasked with stacking blocks on a table on top of each other. One of the actions the robot has is $PickUp(B)$—with the intuitive meaning that the robot will pick up a block B with its actuator. The precondition for this action is $onTable(B) \land \neg on(A, B) \land \neg holding(K)$, meaning that B should be on the table, nothing should be on top of it, and the robot should not already be holding anything else in its actuator. The positive effect of this action is $holding(B)$—the robot is now holding block B. The negative effect is $onTable(B)$—the block is no longer on the table. With action descriptions like this, and state descriptions for a goal and an initial state, planning algorithms can chain actions together in order to find a sequence of actions leading from an initial state to a goal state.

Note that the precondition acts as a selector over which block B will be picked up. In Section 35.4.3, we will discuss how both the truth value of the precondition and an assignment for the variables in the rule, such as which block is chosen for variable B, can be determined at the same time by means of a backtracking algorithm.

35.3.2 Foundation: Tuple Space

Tuple spaces are a way to coordinate distributed systems. Since we do not need to operate a truly distributed system, that is, there are no synchronization issues or accidental data loss, we use a simplified version here. The tuple space provides facilities to store, query, and modify facts used in STRIPS rules, such as $onTable(B)$ from above. Basically, a tuple space can be thought of as a multimap, where the name and the arity (arguments) of a predicate (e.g., onTable/1) are used as keys to map onto all ground facts currently considered being true. Thus, in this form, it only represents positive knowledge under the closed-world assumption, matching STRIPS and enabling negation as failure reasoning.

35.3.3 The Interaction Language Model

A basic interaction script consists of a set of roles and a set of rules. Intuitively, roles define which kind of actors can participate in a script and how many, whereas rules indicate what the actors are supposed to do.

Whenever an actor is participating in a script, it is assigned exactly one role. Multiple actors can be assigned to the same role. An actor may be able to take on different roles.

For example, the old man on the bench may be able to take on the roles citizen, male, elder, and human, but not waiter or tourist (but in the context of a single script instance, he will take on only one role). More precisely, a role consists of the following:

- *Name*: The unique name of the role, such as tourist, waiter, or citizen.
- *Cardinality*: The minimum and maximum number of actors that can take on this role. Role allocation will try to satisfy all cardinalities of the script. If that is not possible, the script will not start. Should any cardinality be violated while the script is running, for example because an actor left, the script will terminate.
- *Flags*: An extensible set of flags that further describes how a role is to be treated at runtime. Most importantly these flags govern whether or not an actor can dynamically take on a role and join the script while it is running, or if any special actions are necessary when an actor is leaving the script, such as sending them a command to move away from the smart location.

We may describe the initial scene between the old man and the tourist with these roles:

- *Elder*: 0..1 dynamicJoin = true
- *Tourist*: 0..2 dynamicJoin = true

Thereby, the script can run with any combination of up to two tourists and one elder. Any role initially unfulfilled can be assigned later dynamically. This permits a variety of different sequences of events; for example, the old man may join the tourist on the bench.

In contrast to roles, rules entail what actors should do once they participate in a script. In a minimal version of this scripting language, rules must consist of at least:

- *Precondition*: The condition that has to hold in order for the rule to fire.
- *Action*: The action an actor should undertake. Note that actions are optional; rules without actions simply apply their effects and can be used to chain more complex effects. In our case, each action identifies a state machine or behavior tree on the lower individual AI level. The degree of abstraction is arbitrary, but we think a reasonable degree is achieved by actions such as "sit down," "go to," or "talk to." Of course, this depends on the concrete game considered.
- *Action parameters*: A list of key-value pairs that are passed to the lower layer that executes the action. For example, movement speed or animation variations often occur as parameters.
- *Addition* (δ^+) *and Deletion* (δ^-): The list of positive and negative effects a rule has. They are applied immediately when the rule fires.
- *Deferred Addition and Deferred Deletion*: Similar to Addition and Deletion, the deferred versions modify the tuple space. However, they are applied only after the action has successfully terminated. If there is no associated action, deferred effects are applied immediately.
- *Termination type*: A rule can be used to terminate the whole script or cause an individual actor to leave the script. The termination type is used to indicate this.

Additionally, we added the following syntactic sugar to simplify common cases:

- *Target*: Most actions have a target, as is implied by the proposition in their name such as goto or lookat. Because these are used so frequently, we treat the target separately instead of using action parameters.
- *Role*: Acting as an additional precondition, the role property of a rule limits the NPCs that can execute a rule to those of the corresponding role.
- *State*: A state also acts as an additional precondition. Only actors currently inhabiting this state can execute this rule. Thereby we overlay the rule-based execution with a simple state machine. It is trivial to formulate state machines using preconditions and action effects; however, a simple state machine greatly reduces the perceived complexity and length of preconditions.
- *Next state*: After successfully executing a rule, an NPC will transition to this state.
- *OnError*: In order to simplify handling of errors stemming from failed actions, a list of facts can be provided to be added if a rule fails.

Treating these notions explicitly simplifies the task of writing scripts, and, in many cases, allows optimizing script execution further. For example, by rearranging rules so that rules of the same state are consecutive in memory, only rules of the current state of an actor have to be evaluated.

Let us consider some simple example rules useful for the bench scenario. First, we need a rule for sitting down:

- **Rule 1**:
    - **Action:** $sit(X)$
    - **Precondition:** $seat(X) \land \neg reserved(X, Y)$
    - δ^+: $reserved(X, .me)$
    - **deferred δ^+:** $sitting(.me) \land timer(.me, .now + randf(2,5)^* .minute)$

The action sit has a target, namely the object to sit on, denoted by the variable X, which is sent as a game object to the individual AI. The implementation of sit may be arbitrarily complex, in this case, it will query the animation system for where to be in relation to X when triggering the sit-down animation, path plan to that point, move, and finally trigger the animation.

The specific game objects that X can possibly refer to at runtime are known by the smart location. Before executing the script, the smart location dumps this information into the tuple space using the predicate seat. The second predicate, reserved, is used to formulate a reservation system inside the tuple space. Note that the keyword reserved does not have any meaning outside of the rule for sitting. The definition of the rule gives meaning to the symbol. The same holds true for the predicates sitting and timer which are used to inform other NPCs that the sitting action has now been completed and to store a timer for future use, respectively. The difference between addition and deferred addition allows us to reserve the seat the moment the action is committed to, while informing other NPCs of the action completion several seconds later.

However, not everything can be solved purely by means of the tuple space, sometimes we need to call into other systems or refer to special purpose symbols. These symbols are prefixed with a dot "." as in *.me*, which refers to the NPC that is currently evaluating the rule. Therefore, the positive effect reserved(X, *.me*) will substitute X with the game object that represents the seat and *.me* with the NPC in question before inserting the resulting tuple into the blackboard. Once the NPCs are sitting, we can drive a simple randomized sequence of talking and listening actions using the following three rules:

- **Rule 2:**
  - **Precondition:** $\neg\text{talker}(X) \wedge .any(Y) \wedge \text{sitting}(Y)$
  - δ^+: $\text{talker}(Y)$

- **Rule 3:**
  - **Action:** $\text{talk}(X)$
  - **Precondition:** $\text{talker}(.me) \wedge .any(X) \wedge X \neq .me \wedge \text{sitting}(X)$
  - **Deferred δ^-:** $\text{talker}(.me)$

- **Rule 4:**
  - **Action:** $\text{listen}(X)$
  - **Precondition:** $\text{talker}(X) \wedge X \neq .me$

Rule 2 does not cause an action; it is merely used to designate a single sitting NPC as the currently talking one by means of the predicate talker. The built-in predicate *.any* unifies its argument with a random participating NPC. The following predicate sitting limits this to a random sitting NPC. The backtracking algorithm achieving this behavior will be discussed in Section 35.4.3.

Rule 3 triggers a talk-action for the designated NPC. Supplying another random sitting NPC as target X, allows for LookAt-IK and other directed animations to take place. After the talk-action finishes, talker is removed, in turn triggering the first rule again. The fourth rule lets us model a listening reaction to the talking action, such as a nod.

Finally, in order to avoid an endless discussion between the NPCs, we add a termination rule that refers to the timestamp introduced in Rule 1, which causes the NPCs to get up and terminate its participation in the script:

- **Rule 5:**
  - **Action:** getup
  - **Precondition:** $\text{timer}(.me, T) \wedge T < .now$
  - **Terminate = true**
  - δ^-: $\text{timer}(.me, T)$ $\text{sitting}(.me)$
  - **Deferred δ^-:** $\text{reserved}(.me, X)$

Note the free variable X in the deferred deletion causes all matching tuples to be removed from the tuple space.

Formally, our query language is limited to conjunctions of literals. A literal is a possibly negated predicate such as reserved(X,Y) or $\neg$talker(Z). Thus, we exclude disjunctions and negations over the scope of multiple literals from the language. Furthermore, the query language also relates to DataLog (Ceri et al. 1989), a function-free declarative language.

That means function symbols are not allowed to occur, thereby greatly reducing the complexity of evaluation compared to other declarative languages, such as Prolog. We can still tolerate function symbols to occur by simply enforcing them to be evaluated immediately when they are encountered, circumventing any costly term manipulation. This allows us to express functional terms such as $.now + randf(2,5) * .minute$ in Rule 1, or $distance(.me, Someone)$ without incurring the cost of term manipulation in a full first-order language. A tool side verification step ensures that this treatment of function symbols is safe, for example, that *Someone* will always be instantiated to an NPC when evaluating $distance(.me, Someone)$.

35.4 Script Execution

A smart location equipped with a script emitter will periodically query a spatial database for NPCs in the vicinity in order to start an interaction scene. Based on the smart location's preference for different scripts, the NPCs found, and the currently loaded scripts, a script is chosen to be executed. From there on, the script is updated regularly in the following way:

- Shuffle all participants. This counters any unintentional bias in the rule set toward the first or last NPC. Any predicate that accesses participants effectively accesses the shuffled list.
- Apply the deferred effect of any action that finished and the OnError list of any failed action.
- For each participant not currently executing an action, find the first matching rule in its state. If found, trigger the action and apply the effect.
- Remove all NPCs from the script that encountered a termination flag.
- Terminate the script if not enough NPCs remain.

Since scripts operate on a local blackboard, each NPC only participates in at most one script at a time, and smart locations have exclusive ownership over their props, multiple script instances can be executed concurrently without the need for thread synchronization.

35.4.1 Role Allocation

Role allocation is the process of assigning actors to roles such that the resulting assignment satisfies all given constraints, such as our cardinalities. In practice, we use additional constraints to reflect that some NPCs, such as families, act as groups and only join scripts together. Since each actor can satisfy multiple roles and each role may require multiple actors, the problem is NP-hard (Gerkey and Mataric 2004). However, the specific problem instances encountered in interaction scripts are typically very small and simple, meaning rarely more than three or four distinct roles and rarely more than five actors. Furthermore, we do not require the resulting allocation to be optimal with respect to some fitness function. Indeed, we can even allow the role allocation to fail occasionally. Thus we can formulate role allocation as a Monte-Carlo algorithm by randomizing its input.

After randomization, role allocation simply assigns NPCs greedily to roles until the lower bound of the respective cardinality is reached. If a role-cardinality cannot be satisfied in this way, the allocation fails immediately. Subsequently, potentially remaining NPCs are assigned until the maximum cardinality is reached or no more NPCs can be added.

35.4.2 Joining Late

Although a smart location is running a script, it will not start a second one to avoid concurrent access to its resources. However, it will periodically query the spatial data base for NPCs in the vicinity that can join the already running script instance. Whether or not this is possible is indicated by the flag "dynamicJoin" introduced in Section 35.3.3. This behavior allows for more dynamic scenes where NPCs come and go, such as street vendors serving pedestrians walking by.

35.4.3 Rule Evaluation

At its core, our rule-based scripting language is declarative in nature. This means that execution and evaluation are often the same. For example, successfully evaluating a precondition will result in an assignment of values to its variables. Rule evaluation is based on two main algorithms: unification and backtracking search.

Unification is an essential algorithm for term manipulation. Given two terms, unification decides whether or not they can be equal and, if so, applies an equalizing substitution. For example, the term $2*X+f(A, B)$ can be unified with $2*A+K$ by substituting X with A and K with $f(A, B)$. For details, consult work on automated reasoning, such as done by Fitting (Fitting 1996).

Since we draw from DataLog and evaluate function symbols immediately, we can simplify unification to three cases: constant to constant, variable to constant, and variable to variable. The first case becomes a simple equality check, and is the only case that can fail. The second case is a pure assignment, and only the last case requires a more work, as the system has to keep track of which variables are unified with each other. We recommend to identify variables with indices and, for each variable, to keep track of the respective variable with the lowest index it has been unified with.

The second algorithm needed, backtracking, is a common method to search for a solution in a structured space, such as a conjunction of literals. Its origins are lost in history, the earliest known application of this algorithm was done by Ariadne to solve Minos' labyrinth (cf. Morford et al. 2013). In essence backtracking explores the state space by successively expanding options and returning to earlier states if it encounters a failure or if it exhausts all options at a particular junction.

Hence, backtracking requires the ability to reestablish a former state in the space explored. In general, this can be achieved with three different techniques: saving the previously visited states, recomputing them from the start, or undoing actions applied. We use a combination of the first two options; we save whatever was assigned to the variables of the rule in the previously visited state, but require any predicate to compute its nth solution from scratch without saving data leading to solution $n-1$. Alternative solutions using scratchpad stack memory are possible, but have not been explored in the context of this work. For further reading on backtracking algorithm we recommend literature discussing DPLL algorithms for SAT solving (Davis et al. 1962), such as (Nieuwenhuis et al. 2004).

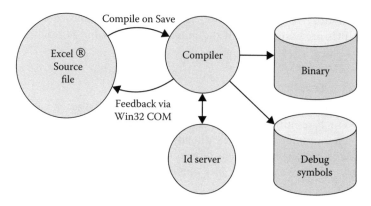

Figure 35.2

The build chain transforms textual scripts into an interpretable binary format.

35.5 Build Chain

The success of any novel scripting methodology depends on its ease of use. We designed the build chain, as shown in Figure 35.2, to provide quick iteration cycles and make use of tools designers are typically familiar with. Scripts are edited in Excel, where table oriented perspective lends itself well to rule-based scripting. Upon saving, a compiler translates the XML source to a binary loadable by the runtime. All identifiers used in the script, such as roles, predicates, and actions are translated to unique 32-bit identifiers by means of an id-server. In order to supply a debug UI with readable names again, a separate file with debug symbols is generated.

35.5.1 Validation

The mathematically grounded properties of STRIPS allow us to detect various scripting errors during compilation and supply feedback directly into the editor. Most notably, we can detect common problems such as:

- Unreachable states.
- Unexecutable rules (specialization of rules of higher precedence).
- Usage of uninstantiated variables.

However, the Turing completeness of the scripting language prevents us from detecting all problems.

35.6 Extensions

The concepts presented here were used heavily during production of *FINAL FANTASY XV*. Naturally, we made adjustments to the original system to accommodate unforeseen needs and situations.

- *Beyond agents*: Although actions of NPCs are easily representable in the language presented, achieving other effects, such as opening a shop UI or reacting to the player clicking an icon was not. Most of these issues relate to the communication with other game systems. We addressed this by wrapping these systems into proxy objects that participate in a script as if they were NPCs. Thus the shop itself becomes an NPC with available actions such as opening and closing specific shop pages. Moreover, these proxy objects push information about ongoing events in their domain into the blackboard. For example, the shop informs the script of what the player is buying or selling. The shopkeeper's reaction can then simply be driven using the blackboard.
- *Templating*: During development, we discovered sets of highly similar scripts being used throughout the game, such as scripts controlling different shopkeepers. The logic within the scripts was almost identical, but various parameters such as motion-sets and shop configurations were changed. We countered this effect by allowing for one script to include another as a base and introduced meta-parameters that the script compiler would replace before creating the binary. Thus we introduced a string templating system in the tool chain. The runtime was completely agnostic about this since it only sees the resulting scripts.

35.7 Conclusion

In this chapter, we presented a novel way of scripting interactions between ambient NPCs using STRIPS rules that modify a blackboard shared by participating NPCs. We described how the necessary information to ground a script in its environment can be supplied by situated objects, namely smart locations, which govern the usage of multiple props. Furthermore, we presented the relevant algorithms for evaluation and role allocation. This approach shifts the modeling focus from the actions of the individual to the interaction between multiple agents and thus significantly simplifies the representation of multiagent scenes encountered in living breathing city scenarios.

The declarative nature of the rule-based approach caused an initially steep learning curve for our designers, but was adopted after a brief transition period. Compared to other scripting methodologies, three advantages became apparent during the development cycle:

- *Locality*: Problems are contained within a single script and thus easier to find.
- *Adaptability*: Scripts adapt themselves naturally to a wide variety of situations.
- *Validation*: The ability of the script compiler to find common mistakes early on greatly reduced iteration time.

References

Blondeau, C. Postmortem: Developing systemic crowd events on Assassin's creed unity, GDC 2015.

Carriero, N. J., D. Gelernter, T. G. Mattson, and A. H. Sherman. The Linda alternative to message-passing systems. *Parallel Computing*, 20(4): 633–655, 1994.

Ceri, S., G. Gottlob, and L. Tanca. What you always wanted to know about datalog (and never dared to ask). *IEEE Transactions on Knowledge & Data Engineering*, 1(1): 146–166, 1989.

Davis, M., G. Logemann, and D. Loveland. A machine program for theorem proving. *Communications of the ACM*, 5(7): 394–397, 1962.

de Sevin, E., C. Chopinaud, and C. Mars. Smart zones to create the ambience of life. In *Game AI Pro 2*, ed. S. Rabin. Boca Raton, FL: CRC Press, pp. 89–100, 2015.

Fikes, R. E. and N. J. Nilsson. Strips: A new approach to the application of theorem proving to problem solving. Technical report, AI Center, SRI International, Menlo Park, CA, May 1971.

Fitting, M. *First-order Logic and Automated Theorem Proving* (2nd Ed.). Springer-Verlag New York, Inc., Secaucus, NJ, 1996.

Forbus, K. Simulation and modeling: Under the hood of The Sims, 2002. http://www.cs.northwestern.edu/~forbus/c95-gd/lectures/The_Sims_Under_the_Hood_files/v3_document.htm (accessed July 5, 2016).

Gerkey, B. P, and M. J. Mataric. A formal analysis and taxonomy of task allocation in multi-robot systems. *The International Journal of Robotic Research*, 23(9): 939–954, 2004.

Morford, M., R. J. Lenardon, and M. Sam. *Classical Mythology* (10th Ed.). Oxford University Press, New York, 2013.

Nieuwenhuis, R., A. Oliveras, and C. Tinelly. Abstract DPLL and abstract DPLL modulo theories, *Proceedings of the International Conference on Logic for Programming, Artificial Intelligence, and Reasoning*. Montevideo, Uruguay: LPAR, pp. 36–50, 2004.

36

Stochastic Grammars
Not Just for Words!

Mike Lewis

36.1 Introduction

Randomness, when carefully and judiciously applied, can be a powerful tool for augmenting the behavior of game AI agents and systems. Of course, purely random behavior is rarely compelling, which is why having some semblance of pattern is important. One way to do this is to simulate *intent*, making AI decisions based on some kind of deliberate design. Many excellent resources exist for creating the illusion of intentional behavior in game AI—and this very volume is not least among them.

However, there are times when it is useful to tap directly into the realm of randomness. Even if it is purely for the sake of variety, a little bit of random fuzz can do a lot of good for an AI character (Rabin et al. 2014). Occasionally, though, there is a sort of confluence of requirements that makes both purely intentional decision-making and heavily randomized decision-making problematic. It is at those times that *structured randomness* comes into play.

Imagine a mechanism for generating sequences of actions. This mechanism can be tuned and adjusted, either at design-time, or on-the-fly at runtime. It creates a controlled blend between predictable patterns and random chaos. That is to say, the mechanism can be tweaked to create arbitrarily "random-feeling" sequences based on completely customizable factors. Again, this can be done statically or dynamically. Moreover, it can generate any kind of structured data. Sound appealing?

Welcome to the world of *stochastic grammars*.

36.2 Formal Grammars

A *formal grammar* is a tool for describing and potentially manipulating a sequence or stream of data. Ordinarily, grammars are used for textual inputs, and operate on sequences known as *strings*. Although historically envisioned by Pāṇini, circa the 4th century BCE, as a tool for rewriting sequences, grammars are also instrumental in recognizing whether or not a string is *valid* according to the rules of the grammar itself (Hunter 1881).

This recognition of validity, along with *parsing*—extracting syntactic structure from a string—is a key component in both natural language processing and computer languages. A compiler, for example, typically uses a tool called a *parser generator* to convert a grammar into code that can parse strings written by those grammatical rules—that is, programs (Brooker et al. 1963).

As an example, Table 36.1 shows a simple grammar that describes the natural numbers.

This grammar uses Extended Backus-Naur Form, or EBNF (Backus 1959, Wirth 1977). Each row of the table describes a *rule*. The third rule, "Natural Number," can be thought of as the starting point for recognizing or generating a natural number. It specifies a *sequence* of symbols, beginning with a nonzero digit. The comma indicates that the following portion of the rule is concatenated with the leading portion. Next, the braces indicate *repetition*. In this case, any digit may appear, and that sub-rule is allowed to apply zero or more times.

Looking at the actual rule for nonzero digits, there is one additional important symbol, the pipe. This indicates *alternations*, that is, that a choice must be made from several alternatives. Each rule also ends in a semicolon, denoting the termination of the rule.

The net result is that the "Natural Number" rule specifies a nonzero digit followed by any number of digits (including zeros). This matches perfectly with the expectation for what a natural number looks like.

However, grammars need not be relegated to use with pure text or numbers. If a string is defined as a set of data *symbols* with some particular set of meanings, virtually any structured data can be defined with a suitable grammar. Allowing these symbols to carry meanings like "punch" or "attack on the left flank" opens the door for much richer applications than mere operations on words.

Table 36.1 Grammar Describing the Natural Numbers in EBNF

Name of Rule	Rule Matches Strings of this Form
Nonzero Digit	1|2|3|4|5|6|7|8|9;
Any Digit	Nonzero Digit|0;
Natural Number	Nonzero Digit, {Any Digit};

36.3 Generating Sequences from a Grammar

Grammars typically have a selected set of *starting symbols* which control the first rule(s) used when creating a new string. How does one choose which rules of a grammar to follow in order to generate a sequence? If the goal is to exhaustively generate as many strings as possible, then the answer is simply "all of them." Sadly, this is not useful for most nontrivial grammars, because they are likely to contain recursive rules that just never stop expanding.

Suppose that each rule of the grammar is augmented with a weight value. As the output is progressively accumulated, there will (probably) be points where more than one rule from the grammar can be applied. In these cases, the next rule can be chosen via a simple weighted random number generation, using the weights from each available rule. This structure is known as a *stochastic grammar* or *probabilistic grammar*.

Supplementing a grammar with this random selection process is akin to describing how "likely" a given generated string might be. If a sequence describes actions taken by an AI agent, the probability weights control that agent's "personality." Some actions—and even subsequences of actions—can be modeled as more "like" or "unlike" that character, and in this way, a sort of preferential action generation process can be constructed.

Take, for example, a ghost wandering a *Pac-Man*-like maze. At each intersection, the ghost can turn left, turn right, continue forward, or reverse directions. Table 36.2 illustrates a simple grammar that describes these possibilities; note the addition of weights to the Direction Decision rule's alternation pattern.

The ghost AI simply needs to generate a string of decisions and pop a decision from the front of the queue each time it enters an intersection. If an "L" decision is retrieved, the ghost turns left; correspondingly, the ghost turns right for an "R." The "F" decision translates to moving forward in the same direction as before, and "B" indicates moving backward. Obviously in some cases a particular decision may not be applicable, so the ghost can simply pop decisions until one is possible. Should the queue become empty, just generate a new sequence and continue as before.

As described in the table, the stochastic grammar will have an equal chance of making each possible selection. However, the "personality" of the ghost can be adjusted to bias toward (or against) any of the options available, merely by tuning the weights of the grammar.

What other sorts of things can be done with a decision-making grammar? Consider a raid boss in a multiplayer RPG. This boss has two basic attack spells: one that makes enemies in a small region vulnerable to being set on fire, and a separate fireball which capitalizes on this vulnerability. Moreover, the boss has a third, more powerful spell that does huge bonus damage to any foe who is currently ablaze.

The naïve approach is to simply cast the vulnerability spell on as many players as possible, then fireball them, and lastly close with the finishing move. Although this is a workable design, it lacks character and can easily be predicted and countered by attentive players.

Table 36.2 Stochastic Grammar to Control a Ghost in a Maze

Name of Rule	Rule Generates these Symbols
Direction Decision	0.25 L|0.25 R|0.25 F|0.25 B;
Navigation Route	{Direction Decision};

Table 36.3 Grammar Producing Attack Sequences for a Raid Boss

Name of Rule	Rule Matches Strings of This Form
Vulnerability Combo	Vulnerability, {Fireball};
Basic Sequence	Fireball, {Vulnerability Combo}, Finisher;
Attack Sequence	{Fireball}, {Basic Sequence};

Instead, describe the available moves for the boss in the form of a grammar, such as that in Table 36.3. One possible sequence generated by this grammar might look like "Fireball × 3, Vulnerability × 5, Fireball × 4, Finisher, Fireball, Finisher." More importantly, given appropriate probability weights for the rules, this grammar will produce different sequences each time the raid is attempted. Although the overall *mechanics* of the fight are intact, the *specifics* vary wildly. That is to say, players know they must come equipped to defend against fire, but the actual progression of the fight is largely unpredictable.

Although arguably the same results could be had with a more sophisticated AI system, it is hard to compete with the raw simplicity and easy configurability of a stochastic grammar. Certainly, there will be applications for which grammars are not the best choice. However, when used appropriately, the ability to generate a structured, semi-random sequence is a compelling tool to have in one's arsenal.

36.4 A Data Structure for Grammars

The actual implementation of code for generating (and parsing) strings is a rich subject. However, it is quite possible to work with simple grammars using basic, naïve approaches to both parsing and generation. Given a suitable data structure for representing the grammar itself, it is easy to start with the trivial implementation and upgrade to more sophisticated algorithms as needed.

Based on the examples so far, some kind of tree-type structure seems well suited to the task of representing the grammar itself. Each rule can be represented as a node in the tree. A "nested" rule can be pointed to as a child node. The nodes themselves can contain a list of parts, with each part being either a sequence of nodes or a list of weighted alternatives to choose from. Within this structure, nodes can be represented using an abstract base class, with derivative classes for sequences and alternations. The actual generated sequence (or input for parsing) can be represented with a container class such as std::vector or equivalent. Each node should have an interface function for generating (or parsing) the substrings for which it is responsible.

Leaf nodes are the simplest case; they will merely append an element to the sequence and return. These nodes represent the *terminals* of the grammar. Next up, sequencer nodes contain a set of node pointers. When they are asked to generate an element, these nodes traverse the container of child nodes in order, asking each one to recursively generate an element. This process can optionally be repeated randomly, so that the sequence itself appears some random number of times in the final output, in keeping with the rules of the grammar.

Alternations, or choices, are where the magic of a stochastic grammar really happens. These nodes store a set of child nodes, like before, but this time each child has an associated weight value. As the node is traversed, *one* child node is selected to be traversed recursively, based on a weighted random selection from the available children. (See the accompanying demo code at http://www.gameaipro.com/ for an example implementation.)

36.5 Streaming Sequences

The approach to generation thus far has focused on creating a finite-length sequence, using random weights to control the length and content of each generated string. However, it can sometimes be useful to generate *infinitely long* sequences as well.

Superficially, this might be denoted by setting a sequence node's weight such that it never chooses to stop repeating. However, there is more to the problem—with the methods described so far, generating an infinite sequence in this way will just exhaust available memory and fail to return anything.

There are two basic approaches to "streaming" an infinite sequence based on a generative grammar. On the more sophisticated side, one might allow *any* sequence node to be infinite, regardless of its position in the grammar/tree. This requires some careful gymnastics to preserve the state of a pass when the output is retrieved midway through.

A hackier alternative is to simply allow only the root node to be infinite. Instead of configuring it as a truly infinitely-repeating node, however, it should be wired up to run exactly once. Then, the grammar simply invokes the root node some random number of times in order to generate a "window" into the current sequence. The resulting output is buffered and can be consumed at any arbitrary rate. Conceptually, the sequence behaves as if it were infinitely long, but the process of generating new subsequences is easily accomplished in finite time.

It should be pointed out that grammars are hardly the only tool for generating such infinite sequences. In fact, if the characteristics of the sequence are *context sensitive*, that is, the upcoming output depends on the value of previous output; an approach like *n*-grams is probably much more useful (Vasquez 2014).

36.6 Grammars as Analogues to Behavior Trees

When considering the design and application of a stochastic grammar, it can be helpful to think of them as limited behavior trees (Isla 2005). As seen earlier, a grammar can often be represented as a tree (although a directed graph is needed in the case where rules form cycles). Each rule in the tree can be thought of as a node in a behavior tree, by loose analogy.

Sequences and alternations map directly to sequence and selection nodes in BTs. The primary distinction is that, for a stochastic grammar, the logic for choosing how to proceed is not based on examining game state, but simply rolling a random number. So a stochastic grammar provides a tool for mimicking more complex AI decisions using a weighted random behavioral pattern rather than something more intentional.

The process for designing a stochastic grammar can closely parallel the process of designing a simple behavior tree. Clearly, the stochastic grammar will make far less deliberate and reactive actions in general, but with careful weight tuning, a fuzzy behavior model can look remarkably similar to a more intentional model.

Choosing to use a grammar over a BT is primarily a matter of considering two factors. First, if the behavior tree is designed to carefully handle contingencies or special cases of world state, it is probably not suitable for replacement with a grammar. Second, the design of the agent being controlled may lend itself to a more randomized behavioral pattern, in which case grammars are an excellent choice. A simple way to recognize this is to check for heavy use of random selector nodes in the behavior tree.

One last potential benefit of the grammar model is that it is cheap to evaluate, since it does not require many world state queries and can operate purely on a stream of random numbers. This makes grammars an excellent tool for simulating large numbers of agents with low-fidelity "intelligence."

36.7 Grammars as Scripting Engine

One of the more powerful ways of looking at grammars is as a tool for generating tiny scripts. If the generated symbols are miniature commands for a scripting engine, grammars define the rules by which those commands can be combined into meaningful programs. Working with this analogy, the goal is to first specify a set of commands that are useful for handling a given AI problem, and then specify a grammar that will produce effective sequences of those commands.

The advantage of using a grammar to generate such script programs is that the scripts themselves need not be static. New scripts can be created on-the-fly as gameplay unfolds. Since the rules for creating a script are defined during the game's implementation, any generated script has a reasonable chance of doing the "right thing"—assuming the rules are suitably constrained.

One way of looking at this is that grammars are a key part of dynamically reprogramming a game's behavior as it is played. As long as a given grammar is well-designed, it will produce new behavioral scripts that are effective within the game simulation itself. Controlling the weights of rules in the grammar yields the power to adjust the "success rate" of any given script on-the-fly. Clearly, the possibilities for this are endless.

Generally speaking, any time an AI system (or other game system!) expresses behavior in terms of sequences of actions, a grammar can be deployed in place of handcrafted scripts. Moreover, given the relationship between grammars and *deterministic finite automatons*, it is possible for any behavior generated by a finite-state machine to also be expressed by a grammar (Zhang and Qian 2013).

There is clearly ample material in a typical game's AI—and, again, other game systems—that could be supplanted by the crafty use of grammars. Grammar-like methods known as *Lindenmayer-systems* (or *L-systems*) are already in popular use for procedural generation of certain kinds of geometry, ranging from trees and rivers to buildings and even entire cities (Rozenberg and Salomaa 1992). Some creative users of L-systems have even explored creating gameplay mechanics based on the technique (Fornander 2013).

36.8 Tuning a Stochastic Grammar

One of the classic methods for computing appropriate weights for a stochastic grammar given a preexisting corpus of sequences is the *inside-outside algorithm* (Baker 1979). This approach computes probabilities of various strings appearing in a given grammar, starting from an initial estimate of each probability. It can then be iteratively applied until a training string's probability reaches some desired point. Indeed, if a corpus of training data is available, this method is the definitive starting point for tuning a grammar.

But what if training data is not available? The primary difficulty of tuning the grammar then becomes generating enough sample outputs to know whether or not the overall distribution of outputs is desirable. Strictly speaking, most stochastic grammar approaches use a *normalized probability* of each rule being selected in the output generation process. This is mathematically elegant but can make it difficult to estimate the overall traits of the grammar, since the human mind is notoriously bad at probabilistic reasoning.

As a compromise, the accompanying demo code does not adhere to a strictly normalized probability model for all of the rules. Some shortcuts have been taken to simplify the tuning process. Namely, *subsequences* have a probability of repeating, which is independently applied after each successful generation of that subsequence. If the random roll fails, the subsequence ends. Further, *alternations* (selections from among several options) employ a simple weighted random scheme to allow the grammar creator to control the relative "importance" of each option.

Although not strictly compliant with the preexisting work on the subject of stochastic grammars, this approach is arguably far simpler to reason about intuitively. More importantly, the tuning process is as simple as generating a large number of outputs, and hand-editing the weights and probabilities of various elements of the grammar to suit.

On an opinionated note, the transparency of the modified stochastic grammar concept is tremendously important. Although probabilistic grammars are typically viewed as a machine learning technique, they need not provoke the negative reaction to machine learning that is so common in game AI circles—because they do not inherently carry the need to give up fine-grained control and intuitive results. Compared with other approaches, the lack of explicit training can actually be a huge boon, since it eschews the "black box" nature of many other learning tools. Designers can rest assured that the grammar will produce *comprehensible* if not directly predictable results.

Moreover, it is trivial to dynamically exploit the direct relationship between weights in a stochastic grammar and the frequency of output patterns. If a grammar produces too many occurrences of some subsequence, the weight for that sequence can simply be decreased at runtime. Of course, the tricky part here is attaching sufficient metadata to the final sequence such that the rules responsible for a particular excessive subsequence can be identified easily. This flexibility (and transparency) is far more cumbersome to build into a system like an artificial neural network or a genetic algorithm.

36.9 Feeding a Grammar with Utility Theory

Another approach to generating weights for a stochastic grammar is to measure them using *utility theory* (Graham 2014). In this technique, the weight of a given node is computed through a scoring mechanism that evaluates how "useful" that node is in a given context. For instance, suppose a turn-based strategy AI has three basic options: attack, reinforce defenses, or expand to new territory. This AI can be given a stochastic grammar for deciding its moves for the next several turns.

Table 36.4 Stochastic Grammar Decides How a Strategic
AI Plays the Game

Name of Rule	Rule Generates these Symbols
Smart Turn	0.4 Attack|0.3 Reinforce|0.3 Expand;
Offensive	Attack, Attack, {Smart Turn};
Turtling	{Reinforce}, {Smart Turn};
Conquest	Attack, Expand, {Smart Turn}, Expand;

When moves are needed, the AI recalibrates the weights of each option based on evaluating the current battlefield. Depending on the grammar it uses, the AI can express various "personality" differences. Consider the example grammar in Table 36.4.

In this model, the AI has three basic personalities to choose from. The Offensive personality will attack two times followed by a series of "smart" choices based on utility. AIs that prefer to "turtle" will reinforce their defenses for an arbitrary period, then make a few "smart" moves. Lastly, expansionistic AIs will attack and expand heavily, sprinkling in a few "smart" turns as well.

The default calibration for "smart" moves has Attack turns slightly preferred to Reinforce and Expand selections—but imagine if the AI could calculate *new* weights for these options on-the-fly. If the utility score for a particular move is exceptionally high, that strategy will dominate the AI's play for several turns. Conversely, if the utility score is low, the AI is less likely to favor that selection.

Ultimately, the result is that AIs will tend to play according to a particular style, but also mix things up periodically with sensible moves based on situational reasoning. A moderate style could even be used which simply does the "smart" thing all the time. More sophisticated play styles can be constructed with almost arbitrary power and flexibility, just by expanding the grammar.

36.10 Conclusion

Stochastic grammars are a widely used tool from natural language processing. They have seen limited use outside that field, despite being applicable to a number of interesting problems, when applied creatively.

By generating sequences of data in a controlled—but still random—fashion, stochastic grammars enable the creation of highly structured—but not perfectly predictable—outputs. Such outputs can be suitable for many game AI and game logic tasks, ranging from design-time procedural content creation to actual on-the-fly behavior controllers.

Although slightly unorthodox in the realm of game AI, grammars offer a much higher degree of designer control than many other machine learning techniques. As such, they are a promising tool for the inclusion in every game AI professional's toolbox.

For those interested in further research, the author highly recommends (Collins).

References

Backus, J. W. 1959. The syntax and semantics of the proposed international algebraic language of the Zurich ACM-GAMM Conference. *Proceedings of the International Conference on Information Processing, UNESCO.* 125–132.

Baker, J. K. 1979. Trainable grammars for speech recognition. *Proceedings of the Spring Conference of the Acoustical Society of America.* 547–550.

Brooker, R.A.; MacCallum, I. R.; Morris, D.; Rohl, J. S. 1963. The compiler-compiler. *Annual Review in Automatic Programming* 3:229–275.

Collins, M. Probabilistic Context-Free Grammars http://www.cs.columbia.edu/~mcollins/courses/nlp2011/notes/pcfgs.pdf (accessed July 10, 2016).

Fornander, Per. 2013. *Game Mechanics Integrated with a Lindenmayer System.* Bachelor's Thesis, Blekinge Institute of Technology. http://www.diva-portal.se/smash/get/diva2:832913/FULLTEXT01.pdf (accessed July 10, 2016).

Graham, Rez. 2014. An introduction to utility theory. In *Game AI Pro,* ed. S. Rabin. Boca Raton, FL: CRC Press, pp. 113–126.

Hunter, Sir William Wilson. 1881. *Imperial Gazetteer of India.* Oxford: Clarendon Press.

Isla, Damian. 2005. *Managing Complexity in the Halo 2 AI System.* Lecture, Game Developers Conference 2005. http://gdcvault.com/play/1020270/Managing-Complexity-in-the-Halo (accessed July 10, 2016).

Rabin, Steve; Goldblatt, Jay; and Silva, Fernando. 2014. Advanced Randomness Techniques for Game AI: Gaussian Randomness, Filtered Randomness, and Perlin Noise. In *Game AI Pro*, ed. S. Rabin. Boca Raton, FL: CRC Press, pp. 29–43.

Rozenberg, Grzegorz; Salomaa, A, eds. 1992. *Lindenmayer Systems: Impacts on Theoretical Computer Science, Computer Graphics, and Developmental Biology.* Verlag/Berlin/Heidelberg: Springer.

Vasquez, Joseph II. 2014. Implementing N-Grams for player prediction, procedural generation, and stylized AI. In *Game AI Pro*, ed. S. Rabin. Boca Raton, FL: CRC Press, pp. 567–580.

Wirth, Niklaus. 1977. What can we do about the unnecessary diversity of notation for syntactic definitions? *Communications of the ACM*, Vol. 20, Issue 11. 822–823.

Zhang, Jielan; and Qian, Zhongsheng. 2013. The equivalent conversion between regular grammar and finite automata. *Journal of Software Engineering and Applications,* 6:33–37.

37

Simulating Character Knowledge Phenomena in *Talk of the Town*

James Ryan and Michael Mateas

37.1 Introduction

There are many examples of stealth and action games that use complicated knowledge, perception, and alertness models to produce short-term NPC beliefs that are a core part of gameplay (Diller et al. 2004, Welsh 2013, Walsh 2015)—here, notable examples include *Thief: The Dark Project* (Leonard 2003), *Fable* (Russell 2006), and *Third Eye Crime* (Isla 2013). Few projects, however, have supported characters whose perceptual systems instantiate memories or lasting beliefs, and there are even fewer examples of the modeling of *fallible* character memory (Ryan 15). Meanwhile, issues of belief—especially false belief—are often central in other fictional media (Palmer 2004). Some games *are* about character beliefs, to be fair, but in these cases beliefs are typically handcrafted, as in *LA Noire* (Team Bondi 2011). In games that do model character knowledge procedurally, the AI architecture that handles such concerns is often called a *gossip system* (Crawford 2004). A classic example of this type of architecture drives the reputation system in *Neverwinter Nights* (BioWare 2002), whereas more recent examples include the rumors system of *Dwarf Fortress* (Adams 2015, Ryan 15) and the beliefs system of Versu (Evans and Short 2014). Frequently, however, gossip systems in games provide only ancillary support to core gameplay. As such, we find that games that are about character beliefs model them with human-authored scripts, whereas games that model such knowledge procedurally tend to do so secondarily to core gameplay.

In this chapter, we present an architecture that, to our knowledge, simulates character knowledge phenomena more deeply than any earlier system has (Ryan 15), all in service of a game that is fundamentally about character beliefs, called *Talk of the Town*.*

Although the game is still in development, the architecture that we present in this chapter is fully implemented. Relative to other gossip systems, like the ones in *Neverwinter Nights* and *Dwarf Fortress*, our system takes a fiercely agent-driven approach, with character knowledge propagating as a result of discrete character interactions. This contrasts the more typical method of abstractly modeling information flow across the gameworld. While the latter approach is more computationally efficient, it would undermine a number of our goals for the *Talk of the Town* player experience, as we discuss in depth at the end of this chapter.

37.2 *Talk of the Town*

Talk of the Town is an asymmetric multiplayer *dwarflike* (a game in the mold of *Dwarf Fortress* [Adams 2015]) that features character knowledge propagation as a core mechanic. In this section, we describe its story, simulation, and our gameplay design; the simulation is fully implemented, but the gameplay layer is currently being developed.

37.2.1 Story

The story that frames gameplay surrounds the death of a very important person in the town in which gameplay takes place. This person had accumulated considerable wealth and produced several descendants who now constitute an aristocracy in the town. Many of these family members had been anticipating the person's death for the inevitably large inheritances that would thereby be disbursed, but in his or her last moments the person apparently signed a document willing everything to a secret lover whose existence had not been known to the family. In one week, the town will gather at a theater to remember the deceased and to witness the reading of his or her will, but the family plans to ascertain the identity of the lover and apprehend this person before the document can ever be delivered to the presiding attorney. Meanwhile, the town is abuzz with rumors about the mysterious lover, whom a handful of witnesses briefly observed on the night of the death.

37.2.2 World Generation

Prior to gameplay, the town is simulated from its founding in 1839, when a handful of families converge on an empty townscape to establish farms, through the death of the central character in the summer of 1979. As in *Dwarf Fortress*, this *world generation* procedure causes a number of structures that are critical to gameplay to emerge bottom-up from the simulation itself. Specifically, these are the town's physical layout (namely the locations of its businesses and homes), its residents' daily routines, and, most importantly, the town's social and family networks that knowledge propagates over. Elsewhere, we provide a detailed account of how character social networks, in particular, are produced (Ryan 16c). Throughout this

---

* The development of *Talk of the Town* is being carried out by a growing team comprising James Ryan, Michael Mateas, Noah Wardrip-Fruin, Adam Summerville, Tyler Brothers, Tim Hong, Joyce Scalettar, and Jill Yeung. Adam Summerville also contributed to the design of the architecture described in this section.

simulation procedure, NPCs act out daily routines across day and night cycles by either going to work, going on errands, dropping by places of leisure, visiting friends and family, or staying at home. Additionally, characters may, for instance, start a business, hire an employee, build a house, marry another character, give birth to a new character, and so forth. NPCs decide what to do by utility-based action selection (Mark 2009). When at the same location (a home or business), characters may interact at probabilities that depend on their relationship and their personalities. From a simple affinity system, continued interaction may breed contempt, friendliness, or romantic feelings (these work unidirectionally and may be asymmetric) (Ryan 16c). The combinatorics of these simple character behaviors over more than a century of game time is enough to generate rich social, family, and work networks by the time that gameplay takes place, at which point around 300–500 NPCs will live in the town.

37.2.3 Gameplay

Talk of the Town's gameplay layer is still being implemented, so in this section we will describe its design. The game is multiplayer and asymmetric: one player, the *lover*, controls the lover character and the other player, the *family member*, controls a member of the deceased person's family. The lover's goal is to go undetected until the will ceremony, while the family member works to ascertain the lover's appearance before that time.*

Gameplay culminates in a scene showing the town's citizens filing into the theater for the will ceremony, during which time the family member must select the person who best matches his or her conception of the lover—if this player selects correctly, he or she wins; otherwise, the lover wins.

The town is represented as an isometric, tile-based 2D world, spanning nine-by-nine city blocks. Each tile contains either part of a street, part of a building (home or business), or part of an empty lot. Players navigate their characters across the town by moving across tiles using directional inputs. When a building is close, the player can click on it to have his or her character enter it. Building interiors are also rendered as tile-based 2D environments, with tiles containing furniture and characters. When an NPC is close enough to the player character, the player can click on him or her to engage in conversation. This is *Talk of the Town*'s core gameplay interaction, since it is how the player will solicit and spread information. Additionally, player characters can patronize certain businesses through dialog interaction with employees—this is critically how the lover can change his or her character's appearance (e.g., getting a haircut at a barbershop or buying glasses at an optometrist).

We are ambitiously aiming for dialog interaction in *Talk of the Town* that is fully procedural, extending our earlier work on *Façade* (Mateas and Stern 2004). Conversations will proceed by turns, with NPCs producing generated dialog and players typing in their dialog in free text. We have already developed a fully implemented *dialog manager*, which is a module that handles conversation flow, updates NPC beliefs according to the semantic content of utterances, and reasons about conversational norms to form content requests on behalf of NPCs (Ryan 16a). Content requests are then processed by a *natural language generation* (NLG) module, which produces NPC dialog on-the-fly; this system is also fully

---

* A given character's appearance is the composite of 24 facial attributes—for example, hair color, hair length, eye color, and nose size—that are inherited from the character's parents.

implemented, with a prototype that allows NPCs to engage in small talk using a pool of nearly three million generable lines of dialog (Ryan 16d).

For *natural language understanding* (NLU)—the task of processing arbitrary player utterances into semantic representations—we are in the early stages of developing an approach that uses deep neural networks (Summerville et al. 2016). NLU is a notoriously difficult challenge, and so we have contingency plans for another dialog-system design in the event that our method does not work well enough; this interface would enable players to construct modular utterances out of dialog components, somewhat in the style of Chris Crawford's Deikto language (Crawford 2007) or *Captain Blood*'s UPCOM interface (Exxos 1988). In any event, deployed utterances will be displayed as speech bubbles emitting from the characters who speak them. By virtue of our dialog manager and NLG module, NPCs may engage in background conversation with one another. If the speech bubbles they emit are in view, the player can eavesdrop on the conversation; we plan to use this both as a storytelling device and a way of improving the believability of background characters (Ryan 16e).

Gameplay will proceed by day and night timesteps that span the week leading up to the will ceremony, with players taking a turn on each timestep. We hope for gameplay to be networked, but we have contingency plans involving local multiplayer and AI opponents. Player turns will be constrained either by a time limit or by a notion of resources (to be spent on a combination of navigation steps, conversation turns, and elapsed time). Between turns, character knowledge phenomena are simulated (see next section), crucially allowing for the propagation of information originating in the player activity of the last turn.

As their character is well-established in the town, the strategy of the family member will be characterized by *management* of the town's knowledge network. This is because the dialog manager reasons about how NPCs will respond (including whether to divulge information) by considering their affinities toward their interlocutors (Ryan 16c). Being quite established in the town, the family member is more likely to encounter NPCs who are comfortable being open with him or her. As such, this player will likely spend his or her turns soliciting town residents for gossip about the lover (whose mysterious identity is the titular *Talk of the Town*). Here, both apparently true and apparently false information are useful. True information obviously helps the family member to ascertain the lover's identity, but patently false information could have actually originated with the lover—a fundamental family-member strategy thus becomes homing in on the sources of apparently deliberate misinformation.

The lover's strategy, then, is to *pollute* the town's knowledge network by changing his or her character's appearance and spreading misinformation about the identity of the mysterious lover (through dialog interaction with NPCs). Given the above, however, it is critical for this player to not pollute the network too extravagantly, because this could lead the family member right to the lover character's identity. One core lover tactic will be using *false flags*, that is, intelligently claiming other characters as the original sources of any misinformation that he or she attempts to spread. We also want the lover to be able to reason about whom exactly to impart misinformation to. As NPCs are more open to characters they know and like, this will promote tactics that require the lover to build up trust relationships with NPCs, so that they will be more likely to believe and propagate misinformation. As noted above, gameplay ends with the town filing into the theater for the will ceremony, at which point the family member must attempt to select the lover from a lineup by clicking on the character that best matches his or her conception of that person.

Broadly, we want the gameworld to feel like it is sprawling with rich NPCs who each have their own unique experiences that are captured by the particular beliefs that they have adopted. In this way, we hope that navigating the town and interacting with NPCs will feel like exploration, but with the depth of the gameworld being expressed more in its character belief structures than in its modest physical size.

37.3 Simulating Character Knowledge Phenomena

Characters in *Talk of the Town* build up knowledge about the world as they go about their daily routines. In this section, we describe our simulation of character knowledge phenomena, including the mechanisms by which knowledge may originate, propagate, deteriorate, and terminate according to the procedures of our architecture.

37.3.1 Overview

People and places in the gameworld have perceptible features, which characters may directly observe to form beliefs about them. Such knowledge may then propagate across characters during social interactions. Critically, character knowledge may also be misremembered (in multiple interesting ways), or be altogether forgotten. All throughout, the system keeps track of belief histories and knowledge trajectories, because we anticipate visualizing summaries of this kind of information at the end of gameplay.

37.3.2 Requirements

Our method has some architectural requirements, which we will list in this section. First, characters must have *perceptible attributes*, meaning attributes that are directly observable by other characters. In *Talk of the Town*, these are mainly physical features, like hair color, but we also model *conditionally* perceptible attributes—for instance, a character's workplace is observable while they are in the act of working.

Next, a *radius of perceptibility* must be modeled, where characters within the radius of another character may observe his or her perceptible attributes. This radius is also used to determine whether a nearby character is close enough to eavesdrop on a conversation, as we will discuss later. As we model space discretely in *Talk of the Town*, we simply say that characters at the same location in town are near enough to perceive one another.

Additionally, system authors must craft a procedure for determining *character saliences*. Character saliences work together with attribute saliences, described next, to determine the probability of knowledge phenomena occurring for a given character and attribute—that is, the probability of a perceptible attribute being observed, as well as the probability of a belief about any attribute being propagated, misremembered, or forgotten. In Section 37.3.6, we explain salience computation in more depth.

Similarly, our architecture uses specified *attribute saliences*, which prescribe how likely given character features are to be observed and to be talked about among characters. In *Talk of the Town*, this specifies, for instance, that a person's hair color is more salient than the shape of her chin.

Finally, authors must also produce a *belief mutation graph*, which specifies how particular character beliefs can mutate, and at what probabilities. We discuss belief mutation in more detail in Section 37.3.8, and Figure 37.3 shows excerpts from the belief mutation graph authored for *Talk of the Town*.

37.3.3 Ontological Structure

As illustrated in Figure 37.1, a character's composite knowledge of the world is structured as an *ontology* of interlinked mental models that each pertain to a single person or place. The interlinking occurs when a character's belief about some attribute of a character or place resolves to some other character or place for whom or which they have another mental model. For instance, a character may believe that a person works at some business in town, and so his or her belief about that person's workplace would itself link to his or her mental model of that business. We use this ontological structure for elegance and convenience, because it allows characters to reason about entities in terms of knowledge they may already have about related entities (rather than by instantiating redundant or potentially inconsistent knowledge). In the case of a character knowing where another character works, this allows the former to reason about, for example, the character's work address in terms of existing knowledge about that place that can be stored and accessed independently of knowledge about the character who works there.

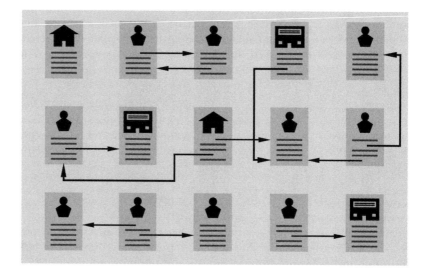

Figure 37.1

An illustration of the *ontological* structure of character knowledge: characters build up mental models of the hundreds of people, homes, and businesses in their towns, each of which might include pointers to other mental models (e.g., a belief about a character's workplace will resolve to a pointer to the mental model for that business).

37.3.4 Mental Models

Characters in *Talk of the Town* form *mental models* about the residents and places in their towns. Each character mental model pertains to a specific individual entity and is structured as a list of *belief facets* that correspond to individual attributes of that entity. A given character attribute will have a *type* (e.g., hair color) and a ground-truth value (e.g., `brown`), but a belief facet corresponding to it will represent a character's potentially false belief about that attribute (e.g., `black`). The attribute types that we have implemented for *Talk of the Town* match the domain and central concerns of the game and are as follows:

- For mental models of characters:
  - *Status*: Condition (`alive` or `dead`), year of departure from the town (if any; e.g., `1972`), marital status (`single`, `married`, `divorced`, or `widowed`).
  - *Age*: Birth year (e.g., `1941`), death year (if any), approximate age (e.g., `30s`).
  - *Name*: First name, middle name, last name, suffix, surname ethnicity (e.g., `German`), whether surname is hyphenated.
  - *Appearance*: Each of the 24 facial attributes that we model (e.g., hair color).
  - *Occupation*: Company (links to mental model of that place), job title (e.g., `bartender`), shift (`day` or `night`), status (`retired`, `employed`, or `unemployed`).
  - *Home*: Home (either an apartment unit or house; links to mental model of that place).
  - *Whereabouts*: Where a person was on a given day or night (links to mental model of that place). This facet is central to the *Talk of the Town* game design, because the lover character is known to have been at the home of the central character on the night of the death.
- For mental models of businesses/homes:
  - *Employees/residents*: Listing of its employees/residents (each links to mental model of a character).
  - *Apartment*: Whether it is an apartment unit (for homes only).
  - *Block*: For example, `800 block of Lake Street`.
  - *Address*: For instance, `613 Fillmore Street`.

We would like to emphasize that these example facet types are only meant to serve as examples, as our method is agnostic to the type of knowledge that it is used to represent. Each facet is structured as a collection of data about the belief. In addition to its *owner* (the character who has constructed the mental model), *subject* (the entity to whom it pertains), and facet type, these data include:

- *Value:* A representation of the belief itself, for example, the string `brown` for a belief facet pertaining to hair color, or the integer `1944` for a facet corresponding to a character's birth year.
- *Mental model:* If the value of this facet resolves to another entity for whom the owner of this facet has formed a mental model, this will point to that mental model. This is how the linking that we have mentioned in earlier examples is handled.

- *Predecessor*: The belief facet that the owner previously held, if any. This allows the system to track supplanted or forgotten character knowledge. As a given chain of predecessors represents a perfect history of an NPC's beliefs about some attribute, we do not plan to give NPCs access to these data.
- *Parents*: If this knowledge originated in information from other characters, this will point to the belief facets of those characters that spawned this current facet. This allows the system to trace the history and trajectory of any piece of information.
- *Evidence*: A list of the pieces of evidence by which the owner of this facet formed and continues to substantiate it; evidence may accumulate as the simulation proceeds. In Section 37.3.5, we outline our evidence typology.
- *Strength*: The strength of this particular belief. This is the sum of the strength of all pieces of evidence supporting it, the determination of which we also explain in Section 37.3.5.
- *Accuracy*: Whether or not the belief is accurate (with regard to the *current* true state of the world).

37.3.5 Evidence

All character knowledge is formed in response to evidence, and may also propagate, deteriorate, or terminate in ways that can be described using pieces of evidence. We will illustrate these details by explaining our evidence typology, which comprises eleven *types* across five categories. This is the most important part of this chapter.

- How knowledge originates:
  - *Reflection*: A reflection represents the case of a character inherently knowing something about himself or herself. We do not spend any computation on actually simulating this phenomenon.
  - *Observation*: When a character directly observes a person or place, he or she may form knowledge about attributes of that entity. Whether knowledge is formed about a particular attribute depends on the salience of the entity and the attribute type, which we explain in Section 37.3.6.
  - *Transference*: If one entity reminds a character of another entity (determined by feature overlap between his or her respective mental models of them), he or she may unconsciously copy beliefs about one to the mental model of the other.
  - *Confabulation*: By confabulation, a character *unintentionally* concocts new knowledge about some entity; this happens probabilistically. The particular belief-facet value that gets confabulated is determined probabilistically according to the distribution of that feature type in the town. For instance, if 45% of characters in the town have black hair, then confabulation of a belief about hair color would have a 45% chance of producing the value `black`.
  - *Lie*: A lie occurs when an NPC *intentionally* conveys information to another character that he or she himself or herself does not believe. We call this a type of origination (and not propagation) because the knowledge in question is *invented* by virtue of the lie—that is, no existing knowledge is propagated by the lie.

- *Implant*: For efficiency reasons, some essential character knowledge will be directly implanted in character minds at the end of world generation, and thus will have no explicit point of origination. We discuss knowledge implantation in depth in Section 37.3.10.
- How knowledge reinforces itself:
  - *Declaration*: Whenever a character delivers a statement, the strength of his or her own belief (being declared by the statement) will slightly increase. That is, the more a person retells some belief, the stronger that belief becomes for him or her, which is realistic (Wilson et al. 1985). By this mechanic, an NPC who frequently tells the same lie might come to actually believe it.
- How knowledge deteriorates:
  - *Mutation*: As an operationalization of memory fallibility, knowledge may mutate over time. We explain this more thoroughly in Section 37.3.8.
- How knowledge terminates:
  - *Forgetting*: To further incorporate memory fallibility, knowledge may be forgotten due to time passing; this is affected by a character's memory attribute and the salience of the facet subject and type.

Characters are not consciously aware of transferences, confabulations, or mutations, and recipients (and eavesdroppers) of lies treat them as statements. That is, the recipient will reason about a lie as if it were a statement (and so the strength of a lie, as a piece of evidence, is equal to that of a statement), but the system will still track that it was in fact a lie, to allow for the presentation of true knowledge trajectories after gameplay. Additionally, each piece of evidence has metadata of the following types:

- *Source*: With a statement, lie, or eavesdropping, this specifies the character who delivered the information. This allows the system to trace the history and trajectory of any piece of information, which is a design goal.
- *Location*: Where the piece of evidence originated (e.g., where an observation or statement took place).
- *Time*: The timestep from when a piece of evidence originated (either a day or night of a particular date).
- *Strength*: The strength of a piece of evidence is a floating-point value that is determined by its type (e.g., a statement is weaker than an observation) and decays as time passes. In the case of statements, lies, and eavesdroppings, the strength of a piece of evidence is also affected by the affinity its owner has for its source and the strength of that source's own belief at the time of propagation.

37.3.6 Salience Computation

When a character observes some entity in the simulation, a procedure is enacted that determines, for each perceptible attribute of the observed entity (as defined in Section 37.3.2), the probability that the character will remember what he or she saw; this procedure crucially depends on the *salience* of the entity and attribute being observed. Salience computation in *Talk of the Town* considers the relationship of an observed character (subject) to the observer (e.g., a coworker is more salient than a stranger), the extent of the observer's friendship with the subject, the strength of the observer's romantic feelings toward the subject, and finally the subject's job level (characters with more elevated job positions are treated as more salient). For places, salience computation currently considers only whether the observing character lives or works at the observed place. Additionally, our salience–computation procedures consult a hand-authored knowledgebase specifying attribute saliences—this was one of the requirements listed in Section 37.3.2. Salience is also used to determine the probability that a character will misremember or altogether forget (on some later timestep) knowledge pertaining to a given subject and attribute—here, the probability of memory deterioration decreases as these saliences grow larger.

37.3.7 Knowledge Propagation

The salience of the subject and attribute type of a piece of information also affects whether a character will pass it on (via a statement, defined in Section 37.3.5). Currently, what subjects of conversation come up in an interaction between two *conversants* is determined by the salience of all entities that either of them knows about (i.e., the sum salience to both conversants). The n highest-scoring[*] entities are then brought up in conversation, with n being determined by the strength of the conversants' relationship and also their respective *extroversion* personality components. This is illustrated in Figure 37.2. For each subject of conversation, the conversants will exchange information about individual attributes of that subject at probabilities determined by the salience of each attribute type. As a character may bring up subjects that an interlocutor does not (yet) know about, our propagation mechanism allows characters to learn about other people and places that they have never encountered themselves. It is even possible for a character to learn about another character who died before he or she was

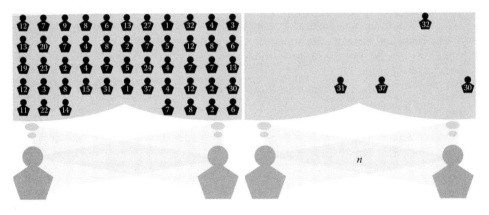

Figure 37.2

An illustration of the procedure by which NPCs decide whom to exchange information about. A pair of conversants score everyone they know about for their saliences to both of them, and then select the n highest scoring (where n is determined by the characters' relationship and personalities) to be the subjects of their knowledge exchange.

---

[*] For greater efficiency, we amortize this computation by keeping track of all pairwise character salience scores as relevant changes to the social state occur.

born; this often occurs when parents tell their children about deceased relatives (who score highly in salience computation due to being related to both conversants).

37.3.8 Fallibility Modeling

As an operationalization of memory fallibility, characters may adopt false beliefs for reasons other than lies. On each timestep after world generation, the four phenomena associated with memory fallibility—transference, confabulation, mutation, and forgetting (see Section 37.3.5)—are probabilistically triggered for character mental models. When this happens, the facets of that mental model are targeted for deterioration at probabilities determined by the character's memory attribute (modeled as a floating-point value inherited from a parent), the facet type (e.g., a whereabouts belief will be more likely to mutate than a first name belief), and the strength of the existing belief (weaker beliefs are more likely to deteriorate). For mutation, the system relies on a handcrafted schema that specifies for a given facet value, the probabilities of it mutating to each other's viable facet value. Figure 37.3 shows excerpts from this schema, which we call a *belief mutation graph*; earlier, in Section 37.3.2, we noted the specification of this graph as an architectural requirement.

37.3.9 Belief Revision

Currently, an NPC will always adopt a new belief on encountering a first piece of evidence supporting it, assuming there is no current belief that it would replace. As a character accumulates further evidence supporting his or her belief, its strength will increase commensurately to the strength of the new evidence. As noted in Section 37.3.5, the strength of a piece of evidence depends on its type; if the evidence has a source, its strength will also depend on the affinity that its recipient has for that character and the strength of the corresponding belief held by the source.

If at any time an NPC encounters new evidence that contradicts his or her currently held belief (i.e., supports a different belief-facet value), the character will consider the strength of the new evidence relative to the strength of his or her current belief. If the new evidence is stronger, he or she will adopt the new belief that it supports; if it is weaker, he or she will *not* adopt a new belief, but will still keep track of

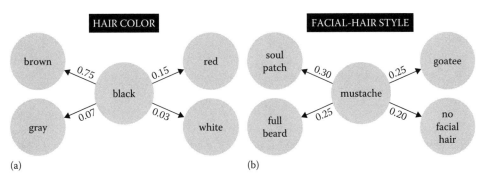

Figure 37.3

Illustrative excerpts from our hand-authored *belief mutation graph*. Probabilities specify how particular beliefs about hair color (a) and facial-hair style (b) might mutate (to model character misremembering).

the other *candidate belief* and the evidence for it that he or she had encountered. If he or she continues to encounter evidence supporting the candidate belief, he or she will update its strength accordingly and if at any time that strength exceeds the strength of the currently held belief, the NPC will adopt the candidate belief and relegate the previously held belief to candidate status. Belief oscillation is possible, as such, but that is an appeal of the design. For an example illustrating how this procedure works, see our earlier paper on the system (Ryan 15).

37.3.10 Knowledge Implantation

In our architecture, procedures related to character knowledge phenomena are expensive. If we enacted them during *world generation*—the period of game time that is simulated prior to gameplay and spans from the town's founding in 1839 up to 1979 (see Section 37.2.2)—we would spend a lot of computation simulating the knowledge of hundreds of characters who would have died long before the period of gameplay. Instead, world generation employs all aspects of the simulation *besides* the ones related to character knowledge (e.g., characters forming relationships, starting businesses) and then terminates one week prior to the death of the central character (the event that kicks off gameplay, as explained in Section 37.2.1). At this point, however, living characters have no knowledge at all—to resolve this, the system employs a procedure that *implants* into each character's mind the knowledge that would believably be ingrained in them. This procedure is illustrated in Listing 37.1.

Listing 37.1. Pseudocode for our *knowledge implantation* procedure, which is carried out at the end of world generation.

```
for resident of town
    implants = []
    for immediate family member of resident
        add immediate family member to implants
    for friend of resident
        add friend to implants
    for neighbor of resident
        add neighbor to implants
    for coworker of resident
        add coworker to implants
    for every other character who has ever lived
        chance = 1.0 - (1.0/salience of that character)
        if random number < chance
            add other character to implants
    for character in implants
        for attribute of character
            chance = attribute salience
            chance += -1.0/salience of that character
            if random number < chance
                have resident adopt accurate belief for attribute
```

37. Simulating Character Knowledge Phenomena in *Talk of the Town*

37.3.11 Core Procedure

After implanting character knowledge, we simulate all character activity, including all knowledge phenomena, for one week of game time (up to the death of the central character). Listing 37.2 shows the operation of this method, with a focus on knowledge-related activity. A variant of the loop is also carried out during gameplay, between player turns.

Listing 37.2. High-level pseudocode for the core procedure of our simulation of character knowledge phenomena.

```
do world generation // See Section 37.2.2
do belief implantation // See Listing 1
while central character still alive // One week of game time
    advance one timestep
    for resident in town
        enact resident routine // Put somewhere in the town
    for resident in town
        for nearby character at same place as resident
            if characters will interact // See Section 37.2.2
                do knowledge exchange // See Section 37.3.7
    for resident in town
        do simulation of fallibility phenomena // See Section 37.3.8
```

37.3.12 Tunable Parameters

Our approach has many parameters that can be tuned for both authorial control and greater computational efficiency. In our implementation, belief mutation is quite expensive, in part because we represent many facet values as strings. Although this aspect of our implementation is currently efficient enough for our needs, it presents a basic opportunity for optimization. Beyond this, mutation rates could simply be turned down (as a way of targeting either greater efficiency or gameworlds with more accurate character beliefs). Other tunable parameters include the salience of characters and attributes; the probabilities of social interactions, eavesdropping, lying, and different kinds of knowledge deterioration; the base strengths of each type of evidence; and more. We currently do have worries about the complexity of interaction between all these parameters; eventually, we may end up simplifying some of these systems.

37.3.13 Some Statistics

A typical *Talk of the Town* will be inhabited by between 300–500 NPCs, each of which will maintain approximately 250–400 mental models; some highly extroverted characters will have as many as 500–600 mental models. Across all his or her mental models, a typical character will own around 800–1200 belief facets by the time gameplay begins. The entire world-generation procedure lasts (on the order of) a few minutes, and the simulation of knowledge phenomena between turns takes about a minute; we expect these durations to decrease as we begin to explore optimization strategies closer to release.

37.4 Discussion

Talk of the Town gameplay would not be possible without the architecture we have presented here. First, as we stated above, a fundamental goal of ours is to provide a gameworld that feels like it is sprawling with rich NPCs who each have unique subjective experiences that are captured by the particular beliefs that they have adopted. If we were to model information flow abstractly, as other gossip systems have done, we would lose all this depth and complexity. Further, we want dialog with NPCs to be a core gameplay interaction—with a coarser, more abstract representation of character knowledge, there would not be much for characters to say. Beyond supporting our intended gameplay esthetic, our architecture critically enables the kind of player strategies that we want to support, which were also detailed above.

First, we want the family-member player to be able to home in on the identity of the lover by investigating apparent sources of deliberate misinformation. This requires information flow to be modeled at a considerable level of fidelity, and it also necessitates the possibility of misinformation propagating from specific sources at specific times. Further, we want the lover to be able to tactfully spread *some* amount of information without making his or her identity obvious, but hitting this sweet spot could be tough with coarser-grained modeling of information flow.

With our approach, we are more confident about signals of deliberate misinformation being readable to both players, because knowledge propagation is modeled at the agent level; intuitively, this fidelity of simulation is more likely to match player expectations than abstract models. Still, we want it to be possible for the lover to be successful at clandestinely propagating misinformation—this requires that benign misinformation also be present in the gameworld, which our architecture supports through its simulation of memory fallibility. Moreover, we wish to support a specific tactic that may underpin the lover's larger strategy of spreading misinformation: the ability to propagate *false flag* sources for his or her own misinformation, meaning characters whom he or she claims told his or her what are in fact his or her own lies. False flags are easily represented in our architecture as metadata attached to discrete character beliefs—namely the *source*, *location*, and *time* attributes of pieces of evidence supporting an NPC's belief—that can be surfaced in generated dialog, for example, *Gary Stuart told me last night at the 3rd Street Diner*.

As our game is still in development, we cannot speak conclusively yet about the success of our architecture from an authorial standpoint. One potentially huge challenge that we anticipate involves balancing the architecture's considerable array of tunable parameters—attribute saliences, mutation rates, and so on. Although *Talk of the Town* is not fully implemented yet, we have actually already used this framework in an award-winning mixed-reality experience called *Bad News* (www.badnewsgame.com, Ryan 16b). Over the course of performing this piece more than one hundred times, we have encountered thousands and thousands of generated character beliefs. Although these beliefs have generally appeared to be well-formed and believable, in early performances we noticed a prevalence of misremembered home addresses, including cases where characters could not remember where their own parents lived. To fix this, we simply turned down the mutation rate for this attribute, which seemed to be a good preliminary indication of the prospects for authorial control in the face of so many tunable parameters. As another fundamental limitation, our method is not very computationally efficient, though in Section 37.3.12 we named a few opportunities for optimization. For *Talk of the Town*, we are not particularly worried about this, because the heavy computation takes place prior to gameplay (generating the town) and between player turns (simulating knowledge phenomena).

It is not easy for us to articulate how this architecture could be utilized for games in mainstream genres. We do think there are probably viable opportunities for this (at least in cases where computational efficiency is not a major concern), but we are more excited about fundamentally new kinds of gameplay experiences that could be made possible by our architecture. Here, we hope that *Talk of the Town*, once completed, will do well to demonstrate the appeal of gameplay surrounding the character knowledge phenomena whose simulation we have described in this chapter.

Acknowledgments

We thank Damián Isla for invaluable feedback that greatly improved this chapter.

References

Adams, T., 2015, Simulation principles from Dwarf Fortress. In *Game AI Pro 2: Collected Wisdom of Game AI Professionals*, ed. S. Rabin. Boca Raton, FL: CRC Press, pp. 519–522.

BioWare, 2002, *Neverwinter Nights*. New York: Infogrames/Atari.

Crawford, C., 2004, *Chris Crawford on Interactive Storytelling*. Berkeley, CA: New Riders Press.

Crawford, C., 2007, Deikto: A language for interactive storytelling. In *Second Person: Role-Playing and Story in Games and Playable Media*, ed. P. Harrigan and N. Wardrip-Fruin. Cambridge, MA: MIT Press.

Diller, D.E., W. Ferguson, A.M. Leung, B. Benyo, and D. Foley, 2004, Behavior modeling in commercial games. *Behavior Representation in Modeling and Simulation*.

Evans, R. and E. Short, 2014, Versu—A simulationist storytelling system. *IEEE Transactions on Computational Intelligence and AI in Games* 6(2):113–130.

Exxos (ERE Informatique), 1988, *Captain Blood*. Lyon: Infogrames.

Isla, D., 2013, Third eye crime: Building a stealth game around occupancy maps. In *Proceedings of the 9th Annual AAAI Conference on Artificial Intelligence and Interactive Digital Entertainment*, October 14–18, 2013, Boston, MA: Northeastern University.

Leonard, T., 2003, Building an AI sensory system: Examining the design of thief: The dark project. *Game Developers Conference*, March 4–8, 2003, San Jose, CA: San Jose Convention Center.

Mark, D., 2009, *Behavioral Mathematics for Game AI*. Boston, MA: Cengage Learning PTR.

Mateas, M. and A. Stern, 2004, Natural language understanding in Façade: Surface-text processing. In *Proceedings of the 2nd International Conference on Technologies for Interactive Digital Storytelling and Entertainment*, June 24–26, 2004, Darmstadt, Germany: Computer Graphics Center.

Palmer, A., 2004, *Fictional Minds*. Lincoln: University of Nebraska Press.

Russell, A., 2006, Opinion Systems, *AI Game Programming Wisdom 3*, Cengage Learning.

[Ryan 15] Ryan, J.O., A. Summerville, M. Mateas, and N. Wardrip-Fruin, 2016, Toward characters who observe, tell, misremember, and lie. In *Proceedings of the 2nd Workshop on Experimental AI in Games*, November 14–15, 2015, Santa Cruz, CA: University of California.

[Ryan 16a] Ryan, J., M. Mateas, and N. Wardrip-Fruin, 2016, A lightweight videogame dialogue manager. In *Proceedings of the 1st Joint International Conference of DiGRA and FDG*, August 1–6, 2016, Dundee, Scotland, UK: Abertay University.

[Ryan 16b] Ryan, J.O., A.J. Summerville, and B. Samuel, 2016, Bad News: A game of death and communication. In *Proceedings of the 2016 CHI Conference Extended Abstracts on Human Factors in Computing Systems*, May 7–12, 2016, San Jose, CA: San Jose Convention Center.

[Ryan 16c] Ryan, J., M. Mateas, and N. Wardrip-Fruin, 2016, A simple method for evolving large character social networks. In *Proceedings of the 5th Workshop on Social Believability in Games*, August 1, 2016, Dundee, Scotland, UK: Abertay University.

[Ryan 16d] Ryan, J., M. Mateas, and N. Wardrip-Fruin, 2016, Characters who speak their minds: Dialogue generation in Talk of the Town. In *Proceedings of the 12th Annual AAAI Conference on Artificial Intelligence and Interactive Digital Entertainment*, October 8–12, 2016, Burlingame, CA: Embassy Suites by Hilton San Francisco Airport - Waterfront.

[Ryan 16e] Ryan, J., M. Mateas, and N. Wardrip-Fruin, 2016, Generative character conversations for background believability and storytelling, In *Proceedings of the 5th Workshop on Social Believability in Games*, August 1, 2016, Dundee, Scotland, UK: Abertay University.

Summerville, A.J., J. Ryan, M. Mateas, and N. Wardrip-Fruin, 2016, CFGs-2-NLU: Sequence-to-sequence learning for mapping utterances to semantics and pragmatics. Technical Report UCSC-SOE-16-11.

Team Bondi, 2011, *L.A. Noire*. New York: Rockstar Games.

Walsh, M., Modeling perception and awareness in Tom Clancy's Splinter Cell Blacklist, *Game AI Pro 2: Collected Wisdom of Game AI Professionals*, 313–326.

Welsh, R., 2013, Crytek's Target Tracks Perception System. *Game AI Pro: Collected Wisdom of Game AI Professionals*, 403:411.

Wilson, R.M., L.B. Gambrell, and W.R. Pfeiffer, 1985, The effects of retelling upon reading comprehension and recall of text information. *Journal of Educational Research*, 78(4):216–220.

SECTION VI
Odds and Ends

38

Procedural Level and Story Generation Using Tag-Based Content Selection

Jurie Horneman

38.1 Introduction

Content selection is something that happens frequently inside games. Abstract data structures need to reference "content"—a mesh, a bitmap, a sound effect, or a line of text—to become something concrete, like an enemy. We must build mechanisms that allow the program to refer to external content, so that nonprogrammers can work without having to modify and recompile code. At the most primitive level, this can just be a filename referring to an external file.

We can do more than simply link entity A to file B, however; we can implement logic to make the selected content depend on dynamic conditions without having to manually spell out every single case. In this chapter, we will look at a simple yet powerful content selection mechanism that uses *tags*. This mechanism can be used for selecting level parts, scenes, events, items, conversations, NPC remarks, audio-visual effects, and more. It is easy to understand and to implement. We will see how and why it works, what the edge cases and pitfalls are, and discuss some alternative or more advanced techniques.

38.2 The Advantage of Simplicity

A simple way to look at content selection is to imagine you have a black box, and you ask it "please give me a piece of content that fulfills the following conditions," and then the black box gives you some content. In *tag-based* content selection these conditions are *tags*, which are represented as simple strings. Behind the scenes you have a pool of content, and each piece of content has been marked up with one or more tags. The algorithm simply looks through the content for pieces that have all of the requested tags, and returns one of them, picked at random (although see Section 38.5 for a more sophisticated approach).

The algorithm is extremely easy to understand. A tag is either there or not; content with the right tags is either there or not. This simplicity is a strength, because of the following:

- It requires little training and documentation.
- It requires little tool support to make the method useable.
- It requires little programmer time to help fix problems, and programmers are typically outnumbered by game designers, artists, sound designers, and so on.
- It does not require people who cross the divides between disciplines (designer-programmers, technical designers, or technical artists).
- It allows people to focus on creating a great game instead of trying to understand complicated systems.

This does not mean that more complicated methods do not have their place, but rather that simplicity has value. But even the simplest method has subtleties, and tag-based content selection is no different.

38.3 Case Study: *Last Mysteries*

In 2010 and 2011, I was part of the team at Mi'pu'mi Games that created *Last Mysteries*, a browser-based multiplayer 2D action role-playing game. Tobias Sicheritz, our technical director, designed a tag-based content selection mechanism to generate dungeons. Our dungeons were 2D arrays where each cell contained a bunch of tags, such as "corridor medieval spooky exit-north exit-west," and we had a number of tagged, hand-created dungeon rooms. The game server would load the 2D array and then find a fitting room for each cell. This is not "classical" dungeon generation: We did not generate dungeon layouts from scratch. Instead, our goal was to be able to design dungeons very quickly.

38.3.1 Dealing with Missing Rooms

What if there is no room with the requested tags? For some content you can simply return null. Perhaps you are asking "does anyone in the party want to say something about the player harassing this chicken?" and it is fine if nobody reacts to it because it does not break the experience or the game.

However, in *Last Mysteries* not finding a room was unacceptable: The player would walk into the void. If the game server could not find a room it would exit. So we had a combination of "hard to test manually" and "catastrophic consequence," and our testing department consisted of just one person.

We solved this problem by writing a medium-sized Python program that read all of the game's data, identified all of the content requests that could be made, and then checked whether those requests could be fulfilled. If not, it would spit out an error. We hooked this into our continuous integration server, and we never had a broken dungeon again. Identifying all the requested tag sets can be tricky, but in our case it was straightforward. As a bonus the tool allowed us to test the content in many other ways. The Expressionist system (Ryan et al. 2015) achieves a similar thing with an automatic, integrated to-do list.

38.3.2 Sparse Content

In a game with dynamic content, it can be helpful for content creators to know where content is sparse. But what does that mean, exactly? For instance, having only one piece of content for a request can be fine if that request is only made once an hour, but terrible if it is made more often. The type of content also plays a role: Spoken text is more memorable and distinctive than a wall texture in the background, and so will suffer more from sparseness.

There is no universal answer to this question, but it is important that you consider and answer it for your particular use case. You can get far with common sense ("The player will be in cells tagged with 'medieval' for a long time, so we need more content there."), but depending on the game you might want to use measurements and statistics, if only to compare reality to the heuristics you used.

Once you know the desired and the actual sparseness, you can display it either in some kind of structure that makes sense for the given content (a table of game events per character showing the number of reactions, say), or with a list showing the "sparsest" content ("number 1: medieval corridors"). Emily Short uses colors to indicate content sparseness in some of her procedural text generation tools.

38.3.3 Optional Tags

In *Last Mysteries* we used a tilde prefix to mark tags that were optional. So we would use "medieval corridor ~spooky" to ask the system: "I would like a medieval dungeon corridor, spooky *if possible*." This made the content selection algorithm slightly more involved. For each piece of content, we had to check whether it had the obligatory tags, and, separately, any optional tags, and select based on that.

We may be tempted to search for the *best* match. But what does that mean? The point of optional tags is to have fallbacks. You can say "If you cannot give me a spooky medieval corridor, just give me any medieval corridor." But if you start packing multiple fallbacks into your tag structure, it becomes unclear what the system should fall back to. For example, when you ask for "spooky ~medieval ~corridor," and there is a "spooky futuristic corridor" room and a "spooky medieval hall" room, which one should the system pick? Is "medieval" more important than "corridor?" Do you add priorities? Do you take content order into account—does earlier content get picked first? Do you look at the number of optional tags a piece of content fulfills? How do you make that truly simple to use?

I recommend picking content from the set that fulfills *any* optional tag, as well as the obligatory tags. This forces users not to be clever. Either something is optional, or it is not. Again, simplicity is a strength. However, depending on the use case, more sophisticated scoring systems can work, as can one of the alternative techniques described later in this chapter.

38.3.4 Excluding Content

Some rooms in *Last Mysteries* had entrances or exits to and from other dungeon floors. The server would start the player in the first room with an entrance, and when the player went to an exit, they would be taken to the next floor, or out of the dungeon altogether.

It was easy to go into the floor description and ask for rooms tagged "medieval" and "entrance." The system would pick the right room. But in the rest of the floor we would ask for rooms tagged "medieval," and this would occasionally lead to entrances being where they should not be, ruining the level flow and causing bugs. A similar problem happened with rooms marked "boss." There was no easy way for us to say "do not pick these rooms."

There are several possible solutions to this problem:

1. Introduce a tag that says "not an entrance, exit, or boss room." Give that tag to all applicable rooms. We did this automatically inside Last Mysteries' export tool—any room request that did not have tags such as "start," "boss," and so on. tags would get a "middle" tag.
2. Make it possible to indicate that a tag must be requested explicitly for the content to be picked. Then tag rooms with, say, "!boss" to mean "boss" must be requested explicitly. The selection algorithm then has to filter out content with explicit tags that are not found in the requested set.
3. If you have a small list of these explicit tags, just treat them as a special case in the selection algorithm. In the case of *Last Mysteries* we only had five.

Solution 1 gives more control to the content creator but involves more tagging, or a magical tag that is never explicitly requested. Solution 2 is less work but complicates the system a tiny bit. Solution 3 is a bit harder to change and slightly more magic. Which solution is best depends on how often you expect these explicit tags to change.

38.4 Case Study: *Mainframe* and Choba

In October 2015, Liz England and I developed *Mainframe* (England and Horneman 2015), a web-based interactive fiction (IF) game for Procjam, a game jam about procedural content generation, using a JavaScript IF system called Choba[*] (Horneman 2016).

Mainframe makes heavy use of tag-based content selection. With Choba, as in any similar choice-based IF system, it is possible to create a link between two scenes, so that an option in one scene takes the player to the second scene. Using *Mainframe*'s XML-based syntax, we would write:

```
<option nextScene="computer_room_introduction1">
Approach the central mainframe.</option>
```

However, Choba can also select another scene using tags and then inject a link to it:

```
<injectOption tags="option, mechanical" />
```

---

[*] Both *Mainframe* and Choba are free and have been released as open source.

This says "find me a scene tagged with 'option' and 'mechanical,' and create an option leading there." Using this, we could express higher level concepts like "give me three options for searching a room with electrical and container elements":

```
<injectOption tags="search, electrical" />
<injectOption tags="search, containers" />
<injectOption tags="search, electrical" />
```

Another use of tag-based content selection simply injects a block of content:

```
<injectBlock tags="mission_desc, act1" />
```

This searches for a block with the tags "mission_desc" and "act1" and inserts it into the scene.

Things got really interesting when we made tag requests dynamic:

```
<injectBlock tags="mdesc, $act" />
```

The "$" prefix indicates the requested tag is a variable, so this command requests a block with the tags "mdesc" and, say, "act1." This runtime evaluation turned out to be immensely useful to allow the game to evolve over time. Depending on certain player actions, the "act" variable is increased, and the game seems to slowly change.

We also used it for a rudimentary injury system. We would occasionally execute:

```
<injectBlock tags="injury, $injury"/>
```

The "injury" variable would start off as "none," and there is an empty block tagged with "injury" and "none." But in certain parts of the game, the "injury" variable could be set to "bleeding_hand," say, and then we had several blocks describing the injury.

Picking some content based on a single dynamic variable can of course easily be done by just using a one-dimensional lookup table, but the advantage of our approach is that we could create both basic and complex mappings quickly and easily in a single line of text.

In *Mainframe*, we used tag-based selection to implement missions, dialog, random remarks, mood text, items, item descriptions, and the injury system. It contains 200 injected scene transitions (using tag-based selection), 249 injected blocks of text, and just 144 standard scene transitions, where the next scene is selected by ID.

38.5 Decks

A subtle aspect of tag-based content selection turned out to be of crucial importance in *Mainframe:* once you have found all pieces of content with the desired tags, which one do you actually pick?

In *Mainframe* we wanted each play-through for each player to be different. We also wanted each piece of content to be seen once before content starts to repeat. Our approach was to shuffle the items with the right tags and then pick the elements in order.

Let's introduce a new metaphor, "decks," that I have found useful in this case, both for the content creator (game designer, writer, etc.) and the implementing programmer. Imagine all pieces of content with a given set of tags as a deck of cards. Immediately, the algorithm to use for picking content becomes very clear: shuffle the deck, then draw. When you are done, shuffle again, so you do not get recognizable patterns.

The metaphor of a deck of cards makes a subtle edge case more prominent. Let us say you want to draw three cards from the same deck, and you do this:

- Draw a card and use it.
- Put the card on the discard pile.
- Shuffle the discard pile if the deck is empty.
- Repeat this three times.

In this case, it is possible to end up with the same card twice, because your deck ran out, you reshuffled, and a card you had already picked ended up in the front of the deck. This is not an esoteric bug: this can happen in *Mainframe*. As a result, it is possible to be in a room with two exits leading to the same place. The correct approach, as you know when you have played board or card games, is as follows:

- Draw cards until you have the desired amount. If the deck becomes empty during drawing, shuffle the discard pile.
- Use all cards.
- Put all cards on the discard pile.

In *Mainframe*, I picked the abstraction "draw a card" and then repeated it three times, instead of picking the abstraction "draw three cards." "Draw a card" is easier to implement, because I only have to consider each draw in isolation. "Draw three cards" is trickier. We can write this:

```
<injectOption tags="option, containers" />
<injectOption tags="option, containers" />
<injectOption tags="option, containers" />
```

in which case it is obvious we need to draw three "cards" from the deck of scenes tagged with "option" and "container." We could instead have used:

```
<injectThreeOptions tags="option, containers" />
```

But we can also write:

```
<injectOption tags="option, electrical" />
<injectOption tags="option, mechanical" />
<injectOption tags="option, electrical" />
```

or add arbitrary if/then logic to these lines. That makes the logic more complex—you need to track what you have drawn from where, per scene. But at least the clear metaphor of a deck makes clear what *should* happen.

It is important to remember when implementing decks that "dealing" a card modifies the deck, and thus the program's state. This also caused problems in *Mainframe*.

One advantage of tag-based content selection is that the content is decoupled from where and how it is used. However, this can also lead to unexpected behavior. For example, in *Mainframe* the selected content can itself select more content, or set variables. Because of this, sometimes when we added a block somewhere, a completely different part of the game broke, because that new block got selected. From a programmer's point of view, it is as if you wrote a function and it crashed your program without you explicitly calling it.

38.6 Other Case Studies

Tag-based content selection has been used in several other games.

38.6.1 Irrational Games

SWAT 4, Tribes: Vengeance, BioShock, BioShock 2, and *BioShock Infinite* by Irrational Games used something very similar to tag-based content selection (Cohen 2005). The system matched audio and visual effects to abstract game events at runtime, by examining the nature of the content involved in the event and then choosing the "best match" effect that artists had mapped for that combination. So, for example, when a gun was fired, the game would figure out what was hit and then trigger a parameterized event, like so:

```
BulletHit(holderOfTheGun, bulletType, materialThatWasHit, meshThatWasHit, …
etc…)
```

It considered things like mesh names, material names, designer-controlled "contexts," and even text tags.

38.6.2 Six Ages

The storytelling game *Six Ages* also makes heavy use of tags (Dunham 2016).

Tags in tag-based content selection are typically inside one big global namespace, and big global namespaces do not scale well. Over time, as multiple people work on a game's content, different subsets of tags may start interfering with each other. *Six Ages* uses tags like this:

```
rumors = [self scriptsWithTag: @"rumor" ofType: type_News];
```

"rumor" is a tag, whereas "News" is a type, another way of classifying content. It may have been possible to implement types using tags, but sometimes it makes sense to introduce stronger typing, to reduce complexity, improve performance, and avoid problems with tags overlapping. The script types in *Six Ages* effectively create namespaces.

Additionally, in *Six Ages* tags can be added dynamically to scenes, and tags can be disabled, meaning content with these tags is no longer selected.

38.7 Extensions and Other Approaches

Tag-based content selection is a simple yet powerful approach, but it does have limitations. Let us look at some ways to extend it, or different techniques that do similar things.

One seemingly promising way to extend tag-based content selection is to allow logical predicates as tags. Instead of tagging something with "medieval," we tag it with "area = medieval," and if that condition is true, that piece of content is selected. After all, some tags are already implicit predicates, such as "mood = spooky." And then why not extend that with logical or comparison operators, such as "health <5"?

This seems a small step but in fact inverts the entire system, because it becomes unclear which "tags" are "requested." The metaphor is no longer "give me some content with the following qualities," it is "here is the entire state of the world, which content fits?" This approach requires a much more sophisticated algorithm to find matches. It will need to go through and evaluate every predicate for every piece of content on every request. It is now effectively evaluating a rule set. This can be done with some combination of intelligent ordering of predicates, shortcut evaluation, caching, and so on, but it is significantly more work, and the question of how to identify the "best" match will become an issue.

As a case in point, I once worked on a project that implemented a simple version of a predicate-based system for text selection. Although the selection algorithm was one line of C#, using Linq, that line took three good programmers a whole day to write, and afterward I still spent more time reasoning about why a given piece of content had been picked than I expected or wanted.

Six Ages uses predicates to *exclude* rather than include scenes. This is considerably simpler in that only a chosen candidate needs to have its condition evaluated.

38.7.1 Valve's Dynamic Dialog System

Rule-based systems have their place. For instance, systems that select audio reactions ("barks") for AI-controlled entities are inherently complex, because they need to react to a lot of different stimuli in complex ways. Tag-based content selection may be too simple. One good approach to look at is Valve's dynamic dialog system (Ruskin 2012), as used in *Team Fortress 2, Left 4 Dead, Portal 2*, and other games. It is based on rules that can query any aspect of the world's state. The advantages of this approach are that it is easy to understand and fairly elegant in design, and can be powerful in practice. From discussions I have had with some studios using this technique, one of the downsides is that it may require a dedicated person, with programmer support, to maintain the rules as they grow in complexity. As an alternative, Paul Tozour (Tozour 04) describes a more complex use of tags, rather than rules, to select animations and audio.

38.7.2 Bioshock Infinite's Gameplay Pattern Matcher

Going even further, *Bioshock Infinite* used a gameplay pattern matcher (Kline 2011) for achievements, NPC AI, quest logic, conversations, scripting logic, and more. Tag-based content selection implicitly recognizes game situations, in the sense that requested tags are a limited proxy for what is happening. *Bioshock Infinite*'s gameplay pattern matcher makes this recognition explicit, and goes beyond simple world state queries into temporal logic. Though it is a fascinating approach, one of the developers noted that nonprogrammers sometimes found the asynchronous nature of its temporal matching hard to conceptualize, and its usability could be improved through better tools. It is significantly more complex than tag-based content selection.

38.8 Conclusion

Content selection is a common activity in game development. Tag-based content selection selects content by comparing a set of tags, that is, strings. This technique is simple to implement and to use. Among other things, it can be used for audio and visual effect selection, for level generation, and for procedural generation of interactive fiction scenes.

Despite its simplicity, there are edge cases that must be considered. There may not be content for a given set of tags, or there may be too little content, which can lead to repetitiveness. Tag structures must be designed with care to make sure unwanted content is not selected by mistake. By making tag requests depend on game state, the game can become more dynamic and responsive. When multiple pieces of content with the same set of tags exist, it is useful to think of the content as a deck of cards from which a piece is "dealt." It may be tempting to use logical predicates or even heuristics instead of tags, but this can make the system much more complex. For some use cases, more complex systems can be appropriate, but tag-based content selection is surprisingly versatile and powerful.

Acknowledgments

Thanks to David Dunham, Sebastian Holzfeind, Christopher Kline, and Borut Pfeifer, for their valuable feedback which greatly improved this chapter.

References

Cohen, T. 2005. Moment of impact: Designing an in-game effects system. *Game Developer Magazine*, pp. 21–28.

Dunham, D. 2016. Scene Tags. http://sixages.com/blog/index.php/2016/05/scene-tags/ (accessed July 11, 2016).

England, L. and J. Horneman. 2015. Mainframe. https://github.com/jhorneman/procjam15/tree/choba (accessed July 11, 2016).

Horneman, J. 2016. The Choba engine. https://github.com/jhorneman/choba-engine (accessed July 11, 2016).

Kline, C. 2011. The future of gameplay authoring. *Presented at Cornell University in 2011.* https://twitter.com/korkyplunger/status/525326773563973632 (accessed July 11, 2016).

Ruskin, E. 2012. AI-driven dynamic dialog. *Presented at Game Developers Conference 2012.* http://assemblyrequired.crashworks.org/ai-driven-dynamic-dialog-at-gdc-2012/ (accessed July 11, 2016).

Ryan, J. O., A. M. Fisher, T. Owen-Milner, M. Mateas, and N. Wardrip-Fruin. 2015. Toward natural language generation by humans. *Proceedings of the Intelligent Narrative Technologies.* http://www.academia.edu/14884597/Toward_Natural_Language_Generation_by_Humans (accessed July 11, 2016).

Tozour, P. 2005. A flexible tagging system for AI resource selection. In *AI Game Programming Wisdom 2*, ed. S. Rabin. Hingham, MA: Charles River Media, pp. 351–359.

39

Recommendation Systems in Games

Ben G. Weber

39.1 Introduction

Players have a large amount of content to choose from across a variety of different game platforms and marketplaces. Some game storefronts now offer thousands of games, and finding relevant content can often be challenging for players. One of the newer ways in which AI is being used is to help players discover content through recommendation systems. A successful recommendation system should suggest content that a player finds relevant and interesting, and that the player would not have otherwise discovered. In games, recommendation systems can be applied to a variety of tasks outside of selling content, including matchmaking systems and dynamic difficultly adjustment (Medler 2008).

The goals for a recommendation system vary based on the system user. For a player, a common motivation for browsing content suggested by a recommender is to find games that closely match the player's preferences. Recommendations can be useful for finding similar titles that do not fit well into existing categories or genres. Another motivation for using recommendation lists is to discover new content that the player would not have otherwise considered. For platform owners that manage a storefront, a common goal is to improve the monetization of players on the system. This can include improving conversion rates, from viewing the store to making a purchase, increasing total daily sales on the platform, and increasing sales for a specific type of content. For game developers, the motivation is to get featured on the recommendation system, to drive additional sales and player engagement.

This chapter will introduce some of the algorithms used to implement recommendation systems and provide examples of systems being used in games. Next, it provides source code examples for setting up a recommendation system using Java, Scala, R and SQL. It concludes by discussing how to test a recommender in offline and online experiments, and options for deploying a recommendation system.

39.2 Recommendation Algorithms

A variety of algorithms are available for suggesting content to players. The best algorithm to use will depend on the number of items in the marketplace, how quickly the marketplace changes, the number of users interacting with the service, and the richness of telemetry collected by the game and platform. An approach that works well for a small, curated game storefront may not transfer well to a marketplace with thousands of titles, millions of users, and constant updates. Additionally, algorithms that use gameplay data to find more relevant content for players, such as a player's favorite class or items in an RPG title, may be too computationally expensive to use in practice.

There are three common types of approaches used for implementing recommendation systems. The first is content-based filtering, which uses information about a specific item, such as game genre, to find related items. The second is collaborative filtering, which uses common purchase patterns across players to make suggestions. The third is model-based approaches that predict a player's likelihood to purchase in order to suggest content. Hybrid approaches can also be used that integrate multiple algorithms.

39.2.1 Content-Based Filtering

Content-based filtering uses only information about an item to suggest related items. This is usually handled through metadata about the item, such as game genre or other item tags. For example, if a user decides to download *Battlefield 4*, a content-based recommendation system might suggest related shooter titles, such as *Battlefield Hardline*. The Steam recommendation system behaves like a content-based system, because it usually suggests content within the same sub-genre. One of the benefits of a content-based system is that it does not need any prior data about the user in order to make suggestions. These systems do not suffer from the cold-start problem, since they do not try to make inferences about users. One of the challenges in using content-based filtering is that accurate metadata or tags need to be created and maintained for the entire catalog.

39.2.2 Collaborative Filtering

Collaborative filtering uses data collected from users and transactions to make inferences about which content users will find relevant. It is therefore making recommendations for you based on the preferences of other users, rather than the genres of the games that you have played. One of the benefits of collaborative filtering is that it can be used to reduce the amount of metadata that needs to be maintained about items in the catalog. For example, instead of specifying a genre for every game on a storefront, you can use data collected from players to determine which games are related.

The collaborative-filtering approach can be used for both item ratings and item rankings. In an item rating system, the goal of the recommender is to predict how a user would rate a game that the user has not yet rated. A system that can accurately model a user's ratings can suggest new games to try by predicting the unrated games the user would rate highest. This is a form of explicit data collection, since the user is assigning scores to items. In an item ranking system, the goal of the recommender is to suggest content that the user is most likely to interact with next. Rather than assign specific scores to items, these types of systems provide an ordered list of content that the user may find relevant. This is a form of implicit data collection, since the user is interacting with the content but not assigning a specific score. Netflix is an example of an item rating system, since it predicts how users will rate new movies, whereas Amazon is an example of an item ranking system, since it suggests related items but does not show explicit scores.

Collaborative filtering can either directly model the relationships between users and items, often referred to as *neighborhood methods*, or indirectly model these relationships using inferred variables (*latent factors*). For direct relationships, user-to-user or item-to-item based approaches can be used. For indirect relationships, solving for the latent factors is treated as a matrix factorization problem and alternating least squares (ALS) is commonly used (Ryza et al. 2015). Apache Mahout provides libraries for user-based and item-based collaborative filtering (Anil 2010), whereas Apache Spark provides an implementation using ALS.

In user-based collaborative filtering, the goal is to find a set of users with similar preferences to the user that needs recommendations. Items that similar users purchased or interacted with are used to generate a list of recommendations. Items from users that are more similar to the user that needs recommendations are given more weight than less similar users. The algorithm works as shown in Listing 39.1. It computes a weighted average for each of the items rated by similar users and returns the items with the highest weighted averages.

Listing 39.1. Pseudocode for User-Based Collaborative Filtering.

```
For every other user V
    Compute the similarity S between U and V
    For every item I rated by V
        Add V's rating for I weighted by S to I's avg. weight
Return the top rated items
```

Item-based collaborative filtering uses a similar approach, but builds recommendations by computing item similarities rather than user similarities. Pseudocode for this algorithm is shown in Listing 39.2. When a user needs a list of recommendations, the system uses prior item ratings and retrieves similar items based on a similarity measure.

Listing 39.2. Pseudocode for Item-Based Collaborative Filtering.

```
For every item I
    For every item J already rated by U
        Compute the similarity S between I and J
        Add U's rating for J weighted by S to I's avg. weight
Return the top rated items
```

In item-based collaborative filtering, item similarity is usually computed based on the overlap of users that interacted with both items I and J. This approach differs from content-based filtering, which computes item similarity based on metadata. This algorithm was used to implement one of the previous versions of Amazon's recommendation system (Linden et al. 2003).

Both item-based and user-based collaborative filtering use similarity measures to select items to recommend. One of the similarity measures that can be used by both algorithms is the *Tanimoto coefficient* (Anil 2010). For user similarity, the coefficient is defined as the overlapping number of items purchased by both users (intersection) over the total number of items purchased by the users (union). It returns a value of 1 for users with the exact same preferences and 0 for users with no overlap. Different similarity measures are useful for different types of recommendations: Pearson correlation and Euclidean distance are commonly used for explicit feedback (item ratings), whereas the Tanimoto coefficient and Log Likelihood are frequently used for implicit feedback (item rankings) (Anil 2010). It's best to experiment with different similarity measures on test data to evaluate which measures work best.

Alternating least squares is another algorithm used for collaborative filtering. It is a model-based approach in which the goal is to associate user and item relationships through latent factors rather than directly representing these associations. Latent factors are variables that are not directly observable, but assumed to have influence on users' preferences for content. This approach uses two matrices: One where each user has k latent variables, and a second where each item in the catalog has k latent variables. ALS is used to solve for these variables, and the resulting matrices can be used to predict how users will rate new content (Koren et al. 2009). This approach is highly scalable and was used by the winning entry in the Netflix prize

39.2.3 Model-Based Filtering

Predictive models can also be used to recommend content for players. One approach that can be used is modeling a user's likelihood to purchase a game, which can be represented as a classification problem. In order to create a recommendation list, a separate classifier needs to be created for each game, and the outputs of the classifiers are used to generate a sorted list of games for a user. One of the benefits of this approach is that if an eager model is used, such as logistic regression (Hastie et al. 2001), then recommendations can be computed very quickly for a user. Some of the drawbacks of this approach are that it requires building a classifier per game in the catalog and may require significant offline training.

In practice other models are often used in order to scale to a large item catalog. One example of a model-based recommendation system used in practice is the Xbox recommender (Koenigstein et al. 2012). This system uses Bayesian inference with a bilinear model, where each user and item is represented as a vector and the inner product of a user vector and item vector predicts the user's affinity for the item.

Another way models can be utilized for recommendations is by identifying different segments, or cohorts of users. For example, one segment of players may prefer RPG titles and purchase a large amount of RPG games and DLC, whereas another segment of players may prefer free-to-play FPS titles. If a model can accurately predict segments for players, then these segments can be used to recommend different content to different groups of players. This approach is often combined with content-based filtering or handcrafted rule sets for a small, curated game catalog.

39.2.4 Algorithm Selection

Depending on the target deployment environment, a variety of different options may be available for implementing a recommendation system. When choosing what approach to use, it is useful to ask the following questions:

1. Is the system generating item ratings or item rankings?
2. How large is the item catalog?
3. Is the metadata for items well maintained?
4. Is there a massive user base with tens of millions of users?
5. Should the recommender include gameplay-specific events?

If the goal of the system is to generate predicted ratings for content, then collaborative is usually the best approach. For item rankings, several options can be well suited. If the item catalog is small, then content-based filtering may be the best approach if accurate and up-to-date metadata is available for the item catalog, such as tags that describe a game. Otherwise, if the catalog is small then model-based approaches such as a classifier per game may be useful. For large item catalogs, collaborative filtering can be useful. In the case of Amazon, with a massive user base, an item-based algorithm was used (Linden et al. 2003). For large user bases where additional information about player behavior should be used for recommendations, such as the favorite class of a player in RPGs, user-based collaborative filtering can be used. ALS provides an approach that can scale to a variety of use cases.

The recommendation algorithm used for the in-game marketplace in *EverQuest Landmark* is user-based collaborative filtering (Weber 2015). One of the unique challenges faced by this title is that user-generated content, published through the Player Studio program, can be sold in the game's marketplace. This resulted in a large item catalog where limited metadata are available to describe items. Additionally, one of the goals for the recommendation system was to incorporate gameplay-based metrics, such as the amounts of different resources collected by a player, when making suggestions for content. User-based collaborative filtering works well for this approach, because the similarity metrics used can incorporate additional features about players, and this approach does not require accurate metadata about items.

39.3 Building a Recommender

There are a variety of open-source tools that can be used to prototype and deploy a recommendation system. This section will present examples for generating a recommended item list using Mahout in Java (Anil 2010), MLlib in Scala (Ryza et al. 15), recommenderlab in R (Hahsler 2011), and directly in SQL. Each of these libraries has evaluation metrics that can be used to measure the performance of a recommender, such as precision and recall metrics. Some of these libraries are better suited for prototyping different system configurations, whereas some are also suitable for deployment in a production system.

39.3.1 Java: Apache Mahout

Mahout is a machine learning library implemented in Java that provides a variety of collaborative filtering algorithms (Anil 2010). Using this library, it is possible to quickly evaluate a variety of recommendation system configurations by combining different algorithms and similarity measures. Mahout can be used on a single machine for prototyping, or deployed to a cluster for a production system. Daybreak Games used this library to test out different recommendation system configurations for the marketplace in *EverQuest Landmark* (Weber 2015).

Mahout implements user-based collaborative filtering with a *UserNeighborhood* class that specifies how similar a user needs to be in order to provide feedback for item recommendations. An example script that generates five game recommendations for user 101 is shown in Listing 39.3. This example uses the Tanimoto similarity measure to find the similarity between users, which computes the ratio of the number of shared games (intersection) over the total number of games owned by the players (union). The script loads game purchase data from a CSV file, which lists game purchases as tuples of User ID and Game ID. This file is used as input to a data model which is then passed to the recommender object. Once a recommender object has been instantiated, the *recommend* method can be used to create a list of game recommendations for a specific user. In this example, the top five game recommendations are retrieved for the user with ID 101. The import statement in this script shows a common directory shared by these classes, to find the fully-qualified class names readers should refer to the Mahout documentation.

Listing 39.3. User-Based Collaborative Filtering with Mahout (Java).

```
import org.apache.mahout.cf.taste.*;

DataModel model = new FileDataModel(new File("Games.csv"));
UserSimilarity s = new TanimotoCoefficientSimilarity(model);
UserNeighborhood neighborhood = new
    ThresholdUserNeighborhood(0.1, similarity, model);
UserBasedRecommender recommender = new
    GenericUserBasedRecommender(model, neighborhood, s);
List recommendations = recommender.recommend(101, 5);
```

An example of item-based collaborative filtering with Apache Mahout is shown in Listing 39.4. The main difference in this example is that a different recommender object is instantiated, and *UserNeighborhood* is not specified. The item-based recommender provides the same *recommend* method that can be used to generate game recommendations. One of the useful classes that Mahout provides not shown in these examples is *RecommenderEvaluator*, which provides functionality for computing the recall and precision of a recommender.

Listing 39.4. Item-Based Collaborative Filtering with Mahout (Java).

```
DataModel model = new FileDataModel(new File("Games.csv"));
ItemSimilarity s = new LogLikelihoodSimilarity(model);
ItemBasedRecommender recommender = new
    GenericItemBasedRecommender(model, s);
List recommendations = recommender.recommend(101, 5);
```

39. Recommendation Systems in Games

39.3.2 Scala: Apache Spark

One of the tools becoming more popular for building recommendation systems is Apache Spark. In fact, many of the single-machine algorithms available in Mahout are being deprecated in favor of Spark. In addition to Mahout, Spark provides a built-in library called MLlib which includes a collection of machine learning algorithms. Currently, ALS is the only implementation of collaborative filtering available in MLlib (Ryza et al. 2015). Although Spark supports multiple languages, the example in this section uses Scala.

A Scala example using MLlib to perform user-based collaborative filtering is shown in Listing 39.5. This script first runs a query to retrieve game purchases in a UserID, GameID tuple format, and then transforms the data frame into a collection of ratings that can be used by the ALS model. Implicit data feedback is being in this example, which is why the *trainImplicit* method is used instead of the *train* method. The input parameters to the train method are the game ratings, the number of latent features to use, the number of iterations to perform for matrix factorization, the lambda parameter which is used for regularization, and the alpha parameter which specifies how implicit ratings are measured. Once the model is trained, the *recommendProducts* method can be used to retrieve a recommended list of games for a user. In this example, five games are retrieved for the user with ID 101.

Listing 39.5. User-Based Collaborative Filtering with MLlib (Scala).

```
import org.apache.spark.mllib.recommendation._

val games = sqlContext.sql("
    select UserID, GameID from GameOwenership
    group by UserID, GameID")

val ratings = games.rdd.map(row =>
 Rating(row.getInt(0), row.getInt(1), 1)
)

val rank = 10
val model = ALS.trainImplicit(ratings, rank, 5, 0.01, 1)
model.recommendProducts(101, 5)
```

39.3.3 R: recommenderlab

If you are more comfortable programming in R, then the *recommenderlab* package provides a great framework for testing out different recommendation systems (Hahsler 2011). An example using this package for user-based collaborative filtering is shown in Listing 39.6.

Listing 39.6. User-Based Collaborative Filtering with recommenderlab (R).

```
install.packages("recommenderlab")
library(recommenderlab)

matrix <- as(read.csv("Games.csv"),"realRatingMatrix")
model <-Recommender(matrix, method = "UBCF")
games <- predict(model, matrix["101",], n=5)
```

The package is available on the CRAN repository and can be installed using the standard *install.packages* function. Once loaded, the package provides a *Recommender* function which takes a data matrix and recommendation method as inputs. In this script, the data matrix is loaded from a CSV file, and the method used is user-based collaborative filtering (UBCF). The *predict* function is then used to retrieve five items for user 101.

39.3.4 SQL

If you have purchase history stored in a database, another option for prototyping a recommendation system is to use SQL directly. This approach can be computationally expensive to use, but can be useful for spot-checking a few results for sampled data. It is also useful in situations where pulling data to a machine running Spark or R is slow or expensive. An example using SQL to perform user-based collaborative filtering is shown in Listing 39.7. In this example, the inner query computes the Tanimoto coefficient between users by finding the ratio in overlapping games divided by total number of games purchased. The outer query returns an average score for each retrieved game. The result set of this query is five game recommendations for user 101.

Listing 39.7. User-Based Collaborative Filtering in SQL.

```
select u. UserID, v. GameID, avg(Tanimoto) as GameWeight
from (
    select u. UserID, v. UserID V_ID,
        count(distinct u. GameID) Overlap,
        Overlap/(u. NumGames + v. NumGames - Overlap) Tanimoto
    from Purchases u
    Join Purchases v
     on u. GameID = v. GameID
    where u. UserID = 101
    group by u. UserID, v. UserID, u. NumGames, v. NumGames
) u
Join Purchases v
    on V_ID = v. UserID
group by u. UserID, v. GameID
order by GameWeight desc
limit 5
```

39.3.5 Evaluating Recommenders

The scripts in this section have provided examples of how to retrieve game suggestions for a specific user. One of the ways to evaluate the quality of a recommender is to use a qualitative approach, in which the output of the recommender is manually examined for a small group of users. Another approach is to use the built-in evaluation metrics included in the different libraries. For example, recommenderlab and MLlib provide functions for computing receiver-operating characteristic (ROC) curves which can be used to evaluate different system configurations.

When evaluating a recommender, it is also a good practice to compare the performance of the recommendation system to other handcrafted approaches, such as a top sellers list. One of the metrics used to evaluate the recommendation system for *EverQuest Landmark* was a holdout experiment, where a single item is removed and the goal of the recommender is to identify the held-out item in as few suggestions as possible. This enabled different Mahout configurations to be tested against hand-authored rule sets. Also, recommender evaluation should not be limited to the prototyping stage. Once put into production, the system should be compared against control groups, such as a top sellers list and other recommendation system configurations.

39.4 Deploying a Recommender

One of the challenges in building a recommendation system for a game is deploying the system so that it can retrieve item recommendations in near real time. A common method for achieving this level of responsiveness is setting up offline and online phases. In the offline phase matrices are precomputed as part of a batch process performed daily, and in the online phase a web service performs a lookup from the most recently precomputed matrix. Using this approach avoids the need to evaluate models in real-time when building game suggestions. Another approach is to set up a streaming recommendation system that computes items for each user in near real-time. For example, Spark can be configured in a streaming mode where new batches of users are evaluated every second. In this configuration, the model needs to be responsive enough to ensure efficient retrieval of recommendation lists. Another approach is to implement the logic for collaborative filtering on the game server. This is similar to the streaming approach, but the response is handled directly by the game server rather than through a recommendation library.

Once a recommender has been deployed, it is useful to measure the performance of the system versus a control group, such as a top sellers list. This can be done through A/B testing where the majority of users interact with the recommendation system, and a holdout set of users serve as the control group and receive suggestions from a top selling items list.

39.5 Conclusion

Recommendation systems have transformed how users discover content and many games are now using these systems in practice. This chapter has provided an overview of common algorithms for building recommendations, provided examples for setting up a system in different languages and environments, and discussed options for deploying a system for a game. Recommendation systems can help improve monetization in a game or marketplace, and also have the potential to help players discover new games to play and find novel content that they would not have otherwise discovered.

References

Anil, R., Owen, S., Dunning, T., and Friedman, E. 2010. *Mahout in Action*. Greenwich, CT: Manning Publications

Hahsler, M. 2011. Recommenderlab: A framework for developing and testing recommendation algorithms. Technical Report. https://cran.r-project.org/web/packages/recommenderlab/vignettes/recommenderlab.pdf (accessed June 19, 2016).

Hastie, T., Tibshirani, R., and Friedman, J. 2001. *The Elements of Statistical Learning: Data Mining, Inference, and Prediction*. New York: Springer.

Koenigstein, N., Nice, N., Paquet, U., and Schleyen, N. 2012. The Xbox recommender system. In *ACM Conference on Recommender Systems*, Dublin, Ireland, pp. 281–284.

Koren, Y., Bell, R., and Volinsky, C. 2009. Matrix factorization techniques for recommender systems. *Computer*, 42(8): 30–37.

Linden, G., Smith, B., and York, J. 2003. Amazon.com recommendations: Item-to-Item collaborative filtering. *IEEE Internet Computing*, 7(1): 76–80.

Medler, B. 2008. Using recommendation systems to adapt gameplay. In *Discoveries in Gaming and Computer-Mediated Simulations: New Interdisciplinary Applications*, ed. R. E. Ferdig. Hershey, PA: IGI Global, pp. 64–77.

Ryza, S., Laserson, U., Owen, S., and Wills, J. 2015. *Advanced Analytics with Spark: Patterns for Learning from Data at Scale*. Sebastopol, CA: O'Reilly Media.

Weber, B. 2015. Building a recommendation system for EverQuest landmark's marketplace. *GDC Talk*. http://www.gdcvault.com/play/1022431/Building-a-Recommendation-System-for (accessed June 19, 2016).

40
Vintage Random Number Generators

Éric Jacopin

40.1 Introduction

It will go like this. You are in a hurry and you need to generate random data structures, so you turn to what your favorite programming language provides—it is C++ after all, how could it hurt you? Or maybe it will sneak up on you. You are prototyping and do not want to worry about implementation details. This graphical tool is so practical and elegant, what could go wrong?

The answer to both questions is `rand()`.

`rand()` can hurt your project because many implementations still use a linear congruential random number generator (LCG), a family of random number generators that were in use as early as 1949 (Lehmer 1949). Many tools still use `rand()` today to generate integers, real numbers, and Boolean values. Such vintage random number generators are still here because they are fast and simple, not because they work well.

The next section presents `rand()`. It explains what an LCG is, how it works, and how it can hurt your project when used to generate random Boolean values, for example. The following section presents better LCGs than the ones built into most current-day compilers. Finally, we present a technique that combines two LCGs to provide randomness you can use. Code for this technique will be provided on the book's website.

40.2 `rand()`: When Randomness Means Cautiousness

In this section, we explain: Why are linear congruential random number generators linear? Why are they congruential? How can we visualize these properties? What about `rand()`, how does it work?

A *linear* congruential random number generator is *linear* because it uses a linear equation to generate the next random number x_n from the previous random number x_{n-1}:

$$x_n = ax_{n-1} + b$$

which gives:

$$x_{n \geq 0} = a^n x_0 + \sum_{i=0}^{n-1} ba^i$$

where x_0 is the *seed* of the random number generator. Consequently, with $a > 0, b \geq 0$ and $x_0 > 0$ we have:

$$\lim_{n \to \infty} x_n = \infty$$

If we choose $a = 2, b = 3$ and $x_0 = 0$ then $x_{15} = 98301$ is the first generated number, which *cannot* be represented with an unsigned 16-bit integer, whereas $x_{29} = 1610612733$ is the largest number, which *can* be represented by a signed 32-bit integer. We obviously need more than just 29 possible random values.

A linear *congruential* random number generator is *congruential* because it frames the generated numbers with the help of a ***mod***ulus operation:

$$x_n = (ax_{n-1} + b) \, \textbf{\textit{mod}} \, m$$

For a positive integer m two integers a and b are said to be congruent modulo m when

$$a \, \textbf{\textit{mod}} \, m = b \, \textbf{\textit{mod}} \, m$$

For example, you can choose $b = a + m$. Consequently, LCGs are periodic random number generators: For some value of n, you will get numbers that have already been generated, in the same order. The following LCG, originally proposed by Derrick Lehmer (Lehmer 1949), has a proven repetition period of 5 882 352:

$$x_n = (23x_{n-1}) \, \textbf{\textit{mod}} \, (10^8 + 1)$$

When $b = 0$ the LCG is called *multiplicative* and one must be careful with the seed, since $x_0 = 0$ will force $x_{n>0} = 0$ (that is, once one value is 0, then all following values will also be 0), which is certainly not random. Consequently, seeds for multiplicative LCGs must be chosen in the range $[1, m)$—that is, at least equal to 1 and strictly less than m. To avoid $x_n = 0$ becoming true for some other generated value, multiplicative LCGs are designed so that only $x_{n-1} = m$ would give $x_n = 0$, which is impossible by definition since all generated values are strictly less than the modulus m.

Both linearity and periodicity of LCGs can be easily visualized by plotting the points made of the pairs (x_{n-1}, x_n) of successive numbers that have been generated; if we further divide the generated numbers by m, we get a normalized plot over the unit range (0,1), of the linear and repetitive behavior of an LCG, as shown in Figure 40.1.

All LCGs repeat themselves for some value of n, including `rand()`. Visualizations for ANSI C (X3J11 1988) and Visual C++ 2015 are shown in Figure 40.2.

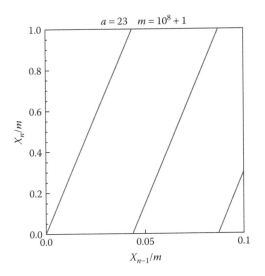

Figure 40.1

$a = 23, b = 0$ and $m = 10^8 + 1$ has a repetition period of 5 882 352.

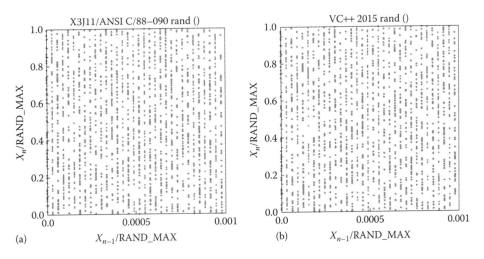

Figure 40.2

(a) `rand()` from ANSI C. (b) Visual C++ 2015's `rand()`.

Here is the portable implementation of `rand()` from ANSI C ($a = 1103515245, b = 12\,345$ and $m = 32\,768$):

```
static unsigned long int next = 1;
int rand(void) /* RAND_MAX assumed to be 32767 */
{
        next = next * 1103515245 + 12345;
        return (unsigned int)(next/65536) % 32768;
}
```

And here is the LCG which is still used by Visual Studio's C and C++ (Lomont 2008):

$$x_n = (214013 x_{n-1} + 2531011) \bmod 2^{31}$$

Note that as $b \neq 0$ for both previous LCGs, the seed x_0 can safely be chosen in the range $(0,m)$ (i.e., greater or equal to 0 and strictly less than m) and $x_{n-1} = 561\,051\,201$ is the only value in the range $(0, 2^{31})$ such that:

$$(214013 x_{n-1} + 2531011) \bmod 2^{31} = 0$$

The ith bit of this LCG has a period of 2^i (L'Écuyer 1990), highlighted in gray in the following ($x_0 = 0$)

$$x_{n \geq 0} \,\&\, 1 = 1,0,1,0,1,0, \ldots$$

$$x_{n \geq 0} \,\&\, 2 = 1,1,0,0,1,1,0,0,1,1,0,0, \ldots$$

$$x_{n \geq 0} \,\&\, 4 = 0,0,1,1,1,1,0,0,0,0,1,1,1,1,0,0,0,0,1,1,1,1,0,0, \ldots$$

$$x_{n \geq 0} \,\&\, 8 = 0,1,0,0,0,1,1,1,1,0,1,1,1,0,0,0,0,1,0,0,0,1,1,1,1,0,1,1,1,0,0,0 \ldots$$

Since $2^{31} = 2^{16+15} = 2^{16} \times 2^{15}$, Microsoft's implementation of `rand()` divides x_n by 2^{16} which deletes the 16 least significant (and most rapidly repeated) bits so that `rand()` returns values strictly less than $2^{15} = 32768 = 1 + \text{RAND\_MAX}$. But the 17th bit nevertheless has a period of 2^{17} and so on for the higher order bits of the numbers generated by `rand()`.

To illustrate one of the common pitfalls of working with `rand()`, we end this section with a discussion on generating random Boolean values. Integer values 0 and 1 are typically used to represent Boolean `false` and `true`, respectively, so it makes sense to generate 0 and 1 values with `rand()` using a modulus operation:

```
bool RandBoolMod(void)
{
        return ((rand() % 2) == 1) ? true: false;
}
```

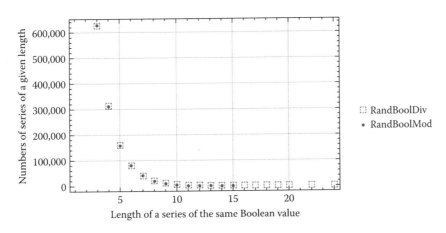

Figure 40.3

Which use of `rand()` do you want to generate Boolean values?

It is also possible to divide `rand()` by (RAND_MAX+1), multiply by 2, truncate the result and return the result as a Boolean value, which is the method used by the Unreal Engine 4:

```
bool RandBoolDiv(void)
{
        int b = (int) ((2.0f * rand()) / (RAND_MAX + 1));
        return (b == 1) ? true: false;
}
```

Both methods are valid; however, as predicted by the discussion above on the periodicity of the ith bit and as shown in Figure 40.3 above, `RandBoolDiv()` will generate longer series of the same Boolean value than `RandBoolMod()`, thus increasing the perception that your game is cheating (Rabin 2004). As a result, on one hand the series of random Boolean values generated with `rand()` has a smaller period than that of a better LCG and on the other hand there are very long subseries with the same Boolean value, that is either `false` or `true`.

40.3 Vintage LCGs You Could Use

Over the years, many empirical and theoretical tests have been developed to assess the performance of LCGs, thus pushing forward the search for better LCGs. We begin with two LCGs reported by NASA as two useful uniform random number generators with very satisfactory performance (Howell and Rheinfurth 82, page 2):

$$x_n = (16807 x_{n-1}) \bmod (2^{31} - 1)$$

$$x_n = (29903947 x_{n-1}) \bmod (2^{31} - 1)$$

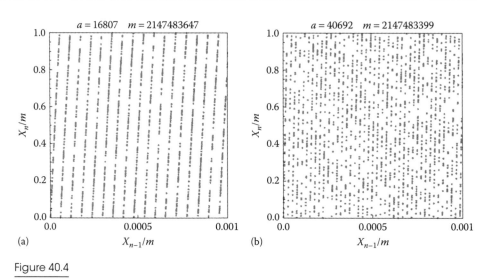

Figure 40.4

(a) Minimum standard LCG. (b) One of the best known LCGs.

The LCG with $a = 16807$ and $m = 2^{31} - 1$ is sometimes considered the minimal standard (Park and Miller 1988) for LCGs and both exhaustive search, and theoretical work has shown that for $m = 2^{31} - 1$, the choice of $a = 16\ 807$ is one of the best possible values (L'Écuyer 1988) for the multiplier a. Other good choices include $a = 742\ 938\ 285$, $a = 950\ 706\ 376$ and $a = 630\ 360\ 016$. An even better option is the LCG:

$$x_n = (40\ 692\ x_{n-1})\ \boldsymbol{mod}\ (2\,147\,483\,399)$$

which is reported to achieve excellent performance (L'Écuyer 1988). Both of these LCGs are visualized in Figure 40.4.

40.4 Combined LCGs: LCGs You Can Use

Although the LCGs in Figure 40.4 are getting better and better, they still suffer from the same inherent problems as rand(). One way to do significantly better is to combine the output of multiple LCGs. Assume two distinct LCGs:

$$x_{1,n} = (a_1 x_{1,n-1} + b_1)\ \boldsymbol{mod}\ m_1$$

$$x_{2,n} = (a_2 x_{2,n-1} + b_2)\ \boldsymbol{mod}\ m_2$$

Here is how to combine $x_{1,n}$ and $x_{2,n}$ into one LCG (L'Écuyer 1988):

$$x_n = (x_{1,n-1} - x_{2,n-1})\ \boldsymbol{mod}\ (m_1 - 1)$$

In theory you can combine as many LCGs as you want (L'Écuyer 1988) (with obvious run-time costs), but two are enough to provide far better performance than one LCG alone.

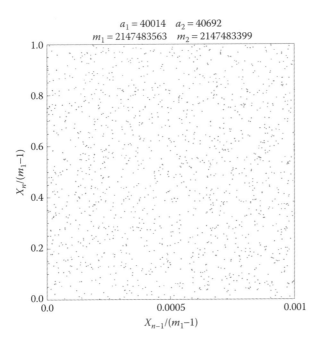

$a_1 = 40014 \quad a_2 = 40692$
$m_1 = 2147483563 \quad m_2 = 2147483399$

Figure 40.5

Combined LCGs for the randomness you should use.

As you can see in Figure 40.5, a combination of two LCGs does not show the linear and congruential properties we have seen in Figures 40.1, 40.2, and 40.4. Although not perfect, combined LCGs achieve the best randomness that LCGs can provide. If you want to keep using vintage random number generators, combined LCGs are the approach that you should use.

The code used to generate Figure 40.5 is available on the website, and can be plugged directly in to your game.

40.5 Conclusion

Let us face it: stop using `rand()`. This can be difficult if not impossible as `rand()` can be hidden in other random functions (such as those built into a third-party game engine), but the effort is worth it. For example, consider combining LCGs as presented in Section 40.4!

Finally, please, take the time to read the papers published on the topic of random number generators for game programming (Lecky-Thompson 2004, Isensee 2001, Jones 2004, Lomont 2008, Rabin 2008), and game artificial intelligence in particular (Freeman-Hargis 2004, Rabin 2004, Rabin et al. 2014).

Acknowledgments

Thanks to Marjan Petkovski for his comments, to Elric Jacquart for generating millions of random numbers, and to Kevin Dill for his work editing this chapter.

References

X3J11. 1988. Draft ANSI C Standard 88-090. http://flash-gordon.me.uk/ansi.c.txt (accessed February 15, 2017).

Freeman-Hargis, J. 2004. The statistics of random numbers. In *AI Game Programming Wisdom 2*, ed. S. Rabin. Hingham, MA: Charles River Media, pp. 59–70.

Howell, L. W. and M. H. Rheinfurth. 1982. Generation of pseudo-random numbers. Nasa Technical Paper 2105, 27 pages. Hampton, VA.

Isensee, P. 2001. Genuine random number generator. In *Game Programming Gems 2*, ed. M. DeLoura. Hingham, MA: Charles River Media, pp. 127–132.

Jones, T. 2004. Zobrist hash using the mersenne twister. In *Game Programming Gems 4*, ed. A. Kirmse. Hingham, MA: Charles River Media, pp. 141–146.

Lecky-Thompson, G. W. 2004. Predictable random numbers. In *Game Programming Gems*, ed. M. DeLoura. Hingham, MA: Charles River Media, pp. 133–140.

Lehmer, D. H. 1949. Mathematical methods in large scale computing units. In *Proceedings of the 2nd Symposium on Large Scale Digital Calculating Machinery*. Harvard University Press, pp. 141–146.

L'Écuyer, P. 1988. Efficient and portable combined random number generator. *Communications of the ACM* 31(6):742–749, 774.

L'Écuyer, P. 1990. Random numbers for simulations. *Communications of the ACM* 33(10):85–97.

Lomont, C. 2008. Random number generation. In *Game Programming Gems 7*, ed. S. Jacobs. Hingham, MA: Charles River Media, pp. 113–125.

Park, S. and K. Miller. 1988. Random number generators: Good ones are hard to find. *Communications of the ACM* 31(10):1192–1201.

Rabin, S. 2004. Filtered randomness for AI decisions and game logic. In *AI Game Programming Wisdom 2*, ed. S. Rabin. Hingham, MA: Charles River Media, pp. 71–82.

Rabin, S. 2008. Using Gaussian randomness to realistically vary projectile paths. In *Game Programming Gems 7*, ed. S. Jacobs. Hingham, MA: Charles River Media, pp. 199–204.

Rabin, S., J. Goldblatt and F. Silva. 2014. Gaussian randomness, filtered randomness, and Perlin noise. In *Game AI Pro*, ed. S. Rabin. Hingham, MA: Charles River Media, pp. 29–43.

Leveraging Plausibility Orderings to Achieve Extremely Efficient Data Compression

Jeff Rollason

41.1 Introduction

Data compression is often blind to the meaning of the data and instead depends on detecting pure, context-free patterns. It is possible, however, to exploit the structured nature of the data to achieve extremely efficient compression. In this chapter, we show how we at AI

479

factory exploited this idea for our mobile Klondike Solitaire game *Solitaire Free* (Solitaire Free 2016), using a very simple approach to achieve compression far in excess of that provided by conventional methods—with final compressed data that were about $100\times$ smaller than the raw data! Given that this was destined for a mobile app, this was a game changer for our team.

The underlying basis of our approach is to exploit the plausibility ordering, an attribute that has been crucial in-game AI for the success of programs such as AlphaGo (Deepmind 2016). We show here how this ordering can be used to yield other benefits, beyond just better gameplay.

41.2 The Core Requirement: A Klondike Solitaire App

Klondike Solitaire (Klondike 2016) is probably the world's most popular solitaire game. In order to build a successful mobile version of the game, we needed to provide the player with a variety of solvable puzzles, ranging from easy to very hard.

By estimation some 15% of Klondike puzzles have no solution (depending on the rule set). The principles needed to solve Klondike are well known but unfortunately not fast enough to randomly create a reliably graded puzzle on-the-fly. Puzzles created this way would tend to be of poor quality and most often unsolvable. Therefore we needed a library of graded puzzles, created in advance.

41.3 Assessing the Space Requirement

Given that runtime puzzle generation was not an option, we set out to create a database of graded puzzles for Klondike. We wanted a puzzle set for each of three difficulty levels. Each puzzle set consists of two rule sets, and each rule set should have 2000 puzzles, so we need to store the solutions for 3 * 2*2000 puzzles. The solutions vary in length, but the longest of them require 198 moves, and the representation for a single Klondike move takes 8 bytes. Thus, the simplest (and worst) solution would require 3 * 2*2000 * 198 * 8 bytes, or over 19 MB just for the puzzles! This is for a mobile app for a consumer market where users fill up their phones with apps, music, and photos. Space is a highly coveted resource. Most of AI Factory's mobile apps are nowhere near this size and they have game code and artwork as well, so clearly this is not an acceptable solution.

Of course this assumes that all solutions require the worst case size of move record, which obviously could be compacted into variable length records. Doing this gives an average record size of 125 instead of 198, which would reduce the overall size to 3 * 2*2000 * 125 * 8 = 12,000,000 bytes, but that is still too much.

41.4 Cutting the Space Requirements, Step 1: Bit Packing

As a first step, we took a look at the move format and saw that the 8-bit bytes are wasteful. There are only 10 move types, so that can be stored in 4 bits. Klondike needs 52 possible cards, which requires 6 bits. The tableau destination needs only 3 bits, and so on. Packing the data more efficiently cut the move record from 8 bytes down to 3, which results in a total size of 4,500,000 bytes. This was looking better, but 4.5 Mb is still quite a bit bigger than the total size of our smallest released product. We can do better…

41.5 Cutting the Space Requirements, Step 2: Table Lookup

The next idea was to replace the coded moves with an index that gives the number of the move in the list of legal moves at that point in the game. This means that the record cannot be decoded without the actual game engine to determine what the move ordering is, as we have reduced a move to a simple index, but this index has no meaning unless we know the order in which the moves are generated in game. This makes the record context sensitive but gives a radical improvement. Each move can now be stored in a single byte, reducing the size to 3 * 2*2000 * 125 * 1 = 1,500,000 bytes.

At this point we might have considered stopping as this is about half of the size of our smallest mobile app, although note that this is just one table, not the complete app. Regardless, we can still do better…

41.6 Cutting the Space Requirements, Step 3: Plausibility + Morse/Huffman Encoding

If we had a strict ordering of the moves by expected quality (a *plausibility ordering*) we could then take advantage of the fact that the distribution of possible move list indices would not be random but rather highly skewed, so that the right move for the solution is much more likely to be near the beginning of the list than near the end. In other words, the first move in the moves list would be expected to be the most common, the second somewhat less common, and so on until we get to the least common move at the end of the list. This would allow us to use a Morse Code-like encoding (Morse 2016) such that the most common index (i.e., 1) would be the equivalent of the letter "E" in Morse, with a single bit representing it, and later moves in the list would take up to 5 bits. This is, of course, essentially a Huffman encoding (Huffman 2016), but we have chosen to express it in terms of Morse Code (which somewhat predates Huffman) as that is a simpler concept with a wider common understanding.

A Huffman encoding could result in a very high level of compression, with an estimated four moves per byte and an overall size of 380 Kb. This would be very small, but a better (and also simpler) solution is possible…

41.7 Cutting the Space Requirements, Step 4: Plausibility + Run-Length Encoding

Examination of the plausibility orderings for the actual solutions showed that the orderings' first move was right most of the time. This offers a better option: To use Run-Length Encoding (Run-length 2016) on the move lists. With this approach a series of nine zeros (i.e., 9 moves where the first move on the list is correct) could be reduced to a single byte of the form 0 × 89 or 128 + 9. Such was the dominance of these first moves that other moves could be left as-is, occupying 7 bits per index.

With this approach, the entire set could be reduced to just 192,160 bytes—and this included the start-up 6 bytes needed for each solution, the random seed (needed to define the card deal), the length of record, and the number of moves. This is storing moves at an astonishing 12.8 moves per byte, ignoring the headers, and 7.8 moves per byte after header overheads. This is almost 100× smaller than the uncompressed data, and makes the point very strongly that plausibility ordering can have a dramatic impact on game database compression.

41.8 An Example Game Record and the Compressed Record

The impact of this method is most easily appreciated by examining a sample solution record. Table 41.1 is the very first game in the database, minus the 6-byte header needed for each solution. This complete 127 move game compresses to the following 3 byte sequence:

```
197,1,185
```

This is dramatically successful, although this particular example is a simple puzzle and thus offers a better chance of high compression than our more complex puzzles do. Nevertheless, it still seems quite remarkable!

41.9 Beyond Data Compression: Plausibility Ordering as an AI Tool

Generation of a good plausibility ordering, in which the early moves are the most likely, is a critical topic. This point was illustrated by the recent success of AlphaGo. Almost certainly key to AlphaGo's success was its capacity to pick an Expert chosen move in the first move ordering 57% of the time, compared to a previous best of 44% by other groups. If this margin had been only, say, 52% then it is quite likely that the human world Go champion, Lee Sedol, would have easily won the match.

To do some simple calculations, consider the impact on a 6-ply sequence: at 57% the chance of taking the "right" line on a rollout of six moves is a healthy 3.4%, but at 44% this figure is a more modest 0.72%. When you project this out to the 20 plies that AlphaGo searched, the divergence in performance is more dramatic: 57% gives you about a 200-fold better chance of hitting the best line the first time.

This feeds back into our chapter in *Game AI Pro* 2, "Interest Search—A Faster Minimax" (Rollason 2015). Again the key to the success of the product *Shotest* (Japanese Chess) was its capacity to get the right move, or at least good moves, to the top of the moves list, in a game with a serious issue with combinatorial search explosions. A good plausibility ordering, combined with the interest search mechanism, allowed *Shotest* to quickly enter the top rankings in Computer Shogi, even though it was authored by a programmer who played a poor game of Shogi! Even a slightly better ordering resulted in a much more efficient and effective tree search.

It is worth pointing out that plausibility ordering, as used in tree search, is not what you would exclusively use to pick a move to play. Its purpose is to provide candidates to explore in a search, so it can afford to make colossal mistakes in its first choice as long as these mistakes are uncommon. Put simply, as long as the search has a high probability of a good choice, a low probability of a terrible choice may have a very limited negative impact. This makes plausibility ordering much easier, since you need not put in the much

Table 41.1 First Solution in the Klondike Puzzle Database

01.	T♣ Tabl->Tabl 5->1 (From 5)	47.	Q♦ Draw
02	4♠ Draw	48.	7♥ Waste->Tabl->4
03.	K♣ Draw	49.	A♦ Waste->Foundation->2
04.	8♣ Draw	50.	Q♦ Waste->Tabl->5
05.	A♣ Draw	51.	4♦ Draw
06.	4♦ Draw	52.	2♦ Waste->Foundation->2
07.	T♦ Waste->Tabl->7	53.	J♥ Waste->Tabl->1
08.	K♥ Draw	54.	8♥ Draw
09.	Q♥ Draw	55.	9♣ Draw
10.	2♠ Waste->Tabl->2	56.	T♠ Waste->Tabl->1
11.	9♣ Draw	57.	?♥ Re-cycle
12.	?♥ Re-cycle	58.	J♣ Tabl->Tabl 7->5 (From 7)
13.	4♠ Draw	59.	3♦ Tabl->Foundation 7->2
14.	K♣ Draw	60.	A♥ Tabl->Foundation 7->3
15.	9♠ Waste->Tabl->7	61.	5♥ Tabl->Tabl 6->7 (From 6)
16.	8♦ Tabl->Tabl 3->7 (From 3)	62.	2♣ Tabl->Foundation 6->1
17.	7♦ Tabl->Tabl 5->3 (From 4)	63.	2♥ Tabl->Foundation 6->3
18.	7♣ Tabl->Tabl 5->7 (From 3)	64.	3♠ Tabl->Tabl 6->5 (From 3)
19.	Q♠ Tabl->Tabl 5->4 (From 2)	65.	6♣ Tabl->Tabl 7->4 (From 4)
20.	J♦ Tabl->Tabl 1->4 (From 1)	66.	T♥ Tabl->Tabl 6->7 (From 2)
21.	8♣ Draw	67.	6♠ Tabl->Tabl 6->3 (From 1)
22.	A♣ Draw	68.	K♦ Tabl->Tabl 4->6 (From 4)
23.	4♦ Draw	69.	3♣ Tabl->Foundation 4->1
24.	K♥ Waste->Tabl->1	70.	3♥ Tabl->Tabl 2->4 (From 2)
25.	2♦ Draw	71.	5♦ Tabl->Tabl 2->3 (From 1)
26.	K♠ Draw	72.	4♣ Tabl->Tabl 4->3 (From 2)
27.	Q♣ Waste->Tabl->1	73.	4♠ Draw
28.	T♠ Draw	74.	4♦ Waste->Foundation->2
29.	?♥ Re-cycle	75.	8♥ Draw
30.	4♠ Draw	76.	K♠ Waste->Tabl->2
31.	6♦ Waste->Tabl->7	77.	Q♥ Waste->Tabl->2
32.	K♣ Draw	78.	J♠ Tabl->Tabl 7->2 (From 3)
33.	9♥ Draw	79.	A♠ Tabl->Foundation 7->4
34.	A♣ Waste->Foundation->1	80.	2♠ Tabl->Foundation 3->4
35.	A♦ Draw	81.	3♥ Tabl->Foundation 3->3
36.	J♥ Draw	82.	4♣ Tabl->Foundation 3->1
37.	Q♥ Draw	83.	5♦ Tabl->Foundation 3->2
38.	T♠ Draw	84.	3♠ Tabl->Foundation 5->4
39.	?♥ Re-cycle	85.	4♥ Tabl->Foundation 5->3
40.	4♠ Draw	86.	5♣ Tabl->Foundation 5->1
41.	5♣ Draw	87.	6♦ Tabl->Foundation 5->2
42.	9♥ Waste->Tabl->4	88.	5♥ Tabl->Foundation 6->3
43.	8♣ Waste->Tabl->4	89.	6♣ Tabl->Foundation 6->1
44.	5♣ Waste->Tabl->7	90.	7♣ Tabl->Foundation 5->1
45.	4♥ Tabl->Tabl 5->7 (From 1)	91.	8♠ Tabl->Tabl 3->7 (From 2)
46.	K♣ Waste->Tabl->5	92.	9♦ Tabl->Tabl 7->1 (From 1)

(Continued)

Table 41.1 (*Continued*) First Solution in the Klondike Puzzle Database

93. 7♠ Tabl->Tabl 3->5 (From 1)	111. 8♣ Tabl->Foundation 6->1
94. 9♣ Draw	112. 9♣ Tabl->Foundation 2->1
95. 9♣ Waste->Tabl->2	113. 9♥ Tabl->Foundation 6->3
96. 8♥ Waste->Tabl->2	114. T♥ Tabl->Foundation 2->3
97. 6♥ Waste->Foundation->3	115. J♥ Tabl->Foundation 1->3
98. 4♠ Waste->Foundation->4	116. J♠ Tabl->Foundation 2->4
99. 5♠ Tabl->Foundation 4->4	117. Q♥ Tabl->Foundation 2->3
100. 6♠ Tabl->Foundation 1->4	118. T♣ Tabl->Foundation 6->1
101. 7♦ Tabl->Foundation 1->2	119. J♣ Tabl->Foundation 5->1
102. 7♠ Tabl->Foundation 5->4	120. Q♣ Tabl->Foundation 1->1
103. 8♠ Tabl->Foundation 1->4	121. K♥ Tabl->Foundation 1->3
104. 8♦ Tabl->Foundation 5->2	122. J♦ Tabl->Foundation 6->2
105. 9♦ Tabl->Foundation 1->2	123. Q♦ Tabl->Foundation 5->2
106. 9♠ Tabl->Foundation 5->4	124. K♣ Tabl->Foundation 5->1
107. T♠ Tabl->Foundation 1->4	125. Q♠ Tabl->Foundation 6->4
108. T♦ Tabl->Foundation 5->2	126. K♠ Tabl->Foundation 2->4
109. 7♥ Tabl->Foundation 6->3	127. K♦ Tabl->Foundation 6->2
110. 8♥ Tabl->Foundation 2->3	

larger effort to avoid rare poor choices. The dynamic of this is significantly different from the needs of the linear evaluation function that might ultimately be responsible for the chosen move.

41.10 Conclusion

This case study shows that plausibility ordering, where better moves are mostly ordered at the top, offers a way to impose a highly structured skew on the data, making it amenable to compression far in excess of what is possible from context-free data compression. Huffman encoding would have allowed the original database of raw solutions to be compressed, but this would have depended on detecting moves common to all solutions. This moves list would have included a relatively vast number of possible moves. However, reclassifying the solutions, not by move content, but by chance of the move being correct, offers a substantially more efficient structure for compression. The complexity of move structure is then completely removed from the database and replaced by a minimalized move index.

In this case our plausibility ordering skewed very heavily to the first move in the list, but another inferior ordering might also perform very well, utilizing either a Huffman encoding or a modified Run-Length Encoding. To get the optimum compression for the latter would probably need some simple hand coding. If the second move had a high chance of being correct then the byte structure might use the top 2 bits, leaving 6 bits for uncompressed moves. This would allow the three top moves to use Run-Length Encoding. If a move sequence of the same positions exceeded 6 bits then it could simply be split into an additional byte for the rare overflow. In our encoding, for example, we might have done better by encoding the top three moves instead of just the top move—but we had already achieved plenty, and time is money!

Of course in more complex distributions the run-length option might simply not work, but the Huffman encoding would almost certainly work in these cases.

References

AlphaGo. https://deepmind.com/alpha-go (accessed June 18, 2016).

Rollason, J. 2015. Interest search—A faster minimax. In *Game AI Pro 2*, ed, S. Rabin. Boca Raton, FL: CRC Press, pp. 255–264.

Klondike (solitaire). https://en.wikipedia.org/wiki/Klondike_(solitaire) (accessed June 18, 2016).

Morse code. https://en.wikipedia.org/wiki/Morse_code (accessed June 18, 2016).

Run-Length Encoding. https://en.wikipedia.org/wiki/Run-length_encoding (accessed June 18, 2016).

Huffman coding. https://en.wikipedia.org/wiki/Huffman_coding (accessed June 18, 2016).

Solitaire Free. https://play.google.com/store/apps/details?id=uk.co.aifactory.solitairefree (accessed June 18, 2016).

42

Building Custom Static Checkers Using Declarative Programming

Ian Horswill, Robert Zubek, and Matthew Viglione

42.1 Introduction

Programmers have developed a wide range of tools for sanity checking their code. Compilers perform type checking and generate warnings about undefined or unused variables. Programs such as Microsoft's FxCop can detect opportunities for optimization, likely bugs such as files that are opened but never closed, and the use of unlocalized strings. These are all examples of *static* checking, as opposed to dynamic checks (such as assertions) that can only verify behavior for a particular run of the program.

Unfortunately, code is only a small part of a game. The rest of the content is composed of a diverse collection of media objects, developed using an equally diverse collection of tools. Many of those tools are purpose-built, whereas others were never specifically designed to operate with one another. As a result, integrity checking of this noncode content, such as:

- Whether a referenced sound file actually exists
- Whether a tag string on an asset is a typo or a valid tag
- Whether all texture files are in the correct format is often limited

487

As a result, these problems are often only found when the problematic asset is used at run-time, resulting in the need for extensive manual testing and retesting.

The barrier to static checking of assets is economic, not technical. Unlike a compiler, whose costs can be amortized over thousands of programmers, the tool chain of a given game is used only by a few people, especially for indie titles. It does not make sense to invest thousands of person-hours in developing a tool that will save only hundreds of person-hours.

Fortunately, writing a static checker does not have to be expensive. In this chapter, we will show you how you can use declarative programming to build your own custom static checkers quickly and easily using a Prolog interpreter that can run inside of Unity3D. This will allow you to write a static checker as a series of statements that literally say "it is a problem if …" and let Prolog do the searching to find instances of the problem.

We have used this technique in two games, a research game, *MKULTRA*, and a commercial game, SomaSim's *Project Highrise*. In both cases, it has saved considerable effort tracking down bugs.

42.2 A Very Brief Introduction to Prolog

We will start by giving you a very brief introduction to Prolog. This will be enough to be able to read the code in the rest of the chapter, but if you want to write Prolog code, then it is worth reading a Prolog book such as *Prolog Programming for Artificial Intelligence* (Bratko 2012) or the first few chapters of *Prolog and Natural Language Analysis* (Pereira and Shieber 2002).

42.2.1 Prolog as a Database

At its simplest, Prolog acts as a fancy database. The simplest Prolog program consists of a series of "facts," each of which asserts that some predicate (relation) holds of some arguments. The fact:

```
age(john, 25).
```

asserts that the age relation holds between john and the number 25, that is, John's age is 25. Note that the period is mandatory; it is like the semicolon at the end of a statement in C. So you can write a simple relational database by writing one predicate per table, and one fact per row, in the database:

```
age(john, 25).
age(mary, 26).
age(kumiko, 25).
…
```

42.2.2 Querying the Database

Having added a set of facts about the ages of different people, we can then query the database by typing a pattern at the Prolog prompt, which is usually printed as ?-. A pattern is simply a fact that can optionally include variables in it. Variables, which are notated by capitalizing them, act as wildcards, and their values are reported back from the match. So if we ask who is age 26, Prolog will reply with Mary:

```
?- age(Person, 26).
Person=mary.
?-
```

Conversely, if we type `age(kumiko, Age)`, we will get back `Age=25`. We can include multiple variables in a query, and Prolog will report back all the different facts that match it. So if we type `age(Person, Age)`, Prolog will report all the `Person/Age` combinations found in the database. However, if a variable appears twice in a query, it has to match the same value in both places. So if we gave a query like `age(X, X)`, it would fail (produce no answers) because there are no `age` facts in the database that have the same value for both their arguments. Queries can also contain multiple predicates, separated by commas, such as in the query:

```
?- age(P1, Age), age(P2, Age).
```

(Remember that the `?-` is the prompt.) Here, the query asks for two people, `P1` and `P2`, who share the same `Age`. Although we might be expecting to get the reply `P1=john`, `Age=25`, `P2=kumiko`, the first reply we will actually get is `P1=john`, `P2=john`, since we never told it `P1` and `P2` should be distinct. We can revise the query to use Prolog's built-in not-equal predicate, `\=`, to get the meaning we intend:

```
?- age(P1, Age), age(P2, Age), P1 \= P2.
```

Prolog has most of the built-in comparisons, you would expect: =, <, >, *etc.* The only thing that is unusual about them is that "not" is notated with \ rather than ! as in C. So not equal is \= instead of != and not X is \+ X rather than !X as in C.

42.2.3 Rules

Prolog also allows you to package a query as a predicate. This is done by providing rules of the form *predicate*:- *query* to your program, for example:

```
same_age(P1, P2):- age(P1, Age), age(P2, Age), P1 \= P2.
```

Again, note the period at the end. This says that `P1` and `P2` are the same age if `P1`'s age is `Age`, `P2`'s is also `Age`, and `P1` and `P2` are different people. You can provide multiple rules and facts for a predicate, and Prolog will test them against your query in the order it finds them in your source file. You can now use `same_age` in your code as if it were a "real" predicate defined by facts, and Prolog will automatically handle queries against it by running the appropriate subqueries.

42.2.4 Prolog as Logical Deduction

So far, we have described Prolog as a kind of database. But we can also think of it as doing inference. Under that interpretation, the program is a set of premises: the facts are just that—facts about what is true; and the *P*: - *Q* rules are logical implications: *P* is true if *Q* is true. The : - operator is logic's implication operator ⇒ (albeit with the arguments reversed), comma is "and" (∧), semicolon is "or" (∨), and \+ is "not" (¬).

A query is a request for Prolog to prove there exists a set of values for the variables that make the query a true statement. Prolog does that by doing a depth-first search of the database to find a specific set of values for the variables that makes the query true. Prolog is not a general theorem prover, however. There are certain kinds of things it can prove and a lot of other things it cannot prove. Moreover, there are a number of places where Prolog programmers have to be aware of the specific search algorithm it uses. Fortunately, we are going to focus on very simple Prolog programs here, so we can ignore the issues of more sophisticated Prolog programming.

42.2.5 Data Structures

So far, we have said little about what kind of data objects Prolog can work with. We have seen the simple strings like john that do not have quotes; Prolog calls these *constants*. We have also seen numbers, and variables. Prolog also supports real strings with double-quotes. And the version of Prolog we use will be able to work with arbitrary Unity objects. More on that later.

Lists are notated with square brackets and can contain any kind of data, including variables. The built-in predicate member (*Element, List*) is true when *Element* is an element of *List*. And so the rule:

```
color_name(C) :- member(C, [red, blue, green, black, white]).
```

says that C is a color name, if it is a member of the list [red, blue, green, black, white], that is, if it is one of the constants red, blue, green, black, or white.

Finally, prolog supports record structures. Instances of structures are notated like constructor calls in C++ or C#, only without the keyword new. So to create a person object, you say person (*fieldValues...*) where *fieldValues...* are the values to fill in for the object's fields. If we wanted to break up the representation of the first and last name components of the people in our age database, we could do it by using structures:

```
age(person(john, doe), 25).
age(person(mary, shannon), 26).
age(person(kumiko, ross), 25).
...
```

Structures are matched in the obvious way during the matching (unification) process, so if we give the query age (person(mary, LastName), 26), we are asking for the last names of people named Mary who are age 26, and it will reply with LastName=shannon.

It is important to understand the difference between structures and predicates. Each statement in your code is a statement about some predicate, either a fact or a rule. In the code above, all the statements are about the predicate age. Each statement tells you that it is true for specific argument values. The person () expressions are not referring to a predicate named person; they are object constructors. But that is purely because the person () expressions appear as arguments to a predicate, not because there is some separate type declaration saying that age is a predicate and person is a data type.

The predicate/data type distinction is determined purely by position in the statement: the outermost name in the fact is the name of the predicate, and anything inside of it is data. In fact, it is common to have data types and predicates with the same names.

42.2.6 Code as Data and Higher Order Code

The fact that code (facts, rules, and queries) and data structures all use the same notation allows us to write predicates that effectively take code as arguments. For example, the predicate `forall`, which takes two queries as arguments, checks whether the second query is true for all the solutions to the first one. For example, query

```
?- forall(person(X), mortal(X)).
```

causes `forall` to find all the X's for which `person(X)`, that is all the people in the database, and for each one, test that `mortal(X)` is also true.* If all the people in the database are also listed as mortal, then the query succeeds. Another example is the `all` predicate, which generates a list of the values of a variable in all the solutions to a query:

```
?- all(X, age(X, 25), SolutionList).
```

finds all the 25 year olds and returns them in its third argument.

Technically, the arguments to `all` and `forall` are structures. But the fact that structures and queries look the same means that we can think of `all` and `forall` as taking queries as arguments.

42.2.7 Calling Unity Code from Prolog

We have built an open-source Prolog interpreter, UnityProlog (http://github.com/ian-horswill/UnityProlog), that runs inside Unity3D. UnityProlog allows you to access Unity `GameObjects` and types by saying $*name*. For example, the query:

```
is_class(X, $'GameObject')
```

is true when X is a Unity `GameObject`. The quotes around the name `GameObject` are needed to keep Prolog from thinking `GameObject` is a variable name. We can then test to see if all game objects have `Renderer` components by running:

```
forall(is_class(X, $'GameObject'),
       has_component(X, _, $'Renderer')).
```

The has_component(O, C, T) predicate is true when C is a component of game object O with type T. Names starting with _'s are treated as variables, so _ is commonly used to mean a variable whose value we do not care about.

---

* Although `forall` is built in, we can also define it by the rule: `forall(P,Q) :- \+(P, \+ Q)`, which says that Q is true for all P if there's no P for which Q is false.

Of course, there are often game objects that are not supposed to have renderers, so a more useful test would be whether all the game objects of a given kind have renderers. Since Unity is component based, we usually test whether a game object has a given kind by checking if it has a given type of component. So we might test if a game object is an NPC by checking if it has an NPC component:

```
npc(X):- has_component(X, _, $'NPC').
```

This says that X is an NPC if it has an NPC component. Now we can update our check to specifically look to see if all NPCs have renderers:

```
has_renderer(X):- has_component(X, _, $'Renderer')).
?- forall(npc(X), has_renderer(X)).
```

Finally, Prolog has a built-in predicate called is that is used for doing arithmetic. It takes a variable as its first argument and an expression as its second, and it computes the value of the expression and matches it to the variable. So:

```
X is Y+1
```

matches X to Y's value plus one. We have extended this to let you call the methods of objects and access their fields. So you can effectively write ersatz C# code and run it using is:

```
Screen is $'Camera'.current.'WorldToScreenPoint'(p)
```

Again, note the single quotes around capitalized names that are not intended to be variables.

42.3 Writing a Static Checker

We now have everything we need to write static checkers. All we have to do is write a predicate, let us call it problem, which is true when there is a problem. We then give it a series of rules of the form problem:- *bad situation*. These literally mean "there is a problem if *bad situation* is the case." To return to our "NPCs should have renderers" example, we might say:

```
problem:- npc(X), \+ has_renderer(X).
```

Now if we give Prolog the query ?- problem, it will automatically find all the NPCs, and check each of them for renderers. If one of them does not have a renderer, the system will reply that yes, there is a problem.

Of course, it is more useful if the system tells us what the problem is. So we will modify the predicate to return a description of the problem the rule has found:

```
problem(no_renderer(X)):- npc(X), \+ has_renderer(X).
```

42. Building Custom Static Checkers Using Declarative Programming

which says, essentially, that "there is a no renderer problem with X, if X is an NPC with no renderer." Now if we ask Prolog if there are any problems, and if the Unity game object fred is an NPC with no renderer, then we should see something like this:

```
?- problem(P).
P=no_renderer($fred)
```

We can add rules for other kinds of problems too. For example, we can check that all cameras are using the correct rendering path with a rule such as:

```
problem(incorrect_render_path(Camera)):-
        Cameras is $'Camera'.allcameras,
        member(Camera, Cameras),
        Camera.renderingPath =\=
            $'RenderingPath'.'DeferredShading'.
```

(the =\= operator is a version of not equals that first runs its arguments using is).

Having generated a set of rules like these for finding problems, we can just add a new predicate for printing a report of all the problems:

```
problems:- forall(problem(P), writeln(P)).
```

This finds all the problems and prints them using Prolog's "write line" predicate.

42.4 Common Problems to Check

Every game has its own data structures and integrity constraints, but here is a list of common types of problems we have found useful to search for.

42.4.1 Object Configuration

One standard thing you might want to do is to look at the different game objects and check to make sure they are configured in some sensible manner. Usually, you will want to do different kinds of checks for different kinds of objects. And since an object's kind is indicated by its components, the basic pattern for these checks will look like this:

```
problem(problem description):-
    has_component(GameObject, Comp, $'Type'),
    Check for bad thing about GameObject and/or Comp.
```

For example, to check that all your particle systems are in layer number 3, you could say:

```
problem(particle_system_in_wrong_layer(GameObject)):-
    has_component(GameObject, _, $'ParticleSystem'),
    GameObject.layer =\= 3.
```

The has _ component line finds all the particle systems and their associated game objects, and the following line checks each one as to whether its layer is 3. Any such objects that are not in layer 3 match this rule, and so are reported as problems.

Alternatively, we might check that all our objects with physics have colliders defined on them:

```
problem(game_object_has_no_colliders(GameObject)):-
    has_component(GameObject, _, $'RigidBody'),
    \+ has_component(GameObject, _, $'Collider').
```

Again, this says, essentially, "it is a problem if a game object with a rigid body does not have a collider."

42.4.2 Type Checking

Suppose your NPCs all have a `nemesis` field, which should be another NPC. Unfortunately, NPCs are game objects, and the only way to know if it is an NPC is to check to see if it has an NPC component, which the Unity editor will not do unless you write a custom editor extension. Fortunately, this sort of type problem is easy to check for:

```
nemesis(C, N):-
    has_component(C, Npc, $'NPC'), N is Npc.nemesis.
problem(nemesis_is_not_an_npc(C, N)):-
    npc(C), nemesis(C, N), \+ npc(N).
```

Here the first rule tells Prolog how to find the nemesis N of a given character C, and the second rule says that it is a problem if C is an NPC, and its nemesis N is not an NPC.

42.4.3 Uninterpreted Strings

Many games make extensive use of strings as identifiers in their data files. For example, Unity attaches a `tag` field to every game object. Tags provide a lightweight mechanism for attaching semantic information to objects, but being uninterpreted strings, the system has no mechanism for detecting typos or other problems with them. Again, we can detect these easily with a problem rule:

```
problem(invalid_tag(O, T)):-
    is_class(O, $'GameObject'),
    \+ member(T, ["tag1", "tag2", …]).
```

where ["tag1", "tag2", …] is the list of valid tags.

Localization is another case where uninterpreted strings can cause issues. Suppose our game uses dialog trees. Characters have a `DialogTree` component that then contains a tree of `DialogTreeNode` objects with fields for the children of the node, and the speech to display. Because of localization issues, we probably do not store the actual speech in the nodes, but instead store a label string such as "Chris professes love for Pat." The label is then looked up in a per-language localization table to get the speech to display.

But what if there is a typo in the label? To check for this, we need to compare all the speeches of all the `DialogTreeNode` objects in the system against the localization table to make sure there are not any typos:

```
problem(unlocalized_dialog(Node, Label)):-
    dialog_node(Node, Label), \+ localization(Label, _).
```

42. Building Custom Static Checkers Using Declarative Programming

That is: there is a problem if a Node has a Label that has no localization. How do we find all the nodes and their labels? We find all characters and their DialogTrees, then walk those trees. That would be something of a pain in C#, but it is easy to do here:

```
dialog_node(Node, Label):-
    has_component(_, DT, $'DialogTree'), Root is DT.root,
    dt_descendant(Root, Node), Label is Node.label.
```

This says Node is a dialog node if it is a descendant of the root of some game object that has a DialogTree component. And we can define a descendant recursively as:

```
dt_descendant(N, N).
dt_descendant(Ancestor, Descendant):-
    Children is Ancestor.children, member(Child, Children),
    dt_dewwscendant(Child, Descendant).
```

The first statement says nodes are descendants of themselves. The second says that a node is a descendant of another if it is a descendant of one of its children.

Not only can we find unlocalized dialog, we can even do a reverse-check to find unused dialog in the localization table:

```
problem(unused_localization(Label)):-
    localization(Label, _), \+ dialog_node(Node, Label).
```

And we can check for the localization string by calling into whatever the appropriate C# code is:

```
localization(Label, Localized):-
    Localized is $'LocalizationTable'.'Lookup'(Label),
    Localized \= null.
```

which says that Localized is the localization string for Label if it is the nonnull result of calling LocalizationTable.Lookup() on the Label. The one problem is that this does not work for reverse lookups. So if we wanted a version that worked for reverse lookups, we could manually do a linear search of the hash table stored in the LocalizationTable class:

```
localization(Label, Localized):-
    HashTable is $'LocalizationTable'.stringTable,
    member(Pair, HashTable),
    Label is Pair.'Key', Localized is Pair.'Value'.
```

This works for both forward and backward searches. There are more efficient ways to code it, but for an offline static check, you may not really care if it takes an extra second to run.

42.5 Case Studies

We have used this technique in two games. The first is a research game called *MKULTRA*. *MKULTRA* uses a number of domain-specific languages for planning, dialog, etc. One of the problems with DSLs is that they often lack basic support for generating warnings about calls to undefined functions, wrong number of arguments, etc. Using the techniques above, we were able to quickly write rules to walk the data structures of the DSLs and check them for integrity, generating error messages as needed.

The other case study is SomaSim's *Project Highrise*. A tower management game that uses its own serialization system. We found that with an afternoon's work, we were able to write a series of rules that found two pages worth of issues. Although an afternoon's work is not nothing, it is less work than would have been required to track down the issues manually. Moreover, they can be rerun each time the assets are changed, saving further work. Moreover, they can be distributed to potential modders, making it easier for them to produce user-generated content, while also reducing the tech support load on the company.

42.6 Conclusion

Modern games incorporate elaborate, ad hoc, asset databases. These databases have integrity constraints that need to be enforced but are often left unchecked due to the cost of writing custom checking code. However, declarative languages provide a cheap and easy way of implementing automated checking. Although we discussed the use of Prolog, other declarative languages, such as SQL, could also be used.

References

Bratko, I. 2012. *Prolog Programming for Artificial Intelligence*, 4th edition. Boston, MA: Addison-Wesley.

Pereira, F. and S. Shieber. 2002. *Prolog and Natural Language Analysis*, digital edition. Microtome Publishing. http://www.mtome.com/Publications/PNLA/prolog-digital.pdf

Index